Introduction to
Computer Law

PEARSON
Education

We work with leading authors to develop the
strongest educational materials in law, bringing
cutting-edge thinking and best learning practice
to a global market.

Under a range of well-known imprints, including
Pearson Longman, we craft high quality print and
electronic publications which help readers to understand
and apply their content, whether studying or at work.

To find out more about the complete range of our
publishing, please visit us on the world wide web at:
www.pearsoned.co.uk

Introduction to
Computer Law

Fifth Edition

David Bainbridge

Professor of Business Law, Aston Business School, Aston University, Barrister, BSc, LLB, PhD, C Eng, MBCS, MICE

PEARSON
Longman

Harlow, England • London • New York • Boston • San Francisco • Toronto • Sydney • Singapore • Hong Kong
Tokyo • Seoul • Taipei • New Delhi • Cape Town • Madrid • Mexico City • Amsterdam • Munich • Paris • Milan

Pearson Education Limited
Edinburgh Gate
Harlow
Essex CM20 2JE
England

and Associated Companies around the world

Visit us on the world wide web at
www.pearsoned.co.uk

_____

First published in Great Britain as *Computers and the Law* in 1990
Second edition published in 1993
Third edition published under the Pitman Publishing imprint in 1996
Fourth edition published under the Longman imprint in 2000
Fifth edition published in 2004

ISBN 0 582 47365 9

British Library Cataloguing-in-Publication Data
A catalogue record for this book is available from the British Library

10 9 8 7 6 5 4 3 2 1
09 08 07 06 05 04

Typeset in 10/12.5 pt Sabon by 3
Printed in Great Britain by Henry Ling Ltd, at the Dorset Press, Dorchester, Dorset

The publisher's policy is to use paper manufactured from sustainable forests.

Contents

Contents

The first edition of this book was published in 1990. It was a relatively slim volume, indicative of the fact that computer law was only really starting to develop as a subject in its own right. Since that time, computer law has grown enormously, reflecting the continual growth of the use of computers and the new and emerging uses that computer technology has been and will be put to. The most noteworthy technological development has, of course, been the phenomenal rise of the Internet, leading to a whole range of issues having legal implications and stimulating legislative responses on a national and international scale. These issues include: the dot.com revolution and the use of the Internet for electronic commerce; challenges to intellectual property rights such as copyright, privacy and freedom of expression issues; the availability of pornographic materials; and the threats posed by hackers and those who write and spread computer viruses. The legal responses have often been quick and proportionate in the light of the threats posed. For example, in the United Kingdom, the maximum penalty in respect of child pornography is now imprisonment for ten years and/or a fine. The need for legal intervention is clear when one considers that the 'I Love You' computer virus was reckoned to have cost a total of $8.75bn. Significant legislative action has come from the European Parliament and Council to ensure that Europe is not disadvantaged by a lack of appropriate regulations and that there is a level playing field in Europe in terms of establishing information society services and carrying out electronic commerce.

What then is computer law? It covers a wide and diverse spectrum, which is reflected in the structure of this book. After a brief introductory chapter, **Part One** of the book concentrates on intellectual property rights. These are the rights associated with creative, innovative and inventive works. Particular areas covered include the protection of computer programs and computer databases, electronic publishing, copyright in the information society and the patenting of software. Design law and trade mark law are also relevant. Design law has been changed recently and it is now possible to register computer graphics and icons as designs. There have been numerous cases involving trade marks on webpages and the registration of famous names as Internet domain names.

Part Two deals with computer contracts and looks at contracts for the writing of software, off-the-shelf software, hardware and website development. There is also a chapter on the liability for defective hardware and software. Particular points of note include a number of recent cases on the court's approach to the reasonableness of terms in computer contracts seeking to exclude or limit liability for defects or breach of performance requirements.

Part Three is new and focuses on electronic contracts and torts. It looks at developments in the formation of contracts over the Internet, electronic commerce and regulations relevant to distance selling, for example, where a person orders a product or service over the Internet. As regards torts, there is a chapter on a range of subjects including libel on the Internet and liability for negligent misstatements. A further issue is the position of intermediaries, such as internet service providers, with respect to illegal material made available or transmitted through their services.

Part Four looks at computer crime, including computer fraud, hacking and associated offences and causing damage to computer programs or data, for example, by the malicious spread of computer viruses or the deliberate erasure of programs or data. There is a chapter on computer pornography and harassing e-mails and a chapter on piracy offences, which are now taken very seriously and carry a maximum prison term of ten years.

The final part of the book, **Part Five**, deals with data protection law. There have been many developments in this field since the previous edition of the book. A large amount of subsidiary legislation has come into force and there have been numerous cases. As the Human Rights Act 1998 has also come into force, many allegations of breaches of data protection law also involve issues connected with the dual rights of privacy and freedom of expression in the European Convention for the Protection of Human Rights and Fundamental Freedoms. There is also a European Directive on privacy and electronic communications, which takes the previous regulations on privacy in telecommunications and extends these to include matters such as unsolicited e-mails and location data in relation to mobile phones.

It has been my intention to make the subject matter accessible and practical, and of interest to students and those involved in the field of computer and information technology, in the widest sense. The fifth edition has been fully updated to take account of new legislation and case law since the previous edition and developments for the future. Each new edition of this book involves a considerable amount of research but this has proved an enjoyable exercise in such a fast-moving, vibrant and important field of study. I hope readers will find the book interesting, stimulating and useful.

Regular updates are available on the book's website: www.booksites.net/bainbridge

I am indebted to those who have helped me in researching for and writing this book. My own students have often asked questions that have driven me to find out more and suggestions from students and practitioners alike have been and always will be most welcome. I would like to thank my wife, Lorraine, for all her help and support and all who have helped with the preparation for and publication of this edition.

I have endeavoured to state the law as it was at 1 September 2003.

David Bainbridge

Computer terms

Algorithm – a structured set of rules or operations defining a logical solution to a problem or a methodology to achieve some end result. An algorithm may be expressed in a flow chart.

Chip – sometimes referred to as 'silicon chip' or, more correctly, integrated circuit. A small piece of semiconducting material, such as silicon, which, with layers of conducting and insulating materials, makes up a micro-electronic circuit incorporating numerous semiconductor devices (such as transistors, resistors and diodes). The contents of some chips are permanently fixed (called ROM chips – Read Only Memory) while the contents of others are volatile and can be changed (called RAM chips – Random Access Memory). Another form of chip is the EPROM – erasable programmable memory. The central processing unit (CPU) of a computer is contained on an integrated circuit; this chip is the 'brains' of the computer and carries out the machine language instructions derived from computer programs.

Compiler – a program which converts a computer program written in a high-level language (source code) into machine language code (object code). The operation is known as compiling and the reverse operation, converting machine language code into a higher level language code, is known as decompiling.

Computer – a programmable machine which can store, retrieve or process data automatically, usually electronically. Section 5(6) of the Civil Evidence Act 1968, now repealed, gave a statutory definition of a computer as 'any device for storing or processing information'.

Computer program – a series of instructions which control or condition the operation of a computer. Programs may be contained permanently in the computer, on integrated circuits, or stored on magnetic disks or tapes, or punched cards, etc. and are loaded into the computer's memory as and when required. A legal definition of 'computer program' is given in the Export of Goods (Control) Order (S.I. 1989 No. 2376) as 'a sequence of instructions to carry out a process in, or convertible into, a form executable by an electronic computer and includes a microprogramme'. However, this definition should not be taken to be of general application. Most statutes having a direct bearing on computer law, such as the Computer Misuse Act 1990, the Copyright, Designs and Patents Act 1988 and the Data Protection Act 1998, do not attempt to define 'computer program'. The United States Copyright Act 1976, as amended, in §101 (the definitions section) defines a computer program as 'a set of statement or instructions to be used directly or indirectly in a computer in order to bring about a certain result'.

Data and database – data comprises information, which may be stored in a computer or on computer storage media such as magnetic disks or CD-ROM. A database is a structured set of data – for example, a list of clients' names and addresses, or a list of employees and their details – typically stored in a computer file. A database is usually associated with computer programs used to store, access, manipulate or retrieve the data contained in it. In terms of copyright and data protection, databases may also include manual systems such as a card index or set of structured paper files. A data warehouse is a massive collection of data, often obtained from various sources and pooled together to form a rich repository of information.

Domain name – the name of a website, being a unique identifier of that website, for example, www.booksites.net. An e-mail address is a personal identifier placed before a website address, for example, anyone@www.booksites.net. Generic top level domains (gTLDs) include .com, .net, .org or .info. There is also a system of country code top level domains (ccTLDs) such as .uk, .de or .fr. Hence, many of the United Kingdom government domains end .gov.uk, such as www.dataprotection.gov.uk, the address of the Information Commissioner. There have been a number of cases where persons have registered domain names similar to the names used by large organisations and then tried to sell them to those organisation for substantial sums of money.

Expert system – a computer system designed to provide advice at, or approaching, the level of an expert. These systems (and other similar systems known as KBS – knowledge-based systems or decision-support systems) usually contain knowledge in a database of rules and facts and details of the internal structure of the knowledge, an inference engine which manipulates and resolves an enquiry from a user, together with a user interface to control interaction with the user including the ability to provide justifications for any advice suggested by the system. The thought of developing expert systems looked very exciting some years ago but, generally, they failed to meet the expectations of researchers in the field. Decision-support and automated decision-taking systems are commonly used though lacking the refinement and sophistication of expert systems.

Facilities management – this is where a contractor takes responsibility for a particular set of operations or functions for the client. It is common in respect of information technology and data processing. For example, a contractor may be appointed to run the client's IT systems. This may require the contractor to develop the IT systems, designing new systems and making recommendations for IT policies and strategies. The facilities management work may be carried out on the client's premises, using the client's equipment and software or it may be carried on off-site at the contractor's premises. Often, when a client first awards a facilities management contract to a contractor, there will be a transfer of staff, equipment and software. Facilities management, sometimes known as outsourcing, is common in relation to the development and maintenance of websites.

Firmware – computer programs, which are permanently 'wired' into the computer, are often referred to as firmware or as being 'hard-wired'. These programs are permanently stored on integrated circuits ('silicon chips').

Fourth-generation language (4GL) – a programming and system development environment. Often used to create and develop applications which include one or more databases. Several databases may be linked together or cross-referenced, being described as relational databases. A fourth-generation language often speeds development time because many routines and procedures (for example, to append and edit records or to print reports) are already built in or may be quickly specified. 4GLs usually have a built-in query language, allowing the user to query the database direct. There is a standard query language known as SQL, sometimes referred to as structured query language.

Hacker – a computer hacker now means a person who gains access to a computer system without permission, usually by guessing or surreptitiously discovering which passwords will allow him access. A hacker may simply inspect the contents of the system he has 'broken into' or may go on to alter or erase information stored in the system or place a computer virus on the system. 'Computer hacker' used to mean a person who was very enthusiastic about computers and who would spend most of his waking hours at a computer terminal.

Hardware – the physical pieces of equipment in a computer system; for example, a computer, printer, monitor and disk drive. Hardware devices usually incorporate software.

High-level language – a programming language which is relatively remote from the computer's machine language. A high-level language statement is equivalent to several machine language instructions. High-level languages often resemble a mixture of written English and conventional mathematical notation and are easier to use for writing and developing computer programs than are low-level languages or machine language. A program in a high-level language is often referred to as a source code program. Examples of high-level languages are BASIC, COBOL, FORTRAN, PASCAL and C.

Low-level language – a programming language which is very close to the computer's machine language. Each instruction in a low-level language has a direct equivalent in machine language.

Machine language – the set of instructions and statements which control the computer directly. Many computer programs are written in high-level languages and have to be converted into machine language code by the use of an interpreter or compiler program. An interpreter produces a temporary translation while a compiler produces a permanent translation into machine language which can be used on its own without the presence of the original program.

Meta-tag – a tag used in HTML (hypertext meta language, the mark up language used to design webpages). Some meta-tags describe the contents of the website and are displayed in a list of 'hits' following a search on the Internet. Others are invisible in normal use, such as keyword meta-tags which are used by search engines to find relevant sites following a search. Sometimes famous names and trade marks have been used without permission in keyword tags for some webpages to increase the likelihood of their being retrieved following a search, with the potential of capturing business or for other deceptive uses.

Object code and source code – a program which must be converted into a different form, such as machine language, before it will operate a computer is known as a source code program. Source code is the version of the program as it is written by the programmer and must be converted, temporarily or permanently, into object code before a computer can execute it. Most commercially available computer programs are distributed in object code form only.

Operating system – a program or set of programs which control and organise the operation of applications programs in addition to managing memory and providing certain facilities such as loading, saving, deleting files, etc. An operating system sets up the computer so that applications programs, such as word processing and spreadsheet programs, can be used. Examples are UNIX and Microsoft Windows.

Shrink-wrap licence – originally, a licence agreement exposed for view under a clear wrapper on the outside of a box containing software in an attempt to draw the licence terms to the attention of the buyer of the copy of the software. This was designed to overcome the problem that it is not possible to introduce new terms into a contract after the contract comes into being. Nowadays, it is more common for the media carrying the software to be in a sealed container carrying a notice to the effect that breaking the seal signifies acceptance of the terms of the licence agreement.

Software – software includes computer programs and data stored in a computer, preparatory design materials and also associated documentation such as user guides and manuals. Software may be obtained 'off-the-shelf', as in the case of popular word processing and spreadsheet packages, or it may be specially written or adapted for a client ('bespoke' software). Applications software is software designed to perform a particular applied function required by the user such as word processing, the preparation of accounts, the design and use of a database or the preparation of a drawing. In contrast, operating system software provides the basic platform upon which applications software can operate.

Spam – unsolicited e-mails, often described as junk e-mails. It is thought that the name derives from the famous Monty Python sketch about Spam (a tinned meat product containing mainly ham, originally an abbreviation of 'spiced ham').

Virus – a program that attaches to other programs and files and is self-replicating and causes damage to computer programs and files. Easily transmitted from computer to computer, often as an e-mail attachment. The damage caused can be considerable with files and programs deleted or modifications made to operating system programs causing a computer to continually crash. Some viruses are specially written to take advantage of weaknesses in operating systems to spread themselves. Some have been spread by automatically forwarding themselves to all the addresses in a person's e-mail address book.

Web-wrap licence – sometimes referred to as a click-wrap licence. A licence agreement used in the context of obtaining software, music or other works in digital form on-line. The usual procedure is for the licensee to signify acceptance of the terms of the licence agreement by clicking on a button on a website at which a copy of the licence agreement is also available for inspection. Normally, the transaction cannot be completed until such positive assent to the licence is given. By these means, the licensor ensures that the licence is incorporated into the contract.

Legal and other terms

Note: legal terms are explained when first introduced in the book but it may help readers who are not lawyers to have a brief glossary of legal and associated terms they may not be familiar with.

Assignment – the transfer of the ownership of a right, for example a copyright. The person transferring the right is known as the assignor and the person acquiring the right is known as the assignee. An assignment need not be in relation to the entire right and may be partial, for example, in respect of certain acts, such as copying but not for the purpose of performing the work in public or rental of copies, or an assignment may be limited geographically, such as the right to make copies and sell those copies in the United Kingdom only.

Brussels and Lugano Conventions and the Brussels Regulation – these Conventions are, in the European Community, largely replaced by a regulation known as the Brussels Regulation govern questions of jurisdiction and the enforcement of judgments in civil and commercial matters. They are important in determining the jurisdiction in which a legal action may be brought and provide for the recognition and enforcement of judgments in the courts of the EC and other EEA countries.

European Court of Human Rights – a judicial body set up under the Council of Europe which hears cases involving rights and freedoms under the European Convention for the Protection of Human Rights and Fundamental Freedoms. Examples include the right to a fair trial, the right to privacy and the right of freedom of expression.

European Economic Area (EEA) – the EEA consists of the countries of the European Community together with Norway, Iceland and Liechtenstein. Some of the European Community legal initiatives apply also to the other EEA countries, for example, the data protection Directive.

European Union (EU) and European Community (EC) – The EU was established by the Treaty of Maastricht 1992. It comprises the 'three pillars', being the European Communities (European Community, formerly the European Economic Community, Euratom and the European Coal and Steel Community), a common foreign and security policy and cooperation in justice and home affairs. In terms of the content of this book, it is the European Community that we are concerned with. EC law has been very influential in the areas of intellectual property rights, e-commerce law and data protection law. There has been significant harmonisation of laws in member states in these fields and there are now also some Community-wide rights, for example, the Community trade mark. At the time of writing there are 15 member states of the EC, being Austria, Belgium, Denmark, Finland, France, Germany, Greece, Ireland (Republic of), Italy, Luxembourg, Netherlands, Portugal, Spain, Sweden and the United Kingdom. A process of enlargement is under way and a number of other countries are likely to join before long (Czech Republic, Estonia, Cyprus, Latvia, Lithuania, Hungary, Malta, Poland, Slovenia and Slovakia).

European Court of Justice (ECJ) and Court of First Instance (CFI) – in the context of the subject matter of this book, the European Court of Justice is important for its judgments in relation to preliminary references where the court is asked to rule upon uncertainties or ambiguities in European Community law, such as where the meaning of a provision in a Directive or Regulation is uncertain. Where such a question arises in a national court, it may (in some cases must) refer the matter to the ECJ. The ECJ's ruling then is applied by the national court to the particular case in hand. The Court of First Instance hears appeals against decisions of the Office for the Harmonisation of the Internal Market (Trade Marks and Designs) (OHIM) in respect of the Community trade mark.

Exhaustion of rights – a doctrine whereby the owner of an intellectual property right such as a patent or a trade mark loses the right to subsequent commercialisation of products subject to the right after those products have been put on the market in the European Community by or with the consent of the owner of the right. For example, the proprietor of a trade mark used for laptop computers might sell 100 of those computers in France. He cannot thereafter use his trade mark rights to stop a third party, who has lawfully come into possession of those particular computers, from further commercialising them such as by importing them into another member state and re-selling them. The doctrine does not apply in relation to products placed for the first time on the market outside the European Community.

Ex parte – a hearing on behalf of someone not a direct party to the action.

Forum non conveniens – a rule of jurisdiction under which a court may decline jurisdiction on the basis that the courts in another jurisdiction are more appropriate to hear the case, because it is more convenient for the parties and it is in the interests of justice.

Injunction – an order of the court, typically requiring a party to refrain from doing something, for example, to stop the defendant continuing to infringe a copyright or disclosing personal data in breach of the Data Protection Act 1998. An important form of injunction is the interim injunction (formerly known as the interlocutory injunction) and which applies until the full trial of the issue at hand. It can be used to prevent continuing damage caused by an alleged wrong, such as an infringement of copyright, until the full trial which might not be recoverable, for example, if the defendant is unlikely to have sufficient assets to pay an award of damages. A balance of convenience is used to determine whether or not to grant an interim injunction. Usually, an interim injunction will not be granted if it would put the defendant out of business.

Licensor and licensee – the licensor grants permission to the licensee allowing him to do certain acts in relation to the subject matter of the licence. For example, the owner of a computer database may grant a licence to an end-user allowing the latter, the licensee, to access the database and retrieve data from it for specified purposes.

Rescission and repudiation – rescission is a remedy whereby a contract is set aside because of misrepresentation. Repudiation occurs where one party to a contract indicates that he will not perform his obligations under the contract. This might occur, for example, where a party repudiates a contract because he considers that the other party is in breach of an important term of the contract entitling the first to repudiate the contract.

Search order – a search order is an order of the court allowing a claimant, in the company of solicitors, to search the defendant's premises for evidence of the alleged wrong and to take copies of or remove alleged infringing material or other evidence as appropriate. Now carefully governed to prevent abuse, its main purpose is the preservation of evidence that might otherwise be destroyed or concealed. Search orders, formerly known as *Anton Piller* orders, are to be distinguished from search warrants under criminal law and other forms of civil search powers, typically provided for by legislation.

Civil procedure terminology

The Civil Procedure Rules 1999 made sweeping changes to civil procedure with the aims of removing differences in procedure between the High Court and the county courts, reducing costs, encouraging the settlement of disputes (with litigation seen as a last resort) and giving the courts more powers of case management. Although a detailed knowledge of civil procedure is not required for an understanding of the material in this book, it might be useful if readers are aware of a few of the changes in terminology which are germane to the subject matter of this book. The new terminology is used throughout the book, even in respect of cases decided or commenced prior to the terminology introduced by the Civil Procedure Rules 1999. Readers should note that the old terminology is still used in other common law jurisdictions, such as the United States and Australia. The changes do not affect Scotland which has a long history of using its own terminology and where, for example, the person bringing an action is known as the pursuer and the person defending is known as the defender.

Terminology under the Civil Procedure Rules 1999 and as used in this book (unless quoted verbatim from a judgment in an older or foreign case)	Equivalent terminology used prior to the coming into force of the Civil Procedure Rules 1999
claimant	plaintiff
claim form	writ or summons
interim injunction	interlocutory injunction
search order	*Anton Piller* order
freezing injunction	*Mareva* injunction

Thus, instead of plaintiff and defendant, it is now claimant and defendant.

Abbreviations

The following list gives the full name of the law reports and other publications for which abbreviated references are used in the text of the book, in line with the usual conventions.

AC	Appeal Cases
AIPC	Australian Intellectual Property Cases
All ER	All England Reports
All ER (D)	All England Reports Digests
ALR	Australian Law Reports
BCLC	Butterworths Company Law Cases
BLR	Building Law Reports
Ch	Chancery (the Chancery Division of the High Court)
CMLR	Common Market Law Reports
Con LR	Construction Law Reports
Const LJ	Construction Law Journal
Cr App R	Criminal Appeal Reports
Crim LR	Criminal Law Review
ECR	European Court Reports
EG	Estates Gazette
EHRR	European Human Rights Reports
EIPR	European Intellectual Property Review
EPOR	European Patent Office Reports
EWCA	England and Wales Court of Appeal cases, suffixed by (Civ) for Civil Division or (Crim) for Criminal Division
EWHC	England and Wales High Court cases, suffixed depending on the Division of the court, for example, (Ch) Chancery Division, (QB) Queen's Bench Division, (TCC) Technology and Construction Court
FCA	Federal Court of Australia
FSR	Fleet Street Reports
HCA	High Court of Australia
HC Deb	Hansard, House of Commons debates
HL Deb	Hansard, House of Lords debates
IRLR	Industrial Relations Law Reports
KB	King's Bench
LEXIS	Computer database of cases and legislation, part of LEXIS-NEXIS service provided in the United Kingdom by LexisNexis Group, part of Reed Elsevier (UK) Ltd
Lloyd's Rep	Lloyd's Reports
Med LR	Medical Law Reports

NI	Northern Ireland Law Reports
QB	Queen's Bench
RPC	Reports of Patent, Design and Trade Mark Cases
RTR	Road Traffic Reports
S Ct	Supreme Court (US)
Sol J	Solicitor's Journal
STC	Simon's Tax Cases
TLR	Times Law Reports
USPQ	United States Patents Quarterly
WLR	Weekly Law Reports

Chapter 1

Introduction

Information technology continues to have an ever-growing impact upon society and the way that society conducts its affairs. Computers have permeated almost every professional, commercial and industrial activity and many organisations would find it difficult, if not impossible, to function without relying heavily on computers. As far as the law is concerned, computers have been a mixed blessing. They have become useful tools, allowing the use of massive legal information retrieval systems, and are of increasing benefit to lawyers in the context of the preparation of documents, administration, accounting and conveyancing and in terms of decision support. Furthermore, the growth of the Internet has brought with it the possibility of accessing a tremendous amount of legal material, including legislation, judgments and *Hansard* and a great deal of foreign legislation and case law. On the other hand, computer technology, by virtue of its unique and volatile nature, has posed novel and complex legal problems. Frequently, the law has been found wanting when dealing with the issues raised by computers and the efforts of the legislators and the courts to come to terms with the technology have sometimes appeared clumsy.

An understanding of the legal issues involved remains of key importance to persons and organisations concerned with information technology, and it is only armed with such understanding that they can satisfactorily address and cater for the legal problems raised by the development and use of computers and computer software. For example, when drawing up a contract for the acquisition of computer hardware or software, the legal implications associated with the technology require careful consideration by lawyers and computer professionals alike. One of the purposes of this book is to bridge the gap between law and computers so that effective legal arrangements can be made for the use and exploitation of computer technology, providing an equitable framework within which the various persons and organisations involved can operate fairly and efficiently. It is hoped that this book can help by indicating various ways of avoiding expensive and lengthy litigation by suggesting suitable legal measures, using the law constructively, as a tool. A practical approach is adopted in the book, giving advice of a proactive and preventative nature. If litigation is inevitable, however, such as when it is suspected that the copyright subsisting in a computer program has been infringed, knowledge of the legal implications should point the way to the most appropriate legal remedies and improve the likelihood of a successful outcome.

Five areas of law of special importance to computer professionals are emphasised in this book: intellectual property (which includes copyright, patents and trade marks), computer contracts, electronic contracts and torts, criminal law and data protection law. Other areas of law are brought into the discussion where appropriate. For example, in negotiating a contract for the writing of software it is important to address the issue of liability for defects and an understanding of the law of negligence is important in this respect. When discussing the practical implications of computer crime the admissibility of computer documents as evidence in a criminal trial must be taken into account.

1

Intellectual property law is important because it is the key to protecting innovation in computer hardware and software in its widest sense. Intellectual property rights, which include copyright, the law of confidence, design rights, trade marks, patents and regulations to protect integrated circuits, are first described in general terms in Chapter 2. These rights provide a basic framework of protection from piracy and plagiarism for computer programs and works created using a computer and works or other information created, stored or transmitted digitally. The enormous scale of computer software piracy resulted in a general recognition of the desirability of effective laws in this area. Special attention is paid to computer software and copyright, the protection of databases, the growing problems associated with electronic publishing and the patentability of software inventions. Intellectual property law has striven to adapt and keep pace with technology to provide the protection necessary but there remain some difficulties which are discussed in detail in Part One, together with suggestions as to how their effects may be mitigated.

Much of the impetus for changes to and the strengthening of intellectual property law comes from the European Community (EC) and the need for harmonised law throughout Europe is very real in the context of rights such as copyright and patent law. This is also true on a wider international scale, resulting from international treaties and agreements, such as the Trade Related Aspects of Intellectual Property Rights, the 'TRIPs' Agreement. As a result, intellectual property law is rapidly changing and there have been numerous European initiatives aimed at dealing with specific issues raised by the use of information technology. A prime example is the European Directive on copyright and related rights in the information society which, *inter alia*, affords specific protection for electronic rights management information (such as a copyright notice and details of acceptable uses of a work made available electronically) and provisions to deal with the circumvention of technological measures designed to protect copyright works. The European and international aspects of intellectual property law are described as appropriate, including likely future changes as they will affect the subsistence and exploitation of rights associated with computer technology.

Part Two of the book is concerned primarily with computer contracts. In terms of the acquisition or modification of computer hardware and software, satisfactory contractual provisions are important to deal with problems which may arise both during the performance of the contract and subsequently. A well considered contract can provide effective machinery for determining responsibilities and resolving disputes without recourse to the courts. The special nature of contracts for the writing of computer software (bespoke software) or for the purchase of software 'off-the-shelf' is discussed together with a description of the implications of licensing and maintenance agreements and the scope and effectiveness of statutory controls on such agreements. Other forms of contractual agreements include 'shrink-wrap' licences and 'web-click' licences and the legal nature of these licences is still not entirely beyond doubt. More lately, website development contracts and website maintenance contracts have come to the fore and raise particular issues. The utility and content of terms in various forms of licence agreements and related contractual agreements are analysed and described in the context of computer contracts.

Electronic contracting is an area that has become very important and is now a settled and major way of doing business, after the initial dot.com euphoria. It is also an area that has attracted significant legislation dealing with issues such as consumer protection and the admissibility of electronic signatures. A number of European Directives have been instrumental in shaping this area of law in Europe and, certainly in the United Kingdom, the push is to facilitate this form of contracting and also in terms of other forms of doing business, such as e-conveyancing and the submission of forms and documents electronically. Another important issue concerns the liability of service providers in the information society, for example, in respect of any illegal material passing through or made available through their services. Applicable law and jurisdiction are also important and there are Regulations and Conventions that provide the rules for determining both of these aspects within Europe but, elsewhere, the position is variable. Liability for electronic torts, for example, defamation on the Internet is also considered in Part Three of the book, which covers electronic contracts and torts.

Computer crime is dealt with in Part Four. It is a major concern to computer professionals, especially when the high incidence of computer-related crime is considered and related to the apparently poor security record of computer systems. At one time, the criminal law was perceived by many computer professionals and financial institutions as lacking teeth and being largely ineffective in the face of some very worrying threats and dangers which could seriously compromise the security of computer systems and undermine confidence in the use of computer technology. Activities which attracted a great deal of attention were hacking (that is, gaining access to a computer system without permission), computer fraud and damaging or erasing computer programs or data. The spread of computer viruses has been alarming and relatively few organisations running large computer systems can claim to have been unaffected. The Computer Misuse Act 1990 was enacted specifically to deal with these problems and to tighten up the law in other areas where computer crime was involved. Three offences were created by the Act and these are described in detail together with the related practical issues in Part Three. Other areas of law which are still useful in the fight against computer crime are also discussed such as the law of conspiracy to defraud, theft and blackmail.

The development of information technology continues to bring problems that have spurred on legislative activity to create new criminal laws or to strengthen existing ones. An example of the former is the introduction of a criminal offence of grooming in chat rooms (contacting vulnerable young people with a view to meeting them for sexual motives). The penalties for child pornography offences have been significantly increased and laws introduced to tackle the problems of noisy neighbours and stalkers have their application in the virtual world also, for example, in the case of threatening e-mails. Jurisdictional issues are also discussed, bearing in mind the international nature of some computer crime, and sentencing practice and guidelines are described where they have been established by the courts.

Part Five deals with privacy and computer data and, in particular, with the provisions of the Data Protection Act 1998 and subsequent developments. It imposes considerable regulation on the processing of personal data on those who decide the means and purposes of the processing (data controllers). The 1998 Act marked a significant change in data protection law in the United Kingdom and gave individuals more rights than they had under the previous legislation, the Data Protection Act 1984; and the rights that individuals had under that Act have been enhanced. As well as a right of access, individuals have rights to prevent processing of personal data relating to them in certain circumstances, and rights in respect of automated decision taking, for example, where computer software is used to make decisions as to whether the individual will be given credit, or other decisions which significantly affect the individual. Data controllers also have to provide individuals with more information than was previously the case. It is obviously important for organisations and individuals processing personal data to know how the new data protection law impacts upon their processing activity, especially as there are a number of criminal penalties in the Act, and the Information Commissioner (previously known as the Data Protection Registrar, then the Data Protection Commissioner) has strong powers of enforcement. A further issue is that the new law, which is the United Kingdom's response to the EC Directive on data protection, has particular provisions to deal with transfers of personal data to countries outside the European Economic Area which do not have an adequate level of protection for personal data. Particular controls have also been brought in to deal with the right to privacy in respect of public telecommunications systems to give individuals rights including in respect of 'cold-calling', 'junk faxes' and capture of telephone numbers. This will soon be extended to other forms of electronic communications such as by e-mail and the Internet in compliance with the EC Directive on privacy and electronic communications.

Data protection is an area where good security is vitally important and obligations are placed on data controllers and those who process data for them such as a computer bureau or company providing information technology facilities management. Indeed, a common thread running throughout the subject matter of this book is the need for good security and good housekeeping systems, the application of which will prevent or minimise many of the legal problems which can result from the use of information technology.

Although the five main areas covered in this book appear to be quite distinct, it should be noted that there is considerable overlap. Contractual provisions can affect copyright issues and vice versa. Computer hackers can interfere with information which is confidential and which may be subject to copyright protection; additionally, hackers can cause difficulties for the owners and managers of computer systems with respect to their responsibilities and duties under the Data Protection Act 1998. There are clear links between electronic contracting and intellectual property and data protection. For example, a commercial website might contain material which infringes copyright and the capture of personal data from a person visiting the site has data protection implications. Employees, working under a contract of employment, may commit computer fraud, commit offences under data protection law and make pirate copies of computer programs, thereby infringing copyright, and so on.

A common theme in this book is the manner in which computer technology affects relationships between individuals in terms of rights and duties. Intellectual property endows rights on the owners of works of copyright or proprietors of patents to exploit their works or inventions while imposing a correlative duty on others not to do certain acts in relation to the subject matter of the rights. Contracts, whether conventional or electronic, are all about reciprocal rights and duties. The criminal law governing computer misuse imperfectly provides rights to computer owners not to have certain acts carried out in relation to the hardware or software while punishing those who fail in their duty to abide by this arm of criminal law. Data protection law imposes obligations on data users and grants rights to individuals who have their personal data stored on computer by others. Thus, an employed computer programmer has a duty not to copy his employer's software without permission, and has duties and rights flowing from his contract of employment. He has a duty not to engage in computer hacking, fraud or similar activities and a right to process personal data stored on his employer's computer in accordance with his contract of employment.

Another theme of a more practical nature is that this book demonstrates the importance of organisations developing policies with respect to the use of computer technology. For example, systems of auditing should be drawn up to check for unauthorised software, to check for computer viruses and fraud, and to verify that the use of personal data is lawful and in accordance with data protection law. Electronic commercial websites need to have clear and accessible terms and conditions of use and privacy policies, providing a good measure of transparency for persons visiting the sites. Policies and procedures should also be drawn up to deal with the acquisition and use of computer software, and educating users and employees should be a priority. Effective and responsible use of computer technology can only come through an understanding of the legal setting in which it takes place.

Checklists, flow charts and tables are included in this book at appropriate places to help with the identification and summarisation of the legal position and to give practical suggestions as to how the effects of the law's shortcomings may be overcome or reduced. In line with standard legislative practice, as confirmed by section 6 of the Interpretation Act 1978, the masculine form, used throughout this book, should be taken to include the feminine form unless the contrary is stated.

PART ONE

Computers and intellectual property

This part deals with the branch of law known as 'intellectual property', which includes copyright law, patent law, trade marks, designs and related areas. The rights associated with intellectual property are of immense importance to those involved in the development, exploitation and use of computer hardware and software, and information technology generally. Legal remedies are available against those who unfairly seek to take advantage of the efforts and investment of someone else. However, the law strives to balance competing interests and the rights given by intellectual property law are not absolute.

Copyright law protects computer programs, databases and other works created using computers or stored in computers. Amending legislation passed in 1985 made it clear that computer programs were protected by copyright law and the current legislation, the Copyright, Designs and Patents Act 1988, confirms that computer programs, preparatory design material for computer programs and databases are literary works for copyright purposes. This Act also uses wide and flexible definitions to make sure, hopefully, that future technological development will not defeat copyright protection.

The law of confidence is a very useful supplement to other areas of intellectual property law and is particularly important in the context of research and development and in matters relating to employees, consultants and freelance workers.

New forms of computer hardware, large or small, usually fall within the province of patent law. Computer programs, as such, are specifically excluded from the grant of a patent but it appears that a program can still be part of a patent application if there is some technical effect which is more than just a software implementation of 'mental steps' or methods of doing business. As a patent is generally considered to be a more desirable form of intellectual property than copyright, there have been numerous attempts to protect computer programs, algorithms and other software inventions by patent law, meeting with varying degrees of success.

Trade mark law, the law of passing off and design law are very important in terms of the commercial exploitation of products, including computer hardware and software. Integrated circuits have their own form of protection by virtue of regulations passed in 1989 which apply an amended form of the design right to semiconductor products.

Chapter 2

Overview of intellectual property rights

Introduction

'Intellectual property' is the name given to legal rights which protect creative works, inventions and commercial goodwill. Basically, intellectual property rights are designed to provide remedies against those who steal the fruits of another person's ideas or work. For example, if a person writes a novel, a piece of music or a computer program, he will be able to take legal action to obtain an injunction and/or damages against anyone who copies the novel, music or program without his permission. In view of the large investment required to finance research, design and development in respect of computer hardware and software, these intellectual property rights are of crucial importance to the computer world. Without such protection, there would be little incentive to invest in the development of new products.

What are these intellectual property rights? Some will sound familiar – for example, *copyright, patents* and *trade marks* – while others will be less familiar – for example, the *law of confidence, design rights* and *passing off*. The scope of these rights differs but sometimes overlaps. Different rights may be appropriate at different times during the lifespan of a product from inception through development to marketing and subsequent modification and updating. Sometimes infringement of intellectual property rights gives rise to criminal penalties (described in Part Four) but, primarily, this area of law falls within the bounds of civil law and it is the civil law with which this part of the book is concerned. At this stage, by way of introduction, it will be useful to describe briefly the various intellectual property rights.

Copyright law

As its name suggests, copyright protects works from being copied without permission. Copyright goes beyond mere copying, however, and extends to other activities such as making an adaptation of the work in question, performing or showing the work in public, broadcasting the work and dealing with infringing copies of the work. The types of works protected by copyright are literary works (including computer programs, preparatory design material for computer programs and databases), dramatic, musical and artistic works, sound recordings, films, broadcasts, cable programmes and typographical arrangements of published editions. Copyright protection has a long duration, the general yardstick being the life of the author (usually, the creator of the work) plus 70 years or, depending on the type of work, 50 or 70 years from the end of the year during which the work was created or published. The major attractions of copyright as a form of protection are that it is free and that no formalities are required; it is automatic upon the creation of the work in question. Additionally, copyright law is practical in nature and has developed to take account of technological changes and advances. In short, most things, if they have been recorded in some tangible form (for example, by writing or printing or by storing the work on a magnetic disk), are protected by copyright, subject to some basic requirements being satisfied. Copyright law is of vital importance to the computer software industry and to people who prepare, record or transmit all sorts of works (for example, literary works such as books, reports, letters or musical works) using computer technology and to those developing or operating websites. Copyright law is governed by the Copyright, Designs and Patents Act 1988, the main provisions of which came into force on 1 August 1989, and subsequent amendments, together with a wealth of case law.

Until the Copyright and Rights in Database Regulations 1997 came into force on 1 January 1998, databases were protected as compilations, being a form of literary work. Now, there are two forms of protection for databases. Those that are 'intellectual creations' have copyright protection as databases, while databases that are the result of a substantial investment are protected by a 'database right' which is of shorter duration than copyright although, strictly speaking, database right is a unique form of right and not a copyright as such though it has some similarities with copyright. The duration of database right is significantly less than for copyright, the basic term for protection being based on 15 years though modifications to a database can result in a new term of protection arising. In many cases, databases will be subject to both rights.

More changes to copyright law are being made to implement the European Directive on copyright and related rights in the information society, including specific provisions aimed at protecting electronic rights management information, such as the names of the copyright author and owner and details of the permitted uses of the work.

Patent law

Patent law is concerned with new inventions such as a new type of computer hardware, or a new process for use in the manufacture of integrated circuits. For an invention to be protected by a patent an application must be made to the Patent Office, an expensive and lengthy process and, if granted, the patent can be renewed for a total period of up to 20 years. Three routes are open to the potential patentee (though the United Kingdom Patent Office must have sight of the application if it is intended to apply elsewhere first): a United Kingdom patent; a European Patent Convention (EPC) patent applying in respect of three or more of the member states of the Convention; or a Patent Co-operation Treaty (PCT) patent designating some or all of the countries covered by the treaty. The choice of countries in which to obtain protection is obviously of fundamental importance and requires careful planning and timing. The relevant statute dealing with patent law in the United Kingdom is the Patents Act 1977. This Act was passed primarily as a response to the European Patent Convention and the basic requirements for patentability are consequently the same in the United Kingdom as in all other members of the Convention.

To be patentable, an invention must be new, involve an inventive step, be capable of industrial application and not be excluded. Most things which are protected directly by copyright law such as a literary work are excluded from patentability; therefore, a new computer program as such cannot normally be protected by a patent. If there is an associated technical effect, however, a patent may be a possibility. For example, a new computer-controlled industrial process may be patentable even though the inventive step resides in the computer program. A patent is the form of intellectual property *par excellence* giving the nearest thing to an outright monopoly although there are provisions in United Kingdom law and European Community law (and United States law) to prevent abuse of patents and other intellectual property rights.

There is a proposed European Directive which may facilitate the patenting of software inventions if they make a non-obvious technical contribution to the state of the art in a technical field. Some countries, such as the United States, have no specific restrictions for patenting software inventions.

The law of confidence

The law of confidence protects information. Unlike copyright and patent law, the law of confidence is not defined by statute and derives almost entirely from case law. The scope of this branch of intellectual property is considerable and it protects trade secrets, business know-how and information such as lists of clients and contacts, information of a personal nature and even ideas which have not yet been expressed in a tangible form (for example, an idea for a new dramatic play, an idea for a new computer program or a new method of doing business by e-commerce). The law of confidence will protect the contents of many databases. However, the major limitation is that the information concerned must be of a confidential nature and the effectiveness of the law of confidence is largely or completely destroyed if the information concerned falls into the public domain; that is, if it becomes available to the public at large or becomes common knowledge to a particular group of the public such as computer software companies. Nevertheless, the law of confidence can be a useful supplement to copyright and patent law as it can protect ideas before they are sufficiently developed to attract copyright protection or to enable an application for a patent to be made. Being rooted in equity, the law of confidence is very flexible and has proved capable of taking new technological developments in its stride.

The law relating to designs

The statutory provisions covering rights in new designs are complicated. Essentially, there are two types of right: *registered designs* and a *design right* which is not subject to registration. The former is available for designs which are new and have an individual character, the latter being measured by the overall impression it produces on an informed user. For registered designs, a 'design' is the appearance of the whole or a part of a product resulting from the features of, in particular, the lines, contours, colours, shape, texture or materials of the product or its ornamentation. For designs subject to the design right, 'design' means the 'design of any aspect of the shape or configuration (whether external or internal) of the whole or part of an article'. This area of law is complex and this is compounded by the fact that the distinction between the rights is not easy to draw, as there is considerable overlap as regards the rights *inter se* and with respect to copyright law.

The durations of the rights are different, being a maximum of 25 years for registered designs and a maximum of 15 years for the design right (but limited to 10 years of commercial exploitation). These rights in designs might be appropriate for items such as a new design for a computer mouse or a new design of laptop computer, keyboard or printer. Design rights and the exceptions to them also have implications for the manufacturers of spare parts, where the design is dictated by the shape of the article with which the spare part must fit or match, as we shall see. The registered design system is important especially in terms of the design of computer hardware as is, to some extent, the unregistered design right. However, the latter is particularly important in relation to the design of semiconductor products as a version of that right protects the topography or layout of such products. The appropriate statutes are the Registered Designs Act 1949 (as amended) and Part III of the Copyright, Designs and Patents Act 1988. The most significant recent amendment, implementing a European harmonising Directive on registered designs took place on 9 December 2001. This made major changes to the United Kingdom law on registered designs.

Recently, a system of Community-wide design rights has been introduced. This provides for a registered design (registrable at the Office for Harmonisation of the Internal Market (Trade Marks and Designs), (OHIM) based at Alicante in Spain) and an unregistered design right of lesser duration.

Trade marks and passing off

Everyone is familiar with trade marks; they are very common and there are many examples in the computer industry: for example, the Apple logo, the terms 'Microsoft' and 'Adobe Acrobat' and the Dell monogram. Trade marks are often in the form of a word (sometimes stylised) or a symbol or both and registration is provided for by the Trade Marks Act 1994. Marks may be registered in respect of goods or services. To be registrable, the mark must be distinctive and capable of being represented graphically. Trade marks are very important as they become associated with successful products and purchasers will often buy or order goods or services by reference to the mark. Marks such as 'Hoover' and 'Hovis' are examples which have become very closely associated with the products concerned. However, trade marks are in danger of being revoked if they become a generic name (common name) for goods or services as a result of the acts or inactivity of the proprietor. The main purpose of trade mark law is to serve as an indicator of trade origin. Thus business goodwill and reputation is protected but this has a secondary effect of also protecting the buying public from deceptive practices.

A related area of law is passing off. This derives from the common law and gives a right of action against anyone who 'passes off' his goods or services as being those of someone else. If a trader uses a particular name or mark or has a particularly unusual method of doing business, he can obtain legal redress against others who use similar names or marks or business methods, especially if there is a serious possibility that the buying public will be deceived and the trader's business goodwill damaged as a result. The law of passing off is independent of trade mark law and will often be useful where a mark has not been registered as a trade mark. For the law of passing off to be effective, however, the trader concerned must have established a goodwill associated with the name or mark or business method. The agreeable alcoholic drink known as champagne affords an example. The French producers of champagne were able to prevent products called 'Spanish Champagne' and 'Elderflower Champagne' from being marketed under those names. In some respects, the law of passing off is wider than trade mark law where, to be registrable, the mark must conform to the requirements of the Trade Marks Act 1994. There is no such restriction with passing off, which can apply to marks which fall outside the scope of trade mark law and can also apply to other aspects of business and marketing.

Both trade mark law and the law of passing off have proved very important in the context of cybersquatting and the Internet generally, for example, in terms of the territorial scope of infringement of a registered trade mark by placing a similar sign on a webpage and the use of trade marks in hidden meta-tags.

Semiconductor Regulations

Integrated circuits, commonly called 'chips' or 'silicon chips', are protected by virtue of the Design Right (Semiconductor) Regulations 1989 which apply a modified version of the design right to semiconductors. They are given 15 years' maximum protection (15 years from creation or 10 years from commercial exploitation). As with the design right generally, there is no requirement for registration in the United Kingdom and there are a number of similarities with copyright law. It is the 'topography' of the chip which is protected, that is, the patterns fixed in or upon the layers of the semiconductor or the arrangement of the layers of the semiconductor product.

Before looking at each of the intellectual property rights in more detail in the following chapters, Table 2.1 summarises the scope, duration and formalities associated with the various intellectual property rights.

Table 2.1   Intellectual property rights – summary

Right	Types of works protected	Examples with respect to computers	Duration	Formalities (UK only)
Copyright	● Original literary, dramatic, musical or artistic works ● Sound recordings, films, broadcasts or cable programmes ● Typographical arrangement of published editions (Computer programs, preparatory design material for computer programs and databases are literary works)	Computer programs and preparatory design material. Databases, other types of work made using a computer or generated by a computer: eg a weather forecast automatically made by a computer linked to weather satellites or a computer-aided design or music made using a computer. Almost any form of work stored digitally	Generally 70 years from the end of the calendar year during which the author dies for the original works and films. For most of the other works the period is 50 years from a specific event	None Copyright is automatic upon the work being created. However, there are tests for subsistence, such as originality or that the work is the author's own intellectual creation
Patent	New inventions including products and industrial processes	New type of printer or computer, new method of making computer 'chips', software controlled industrial process	Renewable up to a maximum of 20 years	Application to the Patent Office to be placed on the register of patents
Confidence	Almost anything of a confidential nature (whether or not stored on computer)	Idea for a new computer program or for a new invention (prior to patent), secret algorithm, lists of customers, business methods, contents of databases	Until subject matter falls into the 'public domain'	None
Registered designs	New designs, having an individual character through the eyes of the informed observer	The appearance of the whole or a part of a product resulting from the features of, in particular, the lines, contours, colours, shape, texture or materials of the product or its ornamentation: eg notebook computer, mouse, computer peripherals and accessories	Initially 5 years renewable by 5-year periods up to a maximum of 25 years	Registration by application to the Design Registry at the Patent Office Application may also be made for a Community registered design
Design right	Original designs, being any aspect of shape or configuration (external or internal) of the whole or part of an article. Applies to functional and aesthetic designs. Spare parts and surface decoration excluded	CD or DVD storage system (partly), keyboard design, mouse, internal components if not commonplace	15 years from creation or 10 years from first marketing	None – automatic as with copyright
Registered trade marks	Any sign capable of being represented graphically which is capable of distinguishing goods or services of one undertaking from those of other undertakings	'Dell, 'Microsoft', 'Oracle', the Apple logo, 'Adobe Acrobat', 'Netscape'	Initially for 10 years and renewable in 10-year periods indefinitely	Application to the Trade Marks Registry
Passing off	Trade names and marks, product 'get-up' or style	Names of software and get-up around which a reputation associated with goodwill has been acquired	Indefinite as long as the name, get-up or style still associated with goodwill (eg by continued use)	None
Semiconductor Regulations (modified design right)	Topography (patterns or arrangements of layers in 'chips')	New design of integrated circuit	15 years from creation or 10 years from commercial exploitation	None

Note: As far as periods for protection are concerned, for copyright, the design right and the Semiconductor Regulations, these periods are measured from the end of the calendar year during which the relevant event occurred, for example, the creation of the work or the death of the author.

Chapter 3

Copyright basics

Note: in Chapters 3 to 7, unless otherwise stated, section numbers quoted refer to the Copyright, Designs and Patents Act 1988, as amended.

Fundamentals

Copyright protects a wide range of works and has developed enormously since its early beginnings as an important intellectual property right. Copyright has a pragmatic approach and it extends to all manner of works regardless of quality, subject to some basic requirements, which are usually easily satisfied. Since the end of the nineteenth century, tables, compilations and even codebooks have been the subject matter of copyright law. During the twentieth century, copyright has flourished and now includes under its umbrella the following: photographs, films, broadcasts, sound recordings, cable programmes as well as computer programs, preparatory design material for computer programs, databases and works stored in or produced by or with the aid of a computer. The first developments in the twenty-first century were to address issues relating to copyright and neighbouring rights associated with the information society. The practical development of copyright has been supported by the judges who have usually been sympathetic to the principle of protecting the results of a person's skill, effort or judgment. As Mr Justice Peterson said in *University of London Press Ltd* v *University Tutorial Press Ltd* [1916] 2 Ch 601:

> ... what is worth copying is *prima facie* worth protecting.

However, this may go too far and the first work must be the result of skill and judgment. As Pumfrey J said in *Cantor Fitzgerald International* v *Tradition (UK) Ltd* [2000] RPC 95:

> ... it is possible that entirely mechanical labour may be saved by copying something produced by entirely mechanical labour, involving no skill.

Taking a photograph of an object will usually require some degree of skill expended by the photographer even if the object photographed is fairly mundane. Skill may derive from the choice of angle, lighting and positioning of the object. These factors may endow the photograph with sufficient skill in its making to attract copyright protection. However, subsequently reducing the object in the photograph to a simplified outline, for example, as use as a watermark on a webpage, will not result in a new work of copyright as it is unlikely that any of the original aspects of the photograph would be carried through into the watermark and it would be unlikely that the process of creating the watermark would require the necessary skill to make it original for copyright purposes. So it was held by Neuberger J in *Antiquesportfolio.com plc* v *Rodney Fitch & Co Ltd* [2001] FSR 23.

Copyright is declared to subsist (that is, 'exist') in the following works by virtue of section 1 of the Copyright, Designs and Patents Act 1988:

(a) original literary, dramatic, musical or artistic works,

(b) sound recordings, films, broadcasts or cable programmes, and

(c) the typographical arrangement of published editions

providing that the requirements for qualification are met: for example, that the author of an original literary work is a British citizen or has certain other nationality or residential qualifications, or that the work was first published in the United Kingdom.

The first category of works is expressed as being original. This does not mean that the work must be unique or special in any way. It is sufficient that the work is the result of the skill or judgment on the part of the creator of the work and that it has not been copied from another work. In other words, it has *originated* from its creator. For one of these original works, the test is qualified and for copyright databases, they are required to be the author's own intellectual creation, as discussed in more detail in Chapter 5. Technically, this should also be the test for computer programs as stated in the European Directive on the legal protection of computer programs, but the United Kingdom did not alter the Copyright, Designs and Patents Act 1988 to that effect when implementing that Directive.

The owner of the copyright in a work is then given the exclusive right to do certain specified *restricted acts* in relation to the work, described below. It is important to appreciate that copyright is a property right and it can be dealt with just as any other form of property. The owner of a copyright is usually the author of the work (the person creating it), except when the work is made by an employee in the course of his employment, in which case his employer will be the first owner, unless otherwise agreed (section 11). There are other exceptions to the basic rule, such as in the case of Crown copyright. The Copyright, Designs and Patents Act 1988 usually refers to the creator of a work as the 'author' of the work, thus a person writing a piece of music is the author of the music and a photographer is the author of his photographs. For sound recordings and computer-generated works, the author is the person who makes the arrangements necessary for the making or creation of the work (section 9), so the author of a report produced automatically by a computer will normally be the person who operates the computer or who manages the computer facilities. In many cases, ownership, as distinct from authorship, will reside with an employer.

The identity of the author is important because the duration of copyright in original literary, dramatic, musical or artistic works (not being computer-generated) is determined by the life of the author, irrespective of ownership. The copyright in such works lasts for 70 years from the end of the calendar year during which the author dies (increased from the life of the author plus 50 years as a result of a European Community Directive on the term of copyright, OJ [1993] L290/9). The duration of copyright in films is now also based on life plus 70 years, measured from the end of the calendar year during which the last of a number of persons, including the principal director, involved in the creation of the film, dies.

The United States also increased its term of protection to 'life plus 70 years' by the Copyright Term Extension Act 1998 but this was subject to a challenge that, in terms of published and existing works, it was unconstitutional as being contrary to the First Amendment (free speech) and the Copyright Clause in Article I, section 8 cl 8 of the Constitution which states that Congress has the power, *inter alia*, to secure to authors for *limited times* the exclusive right to their writing. The Supreme Court rejected these claims in *Eldred v Ashcroft, Attorney General*, 537 US, 15 January 2003. The increase of 20 years' protection for existing works did not prevent the protection being for *limited times* and as the First Amendment and Copyright Clause were adopted closely together this indicates that the view of those framing these provisions was that the limited monopoly provided by copyright was compatible with free speech principles.

If the work is one of joint authorship (a collaborative work in which the contribution of each author is not distinct from that of the other authors), as many computer programs and other computer works will be, the 70-year period starts to run from the end of the calendar year during which the last surviving author dies. This generosity in terms of duration of copyright might seem disproportionate in a fast-moving technology but can be justified on the basis that, generally, copyright does not give a true monopoly. A rough and ready rule of thumb is that copyright does not protect ideas, merely the expression of an idea. For other works, except films where the 70-year period is used, the duration is set at 50 years from the end of the calendar year during which the work was created, broadcast, included in a cable programme service or released, as appropriate. There are exceptions and copyright in typographical arrangements and certain commercially exploited artistic works lasts for 25 years only (other exceptions apply to Crown copyright and Parliamentary copyright). The author's identity may also be important for determining whether a work qualifies for protection. It should be noted, however, that there are two international conventions affording, in effect, reciprocal protection to foreign works of copyright and which also protect United Kingdom works in other countries. In general terms, nationals of other convention countries are afforded the same rights as those of the country in question (see Chapter 14).

The acts restricted by copyright, and which only the owner of the copyright has the right to do or authorise, are set out in section 16. They are:

(a)   to copy the work;
(b)   to issue copies of the work to the public;
(ba) to rent or lend the work to the public;
(c)   to perform, show or play the work in public;
(d)   to broadcast the work or include it in a cable programme service;
(e)   to make an adaptation of the work or do any of the above in relation to an adaptation.

Section 16(ba) was inserted by the Copyright and Related Rights Regulations 1996 to comply with a European Community Directive on rental right and lending right (OJ [1992] L346/61). Section 16(b) was also modified to cover all forms of copyright work.

Infringement

A person infringes the copyright in a work if he does one of these restricted acts or authorises another to do one of the acts in relation to a substantial part of the work without the permission of the copyright owner and such a person may be sued by the copyright owner (or an exclusive licensee of the owner) for the infringement.

The similarities and differences between the first work and the alleged infringement may be important in finding whether the defendant had copied the first work (copying is one form of infringement though all forms of infringement require that some use has been made of the first work). Substantiality is a question of fact but once it is accepted that the defendant's work was copied from that of the claimant, it is no longer relevant to consider the differences between the two works (to do so would be to revisit the question of whether copying had taken place). The question then becomes whether the sum of the parts copied represent a substantial part of the claimant's work. A visual comparison of the two works at this stage is unnecessary and may be misleading. The majority of the House of Lords judges took this view in *Designers Guild Ltd* v *Russell Williams (Textiles) Ltd* [2001] FSR 11, a leading case on copyright infringement set in the context of artistic works, though of wider application. However, Lord Scott of Foscote distinguished a case of altered copying where he suggested that the similarities between the two works could help determine which side of the dividing line, between permissible borrowing of an idea and impermissible piracy, the activity fell, accepting that it is not an infringement of copyright to borrow an idea.

There are certain exceptions to infringement called permitted acts contained in sections 28–77. Copyright is not infringed by 'fair dealing' with a work for the purposes of research or private study or for criticism, review or news reporting or any of the other limited exceptions concerning, *inter alia*, educational and library use. Another permitted act is time shifting, that is recording a broadcast or cable programme for viewing at a more convenient time. This can be relevant in the context of the Internet as there is some authority for the view that information available on a website is classed as a cable programme. This permitted act only applies where the recording is made for private and domestic use and an Internet café which operated a CD burning service for its customers in return for payment of a fee could not rely on the defence (*Sony Music Entertainment (UK) Ltd* v *Easyinternetcafe Ltd* [2003] EWHC 62 (Ch)). This case also confirms that liability for infringement applies even if the person responsible for copying was not aware the work being copied was protected by copyright. The defendant's employees were instructed not to look at the content of the downloaded files they copied on to CDs for customers.

There are also some important exceptions relating to computer programs introduced by the Copyright (Computer Programs) Regulations 1992. These allow for a 'decompilation exception', making back-up copies of computer programs and other lawful uses of a program including error correction. Further specific exceptions relate to databases. There are additional ways of infringing copyright, known as secondary infringements, and there are also some criminal offences which now carry a maximum penalty of a term of imprisonment not exceeding ten years and/or a fine. In broad terms, the secondary infringements and some of the criminal offences apply where the infringer has been dealing commercially with infringing copies, such as by importing, distributing or selling them, and, unlike the primary infringing acts described above, some form of knowledge is required; that is, that the person involved knew or had reason to believe that he was dealing with infringing copies. The criminal offences under copyright law, some of which closely follow the secondary infringements are dealt with separately in Part Four of this book.

Remedies for infringement

If the owner of a copyright successfully sues a person for infringement of that copyright, there are several remedies available. In particular, an injunction, damages or an account of profits might be appropriate and these are provided for by section 96. The basic purpose of an award of damages is to put the claimant in the position he would have been in but for the infringement, as far as a money award can do that. The award should reflect the natural and foreseeable consequences of the infringing acts. Copyright damages may be assessed as the estimated loss resulting from the infringement: for example, the licence fee or royalties that the copyright owner would have expected to receive had he given permission for the acts complained of. For example, if a computer software pirate makes and sells 100 copies of an item of computer software each valued at £500, the copyright owner might expect damages equivalent to a 10 per cent royalty: that is, 10% x 100 x £500 = £5000. However, it is for the claimant to show that he would have made all the sales made by the infringer.

Damages are not available if the defendant did not know or had no reason to believe that the work was protected by copyright. The meaning of 'having no reason to believe that copyright subsisted in a work' requires an objective test: that is, whether the reasonable person, having knowledge of the facts known to the defendant, would have believed that copyright subsisted in the work (see *LA Gear Inc* v *Hi-Tec Sports plc* [1992] FSR 121). An infringer of computer software copyright cannot escape an award of damages merely by turning a blind eye to the question of whether the software is protected by copyright or being indifferent to the possibility. In any case, an account of profits, as an alternative to damages, may be available regardless of the defendant's knowledge and could be awarded even where the person infringing copyright has done so innocently. Of course, software piracy can attract criminal penalties also (see Chapter 31).

Injunctions are very important because they prevent continued or anticipated infringement of copyright. An injunction is a court order requiring the defendant to do something or to refrain from doing something. For example, an injunction would be appropriate to stop a computer software pirate continuing to sell unauthorised copies of computer programs. A particularly useful type of injunction is an interim injunction (previously known as an interlocutory injunction). If a person is sued for infringing copyright, it may be a considerable time before the case comes to trial and, in the meantime, significant damage can be done to the copyright owner's business. This is very relevant in the context of a fast-moving technology like computer technology and, to deal with this problem, the court may be willing to accede to a request for an interim injunction pending the full trial. However, an interim injunction will be granted to a claimant only if there is a serious question to be tried and the claim does not appear to the court to be frivolous or vexatious. Additionally, the balance of convenience must be satisfied, meaning that the damage likely to be done to the claimant if the alleged infringement continues is greater than the harm that will be done to the defendant if the injunction is granted (see *NWL Ltd* v *Woods* [1979] 1 WLR 1294). This balance of convenience is of particular importance if the granting or refusal of an interim injunction would have very serious consequences for either party. In any case, an interim injunction will not usually be granted if the payment of damages by the defendant at the full trial would be an adequate remedy and the defendant is likely to have the means to pay, not being a 'man of straw'.

For an interim injunction to be a possibility, the courts used to require that the claimant showed a serious issue to be tried. However, since the case of *Series 5 Software Ltd* v *Clarke* [1996] FSR 273, the courts have been more willing to consider the relative strengths of the parties' cases as they appear at that stage. If there is material before the court to allow the court to assess the strength of the parties' cases, it should be taken into account in deciding whether or not to grant an interim injunction. In *Series 5 Software*, the defendant removed software belonging to the claimant allegedly in order to encourage the latter to make payment owing to the defendant. The injunctions sought were refused but the judge continued an order for the defendant to deliver up any materials he had which belonged to the claimant. If the defendant had any such materials in his possession and failed to deliver them, he would be in contempt of court.

A distinction between an honest and a dishonest trader might be relevant in determining the terms of any interim injunction and any ancillary relief granted. In *Microsoft Corporation* v *Plato Technology Ltd* [1999] FSR 834, the defendant had sold five copies of counterfeit Windows 95 software infringing the claimant's copyright and trade marks. It was accepted that the defendant had no reason to believe that the copies were counterfeit and an interim injunction was granted restraining the defendant from dealing with software which it knew or ought upon reasonable enquiry to know was counterfeit. The defendant was also required to deliver up all copies in its possession which it knew or ought upon reasonable enquiry to know was counterfeit.

Apart from an award of ordinary damages, the courts also have a discretion to award additional damages under section 97(2), having regard to the flagrancy of the infringement and the benefit accruing to the defendant. This is akin to punitive damages though technically different. Additional damages are suitable in cases where normal damages would not be appropriate: for example, where the defendant has blatantly infringed copyright thinking that he can make a profit far in excess of any normal damages he might have to pay. Another possible use for additional damages is where the claimant has not suffered purely economic loss. This might be the case if the infringement concerned some material which the claimant did not want to publish such as the contents of his diary. In *Williams* v *Settle* [1960] 1 WLR 1072, additional damages were considered suitable when a professional photographer, without permission of the copyright owner, supplied the press with a wedding photograph showing a man who had been murdered.

Additional damages may also be appropriate where a normal award of damages still left the defendant in a favourable position, enjoying the fruits of his infringement, especially where those fruits were non-economic and not recoverable on the basis of an account of profits. Furthermore, such damages could be used to deprive a defendant of the benefit of deliberate wrong-doing when they would not be awarded against someone who did the same thing in innocence. In *Nottinghamshire Healthcare National Health Service Trust* v *News Group Newspapers Ltd* [2002] RPC 49 a photograph of a patient at Rampton Hospital was copied without permission and published by the defendant with a sensationalistic article. An award of £450 for ordinary damages was made together with an award for additional damages to bring the overall total up to £10,000. This was justified on the basis that the defendant had reaped a significant economic benefit from publication of a photograph that was obviously 'stolen' and the lack of an apology, together with the degree of upset to the claimant, which had taken over control of Rampton Hospital and been responsible for the medical records from which the copy of the photograph had been taken without permission.

Recently, claimants seem more prepared to ask for additional damages. In relation to computer software, such damages may be relevant in the case of blatant infringement, for example, by deliberately using someone else's specialised computer software to gain a competitive edge over that other person. Another example is where a person deliberately makes use of another person's database of highly sensitive information. It has been confirmed that additional damages may only be awarded alongside ordinary damages and not an account of profits. A claimant has to elect between damages and an account of profits and cannot ask for both.

In addition to the remedies mentioned above, the claimant may apply to the court for an order for the infringing copies to be delivered up to him or for those copies to be destroyed.

Moral rights

Moral rights were a relatively new concept in the United Kingdom when introduced by sections 77–89 of the Copyright, Designs and Patents Act 1988. These rights, which have long been recognised in some European countries, are independent and distinct from ownership of copyright and give the author of a literary, dramatic, musical or artistic work and the director of a film the right:

- to be identified as the author (or director) of the work,
- to object to a derogatory treatment of the work (for example, if someone rewrites a serious play in the form of a farce without the author's permission), and
- to not have a work falsely attributed to him (this right previously existed under the Copyright Act 1956).

There is also a right to privacy with respect to photographs and films made for private and domestic purposes.

These moral rights last as long as the copyright in the work, with the exception of the false attribution right which lasts for 20 years after the death of the person falsely attributed. The rights are designed to give the creator of the work, who may no longer be the owner of the copyright itself, a degree of control and recognition in respect of the work. By section 103, infringements of moral rights are treated as a breach of statutory duty, injunctions and damages being appropriate remedies. Strangely, there is no provision for additional damages and, presumably, damages will be based on economic loss only. However, the claimant may also have a claim in defamation, particularly in respect of a derogatory treatment of his work or the false attribution of a work.

As computer programs are considered to be literary works, it is surprising that the first two of the moral rights mentioned above are stated not to apply to computer programs. Less surprisingly, nor do they apply to computer-generated works. These exceptions may be justified because of the commercial nature of most computer programs and other software and because of the need to prevent ex-employees attempting to interfere with any future changes to the software they had previously developed. Problems could arise if computer programmers and systems analysts demanded to be recognised as authors, as many computer programs are the result of teamwork, involving many individuals, both in the development of the original program and in subsequent alterations and upgrades.

Moral rights will exist in relation to other forms of original works created using a computer, such as a report or computer-aided design, and in respect of many other types of work stored in a computer in digital form, for example, in a database of artistic works. However, employee-created works are excepted in relation to things done by or with the licence of the copyright owner and the author must positively assert his moral right to be identified. Furthermore, an author may waive his moral rights.

Dealing with copyright

We have already seen that authorship and ownership of copyright are two distinct concepts and that, normally, an employee writing a computer program will be the author of that program but his employer will own the copyright unless they agree otherwise. Frequently, the owner of a copyright will want to use a third party to exploit that copyright for him. It might be more attractive financially to use a publisher to market and sell copies of the work, because the latter will have the marketing expertise and distribution facilities necessary to sell the work in large numbers. The usual way is for the copyright owner to grant a licence to the publisher. In terms of copyright, a licence is a permission to do one or more of the acts restricted by copyright and licences are usually contractual in nature: that is, the publisher will pay a licence fee or royalties in return for the permission. In many cases, the licence will be exclusive, which means that permission will be granted to one publisher only. In the case of marketing computer programs, the copyright owner might grant an exclusive licence to a software publisher who will then grant non-exclusive user licences to 'purchasers' of copies of the program. The users will need licences because loading a program onto a hard disk or into computer memory involves making a copy or adaptation of the program, acts restricted by the copyright. By section 92(1), an exclusive licence must be in writing and signed by or on behalf of the owner of the copyright. No formalities are required for non-exclusive licences but it is sensible to make a written record of the agreement.

Non-exclusive software licences are very common and are used where the copyright owner wishes to retain ownership but wants to allow several or many other persons to use the software. This is the way a great deal of 'off-the-shelf' software is made available. Each person acquiring a copy of the software obtains a licence permitting certain uses. Of course, a licence is only required in as much as the use of software is controlled by copyright but the agreement will include additional terms dealing with other issues such as liability for defects.

Alternatively, the owner of a copyright may *assign* the copyright (that is, transfer ownership of the copyright) to another person and an assignment must be distinguished from a licence. With an assignment, the copyright owner transfers all or part of his rights to another person, whereas a licence is a permission given to another person authorising him to do certain specified things in relation to the copyright work. Furthermore, ownership in copyright can pass under a will or by way of intestacy or as a result of the bankruptcy of the copyright owner. Moral rights cannot be assigned (section 94) but will pass under a will or by way of intestacy (by section 95).

Assignments and exclusive licences, to be effective at law, must be in writing and signed by or on behalf of the assignor (person making the assignment) or licensor (person granting the licence) as the case may be. If these requirements are not complied with the courts may be prepared to use the concept of beneficial ownership or to imply a licence giving the acquirer the right to do what, in the view of the court, was intended by the parties. Nevertheless, it is obviously more satisfactory to make sure that the formalities are complied with.

It is possible to deal with a future copyright; that is, copyright in a work yet to be created (section 91). The prospective owner can assign the future copyright or grant licences in respect of it. These provisions are useful where a self-employed consultant is engaged to create a new item of software. The agreement under which he is engaged should contain a term to the effect that he assigns the future copyright in any work created under the agreement to the person engaging him. This agreement must then be signed by or on behalf of the consultant and, on the work coming into existence, the assignment will automatically take effect. This simple expedient is very important in the software industry, where many persons are self-employed or freelance, and can prevent a bitter dispute later as to ownership of copyright.

Chapter 4

Computer software and copyright

Introduction

Now that the basic principles of copyright law have been described in Chapter 3, the relevance of copyright to computer software can be examined. There are two main areas: the first concerns the protection of computer software and, in particular, computer programs and databases from unauthorised copying; the second concerns works of various types which have been created *by* or *with the aid of* a computer or are stored and accessed or made available electronically. This chapter concentrates on computer programs and the following chapters are concerned with databases, computer-generated works and electronic publishing, and the recent developments in copyright in the information society.

Copyright law protects computer software, whether it be programs, databases, computer files or printed documentation, whereas patent law protects new and inventive forms of computer hardware bearing in mind, of course, that items of hardware often incorporate software. In some cases, software inventions may be patentable providing they produce a technical effect and make a technical contribution to the relevant state of the art. The distinction between hardware and software is sometimes difficult to determine. For example, does a 'dongle' contain a computer program? A dongle is a device which was popular some time ago and which was inserted into a computer port enabling certain programs to be used. Its prime purpose was as a form of copy protection, limiting the use of a program to one computer at any given time. In the Australian case of *Dyason* v *Autodesk Inc* (1990) 96 ALR 57 it was held that the dongle together with the program used to write digital information into it were, in combination, a computer program for copyright purposes. Some confusion as to whether a single word in a computer program was itself a program was resolved in the Federal Court of Australia which held that a single statement in a high-level programming language was not a program but was merely the cipher or key to access a set of instructions: *Powerflux* v *Data Access Corp* [1997] FCA 490. In the United Kingdom there has been some judicial confusion as to whether 'hard-wiring' a computer program in a ROM chip allows the algorithm it represents to be patented (see *Gale's Application* [1991] RPC 305).

Although it is clear that computer software is protected by copyright, current issues concern the scope of that protection and the need to preserve a balance between the rights of the copyright owner and the interests of competitors and what should constitute fair use of existing software. It has already been felt necessary to amend the 1988 Act to achieve that balance (as part of the wider goal of harmonising copyright protection for computer software throughout the European Community). Although the legal protection of computer software has been radically improved, there remain areas of doubt and uncertainty even now that there have been a number of important High Court cases on the infringement of copyright in computer programs. An awareness of these areas will be important for those developing, using and exploiting computer software.

Computer programs

The term 'computer software' includes computer programs, databases, computer files, preparatory design materials, all manner of works stored digitally to be accessed by computer and associated printed documentation such as manuals for users. There has never been any difficulty with regard to printed materials as these have been and continue to be protected by copyright. The protection of computer programs has been less certain and before 1985 it was unclear whether they were protected by copyright. One view was that listings of source code programs were protected as literary works by analogy with codebooks or because they resembled written English to some extent. On the whole, the courts appeared to be sympathetic towards the notion that computer programs were protected. For example, in *Sega Enterprises Ltd* v *Richards* [1983] FSR 73, which concerned alleged copies of the computer game 'FROGGER' (the object of which was to get a frog across a busy road without it being squashed by a lorry), the trial judge was of the opinion that the source code program was protected by copyright and the object code program was protected indirectly as an adaptation of the source code version. However, this was an interim hearing only and the case did not go to a full trial, so the point was not finally decided. Indeed, cases involving copying of computer programs did not seem to get beyond the interim stage, probably because the relief granted by the court at that stage, usually an interim injunction, was sufficient to satisfy the claimant.

There remained serious doubts about computer programs in object code form and these doubts were brought to a head by the Australian case of *Apple Computer Inc* v *Computer Edge Pty Ltd* [1984] FSR 481. In that case, the defendant imported clones of the Apple II personal computer into Australia. His initial claim that his computers, appropriately called 'Wombats', did not contain the Apple operating system and start-up programs was rejected when it was discovered that the programs in the 'Wombat' chips had the names of the Apple programmers embedded within them. The defendant's second line of defence was that the programs were not literary works in the copyright sense, being object code programs. This was accepted by the trial judge but rejected by a 2:1 majority in the Federal Court of New South Wales. However, this decision was unsatisfactory in many respects and the Australian Parliament acted very quickly, passing amending legislation (the Australian Copyright Amendment Act 1984) to put the matter beyond doubt. This did little to assuage concerns in the United Kingdom; it merely highlighted the uncertainty concerning object code programs.

Following considerable pressure from the computer industry, notably from the lobby group FAST (the Federation Against Software Theft), the Copyright (Computer Software) Amendment Act 1985 was passed which made it clear that computer programs were protected as literary works. The Copyright, Designs and Patents Act 1988 follows this approach and places computer programs firmly within the literary work category for the purposes of copyright (section 3) and, now, also databases. It also protects implicitly other forms of works created using a computer or stored in or on computer media. Neither the word 'computer' nor the term 'computer program' is defined in the Act. This is sensible in view of the rapid rate of change in the computer industry as attempts to offer precise definitions would probably prove to be unduly restrictive in the light of technological development. It is better to allow the judges to use their discretion sensibly, permitting a degree of flexibility in this respect. There should be no difficulty in a court deciding that copyright subsists in a program written in assembler language or in a computer program in object code form.

On a European Community scale, it has proved necessary to spell out in detail the scope of exceptions to copyright infringement in relation to computer programs and, to this end, the 1988 Act was amended by the Copyright (Computer Programs) Regulations 1992, as described later in this chapter. The Regulations also specifically place preparatory design material for computer programs in the literary work category. Concerns about the protection of databases by copyright law led to another European initiative, resulting in the Directive on the legal protection of databases (OJ [1996] L77/20). This was implemented in the United Kingdom by the Copyright and Rights in Databases Regulations 1997 which further modified the 1988 Act, adding databases to the literary works category and also created a new database right. Databases are considered in more depth in the following chapter.

Originality and storage

By section 3 of the Copyright, Designs and Patents Act 1988, for copyright to subsist in a computer program it must be 'original' and it must be 'recorded'. For the meaning of 'original', in the main we must turn to case law prior to the Act and section 172(3) confirms that this practice is permissible (this is standard procedure unless it is clear that previous cases no longer represent the law). The requirement of originality is not an onerous one and does not mean that the computer program must be novel or unique in some respect. It merely means that the program has been the result of a modest amount of skill, labour or judgment and that it 'originates from the author' (Peterson J in *University of London Press Ltd* v *University Tutorial Press Ltd* [1916] 2 Ch 601). Compilations of existing information as in a street directory have been afforded copyright protection. In *Macmillan & Co Ltd* v *K & J Cooper* (1923) 40 TLR 186, it was held that, although many compilations have nothing original in their parts, the sum total of a compilation may be original for the purposes of copyright. However, the courts will draw a line somewhere and in *G A Cramp & Sons Ltd* v *Frank Smythson Ltd* [1944] AC 329, a diary which contained the usual information contained in diaries, such as a calendar, tables of weights and measures, postal information and the like, failed to attract copyright protection. The reason given was that the commonplace nature of the information left no room for taste or judgment in the selection and organisation of the material. In the light of these cases, virtually all computer programs will meet the requirement of originality, even if the program comprises little more than an arrangement of commonly used sub-routines, because the selection and arrangement of those sub-routines requires a reasonable amount of skill and expertise.

The European Directive on the legal protection of computer programs required that the test for subsistence of copyright in a computer program was that it was the author's own intellectual creation. Arguably, this is a higher standard than that of originality previously required by United Kingdom law but the test in the Directive was not used in the Copyright, Designs and Patents Act 1988 when it was amended in the light of the Directive. By way of contrast, the test of the author's own intellectual creation in the European Directive on the legal protection of databases was used in respect of databases when that Directive was transposed into the 1988 Act.

In the United States, the expenditure of labour alone is unlikely, without some intellectual contribution, to confer copyright protection on a work (the 'sweat of the brow' doctrine put to rest in the Supreme Court in *Feist Publications Inc v Rural Telephone Service Co Inc* (1991) 111 S Ct 1282; discussed in more detail in the following chapter). It is difficult to conceive of a computer program which does not involve skill and judgment in its creation, in addition to effort. However, standards vary internationally and in Germany it was said that a computer program, to be protected by copyright, must be the result of creative achievement exceeding the average skills used in the development of computer programs (*Sudwestdeutsche Inkasse KG v Bappert und Burker Computer GmbH* (1985) Case 5483, BGHZ94, 276). In other words, a computer program which simply automated an existing process would be unlikely to be the subject of copyright. In the light of the European Community Directive on the legal protection of computer programs, this case must now be viewed as laying down too stringent a test and, indeed, this was confirmed by the Federal Supreme Court of Germany in the *Buchhaltungsprogram* case (unreported) 14 July 1993 which concerned an accounts program.

In the United Kingdom, another requirement for computer programs, and other literary, dramatic and musical works, is that they must be recorded in writing or otherwise (section 3(2)). This has a very wide meaning and 'writing' is defined by section 178 as including:

> ... any form of notation or code, whether by hand or otherwise and regardless of the method by which, or medium in or on which, it is recorded.

Storage of a computer program in a computer memory or on computer storage media such as magnetic disks should present no problems as the above definition in section 178 is sufficiently wide to cover any existing form of storage and any new forms which might be invented in the future. Furthermore, given the spirit of the Act, it is unlikely that the courts will attempt to narrow the concept of 'recording'. It must be noted, however, that the House of Lords has decided that a password held transiently in a computer system was not recorded for the purposes of the Forgery and Counterfeiting Act 1981 (see the discussion of *R v Gold* in Chapter 29). If the only form of existence of a computer program is in a computer's volatile memory, there may be a possibility that, following the *Gold* case, the program will not be considered to be 'recorded'. Nevertheless, because the program will be saved on to a disk or tape before very long, this is unlikely to cause problems in practice. Of course, the program may have been written down by the programmer before entry into the computer or a printout of the program listing may have been taken, in which case the program will be protected anyway. As a matter of interest, the scope of the Copyright (Computer Software) Amendment Act 1985 (now repealed) was possibly wider in that it specifically covered storage in a computer memory.

Preparatory and ancillary materials

Copyright protection extends beyond the computer program itself and will cover written or printed listings of programs, flow charts, specifications and notes. Section 3(1)(c) includes preparatory design material for a computer program in the literary work category. Prior to the Copyright (Computer Programs) Regulations 1992, these materials would generally be protected as literary works although flow charts and diagrams would have been protected as artistic works. The artistic work category of copyright includes paintings, drawings, diagrams, maps, charts and plans which are all protected irrespective of artistic quality. As a result of the Regulations, however, preparatory design materials are deemed to be literary works, irrespective of whether they would have qualified previously as graphic works and, hence, artistic works. In practice, this should not be of any significance although there are some differences in the provisions for literary and artistic works. All these preparatory and other ancillary materials must be original in the sense already discussed. Because copying includes copying by indirect means, it is possible that making an unauthorised copy of a computer program (or screen display) infringes the copyright subsisting in ancillary or preparatory materials in addition to any question of infringement of the program itself or of the screen display.

Of course, manuals and other documentation distributed with computer programs will be protected by copyright, independently of the program itself, as original literary or artistic works, as appropriate.

Restricted acts for computer programs

Of the acts restricted by copyright, three are worthy of special mention as far as computer programs are concerned. These are:

● copying,
● issuing copies to the public, and
● making an adaptation.

All of these restricted acts have a particular meaning which is only partly explained by the language of the Act. Copying and making an adaptation have fairly technical meanings and both of these acts have been extended to take account of computer technology. Copying now has to include electronic copying and also has to countenance the situation where a person copies a computer program but uses a different programming language with the result that the original and the copy bear little, if any, literal similarity when the program listings are compared. If copyright law were unable to control such 'non-literal' copying, it would be too easy to circumvent the protection afforded by copyright. The restricted act of making an adaptation, concerned first of all with translations of literary works and arrangements of musical works, now has to deal with the process of converting source code into object code and vice versa.

Copying

Copying in relation to a literary, dramatic, musical or artistic work means, by section 17(2), reproducing the work in any material form which includes storage in any medium by electronic means: for example, by making a copy of a computer program on a magnetic disk. Additionally, in relation to all forms of copyright work, copying includes making copies which are transient or incidental to some other use of the work (section 17(6)). This implies that the act of loading a computer program into a computer only for the purpose of running the program will be considered to be making a copy of the program, even though this 'copy' will be lost as soon as the computer is switched off. In this way, any unauthorised use of a computer program will infringe the copyright in that program. This is why a licence is required in order to use another person's computer program or database, or indeed, any other work in digital form which will be accessed by computer.

Literal copying

An unauthorised copy of a computer program may be an exact duplicate of such where a disk-to-disk copy is made. The original and copy will be identical. The question of infringement of copyright will be an easy one to deal with and will be limited to an enquiry as to whether the first program is protected by copyright. Almost all computer programs will be subject to copyright as the basic requirements for copyright subsistence usually will be present. As long as the first program is original (in the sense that it originates from its author) and is non-trivial and the qualification provisions are satisfied (or protection is afforded through the international conventions) then the program will be protected. Identical copies of computer programs made without the permission of the copyright owner are, apart from difficulties associated with detection, fairly easy to deal with in terms of the law, both civil and criminal. Software piracy usually falls into this category of copying as does making working copies of computer programs by a licensee in excess of the number permitted by the licence agreement.

Sometimes a person copying a computer program will do further work on the program. This might be to disguise the origin of the program or to improve it, or both. Where this happens, proving copying may be more difficult and requires a consideration of three questions.

- Does copyright subsist in the claimant's program?
- Has the defendant copied parts of the claimant's program?
- Do the parts copied represent a substantial part of the claimant's program?

In practice, the answer to the first question will rarely be in the negative. The second question is more difficult and depends, *inter alia*, on objective similarities and inferences that can be drawn from them. It is further complicated if the same person has been involved in the writing of both programs. The third question, as we have seen, is concerned with the quality of the part taken rather than its overall size relative to the whole. A small but important part of a program will be deemed to be substantial. Indeed, it is arguable that even a tiny part of a computer program could be significant as the program may not operate at all or properly without it! However, in *Cantor Fitzgerald International* v *Tradition (UK) Ltd* [2000] RPC 95, the court held that substantiality must be judged against the program or programs as a whole in the light of the skill and labour expended in the design and coding which went into the piece of code in respect of which the allegation of copying was made. In that case, the defendant admitted copying some 2952 lines of code from the claimant's programs which comprised 77,000 lines of code. The judge found the claimant's case made out in part but Mr Justice Pumfrey went on to say that substantiality was not to be determined by whether the system would work without the part copied nor by the amount of use made of the code in question. These and other issues are considered further in the following important case.

In *IBCOS Computers Ltd* v *Barclays Mercantile Highland Finance Ltd* [1994] FSR 275, one of the defendants, a programmer, wrote a suite of programs and files to handle accounts and payroll for agricultural machinery dealers. He further developed this software for the claimant and when he left the claimant's company, the programmer signed a note agreeing to the fact the company owned the copyright in the software and agreeing not to write competing software for two years. The programmer then wrote another software package, which performed similar functions, for the other defendant. This was not marketed until the two-year period in restraint of trade had expired. Nevertheless, the claimant sued for copyright infringement and breach of confidence. Both suites of programs were written in similar programming languages, being variants of COBOL.

When the code of the two suites of programs was examined, common errors were noticed. These were primarily to do with spelling and punctuation in the comment lines in the programs. The same mistakes tended to occur in the same places. The same piece of redundant code was also present in both suites of programs. The judge, therefore, had little difficulty in finding that there had been copying, showing the usefulness of including deliberate mistakes or redundant elements in copyright works. He also held that copyright subsisted not only in the individual programs but in the whole suite of programs as a compilation because the selection and arrangement of the programs required skill and judgment. On this latter point the judge, Mr Justice Jacob, disagreed with Judge Paul Baker who said, in *Total Information Processing Systems Ltd v Daman Ltd* [1992] FSR 171, that linking several programs together could not constitute an original compilation. In view of the increasing structural complexity of software products, Jacob J's approach should be welcomed by the software industry as strengthening the copyright protection of computer programs.

In the *IBCOS* case, it was held that the defendant had infringed copyright in a number of individual programs in addition to an infringement of the copyright subsisting in the overall structure of the software comprising 335 programs, 171 record layout files and 46 screen layouts. The defendant had argued that similarities were the result of programming style and the reuse of well-known routines but was unable to convince the judge on these points. In other words, the defendant was unable to offer a satisfactory explanation for the similarities. It was also held that the defendant programmer was guilty of a breach of confidence in respect of the claimant's source code programs.

In his judgment, Mr Justice Jacob discussed previous case law and was critical of some aspects of it (see the section on non-literal copying later in this chapter). Some other important points made by Jacob J included:

- Modifying a computer program could give rise to a fresh copyright (presumably if the work in making the modifications was the result of skill or judgment).
- The fact that the program, or parts of it, was constrained by the program's function did not weaken or compromise copyright protection.
- The data division of a COBOL program (being the part defining the variables and database structures) can be a substantial part of a program and a file record, though not a program, could be a compilation.
- Where the evidence clearly indicates copying but the defendant denies this, the court should infer that similarities are the result of copying and not due to programming style unless independent evidence suggests otherwise.

The *IBCOS* case is an important step in the application of copyright law to computer programs. Bearing in mind that preparatory design material is now expressly (and independently) subject to copyright, the width of protection afforded to software is quite

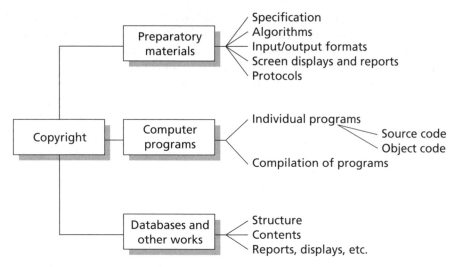

Fig. 4.1 Copyright protection of software package

strong. Figure 4.1 shows this in relation to a typical software package including a suite of programs and data files.

The concept of non-literal copying can strengthen copyright even more. Whether copying is literal or non-literal, however, it should be remembered that infringement of copyright requires use of the first work and creating a similar work independently will not infringe. Writing new accounts software will not infringe any copyrights in existing software packages provided they have not been used in a way that falls within the restricted acts.

In a later case, *Cantor Fitzgerald International* v *Tradition (UK) Ltd* [2000] RPC 95, the main parties were independent bond brokers. A further defendant had been the claimant's managing director but had been dismissed and obtained employment with the first defendant, Tradition (UK) Ltd ('Tradition'). He took a number of other employees of the claimant with him, including programmers who had worked on the claimant's software system. Within a relatively sort period of time, the first defendant had a bond broking software system which the claimant alleged was a copy of its system. Eventually, the first defendant admitted that a small proportion of its software had been copied from the claimant's software.

In finding that the defendants had infringed the claimant's copyright, Mr Justice Pumfrey noted the following points:

- Tradition accepted that the whole of the claimant's software had been loaded onto its computer. This was itself an infringement of copyright.
- The expression of thought in a human language differed to a program for a computer written in a computer programming language. There was a danger in adapting principles developed in the context of traditional literary works and applying them uncritically to computer programs which, although literary works in the copyright sense, had the sole purpose to control the operation of a machine.
- Although every part of a computer program might be essential to its performance, it was too simplistic to regard every part however small as a substantial part of the program. The fact that a program might not function properly or at all without that part did not mean that it was a substantial part of the program.

- The function of copyright was to protect the relevant skill and labour expended by the author of the work and a copyist infringed if he took a part of the work upon which a substantial part of the author's skill and labour was expended.
- A substantial part of the author's skill and labour might reside in the plot of a novel or play and to take it without taking any part of the particular manner of its expression might be sufficient to amount to copying (a case of non-literal copying – see later in this chapter). The architecture of a computer program (either the overall structure of the system at a high level or allocation of functions between various programs) was analogous to a plot and capable of protection if it represented a substantial part of the author's skill, labour and judgment. However, in this particular case, similarities at the architectural level were no more than could be accounted for by fact that both systems were written by the same programmers and, in any case, the claimant did not pursue this aspect. The judge did seem surprised that, although the architecture of the two programs were similar, only around 3.3 per cent of the code of the claimant's program could be detected in Tradition's program code.
- In terms of the decisions taken as to how the programs should be modularised, where the content of each module was largely arbitrary or was not based on considerations concerned with the program as a functional unit but was related to extraneous matters such as the availability and skill of programmers or convenience in terms of debugging and maintenance of the program, it was unlikely, though not impossible, that the skill and labour expended in making such a choice could ever amount to a substantial part of the copyright subsisting in program.
- If the copied program code had been disguised to hide its origins, this showed that the person copying knew what he was doing was wrong and if this was done in blatant disregard of the claimant's rights, this might be the basis of a claim for additional damages.
- The judge accepted that the actual proportion of code copied and used in Tradition's program was very small and Tradition's programmers had wanted the claimant's code as a record of what they had done before. It was intended to build a system which was a substantial improvement on that of the claimant's.

One of the main uses of the claimant's code made by the programmer working for Tradition was to use it for debugging purposes. In such a case, it would be appropriate to calculate damages based on a reasonable fee for the use of code for those purposes.

The facts of this case are not unusual in practice. Computer programmers tend to move from job to job and create similar programs for different clients or employees. It is tempting for them to use earlier programs and designs for programs subsequently. Many programmers build up a toolkit of useful routines and modules to save them time writing them from scratch in the future. It is also likely that programmers working on new programs with functions similar to those they have written before will try to improve upon them and expand their functionality. To draw a line between what is acceptable and what is not is notoriously difficult to do. However, simply making a copy of a previous employer's program without permission infringes copyright as will any subsequent use involving loading the program into a computer. On the other hand, simply remembering the basic ideas and algorithms underlying the programs and writing new programs on the basis of those ideas and algorithms should not infringe copyright (and will not be a breach of confidence unless the functions performed by those programs were in the nature of trade secrets protected by the law of confidence).

On the whole, Mr Justice Pumfrey's judgment in *Cantor Fitzgerald* is sound and builds on the principles expounded by Jacob J in *IBCOS*. The fact that relatively little of the claimant's program code found its way into the defendant's program does not lessen the finding of infringement (providing substantiality is found nonetheless) but might be relevant to the quantum of damages awarded and whether a permanent injunction is granted. On criticism of the judgment is that the judge frequently referred to the author's labour in a way that suggested that it might be sufficient on its own to give rise to copyright. The better view is that the author must expend skill or judgment or both. The test for originality in the European Directive on the legal protection of computer programs was that they must be the author's own intellectual creation (the same applies to copyright databases). Although the Copyright, Designs and Patents Act 1988 was not modified to include this particular requirement for computer programs, it does represent the correct position. It is highly unlikely that a literary, dramatic, musical or artistic work that is the result of labour only will attract copyright protection in the absence of skill or judgment.

Non-literal copying

Copyright does not give a monopoly in basic ideas; what it does is to prevent a person from copying or otherwise using the tangible expressions of ideas made by others in accordance with the acts restricted by copyright. In this way, copyright protects expression not idea though the concept of an idea is not a thing of precision, as Lord Hailsham accepted in *LB Plastics Ltd v Swish Products Ltd* [1979] RPC 551 – it all depends on what you mean by 'ideas'. The level of abstraction is another factor. Taking a basic idea may be acceptable but taking a very detailed plot for a play or novel and re-writing it without copying the actual text of the original play or novel may infringe copyright. Therefore, and bearing in mind those provisos, in principle it is quite acceptable to write a novel about a secret agent in the style of Ian Fleming as long as it does not contain copies of parts of James Bond novels and does not follow closely the events and their sequence, drawing heavily on the character portrayals used in a James Bond novel. The late Ian Fleming did not have a monopoly in tongue-in-cheek, humorous adventures about secret agents licensed to kill, but a novelist might commit the tort of passing off if he changes his name to Ian Fleming or uses the name James Bond or the 007 code in his novel. Copyright protection does not extend, however, to ephemeral things such as skeletal plots for novels or ideas for computer programs unless and until they are recorded in some form or another and, even then, it is the ideas as expressed that are protected, not the underlying concepts. This is a direct consequence of the nature of copyright as set out in the Act.

A literal copy of a computer program infringes copyright if made without the consent of the copyright owner. However, copying is not necessarily limited to duplication of substantial parts and it is possible to copy a computer program in a wider sense. For example, the structure, flow and sequence of operations expressed in a computer program may be copied and, if a different computer programming language is used, a printout of the second program will look dissimilar to a printout of the first program. Should the use of one program to assist with the writing of a second program in such a way be within the ambit of copyright protection even though the codes of the two programs look dissimilar? In other words, should copyright extend to non-literal elements which are not directly perceivable? This question is of such fundamental importance because, if answered in the negative, copyright protection for computer programs would be considerably weakened. This issue is also relevant in the look and feel of websites.

The United States progressed much faster than the United Kingdom in determining this question but the basic legal principles are broadly similar: copyright protects expression but not idea. Nevertheless, expression goes beyond the immediate literal form. For example, in the United Kingdom case of *Glyn v Weston Feature Film Co* [1916] 1 Ch 261, in which it was argued (unsuccessfully) that a film infringed the copyright in a novel, it was acknowledged that copyright can extend beyond the literal text of a book to the dramatic scenes and incidents contained within it.

Because expression may exist at various levels of abstraction (for example, in the program's structure or algorithm) the courts have to be able to distinguish between idea and expression. This has not proved easy and the following United States cases give an indication of the development of tests that may be appropriate. (United States law has no binding effect on the United Kingdom courts but it may be of persuasive authority, particularly in the field of information technology.)

In *Whelan Associates Inc v Jaslow Dental Laboratory Inc* [1987] FSR 1, the programs being compared were designed to assist with the administration of dental laboratories. The same person was involved in the development of each program but they were written in different computer languages: the first was written in EDL and the second, attempting to infiltrate the microcomputer market, was written in BASIC. Thus, there was no substantial literal similarity between the listings of the two programs. The United States Court of Appeals (3rd Circuit) distinguished between idea and expression by reference to the purpose of the program. The purpose of a utilitarian work is the idea of the work whereas everything pertaining to the work which is not necessary to the purpose is expression. If there are several ways of achieving the desired purpose, none of which is necessary to the purpose, then the way chosen is expression and, consequently, protected by copyright.

The purpose of the original program in *Whelan v Jaslow* was to assist in the running of dental laboratories. There were several different methods which could be employed to achieve that same purpose, and therefore the structure of that original program was not essential to the purpose and, hence, the structure was expression and not idea. The purpose itself, being the idea, was not protected by copyright; it is quite acceptable for others to write programs to help with the running of dental laboratories. In this case the structures of the two programs were similar, the programs had a similar look and feel even though written in different computer programming languages and this, coupled with the fact that the same person had been involved in the two programs, raised a strong presumption that there had been copying and, hence, an infringement of copyright. The distinction between idea and expression has been applied in the context of screen displays. In the 'Pac-Man' computer games the maze and dots were deemed to be idea, being necessarily dictated by the program function, but the 'Pac-Man' and 'ghost monsters' characters were considered to be expression as different graphical representations could have been used.

Another important case involved the spreadsheet program Lotus 1-2-3 and a compatible spreadsheet program called VP-Planner. In *Lotus Development Corp v Paperback Software International* 740 F Supp 37 (D Mass 1990), the defendant claimed that he had not copied the Lotus program code but had used a similar menu system to achieve compatibility (especially with respect to spreadsheet files and macros) and to enable people to change to VP-Planner from Lotus 1-2-3 without requiring retraining. The similarities between the programs were the menu command system (two-line moving cursor menu) and the grid system (letters and numbers arranged in a 'rotated L'). It was held by Judge Keeton that the defendant had infringed copyright by copying the two-line moving cursor menu. Various spreadsheet programs used different menu systems showing that the system used by Lotus was expression and not idea. He confirmed, however, that there was no infringement of the rotated 'L' grid as this was idea, it being almost inevitable that a spreadsheet program would use such a system.

In a later spreadsheet case, *Lotus Development Corp* v *Borland International Inc* [1997] FSR 61, in the 1st Circuit Court of Appeals, the decision of Judge Keeton along the lines of his *Lotus* v *Paperback* judgment was reversed by the Court of Appeals which found that the menu command hierarchy in the Lotus 1-2-3 spreadsheet was not a work of copyright. Therefore, by using the 1-2-3 menu command system in its Quattro spreadsheet, Borland had not infringed copyright. The rationale was that the menu command system was a method of operation which is excluded from copyright protection by section 102(b) of the United States Copyright Act. The court likened the menu system to the buttons on a video recorder. The distinction in *Whelan* between idea and expression was considered unhelpful by the court which confirmed that the fact that the Lotus designers could have designed the system differently was immaterial to the question of whether it was a method of operation. The case was then appealed to the Supreme Court but there was no substantive judgment as the court reached a split decision, and the finding of the Court of Appeals stands.

The *Lotus* v *Borland* case can be seen as a further weakening of copyright protection for interfaces (in this case, the interface with the user) and facilitates the pursuit of compatibility in software from an operational point of view. However, it could discourage investment in novel forms of software and major software companies may be encouraged to allow someone else to make the investment in developing innovative software in the knowledge that they can copy the ideas and interfaces to produce similar competing software providing that they do not copy the program code or other protected non-literal elements.

Prior to the *Lotus* v *Borland* case, the authority of *Whelan* v *Jaslow* was already looking shaky and that case had been strongly disapproved of by the United States Court of Appeals (2nd Circuit) in *Computer Associates International Inc* v *Altai* (1992) 20 USPQ 2d 1641. The defendant had produced a program called 'Oscar', a job-scheduling program for controlling the order in which tasks are carried out by a computer. It incorporated a common interface component allowing the use of different operating systems and this part had been added by a former employee of the claimant who had a similar program and interface. The claimant's former employee was very familiar with the interface element (known as 'Adapter') which was part of the claimant's 'CA-Scheduler' program and had even been allowed to take a copy of the 'Adapter' source code home while working on it. When the claimant issued a summons and complaint, the defendant rewrote 'Oscar', using different programmers in an effort to avoid infringing the claimant's copyright in 'Adapter'. The claimant still proceeded even though the defendant had agreed not to challenge an award of $364,444 damages in respect of the earlier version of 'Oscar'. The trial judge held that the later version of 'Oscar' did not infringe the 'Adapter' copyright and the claimant appealed to the Court of Appeals which confirmed the decision of the trial judge.

In a far-reaching judgment, the Court of Appeals laid down a new test for the determination of the question of non-literal copyright infringement, that is, whether there has been an infringement of copyright in non-literal elements such as program structure. The test requires a three-step procedure as follows:

- *Abstraction* – discovering the non-literal elements by a process akin to reverse engineering, beginning with the code and ending with the program's ultimate function. The designer's steps are retraced and mapped. This produces structures of different detail at varying levels of abstraction.
- *Filtration* – the separation of protectable expression from non-protectable material. Some elements will be unprotected being idea, dictated by considerations of efficiency (therefore necessarily incidental to idea), required by external factors (*scènes à faire* doctrine), or taken from the public domain. These elements are filtered out leaving a core of protectable material (this is the program's 'golden nugget').
- *Comparison* – a determination of whether the defendant has copied a substantial part of the protected expression, that is, ascertaining whether any aspect has been copied and, if so, assessing the copied portion's relative importance in respect of the claimant's overall program.

Of course, this test only applies to non-literal copying and the actual code remains fully protected against direct (literal) copying. However, this test is likely to reduce significantly the strength of protection for program structure, menu command systems and interfaces. In many cases, it is possible that, after the process of filtration, there will be no 'golden nuggets' left, that is, no protectable expression, to take forward to the process of comparison. It still remains to be seen what effect this case will have on copyright litigation in the United States. (The judges in the Court of Appeals recognised that their test would be difficult to apply and would need further case law before its application could be predicted with any certainty.) Even more interesting is its effect on copyright law in the United Kingdom, discussed below, although it should be noted that the previous test in *Whelan* v *Jaslow* did not achieve any notable successes in the United Kingdom even though it was used in argument on a number of occasions.

Non-literal copying in the United Kingdom

It was not too long after the *Computer Associates* case that a suitable example of alleged non-literal copying came before the High Court. The facts of *John Richardson Computers Ltd* v *Flanders* [1993] FSR 497 were difficult and provide an object lesson in how not to manage the development of computer software, with scant regard being paid to record-keeping and ownership of copyright. Essentially, the claimant had a computer program for use by pharmacists to print labels for drug prescriptions and to monitor stock levels. The driving force behind the claimant company was Mr Richardson who had originally written a rudimentary program in BASIC and had later engaged computer programmers, both on an employee and consultancy basis and including the defendant, to refine and enhance the program. Eventually it was rewritten in assembly language for the BBC computer (and is referred to below as 'the BBC program').

The defendant wrote a program called 'Chemtec' to perform the same functions as the claimant's program written in QUICK-BASIC for the IBM personal computer. The claimant sued for copyright infringement and breach of confidence though the latter claim was not pursued at the trial. The judge, Mr Justice Ferris, had to consider the claim for copyright infringement in the context of two computer programs written in different languages and bearing no significant literal similarities and with very little English case law to assist him. He identified the following issues raised by the case:

- Does copyright subsist in a computer program?
- If it does, does the copyright in the BBC program belong to the claimant?
- If the above questions are answered in the affirmative, what should the court's approach be to a claim of 'non-literal' copying?
- Are there any objective similarities between the BBC program and the Chemtec program enabling the Chemtec program to be regarded in any respect as a copy of the BBC program?
- Were any such similarities in fact copied from the BBC program?
- Is any copying thus found, copying of a substantial part of the BBC program?

The issue of copyright subsistence was easily dealt with by the judge and ownership of copyright in the BBC program was resolved in favour of the claimant. Although the defendant may have been the legal owner of parts of the program he had written as a self-employed consultant, the claimant was the owner in equity and, as the claimant had joined the legal owner in the action (by suing him), the full range of remedies was available to the claimant should infringement be proved.

After reviewing the English and United States authorities on non-literal copying and discussing the *Computer Associates* case at length, Mr Justice Ferris said that there was nothing in any English decision which conflicted with the general approach adopted in that case. However, he said that, in preference to seeking the 'core of protectable expression' in the claimant's program, an English court would:

- decide whether the claimant's program as a whole is entitled to copyright protection, and then
- decide whether any similarity in the defendant's program resulting from copying amounts to a substantial part of the claimant's program.

Ferris J went on to say that the approach to separation of idea and expression as expounded in *Computer Associates* was appropriate and a similar approach should be adopted in England. This would be relevant to issues of substantiality of copying and originality. Thus, the non-literal elements of a computer program are to be taken into account. In testing for infringement, the judge concentrated on objective similarities in the non-literal elements of the programs and he classified them in four ways:

- similarities that were the result of copying a substantial part of the claimant's program, being the line editor, amendment routines and drug dose codes;
- similarities that were the result of copying but not in relation to a substantial part of the claimant's program – for example, the date option, operation successful, message;
- similarities which may have been the result of copying but which, in any case, did not involve copying substantial parts of the claimant's program – for example, the vertical arrangement of entry prompts;
- similarities that were not the result of copying including the use of the escape key, position of label on screen, etc.

It was held that the defendant had infringed copyright in respect of three non-literal elements. This would mean that it might be a relatively simple matter for the defendant to rewrite the offending parts of his program, notwithstanding any award in damages in respect of the infringement.

The judgment in *Richardson* v *Flanders* attracted a fair amount of criticism. In particular, Mr Justice Jacob in his judgment in *IBCOS* v *Barclays* (a case on literal copying) was particularly critical of a blind allegiance to the United States approach, pointing out that United Kingdom copyright law is different, being based on a different statute. He said that the United States approach was not helpful. It must be noted, however, that Jacob J was dealing with a more straightforward case of copying and the two cases are distinguishable, one being on literal copying (*IBCOS*), the other on non-literal copying (*Richardson*). Consequently, it is possible to reconcile the two cases and the judgments can be seen as complementary. Where *Richardson* is weak is, arguably, in the abstraction to non-literal expression. Furthermore, there was no serious attempt to filter out unprotected elements but this is more likely to be due to differences between United Kingdom and United States law than a failure on the part of the judge.

Finally, it should be noted that the defendant in *Richardson* v *Flanders* had made significant additions and enhancements to his program, which was substantially larger than the claimant's program and had more features. Nevertheless, when comparing programs for copyright infringement it was confirmed that more attention should be paid to the parts claimed to be the same or similar than the other parts of the program. As a result of the *Richardson* and *IBCOS* cases, it would appear that copyright protection for computer programs is at least adequate and there is a reasonable balance between strength of protection and the development of competing programs by others, as is investigated below.

Copying in practice

Has copyright law been developed by the courts to prevent the marketing of look-alike computer programs? Obviously, if a company makes a new type of computer program which proves to be very successful, other companies will want to bring out their own versions in order to gain a share in the market created or stimulated by the first program. Essentially, copyright law does not prevent this as long as the first program is not copied or adapted. Although copying extends to the structure and other non-literal elements of a program this should not prevent competitors bringing out programs to perform similar functions, providing those functions are not novel or, being inventive, are subject to patent rights or are secret and protected by the law of confidence. A line must be drawn somewhere and the following hypothetical examples, involving two software companies Acme and Zenith, indicate where it might be drawn.

Acme developed a program to record and monitor drug dosages to hospital patients and Zenith, shortly afterwards, brought out a similar program.

1 Zenith did not know of the existence of Acme's program. (*No infringement of copyright.*)
2 Zenith knew of the existence of Acme's program but had not seen it in use. (*No infringement of copyright; the function of the program is idea, not expression.*)
3 Zenith had seen Acme's program in use and decided to write a program to fulfil the same purpose, that is, to monitor drug dosages. Zenith did not refer to Acme's program further than this and Zenith developed its own methods of performing the purpose. The structures of the two programs are different in many respects and where they are similar this is the result of coincidence only or because they are constrained by the function. (*No infringement of copyright.*)

4 Zenith buys a copy of Acme's program. Zenith cannot see the source code because the copy is compiled (in object code), but by using the program extensively, Zenith gets a good insight into the workings and structure of Acme's program and, based on this insight, Zenith writes its program (obviously without using a source code listing of Acme's program). Zenith's knowledge of Acme's program is no more than a competent user would achieve. (*Possible infringement of copyright because the structure of Zenith's program is determined by Zenith's familiarity with the structure of Acme's program which Zenith copies indirectly. Copying menu systems, screen displays and other non-literal elements may also infringe Acme's copyright.*)

5 Zenith decompiles Acme's program and rewrites parts of it to make its program, perhaps using a different computer language. (*Definite infringement of copyright; the act of decompilation itself will constitute an infringement of copyright. The 'decompilation' exception to infringement is unlikely to apply here – see later.*)

6 Zenith employs an ex-programmer of Acme who is familiar with the program; this person writes a program for Zenith using copies of listings and flow charts that he retained. Qualitatively substantial parts of the program code are incorporated in the new program. (*Definite infringement of copyright and possible breach of confidence.*)

7 As point 6 above but the ex-programmer of Acme has not retained any materials from his previous employment; he simply uses what he can remember. (*Possible infringement of copyright.*)

The last example lies in a difficult area and is tied up with questions relating to the law of confidence and restraint of trade. Ex-employees frequently cause problems because of the difficulty in reconciling their continuing duty to their ex-employer with the need to be able to obtain other employment. If the ex-employee is not allowed to make use of anything at all from his past experience, he may well be virtually unemployable because what he has done previously is an integral part of his skill and expertise. This question will be considered further in Chapter 9 on the law of confidence. At this stage it needs to be noted that an ex-employee will be able to make use of his skills and what he remembers as long as these are not genuine trade secrets. In terms of writing computer software, a program to automate an existing manual process probably will not be considered a trade secret.

If company B writes a program independently and, by chance, it turns out to be very similar to a program written by company A, there is no infringement of copyright because there has been neither copying nor the making of an adaptation of A's program and both A and B will have a copyright in their respective programs. A substantial similarity between programs, however, can suggest that one has been copied from the other and this can shift the burden of proof to the defendant, especially if there is something else to support the view that copying may have taken place, such as access to the original by the defendant (see *LB Plastics Ltd v Swish Products Ltd* [1979] RPC 551). This means that instead of requiring the claimant to show that copying has taken place, the defendant will have to show that he did not, in fact, copy the claimant's work and such a shift in the burden of proof can be exceedingly onerous to the defendant.

One approach to the question of copying was suggested by the Court of Appeal in *Francis, Day & Hunter Ltd v Bron* [1963] Ch 587, a case concerning an alleged infringement of an old song entitled 'In a Little Spanish Town'. For copying to be proved, the test is as follows:

- there must be sufficient objective similarity between the two works (an objective issue – would the 'reasonable man' consider the two works sufficiently similar?), and
- there must also be some causal connection between the two works (a subjective question but not to be presumed as a matter of law merely upon proof of access).

It is possible to infringe copyright by subconsciously copying a work, although this is probably more relevant to the music industry than the computer industry. Thus the late George Harrison's song 'My Sweet Lord' was alleged to have infringed an earlier song 'He's So Fine', but it is thought that the evidence required to support this proposition would have to be quite strong. Taken to its logical conclusion this might encourage software developers to adopt a 'clean-room' approach, denying access to existing software by the programmers and analysts in an effort to try to prevent accusations of copying. In most cases, this would not be realistic given the likelihood that any skilled programmer would already have a wide knowledge of other software products. Even if it is feasible, there is no guarantee that this would provide a defence to an infringement action. In the New Zealand case of *Plix Products Ltd v Frank M Whinstone (Merchants)* [1986] FSR 63, the defendant asked his designer to design a kiwifruit pack without talking to others in this field and without looking at existing packs. Although there was no direct copying it was held that the copyright in the claimant's packs had been infringed through the medium of the New Zealand Kiwifruit Authority's specification for packs, and the court also seemed to accept the possibility that copyright can be infringed through a verbal description. New Zealand copyright law is very similar to United Kingdom law; but, in the United States, it would be likely that the design features indicated in the specification would be considered to be an unprotectable idea.

The implications of indirect copying (expressly covered by the Copyright, Designs and Patents Act 1988, section 16) are serious for the software industry and care must be taken to avoid such a claim. There is even a case for deliberately making elements in a computer program (including non-literal elements) different from the equivalent part of competing programs if this does not compromise the functionality, usability and attractiveness of the program.

If copyright protection of computer programs is developed by the courts to become too strong, the Act contains safeguards. By section 144(1), following a conclusion of the Competition Commission (previously the Monopolies and Mergers Commission) that there are conditions in licences granted by the owner of copyright in a work restricting the use of the work by the licensee or the right of the copyright owner to grant other licences or where the copyright owner refuses to grant licences on reasonable terms, the Secretary of State or Competition Commission may order that licences are available as of right. Therefore, if a company has a virtual monopoly in a particular type of computer system and charges an exorbitant price for it, the Competition Commission may order that licences are available as of right and anyone will be able to apply for a licence to use the software. The licence fee and other terms of the licence will be decided by the Copyright Tribunal, a body set up to administer licensing schemes. Under section 66, the Secretary of State may order that lending of copies to the public shall be treated as licensed subject to payment of a reasonable royalty or other payments as may be agreed or, failing agreement, as determined by the Copyright Tribunal. Section 66 was amended by the Copyright and Related Rights Regulations 1996. Previously, it was framed in terms of rental rather than lending.

Issuing copies to the public

Under section 18, issuing copies of a work to the public is a restricted act and will infringe copyright if done without the permission of the owner of the copyright. However, the right to control the issue of copies to the public only applies to the first issue of individual copies. Thus, once a particular copy of a computer program has been issued to the public by or with the consent of the copyright owner, he can no longer use that right to control subsequent dealings with that particular copy, apart from rental. The right still applies in relation to un-issued copies. This principle accords with the doctrine of exhaustion of rights in European Community law. Exhaustion would apply where, for example, a software company has sold copies of its programs to one dealer in Germany and, at a lower price, to another dealer in France. A third party might be able to buy copies in France and import them into Germany in order to resell them, undercutting the German dealer. The software company would not be able to use its public issue right to prevent this.

Rental or lending copies to the public

By virtue of section 18A (which was inserted by the Copyright and Related Rights Regulations 1996) the rental or lending of copies of a work to the public is an act restricted by the copyright. This provision applies to literary, dramatic and musical works, to artistic works (except works of architecture and works of applied art) and films and sound recordings.

Making an adaptation

Making an adaptation of a literary, dramatic or musical work is a restricted act. In terms of a musical work, a new arrangement of a song is an adaptation of the original. Changing a cartoon strip into a story told by words only is also an adaptation, as is a translation of a literary or dramatic work. Additionally, for a computer program, making an arrangement or altered version comes within this restricted act. 'Translation' has a special meaning for computer programs, by section 21(4), and includes:

> ... a version of the program in which it is converted into or out of a computer language or code or into a different computer language or code.

If a high-level, source code computer program is compiled (converted) into an object code program, this will be an adaptation of the source code program and, therefore, a restricted act. This provision is aimed at controlling the compilation, decompilation, assembly and disassembly of computer programs – that is, the conversion of source code programs into object code and vice versa as shown in Fig. 4.2. This would seem to be a reasonable activity to be controlled by copyright, especially as reverse-engineering an object code program will make the techniques, ideas and principles underlying a computer program more accessible. As we shall see later, however, under certain circumstances this is expressly permitted under copyright law.

Source code programs are protected by copyright provided they are 'original' – that is, they are the result of skill, labour or judgment. The position is less clear as far as object code programs are concerned because they may not be original in the sense

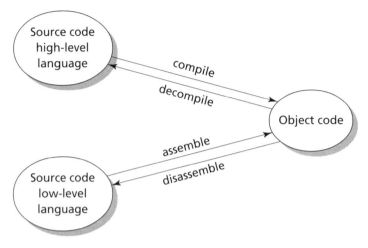

Fig. 4.2 Making an adaptation of a computer program

described above. In most cases, an object code program will have been created by submitting the source code program to a compiler program or assembler program. This process may require little effort or skill on the part of the person creating the object code unless there are several errors detected which need correction before a suitable executable version of the object code is obtained. Even if an object code program is not an original literary work, it will be protected by copyright as an adaptation of such a work and the restricted acts extend to an adaptation as they do to the original work. Thus, it is an infringement of copyright to copy an adaptation of a program or even to make an adaptation of an adaptation.

It could be argued that the meaning of translation is too wide as it seems to catch a version of a source code program written in a different high-level language from that used for the original program, that is, a manual conversion. If a computer program is written using BASIC and someone then rewrites the program in COBOL, the latter will be an adaptation of the BASIC program because it has been converted into a different computer language. To produce a program in a different high-level language, however, is not merely a question of translating the program instructions from one language to another as with spoken languages. The programmer would have to reduce the original program to its underlying concepts and ideas and from those concepts and ideas (not from the computer program itself) develop a new version of the program in another high-level language, as shown in Fig. 4.3.

The differences between the two programs could be as those between Romeo and Juliet and West Side Story and, as a basic principle, copyright should not protect ideas as such, only the expression or recording of those ideas. However, it seems that the new

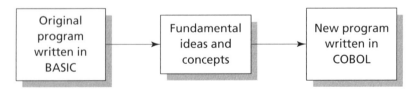

Fig. 4.3 Conversion of a computer program

version of a program in a different high-level language will be an adaptation, regardless of the quite considerable amount of skill and effort required to 'translate' the program in such a way.

Restricted acts apply to a work as a whole or to any substantial part of it (section 16(3)). What is substantial is a matter of fact and the courts will look to quality as well as quantity (see *Hawkes & Sons (London) Ltd* v *Paramount Film Service Ltd* [1934] Ch 593). Therefore, a computer program which includes parts (such as sub-routines) copied from another program will infringe the copyright in that other program if the copied parts represent a substantial part of the original program and they may be substantial if they go to the root of the other program or capture its essence, even though they are small in terms of quantity.

Theoretically, it might seem possible to increase copyright protection by modularising a single program into a number of separate sub-programs which, if each individually is the result of skill, labour and effort, will all be independently protected in addition to any copyright in the suite of programs as a compilation. Substantiality, in terms of infringement, will be measured by comparison with a sub-program rather than the unified whole. However, there are limits to this and the part copied must represent a substantial part of the author's skill or judgment used in creating that part. Furthermore, the judgment in *Cantor Fitzgerald International* v *Tradition (UK) Ltd* [2000] RPC 95, discussed earlier in this chapter, suggests that it is unlikely that decisions made in respect of how to modularise a program or suite of programs will, *per se*, be the result of sufficient skill or judgment for the purposes of copyright subsistence.

Exceptions to copyright infringement

When it was decided to classify computer programs as literary works for copyright purposes, the usual exceptions to copyright infringement applied. The Act contains a great many exceptions, called the 'permitted acts': for example, fair dealing for research or private study or for criticism, review or news reporting. In order to provide for uniform protection of computer programs throughout the European Community, Council Directive 91/250/EEC on the legal protection of computer programs was published in 1991 (OJ L 122, 17.05.1991, p.42). United Kingdom law was already well developed and complied with most of the Directive's provisions. However, because some aspects of United Kingdom law were somewhat vague and ill defined (for example, the meaning of fair dealing) it was decided to tighten up some of the exceptions to copyright infringement, the necessary changes to the 1988 Act being made by the Copyright (Computer Programs) Regulations 1992. In terms of the permitted acts, three particular issues were addressed:

- 'decompiling' an existing computer program for interoperability;
- making necessary back-up copies;
- copying and adapting including error correction.

These three important exceptions to copyright infringement are described and examined below. It should be pointed out that the previous law probably covered the above acts in most circumstances. For example, fair dealing for research purposes might have allowed decompilation to achieve interoperability, though fair dealing for research pur-

poses will very soon be limited to non-commercial purposes as a result of implementing the European Directive on the harmonisation of certain aspects of copyright and
related rights in the information society (see Chapter 8). Implied licences might have
been appropriate in some cases involving error correction and back-up copies. One further point is that, in addition to statutory defences to copyright infringement, there is
a defence of public interest – for example, if it is in the public interest that a program
listing is published. This might apply to code used by 'hackers' to penetrate computer
systems or computer viruses because publication would assist managers of computer
installations in their attempts to combat computer hacking and the spread of viruses.

Decompilation of computer programs

'Decompilation' is used in a wide sense and defined in section 50B as converting a copy
of a computer program expressed in a low-level language into a version expressed in a
higher-level language and extends to copying incidental to such conversion. The restricted act of making an adaptation includes decompilation and infringes copyright unless
allowed by the decompilation permitted act. The normal fair-dealing provisions, as
amended, apply otherwise. By section 50B(1), a lawful user (being a person having a
right under a licence or otherwise to use the program: section 50A(2)) may decompile
the program if necessary to obtain the information necessary to achieve the interoperability of any independently created program with the decompiled program or another
program. In other words, it is permissible for a lawful user to decompile or disassemble a computer program to determine its interfaces if this is a necessary step in creating
a new program which will interoperate (interact) with that or some other program.

Typically, a software developer might want to write a word processing program
which will be compatible with another company's spreadsheet program so that data
and files can be passed between the two programs (see Fig. 4.4). This form of compatibility is certainly desirable and should not cause any great concerns, unless the spreadsheet company was hoping to make its own compatible word processor in the future.
Once the compatible interoperable program has been created there seems no reason

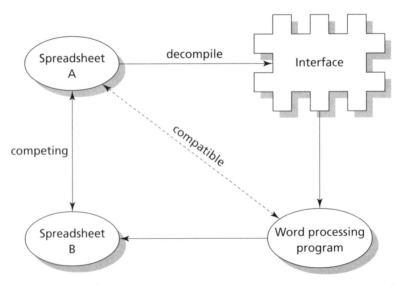

Fig. 4.4 Decompilation of a computer program

why the interface details cannot be used subsequently to create competing, replacement programs as long as there is not a substantial copy made of the code in the original program, as indicated in the figure.

The Copyright, Designs and Patents Act 1988, as amended, attempts to deal with this situation by making the use or supply of the information for any other objective, or in the development, production or marketing of any computer program substantially similar in its expression to the original program, an infringement of copyright (section 50B(2)). However, reuse of interface details will not necessarily result in a substantially similar expression and, in the example in Fig. 4.4, the expression (program listings and structure) may be quite different. Interface details may be qualitatively insubstantial; after all the program is a spreadsheet program, not an interface program, and may be written in different code to achieve the same purpose. In practice, these provisions will be very difficult to apply but the preamble to the Directive may give some assistance as it talks about the European Community being fully committed to the promotion of international standardisation. The only other proviso is that the creation of the second spreadsheet program should not have been in the contemplation of the licensed user when decompiling the original program, otherwise the permitted objective of decompilation might be compromised. The permitted act of decompilation does not apply if the information required has been previously readily available (section 50B(3)): for example, the interface details have been published or made available at reasonable cost. A further point is that there is no need to rely on the right unless the decompilation is carried out to a substantial part of the original program (there is no infringement to excuse otherwise). The decompilation permitted act cannot be prohibited or restricted by a term in a licence agreement, any such term being void and unenforceable at law (section 296A).

Back-up copies of computer programs

It is essential that back-up copies of computer programs be made. A back-up copy will be needed if the original copy of the computer program becomes damaged or corrupted in any way. The original may be physically damaged, for example, if the surface of the magnetic disk or compact disc on which the program was delivered has been scratched or damaged in other ways. The original program, if stored on re-writeable media, may become contaminated with a computer virus. If a computer program has been obtained for use in a commercial environment, whether it is a word processing package, accounts system or spreadsheet, the chances are that the software will fail at the worst possible moment. If a back-up copy is available, a potential disaster can be averted and the urgent document, spreadsheet or whatever can still be completed on time.

The Act, as amended, makes specific provision for the making of back-up copies of computer programs. Before the amendments made by the Copyright (Computer Programs) Regulations 1992, there was no such provision although the courts may have been prepared to imply an appropriate term into a software licence where the making of a back-up copy was reasonably necessary to the use of the program in question. Of course, many software companies make express provision for the user to make a back-up copy. It is common for the installation instructions to ask the licensed user to make a copy of the program first and use this as the working copy, placing the original disks in a safe place in case the working disks become damaged or corrupted in some way. Alternatively, the software is delivered on a compact disc and copied to the computer's hard disk, the compact disc being available for re-loading in the future if the hard disk copy becomes corrupted in some way.

Section 50A states that copyright is not infringed by a lawful user making an additional copy of a computer program for back-up purposes if doing so is necessary to the lawful use. This right cannot be taken away by any terms in a licence agreement but there may be some difficulty with deciding when making a back-up copy is truly necessary. It might not be so if a licence agreement includes terms to the effect that the licensor will himself make a further copy available to the licensee in the event of failure of the original copy.

The Act recognises the possibility that back-up copies may have been made. Section 56 deals with transfers of works in electronic form and the position with respect to copies which are not transferred along with the original software. This is best described by way of an example. A business, Acme Ltd, obtains a word processing package (WORDY); the licence agreement allows the making of one back-up copy. Acme uses WORDY and makes two copies of it, one as a back up and one for use on another computer. Two years later, Acme decides to obtain some new computers and a more powerful word processing program. It looks at the WORDY licence and sees that the licence does not prevent the transfer of the package to someone else. Acme assigns its licence to use WORDY to the Zenith Co and transfers the original copy of the program plus the single back-up copy. By section 56, Acme was permitted to transfer the software because there were no express terms in the licence agreement prohibiting this, but it should have transferred all copies of WORDY. By section 56(2), the copy it has retained is treated as an infringing copy and leaves Acme liable to the owner of the copyright in the word processing programs. Additionally, because Acme made two copies instead of the one permitted under the licence agreement, it was in breach of that agreement and, depending on the terms in the licence dealing with breach, it might find that the licence was brought to an end and that the purported transfer to Zenith was void.

Miscellaneous exceptions and error correction

By section 50C, a lawful user is permitted to copy or adapt a computer program providing that it is necessary for his lawful use and not prohibited by the agreement regulating the use (for example, a licence agreement). Section 50C(2) provides a specific example of when this may be necessary, that is, where it is for the purpose of error correction. A licence agreement may specifically prohibit error correction so that all this provision does is to raise a presumption in favour of the lawful user. For example, if disassembling a computer program in order to correct errors is necessary to the lawful use and there are no express terms prohibiting this, then it can be done without infringing copyright. Again, the meaning of 'necessary' may be at issue but the important factor is that the presumption can be and, in many cases in practice, will be cancelled out by express terms. A number of software companies are reluctant to allow licensees or third parties to modify programs. Any such modifications could be carried out badly, resulting in unfavourable publicity for the software company through no fault of its own.

Even though a licence agreement may prohibit error correction by the licensee or a third party, it is possible that other areas of law may apply to defeat the prohibition. The common law principle of non-derogation from grant was used in *British Leyland*

Motor Corp Ltd v *Armstrong Patents Co Ltd* [1986] AC 577 to stop British Leyland enforcing its copyright in drawings of exhaust systems for cars to prevent a free market in spare parts. The same argument holds true for computer programs. A licensee should have access to a free market in maintaining the programs and there are signs that judges are likely to accept this possibility in at least some situations.

European Community competition law may also impinge on terms prohibiting error correction by anyone other than the licensee on the basis that this is restrictive of trade between member states under Article 81(1) of the Treaty of Rome. Alternatively, where the licensor is a major software company, a restriction on third party maintenance could be seen as an abuse of a dominant position under Article 82. United Kingdom competition law also has equivalent provisions under the Competition Act 1998. The major difference is that the European Community provisions apply where the activity concerned may affect trade between member states or competition within the Community whereas, the Competition Act controls relevant activities where the effects are within the United Kingdom. Competition law provisions are described in more detail in Chapter 14.

Section 296A(1) of the Copyright, Designs and Patents Act 1988 makes any term or condition in an agreement void in so far as it purports to prohibit or restrict the use of any device or means to observe, study or test the functioning of a computer program in order to understand the ideas and principles underlying any element of the program. This reinforces the idea/expression dichotomy but is unlikely to be welcomed by software producers. It would, for example, excuse the form of reverse engineering used in the *Dyason* v *Autodesk* case (measuring the electrical signals passing between the dongle and the computer program).

The exceptions apply to new programs and programs in existence at 1 January 1993 (the commencement date for the new Regulations). Agreements and terms or conditions in agreements entered into before 1 January 1993 were unaffected, however. For example, a term prohibiting making a back-up copy in a pre-1993 agreement will not be made invalid by reason of the changes brought about by the Regulations even if the making of a back-up copy is deemed to be necessary to the lawful use of the program.

Employees and freelance programmers

The author of a work is the first owner of the copyright in the work. An exception which applies to literary, dramatic, musical or artistic works is where the work is made by an 'employee in the course of his employment', in which case the employer becomes the first owner of the copyright in the work, subject to a contrary intention (section 11(2)). This raises the following questions.

- Who is an employee?
- What is the position regarding freelance computer programmers and consultants?
- What is the meaning of 'in the course of employment'?

The Copyright, Designs and Patents Act 1988 does not specifically define these terms but states that 'employed', 'employee', 'employer' and 'employment' refer to employment under a contract of service or apprenticeship (section 178). The question of ownership of computer programs written by freelance staff will be considered first.

Freelance staff

It is not always easy to identify when a person is an employee and when he is not; various tests have evolved and some concern questions of 'control'. These tests include whether the 'employer' can tell the person what to do, when to do it and how to do it. Does the 'employer' provide the person with time off for holidays, sick pay or a pension? Does the person have to correct unsatisfactory work in his own time and at his own expense? How is income tax paid? In many cases the question will be answered by looking at the terms of the contract between the parties although a description of the parties as 'employer' and 'employee' is not conclusive. In many cases, freelance staff, hired to perform a particular task such as writing or modifying a specific computer program, will be deemed to be self-employed. The consequence of this is that the copyright in any program so written will, *prima facie* and in the absence of any agreement otherwise, belong to the freelance programmer.

It is essential, therefore, when employing freelance staff, or anyone else who is not employed under a permanent contract of employment, to make contractual provision for determining ownership of copyright. The organisation hiring the programmer or consultant may want to own the copyright so that it can exploit the resultant program itself, or it may simply want to prevent its competitors from obtaining a copy of it. In either of these situations the contract should specifically state that the ownership of the copyright belongs to the organisation and not to the programmer and, furthermore, there should be a written assignment of copyright, signed by the freelance programmer. Of course, the fee charged will probably be greater as a result because the freelance programmer might have envisaged making use of the program elsewhere; he may know of other businesses which would be interested in what he produces. On the other hand, if the commissioning organisation does not itself contemplate commercially exploiting the software or preventing others from using it, then it is important that a term is included in the contract granting a licence for the continued use of the program.

If the contract is silent on such matters, the freelance programmer may later decide to test his ownership of the program by offering it to others or, worse still, claim that, as owner, he will permit the continued use of the program only on payment of a licence fee. These difficulties may arise especially when the program in question turns out to be more useful and successful than the parties originally envisaged. There is a danger that a freelance programmer will try to hold his client to ransom if he later realises that the value of the software he has produced is out of all proportion to the payment he received for writing it.

Unfortunately, not all 'freelance staff' are self-employed and some are employed by an agency. In this case the same precautions apply and it is even more important to deal with ownership of copyright, otherwise the agency (as employer) could turn out to be the first owner of the copyright.

It became common for computer software professionals to set up small limited companies or partnerships, perhaps with a spouse as co-director or partner. This was advantageous for the purposes of calculating tax liability. However, where the circumstances are such that the individual would otherwise be deemed to be an employee of the client, for example, where he or she works for a single client for a prolonged period of time, such persons are now deemed as employees for tax purposes. In such cases, the distinction between self-employed consultants and employees has become blurred by the changes to tax law made by the notorious IR 35 'anti-tax avoidance' provisions in the Finance Act 2000. The basic difference between a self-employed consultant and an employee is that the former works under a *contract for services* whereas employees work under a *contract of service*.

In *Synaptek Ltd* v *Young (Inspector of Taxes)*, *The Times*, 7 April 2003, a consultant software engineer carried out work under the auspices of a company, the only directors being the engineer and his wife. He carried out work for a government department for a period of six months. It was held that the tax commissioners were correct in deciding that, had the engineer worked directly for the government department, he would have been an employee. A number of factors were put forward in favour of a finding that the contract was a contract for services rather than a contract of service. They were that the client had only limited control of the time and manner in which the engineer performed his duties, his company provided training and computer facilities at his own premises, the contract with the client contained provisions dealing with intellectual property rights and the engineer was required by the client to provide professional indemnity insurance. On the other hand, the minimum working hours were broadly equivalent to a normal working week, the engineer's only financial risk was that the client might become insolvent (extremely unlikely in the particular circumstances), the duration of the contract was six months, the engineer worked with other staff of the client and his work was sufficiently integrated with the other workers for him to have a line manager and the fact that he agreed to comply with the client's instructions. On balance, the court thought that the commissioners had not been mistaken in law and confirmed that the IR 35 provisions applied.

The decision in this case, makes it very difficult to predict whether a person, working on their own behalf or under the auspices of a company or partnership, is an employee of the client. What, for example, if the software engineer worked for the client for only three months or worked more irregular hours or where the work was not integrated with that of employees of the client? This makes it even more important to expressly provide for ownership of copyright and any other intellectual property rights subsisting in the programs and other items of software created by the person engaged by the client.

The employee and the course of employment

As regards persons who can safely be classified as employees, their employers cannot safely assume that they will own the copyright in everything produced by those employees. For example, if an employee writes a computer program to help with his work, for example, as an accountant, but he is not employed as a computer programmer, his job is not to write computer programs and an employer cannot necessarily assume that he owns the copyright in that particular program. A lecturer normally owns the copyright in any book or article he writes because he is primarily employed as a teacher and not as a writer of books and articles, even though his employer may encourage this. A person employed as an accountant who writes a computer program to help with the production of financial accounts will own the copyright in that program if he wrote it in his own time, using his own equipment. Initially, this may create no problems because the accountant may have been motivated by interest and a desire to improve his own efficiency at work but problems could arise later if the accountant moves to another firm or discovers that his program is commercially viable. If an employer is faced with the situation where an employee has, in his own time and using his own equipment, developed a useful computer program, then the employer should immediately try to reach agreement as regards questions of ownership and use of the program with the employee concerned, rather than allowing the program to be used without such agreement.

If an employee has produced a computer program outside the normal course of his duties, but has used his employer's equipment or done it during the hours of his employment, the ownership of copyright is more difficult to predict, although it is more likely that the employee will be treated as owner. Even here, however, it is wiser to seek agreement at the outset rather than leave matters until there is some disagreement about the continued use or exploitation of the program. Employers should consider the introduction of, or extension of, a 'suggestions' scheme to include computer programs or systems written by staff who are not employed to do this, with effective rewards and suitable provisions as regards ultimate ownership.

Programming languages and instruction sets

A computer program is written using a specific computer programming language. Languages vary enormously from the basic instruction set of the central processing unit to 'fourth-generation' languages and languages used for programming logic. A great deal of skill, imagination and effort goes into the design of a new programming language and the development of new languages will be encouraged if some form of protection is afforded to them. However, the exercise of rights in languages could seriously interfere with the licensing and distribution of computer programs and data-bases. In principle, there is a strong argument for saying that programming languages are ideas and, as such, cannot be protected by copyright. Therefore a person who writes an original program in COBOL infringes no copyright in the process of writing the program. There is an analogy with natural language and it would be ridiculous to suggest that writing an article or report using 'Esperanto' infringed any copyright subsisting in the language. Of course, making an unauthorised copy of an Esperanto–English dictionary would infringe copyright, if only that subsisting in the typographical arrangement.

The European Council Directive on the legal protection of computer programs recognises that programming languages, at least to the extent that they comprise ideas and principles, should not be protected by copyright. Given that this is so one might wonder wherein lies the incentive to create a new language. The answer lies in the fact that, usually, the program, once written, can only be run on a computer if it is converted into object code whether temporarily, using an interpreter program, or permanently, using a compiler program. The licensing of these interpreter and compiler programs, together with appropriate documentation describing the syntax, semantics and use of the language, is the method by which financial reward is usually sought. These programs are, of course, protected by copyright. However, the obsession in the United States of withholding copyright protection from ideas including features of programs dictated by function might have the drastic effect, if taken to its logical conclusion, of robbing interpreter and compiler programs of copyright protection.

Some languages and program development tools (languages in a wide sense including expert system shells) require 'run-time' licences to be acquired before application programs and systems may be distributed. These generally permit the copying and distribution of a cut-down version of the language, tool or shell sufficient to run the application.

A computer's instruction set represents a language at its most basic level and, at this level, it is nearest to idea and, when used to write small programs, it has been argued that there is a merger of idea and expression – in which case protection will be denied. This happened in the United States case of *NEC Corp* v *Intel Corp* (1989) 10 USPQ 2d where it was held that Intel's microcode programs were dictated by the instruction set of the microprocessors and, as there were no alternative ways of expressing the ideas incorporated, reverse analysis of the microcode programs did not infringe copyright. However, it was also accepted that such programs could be protected if not dictated by idea.

In the United Kingdom, the question of copyright protection for an instruction set was considered in *Microsense Systems Ltd* v *Control Systems Technology Ltd* (unreported) 17 June 1991, Chancery Division. The claimant made traffic control systems and controllers for pelican crossings, which were programmed using a set of mnemonics (a set of three-letter symbols) which were in turn used to monitor the controllers. The defendant made similar controllers and used a total of 49 of the claimant's mnemonics arguing that there was no copyright in them because, once the functions had been decided, there was no room for skill and labour in devising the mnemonics. This was an interim hearing so no final decision was taken but the judge thought that there was an arguable case that the list of mnemonics was protected by copyright because of the work in designing the controller in the first place. This seems to contradict the *NEC* v *Intel* case although, being an American case, it is not binding on the United Kingdom courts. However, the defendant's argument that the list was effectively idea reflects the desirability of standardisation in traffic controllers as, otherwise, there could be catastrophic mistakes.

Devices to overcome copy-protection

At the time of writing, the European Directive on the harmonisation of certain aspects of copyright and related rights in the information society should have been transposed into United Kingdom law by 22 December 2002 but this has not yet happened. The legislative changes necessary to comply with the Directive are proving to be complex and difficult. It is likely that this section relating to devices designed or adapted to overcome copy-protection will remain more or less as they are described below with the exception that the statutory provisions under section 296 of the Act will be restricted to computer programs only rather than any form of copyright work issued to the public in electronic form. A whole raft of other provisions will be introduced for other forms of copyright work where effective technological measures are used to protect the work. These are described in Chapter 8 on copyright in the information society. Therefore, when reading the remainder of this section, bear in mind that these particular provisions are likely to be limited to computer programs only in the very near future.

Some computer programs were marketed in a form that makes them difficult to copy. Almost inevitably, devices and software designed to overcome these attempts at copy-protection soon appeared on the market, to the intense irritation of the software industry. A distinction must be made at this stage between things that can be used to make unauthorised copies of programs, but which also have legitimate uses (for example, computers with two disk drives and cassette players with twin tape decks) and things specifically designed to overcome copy-protection, such as software to be used to copy other software which has been copy-protected. Where a device or software has lawful uses, it would obviously be unsatisfactory to ban its sale. The music industry tried to interfere with the sale of twin-cassette music centres in *CBS Songs Ltd* v *Amstrad Consumer Electronics plc* [1988] AC 1013, on the basis that, by the sale and advertising of these machines, Amstrad was inciting the public to infringe copyright. The fact that the machines made by Amstrad had other legitimate uses, such as making copies of the purchasers' own music or of works not protected by copyright, was important, even though it was obvious that the largest use would involve copyright infringement. Nor was Amstrad authorising infringement.

There can be little sympathy, however, for firms who make devices or software deliberately designed to permit the copying of works which are copy-protected. The sole purpose of these devices and software is to enable copy-protection to be overcome. By section 296 of the Copyright, Designs and Patents Act 1988, devices or means specifically designed or adapted to circumvent copy-protection of works issued to the public in electronic form are controlled by treating the making, importation, sale or hire, possession in the course of business, etc. of such devices or means as an infringement of copyright. Furthermore, publishing information to enable or assist the circumvention of copy-protection is similarly treated. The use of the phrase 'devices or means' should be wide enough to cover both hardware devices and software methods designed to overcome copy-protection. Computers with dual disk drives and twin tape cassette machines are not caught by these provisions because they are not 'specifically designed or adapted to circumvent copy-protection'. Similarly, normal copying programs which come with a computer operating system are within the law because they are designed to be used legitimately, to take back-up copies of programs and data files. Indeed, such programs will usually fail to copy computer programs that are copy-protected. A difficulty with this provision is that it is enforceable only by the person issuing copies of the copy-protected work in question to the public and then only if the person making, importing, selling or hiring, etc. the device, means or information knows or has reason to believe that it will be used to make infringing copies.

Implications of software copyright law

The scope of copyright law in relation to computer software in general and computer programs in particular has become more certain in the last couple of years or so. Consequently, a number of practical recommendations can be made to software developers.

- Do not copy screen displays, menus, program structure, database structure, the look and feel of websites or other non-literal elements of software.
- Even if some element of new software is likely to be 'dictated by function', create it independently and retain all the preparatory materials in respect of it.
- Prepare, date and keep preparatory materials for all items of software.
- Insert deliberate mistakes or redundant code or entries into programs, databases and other works.
- Be aware that copyright extends to a compilation of individual programs and/or data files.

- Make sure employees do not use materials or confidential information belonging to previous employers.
- Obtain a signed written assignment of copyright in respect of works to be created by self-employed programmers or consultants.
- Check licence agreements for void terms in respect of decompilation and making back-up copies of computer programs and void terms in respect of databases.
- Make sensible arrangements for error correction of computer programs.

In general terms, copyright law does not protect the function of a program. It will be perfectly legal to write a program that performs the same function as an existing program provided the function itself is not protected by the law of confidence and the first program is not used in a manner which falls within the acts restricted by the copyright: for example, to be copied and then modified to create the new program or used to test the new program. However, where the same person is involved in writing the first and second programs a great deal of care must be taken to be able to rebut any presumption of copying that is likely to be raised in any action for infringement of copyright.

Chapter 5

Copyright and databases

Introduction

Until changes to copyright law which took effect on 1 January 1998, it was generally accepted that computer databases were protected by copyright as literary works as they could be considered to be compilations. This was, of course, without prejudice to any individual copyrights subsisting in the individual items or works contained within the database. For example, consider a database of modern romantic poems. Each poem would be protected by copyright as an original literary work and, providing sufficient skill, labour or judgment was expended in selecting and arranging, indexing or annotating the poems, there would be a separate copyright in the database as a whole. There could be other copyrights also, such as in respect of any index, cross-referencing system or annotations. Some of these elements could be protected as non-literal elements such as, for example, any hypertext links or the indexing system itself.

There was some doubt about whether a database of artistic works could be a compilation as literary works are defined in section 3(1) of the Copyright, Designs and Patents Act 1988 in terms of works which are written, spoken or sung. It is arguable that this does not apply to most forms of artistic works. An exception is a circuit diagram which, according to Mr Justice Jacob in *Anacon Corp Ltd* v *Environmental Research Technology Ltd* [1994] FSR 659, was also a literary work because it was intended to be read by the person making a circuit board in accordance with the diagram. Mr Justice Laddie agreed with this in *Electronic Techniques (Anglia) Ltd* v *Critchley Components Ltd* [1997] FSR 401. However, he said that, when considering a circuit diagram as a literary work, the graphic elements must be ignored and, that being so, the work could not be a literary work as it was little more than a list of five or six components. In other words, the circuit diagram was not sufficiently substantial for copyright as a literary work.

The legal protection of databases was significantly changed by the Copyright and Rights in Databases Regulations 1997 which came into force on 1 January 1998. The Regulations were made in order to comply with a European Directive on the legal protection of databases (96/9/EC, OJ L 77, 27.03.96, p.20). A particular concern, following developments in the United States in the *Feist* v *Rural Telephone* case (discussed below), was that some databases that might be commercially valuable would fail to attract copyright protection in some member states of the European Community. Thus, a dual approach to protection was taken in the Directive. First, providing a database can be regarded as an intellectual creation, it will have copyright protection. If the database can be regarded as the result of a substantial investment, it will attract a right, referred to in the Regulations as a 'database right' which was introduced into the United Kingdom by the Regulations. Of course, in many cases, databases will enjoy both a copyright and a database right (as well as separate rights in the constituent parts in some cases) but the database right was designed specifically for valuable databases which failed to reach the requirements for copyright protection.

In this chapter, the new provisions for databases are described. However, first it will be useful to look at the basic position before the changes brought about by the Regulations and the position in the United States.

Copyright in a database before 1 January 1998

Databases were not expressly mentioned in the Copyright, Designs and Patents Act 1988 but were potentially protected by copyright as compilations, provided they were original. Copyright might have subsisted at two levels if the database was a collection of individual works, as mentioned earlier. Each work may be subject to copyright but, on a higher level, there may be a separate copyright in the database as a whole if the selection and arrangement of materials contained within it is the result of a modicum of skill or judgment. This is similar to the copyrights found in the *IBCOS* case discussed in Chapter 4. It appeared that most databases would have had copyright protection providing they were the result of a minimum amount of skill, labour or judgment. Traditionally, the threshold for copyright protection in the United Kingdom was relatively low in comparison, for example, to German copyright law which requires a work to be a personal intellectual creation (German Copyright Act 1965, section 2(2), as amended). This appeared to be a higher standard than that required in the United Kingdom where copyright law developed in a very pragmatic manner.

Consider a database comprising details of a company's customers. Say that the information stored includes names and addresses of existing and potential customers together with details of the customers' operations and views on the customers' creditworthiness, payment facilities, discounts, etc. This database would have been protected by copyright in the United Kingdom because it required skill and judgment in the design of the structure of the database (that is, the design of the number and type of fields and their length) and in the selection of the information to be entered. Thus the structure of the database and the information contained within it would have been forms of expression for copyright purposes.

This should be contrasted with a database containing simply the names and addresses of all a company's customers because there is no selectivity or judgment (or very little) in the decision as to what should be included and relatively little skill in designing the structure of the database. This would be similar in principle to *G A Cramp & Sons Ltd v Frank Smythson Ltd* [1944] AC 329, discussed in Chapter 4, in which copyright was denied to a small collection of tables of information at the front of a simple diary because the commonplace nature of the information left little room for judgment in the selection and organisation of the information. If the creation of a database was the result of a great deal of effort alone, with little judgment in the design of the database or in the selection of material (for example, a telephone directory stored in a computer database or a directory of postcodes), it was debatable whether it would attract copyright protection. However, the United Kingdom law traditionally has been generous and compilations of non-original matter have been protected providing that some judgment at least has been expended in their making (see *Macmillan & Co Ltd v K & J Cooper* (1923) 40 TLR 186). In reported cases on copyright and databases, including some on the copyright in a database of lawyers, the question of whether the databases were protected by copyright was not put into issue; see, for example, *Waterlow Directories Ltd* v *Reed Information Services Ltd* [1992] FSR 409.

The United States and the 'sweat of the brow' principle

The 'sweat of the brow' principle, affording copyright protection to works which are the result of labour only, was roundly rejected in the United States Supreme Court in *Feist Publications Inc* v *Rural Telephone Service Co Inc* (1991) 111 S Ct 1282. In that case, it was held that the 'white pages' in a typical telephone directory were not protected by copyright because of a lack of creativity, as they did not owe their origin to an act of authorship. The court did recognise, however, that a compilation of facts could be the subject of copyright because the author has to choose which facts to include and in what order to place them. The court went on to suggest that the 'yellow pages' section of a telephone directory was protected because of the presence of original material such as drawings in advertisements. There is also some skill in devising the classification system used. Subsequently, however, it was held in the United States that taking a large amount of data from a classified directory did not infringe copyright (see *Bell South Advertising & Publishing Corp* v *Donnelley Information Publishing Inc* (unreported) 2 September 1993, 11th Cir). It is fair to say that the position in the United Kingdom has probably been more generous to database compilers and it has been accepted that headings in a trade catalogue are protected by copyright. The United States Constitution gives a clue to the more rigorous approach there as it states the object of copyright is 'to promote the progress of science and the useful arts' (Article 1, Section 8, cl 8). This would appear to be incompatible with rewarding acts of labour only.

Protection of databases on or after 1 January 1998

In view of problems such as that highlighted in *Feist* v *Rural Telephone* and bearing in mind even telephone directories and directories of postcodes can be commercially valuable – for example, by being sold on compact discs – it was considered important to improve the protection of databases on a European scale. Another factor was that standards of protection varied throughout Europe and there was a need for harmonisation of national laws. The model of protection adopted was to provide for a standard copyright treatment for databases requiring skill or judgment in their making but, in addition, to introduce a new *sui generis* right specifically aimed at providing shorter-term protection for databases that might not meet this standard but which were, nevertheless, the result of a substantial investment which would be prejudiced if such databases had no protection.

The new copyright and the database right apply equally to both electronic and non-electronic databases, in line with the general approach of the European Commission not to distinguish between electronic and manual databases. Both of the new rights are without prejudice to copyright in the contents. Thus, where a database contains individual works of copyright, those works will retain their own copyright in addition to any copyright or database right in the database as a whole. For example, consider a database of recipes. If a person copies one of the recipes without permission, he will infringe the copyright in it. If he copies several recipes without permission, he will infringe the copyright in each individual recipe as well as infringing the copyright in the database and/or the database right, depending on whether one or both subsist, subject to the question of whether the recipes copied represented a substantial part of the database.

It should also be noted that the moral rights have not been affected by the changes and, consequently, an author of a copyright database may have moral rights in respect of it although there are no moral rights in respect of a database only protected by the database right (ignoring any copyrights in the constituent parts) and music collections on compact discs are expressly excluded from these new provisions. They will continue to be treated as compilations for copyright purposes.

First, the copyright protection of databases is considered, followed by an examination of the new database right.

Copyright in databases

Section 3(1) of the Copyright, Designs and Patents Act 1988 is amended and 'database' is added to the non-exhaustive list of works that are literary works. Databases are then excluded from compilations and there are now some differences as to how databases and compilations are treated by copyright law. Of course, many of the provisions are the same for both but it should be noted that there is a difference in the fair dealing provisions and there is a special non-derogation from grant provision, preventing undue interference with the rights of lawful users of databases.

The precise nature of the original works of copyright is not expressly defined in the Act but there is now a detailed definition of 'database', following that in the Directive. Section 3A was inserted into the Act which defines 'database' as

> ... a collection of independent works, data or other materials which-
> (a) are arranged in a systematic or methodical way, and
> (b) are individually accessible by electronic or other means.

The use of the phrase 'other means' shows that the provisions apply equally to non-electronic databases and this is confirmed in the recitals to the Directive. A card index will be a database for copyright purposes. Although the Act, as modified, is silent on the point, the Directive makes it clear that the copyright protection for a database does not extend to any program used in the making or operation of an electronic database. Of course, computer programs are separately protected as another form of literary work.

Unlike the other original works, a gloss is added to the test of originality and a database is original for copyright purposes if and only if, by reason of the selection or arrangement of its contents, the database constitutes the author's own intellectual creation; section 3A(2). This is equivalent to the German approach to copyright and seems to be a much stricter requirement than that which existed before 1 January 1998. However, this is not to prejudice pre-existing databases and, where a database was created on or before 27 March 1996 (which was the date on which the Directive as adopted was published) and was protected by copyright immediately before 1 January 1998, that copyright will continue for its full term (that is, 'life plus 70 years'), even if it does not qualify for copyright protection under this new test for originality.

The usual restricted acts apply to databases as they do for literary works generally except that the restricted act of making an adaptation is redefined for databases in terms of an adaptation being an arrangement or altered version or a translation of the database. Examples of these are:

- a version in which the information contained in the database has been sorted into a different order (arrangement);
- a version in which some of the information is suppressed or deleted (either records or fields or both) (arrangement or altered version);
- a version in which the database is converted to be used with a different program to access the contents or it is converted from 8bit to 7bit code or it is imported into a word processing or spreadsheet program (altered version or translation).

The Directive left member states with some discretion as to which permitted acts they applied to copyright databases. The approach in the United Kingdom was to apply the traditional permitted acts that apply to literary works, with the exception of fair dealing for research and private study where two specific changes were implemented for databases. A new subsection (1A) was inserted into section 29 which, in respect of fair dealing for research or private study, requires the source to be indicated. Furthermore, under section 29(5), it is not fair dealing to do anything in relation to a database for a commercial purpose. This is in line with the imminent changes to be made to fair dealing generally.

Section 50D was inserted into the Copyright, Designs and Patents Act 1988. This applies to any person having a right to use a database or part of a database. Such a person does not infringe copyright if, in the exercise of that right, he does anything which is necessary for the purposes of his access to and use of the contents of the database (or part of the database). This prevents a person licensing a database to another including terms in the licence agreement which purport to hinder access to and use of the database. It is essentially a non-derogation from grant provision. It is clear from this provision that a database may be made available in such a way that a licensee may be restricted to part only of the database. The restriction may be in terms of certain records or certain fields. For example, in a database of potential customers, a licensed user may be restricted to customers living in the South of England only or it may be that the user can retrieve names and addresses only and not data relating to individuals' financial standing. The right under section 50D cannot be prohibited or restricted and section 296B makes void any term or condition in an agreement in so far as it purports to prohibit or restrict those acts permitted under section 50D or any act necessary for the exercise of the rights granted by the agreement.

The database right

The Copyright, Designs and Patents Act 1988 was not amended to include the provisions relating to the database right. Instead it is provided for separately in Part III of the Copyright and Rights in Databases Regulations 1997.

The database right, described in the Directive as a right *sui generis*, was designed to protect the investment in obtaining, verifying or presenting the contents of a database. It is of limited duration compared to copyright but the right is not restricted to non-copyright databases and many databases will be subject to both copyright and the database right. As with the copyright provisions, the database right is unaffected if the database contains works which are themselves subject to copyright. Take, for example, a database of original maps or charts which required the exercise of skill and judgment (assuming that this test is the same as 'author's intellectual creation') and which was also a substantial investment, for example, in the presentation of its contents. The individual maps or charts will be works of copyright; the database as a whole will be a work of copyright and it will also be subject to the database right.

Definitions

The database right is a right given to the maker of a database to prevent the unauthorised extraction or reutilisation of the contents of a database. To understand this basic right, it is important to look at the definitions in the Regulations which are set out below. However, it must be noted that the meaning of 'database' is the same as applies to databases subject to copyright. The definitions are contained in regulation 12, although the fine detail of some of them occur in other parts of the Regulations as indicated:

- 'database right' is defined in regulation 13(1) as a property right which subsists in a database if there has been a substantial investment in obtaining, verifying or presenting the contents of the database;
- 'investment' includes any investment, whether of financial, human or technical resources;
- 'substantial', in relation to any investment, extraction or reutilisation, means substantial in terms of quantity or quality or a combination of both;
- 'insubstantial' is relevant to infringement and, under regulation 16(2), the repeated and systematic extraction or reutilisation of *insubstantial* parts of the contents of a database may amount to the extraction or reutilisation of a substantial part of those contents;
- 'extraction', in relation to any contents of a database, means the permanent or temporary transfer of those contents to another medium by any means or in any form;
- 'reutilisation', in relation to any contents of a database, means making those contents available to the public by any means;
- 'maker' is defined in regulation 14(1) as the person who takes the initiative in obtaining, verifying or presenting the contents of a database and assumes the risk of investing in that obtaining, verification or presentation, such acts constituting the act of making the database. The basic rule is that the maker will be the first owner of the database right. Where a database is made by an employee in the course of his employment, the employer is regarded as the maker of the database and there is provision for Her Majesty to be regarded as the maker of a database where it is made by an officer or servant of the Crown in the course of his duties (Parliamentary database right is also provided for);
- 'jointly' in relation to the making of a database is defined in regulation 16(2) in terms of two or more persons who act in collaboration in taking the initiative and assuming the risk of investing; however, unlike the case in copyright law, there is no requirement that the contribution of each is not distinct.
- 'lawful user', in relation to a database, means any person who (whether under a licence to do any of the acts restricted by any database right in the database or otherwise) has a right to use the database.

A few points can be made about these definitions. First, the fact that the right is a property right (as is copyright, of course) should come as no surprise. The meaning of 'substantial' is slightly different from that generally accepted (though not defined) for copyright purposes, because quality, quantity or both are factors, whereas for copyright purposes attention tends to focus primarily on quality rather than quantity. However, that is not to say that the proportion of the work taken can never be a factor in determining infringement. A curious provision is that continuing to take or make available insubstantial parts may amount to a substantial taking or making available. This is to prevent any doubt as to whether such action would infringe the database right, though this provision has proved difficult to apply in practice. There is some doubt under copyright law as to whether the repeated taking of insubstantial parts can infringe although it would seem sensible to view such taking as a connected series of takings and view them cumulatively, in the round.

The meanings of 'extraction' and 'investment' are quite wide. In particular, the latter is not restricted to financial investment and covers a situation where a person spends time and effort in making a database or simply where technical resources are tied up. This could be the situation where a central computer is dedicated to receiving information from remote users who submit information to the computer which is automatically collated and entered into a database. As substantiality is a factor in the investment, it is possible that the skill of any person involved or the power or technical advancement of equipment used could be relevant in determining whether the right subsists. The meaning of 'reutilisation' is directed to making the contents available to the public rather than simply making use of the contents for one's own purposes, although this would almost certainly involve an infringing act of extraction first. There may also be infringements of any copyright in the underlying works included in the database, where such copyright exists.

Lending a copy of a database (not for direct or indirect commercial advantage) by an establishment accessible to the public does not constitute extraction or reutilisation of the contents of a database but this exception does not extend to making available for on-the-spot reference use which could, therefore, fall within the meaning of extraction or reutilisation.

The doctrine of exhaustion of rights within the European Economic Area (EEA) applies to copies sold within the EEA by or with the consent of the owner of the database right to the extent that any subsequent sale of *those* copies does not constitute extraction or reutilisation of the contents of the database. Therefore, if a person lawfully buys a copy of a database, that person can resell that copy elsewhere in the EEA without infringing the database right. The fact that a database has been made available online for consultation by members of the public does not, however, exhaust the maker's right of reutilisation. It is only sale of copies, for example, on compact discs, that exhausts any right to control resale of those copies.

Qualification

For the database right to subsist, it must satisfy the qualification requirements. These are set out in regulation 18, and require that, at the 'material time', the maker (or at least one of them where there are joint makers) be:

- a national of an EEA state (or habitually resident in the state),
- a body incorporated in an EEA state, having its central administration or principal place of business in an EEA state or registered office in the EEA and the body's operations linked on an ongoing basis with the economy of an EEA state, or

- a partnership or other unincorporated body formed under the law of an EEA state, having at that time its central administration or principal place of business within the EEA.

The 'material time' is the time when the database is made or, if this extended over a period of time, a substantial part of that period. The qualification requirements do not apply in the case of Parliamentary database right although there is no express exception for Crown database right.

Duration

The Directive emphasised that the right is to be limited in time, subject to a new right arising if a database undergoes substantial change, and the term of protection afforded by the database right is stated in regulation 17 as 15 years from the end of the calendar year during which the making of the database is completed; although, if it is made available to the public before the end of that period, the right will continue to endure for 15 years from the end of the calendar year during which it was first made available. Of course, many databases are subject to continuing or periodic modification. Thus, a new period of protection arises if changes to the database are substantial and this *includes* any substantial change resulting from an accumulation of successive additions, deletions or alterations, which would result in the database being considered to be a substantial new investment. The wording of the regulation does not limit this to additions, deletions or alterations and substantial investment in verifying the contents or presenting them in an improved manner should suffice in appropriate circumstances.

Thus, a new database right might arise simply because the maker has redesigned his software to improve the presentation of the contents of the database, or has put resources into checking the accuracy of the contents. For example, in the case of a database of customers, the owner has sent out a mailing asking for confirmation of the details of individuals and made corrections to the database as appropriate.

If the database in question was made on or before 1 January 1983 and the database right subsisted in the database immediately on 1 January 1998, the database right will last for 15 years beginning with 1 January 1998.

Infringement

Infringing acts are defined in regulation 16 in terms of the extraction or reutilisation of all or a substantial part of the contents of the database without the consent of the owner. Reflecting the special nature of databases and the damage that may be done to the owner's interests by a systematic course of unauthorised use of small parts of the database, the repeated and systematic extraction or reutilisation of insubstantial parts of the contents of a database *may* amount to the extraction or reutilisation of a substantial part of those contents.

The first reported case to involve the database right was *Mars UK Ltd* v *Teknowledge Ltd* [2000] FSR 138 in which the claimant designed and made coin operated machines which contained discriminators designed to detect whether or not a coin was genuine. The claimant brought out a new discriminator known as 'Cashflow' which was programmed for new coin data and contained an EEPROM (electronically erasable programmable read only memory) which could be reprogrammed in the future with new data. This was important so as to allow the discriminator to be recalibrated to accept new types of coin and reject new forms of blanks or foreign coins. The claimant wanted to keep to itself the work of reprogramming these EEPROMs and the data contained within them was encrypted. The defendant managed to overcome the encryption and was then able to recalibrate Cashflow machines itself. The claimant commenced proceedings for infringement of copyright and the database right in the computer programs and data in the computer chips in the discriminators. Breach of confidence was also alleged but this claim failed, for which see Chapter 9.

The defendant eventually admitted infringing copyright in the computer programs and algorithms and copyright and database right in the data, subject to a *British Leyland* defence. In *British Leyland Motor Corp Ltd v Armstrong Patents Co Ltd* [1986] AC 577, the defendant made exhaust systems for the claimant's motor cars without permission. It was held that this had been a technical infringement of the copyright subsisting in the drawings of the exhaust systems but that copyright would not be enforced as individuals buying the motor cars had a right to access a free market in spare parts. This so-called spare parts defence has been largely overtaken by the Copyright, Designs and Patents Act 1988 which contained express provisions to permit the making of spare parts subject to design rights and, effectively suppressed copyright in drawings as a means of protecting industrial designs.

Mr Justice Jacob doubted whether recalibration of discriminators fell within the *British Leyland* spare parts defence anyway but considered the situation if it did. He noted that no provisions equivalent to a spare parts defence were contained in the European Directives on the legal protection of computer programs and databases nor was there any overriding public policy in having such a defence in this context. Although the Directive on the legal protection of databases permitted individual member states to adopt defences traditionally authorised under national law, Parliament had chosen not to expressly adopt any such defence and it would be wrong for judges to introduce such a defence. Although the *British Leyland* defence has all but disappeared, and its further development has been effectively censured by the House of Lords in *Canon Kabushiki Kaisha v Green Cartridge Co* [1997] AC 728 where it was held that a refiller of toner cartridges for photocopies and laser printers could not avail itself of the defence. However, the defence may yet have a residual role to play in very limited circumstances such as in terms of software maintenance.

In terms of 'insubstantial infringement', the Directive stated that the repeated and systematic extraction or reutilisation must imply acts conflicting with a normal exploitation of the database or be unreasonably prejudicial to the legitimate interests of the maker of the database. One way of looking at repeated insubstantial takings is to view them as a continuing act and as equivalent to a substantial taking by accumulating them. However, it seems clear that what is intended is that an accumulation of insubstantial takings could infringe even if, when accumulated, they still do not amount to a substantial part of the database, otherwise there would seem little point in including this provision. But there is some doubt about the precise meaning and scope of infringement by repeated and systematic taking of insubstantial parts of the contents of a database.

The scope of infringement by insubstantial taking was an important issue in *British Horseracing Board Ltd v William Hill Organisation Ltd* [2001] RPC 612. The claimant (BHB) maintained a database containing details of racehorse owners, racing colours, trainers and jockeys and pre-race information, such as the runners and riders for a given race. Nearer the date of the race, this pre-race information was updated and expanded to include, *inter alia*, the time of the race, sponsor, weights and stalls the horses start the race from. The cost of obtaining the data, verification and presentation of the data cost around £4m per annum. This was certainly a substantial investment for the purposes of the database right.

BHB granted licences allowing subscribers to make use of the information contained in the database. Up-to-the-minute details of races, including times, declared runners and jockeys, distance of race were made available to subscribers in electronic form and to a company, Satellite Information Services Ltd (SIS), which transmitted data from the database to its own subscribers in a form known as a raw data feed (RDF).

The defendant was a well-known bookmaker which established an internet site and an enhanced version went on-line during 1999. This permitted on-line betting with real time changes in odds being offered. The defendant's website contained information identical to that in the BHB database and BHB claimed that much of the information on the website was obtained via the SIS RDF and the defendant was not licensed to do this. BHB alleged that its database right had been infringed by the defendant, first, by the extraction or reutilisation of a substantial part of the database and, secondly, by the repeated and systematic extraction of insubstantial parts of the contents of the database.

Laddie J accepted both allegations and found that the defendant had infringed the database right in both ways. He held that whilst the quantity and quality of what is taken must be looked at in combination, the significance of the information taken to the alleged infringer can throw light upon whether that part was an important or significant part. In this case, the defendant made use of the most recent and core information in the database and relied on the accuracy and completeness of the information. This was a reflection of BHB's investment in obtaining and verifying the contents of the database. Therefore, the defendant had taken a substantial part of the database.

The defendant had taken information from the database on a day-by-day basis. This conflicted with the normal exploitation of the database by BHB and was unreasonably prejudicial to BHB's legitimate interests, applying the test as set out in the Directive (the implementing Regulations do not specifically refer to these tests). Therefore, Mr Justice Laddie confirmed that the defendant infringed by the repeated and systematic extraction and reutilisation of the database. He considered that the defendant's acts undermined a significant part of BHB's exploitation of the database. An argument that each day the database was a different database because of changes made to it so that there was only a taking of an insubstantial part from a sequence of databases was rejected as such an interpretation would mean that otherwise this form of infringement would rarely apply because most databases are subject to constant revision. Approximately 800,000 entries were made annually to BHB's database. It would be impossible to say just how many new databases were created each year.

The defendant appealed to the Court of Appeal (*British Horseracing Board Ltd* v *William Hill Organisation Ltd* [2001] EWCA Civ 1268) which noted that a narrower interpretation of the database right had been taken in Sweden and the Netherlands. The Court of Appeal referred some questions to the European Court of Justice for a preliminary ruling and, pending that ruling, discharged the injunctions imposed in the High Court. Unfortunately, the questions submitted to the European Court of Justice have not yet been published and it may be some time before a preliminary ruling is handed down. Alternatively, it may be that a settlement has been reached between the parties making the reference no longer necessary.

Either way and bearing in mind the commercial significance of databases, it is important that there should be little doubt as to the scope and extent of the database right as a form of protection. There is no great difficulty in respect of copyright data-bases as there is a wealth of copyright law relating to literary works available to apply to copyright databases. This is not the case with the database right and the only two significant United Kingdom cases thus far have failed to produce any real guidance. The Directive itself provides the basic test. Does the defendant's unauthorised use of the database in question conflict with the owner's normal exploitation of it and unreason-ably prejudice the legitimate interests of the owner? In other words, is it a case where, based on normal and honest commercial practices, a disinterested but objective onlooker would think it only fair that the use complained of ought to be paid for by means of a licence agreement?

Exceptions to infringement

There are a number of exceptions to infringement. Regulation 19 contains a 'non-dero-gation from grant' provision which prevents the owner of the database right interfer-ing with the subsequent use of insubstantial parts by a lawful user such as a person having access under a licence agreement. A lawful user of a database, which has been made available to the public, cannot be prevented from extracting or reutilising insub-stantial parts of the database for any purpose. Any term in an agreement, under which the right to use a database or part of a database has been granted, which attempts to prevent this is void. Regulation 20 contains a fair dealing exception to infringement. Where the database has been made available to the public in any manner, fair dealing with a substantial part of the contents does not infringe if:

- the part is extracted by a person who is otherwise a lawful user,
- it is extracted for the purposes of illustration for teaching or research (but not for a commercial purpose), and
- the source is indicated.

This differs from the fair dealing provisions for conventional literary, dramatic, musi-cal or artistic works where there is no requirement that the person is otherwise a lawful user. However, those provisions in section 29 of the Copyright, Designs and Patents Act 1988 do not specifically state that the part dealt with has to be a substantial part of the work. In reality, however, section 29 can only apply where the part taken is sub-stantial otherwise there can be no infringement in the first place and no need to rely on section 29.

Further exceptions are set out in Schedule 1 to the Regulations and relate to parlia-mentary and judicial proceedings, Royal Commissions and statutory inquiries, material open to public inspection or on official register, material communicated to the Crown in the course of public business, public records and acts done under statutory authority. These mirror the equivalent permitted acts for copyright. However, apart from these exceptions and those mentioned above, none of the other permitted acts that apply gen-erally to literary works under copyright apply to the database right. For example, there is no provision for fair dealing for criticism or review or for reporting current events.

Where it is reasonable to assume that the database right has expired and the identity of the maker (or each of the makers in the case of a database made jointly) cannot by reasonable enquiry be ascertained, the right will not be infringed by the extraction or reutilisation of a substantial part of the contents: regulation 21. It is important, there-fore, for the owner of databases to indicate the identity of the maker on copies of the database and the year during which it was first published. If the database is made available on-line, this information should appear on the title screen or other appropriate place. This is also worth doing so as to raise useful presumptions as discussed below.

It should be noted that it is the identity of the maker which is important, not that of the owner, where the maker and owner are not the same person. This is similar to copyright where it is the identity of the author which is crucial. However, unlike copyright, the duration of the database right is not dependent on the life of the maker and is fixed by the act of making or first publication. Of course, it may be dangerous to rely on this and other permitted acts which relate to the database right, as the database and/or its contents may be subject to copyright. Such copyright, where it subsists, is independent of and not prejudiced by the database right. Where copyright subsists in the database or its contents, a person using a database must ensure that the agreement under which he is using it extends to the appropriate use of copyright materials. A person relying on the exceptions to infringement of the database right must also check to make sure that his intended use is also covered by the exceptions to copyright infringement. For example, if a person who has the right to use a database wants to extract any part for the purpose of illustration for teaching, he should confirm that he can rely on the equivalent permitted acts in relation to teaching which apply to copyright works if the part extracted is protected by copyright unless, of course, his right to use the database covers this.

Presumptions

There are some presumptions which apply to the database right and which may be helpful to the owner in an action for infringement. They are not dissimilar to the equivalent presumptions which apply in relation to copyright works. Under regulation 22, where a name purporting to be that of the maker of the database appears on copies of the database as published, it is presumed that that person is the maker and the database was not made in circumstances where the employer would be the first owner and is not Crown or parliamentary database right. Where copies of a database as published bear a label or mark stating that a named person was the maker and that it was first published in a specified year, the label or mark shall be admissible as evidence of those facts and presumed correct until the contrary be proved.

Where a database has been made jointly, these provisions apply in relation to each person alleged to be one of the makers. Under copyright law, the usefulness of the equivalent presumptions was seen in the case of *Microsoft Corp v Electrowide Ltd* [1997] FSR 580 where, in the absence of any evidence submitted by the defendant, the Microsoft Corporation did not have to prove that it owned the copyrights subsisting in software such as 'Windows 95'.

Other provisions

The provisions which apply to dealing with rights in copyright works, the rights and remedies of the owner of copyright and of an exclusive licensee under the copyright are all applied without modification to the database right. Thus, assignment of the database right must be in writing and be signed by or on behalf of the assignor and exclusive licences are required to be in writing and be signed by or on behalf of the owner of the database right. This is helpful and where the database and/or its contents are also protected by copyright a simple form of words can be used. For example, an assignment may use the phrase 'I hereby assign the copyright and database right subsisting in [the database] and the copyright subsisting in its contents' or, more simply, 'I hereby assign all the rights subsisting in [the database] and its contents', assuming that the contents are not subject to other rights owned by third parties.

Remedies are the same as for copyright and include damages, injunctions, accounts or otherwise as is available for infringement of any other property right, and additional damages are also possible in the case of flagrant infringement. Exclusive licensees have rights concurrent to those of the owner and may bring an action themselves. As is usual, the owner would be expected to be joined in the action, for example, as co-claimant or defendant.

Schedule 2 to the Regulations contains provisions for licensing the database right and deals with licensing schemes, licensing bodies and referral of licensing schemes to the Copyright Tribunal. These provisions are equivalent to those in sections 116–129 and 144 of the Copyright, Designs and Patents Act 1988 which apply to copyright works. The jurisdiction of the Copyright Tribunal is enlarged accordingly to give it jurisdiction over the database right.

Database structure

As the non-literal elements of a computer program, including its structure, can be protected by copyright, it would seem sensible to assume that the structure of a database can also be protected by copyright. However, in *Total Information Processing Systems Ltd v Daman Ltd* [1992] FSR 171, it was held that the field and record specifications as expressed in the data division of a COBOL program were not protected because, in this form, the information did not form a substantial part of the computer program as a whole. This part of the program defines the structure of the database in addition to setting out the variables and their nature and format. In the second edition of this book the author submitted that this approach was wrong and that it would be better to consider the database structure as a form of expression in its own right and not as part of the computer program. This would accord with common sense because, in many cases, a great deal of work involving skill and judgment is expended in the design of database structure. Indeed, subsequently in *IBCOS Computers Ltd v Barclays Highland Mercantile Finance Ltd* [1994] FSR 275, Mr Justice Jacob made a number of criticisms of the judgment in the *Total Information Processing Systems* case and he said that there may well be a considerable degree of skill in devising the data division of a program and so it would be considered to be a substantial part of a program as a whole.

In an earlier case, *Computer-Aided Systems (UK) Ltd v Bolwell* (unreported) 23 August 1989, Chancery Division, the mere fact that a new program had file compatibility with an earlier program written by the same people failed to impress the judge who considered the claimant's application for inspection of the defendant's program to be nothing more than a 'fishing expedition'. There was no evidence of copying and the two programs were written in different languages, the original being written in COBOL, the latter one being written in a fourth-generation language called PROGRESS. The structure of the databases in terms of input and output formats must have been identical or similar but this did not seem to be sufficiently argued; instead the claimant concentrated on an argument that the structure of the two programs must have been similar. Alternatively, the fact of file compatibility could have been the result of a 'filter', a program which converted the file structure from one format to another.

Although the Copyright and Rights in Databases Regulations 1997 make no mention of the structure of a database, recital 15 to the European Directive on the legal protection of databases states that copyright protection should cover the structure of a database. The only major requirement for protection, therefore, apart from the qualification provisions (for example, that the author was a British citizen at the time of creation or that the work was first published in the United Kingdom), is that the database is an 'intellectual creation'. If it is and someone copies the database structure but not its contents without the permission of the owner, this will infringe the copyright if the database structure represents a substantial part of the database in terms of the skill or judgment expended by its creator. It should not be necessary to demonstrate that the database structure, as opposed to the database as a whole, is an intellectual creation. It would seem that if a database is subject to the database right only, its structure is not protected by that right. In order to further strengthen protection of databases, whether protected by copyright or the database right or both, the author or maker should retain copies of preparatory design materials such as diagrams, layouts and specifications. It is possible that anyone copying the structure of a database will indirectly infringe the copyright subsisting in such materials.

Chapter 6

Computer-generated works

Introduction

The Copyright, Designs and Patents Act 1988 expressly recognises that works produced by or with the aid of a computer are worthy of copyright protection. Such works were protected before the 1988 Act but there were difficulties in determining the identity of the author of the work for copyright purposes. Grids of random numbers selected by computer for a newspaper competition called 'Millionaire of the Month' were held to be protected by copyright in *Express Newspapers plc* v *Liverpool Daily Post & Echo plc* [1985] 1 WLR 1089. Arguments that there was no human author and, consequently, the lists of numbers drawn by the computer were not protected by copyright were rejected by Mr Justice Whitford who said that such a claim was as silly as saying that a pen could be the author of a literary work. The human expertise in computer-derived works could be found to reside in the programs which, in this case, produced the lists of random numbers.

In works produced by or with the aid of a computer, human skill can reside in the person who enters information into the computer to produce the output or in the programmer who writes the program used or a combination of them both. Section 178 of the Act defines a work as 'computer-generated' when it is generated by a computer in circumstances such that there is no human author of the work. Section 9(3) states that, in the case of a literary, dramatic, musical or artistic work which is computer-generated, the author is the person by whom the arrangements necessary for the creation of the work are undertaken. This will generally mean that the person who has control of the computer will be the author of any computer-generated work. These two definitions are tautologous when taken together: a computer-generated work is one created in circumstances such that there is no human author but if we attribute authorship to a human it cannot be computer-generated. The only way round this dilemma is to determine authorship *after* the creation of the work but this seems illogical. Normally, creation and attribution of authorship are coincident in time.

The approach taken in the Act can lead to difficulties because in many cases of works produced *with the aid of a computer* it will not be possible to say with any certainty whether the work has a human author. At one end of the spectrum a work will be produced using a computer as a tool, just as a writer uses a pen or a typewriter, while, at the other end, the computer will produce its works with little or no direct human effort. Neither of these situations should cause any great difficulty, but in between these two extremes lay a great many types of work which are the result of a modest amount of direct human input and classifying such works will not be easy. In order to consider this question further, works which involve computers in their production will be categorised as follows:

- works created using a computer,

- works created by a computer, and
- intermediate works.

In all these cases 'computer' means a programmed computer.

Works created using a computer

Examples of works which fall into this category are: documents produced using a word processing system; CAD (computer-aided designs) such as plans for a house or a new car body panel; music written using a program designed to assist with the composition of the music (as opposed to a program designed to write music); and an accounts report created using a spreadsheet program. In all these cases, the person operating the system is using the computer to achieve the results that he wishes to obtain. The programmed computer is merely a tool that allows the operator to use his creativity and imagination to the fullest extent and efficiency. Such works are not computer-generated; the skill and expertise (or at least the greatest part of these) derives from the user of the system. Word-processed documents, drawings, music and reports produced using packages which facilitate the making of these works are protected by copyright as original literary, dramatic, musical or artistic works in their own right. Indeed, section 51 of the Act recognises that copyright can subsist in data stored in a computer representing a design as a form of design document.

The person using the computer to create the work provides the expertise necessary for the making of the work and is, for copyright purposes, the author of the work. That expertise may be applied directly or indirectly: for example, a person writing a report may draft it out on paper and then hand it to a word processor operator who enters it into the computer. In these circumstances, the author is not the operator but the person writing the report. It is similar to the process of amanuensis in which a person dictating a letter will be the author of that letter; the person who writes the dictation down is merely his agent.

The person who wrote the computer program used to assist in the creation of the types of works described above has no rights in the work because, although the programmer may control or influence the *format* of the finished work, he has no control or influence on the *content*. The fact that many works in this category may be produced directly using a computer before any other tangible form exists presents no serious problems because these works will exist, in terms of copyright protection, the instant they are recorded; that is, as soon as they are stored on a computer disk or printed out on paper.

Works created by a computer

These works, which may be literary, dramatic, musical or artistic, are those in which there is 'no human author' (section 178). This implies that the direct degree of human intervention in the making of the work is lacking or minimal. Examples include:

- the automatic generation of weather forecasts by a computer communicating with satellites;
- the selection of lists of random numbers for a competition or for the Premium Bond draw;

- programs which produce artistic designs or music automatically, being based upon a set of rules or algorithms built into the program;
- a program designed to simulate some particular environment, such as climate, monetary systems, battle scenarios, etc. and to produce reports based on that simulation;
- works resulting from the application of fractal theory (it is claimed that fractal theory has a growing number of industrial and commercial uses, for example, to accurately measure a coastline; Glasser, D 'Copyrights in Computer-generated Works: Whom if Anyone do we Reward?' (2001) Duke L & Tech Rev 0024).

Many of these systems operate with no human effort or skill apart from switching the equipment on and checking that there is sufficient paper in the computer printer or plotter and so on. The human operator has very little or no control over the *format* or *content* of the output produced by the computer. The author of such a work is the person who makes the arrangements for the work to be created. Therefore, if a business organisation buys and installs computer equipment and software to produce such works, that business organisation will be regarded as the author and, as a result, the first owner of the copyright in the work. The Act contemplates non-human authors as, by section 154, an author can be a qualifying person if, *inter alia*, it is a body incorporated in the United Kingdom, such as a limited company. In the case of an unincorporated body, such as a partnership, the partners will be considered to be the joint authors of the work. As, theoretically, a company can be an author of a computer-generated work, there has to be a special rule for determining the duration of copyright in such works: the copyright expires at the end of the period of 50 years from the end of the calendar year in which the work was made; section 12(7).

Interestingly, and controversially, the Act appears to ignore the skill and expertise of the person or persons who wrote the computer programs used to generate these works. It could be argued that the computer programmer whose skill lies behind the computer output should have some recognition of authorship. However, this could cause difficulties because a person obtaining a computer program would expect to own the copyright in anything produced using the program, and any provisions sharing the ownership of the copyright between the user and the programmer could result in an undesirable fetter on the subsequent use of information and reports generated by the computer. The owner of the copyright in the computer program, suddenly realising that he has rights with respect to the output generated from using the program, might attempt to interfere with the subsequent use of that output in the hope that he will be able to negotiate a fee for his permission.

A concept, as yet untested in the courts, is that there is no such thing as a computer-generated work; that is, a work without a human author. After all, the argument that a list of numbers drawn at random by a programmed computer had no human author was rejected, as we have seen, in the *Express Newspapers* case. The approach adopted by the Copyright, Designs and Patents Act 1988 is a utilitarian one but it does not reflect the reality of the situation as it fails to recognise that all computer output is the result, albeit in many cases the indirect result, of human skill and effort. It would have been better if the programmer's skill were recognised making him the author or joint author of 'computer-generated' works. The practical difficulties resulting from this could be assuaged by raising a presumption that ownership of copyright would lie with the licensee, the ultimate user, of the computer program, subject to any agreement to the contrary.

Intermediate works

These works lie in the area between computer-generated works and works made using the programmed computer as a tool. The *content* of the output produced is the result of the skill and effort of the person using the computer *and* the skill and effort of the person who wrote the computer program and/or the person who produced any database used in conjunction with it. There are many examples of these intermediate works, such as a specialised accounting system for a particular type of business, builders' estimating systems, or a music synthesiser designed to produce music from a basic framework of notes entered by the user and expert and decision-support systems.

A great deal of specialised software falls into this category where the skill required to produce the finished results is contained partly within the program, the remainder being provided by the user of the computer system. In some systems, the skill may come from more than two sources. For example, consider a computer system designed to be used to estimate the cost of building work. The system itself will comprise a suite of computer programs, which include routines to provide analyses and breakdowns of the costs derived, and a database of standard prices, based on sets of resources and labour outputs. The person using the system to work out the cost of a building brings a substantial degree of skill by deciding whether the standard prices are applicable and, if not, by building up new prices and entering them into the database. As Fig. 6.1 shows, the resulting computer output has three sources of expertise: that of the programmer, of the persons responsible for developing the database of standard prices, and of the person using the system. Who is the author of the finished work? Because the person using the system brings an amount of skill to the task, it would not be unreasonable to suggest that he is the author. Indeed, the user has the most direct link with the finished product and has ultimate control but may, nevertheless, rely to a great extent on the programs and information contained in the database. It could be argued that the finished work is partly created by human author and partly computer-generated. Alternatively, all three persons – programmer, database developer and user – might be considered to be joint authors. In the absence of any clear guidance in the Act and until we have a judicial precedent which clarifies the meaning of 'computer-generated', it is important that contractual provisions are made to cover the ownership of rights in the output of such intermediate works. In some cases, because all the persons involved are employees of the company developing and using the software, there will be little difficulty, but if outsiders are involved at any stage, terms should be inserted in contractual agreements dealing with ownership and use of the computer output.

The same considerations apply to expert and decision-support systems. These computer systems, which are intended to emulate the thought processes, analytical

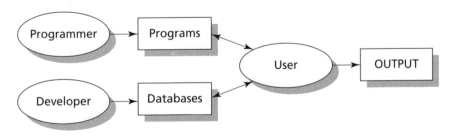

Fig. 6.1 Authorship of intermediate works

reasoning and advice of experts, contain a great deal of skill and expertise within the systems themselves. An expert system, in basic terms, contains three main elements: a knowledge base (rules and facts provided by experts), an inference engine (a computer program which manipulates the knowledge base and applies it to a particular problem) and a user interface to make the system 'user-friendly' and to provide explanations of the reasoning adopted and advice given by the expert system. When an expert system is used to produce some advice or a report, the expertise underlying the output comes from the following sources:

- the experts who provided the knowledge;
- the persons (sometimes called 'knowledge engineers') who refined the knowledge and formalised it so that it could be installed in the knowledge base;
- the persons who wrote the inference engine and the user interface (or adapted existing ones); and
- the user of the system.

The user of the system provides expertise because he will have to understand and respond to the system, and he will have to interpret the questions asked by the system and know what the scope and limitations of the system are. At this stage, most if not all expert and decision-support systems cannot be used by naive users; a reasonable general knowledge of the area of expertise covered by the system (its knowledge domain) is essential if the output produced is to be taken seriously, just as the scope, limitations and difficulties presented by a new piece of legislation can only be predicted with any certainty by a lawyer and, even then, not always correctly.

What will the law make of the output of expert and decision-support systems when it comes to deciding the authorship and ownership of the copyright in that output? To argue that it is computer-generated and has no human author runs counter to common sense. To say that the user of this system is its sole author might be convenient but is unrealistic. To attribute authorship to the experts and knowledge engineers who developed the knowledge base is unsatisfactory because they cannot predict how the system will be used and what responses will be made by the user; they have no control over its use. In reality, all the persons listed above are the joint authors, in differing proportions, of the output resulting from the use of the system. It must be said, however, that, if the courts follow this interpretation, it will lead to all manner of complications regarding the commercial use of expert systems and other 'intermediate' systems. Although the courts might be willing to imply terms – for example, that the licensee or 'purchaser' of such systems owns the copyright in any output – it is obviously more sensible to recognise the difficulties associated with this part of the Act and to make suitable contractual provision for ownership (as opposed to authorship) of computer output. Better still, the provisions relating to computer-generated works ought to be repealed. It is notable that the United States has no provisions for determining the authorship of computer-generated works and that does not seem to have caused any particular problems in practice though there are some concerns, particularly as utilitarian works are less likely to attract protection under United States copyright law.

In spite of the doubtful value and uncertainty surrounding the authorship of computer-generated works, it is surprising that, to the best of the author of this book's knowledge, there are no cases (reported or otherwise) in the United Kingdom on the authorship of computer-generated works following the commencement of the Copyright, Designs and Patents Act 1988. Incredibly, the only two cases on this issue were decided under the previous legislation, the Copyright Act 1956, which had no provisions whatsoever on the matter. There may be a number of explanations for this. Either the provisions are well understood and work effectively in practice (which seems unlikely) or the question of ownership of computer-generated works or intermediate works has been dealt with by way of licences and assignments. Another possibility is where several persons might have a claim to authorship, they are all employees of the same employer. A final possibility is that the software industry has not yet woken up to the potential uncertainties regarding authorship. It may simply need just one case where the output from an intermediate work proves to be very valuable commercially in a situation where ownership has not been fully tied up that we see some serious litigation in this area.

Chapter 7

Copyright and electronic publishing

Introduction

All manner of works can be stored and made available electronically. Literature, music, works of art, audio-visual works and industrial designs can all be represented in digital form. Even three-dimensional works and moving images can be expressed digitally and, using appropriate software, displayed on screens, copied, manipulated or transmitted anywhere in the world 'at the touch of a button'.

The ease with which all forms of creative expression can be exploited digitally has far-reaching consequences as regards the dissemination of information and has opened up the exciting prospect of a global information village. The term generally accredited to Al Gore, the then Vice-President of the United States, of 'The Information Super-Highway' is very apt to describe the technology, and the rate at which the largely unregulated Internet has grown and continues to grow is impressive. Another recent phenomenon is the growth of multimedia technology offering large storage of a wide variety of works on a single disk, such as a compact disc (CD) or digital versatile disk (DVD). Typically, a CD or DVD may contain film, music, photographs, text and the spoken word, a collection of disparate works, each of which may be subject to copyright and may incorporate other rights such as rights in performances.

It is unsurprising that these new technologies pose considerable challenges to copyright law and the traditional role of copyright, which has only recently come to terms with the computer program and database. Already there are serious issues relating to balancing controls over the access and use of works and freedom of speech.

In the United States, a corporation which owned the copyright in certain works created by L Ron Hubbard, the founder of the Church of Scientology, sued a former member who placed extracts of the works on the Internet for infringement of copyright and trade secret violations (BBC2, *The Net*, 15 May 1995). It seems that the access provider was also threatened with legal action and that members of the Church sent cancel messages on the Internet to delete previously posted messages about the Church. The former member of the Church responsible for placing the works on the Internet, Dennis Erlich, said, 'We're using 18th and 17th century law to define what goes on in a 21st and 22nd century medium.' As a matter of note the defences of fair dealing and public interest were available to a defendant who had reproduced extracts of Mr Hubbard's writings in the United Kingdom in paper form (see *Hubbard v Vosper* [1972] 2 QB 84).

This chapter looks at the particular implications for electronic publishing. The following chapter concentrates on the European Directive on the harmonisation of certain aspects of copyright and related rights in the information society (subsequently referred to as the 'Directive on copyright in the information society'). Certain provisions of this Directive are supplementary to the subject matter of this chapter, particularly in respect of electronic rights management information and technological measures aimed at protecting works from unauthorised use and, to that extent, the following chapter should be referred to when reading this chapter.

Before looking at the copyright implications of these new forms of information dissemination, it is worth looking at what is meant by electronic publishing.

What is electronic publishing?

The term 'electronic publishing' is lacking in precision and it is by no means clear what it encompasses. For example, it could include publication by one of the following methods:

- sale, rental or lending of a physical carrier containing a copy of the work or works in question – for example, CD, DVD, magnetic disk or magnetic tape;
- by means of communications networks – for example, the Internet, other on-line facilities or intranets; or
- by means of a broadcast, whether or not encrypted and whether or not in digital form – for example, CEEFAX.

All these three forms of electronic publishing are capable of copyright subsistence. In all cases, the individual works so made available may be subject to copyright and, in some cases, there will be other copyrights, such as that in the broadcast or cable programme. Additionally, there may be a further copyright in the form of a compilation.

It should be noted that, for copyright purposes, the word 'electronic' has a particularly wide meaning, by section 178 of the Copyright, Designs and Patents Act 1988, as being 'actuated by electric, magnetic, electro-magnetic, electro-chemical or electro-mechanical energy' and the term 'in electronic form' means in a form usable only by electronic means. However, even this width of definition may be incapable of keeping up with technological change. Would the above definitions be appropriate in relation to a liquid DNA computer described by Alexander (Alexander, G, 'DNA holds key to explosion in computer power', *The Sunday Times*, 30 April 1995, p.29)? Nevertheless, it is clear that the definitions of 'electronic' and 'in electronic form' apply to CD, DVD, laser disk, magnetic disk technology and other forms of storage presently in use such as memory cards used in digital cameras. This is important as, under section 17(2), copying includes storage in any medium by electronic means. The Act has specific provisions for broadcasts and cable programmes and some forms of on-line publishing would be deemed to be cable programme services. Information made available over the Internet has been considered to be a cable programme or part of a cable programme.

This chapter concentrates on publication by means of multimedia and the Internet. It also looks at the potential liability of internet service providers (ISPs) for copyright infringement.

Multimedia

A CD or DVD typically may contain a whole range of works. For example, a multimedia product on the topic of romantic poems may include among other things:

- the text of poems to be displayed on screen;

- the sound of poems being recited;
- a commentary comprising an oral and/or textual description of material relating to the poets and their poems;
- film sequences showing the poets at work or relaxing;
- photographs of the poets' birthplaces, homes, relatives and acquaintances; and
- introductory and background music.

A feature of multimedia is that the person using the product can move about it at will. The information is, therefore, structured and may have hypertext links. In terms of copyright subsistence, all the works above may be subject to copyright in addition to the whole as a compilation or database. The following example gives some idea of the complexity of rights in such a work.

MultiMega, a multimedia publisher, decides to produce a DVD containing selected poems written by Andrew, Belinda and Clarence. Andrew is still alive, Belinda died some 20 years ago and Clarence has been dead for 80 years. Diana, a famous self-employed literary critic has been commissioned by MultiMega to select the poems to include in the DVD and to write some material giving a critical appraisal of each poem. MultiMega's editing manager, Edward, selects some music written by Frances, who died 62 years ago, to use as background music. George, an actor, is commissioned to recite the poems in front of a studio audience. A selection of modern photographs of the poets' homes and favourite haunts, taken by Harriet, is to be included in the work, with her permission. There is also some old footage of Belinda being interviewed live on ICE television. MultiMega's employees created the computer programs to access and display the works and the hypertext links.

Assuming that there has been no subsequent transfer of the various copyrights except on the death of a copyright owner, the following permissions will be required by MultiMega:

- a licence from Andrew and from Belinda's estate (as she is now deceased) allowing for the copying, performance and issue to the public of their poems;
- an assignment (or exclusive licence) from Diana in respect of the compilation copyright and the material she has written;
- an exclusive licence from George in respect of his live performance and that of the recording company which first recorded the performance (these are rights in performances, such rights being similar to copyright, often described as neighbouring rights); and
- a licence from ICE in respect of the broadcast.

No permission is required in respect of Clarence's poems which are now out of copyright but care must be taken as far as Frances's music is concerned as the copyright in it might be revived as a result of the extension of the term of copyright to life plus 70 years (this will be so if her music is still protected in any member state of the European Community). As Edward presumably is an employee, none of his efforts will result in a copyright that belongs to him rather than MultiMega. Another problem for MultiMega is that some of the persons involved will have moral rights (in particular, Andrew, Diana and Harriet), and it must take account of moral rights, either by acknowledging the authors or seeking a waiver in respect of the right to be identified. It is clear that, in most cases, obtaining the necessary permissions for a work of multimedia will be difficult, drawn out and, probably, expensive!

The changes to copyright in relation to databases result in the ensuing multimedia product probably being considered to be a database rather than a compilation. The definition of a database is a collection of independent works, data or other materials which are arranged in a systematic or methodical way and are individually accessible by electronic or other means. This would certainly seem to be the case with MultiMega's DVD. However, one proviso is that it may be that not all the works included are 'individually accessible'. For example, a particular piece of music may be played only when a specific film sequence is accessed and it may not be possible to access that music entirely on its own. This may seem overly pedantic but, if the DVD does not qualify as a database, it almost certainly will as a compilation. As far as copyright is concerned, there is very little difference between copyright in a database and copyright in a compilation. But, databases must be personal intellectual creations to attract copyright whereas the requirement for originality for compilations is not further qualified. The other main difference is that fair dealing for the purposes of research or private study in respect of databases requires an indication of the source and does not extend to research for a commercial purpose. (However, this soon will be the same for other literary, dramatic, musical and artistic works as a result of the forthcoming implementation of the Directive on copyright in the information society.) There is also a provision protecting the carrying out of any act necessary for access and use of the contents of a database by a person having a right to use it.

On balance, it seems most likely that such DVD and CD products will be classified as databases, except in the case of music compilations which are excluded by the Directive on the legal protection of databases: these continue to be protected as compilations. If a DVD or CD like that made by MultiMega is a database, the next question is whether it is a copyright database or whether it is only subject to the database right. As seen in the preceding chapter, this is a question as to whether its making was the result of a personal intellectual creation and/or whether it required a substantial investment. In the above example, it is possible that both of these rights subsist. Of course, whether the entire work is classed as a copyright database or one subject to the database right or both does not affect the copyright and other rights subsisting in the individual works and performances contained within it.

A further issue is whether the hypertext links built into the software are protected by copyright. These may be considered to be a structural element of the database protected as a non-literal element. As the Directive on the legal protection of databases makes clear, the protection of copyright databases extends to their structure. It seems entirely reasonable to assume that a person copying the structure of hypertext links from one multimedia product to another, different, product may infringe the copyright in the first if those parts taken represent a substantial part of the first, providing it is a copyright database. Of course, it would be rare that much would be gained simply by copying the structure of hypertext works alone.

The Internet

Publishing works on the Internet looks very attractive at first sight. It is a really effective way of making a work available to a wide audience at minimal expense. Many academic writers were quick to seize the opportunity to spread their work on a world-wide scale. A number of academic journals are now appearing on-line and while many

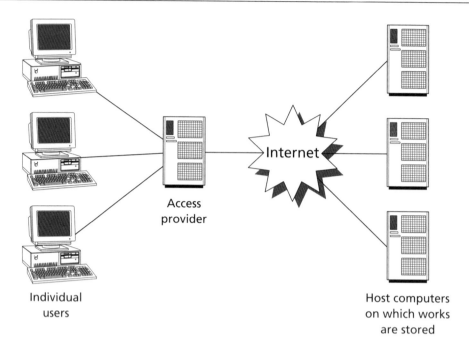

Fig. 7.1 The Internet

authors may be happy to distribute their work in this way, without recompense, there are large numbers of authors who depend on the income they receive from publishing their work, as do their publishers. There is a view, still held by some, that the Internet is equivalent to the public domain and anything available there should be freely copied and used. This view is misguided.

Typically, individuals gain access to works on the Internet, which are stored on host computers, via an access provider (see Fig. 7.1).

The Internet itself is, basically, made up of public telecommunications systems which are used to carry information from host computers. The technology makes use of the most effective path through the system at the time of transmission, re-routing to avoid busy lines. No one is in overall control of the Internet.

Individual works available on the Internet will normally have their own copyright which may well be a foreign copyright. They may also be subject to other rights such as moral rights, performance rights and recording rights. Contrary to the view that the Internet is equivalent to the public domain, this does not affect the fact of subsistence of copyright and other rights. A copyright owner may choose to make his work available freely but it will remain a work of copyright and will not affect the copyright position of other works. It is advisable for owners of copyright works to make it clear whether the work can be printed or downloaded or used in other ways. Whilst it is almost impossible to police the use of works on the Internet the copyright position, including moral rights, should be spelt out. In fact, the Directive on copyright in the information society provides for specific protection for such information, as described in the following chapter.

Under United Kingdom law, apart from any copyright in the individual works, databases or compilations of works, there may be separate copyrights as cable programmes included in a cable programme service. This is defined by section 7(1) of the Copyright,

Designs and Patents Act 1988 as a service consisting wholly or mainly in sending visual images, sounds or other information by means of a telecommunications system, otherwise than by wireless telegraphy, for reception:

(a) at two or more places (whether for simultaneous reception or at different times in response to requests by different users), or
(b) for presentation to members of the public.

It seems clear that information available via the Internet falls within (a) above. There are a number of exceptions (including systems which are predominantly interactive such as electronic mail). There are difficulties, however, with applying cable programme copyright to the Internet. This form of copyright was intended to be the equivalent to the broadcast copyright for providers of cable television. In this sense it works well but, by section 9(2)(c), the author of a cable programme is the person providing the cable programme service in which the programme is included. The question here is: who is the person providing the service? As no one person is in overall control this is not easily answered. The access provider who arranges connection to the Internet does not, in reality, provide the service in which the programmes (or works) are included. Rather, the service provider is a facilitator rather than a provider.

The first case on the copyright nature of the Internet was heard in Scotland. It involved webpages of the *Shetland Times* on which extracts of news items appearing in printed editions of its newspapers were placed. It was hoped that advertisers would want to advertise on the front page of the website. The defender, Dr Jonathan Wills, operated a website called *The Shetland News* on which he had placed verbatim headlines from the *Shetland Times*. Anyone accessing these headlines could, by clicking the mouse button on them, gain access to the news items on the *Shetland Times* website, by-passing the front page with its advertisements. It was claimed that the copyright in the headlines had been infringed. In *Shetland Times Ltd* v *Dr Jonathan Wills* [1997] FSR 604, in the Outer House of the Court of Session, Scotland, Lord Hamilton granted an interim interdict (injunction). He said that it was arguable that the copyright in the headlines had been infringed by including them in a cable programme service. He also said it was at least arguable that operating a website was operating a cable programme service within section 7(1) of the Copyright, Designs and Patents Act 1988 (see above).

There is an exception in section 7(2)(a), where an essential feature of the service is that it is interactive. However, Lord Hamilton did not accept that this provision applied to save the defender as, although persons accessing the website could send messages and communicate with the *Shetland Times* via the Internet, this was not an essential feature of the service. Alternatively, that part of the service was severable, leaving the remainder of the service to be classed as a cable programme service. An appeal was lodged but the parties settled the dispute before the appeal got properly under way. That being so, it is not beyond doubt whether operating a website is within the meaning of operating a cable programme service, although that does seem to be the most appropriate form of copyright.

Later decisions have reinforced the view that operating a website is within the meaning of providing a cable programme service for the purposes of copyright law. For example, in *Sony Music Entertainment (UK) Ltd* v *Easyinternetcafe Ltd* [2003] EWHC 62 (Ch), the judge thought that that this was correct although he did not have to decide the matter. In that case, the defendant provided a CD burning service in its internet café such that customers could save music and other works downloaded from the Internet into a personal directory, from where an employee of the defendant could copy the works onto a CD on payment of a fee by the customer. The employee was told not to look at what had been downloaded. This was held to infringe copyright, the fact that the defendant was not aware of what was being copied was no defence as copyright is infringed simply by carrying out one of the restricted acts, knowledge being irrelevant (although it could affect the availability of damages). It would seem that the defendant could also have been liable on the basis that it had authorised infringement by the customer who would subsequently play the music but this point was not argued.

The defendant then argued that the copying onto CDs was within the 'time-shifting' defence under section 70 of the Copyright, Designs and Patents Act 1988 which provides that the making for private and domestic use of a recording of a broadcast or cable programme solely for the purpose of enabling it to be viewed or listened to at a more convenient time does not infringe any copyright in the broadcast or cable programme or in any work included in it. If the Internet was a cable programme service, then, potentially, this defence could apply but Mr Justice Peter Smith held that the copying was not done by the defendant for private and domestic use as customers were charged for this service.

If operating a website is operating a cable programme service, this has important consequences. A cable programme is defined as 'any item included in a cable programme service' by section 7(1) of the Copyright, Designs and Patents Act 1988. As a cable programme service consists wholly or mainly in sending visual images, sounds or other information and infringement extends to including a cable programme in a cable programme service, this could mean even very small items, normally regarded as too small or trivial to attract copyright protection otherwise, could be protected. In particular, an item of 'information' could be quite small. It should be sufficient to convey something (a dictionary definition of 'information' is 'something told, knowledge, items of knowledge') and it is likely that even a small newspaper headline could do this. Somewhat controversially, in the *Shetland Times* case, Lord Hamilton considered that the headlines were literary works in their own right. Normally these would be considered too small for copyright protection and, in the past, phrases such as 'Beauty is a social necessity, not a luxury' and 'The man who broke the bank at Monte Carlo' and words such as 'EXXON', 'Kojak' and 'Elvis' have been held not to be works of copyright. However, if a generous view is taken of 'information', very trivial things could be protected by virtue of cable programme copyright. Apart from continuing doubts as to the copyright status of the Internet as a service (notwithstanding that individual works placed on webpages will, in most cases, have their own independent copyright) there are other serious problems for copyright in 'cyberspace' such as:

- powerful copyright owners may use bullying tactics, obtaining or threatening injunctions against individuals and, more seriously, against access providers;
- it becomes impossible to control copying and unauthorised use of works (copies can be made on disk virtually instantaneously – much cheaper and quicker than photocopying); and
- the international dimension is a nightmare in terms of policing, jurisdiction and acting against infringers.

Until recently, there has been an emphasis on the medium on which a work is stored with too little appreciation of the nature of copyright. For example, a book comprises two separate and distinct property rights. The paper, ink and binding together make an item of tangible property, a good or personal chattel. The work contained within the book and expressed therein is subject to a copyright which is a form of intangible property. There has been insufficient focus on the existence of the intangible right that is copyright and, with the advent of the Internet, freeing the copyright from its medium, like releasing the genie from the bottle, may yet have interesting and possibly unexpected consequences.

Licensing

When it is required to commercially exploit works published electronically (whether by cable, broadcast or in multimedia products) it is usual for access to be provided by means of a licence agreement. A licence is necessary because accessing the works will involve an act restricted by copyright. For example, retrieving a document from a database of documents will require a copy to be made in the computer's memory and the copyright owner's permission to do this must be obtained. This is not so with traditional paper materials. Taking a book from a library shelf and reading it does not require any acts to be done which are restricted by copyright. Any use of a work involving computer technology will require copies to be made even if they are only transient. By section 17(6) of the Copyright, Designs and Patents Act 1988, it is an infringement of copyright to make a transient copy.

The use of licence agreements brings contract law into play in addition to copyright law. A licence agreement will contain terms concerning the use of the work and may impose restrictions going beyond copyright. Typically, a licence may specify the acts that may be done in a negative way by stating what may not be done. For example, a licence for the use of a multimedia product stored on a CD or DVD may state that the licensee shall not duplicate the CD or DVD or print out any of the works contained in it or download any of those works apart from viewing on a screen. If the product is available with an updating service there may be a term requiring that old copies are destroyed or returned to the licensor. The licence may also require that the licensee place notices near computer terminals warning of copyright infringement. Failure to abide by the terms of the licence will be a breach of contract and, in many cases, also an infringement of copyright.

There are important international differences in the protection of creative works. For example, the United Kingdom does not yet provide for an artist's resale right as applies in France. This can make the identification of rights and obtaining the permissions required very difficult, especially with a product such as multimedia. The person acquiring a multimedia product, particularly for business purposes, should satisfy himself that all the relevant permissions have been obtained and provided for in the licence and should check that the licence agreement also contains an indemnity. If it turns out that a relevant permission has not been obtained, the licensor should indemnify the licensee against any claims arising and which are directed at the licensee. An example of the difficulty that might be experienced is whether a consent that had been obtained 40 years ago in respect of playing music from a vinyl sound recording in public would now extend to incorporating the music in a multimedia product. Peggy Lee obtained some $3.8m in an award of damages resulting from an action against Walt Disney. She claimed that her original agreement with Walt Disney for her work on *Lady and the*

Tramp did not extend to selling videos of the film. Video had not been invented at the time! (*The Times*, 7 October 1992, p.16.)

On-line databases are now well established and, usually, made available through a subscription in the form of a licence agreement. In addition to paying an annual fee, it is not uncommon for each search of the database to be charged individually. An interesting feature of an on-line database is that the provider can keep an exact record of the use of the database and can charge a sum reflecting the precise use that has been made of the database by the subscriber. The ability to monitor use in this way will have increasingly significant implications in the future.

An on-line database may comprise a number of copyrights as is the case with CDs and DVDs. Taking LEXIS as an example, a database containing the full text of legislation and cases, the legislation is, in the United Kingdom, a work of copyright which belongs to Her Majesty (Crown copyright). The cases contain court judgments each of which comprise catchwords, a headnote and the judgment itself. The copyright in the catchwords and headnote will belong in the first instance to the organisation employing the law reporter (or reporter himself if self-employed) but the judgment will be Crown copyright on the basis that a judge is probably a servant of the Crown who writes the judgment in the course of his duties; section 163. The database maker will have a copyright or database right or both in the database as a whole and will have been permitted to enter the individual materials into the database under licence agreements. The licence under which the subscriber is permitted to use the database will restrict that use, particularly in terms of downloading and copying.

Other questions are raised in relation to databases. For example, is a particular database protected by copyright or by the database right or both? How is substantiality determined in relation to a database? Is the copyright in a database refreshed from time to time as it evolves and undergoes changes? At what stage does an aggregation of incremental changes give rise to a fresh copyright or database right?

Collecting societies such as the Performing Right Society, the Copyright Licensing Agency and Newspaper Licensing Agency assist in the exploitation of copyright by increasing the accessibility of works and allowing a certain amount of copying or playing while providing copyright owners with income. These societies are, in general terms, just coming to grips with the fact that organisations are more likely to prefer to copy works available on-line and to disseminate them on-line to staff or students, for example, by means of an intranet. The Copyright Licensing Agency's main type of licence still only allows photocopying from paper to paper although it does run a Higher Education Digitisation Licensing Scheme which allows scanning from certain paper publications to make information available to staff and students of educational establishments over a network. However, permission must be sought individually each time it is desired to make part of a work available in this way. The Educational Recording Agency allow staff at educational establishments to record radio, television and cable output of its members to show to students in that establishment. A similar arrangement applies to Open University materials.

The Newspaper Licensing Agency is very important as a means of distributing press cuttings to staff in a company or firm. This does allow digital copying under one of its schemes. Of course, in all these cases, the licences only apply to works of publishers, recording companies, broadcasters and the like which are members of the relevant schemes. The licence fees paid by subscribers form the basis of payments made to members. These licensing schemes are likely to increase in importance and in terms of the range of works covered. For many authors and publishers, for example, they already are a significant source of income. The Public Lending Right Scheme is a scheme which distributes money provided by the government to authors of books to compensate them for borrowing of the books from public libraries. At this stage, the scheme only applies to books in paper form.

Special copyright problems posed by electronic publishing

Apart from the issues identified above, there are a number of specific problems that may result from the widespread use of electronic storage and publishing of works. These problems relate to digitisation, typographical arrangements, electronic publication of old works and the liability of 'facilitators', persons or organisations (such as libraries) which make electronically published works available to end users and, especially, internet service providers (ISPs). These are considered below.

Digitisation

Some doubts have been expressed as to whether digitising (storing in digital form) is within the restricted act of copying for copyright purposes. In *Anacon Corp Ltd* v *Environmental Research Technology Ltd* [1994] FSR 659, the defendant had used the claimant's circuit diagram to create a printed circuit board. As an intermediate step, the defendant made a net list (a list of the electronic components with details of their interconnection) from the circuit diagram. Although a circuit diagram is, *prima facie*, an artistic work, the judge held that it was not an infringement of the copyright in the circuit diagram as an artistic work because the circuit board did not look like an artistic work. He said that it was the visual significance of an artistic work that mattered.

On this basis, making a digital copy of an artistic work will not infringe as the digital copy will not look like the original work or, for that matter, any artistic work. Previous case law under the Copyright Act 1956 supports this view but the Copyright, Designs and Patents Act 1988 contains a provision that clearly contradicts this approach. Section 17(2) states that copying a literary, dramatic, musical or artistic work 'includes storing the work in any medium by electronic means' – a phrase that was not mentioned by the judge, Mr Justice Jacob. Of course, the words of the statute, if they are clear and unambiguous, which they are, prevail. Therefore, that part of the judgment dealing with infringement of copyright in artistic works must be read with caution.

Jacob J overcame this apparent (and mistaken) limitation by holding that the circuit diagram was also a literary work because it was intended to be read. A person making a circuit board would have to read the information contained in the diagram, which also included written information such as the rating of components. By doing so and creating a net list, the defendant had reproduced the literary work in a material form.

The definitions of sound recordings, films, broadcasts and cable programmes are very wide and, for these works, converting or storing the work in digital form should present no particular problems. For example, by section 5(1) a 'film' means 'a recording on any medium from which a moving image may by any means be produced'. Of course reproducing a work from a digital recording will normally infringe copyright if done without the copyright owner's licence and this is so even if any intervening act does not infringe; see section 16(3). For example, say that Mary in London buys an L S Lowry print (L S Lowry died during 1976 and his paintings are still in copyright). Mary scans the print into her computer, converting it into digital form, say as a JPEG file. She then sends the file as an e-mail attachment to Thomas in Cardiff who then downloads the file and opens it so he can view the image on screen and then he prints it out on paper. Neither Mary nor Thomas has the permission of L S Lowry's estate to do any act restricted by copyright. By section 17(2), by scanning in the image and storing the work electronically, Mary has infringed copyright. Transmitting the work digitally does not infringe as the transmission is only sent to Thomas and does not make the work available to the public. As the image was sent as an e-mail attachment rather than placed on a website, there is no infringement on the basis of it being included in a cable programme service. However, Thomas infringed the copyright, first by downloading (making a copy in electronic form) then by viewing the image (making a transient copy) and then by printing the image on paper (making a permanent copy). The fact that an intervening act (transmission as an e-mail attachment) did not infringe does not break the chain as far as Thomas is concerned. Mary will probably be liable also for the infringing acts of Thomas because infringement includes authorising another to do any of the acts restricted by copyright. This is shown diagrammatically in Fig. 7.2. It is interesting to note that Thomas infringes the copyright simply by downloading the image (or even by viewing on screen without first saving the file to disk) as there is no defence of innocent infringement. Thus, it is possible to infringe copyright by opening or saving a file without any knowledge of the contents. The harshness of this rule is that, although there is a technical infringement, damages will not be available to the copyright owner unless the person in question knows or has reason to believe that the copy is an infringing copy.

It is arguable that because of the weak link in the above acts (transmission other than by way of a broadcast or cable programme service) there should be a strengthening of the Copyright, Designs and Patents Act 1988 in this respect. Though it should cause no particular difficulties within the United Kingdom, it could if a copy of the work is obtained lawfully already in digital form and it is then transmitted to another country. On the face of it, the person transmitting the work from the United Kingdom does not himself infringe copyright. Liability might still accrue, however, on the basis that he has authorised the infringement by facilitating it. In such a case, it is doubtful whether there would be an infringement of United Kingdom copyright but there could be liability in

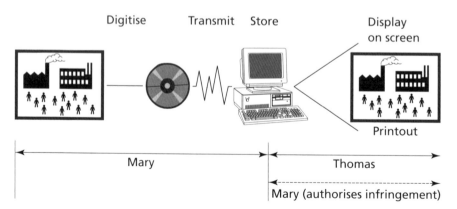

Fig. 7.2 Infringement of copyright in a digital work

the country where the copying actually takes place for authorising copying in that country. This assumes that the work in question has copyright protection in that country. Infringement by authorisation is considered later in this chapter in the context of ISPs.

Typographical arrangements of published editions

Typographical arrangements of published editions are protected as a distinct form of copyright (section 1(1)(c) of the Copyright, Designs and Patents Act 1988). This copyright gives protection to publishers of literary, dramatic and musical works irrespective of the copyright subsisting in those works as such. Thus a new publication of a new play will have two copyrights: the play which, as a dramatic work, will be protected for the life of the author plus 70 years and the typographical arrangement, the copyright of which will endure for 25 years from the end of the calendar year during which it was first published (section 15).

The typographical arrangement copyright is particularly useful to a publisher of a work which is itself out of copyright. For example, if a publisher decides to publish a document containing a collection of the writings of Charles Babbage (1791–1871) he will be able to sue someone who photocopies the document without permission on the basis of the copyright in the typographical arrangement even though the copyright in the writings as literary works expired some time ago. Of course, if the publisher engages an author to select and arrange Babbage's writings and to add a commentary there will arise additional new copyrights in the commentary, providing it is more than trivial and, potentially, in the work expended on the selection and arrangement resulting in a compilation copyright.

The purpose of copyright in typographical arrangements is to protect the publisher's work in selecting the typeface, margins, headings, spacing and other typographical details; in other words, the layout of the print on the page. This is all well and good in the context of print on paper but what is the position where the work in question is published electronically? To take an example, say that Charles decides to store the entire known works of William Shakespeare (1564–1616) on computer disk. Copyright in Shakespeare's works expired some centuries ago and, as the entire known works are to be stored, it is unlikely that there is any copyright in the whole as a database because, on the basis of *G A Cramp & Sons Ltd v Frank Smythson Ltd* [1944] AC 329, there is no room for skill and judgment in selecting the materials to include. The requirement that a copyright database must be the *author's own intellectual creation* adds weight to this argument. For the sake of this example, it is assumed that the individual works are not entered in any particular order or subject to a newly devised classification system.

For copyright to subsist in a typographical arrangement, the following requirements must be met:

- the arrangement must qualify for United Kingdom copyright or, in the case of a foreign national, United Kingdom copyright has been extended to nationals of that country (this will not usually be an issue),
- it must not simply be a reproduction of the typographical arrangement of a previous edition, and
- it must be applied to a published edition of the whole or part of one or more literary, dramatic or musical works (section 8).

The last point is doubtful in terms of electronic publishing. The phrase 'published edition' is not defined in the Act other than as above although it is reasonable to suppose that the meaning of 'publication' will be relevant. This is defined in section 175 as issuing copies to the public and includes, in the case of a literary, dramatic, musical or artistic work, making it available to the public by means of an electronic retrieval system. Thus, electronic publishing of the original works of copyright is specifically covered, but typographical arrangements are not mentioned. Even if it does extend to typographical arrangements, there may be further difficulty with the word 'edition'. This reflects traditional publishing but may be inappropriate in the context of, say, a database which is continually being updated. Certainly, when a database is first made available to the public that could be said to be its first edition. But when does a second or subsequent edition exist? Does the owner of the database have to change the font, point size, margins, etc. to obtain a new typographical arrangement copyright? 'Typographic arrangement' is not defined in the Act and this may allow the courts to take a flexible view and to confirm, if the need should arise, that it applies to the layout of text or musical notation on a screen and/or the details of font, spacing, page and style setting, etc. embedded within the relevant computer file containing the work. That there are doubts about typographical arrangements of published editions in the context of electronic publishing is regrettable. Perhaps there should be a new electronic document format copyright which would extend not only to the choice of fonts, margins, page settings and such like but also to protect the work involved in creating hypertext links and other structural or indexing systems used in computer documents. Electronic publishers should not be disadvantaged compared to traditional paper publishers.

Returning to our example, if Charles sells CDs containing the works of Shakespeare, even if his electronic arrangement is deemed to be a typographical arrangement of a published edition, this will not enable him to take legal action to prevent someone copying out the works in a different form, for example, by handwriting or converting the file into a text only file, resulting in the loss of most or all of the formatting. Converting the format by changing details such as font, point size, margins, etc. to produce a different format will not infringe copyright as the restricted act of making an adaptation does not apply to typographical arrangements of published editions. Thus Charles may have limited protection only and the situation should be the same if he makes the works available to the public on-line.

It has already been noted that a copyright might arise if Charles has to expend skill or judgment in selecting what to include and in arranging the individual works, perhaps using a classification system based on type of work: tragedy, love sonnet, etc. Certainly, if he adds commentary and criticism that itself should attract copyright. The position is less clear where Charles has carried out extensive research in an effort to get to the precise wording of Shakespeare's works as written, correcting errors in known texts. Can there be a copyright in correcting mistakes in old works? It would seem reasonable to reward the skill and judgment expended by Charles but if he succeeds in recreating the true text as written by Shakespeare that would produce the anomaly of resurrecting a long extinct copyright!

Clearly, there are problems with typographical arrangements in electronic publishing. Although it is entirely reasonable to accept that the provisions protecting typographical arrangements also ought to apply to the format of electronically published works it is far too easy to copy the work without the format. For example, a word processed document which has been carefully set out and formatted to look attractive on a computer screen or as printed and has numerous font changes, indents, headings, etc. can simply be converted to ASCII code to avoid infringing the copyright in the typographical arrangement. Some word processors have 'style sheets' which determine the format and layout of the document. Could these be deemed to be typographical arrangements? The difficulties are amplified where the copyright in the work itself has expired because of its age.

Apart from the above uncertainties in relation to typographical arrangements of published editions in works made available electronically, a decision of the House of Lords indicates that this form of copyright protection might be fairly limited and can only apply in respect of a whole edition and not parts of it. Therefore, to infringe by taking a substantial part, this must be viewed in relation to the entire edition. In *Newspaper Licensing Agency Ltd v Marks & Spencer plc* [2002] RPC 4, the defendant made unauthorised copies of newspaper cuttings and distributed these to some of its staff. It was held that an edition, for these purposes, means the whole of the composite work 'between the covers'. Infringement of a typographical arrangement of a published edition depends not upon the proportion of the part taken in relation to the whole but requires that the presentation and layout of the edition has been appropriated. This is a result of considering why this form of protection was introduced which was, in the context of a modern newspaper, to protect the skill and labour in its overall design. The House of Lords said that it would be unlikely that the skill and labour which has gone into the creation of the typographical arrangement would be expressed in anything less than a full page. The defendant, which had taken press cuttings which it had re-arranged to fit onto a sheet of A4 did not infringe. The cuttings did not resemble the newspapers from which they were taken nor could they be regarded as having newspaper-like qualities.

Even if typographical arrangement copyright does apply to electronic publication, it would seem to be fairly restricted. For example, in terms of a website, a substantial part of the skill and labour going into the overall design of at least one webpage would have to be taken. Simply copying extracts from a number of different pages and pasting them together into a new file would be unlikely to infringe this form of copyright although, of course, any literary copyright in the content of the webpages would be likely to be infringed. A further limitation to typographical arrangements is that they only apply to literary, dramatic and musical works, not to artistic works.

Legal liability of internet service providers

Internet service providers (ISPs) facilitate access to material on the Internet. Through their agreements with persons to whom they provide access, ISPs have some measure of control, for example, by requiring the client to adhere to copyright law and not to make infringing material available to others, whether on a webpage or by transmitting by e-mail. ISPs may even seek indemnities from their clients for copyright infringement attributable to their actions. Nevertheless, ISPs may be vulnerable for copyright infringement in a number of ways:

- by being secondary infringers,
- by authorising infringement, or
- by joint infringement.

These are considered below as is the defence available to ISPs and other information society service providers in respect of illegal material generally (not just in terms of copyright). These defences result from the European Directive on certain legal aspects of information society services, in particular electronic commerce, in the Internal Market (the 'Directive on electronic commerce') (2000/31/EC, OJ L 178, 17.07.2000, p.1) and apply where the service provider acts as a mere conduit for the material or in connection with caching or hosting. This defence, which is of wider application, is also considered in Chapter 26.

Secondary infringement

Under section 24(2) of the Copyright, Designs and Patents Act 1988 it is an infringement of copyright to transmit a work, without the licence of the copyright owner, by a telecommunications system knowing or having reason to believe that infringing copies will be made by means of the reception of the transmission in the United Kingdom or elsewhere. Although it matters not where the reception takes place, the definition of 'infringing copy' provides territorial constraint as, in relation to infringing copies made outside the United Kingdom, the copy must either have been imported or is proposed to be imported into the United Kingdom. Also, had it been made in the United Kingdom that would have been an infringement of the copyright in the work or a breach of an exclusive licence agreement relating to the work.

A serious limitation is that the transmission must be otherwise than by broadcasting or inclusion in a cable programme service. As discussed above, the *Shetland Times* case is authority for the view that operating a website is within the meaning of operating a cable programme service. If this is confirmed, then this form of infringement does not apply to those parts of the service deemed to be cable programme services. However, parts of the service intended to be interactive, such as e-mail or bulletin boards, may still be caught by section 24(2) as these will fall within the express exception to cable programme services.

If a person who subscribes to an ISP gains access to an infringing work of copyright, that person will infringe copyright by making a copy, whether transient or otherwise. Innocent copying still infringes, although innocence may be a factor in whether damages are available. However, an ISP will infringe under section 24(2) only if he has reason to believe that infringing copies will be made by means of the reception of the transmission in the United Kingdom or elsewhere. This is an objective test. Would a reasonable person, with knowledge of the facts known to the alleged infringer, have reason to believe infringing copies would be made?

Authorising infringement

Section 16(2) of the Copyright, Designs and Patents Act 1988 states that copyright in a work is infringed by a person who, without the licence of the copyright owner does, *or authorises another to do*, any of the acts restricted by the copyright. If the act which infringes is done in the United Kingdom, it does not matter if the authorisation comes from elsewhere. In *ABKCO Music & Records Inc v Music Collection International Ltd* [1995] RPC 657 a Danish company granted a licence to an English company to make and issue to the public recordings of the claimant's sound recordings in the United Kingdom and Eire. It was held that it did not matter where the authorisation was given as long as the restricted act was carried out within the jurisdiction of the United Kingdom courts. Thus, if an Australian ISP authorises someone in the United Kingdom to make infringing material available on the Internet, the ISP is caught by section 16(2) and is liable for the infringement together with the person responsible for making the material available.

It is important to understand what is meant by authorisation. It has been construed by the courts in a fairly wide sense and turning a blind eye can amount to authorisation. Indifference or even failing to inform persons of the implications of copyright law may suffice. In *Moorhouse* v *University of New South Wales* [1976] RPC 151 a failure to inform users of a library with photocopying facilities as to copyright law and to supervise the use of the copiers was held to be authorising infringement of copyright. In the United Kingdom, judges have equated authorisation with '... the grant or purported grant, which may be express or implied, of the right to do the act complained of'.

An ISP could be said to authorise infringement if it fails to inform its clients of copyright law and the need to avoid infringement of copyright. It is possible that an even stronger duty could be placed on an ISP, for example, a positive duty to check material made available through its service. This may require spot checks or sampling of material made available through its service by its clients. However, the specific defence available to ISPs in respect of illegal material, discussed later, generally does not require vigilance on the part of the ISP.

Joint infringement

It is possible that an ISP could be claimed to be a joint infringer along with the client responsible for making infringing material available through its service. Joint infringement occurs where two or more persons act in concert pursuant to a common design to infringe. In terms of stereo equipment having dual cassette tape players, in *Amstrad Consumer Electronics plc* v *The British Phonograph Industry Ltd* [1986] FSR 159, it was held that supplying machines which would be likely to be used to unlawfully copy pre-recorded cassettes subject to copyright protection was not authorising infringement of copyright. The supplier had no control over the way the machines were used once sold.

In the case of ISPs, things are different. They do have some control. They can monitor and check what is being made available through their service. They can erase or block infringing material. The problem they have is that the sheer volume of material involved makes effective control and policing almost impossible. The best they can do is to warn their clients about the dangers of copyright infringement. But if they encourage, even implicitly, a disregard for copyright laws, this could be seen as authorisation or even joint infringement. A sensible approach for an ISP is to inform their clients and to carry out a reasonable level of policing and checks on what material is being made available and transmitted through their service, the only difficulty being that they may then be accused of invasion of privacy.

What has been said above in relation to ISPs also applies to others who facilitate access to material over the Internet. Thus, libraries with on-line facilities or employers who allow or encourage employees to make use of the Internet should be careful as regards copyright infringement by their clients or employees. Education and vigilance seem to be the key words in respect of the Internet.

ISPs and illegal material

Tremendous amounts of information pass through and are stored on the computers of ISPs. It is impossible for them to check everything that passes through, is stored, temporarily or permanently on their computers or is otherwise accessed through their services. As there was some concern about disparities between the laws of member states of the European Union in terms of e-commerce generally, it was decided to harmonise this area of law and one of the issues that was dealt with by the Directive on electronic commerce was the potential liability of information society service providers for any illegal material that passed through or was stored on their computer systems. The head of one ISP had been prosecuted in Germany in respect of pornographic images made available through the ISP's services. The decision was taken to provide information society service providers, which include ISPs, with a defence, not just in respect of pornographic images but also in terms of illegal material generally. These provisions, which were implemented in the United Kingdom by the Electronic Commerce (EC Directive) Regulations 2000, came into force on 21 August 2002 (with the exception of regulation 16 which modified the law relating to Stop Now Orders which came into force on 23 October 2002). The defences relevant for ISPs apply to all forms of illegal material and this covers material infringing copyright and other intellectual property rights. It is in terms of copyright and liability for infringement of copyright that this section is directed. For a more general in-depth view of these regulations, see Chapter 26.

Under regulation 17 (the 'mere conduit' defence), where the service consists of the transmission in a communication network of information provided by a recipient of the service or the provision of access to a communication network, the service provider will not be liable for damages or other financial remedy if it did not initiate the transmission, did not select the receiver of the transmission and did not select or modify the information contained in the transmission. Automatic, intermediate and transient storage is permitted provided it is for the sole purpose of the transmission and the information is not stored for longer than necessary for that transmission.

Regulation 18 applies to caching (that is, temporary storage for quick access). The service provider will not be liable for damages or other pecuniary remedy if the sole purpose is to make more effective the onward transmission of the information to other recipients of the service upon their request. The service provider must not modify the information and comply with conditions on access to the information and with any rules regarding the updating of the information, specified in a manner widely recognised and used by industry. Furthermore, the service provider must not interfere with the lawful use of technology, widely recognised and used by industry, to obtain data on the use of the information and must act expeditiously to remove or to disable access to the information he has stored upon obtaining actual knowledge of the fact that the information at the initial source of the transmission has been removed from the network, or access to it has been disabled, or that a court or an administrative authority has ordered such removal or disablement. In other words, once the service provider knows that the information has been removed or disabled at source or a court has so ordered, the service provider must remove or disable access to that information.

Regulation 19 applies to storage of information supplied by the recipient of the service (for example, where the service provider hosts a subscriber's webpages). Again, the service provider will not be liable for damages or any other pecuniary remedy if he does not know (actual knowledge is required) of unlawful activity or information and, where a claim for damages is made, is not aware of facts or circumstances to put him on notice that the activity or information was unlawful. If the service provider obtains such knowledge or awareness, he must act expeditiously to remove or to disable access to the information. A further requirement for the defence to apply is that the recipient of the service (that is, the person subscribing to the service) was not acting under the authority or the control of the service provider.

Actual knowledge, for the purposes of regulations 18 and 19 is a matter of taking into account all matters which appear to the court in the particular circumstances to be relevant. This may include whether a service provider received notice from any person through a means of contact required to be made available by the service provider (for example, e-mail address) and the extent to which the notice includes the full name and address of the sender, details of the location of the information in question and details of the unlawful nature of the activity or information in question.

The mere conduit defence is a complete defence if the conditions apply. However, in respect of the caching and hosting defences, they do not provide complete immunity to a copyright infringement action (nor in respect of other civil wrong) but operate to protect the service provider for a claim in damages or for some other pecuniary remedy, such as a claim for an account of profits. The service provider may still be subject to a finding of infringement (again, noting that innocent infringement is no defence) but the only appropriate remedy available to the copyright owner would be an injunction which may, in such circumstances, require the service provider to remove the offending material.

In the Directive on electronic commerce, Article 15 states that the service provider does not have a general obligation to monitor the information he transmits or stores, or any general obligation to actively seek facts or circumstances indicating illegal activity.

The future

It is arguable that the mass storage of all manner of works on electronic media will create insuperable problems for copyright law. Until not too long ago copies of copyright works were only available as stored in or on some tangible item, for example, a book, disk, oil on canvas, magnetic tape and so on. Now, as we have now entered an information cyberspace, these tangible items are no longer necessary to the distribution or use of copyright works and there are unprecedented challenges ahead for copyright law, notwithstanding European and other initiatives to address the challenges of the information society. However, in the past, copyright law has proved itself to be capable of adapting to protect new forms of technological expression such as the photograph, sound recordings, broadcasts, cable programmes and computer programs. Technology is both a threat to copyright law and its potential saviour. For example, developments in cryptography, the increasing power of computers to monitor and record the use and copying of copyright works and to extract payment by electronic funds transfer and to precisely distribute that income among the plethora of right holders must not be under-rated. Authors and copyright owners will be reimbursed for the actual use made of their work. This could diminish the role of the traditional publisher. Authors of works of copyright instead may deal directly with the providers of electronic databases and internet access providers. Agents may become more important, being persons who will negotiate the best deals for authors to enable the work to be made available by the most effective providers.

Collecting societies such as the Copyright Licensing Agency may have a role to play in the above developments. One danger of the technological control of works of copyright is that the permitted acts under copyright law may be reduced to vanishing point as access may be denied without the appropriate licence fee being paid. This is a serious issue and could distort the balance of copyright between the rights of authors and owners on the one hand and users of copyright material on the other, as set out in the Berne Copyright Convention. Because of this we can expect that compulsory licensing provisions and licensing schemes will be extended more and more into the copyright field. The Commission of the European Communities has not entirely ruled out the need for compulsory licensing in the area of copyright. In the end, it may be that limited access to a work, broadly in line with the existing permitted acts under copyright law, may become a precondition to the enforcement of copyright against infringers. One thing that is certain is that copyright law is facing unprecedented challenges and it will be interesting to see how it develops. At the end of the day, however, given the power of technology to make works available anywhere at any time, the main issues may be concerned more with policing copyright and bringing pressure to bear on countries with weak or unenforced copyright laws.

Chapter 8

Copyright in the information society

Introduction

During December 1996 a Diplomatic Conference was held under the auspices of the World Intellectual Property Organisation (WIPO). This resulted in the adoption of two new Treaties, the 'WIPO Copyright Treaty' and the 'WIPO Performances and Phonograms Treaty'. The Treaties updated the international protection for copyright and related rights significantly, especially in respect of the implications of the digital age and the need to improve the fight against piracy on a world-wide basis. By the time most of the member states of the Community had signed the Treaties a Directive was adopted by the European Parliament and the Council containing provisions for implementing the Treaties. It was perceived as particularly important to harmonise copyright (and related rights) in the context of the information society to increase legal certainty and to provide a high level of protection to stimulate investment in creativity and innovation, including the network infrastructure.

Directive 2001/29/EC of the European Parliament and of the Council of 22 May 2001 on the harmonisation of certain aspects of copyright and related rights in the information society (2001/29/EC, OJ L 167, 22.06.2001, p.10) was required to be implemented by member states by 22 December 2002. The United Kingdom, in common with most of the other member states, failed to meet this deadline. At the time of writing, the United Kingdom government has some draft regulations to make the necessary changes to the Copyright, Designs and Patents Act 1988 but, apart from their complexity, these are proving controversial.

As the final form of the United Kingdom amending legislation is not yet known, this chapter will concentrate on the provisions of the Directive (of course, the changes to United Kingdom law should be an accurate reflection of the provisions in the Directive). Towards the end of the chapter, the draft proposals to comply with the Directive will be briefly described. The final form of the changes to United Kingdom law will be covered by one of the updates on the accompanying website (www.booksites.net/bainbridge).

The European Directive

The scheme of the Directive is to provide for specific rights designed to take full account of electronic publication, storage and dissemination and also contains other measures addressed at the problems of piracy. The rights provided by the Directive are:

- a reproduction right which extends also to temporary reproduction,
- a right of communication to the public of copyright works and a right of making available to the public other subject-matter, and

- a distribution right.

As far as these rights are concerned, United Kingdom legislation already provides for these rights in most cases but there are some shortcomings and uncertainties which hopefully will be eradicated by the changes to be made to the Copyright, Designs and Patents Act 1988.

In terms of directly facing up to the challenges of piracy two other measures are included in the Directive, being:

- the provision of adequate protection against the circumvention of technical measures designed to prevent or restrict unauthorised acts in respect of works or other subject-matter, and
- the provision of adequate protection for electronic rights-management information.

Of these measures, there are already provisions dealing with circumvention of copy protection in the United Kingdom Act but these apply only in respect of computer programs, films and sound recordings. The Directive extends protection to other forms of works and, again, amendment of the 1988 Act is required. The final measure relating to electronic rights-management information is entirely new and will require the introduction of new remedies in respect of anyone interfering with such information or distributing works where such information has been removed or altered.

The Directives on the legal protection of computer programs, rental and lending rights, term of protection of copyright, satellite broadcasting and cable retransmission and the legal protection of databases are unaffected apart from some minor technical modifications.

Reproduction, communication and distribution rights (Articles 2–4)

Copyright law in the United Kingdom and other member states already provides for these rights but there is some doubt about the scope and extent of them, particularly in respect of rights related to copyright such as rights in performances. It is likely that in the United Kingdom some fine tuning of the Copyright, Designs and Patents Act 1988 will be needed, although the draft Regulations presently available make a significant change by assimilating cable programme services with broadcasts, two forms of transmission that have been treated quite separately in the past, although it must be said that the distinction has been somewhat artificial. However, the scope of infringement is different and the Regulations will have to address this.

Exhaustion of rights is an important principle that applies generally to copies of works put into circulation by or with the permission of the owner of the relevant intellectual property rights. The owner of those rights cannot exercise them so as to prevent any subsequent commercial dealings in those copies. Therefore, where the owner of a copyright work has sold copies of that work, he cannot enforce his copyright to prevent the re-sale or export of those particular copies. The Directive makes it clear that the principle does not apply where the work or performance, etc. has been made available to the public electronically on-line. It is limited to situations where the owner has put into circulation copies of his work on tangible media and, of course, even then, it only applies to the particular copies put into circulation by the owner of the relevant intellectual property right.

Exceptions and limitations to rights

Article 5 of the Directive contains a number of exceptions and limitations to the above rights. Only the first, provided for in Article 5(1) is mandatory. This applies to temporary acts of reproduction having no economic significance. These are excepted from the reproduction right where transient or incidental and an integral part of a technological process, the sole purpose of which is to enable (a) the transmission in a network between third parties by an intermediary or (b) a lawful use of a work. For example, internet service providers who act as a conduit for the onward transmission of a work from one person to another do not infringe the reproduction right providing they do not go beyond this. Such reproduction as is necessarily associated with lawful use is also outside the reproduction right. Any other form of transient or incidental copying is not excepted.

Paragraphs 2 and 3 of Article 5 provide for a number of optional exceptions or limitations. These diverse exceptions and limitations include reproduction on paper provided the owner of the right receives fair compensation, reproduction and dissemination by the press, teaching and non-commercial research, private study, criticism or review, uses for disabled persons, public security, caricature, parody or pastiche and use in cases of minor importance providing the use is analogue and does not affect the free circulation of goods or services within the Community. Fair compensation payable to the owner of the relevant right is required in some cases and an acknowledgement of the source and the author's name is required in some cases. Of these optional exceptions and limitations, the United Kingdom government's stated approach is to attempt to maintain the existing exemptions as far as possible. Generally, equivalent provisions will be made in respect of rights in performances.

In line with Article 13 of the Trade Related Aspects of Intellectual Property Rights Agreement and Article 10 of the WIPO Copyright Treaty, Article 5(5) in the Directive contains the 'three-step test' which requires that the exceptions and limitations should:

1 only be applied in certain special cases,
2 not conflict with a normal exploitation of the work or other subject matter, and
3 not unreasonably prejudice the legitimate interests of the owner of the right in question.

This applies to all the permitted acts under copyright or related rights or other subject matter (such as the database right) which relate to reproduction, communication to or making available to the public or distribution. Consequently, a number of the other existing permitted acts will have to be re-assessed in the light of this test. One likely consequence is that fair dealing for research or private study is likely to be limited to non-commercial research for all forms of works or other subject matter, as is already the case with databases, whether protected by copyright or the database right.

Protection of technological measures

Article 6 of the Directive requires member states to provide adequate legal protection against the circumvention of any effective technological measures which the person concerned knows, or believes on reasonable grounds, that he is pursuing that objective. Adequate legal protection must also be provided against the manufacture, import, distribution, sale, rental, advertisement for sale or rental, or possession for commercial purposes of devices, products or components or the provision of services which:

- are promoted, advertised or marketed for the purpose of circumvention of, or
- have only a limited commercially significant purpose or use other than to circumvent, or
- are primarily designed, produced, adapted or performed for the purpose of enabling or facilitating the circumvention of,

any effective technological measures.

A 'technological measure' is any technology, device or component designed to prevent or restrict acts not authorised by the owner of the relevant rights, which include copyright, related rights and the database right. A technological measure is effective where the use of the work or other subject matter is controlled by access controls or protection processes such as encryption, scrambling or other transformation or a copy-control mechanism which achieves the protection objective. Measures must be taken by member states to ensure that the use of technological measures do not compromise certain of the exceptions and limitations to the rights granted by the Directive in the case of a person who has legal access to the work or other subject matter in question. Having legal access is not necessarily the same as having access to the work by virtue of being a licensee. For example, a student at an educational institution may have legal access where the institution has an electronic database under a licence that allows access by staff and students. One of the existing permitted acts, under section 36 of the Copyright, Designs and Patents Act 1988, allows educational establishments to copy by reprographic copying (defined to include electronic copying) up to 1 per cent of a published literary, dramatic or musical work in any one period of three months for the purposes of instruction providing no licensing scheme exists that would apply to such copying. At the present time, the development of licensing schemes to cover works available on-line has a long way to go and most works and other materials available electronically are not yet subject to licensing schemes. Where works are available electronically, technological measures could be adopted by the licensor to prevent such copying. According to the Directive, member states must take appropriate measures to ensure that owners of the rights ensure that the relevant persons may still benefit from certain of the exceptions and limitation to the rights, unless the owners of the rights do this voluntarily. In practice, it will be difficult to see what measures could be adopted by member states to protect these exceptions and limitations should technological measures be used to compromise them.

Compared with the provisions in the Act concerning the circumvention of copy protection, Article 6 of the Directive on technological measures represent a significant expansion, applying to all works of copyright, rights in performances and the database right. They may also apply in relation to the publication right as this can be described as a right related to copyright. The Directive does not state what form adequate legal protection should take. It is likely that civil and criminal sanctions will be adopted in the United Kingdom. At the present time, circumvention of copy protection applied to computer programs, films and sound recordings give a civil remedy only to the copyright owner. However, the existing provisions relating to circumvention of computer programs should remain as Article 1 states that the Directive should be without prejudice to the Directive on the legal protection of computer programs. This could lead to a situation where overcoming technological measures applied to a database attracts criminal liability but not where the measures have been applied to a computer program.

Electronic rights management information

Many works that are published have copyright notices attached to them. The common form of notice is:

© **Name of copyright owner, year of publication.**

Other information may also be printed on copies of the work such as the fact that the author asserts his or her moral rights and a description of the permitted uses of the work. In terms of paper publications, it is not always easy to remove this information without making its removal obvious such as by tearing the page containing the information from a book or by scratching off the copyright or performance rights notice from the surface of a CD. Where the work is published on-line, it may be an easy matter to copy the work, remove the notices and then upload the work on a website. Anyone accessing the website might think, in the absence of any such notices, that the work is in the public domain or that there are no restrictions on what uses may be freely made of the work. By protecting copyright and other notices from removal or alteration, it is hoped that the rights of owners and authors might be better respected and safeguarded. This is what the Directive seeks to achieve by its provisions on electronic rights management information.

Article 7 of the Directive requires member states to give adequate legal protection to electronic rights management information. 'Rights management information' is defined as any information provided by rightholders which identifies the work or other subject matter, the author or any other rightholder, or information about the terms and conditions of use and any numbers or codes representing such information ('rightholder' being the owner of the relevant right, such as a copyright or database right). Protection must be afforded against a person knowingly performing without authority:

- the removal or alteration of any electronic rights management information, or
- the distribution, importation for distribution, broadcasting, communicating or making available to the public works or other subject matter from which such information has been removed or altered without authority

if, by doing so, the person concerned knows, or has reasonable ground to believe, that by doing so he is inducing, facilitating or concealing an infringement of any copyright, related rights or database right.

The protection applies where the information is associated with the work or appears in connection with the communication to the public or a work or other subject matter.

The moves towards standardisation of rights management information systems is progressing and the recitals to the Directive make it clear that global standards should be aimed for and owners of rights in works and other materials made available electronically should be encouraged to mark their works and other subject matter with rights management information as described above together with information as to their authorisation. Where such systems also monitor access and usage patterns of the work in question, proper regard must be had to data protection law, where any personal data relating to users is obtained, in particular in respect of appropriate privacy safeguards. The Directive clearly envisages the use of very sophisticated electronic rights management information systems, adopting technical measures that go way beyond a simple notice placed on the work.

Proposed changes to the Copyright, Designs and Patents Act 1988

During 2002, the Patent Office published a consultation paper on the Directive (EC Directive 2001/29/EC on the Harmonisation of Certain Aspects of Copyright and Related Rights in the Information Society: Consultation Paper on Implementation of the Directive in the United Kingdom, Patent Office, 7 August 2002). It was clear from the consultation paper, which included proposals to modify the Copyright, Designs and Patents Act 1988 to implement the Directive, that making the necessary changes would be very complex and a matter of some controversy. As a result, at the time of writing, a draft of the Regulations modifying the Act has still not been published, even though the Directive was supposed to be transposed into national law before 22 December 2002. To give a flavour to the United Kingdom's possible response, some of the proposals in the consultation paper are summarised very briefly below. A caveat must be added however as it is likely that the Regulations, when finally laid before Parliament, may contain some differences compared to the proposals outlined below.

The main changes to the Copyright, Designs and Patents Act 1988 as set out in the consultation paper are:

- the distinction between broadcasts and cable programmes will disappear with the non-interactive aspects of cable programmes being assimilated into a new definition of broadcasts;
- that copying of performances covers transient and incidental copies will be clarified;
- existing section 20 which covers infringement by broadcasting or inclusion in a cable programme service will be replaced with a new section 20 covering infringement by communication to the public and will extend also to on-demand and interactive services and an exclusive on-demand right will be granted to performers and the performer's existing right to an equitable remuneration in respect of public performances and broadcasts will be extended to cover other forms of communication to the public such as by an on-demand or interactive service;
- no changes are required to comply with the distribution right;
- except for Article 5(1), the United Kingdom will attempt to maintain existing exceptions and limitations on rights in as much as these do not contravene the Directive: however, some changes will be made;
- civil and criminal remedies will be available in respect of technological measures adopted to prevent or restrict unauthorised access and search warrants and forfeiture will also be available;
- only civil remedies will be available in respect of electronic rights management information;
- the civil rights in respect of technological measures and electronic rights management information will be granted to the owner of the relevant right and to the person issuing or communicating the copies to the public.

Summary

Implementing the Directive will bring welcome harmonisation to the protection afforded to works and other materials stored and made available electronically, particularly in respect of on-line services and the Internet generally. Harmonisation is very important in Europe as, otherwise, the Internal Market would be in danger of fragmentation. The fact that complete harmonisation of the exceptions and limitations to the rights is a reflection of present disparities between member states in the exceptions and limitations to copyright generally. These disparities reflect traditional differences as between copyright laws in the countries of Europe. For example, in some countries, it is not an infringement of copyright to make a parody of another work though this is not within the United Kingdom's permitted acts under copyright law.

This Directive is the latest in a long line of Directives that have modified the law of copyright and related rights. In some respects, this is the most ambitious copyright Directive of all and some of its provisions, though they seem straightforward at first sight, will prove difficult to integrate into what is already a very complex area of law. Furthermore, some of the changes are fairly radical and there is likely to be some ongoing controversy and some uncertainty as to the precise nature and scope of some of the rights and other measures in the Directive. In the United States, the Digital Millennium Copyright Act 1998 which, *inter alia*, implemented the WIPO Copyright and Performances and Phonograms Treaties, has caused much controversy over the equivalent measures aimed at the prevention of circumvention of technological measures to protect copyright works. It has been claimed that these provisions are contrary to the United States Constitution by impinging on freedom of speech. For example, under the Act publishing information about encryption techniques could attract criminal liability.

Chapter 9

The law of confidence

Introduction

The law of confidence is concerned with the protection of secrets whether they are trade secrets, secrets of a personal nature or concerning the government of the country. The fundamental rationale underlying the law of confidence is that it can prevent a person divulging information which has been given to him in confidence, on an express or implicit understanding that the information should not be disclosed to others or otherwise used by the recipient of the information. Alternatively, if the information has already been disclosed or used in breach of confidence, damages may be awarded against the person divulging or using the information. The roots of the law of confidence lie in equity and it is almost entirely based on case law, though now it is modified by the rights of privacy and freedom of expression in the European Convention for the Protection of Human Rights and Fundamental Freedoms. It is given statutory recognition in the Copyright, Designs and Patents Act 1988, section 171, which states:

> ... nothing in this Part [the part dealing with copyright] affects ... the operation of any rule of equity relating to breaches of trust or confidence ...

Although of older pedigree, the modern law of confidence developed in the nineteenth century and then lay relatively dormant until the middle of the twentieth century. It soon became clear that breach of confidence was actionable *per se*, and did not require a contractual relationship between the parties. An important case, *Prince Albert* v *Strange* [1849] 1 Mac & G 25, helped to establish this area of law and concerned etchings made by Queen Victoria and her consort, Prince Albert. The Queen and Prince made etchings for their own amusement, intended only for their own private entertainment, although they sometimes had prints made to give to friends. Etchings were sent to a printer to make some impressions and someone surreptitiously made copies which he passed on to the defendant who intended to display them in an exhibition which the public could attend on payment of an admission charge. It was held that relief would be given against the defendant even though he was a third party. He had argued that the prints were not improperly taken but it was said that his possession must have originated in breach of trust, confidence or contract and, therefore, an injunction was granted preventing the exhibition.

The law of confidence can be a very useful adjunct to other intellectual property rights. Copyright protects the expression of an idea, but the law of confidence is wider and can protect the idea itself. In *Andersen Consulting* v *CHP Consulting Ltd* (unreported) 26 July 1991, Chancery Division, a case concerning a dispute about maintenance of computer software by third parties, it was said by Mr Justice Harman that confidence is frequently used in connection with copyright material as it is:

... of course notorious that copyright protects only the expression of ideas and does not protect the idea itself ...

The law of breach of confidence can supplement copyright and patent protection especially in the early stages when there is nothing tangible or substantial enough for copyright law or patent law to protect. Additionally, the law of confidence can be useful for certain types of secrets for which other rights are inappropriate such as secret recipes, research techniques or industrial processes.

Basic requirements

A good working formula for the application of the law of confidence was laid down in *Coco* v *AN Clark (Engineers) Ltd* [1969] RPC 41, by Mr Justice Megarry (as he then was). This involved a moped engine designed by the claimant who entered into informal negotiations with the defendant; no contract was executed. Megarry J held that the defendant owed the claimant an obligation of confidence (although he doubted the confidential quality of the information) and said that, apart from contract, an action for breach of confidence will require three elements:

1 The information must have the necessary quality of confidence about it.
2 The information must have been imparted in circumstances importing an obligation of confidence.
3 There must be an unauthorised use of that information to the detriment of the party communicating it.

The third of these elements is self-evident, but the first two require further discussion.

Quality of confidence

To be protected by the law of confidence, the information must have a quality of confidence about it. If the information is commonplace or is common knowledge to a class of persons (for example, it is well known to computer programmers) or to the public at large, it cannot be confidential; instead, it will be considered to be in the public domain. Often, it will be obvious whether the information is or is not confidential. The concept of confidentiality was considered in the case of *Thomas Marshall (Exports) Ltd* v *Guinle* [1976] FSR 345, in which the defendant, who was the managing director of the claimant company, resigned half-way through his ten-year service contract to set up a rival business. The information involved sources of supply and the names of officials and other contacts in Europe and the Far East. Megarry VC found for the claimant and he said that four elements were necessary in testing for confidential quality.

1 Release of the information would injure the owner of the information or benefit others.
2 The owner must believe the information to be secret and not already in the public domain.
3 The owner's belief in 1 and 2 above must be reasonable.
4 The information must be judged in the light of usages and practices of the particular trade or industry concerned.

To come within the scope of the law of confidence, the information does not have to be particularly special and, as in the above case, ordinary and mundane information can be the proper subject matter of confidence as long as it is private to the person who has compiled the information, even though others could gather similar information if they took the trouble to do so. In this way, the law of confidence prevents others from gaining benefit from the work of the person who accumulated the information in the first place. As a result, a great deal of material related to the running of a business will fall within the ambit of the law of confidence. Examples of information relevant to computers which may be the subject matter of confidence include:

- ideas for a new or improved computer system, hardware and software (programs, databases or other works in digital form) and research and development work generally;
- details of existing computer systems as would be known by computer analysts or programmers or even users of the system (in terms of users, the system would have to be uncommon in some respect);
- lists of customers or sub-contractors and associated information – for example, what services they perform, what their credit rating is. Information stored in computer databases is often confidential;
- a company's strategy for future research and development, production and marketing.

Usually, software companies treat their source code programs as being confidential and, in most circumstances, only make available to clients object code versions of the programs. It is generally accepted that source code programs are confidential unless published. In *Cantor Fitzgerald International* v *Tradition (UK) Ltd* [2000] RPC 95, the defendant made use of the claimant's source code programs when developing its own bond-broking software. It was held that the claimant's copyright had been infringed by the defendant which had loaded the claimant's programs into its computers and had adapted some of the claimant's modules in its own programs. Accepting that the source code was confidential, the judge confirmed that the defendant's use of the claimant's programs for the purposes of debugging its own programs was a breach of confidence. Some of the techniques and 'wrinkles' developed by the defendant's programmers whilst they were employed by the claimant were held not to be trade secrets as such and were the sort of thing an ex-employee would be expected to be free to use after cessation of his employment, in the absence of a covenant in restraint of trade. However, had the programmers disclosed this sort of information to a third party during their employment by the claimant that would have been a breach of their employment contracts and a breach of confidence.

Obligation of confidence

An obligation of confidence will not be imposed on everyone. A person who is given confidential information and is unaware of its confidential nature (and has no reason to be aware) will be able to use the information freely. This is a major weakness of the law of confidence as it is largely ineffective against innocent third-party recipients of the information. For example, if A tells B something in confidence and B (without A's permission) passes the information on to C, who has not been told that it is confidential and the circumstances are such that an obligation of confidence cannot be imputed to C, then C will be able to use the information freely although B himself can be prevented from using the information or divulging it further. However, it may still be possible for A to obtain an injunction against C in respect of future disclosure or use by C if the information has not yet entered the public domain. C will not, of course, be liable for any acts that he may have carried out innocently before notification that B had divulged the information in breach of his obligation of confidence to A.

Obviously, an obligation of confidence can arise by express agreement: for example, where a self-employed freelance computer programmer is engaged to carry out some work under a contract which contains a term stating that the programmer will not use or divulge details of the client's business. An obligation of confidence may also be implied by the courts where there is a duty of good faith as in the relationship between a client and a solicitor, patent agent or bank manager. Another situation where the obligation will be imposed is where a person discusses his ideas with business organisations with a view to the commercial exploitation of those ideas: for example, if a computer analyst has an idea for a new computer system and discusses that idea with software houses interested in developing and marketing the system.

Using technical means to make it difficult to gain access to confidential information will not necessarily be sufficient to impose an obligation of confidence. In *Mars UK Ltd v Teknowledge Ltd* [2000] FSR 138, the claimant designed and manufactured mechanisms for receiving coins in vending machines and the like. The mechanisms contained computer programs, algorithms and databases of acceptable parameters for coins (to distinguish genuine coins from foreign coins and blanks). The programs, algorithms and databases where stored in encrypted form on EEPROM computer chips ('electronically erasable programmable read only memory). These could be recalibrated with new data. When the defendant reversed engineering the chips so that it could offer a re-calibration service, it was claimed that this was a breach of confidence (apart from breach of copyright and database right; see Chapter 5). As the machines containing the mechanisms were freely available and on the market, the encrypted information did not have the necessary quality of confidence about it. There was nothing to prevent a purchaser of the machines from dismantling them to find out how they worked and the fact that the information was encrypted did not, *per se*, impose an obligation of confidence. Of course, it might have been different if an express obligation of confidence had been imposed on persons acquiring the machines but there is some doubt that even that would be effective unless the contract under which the ownership of the machines passed imposed duties not to dismantle the machines or reverse engineer the chips inside them. This might not be enough, however, to impose an obligation on third parties, perhaps who obtained the machines after subsequent re-sale.

In *Douglas v Hello! Ltd* [2003] EWHC 786 (Ch), Michael Douglas and Catherine Zeta-Jones, the famous film stars ('the Douglases') were married in the New York Plaza Hotel. They had made a contract with the proprietor of OK! Magazine, granting it exclusive rights to publish and syndicate photographs of the wedding and reception. Photographers were engaged by the Douglases and, under the contract, they were responsible for ensuring that no other photographs were taken. Very rigorous security arrangements were put into place to restrict those attending to invited family and friends, to prevent unauthorised photographs being taken and to preserve the exclusivity of the photographs to be given to OK! Magazine. The Douglases were each paid £500,000 together with a share of any income from syndicating the photographs made by OK! Magazine in excess of £1m. As part of the arrangement, the Douglases were to select which photographs would be published and syndicated by OK! Magazine.

Unknown to the Douglases, a paparazzo photographer had somehow gained access to the event and he surreptitiously took a number of photographs of the couple, most of which were poor quality and blurred. The photographs found their way to the owners of Hello! Magazine and arrangements were made to publish the photographs in the next issue. When the Douglases found out about the planned publication of the unauthorised photographs, they obtained an injunction preventing publication but this was lifted by the Court of Appeal and publication took place. In the ensuing action in the Chancery Division of the High Court, numerous claims were put forward by the Douglases and OK! Magazine, including a claim for breach of confidence. In holding that the defendants had been guilty of a breach of confidence, Mr Justice Lindsay confirmed that, in a situation where it had been made clear, expressly or impliedly, that photographs were not to be taken by the guests, their actual or imputed knowledge was sufficient to impose a duty of confidence upon them, even though there were in excess of 300 guests. That duty also extended to the defendants. By the strict security arrangements, which included searching guests for cameras and camcorders the Douglases had sent a message to the guests which placed them under a duty of confidence.

Mars UK Ltd v *Teknowledge Ltd* was not mentioned in the *Douglas* case (nor in the Court of Appeal earlier) and it is hard to reconcile the two decisions in respect of an imposition of a duty of confidence. It could be argued that encrypting information to make it very difficult to access sends a similar message to that of letting persons attending a wedding ceremony and reception know in clear terms that they are not allowed to take photographs.

Employees

The employee–employer relationship is a special case and may be governed by express terms, as incorporated in the contract of employment, or implied terms or both. Generally, the duty of confidence owed by ex-employees will be less than for current employees who should always act in their employer's best interests. A present employee must respect the confidentiality of his employer's information even to the extent that he should not pry into information he has been told not to look at. In *Denco Ltd* v *Joinson* [1991] IRLR 63, an employee who had a right of access to certain information in his employer's computer system used another employee's password to gain access to other parts of the computer system – something he was not entitled to do. It was held that the employer was entitled to dismiss the employee summarily for his unauthorised use of the password.

Ex-employees have to make a living and much of the ex-employee's skill will involve what he learnt while in his previous employment, thus providing the courts with a dilemma. In many cases, to complicate matters, there may be an overlap with copyright law. However, the courts have developed rules for resolving the conflict which strike a reasonable balance between the interests of employee and employer alike.

When there are no express terms, the employer will not be protected to any great extent. If the ex-employee simply remembers details of some of the previous employer's customers, there is nothing to stop him using this information. Of course, it would be different if he deliberately memorised the customers' names or made a copy of them. In the absence of an express term in the contract of employment dealing with confidentiality, it was said, in *Printers and Finishers Ltd* v *Holloway* [1965] RPC 239, that there would be nothing improper in the employee putting his memory of particular features of his previous employer's plant at the disposal of his new employer. Even if there is an express term the employer would have to show that the information was over and above the employee's normal skill in the job and amounted to a trade secret. The nature of a trade secret was considered in *Lansing Linde Ltd* v *Kerr* [1991] 1 WLR 251, in which it was recognised that it was not confined to secret formulae or processes but could, in appropriate cases, extend to names of customers and the goods which they buy.

In *Northern Office Microcomputer (Pty) Ltd* v *Rosenstein* [1982] FSR 124, a South African case, the problem of where to draw the line between the employer's and employee's interests was considered. In this case, a computer programmer developed a computer program which was similar to one he had written for his previous employer. The case involved copyright matters in addition to the law of confidence and is notable in that the court recognised that computer programs were protected by South African copyright law as literary works. The trial judge agreed that the computer programs were protected by confidence but said that the protection should be of a limited nature. Although the defendant programmer would not be allowed simply to copy the programs in question, he would not be required to 'wipe clean the slate of his memory' because to do so would unduly restrict his use of his own training, skill and experience. There would be nothing, in principle, to prevent an ex-employee computer programmer writing a similar program by the exercise of his own mental effort provided he did not simply plagiarise his previous employer's program. To some extent, an important factor is the computer program itself, whether it is a commonplace program, carrying out mundane operations, or whether it is designed to do something novel, that is, whether the purpose of the program can be said to be in the nature of a trade secret.

In many cases, the employer's 'trade secrets' may be no more than the result of the application by an employee of his own skill and judgment, but if the employee was engaged specifically to produce that information then it can still amount to a trade secret. If the material were commonplace, however, there would be nothing to stop an ex-employee deriving the same or similar material again as long as he did not simply copy his employer's material. In such circumstances, all that would be protected would be the employer's 'lead time', the advantage of getting his product to the market place first.

An important case laying down principles which can be applied to the employer–employee relationship was *Faccenda Chicken Ltd* v *Fowler* [1986] 1 All ER 617. The employer's business was supplying fresh chickens and it was alleged that the employee had made wrongful use of sales information such as customers' names and addresses. The employer's action failed, but the following guidelines were laid down in the Court of Appeal.

1 If there is a contract of employment, the employee's obligations were to be determined from the contract.
2 If there were no express terms, the employee's obligations would be implied.
3 While still in employment, there was an implied term imposing a duty of good faith. This duty might vary according to the nature of the contract of employment but would be broken if the employee copied or deliberately memorised a list of customers.
4 The implied term imposing an obligation on the employee after the termination of his employment was more restricted. It might cover secret processes and trade secrets.

5 Whether information fell within this implied term to prevent its use or disclosure by an ex-employee depended on the circumstances, and attention should be given to the following:

- the nature of the employment;
- the nature of the information;
- whether the employer stressed the confidential nature of the material;
- whether the information could be easily isolated from other material the employee was free to use.

An ex-employee is thus allowed to make use of his own memory of the work he has carried out in his previous employment unless it involves genuine secrets or is covered by an express term in the contract of employment. Computer programmers and analysts will be allowed to make use of programming techniques and skills which they have learnt and which have become part of their own skill and experience, unless there is something very special about them or they have expressly agreed not to make further use of them. However, a very restrictive express term which tries to prevent an ex-employee making use of mundane skills will be struck out by the courts as being in restraint of trade. The same fate will await any terms which restrict the ex-employee's future employment prospects to any great extent – for example, a term which states that a computer programmer cannot work for computer software companies in the United Kingdom for five years following the termination of his employment. Such restrictive terms will be upheld by the courts only if they are reasonable, such as when a computer programmer working for a bank agrees not to work for another similar bank within a five-mile radius for the first year following the termination of his employment. The purpose of a covenant in restraint of trade should be to protect the employer's legitimate interests rather than simply preventing competition. Essentially, to be enforceable, the term should be aimed at protecting the employer's genuine business interests rather than trying to prevent lawful competition.

It is not easy to lay down an all-purpose formula based on time and geographical area as each case will turn on its own facts. For example, in *Office Angels Ltd* v *Rainer-Thomas* [1991] IRLR 214, it was held that a covenant precluding an ex-employee from opening an employment agency anywhere in an area only within a 1000-metre radius of the previous employer's agency for a period of only six months was inappropriate and would do little to protect the employer's interests because clients usually placed orders over the telephone and the geographical location of the office was of no consequence to them. In that case, the Court of Appeal also confirmed that, where a covenant in restraint of trade was ambiguous, the narrower construction would be taken. This is even more so where organisations are engaged in e-business and trade online. Geographic area is largely irrelevant in terms of deciding whether a covenant in restrain of trade is or is not reasonable.

Computer hackers

A computer hacker is a person who gains access to a computer system without permission. Computer hackers pose a serious threat to the security of computer systems and some of the activities in which they engage are potentially criminal in nature. These activities are fully discussed in Chapter 29. However, computer hackers also might be liable under the law of confidence, depending on the circumstances. If a hacker gains access to confidential files stored on a computer, it is just possible that the law of confidence might be used to prevent the hacker from making use of the information assuming, of course, that the hacker can be identified. In many cases, information stored in computer systems is highly confidential. It might, for example, concern medical records, creditworthiness, employment or lifestyle details. But will an obligation of confidence attach to a computer hacker? The case of *Prince Albert* v *Strange*, discussed above, suggests that an action might lie in breach of confidence even if the information was obtained surreptitiously. The court in that case was quite happy to imply an obligation of confidence even though it was not possible to say how the confidential information (that is, the prints taken from the engravings) came into the defendant's hands. It could only be assumed that the prints had been obtained in a clandestine manner. In principle, this is very similar to the position of a computer hacker. The case of *Douglas* v *Hello! Ltd* [2003] EWHC 786 (Ch), discussed above, reinforces this notion. A hacker must know that there is a strong possibility that the information he accesses will be confidential and, therefore, he will be fixed with an obligation of confidence. If the information turns out to have a quality of confidence, then there is no reason in principle why the hacker should not be sued for breach of confidence if he uses that information or discloses it to others.

If the information is accidentally overheard or intercepted in circumstances where the owner of the information utters it or transmits it by insecure means (for example, by telling it to someone in a crowded room or by transmitting the information by a public telecommunications system) an obligation of confidence might not be imposed on the person obtaining the information in this manner. In *Malone* v *Metropolitan Police Commissioner* [1979] Ch 344, information overheard during an authorised telephone tapping operation by the police was held not to have been disclosed in confidence. However, the law on the matter of unauthorised interception of information is not clear. In most circumstances, unless authorised by a judge or senior police officer, an offence may be committed under the Regulation of Investigatory Powers Act 2000.

Public interest defence

Disclosure of confidential information can sometimes be justified as being in the public interest. This might be the case, for example, where a person discloses information which shows that an illegal activity is taking place, such as where a number of companies are involved in price fixing or where a radar device used by the police to catch speeding motorists is inaccurate. However, it must be noted that what is interesting to the public is not necessarily in the public interest. This is particularly so in respect of famous persons and, although those who seek publicity and foster a particular image of themselves to the public, must expect publication of information tending to show this image is false, a line has to be drawn even so. In *Naomi Campbell* v *Mirror Group Newspapers plc* [2002] EWCA Civ 1373, the defendant published a story about how the famous fashion model had undergone treatment for drug addiction. Previously, she had denied being addicted to drugs. The Court of Appeal accepted that a journalist must have a certain latitude when deciding what to publish. Although it was not permissible to publish everything about an individual's life, in this case, it was acceptable to publish a photograph of the model leaving a drug rehabilitation clinic and details of her treatment. However, the court acknowledged that it was still early days when deciding issues of breach of confidence in the context of the balance between the right of privacy in Article 8 and the right of freedom of expression in Article 10 of the

European Convention for the Protection of Human Rights and Fundamental Freedoms, the Convention only being brought into force in the United Kingdom on 2 October 2000.

Public interest and freedom of expression were used as defences in *Douglas v Hello! Ltd* [2003] EWHC 786 (Ch), discussed earlier in this chapter. The court accepted that the law of breach of confidence has been somewhat modified by the adoption of the above Convention rights but there is no separate right to privacy. The law of confidence, as amended by these rights, is the appropriate means to protect privacy. Mr Justice Lindsay rejected the defence, that by publishing their own selected photographs of their wedding, Michael Douglas and Catherine Zeta-Jones had waived their right to prevent publication of surreptitiously taken photographs. Whilst a public interest defence would apply to publication of information about personalities who had promoted a false image of themselves, to 'put the record straight' (as in the *Naomi Campbell* case), the claimants here had done no such thing. Further, the right of freedom of expression was subject to, *inter alia*, conditions or restrictions prescribed by law. That was the case here. In any case, the defendants had violated the Privacy Code of the Press Complaints Commission, something which, under section 12 of the Human Rights Act 1998, must be taken into account.

Remedies for breach of confidence

The most important remedy for breach of confidence is an injunction preventing the use or disclosure of the information. If the information has been divulged to sufficient people so that it can be said to be no longer confidential, an injunction will not be of any help; it would be like locking the stable door after the horse has bolted. If this has happened and the information has been used to the detriment of the person to whom it 'belongs', however, damages will be available against the person responsible and a limited injunction may be granted against that person.

As an alternative to damages, an account of profits may be available and this may be more advantageous to the claimant, especially if the defendant has made substantial profit from his use of the information. Being an equitable remedy it is discretionary and the claimant must have 'clean hands' and have acted promptly in enforcing his rights. An example of the use of this remedy is the case of *Peter Pan Manufacturing Corp v Corsets Silhouette Ltd* [1963] RPC 45, which involved the use of confidential information, after the expiry of a licence agreement, in the manufacture of brassières. The claimant asked for the whole of the profits on the brassières but the defendant said that the account of profits should only be based on the profit resulting from the wrongful use of the confidential information; that is, the profit relating to the parts of the brassières incorporating the confidential information. The difference between the two sums was substantial and the claimant was awarded the higher sum because the defendants would not have been able to make the brassières at all without using the confidential information.

It can be seen that the law of confidence is very useful at an early stage when ideas are being formulated and discussed. Although the law of copyright gives some protection at this stage by protecting plans, specifications and notes, the protection does not extend to the ideas behind them. Confidence is particularly important during the development of inventions before they are granted patents because a patent will be refused if details of the invention have been made available to the public, as we shall see. In the computer industry, as with any other, ideas have to be discussed with various persons and organisations with a view to raising finance and granting licences to use or reproduce the resulting invention or copyright work. Many licences for the use of patented inventions include permission to use 'know-how', the confidential information needed to work the invention to best effect. Some licences may be purely for know-how where there is no patent involved. In most circumstances, during negotiations, an obligation of confidence will be implied but it is sensible to impose it expressly in writing, for example, by stating that the information is confidential and must not be used or disclosed to anyone else without the owner's express written permission.

Court orders and breach of confidence

Apart from the usual orders for injunctions and delivery up of confidential information taken illegally, the courts may have to consider other forms of order such as an order for disclosure of the identity of the person responsible for passing on confidential information to a third party who publishes the information. Where information has been divulged in breach of confidence and there is a danger that there will be more such breaches in the future, this could be a factor in whether a court identifies the person responsible. In *Ashworth Security Hospital* v *MGN Ltd* [2003] FSR 17 an unknown person who presumably worked at the hospital disclosed confidential information taken from a hospital database about Charles Brady to the defendant, Mirror Group Newspapers. The hospital sought an order forcing the defendant to identify the culprit who might be in breach of his contract of employment, in breach of confidence, notwithstanding any criminal offences under the Data Protection Act 1998. It was argued that ordering that the defendant identify the person responsible for the disclosure of information was a breach of the right of freedom of speech under Article 10 of the European Convention for the Protection of Human Rights and Fundamental Freedoms. However, the Court of Appeal and the House of Lords confirmed that the order was lawful and did not breach Article 10. In particular, Article 10(2) permits derogation from the basic principle, *inter alia*, to prevent the disclosure of information received in confidence. The House of Lords held that the disclosure of patients' records from a secure hospital was an exceptionally serious matter and, to deter further disclosures in the future, it was necessary, proportionate and justified to order disclosure of the source so that he could be punished. Section 10 of the Contempt of Court Act 1981 was not incompatible with the Convention. Section 10 prevents a court from ordering such disclosure except in the interests of justice, national security or the prevention of crime and disorder.

If it is suspected that a person has taken copies of confidential information or copyright material, for example, on magnetic or optical media, there may be a suspicion that the information will be erased or destroyed once the defendant is aware that legal proceedings are likely to be initiated against him. The 'without notice search and seizure order' (formerly known as an *Anton Piller Order*) may be particularly valuable in this respect and has the purpose of preserving evidence where there is a danger it may be destroyed. In *Elvee Ltd* v *Taylor* [2002] FSR 48 some ex-employees of the claimant, a company designing computer graphics, left to join another company (which had been incorporated whilst two of the defendants were still employed by the claimant). It was later discovered that about 200 blank CDs belonging to the claimant were missing. The claimant thought that data relating to its customers which was confidential or subject to copyright had been copied by the defendants and, fearing the evidence would be destroyed, sought a without notice search and seizure order against the defendants' company. A specialist data recovery company was engaged by the claimant and made images of the computer hard disks at the defendants' company's premises. An application by the defendant to discharge the order on the grounds of a material non-disclosure was refused. The judge making the original order had not been told about the fact that, in parallel proceedings, the defendants had entered a defence and counter-claim. A further reason was that the judge who granted the order was in the Queen's Bench Division and he should have been told that such an application in an intellectual property case should be made to the Chancery Division.

Summary

The law of breach of confidence is a useful ally to other intellectual property rights and can also prove very important in its own right. Almost every organisation, whether of a private or public nature, and consultants, have and use confidential information. This area of law is particularly relevant to the computer industry and any organisation involved in information technology. All manner of works and information can be protected by the law of confidence, such as source code programs, databases and other works stored in digital form, and design materials for such materials. It also covers general business information such as customer details, business plans and such like.

A serious challenge to maintaining confidentiality is the ease with which confidential information stored electronically, as much of it now is, may be copied, transmitted and disseminated, particularly with the advent of CD and DVD writers. This fact alone makes it imperative for owners of confidential information to properly monitor its use and disclosure. Employees represent a significant threat in this respect and there are many examples of ex-employees taking away copies of confidential information as their employment is coming to an end. In many cases, this information is used to develop competing software or to target clients and customers of the previous employer. Computer programmers and software developers generally, whether employed or self-employed are frequently subject to covenants in restraint of trade. These covenants are effective only if reasonable and if they do not unduly interfere with the individual's ability to exercise his trade or profession elsewhere. Furthermore, they must be designed to protect the employer's or client's legitimate interests and not aimed at preventing or restricting competition. In other cases, where confidential information is being disclosed to another, it is always useful to impose an express duty of confidence as the courts cannot be relied upon to impose a duty in some cases.

Chapter 10

Patent law

Introduction

Patents are granted for new, non-obvious inventions that have an industrial application. A patent is a very desirable form of intellectual property because it gives to the owner a monopoly in his invention, enabling him to exploit the invention for a number of years to the exclusion of all others (subject to provisions designed to prevent abuse of the monopoly granted). Patent law has a long history and has developed as a means of protecting innovation, which has a benefit to innovator and public alike. Inventors are encouraged to invent and investors are more likely to risk money in the development of new inventions if a monopoly right is available for inventions. Society reaps a benefit because the invention will eventually fall into the public domain and because, in the meantime, commercial enterprise is stimulated.

The availability of patents for software inventions has been a subject of some controversy. A particular problem in Europe is that there is an exclusion from patentability that prevents the patenting of computer programs *as such*. Other exclusions, such as the presentation of information, business methods and mental acts impact on forms of software other than computer programs. A further issue is the fact the some countries, notably the United States, freely grant patents for software inventions and there is no equivalent exclusion on patenting computer programs or other forms of software. As a great deal of software is made available and exploited on a global basis, for example, on e-business websites, a more serious criticism of the United States approach is that the United States Patents and Trademark Office seems to be far too liberal in the granting of software patents and it is suspected that a great many software patents are invalid for lack of novelty or inventive step. As one might guess, challenging a patent in the United States is a daunting and potentially very expensive exercise for organisations and individuals based outside the United States. The patentability of computer programs in particular has been reviewed in Europe and it is likely that some changes will be made in the future to patent law in Europe, which may facilitate the obtaining of patents for computer programs. These proposals are outlined towards the end of this chapter.

Basic considerations

There are two types of patentable invention – a product invention and a process invention – and it has been said that an invention is a new way of making something old or an old way of making something new. A patentable invention could relate to a new piece of computer hardware such as a new and inventive input device such as a scanner, a new type of output device such as a more efficient flat-screen display or a new form of storage medium or it could be a new way of making integrated circuits or flat screens. There have been many patent applications for computer hardware and other electronic materials: for example, the invention of the printed circuit board, the transistor and the integrated circuit have all been patented. Sometimes, other forms of protection may be available such as design law or copyright. If the invention fails to meet the rigorous standards required for patentability, these and other forms of protection may still be available. For example, the design right may protect a new layout of components on a printed circuit board even if there is no inventive step for patent purposes. Subject to a general but not complete exclusion, some computer programs and other software inventions may be patentable, such as a digital image processing system or a computer program which, when run in a computer, controls an industrial process.

Fundamentally, the inventor (or more usually, the employer of the inventor) applies for a patent to the Patent Office in London, whether the inventor wants a United Kingdom patent or one which extends to other countries as well. If the application is successful, a patent will be granted for four years initially and may be renewed, annually, up to a maximum of 20 years from the date the application is first filed (the priority date). The renewal fees become progressively steeper throughout the life of the patent and most patents do not run the full 20 years.

Obtaining a patent is a complex, expensive and lengthy process and the services of a patent agent are desirable because the drafting of the patent specification and claims is extremely important as regards the future scope of the patent. Until the Copyright, Designs and Patents Act 1988, only a registered patent agent or a solicitor could act for gain as an agent for persons seeking patents, but now anyone can do this as long as he does not describe himself as, or hold himself out to be, a 'patent agent' or 'patent attorney'. In view of the complicated nature of the process, however, the person applying for a patent would be well advised to satisfy himself as to the ability of his agent. In some circumstances, it may be preferable simply to keep the idea secret and rely on the law of confidence; this costs little or nothing and there is no requirement that the invention must eventually fall into the public domain. Examples of the effectiveness of this approach are the recipes and processes used in many familiar drinks and foodstuffs. In many cases, however, the invention cannot be kept secret, especially if articles made to the invention are to be marketed commercially or if a large number of employees know of the invention, in which case a patent is the only realistic way of protecting the invention.

Procedure

The ponderous patent application process seems to be unsuited to a fast-moving technology as it can take several years from initial application before a patent is finally granted. The procedure for obtaining a patent in the United Kingdom is as follows.

1 The application is filed together with a specification describing the invention, an abstract (the title for the invention and concise summary) and the claims (defining the scope of the monopoly claimed). Drawings will usually be included in the specification.
2 The Patent Office will carry out a search for patents and other documents which may be relevant to the invention. Typically, this will find previous patents in the same field which might have a bearing on the patentability of the invention. It is common for the application to be amended following the search.

3 Eighteen months following the first filing of the patent it is published. This is referred to as 'A' publication.
4 The Patent Office examiners then carry out an extensive examination of the patent application to check for conformity with the requirements of the Patents Act 1977. Again, some amendments may be necessary at this stage, though it should be noted that the monopoly claimed cannot be widened.
5 Finally, the patent will be granted (all being well) and it will be published again – 'B' publication.

The procedure is shown in Fig. 10.1. It is greatly simplified and assumes no problems are encountered. Since 1995, the United Kingdom Patent Office has offered a speedier procedure whereby the applicant can request a combined search and examination and earlier publication. This procedure may be suitable for straightforward applications but is unlikely to be appropriate for software inventions.

The proprietor's monopoly dates back, effectively, to the date of 'A' publication. Although he cannot bring legal proceedings for infringement of the patent until the time that the patent is granted, he will be entitled to damages in respect of any infringement carried out after that publication.

The date when the patent application is first filed becomes its priority date. As a result of international conventions, the applicant may make further applications in convention countries within the next 12 months and the novelty of the invention will still be judged as at its priority date, nothing which has been made available to the public in that period will be taken into account in determining whether the invention is new. The later filings will be given the priority date of the first filing date. Thus, the applicant has 12 months to decide in which other countries he wishes to obtain a patent.

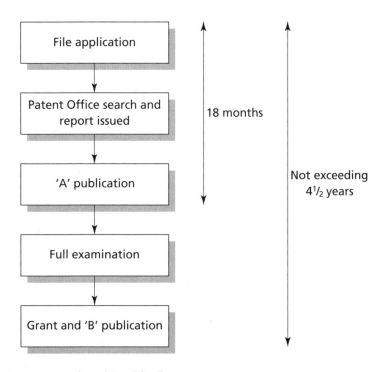

Fig. 10.1 Patent procedure (simplified)

Two international conventions – the European Patent Convention and the Patent Co-operation Treaty – facilitate the obtaining of patents in a number of other countries.

The main legislation governing patents is the Patents Act 1977 and the Patents Rules 1995. The 1977 Act was passed to bring United Kingdom patent law in line with the European Patent Convention (EPC) to which the United Kingdom is a member. Presently, all the European Community member states belong to the EPC together with a number of other countries including Switzerland, Cyprus, Turkey, Hungary and the Czech Republic. At the time of writing there are a total of 27 members of the EPC. Following a single filing and search and examination process, once granted an EPC patent devolves into a bundle of national patents for countries nominated by the applicant, not being less than three countries.

The EPC is not a European Community institution although the European Patent Office (EPO) will administer the proposed Community Patent Convention, providing a Community-wide patent system, when it comes into force. This system was first on the drawing board in the 1960s but still has not yet come to fruition. In many respects this is a great pity as the availability of a single patent in force in all the member states of the European Community (and possibly wider) is very attractive and could prevent some of the difficulties of enforcing equivalent national patents for the same invention across a number of countries. A basic rule of jurisdiction is that, if in patent litigation the validity of the patent is challenged, only the courts in the country where the patent is registered have jurisdiction to hear the case. If, for example, a company owns a number of national patents covering the same invention and they are being infringed in, for the sake of argument, six countries by defendants that are economically linked to each other (such as a group of companies or in the case of a parent company and subsidiary companies) the owner of the patents will have no option but to commence proceedings in each of those countries unless the validity of each national patent is not challenged. Normally, however, a defendant will raise issues of validity, after all, if he can show that the patent is not valid or not valid in relevant respects, that provides a complete defence to an infringement action.

It is normal for a company based in the United Kingdom or a person resident in the United Kingdom to file at the United Kingdom Patent Office first before applying elsewhere. In fact, it is an offence to file an application outside the United Kingdom less than six weeks before filing an application in respect of the same invention in the United Kingdom or where security directions have been issued or unless the Comptroller gives written permission allowing application elsewhere otherwise.

In addition to the Patents Act 1977, there are a number of rules and regulations dealing with details such as registration procedure, fees and the Patents County Court in London. The Comptroller of Patents also has jurisdiction to hear certain patent disputes if the parties are willing and to hear other matters, such as determining who should be the true proprietor or whether an employee inventor should be awarded compensation for an invention belonging to his employer which is of outstanding benefit to the employer.

Not all inventions are capable of supporting a patent. The Patents Act 1977 lays down several requirements which must be satisfied before a patent can be granted and, furthermore, certain things are specifically excluded from patentability. The basic requirements for the grant of a patent will now be explained, followed by a consideration of the exclusions and their impact, especially with respect to computer software.

Basic requirements

The basic requirements for the grant of a patent are stated in section 1(1) of the Patents Act 1977 as follows:

A patent may be granted only for an invention in respect of which the following conditions are satisfied, that is to say:
(a) the invention is new;
(b) it involves an inventive step;
(c) it is capable of industrial application;
(d) the grant of a patent for it is not excluded by subsections (2) and (3) below ...

The exclusions referred to in (d), which include computer programs, will be considered later but first the interpretation of the first three conditions will be examined.

New invention

The word 'invention' is not defined in the Act but its meaning is really a matter of common sense and it can be used in a fairly wide sense. It is obvious that a patent should not be granted for anything which is not new, which is already in the public domain, otherwise the grant of the patent could make illegal an act which was previously legal. For example, if a company has been making integrated circuits by a special process for several years but failed to apply for a patent, a second company which uses the same process, perhaps coincidentally, and applies for a patent for the process will be refused a patent on the grounds that the invention is not new unless the first company's use of the process was not such as to make it available to the public. In that case, the second company may be able to obtain a patent for the process but there is a special defence for the first company under section 64 of the Patents Act 1977 and it will be allowed to continue to use the process. The same would apply if the first company had not necessarily used the process before the application for a patent had been filed but had made serious and effective preparations to use the process by the filing date.

Section 2 of the Act expands on the meaning of 'new' and says that an invention is new if it does not form part of the 'state of the art'; this expression comprises all matter which has been made available to the public in the United Kingdom or elsewhere, by written or oral description, by use or in any other way. Matters contained in patent applications having earlier priority dates are also included even if they had not been published by the date of first filing of the application in question. There is no need for the invention to have been made widely available to the public and, in *Windsurfing International Inc* v *Tabur Marine (GB) Ltd* [1985] RPC 59, it was held that a 12-year-old boy, who had made his own sailboard which he used at Hayling Island on summer weekends, had made the invention available to the public with the effect that a patent later granted to the claimant for a sailboard was declared invalid after the defendant had challenged its validity on the grounds of lack of novelty and lack of inventive step.

The inventor must resist any temptation he might have to publish details of his invention before the first filing date (the priority date), otherwise he could inadvertently add his invention to the state of the art and anticipate his own patent. Similarly, the inventor must be careful when discussing his invention with potential manufacturers and the like and the law of confidence is very important at this stage. However, if details of the invention are disclosed by a person acting in breach of confidence or who has obtained details unlawfully, that disclosure will be disregarded in determining the state of the art if such breach occurs no earlier than six months preceding the filing of the patent.

As technology advances and the pool of knowledge in the public domain grows, it is increasingly difficult to devise something which is absolutely 'new'. Indeed, it is not an easy task to find out if the invention has been anticipated and is already part of the state of the art, given the massive world-wide volume of published work, and it is possible that a publication which anticipates the invention will not be discovered. If that material is subsequently found and shows that the invention was not new when the patent was applied for, the patent is in danger of being revoked. A number of patents may be on shaky ground as far as novelty is concerned if sufficient time and effort were expended on trying to trace anticipatory materials or prior use. This is particularly the case in respect of software inventions where the size of the prior art is enormous. A person who is being sued for infringing a patent will try to find such material and, in the case of a challenge to a software patent, the enquiry is likely to go far beyond looking at prior patents and will cover other published material and software products put on the market prior to the first filing date of the software patent.

Inventive step

By section 3 of the Patents Act 1977 an invention involves an inventive step if it is not obvious to a person skilled in the art. This test, known as the 'notional skilled worker test', takes account of the complexity of technology, hence the reference to a skilled person rather than the ubiquitous reasonable person, so often used as a benchmark by judges. The reason is that a great many 'inventions' would not be obvious to a layperson but would be to someone who knew something of the technology involved. It has been accepted that the 'skilled person' may be a team of highly qualified research workers such as a team of systems analysts, software development engineers and computer programmers. When it comes to applying the test, the skilled person is not endowed with any inventive faculties himself, a somewhat artificial premise, but to hold otherwise would mean that all inventions could be deemed to be obvious and not patentable.

'Obvious' has no special meaning but is judged by looking at the invention as a whole and considering the entire state of the art. Whether the invention is obvious is a question of fact. In the *Windsurfing* case discussed earlier in connection with novelty, Lord Justice Oliver suggested the following four-stage test for determining whether an invention is obvious.

1 Identify the inventive concept embodied in the patent.
2 The court then assumes the mantle of the normally skilled but unimaginative person in the art at the priority date of the patent and imputes to him what was, at that date, common general knowledge in the art.
3 Identify what, if any, differences exist between that knowledge and the patented invention.
4 Consider whether, without knowledge of the invention, those differences constitute steps which would have been obvious to the person skilled in the art or whether they require any degree of invention.

When considering whether an invention contains an inventive step, the danger of using hindsight must be avoided. It is so easy for expert witnesses and, sometimes, the judge, to fall into that trap. What might seem obvious now with the benefit of hindsight might not have seemed obvious at the time the application for the patent was filed. Step 2 of the *Windsurfing* test guards against this danger by reminding the judge to put himself in the position of the skilled person *at the priority date* of the patent.

Commercial success is a factor which can be taken into account in determining obviousness though it is not conclusive. In *Technograph Printed Circuits Ltd* v *Mills & Rockley (Electronics) Ltd* [1969] RPC 395, a case involving a patent for a method of making printed circuits, Harman J said:

> It was objected that in fact it was not until ten years after the invention was published that it was commercially adopted ... and it was argued from this that it was not a case of filling a long felt want. I do not accept this argument. In the years immediately following the war, manufacturers could sell all the machines they wanted using the old point-to-point wiring and had no need to trouble themselves with anything better.

Computer technology spreads into all kinds of other technologies and this may lead to patentable inventions and, even though the computer technology used itself is not new, the application of the technology to provide a solution to a technical problem may be new. In principle there is nothing to prevent the application of well-known technology to a particular problem being the proper subject matter of a patent. This may not be obvious if there has been a major problem and a solution has evaded many attempts to reach it. Again, the commercial success of the invention is a useful guide. In *Parks-Cramer Co* v *G W Thornton & Sons Ltd* [1966] RPC 407, the invention was a method of cleaning floors between rows of textile machines. There had been many unsuccessful attempts to find a satisfactory solution but none of them, unlike the present invention, actually worked. Essentially, all the invention consisted of was an overhead vacuum cleaner which moved back and forth between the textile machines and which had attached to it a long vertical tube, reaching almost to the floor. It was argued that this was obvious because 'every competent housewife' knows that dust can be removed from a floor by the passage of a vacuum cleaner. This argument was rejected and the patent was held to be valid as the many unsuccessful attempts by inventors to find a solution coupled with the immediate commercial success of the present invention denied the possibility of a finding of obviousness.

The courts have to draw a line somewhere when it comes to obviousness although it is difficult to lay down hard and fast rules. It is clear, however, that there must be a sufficient inventive step and merely taking two older inventions and sticking them together, described by patent lawyers as a mere collocation, will not necessarily be regarded as an inventive step. However, in *Storage Computer Corp* v *Hitachi Data Systems Ltd* [2002] EWHC 1776 (Ch), a case involving patents for a system for compensating for and overcoming hard errors common in writing to and reading from computer hard disks, Mr Justice Pumfrey confirmed that there is no separate law of collocation. The statutory test, being whether the invention is obvious to a person skilled in the art, remains the same. In some cases, it may well be inventive to combine two separate pieces of prior art.

Industrial application

Another requirement for the grant of a patent is that the invention must have an industrial application but this is widely defined by section 4 of the Patents Act 1977 which states that the invention must be capable of being made or used in any kind of industry, including agriculture. However, a method of treatment of the human or animal body by surgery or therapy or a method of diagnosis practised on the human or animal body is not capable of industrial application although this does not prevent the patenting of drugs to be used in any such treatment or diagnosis.

The need for industrial application shows the practical nature of patent law, which requires that the invention should be something which can be produced or that it relates to some sort of industrial process.

Examples of refusal on the grounds that the invention does not have an industrial application are rare, but one example is provided by *Hiller's Application* [1969] RPC 267. This case concerned an improved plan for underground service distribution schemes for housing estates; that is, the layout of the gas, sewerage and water pipes and electricity cables. It was held that this could not constitute a 'manner of manufacture' (the phrase used instead of 'industrial application' prior to the 1977 Act). Therefore, if someone develops a new form of layout for the components in a computer or a new configuration for printed circuit boards, these are unlikely to be granted patents. However, the layout of components and the configuration of a printed circuit board may be protected by copyright through any drawings which have been made indicating the layout or by the design right. Methods or principles of construction are excluded from the design right.

Exclusions from patentability

Several things are excluded from the scope of patent law. Section 1(2) of the Patents Act 1977 contains those which can generally be classified as coming within the scope of copyright law or the law of confidence and, in that context, computer programs are of particular interest. (Section 1(3), as amended, excludes inventions the commercial exploitation of which would be contrary to public policy or morality.) Section 1(2) of the Act states that the following are not inventions for the purposes of the Act:

(a) a discovery, scientific theory or mathematical method;
(b) a literary, dramatic, musical or artistic work or any other aesthetic creation whatsoever;
(c) a scheme, rule or method for performing any mental act, playing a game or doing business, or a program for a computer;
(d) the presentation of information;
but the foregoing provision shall prevent anything from being treated as an invention for the purposes of this Act only to the extent that a patent or application for a patent relates to that thing *as such* [emphasis added].

Note that the above exceptions only apply to the extent that a *patent relates to that thing as such*. This means that these particular things mentioned in the above list of exclusions can be protected by patent indirectly if they are part of a patent application which includes other elements which are patentable in their own right. For example, a computer program *as such* to control the temperature of a furnace cannot be patented (it will, of course, be protected by copyright). If an application is made to patent a computer-controlled furnace, however, it may well succeed and be granted a patent.

Computer programs

The exclusion from patent of computer programs reflects international trends. Copyright is seen as the proper vehicle for the protection of computer programs although, when the current Patents Act was passed in 1977, it was far from clear whether copyright did protect computer programs. Even before the 1977 Act, computer programs were not generally patentable *per se*, but there were cases, both in the United Kingdom and in the United States, where computer programs have been granted patents indirectly, usually as being part of a piece of machinery or an industrial process. For example, in *Diamond* v *Diehr* [1981] 209 USPQ 1, the United States Supreme Court confirmed that a computer-controlled process used in rubber curing was patentable. Since that time, the United States has become much more liberal in granting patents for software inventions generally, as discussed later in this chapter.

In *Gever's Application* [1970] RPC 91, data processing apparatus was arranged to work in a certain way associated with punched cards inserted into it. The purpose of the apparatus was to file world trade marks in such a way that they could be easily produced to check for similarity and prior registration. The patent application, which concerned a piece of machinery which functioned in a certain way because of the punched cards, was allowed to proceed. The cards were described by the judge as a 'manner of manufacture' because he thought that a punched card was analogous to a cam for controlling the cutting path of a lathe. This was distinguished from a card which merely had written or printed material on it, intended to convey information to the human eye or mind, and not meant to be ancillary to some machine by being specially shaped for that purpose. However, because of subsequent technological developments, integrated circuits, magnetic disks and tapes and optical character readers now are used to enter information into a computer or to store the programs which control the computer. The analogy with a mechanical process no longer rings true and it is unlikely that this case will be followed.

In another case, *Burrough's Corporation (Perkin's) Application* [1974] RPC 147, computer programs controlled the transmission of data to terminals from a central computer (a communications system). The system, including the computer programs, was held to be the proper subject matter of a patent because the programs were embodied in physical form; they were 'hard-wired' – permanently embedded in the electronic circuits of the equipment. In many respects the significance of the physical form of a program, whether hard-wired on a silicon chip or stored on magnetic disks, is an irrelevance and should not affect patentability.

The distinction between modes of storage and their effect on patentability was considered more recently in *Gale's Application* [1991] RPC 305, concerning an application for a method of calculating square roots by program instructions contained in a ROM chip. The Comptroller of Patents, Designs and Trade Marks rejected the application but the applicant's appeal to the Patents Court was allowed by Aldous J who said that the claimed invention related to a product (the ROM chip) and was, therefore, patentable. He then said that the program would not have been patentable had it been stored on a floppy disk. This decision would have had the effect of making a software designer's choice of storage medium crucial to the question of patentability but it was, fortunately, quickly overruled in the Court of Appeal where Lord Justice Nicholls said:

> It would equally be nonsense, if a floppy disc containing a computer program is not patentable, that a ROM characterised only by the instructions in that program should be patentable.

The Court of Appeal's decision conforms to common sense and the simple expedient of hard-wiring a computer program should not, *per se*, make the program patentable. Something else must be present such as a technical effect.

Technical effect

Two alternative approaches have been made to the question of the patent protection of inventions which include a computer program. The first is that the patent application should be considered without the contribution of the excepted thing. For example, if a machine includes a computer program it is then a question of whether the machine, without taking the computer program into account, adds anything to the state of the art. Does the machine, ignoring the computer program, meet the requirements for patentability? If the only novel and inventive step concerns the computer program itself, then the machine as a whole is not patentable. The case of *Re Merrill Lynch, Pierce Fenner & Smith Incorporated's Application* [1988] RPC 1, illustrates this approach. The invention related to an improved data processing system for implementing an automatic trading market for securities. The system received and stored the best current bids, qualified customer buy and sell orders, executed orders as well as monitoring stock inventory and profit. The Principal Examiner of the Patent Office rejected the application for a patent and the appeal against his decision was dismissed. On appeal to the Patents Court, it was held that where an invention involves any of the excluded materials in section 1(2), the proper construction of the qualification in that subsection requires that the Patent Office enquires into whether the inventive step resides in the contribution of the excluded matter alone. If the inventive step comes only from the excluded material, then the invention is not patentable because of section 1(2). The judge, Falconer J, said that the novel and inventive effect must reside outside the computer program even though it may be defined by the program.

In a further appeal to the Court of Appeal (*Merrill Lynch's Application* [1989] RPC 561), the approach of Falconer J was qualified and that taken by the European Patent Office (EPO), as described below, was approved. However, the Court of Appeal still confirmed that the invention in *Merrill Lynch* was not patentable but on the grounds that there was no technical effect, the operation being entirely software based.

In *Vicom Systems Incorporated's Patent Application* [1987] OJ EPO 14, a different approach to that of Falconer J was taken. This case concerned an application to the EPO and the invention was a new digital image processing system, the process steps being expressed mathematically in the form of an algorithm. It was held that this claim was allowable. It was said that if a claim is directed to a technical process which is carried out under the control of a program (whether implemented in the hardware or the software), then the claim cannot be regarded as related to a computer program as such. It is an application of the program for determining the sequence of steps in the process and it is the process for which protection is sought. In the present case, the subject matter of the invention was the practical application of a computer program, the technical effect resulting from the operation of the programmed computer and not the computer program itself. The EPO's approach has been followed and approved subsequently by the English courts. In *Genentech Inc's Patent* [1989] RPC 147, it was held, *inter alia*, in the Court of Appeal that a patent which claimed the practical application of a discovery did not relate to the discovery as such and was not excluded by section 1(2) of the Patents Act 1977 even if the practical application might be obvious once the discovery had been made. *Gale's Application* [1991] RPC 305, discussed above, confirms this as the correct approach.

It would seem that the technical effect does not have to be external to the computer and, in principle, operating systems are patentable because they determine how a computer operates technically. Indeed, there are patents in the United Kingdom and the United States in respect of operating systems including the recently litigated data compression software. With applications programs it is more difficult to achieve a technical advance and, in *Wang Laboratories Inc's Application* [1991] RPC 463, an application for a patent for an expert system shell was rejected because there was no new technical effect. Aldous J said that the computer (being a conventional machine) and the program combined did not produce a new computer. In *Hitachi Ltd's Application* [1991] RPC 415, an application in respect of a compiler program was rejected by the Patent Office as being no more than an application for a computer program as such.

While a patent will be refused for a computer program as such (or any of the other exceptions in section 1(2) for that matter) it will be allowed if the purpose of the program is to bring about some technical effect and it is that effect which is the subject matter of the patent application. The subject matter should make a technical contribution to the state of the art.

For a while, the EPO remained loyal to the technical effect approach. Another example was provided by the case of *IBM/Card Reader* [1994] EPOR 89, in which the Technical Board of Appeal dismissed an appeal against a refusal to grant a patent in relation to an invention whereby an automatic card-reading machine could read any card. This would allow the use of any bank card with a machine such as an automated teller machine (ATM or cashpoint machine) to carry out a transaction. The Board of Appeal confirmed that the subject matter of a patent must have a technical character and be industrially applicable. It also went on to say that applying technical means to perform a business activity does not mean that the business activity has a technical character and is thus an invention. It should be noted that a method of doing business is also excluded under the EPC and section 1(2) of the Patents Act 1977.

The approach of the EPO to the patentability of computer programs and software-related inventions has been modified by decisions in a number of cases. One example is *IBM's Application* [1999] RPC 861. IBM applied to patent a data processing system used to display information in windows such that any information displayed in one window and obscured by a second window is moved automatically to a new position so that it was no longer obscured. The first few claims concerned the process and had been accepted by the EPO as having a technical effect but some subsequent claims were rejected. Some of these focused on a computer program product (that is, a storage device on which the program was stored) and which, when run, caused the computer to execute the process.

The board of appeal at the EPO held that a computer program product was not excluded, *per se*. It confirmed that computer programs must have a technical character, for example, in the effects resulting from the running of the program, to be patentable. Furthermore, a claim for a computer program product may have a technical character resulting from the potential technical effect which will be revealed when the program is run on a computer. The same applies to the apparatus adapted for carrying out the technical effects. Therefore, in principle, a patent may be available for:

- a computer program which has a technical character because, when run, it causes technical effects,
- a computer when so programmed to create those technical effects, and
- a computer program product containing the program which, when run in a computer, creates the technical effects.

The United Kingdom Patent Office modified its practice in conformity with this decision very soon after it was published.

It is submitted that the approach of the EPO is correct and accords with the basic historical nature of a patent. Although the European Patent Convention (EPC) does not define an invention as such, it seems reasonable to assume that the practical application of an invention will be to cause technical effects to take place. England's first patent legislation was the Statute of Monopolies 1623 which allowed patents for any new manner of manufacture, a phrase which was used right up to the 1977 Act. Insisting on a new technical effect whether inside or outside the computer is entirely consistent with that phrase and its replacement 'industrial application'.

Mental steps, business methods and other excepted matter

The operation of a novel computer program may produce a technical effect which is itself caught by the exceptions to patentability as in the *IBM/Card Reader* case above where it was held that the technical effect was a method of doing business. Another exception is a scheme, rule or method of performing a mental act and it seems that simply programming a computer to carry out something that can be performed by the human intellect will not be patentable. For example, in *Re The Computer Generation of Chinese Characters* [1993] FSR 315, an application for a patent in respect of a method of storing, processing, displaying and printing Chinese characters was turned down in Germany. It was said that the subject matter neither solved a technical problem by a technical method nor did it make a technical contribution to the state of the art.

Similarly, in the United Kingdom, a patent was refused for a software means of identifying ships by comparing the silhouette of an unknown ship with a database of ships' silhouettes in *Raytheon Co's Application* [1993] RPC 427. The fact that the equivalent mental act in the human mind would not be a deliberate conscious process did not bring the application out of the exception. Recognition of shapes by humans is almost instantaneous, whereas a computer program doing this would be based on algorithms that may operate quite differently, in logical terms, to the human brain. The deputy judge was not prepared to read the exception in a narrow sense. Thus, it appears that a computer program that simply does something that can be done by mental acts in the human brain will not be patentable even though the program may do it differently and in a totally new way. The same must apply to the other exceptions such as methods of doing business.

The mental steps doctrine has become even more ingrained in United Kingdom patent law. *Fujitsu Ltd's Application* [1997] RPC 610 involved an application for a patent in relation to software which was developed to help chemists design new chemical compounds. A computer screen displayed the crystalline structure of two known chemicals and these images could be rotated and manipulated so as to align one face of one crystal to be aligned with the complementary face of the other crystal. This then formed the blueprint for a new hybrid 'designer' chemical.

It was held that the application was for a method of performing a mental act as such. In the Court of Appeal, Lord Justice Aldous rejected the submission that, as it was not possible to perform a mental act using a computer, a claim for a method of using a computer could not be a claim to a method of performing a mental act. He stressed that it was important to look at the substance of an application. Thus, a claim for a computer program operating in a particular way is no more than a claim to a computer program. Furthermore, a claim to a method of carrying out a calculation, which is a method of performing a mental act, can never become more patentable simply because the calculation is being performed by a computer rather than being done manually on a piece of paper.

It was also accepted by the Court of Appeal that the application was for a computer program as such and not patentable on this ground also. The invention used a conventional computer to do what was previously done using plastic models. The only advance was that of using a computer to enable the result to be portrayed more quickly. Aldous LJ said that this was just the sort of advantage to be obtained by the application of a computer program. In other words, there was nothing special in it.

In the context of computers, the exception for methods of doing business and performing mental acts is potentially very wide. Many programs automate business methods that were carried out previously without the use of computer technology or operations that used to be performed by the human mind, even if a computer does it on the basis of completely different algorithms. Although not really discussed in the *Fujitsu* case, it was highly arguable that the application would also have failed for lack of novelty (the exercise was done before but by using physical models) or through lack of inventive step. It is fairly obvious that advantages can be achieved by automating existing processes. This is why most computer programs would fail to be patentable. However, there are some programs that make new and effective technical contributions and it is for these that the patent system is important. Incidentally, the Fujitsu patent appears to have been granted in Japan.

Fujitsu also failed to obtain a patent for an invention involving a reservation management system for scheduling meetings based on an algorithm to resolve conflicting reservation requests which were based on a number of criteria and which would, if appropriate, reschedule a particular meeting. Further embodiments of the invention concerned prioritising queues processed by computer and the management of database entries designed to prevent mutually exclusive entries in the database. In *Fujitsu Limited's Patent Application* (unreported) 23 August 2000, in the Patent Office, the hearing officer held that the invention was a method of doing business and, although he accepted that automating the system would make it quicker, more accurate, more easily accessible to users and, in a network version, more widely available, these were the usual benefits of computerisation. There was nothing to produce a new technical result. The hearing officer also confirmed that he considered the invention also to be excluded as a program for a computer.

If a computer program, when run in a computer, produces a new and inventive effect which is itself excluded from patentability, does this mean that a patent cannot be granted under any circumstances? This certainly seems to have been the approach in the United Kingdom but later cases at the EPO suggest it may be a matter of precisely what is claimed, for example, a business method or an apparatus to perform that business method. In *Controlling Pensions Benefits System/PBS* T-0931/95, 8 September 2000, the Board of Appeal confirmed that it was implicit that an invention had to have a technical character to be patentable. The board further stated that methods only involving economic concepts and practices of doing business are not inventions for the purposes of the EPC and a feature of a method which concerned the use of technical means for a purely non-technical purpose and/or for processing purely non-technical information does not necessarily confer a technical character to such a method. However, an apparatus constituting a physical entity or concrete product, suitable for performing or supporting an economic activity, is an invention within the meaning of the EPC. The Board then rejected the notion that the question of whether the invention made a technical contribution to the art was relevant to whether it was an invention for the purposes of the Convention (though, of course, it might be relevant to whether it was new or involved an inventive step).

This case and others at the EPO show a distinct trend towards liberalising the patentability of computer programs and other software inventions, even if the effects produced are themselves within the specific exceptions. This is more in line with practice in the United States, where there are no exceptions for computer programs as such and business methods are also patentable, and the Agreement on the Trade Related Aspects of Intellectual Property Rights (TRIPs Agreement) Article 27(1) of which states that patents should be available in any field of technology. Taken to its extreme, this could mean that every computer program has a technical character and is patentable provided novelty and inventiveness are present. By accepting that computer programs have a technical character, *per se*, apart from making computer programs fulfil the requirement of being inventions, they also should meet the requirement of industrial application. The growing ease of obtaining patents for software inventions may be given a further boost by a proposed Directive on the patentability of computer-implemented inventions, discussed in the next section.

Proposed software patents Directive

In the United States of America software patents are readily granted, many for inventions in the field of e-commerce, which seem to be clearly invalid for lack of novelty or inventive step or both (*The Economic Impact of Patentability of Computer Programs*, Intellectual Property Institute, London, March 2000). The question of novelty in the United States is made more complex because inventors there are allowed one year's period of grace between making the invention and filing the application. Although the position in the United States, particularly as regards the practices in the United States Patent and Trademark Office, is unsatisfactory, it has been noted that the ready availability of patents for software inventions has had a very positive impact on the growth of the software industry there. Another important consideration is that the TRIPs Agreement does not expressly excluded computer programs as such.

With all this in mind, the European Commission considers it important to make change to patent law in Europe. On balance, the Commission believes that the effects of making it somewhat easier to obtain patents for software inventions will be positive and will help small and medium sized enterprises particularly. Furthermore, the opportunity should be taken to better harmonise patent law in Europe and the Commission published a proposal for a Directive on the patentability of computer-implemented inventions COM(2002) 92 final, 20.02.2002. This will require member states of the EPC to agree to changes to the Convention. In particular, Article 52(2)(c) would have to be modified by deleting computer programs as such from the list of non-patentable inventions. Member states would also be required to modify their domestic patent legislation accordingly.

Article 3 of the proposal requires that computer-implemented inventions be considered as belonging to a field of technology. A 'computer-implemented invention' is, under Article 2, any invention the performance of which involves the use of a computer, computer network or other programmable apparatus and having one or more prima facie novel features which are realised wholly or partly by means of a computer program or computer programs. The use of the phrase prima facie means that it will not be necessary to establish *de facto* novelty by carrying out an extensive search. What is intended is that the presence of a technical contribution will be assessed by consideration of whether the invention contains an inventive step rather than a consideration of novelty. This is pragmatic bearing in mind the difficulty in carrying out searches for prior art in the field of software but may result in some of the problems of the United States system. A further definition is that of 'technical contribution' which means a contribution to the state of the art in a technical field which is not obvious to a person skilled in the art.

Article 4 of the proposal sets out the criteria for patentability as follows:

- A computer-implemented invention is patentable on the condition that it is susceptible of industrial application, is new, and involves an inventive step.
- A computer-implemented invention must, as a condition of involving an inventive step, make a technical contribution.
- The technical contribution is to be assessed by consideration of the difference between the scope of the patent claim considered as a whole, elements of which may comprise both technical and non-technical features, and the state of the art.

The first condition simply repeats the basic test in the EPC and the requirement for technical contribution can be seen as a gloss on the basic test for patentability. In respect of inventions not containing any other excluded subject matter such as a method of doing business, the need to expressly specify technical contribution is not required, for example, in the case of a computer-controlled aircraft landing system.

The third condition is consistent with decisions before the EPO such as *Koch & Sterzel/X-ray apparatus* [1988] EPOR 72 in which the board of appeal held that an invention must be assessed as a whole and the inclusion of non-technical matter does not detract from the technical character of the invention as a whole.

The explanatory memorandum to the proposed Directive states that a computer-implemented invention which lies in one of the remaining excluded fields (for example, a method for doing business or the presentation of information) may still be patentable even if it contains a non-obvious technical contribution. However, if the contribution to the state of the art resides wholly in non-technical matter the invention will not be patentable. The memorandum continues by stating that a technical contribution may come from:

- the problem underlying, and solved by the claimed invention;
- the means, that is the technical features, constituting the solution of the underlying problem;
- the effects achieved in the solution of the underlying problem;
- the need for technical considerations to arrive at the computer-implemented invention as claimed.

Article 5 makes it clear that the patent may be granted in respect of products or processes. Therefore, a programmed computer, a programmed computer network or other programmed apparatus, a process carried out through the execution of software by such a computer, computer network or apparatus may be claimed.

Where a computer-implemented invention is patented, there will be an inevitable overlap with the copyright subsisting in that software. There may also be an overlap with the database right. Taking note of the exceptions to infringement of copyright in computer programs, originating from Directive 91/250/EEC on the legal protection of computer programs (OJ L 122, 17.05.1991, p.42), Article 6 states that, in particular, the provisions relating to decompilation and interoperability are not affected by the proposed Directive. Thus, acts of decompilation in accordance with the computer program Directive will not infringe any patent granted for an invention implemented by the program concerned. Article 6 also includes the protection afforded by provisions concerning semiconductor topographies and trade marks. There is no mention of the database right, or copyright in respects to items of software other than computer programs; surely this is an oversight.

It has already been noted that there are a large number of patents in the field of e-commerce in the United States. E-commerce may be further prejudiced by the grant of even more patents for software inventions, bringing about the possibility of infringing patents in a host of other jurisdictions simply by having a commercial web presence. However, the European Commission claims that the situation will be much more satisfactory in Europe which has a very effective opposition procedure for patents (anyone may oppose the grant of a patent) and anyone may, without becoming a party to any hearing or court action, make observations concerning a patent application. These considerations should prevent or minimise patents being granted for software inventions that may be invalid, apart from the rigorous search and examination procedures in Europe compared with the United States.

Infringement

A patent is infringed if a person does one of certain things in relation to the invention in the United Kingdom without the permission of the proprietor (owner) of the patent. Section 60 of the Patents Act 1977 defines what does and what does not constitute infringement. The nature of the infringement depends on whether the invention is a product (for example, a new type of computer printer) or a process (for example, a new method of making integrated circuits). If the invention is a product, the patent is infringed by making, disposing of or offering to dispose of, using, importing or keeping the product. Similar provisions apply to a process: for example, using the process infringes but, additionally, the patented process may be infringed by using or disposing of, etc. any product obtained directly from that process. Another difference between products and processes relates to the knowledge of the infringer. For a process, knowledge that a patent is being infringed is required. However, 'knowledge' is used in a special way and a person can still be deemed to have the requisite knowledge if it would be obvious to a reasonable person that a patent was being infringed. There is no requirement for knowledge as regards a product and, therefore, in the absence of a defence, liability for infringement is strict.

Under section 60(2), a patent is also infringed if a person supplies or offers to supply some other person with any of the means, relating to an essential element of the invention, for putting the invention into effect. Knowledge is required in that the person supplying knows, or it is obvious to a reasonable person, that those means are suitable for putting the invention into effect and that person so intends. This 'supplying the means' infringement is useful as it applies to persons who supply products in kit form. For example, if a person supplies a computer in kit form which, when assembled, infringes a patent, then the supplier of the computer kit infringes the patent even if he is just an intermediary as long as he has the requisite knowledge. This prevents a possible loophole in patent law such as where a person imports components made in a foreign country to be sold as a kit. The person assembling the kit computer will not be liable under patent law, however, if he assembles and uses the computer privately and for non-commercial purposes. To give a practical example of infringement, consider the following situation:

An inventor **A** has invented a new type of computer 'chip' and a new process which will be used for making those chips. He has taken out patents for the process and for the chips. **B** finds out about the process and decides to build a similar process for making these computer chips. **B** asks **C** to supply equipment which is essential to the process. **B** then makes some computer chips and sells them to **D**, a trade supplier. The position is:

B, if he knows, or it would be obvious to a reasonable man, that the process was patented, has infringed the patent for the process. Even if **B** had no actual knowledge it would be most likely that he would be fixed with knowledge on the basis of the reasonable person test. (Patent specifications are available for public inspection – would a reasonable man check first?)

B has infringed the patent for the computer chips even if he did not know or could not be expected to know of the patent.

C has infringed the patent for the process if he knows, or it would be obvious to a reasonable person, that the equipment he supplied was suitable for putting the process into effect and the equipment was intended to do so.

D infringes the patent for the computer chips, regardless of knowledge.

The fact that some infringements do not require any form of knowledge may seem unduly harsh, but knowledge is required for some of the remedies and the situation is not as inequitable as it might appear, bearing in mind the need to protect the patent.

Variants and the *Catnic* test

Often another person will make use of the subject-matter of the invention but there may be some minor differences compared with the invention itself, for example, where the second is a variant of the first. The question then is whether the second infringes the first invention, does it fall within the penumbra of protection afforded by the patent? To determine whether there has been an infringement the claims, interpreted in accordance with the specification and any drawings, must be examined to determine the scope and limits of the invention as protected by the patent. Although judges tend to interpret Acts of Parliament and legal documents literally (unless this leads to an absurd result), patent specifications are interpreted purposively; that is, in line with the presumed intention of the person who wrote it.

In *Catnic Components Ltd* v *Hill & Smith Ltd* [1982] RPC 183, the claimant obtained a patent for a load-bearing lintel, the main strength of which came from a vertical metal rear face. The specification and claims in the patent referred to the rear face as being vertical. Claim 1 described the rear face as '... a second rigid support member extending vertically from or from near the rear edge of the first horizontal plate ...'. The defendant made a similar lintel but with a rear face inclined at six degrees from the vertical. The House of Lords, adopted a test which has since been refined into a three-stage test which can be briefly summarised as follows:

1 if the variant does not have a material effect on how the invention works, and
2 this would have been obvious to a skilled person at the time of publication of the specification, and
3 the skilled person would understand that the proprietor of the patent did not intend to limit his invention to the strict wording of the claim,

then the variant infringes the patent.

Effectively, the House of Lords interpreted the relevant claim by taking the word 'vertical' to mean, in effect, 'vertical or nearly vertical' and held that the patent had been infringed. The important feature was the metal rear face, the purpose of which was to support the load. The defendant's slightly sloping rear face had a minimal impact on the load-bearing qualities of the lintel. This approach is in line with both common sense and prevents others from flouting patent law by making minor changes to details of an invention while retaining the underlying principles involved, and is justified on the basis that patent specifications and claims are directed to technical people, not lawyers. It also shows the different scope of patent law compared with copyright law, because patent law can protect purpose and the embodiment of a principle whereas, generally, copyright law cannot. The so-called *Catnic* test survived an attack upon its validity during 1995 when it was claimed by one judge to be inappropriate under the 1977 Act, *Catnic* being a case under the Patents Act 1949, and that the provision in the EPC should be used instead where an approach to interpretation of patent claims based on a middle way between a strict literal meaning and using the claims as a guideline only. This should give an interpretation that combines fair protection for the proprietor with a reasonable degree of certainty for third parties (the Protocol on Article 69 of the Convention). However, very soon afterwards, the Court of Appeal confirmed that the *Catnic* test was still useful and was the United Kingdom's practical application of the Convention test. The *Catnic* test continues to be used in almost all cases involving an interpretation of patent claims.

A recent example of the use of the *Catnic* test, as refined, in the context of computers was *Storage Computer Corp v Hitachi Data Systems Ltd* [2002] EWHC 1776 (Ch) which concerned patents for a system for compensating for and overcoming hard errors common in writing to and reading from computer hard disks. The defendant used a system which was a variant of that described in the first patent (the second patent was held invalid in its entirety). However, there were some differences in how the claimant and defendant's inventions worked even though they did the same thing. In particular, the claimant's invention used a dedicated disk to write parity blocks to, whereas the defendant's system used distributed parity (writing parity blocks to different disks). This resulted in the variant having, in fact, a material effect on how the invention worked. Even if it did not, Mr Justice Pumfrey held that the claimant had made it clear in his claims that an essential element of the invention was that it used a fixed parity disk. Therefore, the defendant did not infringe the patent. In any event, it was also held that the first two claims of the first patent were invalid for lack of inventive step.

Patent infringement and the Internet

The Internet presents two particular problems in the case of software patents. First, the use in the United Kingdom of a software invention on a webpage or an offer to deliver software advertised on a webpage (whether or not delivered on-line) could infringe patents in other jurisdictions even if there are no relevant patents in the United Kingdom. Bearing in mind the apparent ease with which some dubious software inventions are granted patents in the United States, there are serious dangers of infringing software patents there from web-based activities in the United Kingdom. If readers think this fanciful in the extreme, the author suggests looking up US patent number 4,646,250 for a data entry screen and US patent number 6,272,493 for a system and method for facilitating a windows based content manifestation environment within a WWW browser.

Infringement of a patent includes using a patented product or process and offering to sell a patented product or process in the relevant jurisdiction. Thus, taking the above example, collecting data using a similar design of data entry screen could infringe in the United States as could using windows in a web browser. Placing an advertisement on a webpage for a product and including a reference to a price in US$ could infringe. For a court in the United States to accept jurisdiction, however, the particular activity would have to be targeted at individuals in the particular state where legal proceedings are commenced. If patent infringement was found in a United States court against a person resident in the United Kingdom who has no physical presence in the United States, the proprietor could find it very difficult to enforce that judgment in the United Kingdom, unless the defendant put in a defence to the action in the United States. The proprietor would have to ask a court in the United Kingdom to enforce the judgment which it would be unlikely to do if the defendant put in an appearance and challenged the validity of the patent in question. These difficulties of enforcement do not apply to European countries and most Commonwealth countries and a few others because of Conventions and Regulations covering jurisdiction and the enforcement of judgments.

As patent rights are territorial in nature, to infringe a United Kingdom patent, the infringing act must be done within the territory of the United Kingdom. A rudimentary application of this simple rule in the context of computer networks and the Internet could result in a person who puts to work a software invention without permission escaping an infringement action by placing the most significant part of the invention outside the territory of the United Kingdom. However, in such a case a sensible approach is to consider where the person or persons making use of the invention are located. In *Menashe Business Mercantile Ltd* v *William Hill Organization Ltd* [2002] RPC 47, Dr Julian Menashe was the proprietor of a patent in respect of a system for playing an interactive casino game. The patent claimed a computer terminal connected to a host computer by communication means. For example, a gambler could use his own computer to access the host computer on which the gambling software was located by means of the Internet. Menashe Business Mercantile Ltd had an exclusive licence to work the patent.

The defendant was a bookmaker who decided to operate a gaming system. Gamblers were supplied with CDs containing a computer program which they installed on their own computers. This enabled the gamblers' computers to communicate via the Internet with the defendant's host computer which was situated first in Antigua and, later, in Curaçao. The claimants sued the defendant on the basis of section 60(2) of the Patents Act 1977 alleging that the defendant had supplied and/or offered to supply in the United Kingdom the means, relating to an essential element of the invention, for putting the invention into effect, knowing or where it would be obvious to a reasonable person in the circumstances that those means were suitable for putting, and were intended to put, the invention into effect in the United Kingdom. The defendant argued that it did not infringe the patent because its host computer and part of the communication means were situated outside the United Kingdom. The court had to determine a preliminary question concerning whether the fact that the host computer and part of the communication system which were located outside the United Kingdom was a defence to an infringement action under section 60(2).

The Court of Appeal noted that infringement of a patent under section 60 can only occur if a person does an act within the United Kingdom without the proprietor's consent. However, that does not assist with the meaning of the phrase in section 60(2) '. . . to put, the invention into effect in the United Kingdom'. The court said that where the invention is an apparatus what is required is that the means are intended to put the apparatus into effect so that the apparatus becomes effective. Therefore, in the present case, the means, being the CDs, must be suitable for putting the apparatus into a state of effectiveness: that is, to put it into an infringing state in the United Kingdom. The Court of Appeal held that where an invention is an apparatus, it is irrelevant to the question of infringement if part of the apparatus is situated outside the United Kingdom and it is wrong to apply old notions of location to inventions such as that in the present case. The answer in such a case is to consider who is making use of the system and where he is located when he makes that use. As the gamblers used the system in the United Kingdom they could be said to use the host computer in the United Kingdom even though it was situated outside the United Kingdom. Therefore, supplying gamblers with CDs in the United Kingdom to enable them to use the gambling system was supplying the means relating to an essential element of the invention, intended to put the invention into effect in the United Kingdom and was not a defence to an infringement action under section 60(2).

This is a very sensible decision and overcomes the danger of defendants avoiding infringement by taking a significant part of an invention outside the jurisdiction of the United Kingdom and relying on cross-border problems. Similar circumstances are likely to become more common, especially with the potential growth in numbers of software patents which will have a relevance to activities carried out over the Internet.

Defences and remedies

There are certain defences or exceptions to infringement set out in section 60(5) of the Patents Act 1977: for example, if the act is done privately and for non-commercial purposes or for experimental purposes (on the basis that the proprietor's interests are not harmed by such use). It has long been accepted that there is a right to repair defence at common law. This might be applicable where an error in a software invention has been discovered. However, the House of Lords has confirmed that this defence is very narrow and does not allow a patented product to be rebuilt. There are some other defences, such as use on certain aircraft or ships temporarily or accidentally in the United Kingdom and some special defences in relation to agriculture.

A patent, once granted, can be revoked if it is subsequently shown to fail to meet the requirements for patentability: for example, it was not novel at the priority date or does not involve an inventive step, or if it was not granted to the person entitled to it. The fact that a patent has been granted by the Patent Office is not conclusive proof that the invention has satisfied all the requirements and the discovery of a prior publication disclosing the invention can result in the patent being revoked. Often, a person sued for infringement of a patent will attack the validity of the patent. As far as the alleged infringer is concerned, this can be a useful ploy as the proceedings will be drawn out and the proprietor of the patent will be put to extra expense in defending his patent. Although the validity of patents is frequently brought into issue by defendants, only a handful of patents are revoked each year.

The remedies available for infringement of a patent are injunctions, delivery up or destruction of infringing articles, damages or an account of profits and a declaration that the patent is valid and infringed by the defendant. Damages and accounts of profits are alternatives. If the defendant proves that he was not aware and had no reasonable grounds for supposing that the patent existed, then neither damages nor accounts of profits are available. If a product carries the word 'patent' or 'patented' or similar, this does not automatically mean that the defendant knows of the patent unless the number of the patent also appears on the product concerned. This enables anyone to look up and inspect the patent specification to determine its scope.

The proprietor of a patent must be careful how he warns alleged infringers. There is a remedy under section 70 in respect of groundless threats of infringement proceedings. A person aggrieved by the threat may bring an action, unless the person making the threat can show that the acts in respect of which the threats were made were or would constitute an infringement of the patent, and the patent is not shown to be invalid by the person bringing the action. The remedies available are a declaration that the threats are unjustified, an injunction against a continuance of the threats, and damages for any loss sustained by the person aggrieved who has brought the action. Groundless threats actions do not apply to all forms of infringement (making or importing a product or using a process) and simply notifying any person of the existence of the patent does not constitute a groundless threat.

An example where a groundless threats action might be appropriate is where it is alleged that a computer imported into the United Kingdom by Acme Importers Ltd infringes a United Kingdom patent belonging to Esoteric Computers plc. The computers are sold by Acme to Krafty Computer Sales Ltd, a retail outlet. Esoteric send a letter to Krafty threatening to sue Krafty unless it ceases selling the computers forthwith. Krafty will be 'a person aggrieved' and so may Acme, if Krafty stops buying computers from Acme. Either should be able to bring an action for groundless threats and will be entitled to remedies unless Esoteric can show that the sale of the computers infringes the patent and, if a challenge has been made on the validity of the patent, or any relevant part of it, that it is valid.

Miscellaneous provisions

Certain other provisions contained in the Patents Act 1977 are worthy of brief mention. An invention may be potentially very beneficial but might also destroy or seriously undermine an existing business: for example, a car engine that does 200 miles to a gallon, or an everlasting light bulb. To prevent the proprietor sitting on his patent, deliberately failing to use it, section 48 of the Act allows any person to apply for a compulsory licence under the patent, after the expiry of three years from grant if, for example, the patent is not being worked or some abuse is being made of the patent monopoly such as if the product is not being made available at reasonable terms.

An employee who, in the course of his employment, has made an invention which belongs to his employer may be awarded compensation to be paid by the employer if the patent is of outstanding benefit to the employer (section 40). This provision is seldom used, perhaps because reasonable employers reward such employees sufficiently well so that they do not apply for compensation. However, it is clear that the benefit must be truly outstanding if the employee is to stand any chance of obtaining compensation. The author is not aware of any examples of compensation awarded under section 40.

Utility model

There are plans for a new form of protection in the United Kingdom which is called the utility model and is like a lesser version of a patent, sometimes referred to as a 'petty patent'. This new right will come about through moves to harmonise this form of protection throughout the EC; Proposal for a Directive for the protection of inventions by a utility model, COM (97) 691, OJ C36, 03.02.1998, p.13. An amended proposal was published in 2000 (COM (1999) 309 final, OJ C 248, 29.08.2000, p.56). Only three member states do not have any equivalent form of protection, these being the United Kingdom, Luxembourg and Sweden. In its original form, computer programs were excluded from protection by the utility model, but as a result of the amended proposal, computer programs will be appropriate subject matter for protection, providing they are new, involve an inventive step and are suitable for industrial application. The test for inventive step is that, compared to the state of the art, the invention presents an advantage and is not obvious to an expert in the field. This will surely be a nightmare to interpret and apply in practice. Protection will be for up to ten years and the harmonised utility model is intended to be implemented no later than two years after the Directive as adopted has been published in the *Official Journal*.

Summary

In the past, it had been argued that a special, hybrid type of right should be introduced for computer programs, something between a patent and copyright. This would give a monopoly in the program, thus protecting the underlying ideas more effectively than copyright, but the right would last for a shorter period than a patent, say five or seven years maximum. In the end, however, the approach in most countries has been to provide both copyright protection and, up to a variable extent, patent protection.

There are a number of arguments for and against the grant of patents for software inventions. Patents enable small and start-up companies, so important in the software industry, to get very effective protection for their inventions and, in the United States, many such companies have grown very quickly on the back of their patents. Although copyright provides a reasonably good degree of protection to computer programs and other items of software, it is not a true monopoly protection and requires proof of access and use of the protected work on the part of the infringer. However, patents take a long time to acquire, particularly in European countries, and are expensive if protection is required in more than just a handful of countries. It may be several years before legal proceedings can be commenced against an alleged infringer and, even then, patent litigation can prove prohibitively expensive. Other difficulties in terms of software patents include the search for prior art which can never be exhaustive, leaving the patent vulnerable to attack on the basis of prior art not discovered by the applicant or the Patent Office. A significant danger of patents is that large powerful companies can use their patents to frighten off smaller companies which do not have the resources or willingness to get involved in complex, lengthy and expensive patent litigation. Nevertheless, it seems certain that patenting of software inventions is here to stay.

In a case where a powerful patent proprietor is using his patent in an abusive fashion, apart from remedies under patent law, in particular a groundless threats action, competition law may be relevant. Article 82 of the EC Treaty (the Treaty of Rome) covers abuses of dominant positions and there is an equivalent provision applying to situations where trade within the United Kingdom is or is likely to be affected under section 18 of the Competition Act 1998. Apart from giving the European Commission or Director General of Fair Trading, as the case may be, the power to fine the company abusing its dominant position within the market, these provisions can be used as a defence in proceedings brought by the dominant company. However, bearing in mind the possible penal consequences of a finding that there has been an abuse, although the defendant has the civil standard of proof (on a balance of probabilities), the evidence submitted by the defendant must be subject to careful scrutiny, especially in an action for summary judgment. So it was held in *Intel Corp* v *Via Technologies Ltd* [2003] FSR 12, in which the claimant brought an action for summary judgment for infringement of the patents associated with the Pentium 4 computer microprocessor. After failing to agree a licence with Intel for the manufacture of microprocessors having the Pentium 4 technology, the defendant manufactured microprocessors compatible with the Pentium 4. The defendant put up competition law defences. In granting summary judgment for the claimant, the judge said that it might be an abuse of process to bring a legal action for the purpose of harassing a competitor but this would only be in very exceptional cases and there was no basis for this in the present case.

It has been noted that, at present, the position in Europe is significantly different to that in some other countries, most notably the United States. However, the EPO, in its more recent decisions, appears to be taking a more generous approach to the patentability of computer programs and it now appears that changes may be made to the EPC to facilitate the granting of patents for software inventions on a wider scale than was previously the case. These developments also impact on patent law in the United Kingdom as the relevant provisions of the Patents Act 1977 on the requirements for patentability are stated by section 130(7) of that Act to have, as nearly as practicable, the same effects as the corresponding provisions of the EPC.

With all these changes and the possibility that the Community Patent Convention might eventually come into being, patent law looks like it is subject to exciting though uncertain times ahead. The latest proposal for the Community Patent Convention was published in 2000 (proposal for a Council Regulation on the Community Patent, COM(2000) 412 final, OJ C 337, 28.11.2000, p.278). First mooted in the 1960s, it seems incredible that we still await this Convention.

Chapter 11

Trade marks and passing off

Trade marks

Marks have been used to identify the makers of goods for thousands of years. Individual marks become associated with a particular product and with the quality of that product. As regards the value of a trade mark to a trader (for example, a manufacturer of goods or a provider of services), two factors are important: the buying public's familiarity with the mark and its experience of reasonable quality or value for money in the past associated with the mark. A trade mark, which is used with a successful product, is of tremendous value to the owner of the mark and he will want to prevent others from using the mark or a similar one to capture some of his trade. From the perspective of a consumer, the association between a trader (referred to as an 'undertaking' in the legislation) and his goods or services allows the consumer to repeat a buying experience that has proved positive or to avoid repeating one that has proved unsatisfactory.

The primary function of a trade mark is to distinguish the goods or services of one trader from those of other traders, that is, to act as a 'badge of origin'. By fulfilling this function, trade mark law serves two main purposes: first it protects the goodwill and reputation which a trader has built up around the mark involved and, second, it prevents the public from being deceived as to the origin of goods or services. Trade mark law establishes a property right in the mark in question and requires that the mark be used (failure to use a mark for five or more years may result in it being revoked).

A trader who makes or sells goods or provides services may register a sign as a trade mark for specified goods or services in one or more classes of goods or services. This will give the owner of the mark a monopoly in the use of that mark in the goods or services for which the mark has been registered. There are a total of 34 classes of marks for goods (for example, chemicals, electrical goods and scientific apparatus, vehicles, clothing, fancy goods and smokers' articles) and a further 11 classes for services (for example, advertising and business, insurance and financial, telecommunications, transport, education and medical services). Trade marks for computers and software may be registered in Class 9 which includes data processing equipment and computers. A person providing services by designing and developing computer hardware and software would register a mark in Class 42 which includes installation, maintenance and repair of computer software, computer consultancy services, website design and keeping registers of domain names. Providing access to internet or portal services is covered in Class 38 which applies to telecommunications.

If anyone else uses the mark, or one deceptively similar, in the course of trade without the owner's permission, that person can be sued for infringement of the trade mark. Depending on the circumstances, a criminal offence may also be committed, as mentioned in Chapter 31. The remedies available to the owner of the trade mark are as usual: injunctions, damages or an account of profits as an alternative to damages, plus removal of offending marks. The infringing articles may be ordered to be destroyed if the offending marks cannot be removed.

In the computer industry, the power of trade marks can readily be seen as, in a relatively short space of time, names such as 'Apple', 'IBM', 'Oracle', 'Java', 'Windows' and 'Microsoft' became very well-known names. Trade marks are especially important in a fast-moving industry and it is very comforting to buy goods with familiar names when so many products and businesses come and go in rapid succession, as happened with microcomputers in the early 1980s. A familiar name or mark is very influential as many who buy computer hardware and software will look for a product which is likely to be of reasonable quality and will be supported in years to come. There have been few examples of trade mark infringement in the world of computers and most counterfeiters have used different names or marks: for example, copies of the Apple computer imported into Australia were called 'Wombats'. Other Apple look-alikes have been called 'Pineapples' and 'Microprofessors'. Perhaps this is a testimony to the effectiveness of trade mark law.

Until 1994 trade mark law was provided for by the Trade Marks Act 1938 which was widely recognised as being difficult, outdated and obscure in parts. The present law is contained in the Trade Marks Act 1994 which is a result of a European Directive harmonising trade mark law (First Council Directive 89/104/EEC of 21 December 1988 to approximate the laws of the member states relating to trade marks, OJ L40, 11.2.1989, p.1). The 1994 Act marks a significant change in trade mark law and only a little of the case law under the 1938 Act and previous trade mark legislation is still relevant. Although the 1994 Act was seen as a welcome and much awaited improvement of trade mark law, that Act and the Directive have not been without their difficulties and together, they have generated an impressive amount of case law before the courts in the United Kingdom and the European Court of Justice.

Community trade mark

Apart from the national systems of trade marks (substantially but not completely harmonised by the Directive), there is also a Community trade mark which gives the proprietor of the trade mark a single registration at the Office for Harmonisation of the Internal Market (Trade Marks and Designs) (OHIM) which has effect throughout the European Community, described as having unitary effect, that is, validity throughout the Community. The OHIM commenced accepting applications to register Community trade marks on 1 January 1996 and the provisions governing the registrability of a Community trade mark are, to all intents and purposes, the same as those applicable to the harmonised trade mark in the United Kingdom. The OHIM has its own Boards of Appeals to hear appeals against decisions of the trade mark examiners at the OHIM. Subsequent appeals are brought before the European Court of First Instance from where appeals may be brought before the Court of Justice of the European Communities (the European Court of Justice). In terms of trade mark law in member states, references for preliminary rulings on the interpretation of the harmonising Directive are submitted to the European Court of Justice. This is where there is some doubt as to the meaning of a provision in the Directive arising in a national court.

Although the main aspects of the Community trade mark look very similar to those for the harmonised national trade mark systems, it has been made clear that it is a completely separate system and decisions in cases on the harmonised national trade marks before the national courts and the European Court of Justice are not binding on the OHIM. Nor is it bound by decisions taken in national trade mark offices, such as a decision to permit or reject registration of a particular type or form of mark, such as an olfactory mark.

From a trader's point of view, the Community trade mark is a very attractive proposition, a single registration giving validity throughout the Community. However, in some cases, whilst a trade mark might be registrable in some member states, it may not be in others because of pre-existing conflicting national registrations or other rights. Such a position could prevent the OHIM accepting registration. In practice it is not uncommon for traders based in one of the member states to apply to register in their own country and at the OHIM. Registration in some other countries may be facilitated by use of the Madrid System which allows registration in a number of specified countries. The Madrid System comprises an Agreement and a Protocol, each with over 50 members. At the present time, the United Kingdom is party to the Protocol only.

What is a trade mark?

By section 1(1) of the Trade Marks Act 1994, a trade mark is:

> ... any sign capable of being represented graphically which is capable of distinguishing goods or services of one undertaking from those of other undertakings.

It goes on to say that a trade mark may, in particular, consist of words (including personal names), designs, letters, numerals or the shape of goods or their packaging. This definition is much wider than that in the 1938 Act, under which an application to register the Coca-Cola bottle as a trade mark failed in *Re Coca-Cola Co's Application* [1986] 2 All ER 274. The new definition allows the registration, potentially, of music and shape marks. Even a small number of smells marks have been accepted for registration though this is very controversial and the better view is that they are not registrable as it is not possible to represent them graphically with sufficient precision. There should be no difficulty for software companies to register marks embedded in software such as a moving image produced on a screen when a computer game is being loaded together with any associated distinctive musical motif, computer icons and other computer-generated images, providing the requirements for registrability are satisfied.

The threshold for registration was simplified by the 1994 Act. Previously, under the 1938 Act, there were two parts to the register of trade marks. Part A was for marks adapted to distinguish the goods of one trader from those of other traders while Part B was for marks which were capable of distinguishing, a lower standard which offered less protection. Now the lower requirement 'capable of distinguishing' applies to all marks and the nonsense of a two-part register was abolished. In *Davies v Sussex Rubber Co* (1927) 44 RPC 412, a case involving 'Ustikon' for stick-on rubber soles for shoes, it was said that a mark was capable of distinguishing if it would become distinctive through use; in other words, if it was not incapable of becoming distinctively associated with the goods of the trade mark proprietor.

This approach was accepted as also being appropriate under the 1994 Act in *AD2000 Trade Mark* [1997] RPC 168. In that case an application to register AD2000 as a trade mark failed. A combination of two letters and four numbers could be capable of distinguishing if it was idiosyncratic. However, that was not the case here as AD2000 naturally referred to the year 2000 and was not idiosyncratic. Mr Geoffrey Hobbs QC, the

Appointed Officer hearing the case, refused to be swayed by the fact that the word 'MIL-LENNIUM' had previously been accepted for registration as a trade mark.

Unregistrable marks

The fundamental purpose of a trade mark is to distinguish goods or services of one undertaking from those of other undertakings. In other words the mark must serve as an indicator of trade origin. If it does not do this, it is not registrable. For example, 'TARZAN', 'ELVIS' and 'ELVIS PRESLEY' were held to be unregistrable. By the time the applications were received, these names were so well known as 'household' words that they could not serve the function of indicating a connection in the course of trade between a trader and his goods. Although 'three-dimensional' signs are now potentially registrable, the same principle applies. In *Philips Electronics NV v Remington Consumer Products Ltd* [2003] RPC 2, a registration as a trade mark of a representation of a three-headed electric razor was declared invalid, *inter alia*, because it denoted function rather than trade origin. A specific ground for refusal of registration is where the sign in question consists exclusively of a shape necessary to obtain a technical result. That was so in this case. The European Court of Justice confirmed that a shape mark was still unregistrable on this ground even if it could be shown that other shapes could be used to achieve the same technical result. This remained so even if the sign in question had become highly distinctive by the use made of it and was recognised by most consumers as being associated with a particular trader.

Apart from the basic requirement that a trade mark must serve as a badge of origin, there are two types of grounds for refusal of registration – absolute grounds and relative grounds – the latter being so called because refusal depends on the mark's similarity with other marks. The absolute grounds for refusal are, by section 3 of the Trade Marks Act 1994, where the sign or mark in question:

- does not satisfy the requirements of section 1(1), (is not capable of graphical representation or not capable of distinguishing goods or services of one undertaking from those of other undertakings);
- is devoid of any distinctive character;
- consists exclusively of signs or indications which serve in trade to designate the kind, quality, quantity, intended purpose, value, geographical origin, time of production of goods or rendering of services, or other characteristics of goods or services (in other words, they are descriptive or laudatory (words of praise) – for example, 'Superb Computers' or 'Cheap Software' or 'Yorkshire Computer Services' or 'Personal Computers' or 'Internet Services';
- consists exclusively of signs or indications that have become customary in the current language or in the *bona fide* and established practices of the trade – for example, 'Software Bug' or 'Website' or 'Applet';
- consists exclusively of
  - a shape which results from the nature of the goods themselves – for example, the shape of a silicon chip, or
  - the shape of goods which is necessary to obtain a technical result – for example, the shape of a CD, or
  - the shape which gives substantial value to the goods (it is very difficult to know where the boundaries of this exception lie though a possible example is a computer mouse with a new ergonomic shape);

- is contrary to public policy, accepted principles of morality or deceptive (for instance, as to the nature, quality or geographic origin of the goods or services) – for example, where a dating agency that does not possess or use a computer wishes to register the mark 'ComputaDate'.

Also excluded are certain flags and emblems. Nor will a mark be registered if it was applied for in bad faith, such as where a tobacco company registered 'Nerit' to try to protect its 'Merit' mark. 'Merit' is a laudatory word and not registrable. The 'Nerit' mark was ordered to be removed from the register of trade marks.

The meaning of 'bad faith' under the 1994 Act was not entirely clear. In *Road Tech Computer Systems Ltd* v *Unison Software (UK) Ltd* [1996] FSR 805, the claimant traded in computer software for the transportation business and was the registered proprietor of the trade mark 'Roadrunner', which was registered in respect of 'computer software and programs; all included in Class 9 but not including any such goods relating to birds'. The reason for the latter exception was that an American bird, the paisano, is also known as a roadrunner. The defendant claimed that the registration was not *bona fide* as the claimant had no intention of using the mark. The claimant argued that bad faith was more restrictive and required dishonesty. The judge pointed to the difficulty of determining the meaning of bad faith under the 1994 Act, which was not helped by looking at the Directive. Accordingly, he granted the defendant leave to defend the claimant's action for infringement as he considered that the claimant's argument was not sufficiently clear to allow it summary judgment against the defendant. He added that if the hearing had been a full trial, he would have considered referring this issue to the European Court of Justice for a preliminary ruling.

More recently, in *Gromax Plasticulture Ltd* v *Don & Low Nonwovens Ltd* [1999] RPC 367, Mr Justice Lindsey, whilst avoiding formulating a comprehensive definition said that bad faith plainly includes dishonesty and some dealings that 'fall short of the standards of acceptable commercial behaviour observed by reasonable and experienced men in the particular area being examined'. This case has become the authority for the meaning of bad faith in trade mark cases.

Applying to register a trade mark, having no intention to use the mark in respect of the goods or services applied for, could give rise to an allegation of bad faith. The form used to apply to register a sign as a United Kingdom trade mark carries a declaration that the trade mark is being used by applicant or with his consent in relation to the goods or services covered by the application or that there is a *bona fide* intention that it will be so used. Another form of bad faith could be where a person applies to register as a trade mark a name or mark already used by an established trader who has failed to register the name or mark himself, perhaps in the hope of selling the registration to the trader. An extreme example was in the case of *Baywatch Trade Mark Application* (unreported) 12 November 1999. The applicant had nothing to do with the producers and owners of the rights in the Baywatch television series, Baywatch Production Company, but applied to register the name in respect of various fast-food items. When challenged, the applicant offered to sell the trade mark for £15m plus royalties. The production company opposed the application and it was held to be unregistrable, *inter alia*, on the ground that the application was made in bad faith as the applicant failed to convince the hearing officer that he had a *bona fide* intention to use the mark. The applicant claimed that he intended to use the mark with a restaurant he intended to open but he failed to adduce convincing evidence of business plans to that effect.

The relative grounds of refusal of registration are set out in section 5 of the Trade Marks Act 1994 and depend on the relationship of the mark applied for and earlier trade marks, or other rights. First of all, a trade mark will be refused registration if it is identical to an earlier trade mark and the goods or services for which the trade mark is applied for are identical to those for which the earlier trade mark is protected. If this is the case, registration will be refused without having to prove anything else, such as a likelihood of confusion. Where the trade mark applied for is identical to or similar to the earlier trade mark and is to be used for similar goods or services, or where the trade mark applied for is similar to the earlier trade mark and is to be used for identical goods or services (in other words, where there is not identity of trade marks *and* goods or services), then it will not be registered if there exists a likelihood of confusion on the part of the public. A likelihood of confusion is stated to include a likelihood of association but this seems to add little or nothing to the test and it has been confirmed that there must be confusion as to the origin of the goods or services. The fact that seeing a trade mark applied to goods might bring another trader to the mind of a consumer without causing the consumer to be misled as to the origin of the goods is not enough. In terms of deciding whether two trade marks are identical, the fact that there are minor changes or additions does not prevent the marks being identical for these purposes if they incorporate differences that are so minor as to go unnoticed by the average consumer. Some latitude in whether goods or services are identical is also possible.

A further relative ground for refusal of registration is where the trade mark applied for is identical or similar to an earlier trade mark and is to be used for goods or services which are not similar to those for which the earlier trade mark is protected where the earlier trade mark has a reputation in the United Kingdom (or European Community in the case of a Community trade mark). However, for this to apply, the use of the mark applied for must be such, without due cause, as to take unfair advantage of or be detrimental to the distinctive character or repute of the earlier trade mark. An example might be if someone other than the Microsoft Corporation applied to register 'Windows XP' for double-glazing. Although this ground for refusal is in terms of goods or services that are not similar, the European Court of Justice has ruled that the equivalent provision in the harmonising Directive applied also to similar goods or services; *Davidoff & Cie SA* v *Gofkid Ltd*, Case C-292/00, 9 January 2003.

For the purposes of the above relative grounds for refusal, an earlier trade mark means one which is a United Kingdom registered trade mark, a Community trade mark or one entitled to protection under the Paris Convention for the Protection of Industrial Property or the World Trade Organisation, being a trade mark well-known in the United Kingdom even though the person to whom the mark belongs does not carry on business in the United Kingdom and does not have any goodwill there.

The further relative grounds for refusal of registration are based upon the relationship with signs and trade marks protected by other rights, such as copyright, design right or registered designs. Registration will be refused if the use of mark applied would be liable to be prevented by virtue of any rule of law, in particular, the law of passing off.

Rights and infringement

The registered proprietor of a trade mark has, by section 9 of the Trade Marks Act 1994, the exclusive right to use the mark in the United Kingdom. Use of a sign by another without the proprietor's consent will infringe if within section 10. The use complained of must be in the course of trade. For the purposes of infringement, a person is taken to use a sign in a number of situations including fixing it to goods or their packaging, offering or supplying services, offering or exposing goods for sale, importing or exporting under the sign or using it on business papers or in advertising.

With that in mind, the infringing acts set out in section 10 closely follow the relative grounds of refusal that apply in respect of earlier trade marks (except now the reference is to registered trade marks). Using a sign identical to a registered trade mark in relation to identical goods or services infringes *per se*. Where there is not complete identity of the sign and the registered trade mark *and* the goods or services then infringement depends on the existence of a likelihood of confusion. Trade marks having a reputation in the United Kingdom are infringed if a sign identical or similar to the trade mark is used for different goods or services (and apparently now also similar marks in the light of the *Davidoff* case above) where that use, without due cause, takes unfair advantage of, or is detrimental to, the distinctive character or repute of the registered trade mark.

In respect of whether goods or services are similar, Mr Justice Jacob laid down some guidelines based on an old test under the 1938 Act which he said was still applicable under the 1994 Act. In *British Sugar plc v James Robertson & Sons Ltd* [1996] RPC 281, he said that respective uses and users, the physical nature of the goods or services, the respective trade channels, whether goods are sold alongside each other in supermarkets and the extent to which the goods compete are all useful factors to consider.

Practice as developed at the Trade Mark Registry may also be a factor. In *Avnet Inc v Isoact Ltd* [1998] FSR 16, the defendant used the word 'Avnet' for his internet service for the aviation industry. This service also allowed subscribers to place advertisements on their own webpages. The claimant had registered 'AVNET' for advertising and promotional services and complained of the defendant's use of the word. However, summary judgment was refused. An important factor was that, at the time, Registry practice was to classify the claimant's activities and defendant's activities in different classes of the trade marks register.

Comparative advertising occurs where a trader advertises his goods or services in comparison with those of another trader in a way which includes a reference to that other trader's registered trade mark. It used to infringe under the 1938 Act and may still do so under the 1994 Act. However, under section 10(6) of the 1994 Act comparative advertising will not infringe if it is in accordance with honest practices in industrial or commercial matters. Otherwise, it will infringe if, without due cause, it takes unfair advantage of, or is detrimental to, the distinctive character or repute of the trade mark.

Under the 1938 Act the case of *Compaq Computer Corp v Dell Computer Corp Ltd* [1992] FSR 93 gives an example of comparative advertising. Dell advertised its computers with a photograph showing its computer and a Compaq computer with both makers' names (including the word 'Compaq', a registered trade mark) and the price of the machines. The claimant, Compaq, sued for trade mark infringement, passing off and trade libel. The court granted an interlocutory injunction to Compaq. It was at least highly arguable that Dell infringed the Compaq mark through its advertising. However, there was some doubt as to whether the Compaq mark should have been accepted for registration because of its phonetic similarity with 'Compact', an everyday word.

The 1994 Act marked a sea change in legal responses to comparative advertising and it was not long before traders were exploring the boundaries of what was permissible.

In *Barclays Bank plc* v *RBS Advanta* [1996] RPC 307, the defendant advertised its new credit card by reference to the Barclaycard trade mark with a list of features comparing both cards. Of course, the features selected were designed to show the defendant's card in the best light. The judge said that it was for the proprietor of the trade mark to show that the use was not in accordance with honest practices. Further, persons reading the advertisement would realise that the advertiser would be selective in choosing which features to compare and would also expect a certain amount of hyperbole. What an advertiser can get away with would depend to some extent on the nature of the goods or services concerned.

In *Vodafone Group plc* v *Orange Personal Communications Ltd* [1997] FSR 34, where the defendant advertised by stating that on average subscribers would save £20 per month by switching to its service, the judge accepted that the public would expect some elasticity of price and usage in relation to the quoted average saving. However, if the information is clearly untrue or misleading, comparative advertising is likely to infringe as in *Emaco & Aktiebolaget Electrolux* v *Dyson Appliances* [1999] EWHC 260 (Patents).

Remedies for trade mark infringement are, by section 14, damages, injunctions, accounts or otherwise. There are also orders for delivery-up, erasure or destruction.

Exceptions to infringement

There are a limited number of exceptions to trade mark infringement which may be set up as a defence. They include, by section 11:

- use by a person of his own name or address;
- use of indications of the kind, quality, quantity, intended purpose, value, geographical origin, the time of production of goods or rendering of services, or other characteristics of goods or services;
- use, where it is necessary, to indicate the intended purpose of a product or service, in particular, as accessories or spare parts (for this and the exceptions above to apply, the use must be in accordance with honest practices in industrial or commercial matters); or
- use of an earlier right (such as an unregistered mark protected by the law of passing off) in a particular locality.

The third exception (actually, its equivalent under section 4(3) of the Trade Marks Act 1938) was considered in *IBM Corp* v *Phoenix International (Computers) Ltd* [1994] RPC 251. Phoenix supplied computer equipment including 'reworked' memory cards which contained IBM components. Phoenix advertised these cards as 'IBM manufactured' and IBM sued for trade mark infringement and for passing off. Phoenix argued, as far as the trade mark infringement was concerned, that it had IBM's implied consent or that the use indicated that the boards were adapted from IBM components. The judge refused to strike out this defence. However, this does not mean that the defence would succeed at a full trial. The wording of section 11 in the 1994 Act is much simpler and, provided the use of the mark in such cases is necessary to indicate the intended purpose (for example, that the cards will work in IBM mainframe computers) and such use accords with honest practices, the defence ought to succeed. It is submitted that the use of the phrase 'manufactured from IBM components' would be more likely to be acceptable than simply 'IBM manufactured'.

As with patents (and designs) there is a remedy in respect of groundless threats of infringement proceedings. This was introduced into trade mark law by the 1994 Act. An example of a successful action was *Prince plc* v *Prince Sports Group Inc* [1998] FSR 21 in which the defendant, a United States company with a United Kingdom registration in respect of the word 'Prince', threatened the claimant, which had registered 'prince.com' as its Internet name, with litigation if it did not transfer the domain name to the defendant. The court held that the threats were unjustified and granted an injunction against their continuance.

Registration of a trade mark

Initial registration of a trade mark is for ten years and the renewal period is also ten years (under the old law the periods were seven years and 14 years respectively). There is no upper limit to the duration of a trade mark, which can be renewed again and again providing it has not suffered a period of non-use of five or more years. Many of the trade marks first registered under the Trade Marks Registration Act 1875 (the first Act allowing registration of trade marks) are still registered and in use today, demonstrating the importance of trade marks, including Britain's Number 1 trade mark, the BASS 'red triangle' mark.

Following receipt of the application, it is examined by the Trade Marks Registry to determine whether it is acceptable under the Trade Marks Act 1994. If it is it will be advertised in the *Trade Marks Journal*. This allows others to object to the application by raising grounds of opposition to registration or by making observations. Opposition must be filed within three months of the publication of the trade mark in the journal. It is planned that only the proprietors of earlier marks or rights that are alleged to conflict with the application will be able to oppose an application on the basis of the relative grounds of refusal. If an opposition is filed then, providing that neither the application nor opposition is withdrawn or the parties agree to settle, there will be opposition proceedings where it will be decided whether or not the opposition succeeds and, if it does succeed, to what extent. The most common grounds of opposition are on the basis that the mark applied for is identical or similar to an earlier trade mark and is intended to be used for identical or similar goods or services. Bad faith is frequently used also but does not succeed very often.

The fee for registration is £200 covering goods or services in one class of goods or services. For each additional class the fee is £50. The renewal fee is £200 for one class and £50 for each additional class. The fee for filing an opposition to a trade mark application is £200.

Trade marks and the Internet

A number of issues have arisen in relation to trade marks and the Internet, in particular where trade marks have been used on websites. Before looking at these issues in detail, it is worth making a few points about trade marks which apply generally to trade mark law, whatever the country. First, trade mark rights are territorial. They apply only in the country or geographic area of registration. Thus, a United Kingdom trade mark grants rights that can be infringed only by acts carried out within the territory of the United Kingdom. A Community trade mark can only be infringed by acts carried out within the

European Community, and so on. Secondly, infringement of a trade mark requires the offending use to be in the course of trade or business. A final point is that the fact a trade mark appears as an image on a screen display rather than in physical or printed form does not affect its inherent ability to infringe a registered trade mark, though determining whether it does or does not infringe may involve a modified assessment of the factors normally taken into account. These points then must be considered in the light of the practical implications of the Internet. Placing text or images or, for that matter, anything else on a website potentially makes it available everywhere unless, of course, access is restricted by passwords or other techniques to limit access. Does the fact that the Internet knows no physical boundaries bring real and serious risks of content placed on websites infringing registered trade marks all over the world? Another aspect is that websites use meta-tags and, in particular, keywords used by search engines which are hidden from visitors to websites. Even though not visible in normal use, can meta-tags infringe trade marks? Finally, does a virtual image have the same impact on a consumer when deciding whether there is a likelihood of confusion?

Jurisdiction – potential world-wide infringement?

To infringe a registered trade mark, the offending sign or mark must be used in the course of trade. In other words, it must be used as a trade mark. Furthermore, that use must be use within the territory in which the trade mark is registered. The use must, therefore, be targeted at consumers within the territory where the trade mark has legal effect. The United States was the first to address this issue. This is not surprising as a United States trade mark has effect throughout the territory of the United States but an action for infringement will be commenced in a state where infringement is alleged to have occurred. In *Zippo Manufacturing Co v Zippo Dot Com Inc* 952 F Supp 1119 (WD Pa 1997), the claimant made cigarette lighters and sued the defendant which operated a web-based subscription news service on the ground of trade mark dilution by its use of zippo.com and other domain names. The claimant sued in the state of Pennsylvania, where it was established, and the defendant argued that the courts there did not have jurisdiction as its principal place of business was in California and it had no physical presence in Pennsylvania. The court in Pennsylvania rejected that argument as the defendant had several thousand subscribers in that state and actively sought business there. The use of the zippo name was targeted there by the use of the domain name. In deciding this preliminary issue, the court developed a useful test, called the 'Zippo sliding scale'.

At one end of the scale, a defendant has an interactive website and makes contracts with residents within the particular jurisdiction. This involves the knowing and repeated transmission of files over the Internet. In such a case, the defendant is clearly doing business and is using the trade mark for trade mark purposes within that jurisdiction. At the other end of the scale, the website is passive in nature. This is where the person responsible for the site has done no more than to post information on it which, although accessible by persons within the jurisdiction concerned, is not associated with commercial activity. The trade mark is not used in a trade mark sense. There is a middle ground, however, where the website is interactive and where the user can exchange information with the host computer. In such cases, it is a question of looking at the level of interactivity and the commercial nature of the website to decide whether the trade mark is used in a particular jurisdiction.

The first United Kingdom case to look at this issue was *800-FLOWERS Trade Mark* [2000] FSR 697 in which an American company applied to register '800-FLOWERS' as a trade mark in respect of receiving orders for flowers and transferring them to florists. The application was opposed. At first instance, it was submitted that simply placing a sign on a website could infringe trade marks anywhere in the world. This was because the sign was used in an 'omnipresent cyberspace' and was 'putting a tentacle' into the computer of every person who visited the website. In rejecting that argument, Mr Justice Jacob gave the example of a fishmonger from Bootle, Lancashire who advertised on his own website for local delivery. This could not be seen as aimed at persons all over the world and anyone using a search engine who accessed the site would quickly realise it was not intended for him or her unless they lived in a reasonable proximity of the fishmonger's shop. It is a fact of the Internet that using a search engine will inevitably retrieve irrelevant hits.

Later, in *Euromarket Designs Inc* v *Peters and Crate & Barrel* [2001] FSR 288, Jacob J had a further opportunity to consider the matter. In that case, the American claimant company had a chain of stores in the United States operating under the name 'Crate and Barrel'. It had registrations of the name as a trade mark in the United Kingdom and as a Community trade mark. The defendant owned a shop in Dublin which sold furniture and household items and used the name Crate and Barrel for the shop and advertised in a magazine and on its website using the Crate and Barrel name. There was no evidence to show that the defendant had actively sought business in the United Kingdom. The claimant sought summary judgment for infringement of its trade mark, even though it did not have any real trade in the United Kingdom.

Section 9(1) of the Trade Marks Act 1994 states that the exclusive rights in a trade mark are infringed 'by use of the trade mark in the United Kingdom without [the proprietor's] consent'. The claimant argued that this suggested that mere use without consent in the United Kingdom infringed. However, Jacob J rejected this saying that section 9(1) simply adds a gloss to the infringing acts in section 10 to the effect that the acts within section 10 must be without the proprietor's consent. This means that section 9 does not stand on its own and provides for infringement on the basis of use, *per se*, without consent. This would run contrary to the harmonising Directive which has no equivalent to section 9(1).

Jacob J looked at the practical reality of websites and the fact that many are visited following a search which usually results in lots of irrelevant hits. If the defendant was using Crate & Barrel in the United Kingdom in the course of trade, bearing in mind there was no evidence of actual trade or an intention to trade in the United Kingdom, potentially it was using the name in every country in the world. However, there must be a distinction between active and passive use on a website and the terminology of the Internet supports this. When a person gains access to a website, he is said to go to the site or to visit the site. At this stage use of any trade mark on a website is passive only. Jacob J approved of the submission that using the Internet to visit a website was like the user focusing a super-powerful telescope on the site concerned. Without evidence of commercial activity in the United Kingdom, the defendant could not seriously be said to be using the Crate & Barrel trade mark in the course of trade in the United Kingdom. Of course, this would be different if the defendant had built into the website a facility for visitors to place orders, especially if prices in pounds sterling were displayed and it was clear that delivery to the United Kingdom was possible.

This approach was followed in Scotland in *Bonnier Media Ltd* v *Greg Lloyd Smith and Kestrel Trading Corp* (unreported) 1 July 2002. The defender registered domain names which were variations of the names used by the pursuer. Although the judge accepted that operating a website has the potential for infringement all over the world, it does not follow that infringement occurs in every country in the world. It is a question of considering the content of the website and the commercial or other context in which it operates. On the facts, the defenders had announced an intention to offer on-line services of interest in Scotland and similar to those offered by the pursuer. The defenders' planned activities would have their main impact in Scotland and that impact would be commercially significant. Therefore, the Scots courts had jurisdiction.

The *800-FLOWERS* case, discussed earlier, went to the Court of Appeal (*800 FLOWERS Inc* v *Phonenames Ltd* [2002] FSR 12) where the approach of Jacob J was accepted as correct in general terms. Lord Justice Buxton said:

> There is something inherently unrealistic in saying that A 'uses' his mark in the United Kingdom when all that he does is to place the mark on the internet, from a location outside the United Kingdom, and simply wait in the hope that someone from the United Kingdom will download it and thereby create use on the part of A ... the very idea of 'use' within a certain area would seem to require some active step in that area on the part of the user that goes beyond providing facilities that enable others to bring the mark into the area. Of course, if persons in the United Kingdom seek the mark on the Internet in response to direct encouragement or advertisement by the owner of the mark, the position may be different; but in such a case the advertisement or encouragement in itself is likely to suffice to establish the necessary use.

To infringe a trade mark in a particular jurisdiction, an identical or similar sign must be placed on a website by someone who is actively pursuing a commercial activity in that jurisdiction.

Meta-tags

Webpages on the Internet contain meta-tags. These are HTML (Hyper-Text Mark-up Language) tags that do not affect the normal appearance of the webpage with which they are associated but have a number of uses such as describing the contents of the webpage when it is retrieved in a list of 'hits' following a search. Another form of meta-tag is the keyword meta-tag. In this a list of keywords is placed which will be used by search engines looking for sites that match the search criteria. When a person builds a webpage in HTML it is sensible to include appropriate keywords which will attract hits from persons carrying out searches who will be interested in the material on that webpage and other pages linked from there. Persons carrying out searches and visiting websites do not see the keyword meta-tags as they are visible only when the page is viewed as source code, which a person visiting a website is unlikely to do, although it is relatively easy to do this by using the right mouse button when the relevant webpage has been retrieved. It might be tempting, therefore, for a person building a commercial website to include trade mark names belonging to rival traders in an attempt to divert visitors to that site rather than a rival's site. Can such use of a trade mark infringe even though consumers visiting the site do not see the trade marks?

As is often the case, the question first arose for consideration by the courts in the United States. In *Playboy Enterprises Inc* v *Calvin Designer Labels* 985 F Supp 1220

(ND Cal 1997) the defendant inserted the claimant's trade marks 'Playboy' and 'Playmate' in meta-tags. Although invisible to persons visiting the defendant's website, this was held to infringe the trade marks. However, to infringe, the use must be use as a trade mark. In *Playboy Enterprises Inc* v *Welles* 7 F Supp 2d 1098 (SD Cal 1998), the defendant, the model Terri Welles advertised the fact that she was a former Playmate of the Year. This was held not to infringe as the use of the trade marks was minimal and there were a number of disclaimers on the website. Her use of the trade marks was a descriptive use and was her way of indexing the content of her website.

The first case in the United Kingdom on the use of trade marks in meta-tags was *Roadtech Computer Systems Ltd* v *Mandata Ltd* [2000] ETMR 970, where the defendant inserted the claimant's trade mark 'Roadrunner' and its name 'Roadtech' in meta-tags. Before the trial, the defendant removed the names from the meta-tags but the court confirmed that this use of a trade mark infringed and that the defendant was also guilty of passing off. In *Pfizer Ltd* v *Eurofood Link (UK) Ltd* [2001] FSR 3, the defendant which marketed a drink called 'Viagrene', included the claimant's registered trade mark 'Viagra' in the keyword meta-tags. However, the court did not need to find that this infringed as it was held that there had been an infringement by the use of 'Viagrene' in connection with the drink.

Finally, in *Reed Executive plc* v *Reed Business Information Ltd* [2003] RPC 12, the claimant ran an employment agency and had registered the name 'REED' as a trade mark in respect of employment agency services. The defendant companies commenced a recruitment website (totaljobs.com) and used the name 'REED' in its meta-tags. To infringe, the offending sign must be *used* in the course of trade. Mr Justice Pumfrey, accepted that invisible use of a trade mark was 'use' for the purposes of infringement. Although he did not mention it, section 103(2) of the Trade Marks Act 1994 states that use includes use otherwise than by means of a graphic representation and, providing the use is in the course of trade, there seems no reason to take a restrictive view of the meaning of use. A possible way of looking at the question of whether an invisible use is caught is to look at the effect of that use. If it has real and commercial effects than that should be sufficient, for example, if the invisible use is such as to divert potential customers from the trade mark proprietor's site.

A further issue in the case was whether the defendants could rely on an 'own name' defence. Section 11(2) of the Act, *inter alia*, provides that a trade mark is not infringed by the use of a person of his own name and address unless the use is not in accordance with honest practices in commercial or industrial matters. This defence was potentially available to the defendants as their company names also included the name 'Reed'. However, Mr Justice Pumfrey confirmed that the use made by the defendant went beyond the own name defence as it would cause search engines to rank the site more highly than would be the case if visible use of the defendants' names only was made. He said that '[a]n invisible use would not, it seems to me, satisfy the requirements of s.11 because of its invisibility'.

To summarise, the position seems to be that using a trade mark name without the proprietor's consent in meta-tags can infringe the trade mark, providing it falls within the scope of the infringing acts (for example, used in the course of trade, identical or similar to the trade mark and used in relation to identical or similar goods and services). This is plainly so if the trade mark is used in the description meta-tag and displayed when the site is retrieved in a list of hits. This applies even if the trade mark is invisible as in a keyword meta-tag or used in another invisible manner, for example, by the use of black characters on a black background. These operations, sometimes referred to as spamdexing, will be deemed to be unfair and will almost certainly deprive the person responsible of any of the defences in the Act, such as the 'own name' defence. Otherwise, the scope of infringement is not widened by invisible use as opposed to visible use. Use otherwise than use in a trade mark sense, to indicate origin of the goods or services, will not infringe.

Banner advertisements and reservation of keywords

A related issue is the reservation of keywords with search engines which trigger banner advertisements. In the *Reed* v *Reed* case above, the defendants had reserved a number of keywords with some search engines. These words did not include 'Reed' but included words such as 'job', 'jobs', 'vacancies', 'careers' and 'employment'. Carrying out a search using any of these words automatically triggered the display of banner advertisements. Clicking on the banner advertisements took the user directly to the defendants' website. Some of these banner advertisements were described as fake search results in that they showed the words typed in by the user, for example:

'"JOB VACANCIES" MATCH FOUND – 1 SITE *****', and
'"JOB AGENCIES" MATCH FOUND – 1 SITE *****'

The fake search results also carried a phrase, such as 'I'm a designer lost in the world of accountancy' and the domain name totaljobs.com in an oval outline. It was, however, fairly clear that they were banner advertisements and not genuine search results.

The judge held that this did not infringe. The defendants had not reserved the word 'Reed' with any search engines and the fact that reserving words like 'jobs' would mean that a user might type in 'Reed jobs' and be taken via the banner advertisement to the totaljobs.com site was not use of the word 'Reed' by the defendants. Such use was by the person entering the search.

Likelihood of confusion and websites

For some forms of trade mark infringement, it must be shown that the use complained of is such as to cause to exist a likelihood of confusion on the part of the public. This is where there is not complete identity of the sign and the trade mark or the goods or services for which the sign has been used and the goods or services covered by the registration. The way in which this is tested is to consider the question from the viewpoint of the average consumer of the relevant goods or services and who is taken to be reasonably well-informed and reasonably circumspect and observant but who rarely has the opportunity of comparing the marks side by side and relies instead on his somewhat imperfect recollection of them. The visual, aural and conceptual similarities of the sign and the trade mark are assessed globally by reference to the overall impression made by them. Furthermore, a greater similarity between the sign and the trade mark might be offset by a lesser similarity between the goods or services in question and *vice versa*.

Based on the above and other guidelines, most of which emanate from the European Court of Justice, the national courts and trade mark offices now have a reasonable amount of experience in applying such tests and guidelines in relation to conventional forms of trade marks, for example, as fixed to goods or their packaging or as used in newspaper and magazine advertisements. But it is debatable whether such approaches to the likelihood of confusion are the same or have similar outcomes in the case of signs placed on websites which are similar to registered trade marks.

In the United States, in *Brookfield Communications Inc* v *West Coast Entertainment Corp* 174 F 3d 1036 (9th Cir 1999) the claimant owned databases of information concerning the entertainment industry. It had previously used the name 'MovieBuff' but without having registered it as a trade mark. Later, the claimant wanted to register 'moviebuff.com' as its domain name but discovered that it had already been registered as a domain name by the defendant so it registered 'moviebuffonline.com' as its domain name instead. Subsequently, the claimant registered 'MovieBuff' as its trade mark used for its database and sued the defendant for infringing the trade mark by offering a database in a similar field on its website. The United States Court of Appeals held that the defendant infringed the trade mark. The judge cautioned against rigidly applying previously accepted tests for infringement in the context of the Internet. He went on to say that 'web surfers are more likely to be confused as to ownership of a website than the traditional patrons of a brick-and-mortar store would be of the store's ownership'. The fact that both parties used the Internet as a marketing tool and provided access to their respective databases on line was likely to increase the likelihood of confusion. This factor was also influential in *GoTo.com Inc* v *Walt Disney Corp* (unreported) 27 January (9th Cir 2000) where the defendant's use of a sign similar to the claimant's registered trade mark infringed it.

The significant difference between the Internet and traditional 'brick-and-mortar' establishments is that there are fewer clues to help the consumer discriminate between different traders. This is exacerbated by the fact that many websites are relatively transient and web-traders can appear and disappear with greater rapidity than conventional traders having a physical presence such as offices, factories, retail outlets or simply goods stacked on supermarket shelves. A further factor is that it is not always possible to confirm the location of a web-trader, for example, where a country-neutral domain name is used. On the other hand, it is likely that most people ordering goods or services over the Internet will exercise a greater degree of caution because of the increased dangers of fraud and scams or being deceived as to origin, ending up being supplied with sub-standard goods or services.

Passing off

In many ways, the law of passing off is a common law version of trade mark law although of older pedigree. Passing off protects business goodwill and safeguards the public from deception by giving a right of action against anyone who tries to pass off his goods or services as those of someone else. One trader might try to 'cash in' on the goodwill and reputation of another trader by dressing up his goods in such a way that they look like those of that other trader. There is a large overlap between trade marks and passing off and it is not unusual for a legal action to involve both passing off and trade marks. The law of passing off is particularly useful if there is no registered mark to be infringed; perhaps a trader or manufacturer has used a mark for several years without registering it as a trade mark. The mark may fail to qualify for registration or the act complained of might fall outside the scope of trade marks – for example, if it relates to the format of an advertising campaign.

The following example shows the application of passing off. A computer retailer has been operating for three years under the name of 'Computer Equipment Sales' and has a chain of stores in the South of England. The retailer has acquired a reputation for low prices and efficient service. Recently, another retailer has opened a store in the South of England and uses the name of 'Computer Equipment Sales and Service'. Neither name is registered as a trade mark; in fact the names would be refused registration because they are too descriptive of computer retailing generally and would make it difficult for other traders to describe their business activities. As there is a danger that people will be confused and might buy from the second retailer thinking that they are buying from the first, if he has built up sufficient goodwill, the first should be able to obtain an injunction preventing the second retailer from continuing to use the name he has chosen. If the first retailer has only been in business a short time before the second retailer opens his store then it is unlikely that anything can be done. This is because there has not been sufficient time to build up goodwill connected with the name and, hence, there is little danger that the public will be confused. Similarly, if the second trader's store was in North Wales, it would be unlikely that the first trader's business would be affected, unless his goodwill extends to that location, for example, because he advertises nationally.

Basic requirements for a passing-off action

Before the claimant can suffer the type of damage caused by passing off, he must have a reputation associated with goodwill. He must be able to show that his name, mark, get-up or something else which is distinctive about his business will be associated with his goods by the public. If a trader has just started in business he will not succeed in a passing-off action but a newly registered trade mark has immediate protection. However, the necessary reputation could be obtained relatively quickly by an intensive advertising campaign on a national scale.

The ingredients necessary to a successful passing-off action were described in *Erven Warnink Besloten Vennootschap v J Townend & Sons (Hull) Ltd* [1979] AC 731. The claimants made a liqueur called advocaat which came to be well known. It was made from brandewijn, egg yolks and sugar. The defendants decided to enter this market and they made a drink called 'Keeling's Old English Advocaat' which was made from Cyprus sherry and dried egg powder, an inferior but cheaper drink. This captured a large part of the claimants' market in the United Kingdom. It was held that, because of the reputation the claimants' product had gained, it should be protected from deceptive use of its name by competitors even though the goodwill was shared by several traders. There was a misrepresentation made by the defendant calculated to injure the claimants business or goodwill and an injunction was granted in favour of the claimants. Lord Diplock laid down the essentials for a passing-off action as:

- a misrepresentation,
- by a trader in the course of trade,
- to prospective customers of his or ultimate consumers of goods or services supplied by him,
- which is calculated to injure the business or goodwill of another trader, and
- which causes actual damage to a business or goodwill of the trader by whom the action is brought.

Lord Oliver, in *Reckitt & Colman Products Ltd* v *Borden Inc* [1990] 1 All ER 873 (which involved the Jif Lemon and a competing lemon-shaped container for lemon juice), usefully condensed the test for passing off into the presence of the claimant's goodwill, a misrepresentation as to the goods or services offered by the defendant and damage or likely damage to the claimant's goodwill.

Normally, one would expect damage in the form of lost sales as a result of the defendant's misrepresentation. However, it also extends to damage to the claimant's goodwill itself such as where its unique character is eroded. This happened in *Taittinger SA* v *Allbev Ltd* [1993] FSR 641, in which the defendant produced a sparkling non-alcoholic drink which he called 'Elderflower Champagne'. It was sold for £3.50 in green bottles which resembled champagne bottles. It was held that this was passing off. Although it was unlikely that many would be deceived, the use of the name champagne in this way would reduce its distinctiveness and, hence, injure the champagne manufacturer's goodwill. Although this case has not been overturned, doubts have been expressed about it as it could be perceived to be an undesirable extension of passing off.

The misrepresentation

The misrepresentation is not necessarily limited to an exact copy of the name or get-up. It may be sufficient if it unfairly imputes a quality into some product or service, such as where a new trader uses another, established, trader's name or mark. An important factor is whether the buying public will be deceived by this unauthorised use of another's name. In deciding this it is not necessary to consider whether members of the public who are knowledgeable about the product are deceived; it may be sufficient if members of the public who have very little knowledge of the product concerned are likely to be deceived (see *J Bollinger* v *Costa Bravo Wine Co Ltd (No. 2)* [1961] 1 All ER 561, where an injunction was granted to prevent the use of the name 'Spanish Champagne').

As mentioned earlier, a misrepresentation does not have to be confined to a name or mark. The tort of passing off is wide enough to encompass other descriptive material such as slogans and visual images associated with an advertising campaign if this material has become part of the goodwill of the claimant's product. The test is whether the claimant has acquired an intangible property right for his product deriving from the distinctive nature of this material which is recognised by the market. In applying the test, the courts have to bear in mind the balance between the claimant's investment in the product and the protection of free competition.

In one respect, Lord Diplock's judgment is misleading. He spoke of the misrepresentation being calculated to injure. This suggests that passing off must be deliberate. However, this is not necessary and innocence is not an absolute defence although it may influence the remedies granted.

The misrepresentation may come about by modifying an image of a famous person to suggest that the person concerned is endorsing or recommending a particular product or service. In *Edmund Irvine* v *Talksport Ltd* [2003] EWCA Civ 423, Eddie Irvine, the well-known Formula 1 racing driver complained about the defendant's promotional campaign which included a photograph of Eddie Irvine. The defendant had permission to copy the photograph but had doctored it. Originally, the photograph showed Eddie Irvine holding a mobile telephone but it had been replaced by an image of a portable radio on which the words 'Talk Radio' could be seen. At first instance, Mr Justice

Laddie confirmed that Eddie Irvine had goodwill which could be protected against a false claim that he endorsed the defendant's products. The Court of Appeal upheld the judge's finding as to passing off but increased the award of damages from £2000 to £25,000. Doctoring images on webpages so as to suggest someone endorses a particular product will undoubtedly be passing off. What is not clear, however, is the position where the famous person is deceased, although there may be issues of copyright in the original photograph of film used.

Common fields of activity

If the traders in a passing-off action operate in different fields of activity, it will usually be assumed that there is less danger of confusion and thus less danger of damage to the claimant. For example, in *Granada Group Ltd* v *Ford Motor Company Ltd* [1973] RPC 49, the Granada television group could not prevent the Ford Motor Company calling one of their cars a Ford Granada; the court held that there was no danger of confusion because of the different fields of activity – namely television and cars. However, in *Lego UK Ltd* v *Lego M Lemelstrich Ltd* [1983] FSR 155, the Lego company, which makes children's construction kits comprising coloured plastic bricks, was granted an injunction against the manufacturers of coloured plastic irrigation material preventing them using the name 'Lego' as part of the description of the material. The claimant was able to show that there was a real danger of confusion and damage to its goodwill.

The claimant in *Silicon Graphics Inc* v *Indigo Graphic Systems (UK) Ltd* [1994] FSR 403 supplied computer work-stations for computer-aided design under the 'Indigo' mark and had 3 to 5 per cent of the top end of the pre-press market, that is the market for all stages in the printing process prior to actual printing. The defendant made printing equipment under the Indigo name and although the claimant did not make printers it sued for trade mark infringement and passing off and applied for an interlocutory injunction. As far as passing off was concerned the claimant based its claim on a natural future extension of its business into the manufacture of printers. The judge accepted that there was a triable issue on passing off but, on the balance of convenience, refused the injunction requested.

There is no copyright in a fictitious name and an action in passing off is unlikely to be of much help if the defendant uses that name in relation to different goods or services. The test, as always, is whether the public is likely to be deceived by the use of the name, and in applying this test it is important to consider the fields of activity involved: do the two parties operate in the same or different fields? In the past, judges have not assumed that the public has a detailed knowledge of character merchandising. An example is provided by the case of *Wombles Ltd* v *Wombles Skips Ltd* [1977] RPC 99. Wombles were fictitious animals from a TV series noted for their cleanliness, and for cleaning up litter and putting it to good use. The claimant company owned the copyright in the books and drawings of the Wombles, and their main business was granting licences so that manufacturers, in return for a fee, could use the Womble characters to promote their goods. They granted one such licence for waste-paper baskets. The defendant formed a company to lease builders' skips for rubbish. After considerable thought, and remembering the Wombles' clean habits, he decided to call his company Wombles Skips Ltd. In finding for the defendant, the court held that there was no common field of activity and, therefore, no danger of confusion. However, some judges do seem prepared to accept that the public are now more aware of character merchandising and there may be a change in this aspect of passing off before too long.

As technology moves on, sometimes two distinct fields of activity may converge. In *Nad Electronics Inc* v *Nad Computer Systems Ltd* [1997] FSR 380, the claimant sold high quality hi-fi systems and the defendant sold computers. Developments in computer technology have resulted in modern personal computers being equipped with compact disc drives capable of playing music CDs. As the fields of audio entertainment and computers are converging, the judge held that the defendant was liable in passing off. An important factor was that the parties' respective goods were similarly advertised and were sold alongside each other in retail outlets.

Internet domain names

Every Internet domain name must be different to every other one. However, computers can distinguish the smallest changes, so inserting another character such as a hyphen will result in two potentially usable and distinct domain names: for example, smithjones.com and smith-jones.com. Another distinct domain is smithandjones.com. If close names are registered by traders, it is highly likely there may be confusion on the part of persons accessing the relevant Internet addresses. There is a distinct possibility of passing off where traders are using similar domain names.

Although dispute resolution procedures are now in place, resolving many potential legal conflicts without recourse to the courts, it has been the practice of domain name registries to accept applications to register domain names on a first-come, first-served basis without any consideration as to whether the applicant had the right to register the name. Individuals have registered names such as 'mcdonalds.com', 'mtv.com' and 'harrods.com'. Such registrations may have been made in order to sell the addresses to the relevant organisations but, in the United Kingdom, the law of passing off has proved valuable in respect of such practices.

In *Pitman Training Ltd* v *Nominet UK* [1997] FSR 797 two companies, at the time of the case distinct from each but sharing a common origin, had similar names: Pitman Training Ltd and Pitman Publishing. The case concerned the right to the domain name 'pitman.co.uk'. Pitman Publishing, which was the second defendant, successfully applied to register that name but did not make use of it for a period of time. Due to an error, the name was re-allocated to Pitman Training Ltd. Pitman Publishing complained when it found out and the name was re-allocated to Pitman Publishing. Pitman Training Ltd commenced proceedings, wanting the name transferred back to it, claiming, *inter alia*, that its use by Pitman Publishing was passing off. However, this failed to impress the judge who thought it highly unlikely that the public would associate the domain name with Pitman Training Ltd. Rather, it was more likely to think it belonged to Pitman Publishing as it had been trading under that name for nearly 150 years. An additional factor was that, when the Pitman companies were sold off in 1985, there was an express agreement that Pitman Training Ltd would not use the word Pitman without the word 'Training'.

In another case, a company with no connection to Harrods (the famous store in Knightsbridge) registered 'harrods.com' as a domain name. Use of the name was suspended pending the outcome of the dispute resolution procedure provided by the registration body in the United States but, in the meantime, Harrods launched an action in England for passing off and trade mark infringement: *Harrods Ltd* v *UK Network*

Services Ltd [1997] EIPR D-106. Summary judgment was granted and the defendant was ordered to release the domain name to the claimant.

In a subsequent case, *Marks & Spencer plc v One in a Million Ltd* [1998] FSR 265, five actions were brought by well-known organisations, each of which had substantial goodwill, against the defendant which was a dealer in Internet domain names. It had registered names such as 'bt.org', 'sainsbury.com' and 'marksandspencer.co.uk'. The defendant wrote to the organisations offering to sell the domain names. The judge considered that threats of passing off and trade mark infringement were made out and he granted injunctions ordering the defendant to transfer the domain names to the claimants.

The defendant's appeal to the Court of Appeal was dismissed; *British Telecommunications plc v One in a Million Ltd* [1999] RPC 1. It was confirmed that the court had jurisdiction to grant relief where a defendant had or was intending to transfer an instrument of fraud to another. It was said that the registrations, described as blocking registrations, were made for the purposes of obtaining money from the owners of the goodwill attached to the names and that the domain names were instruments of fraud as the only realistic use of the names, other than by the owners of the goodwill attaching to them, would result in passing off. Similar activities in relation to company names in another case were described by the judge as a 'scam'.

A manager of a civil engineering company registered easyRealestate.co.uk to use as a cut-price web-based estate agency. He approached the founder of the easyJet airline and associated companies such as easyRentacar hoping to induce him into entering a partnership and providing capital to help get the web-based estate agency up and running. In *EasyJet Airline Co Ltd v Dainty (t/a easyRealestate)* [2002] FSR 6, summary judgment was granted to the claimants. The defendant was ordered to transfer the domain name to the claimants as it was accepted that he had intended to take advantage of the goodwill of the claimants by choosing a name and design of website that was similar to that of the claimants. Although it was accepted that the claimants had no rights in the word 'easy', *per se*, coupling it with a word describing the service offered, using it in lower case as a prefix with a word starting with an uppercase letter and using the same livery colours as the claimants all suggested that the defendant had copied the claimants' get-up when he commissioned the design of his website. Again the judge accepted that the domain name, in the hands of the defendant was an instrument of fraud and the order requiring its transfer to the claimants was appropriate. However, as the defendant had only done minimal, if any, business through the website, there would be no award of damages as such an award, in favour of a very large organisation, could be seen as oppressive. An interesting aspect of the judgment is that the judge did not consider the use of the domain name alone, without taking the other factors into account, was such as to inherently lead to a conclusion of passing off. It was by looking at the circumstances and the perceived intention of the defendant that convinced the judge that the domain name was a 'vehicle of fraud'.

It is clear that the courts will not look sympathetically at persons who register famous names as domain names with the intention of selling them for large sums of money. The law of passing off is appropriate, though at the time there may not have been any actual use of the name. The threat of passing off if the intended buyer does not accede is very real where someone registers a name in bad faith. However, real difficulties still may arise, for example, because of the international nature of the Internet. What if an American company, having a website site in the United States accessible from the United Kingdom, has a very similar name for its Internet address to that of an English company having an established goodwill? Furthermore, what if a sole trader whose name happens to be John Sainsbury wishes to register john-sainsbury.com as his domain name?

As mentioned earlier, there is now an effective dispute resolution system in place to deal with disputes as to the right to own a domain name. It is the Internet Corporation for Assigned Names and Numbers (ICANN) which developed a Uniform Domain Name Disputer Resolution Policy (UDRP Policy) to settle disputes by a registrant and a third party claiming the registration is abusive in relation to the gTLDs (generic Top Level Domains) .com, .net, .org, .biz, .info and .name and in respect of ccTLDs (country code Top Level Domains) in respect of those countries which have adopted the policy on a voluntary basis. The World Intellectual Property Organisation operates the ICANN UDRP.

The United Kingdom is not one of those countries that has adopted the UDRP Policy in respect of the .uk ccTLD but Nominet UK has a dispute resolution policy and procedure for dealing with complaints by third parties against registration of domain names. In other countries that have not adopted the UDRP Policy in respect of ccTLDs, complaints have to be directed to the relevant domain name registry. The general rule is that dispute resolution procedures can only be implemented by a third party objecting to registration and not, for example, by a person who, having registered a domain name, has been threatened with legal action if he fails to hand over the domain. Nor can the system be used to submit complaints against the registrar. Making a complaint or responding to a compliant does not prevent the commencement of legal proceedings.

Remedies for passing off

The available remedies are injunctions, including interim injunctions, and damages. An account of profits may be available as an alternative to damages. The damages are assessed by considering the harm done to the claimant's goodwill and the lost sales of the claimant's goods as a result of the passing off. The most desirable remedy is an injunction, preventing the other person or business from continuing to use the claimant's established name, get-up or style.

Trade libel

An action related to passing off is trade libel, usually referred to by lawyers as malicious falsehood. This is the commercial equivalent of defamation and an example is where a person publishes untrue information concerning the quality of a trader's goods. In terms of computer technology, trade libel would occur if someone falsely claimed that a particular software dealer was trading in pirated software or was in financial difficulties or that a software house's products were defective or would not operate on a particular make of computer. Of course, the information must be false and must be published or stated maliciously. This means made without good cause or excuse and could extend to a reckless statement. In *Compaq Computer Corp* v *Dell Computer Corp Ltd* [1992] FSR 93, discussed earlier in this chapter, it was held that there was an arguable case of trade libel because the computer systems compared were materially different and the representations as to price were misleading and not justified.

However, the requirement to prove malice reduces the frequency with which trade libel actions are brought.

Embarking upon a comparative advertising campaign can precipitate an action for malicious falsehood, if malice can be shown and if the information used is palpably false. In *DSG Retail Ltd* v *Comet Group plc* [2002] FSR 58, the defendant ran an advertising campaign claiming that it had a price guarantee and would always under-cut competitors' price-cutting promotions. This campaign was held to be an attempt to denigrate competitors' goods or services and contained clear references to the claimant. Further, the defendant's claims were deceptive in that its stores were instructed to lower marked prices only if challenged by customers. Thus, the statements were false and the defendant knew this. The tort of malicious falsehood requires that the statement is made with knowledge of its falsity or recklessness as to its truth. The judge accepted that the defendant knew full well that the statements were false and confirmed the injunction previously granted.

Chapter 12

Designs

Introduction and background

Design law was originally concerned with the protection of designs applied to articles, for example, a new design of furniture, telephone, lamp, linen, cutlery, writing instrument, etc. The scope of articles for which designs could be protected was enormous but, apart from being able to protect new designs applied to hardware, design law had little relevance for the computer industry and information technology generally. Until 1 August 1989, designs could be protected only if registration was applied for and the maximum duration was 15 years' protection. The protection was quite strong and it was in the form of a monopoly protection so that the right could be infringed by someone who independently made an article, in respect of which the design had been registered, to the registered design or one not substantially different from it. Unlike copyright, the proprietor of a registered design did not need to show that his design had been copied or the person alleged to infringe had obtained some other form of access to his design.

Very significant changes were made to design law by the Copyright, Designs and Patents Act 1988, the relevant provisions of which came into force on 1 August 1989. To some extent, these changes were influenced by the fact that designs which did not meet the requirements for registration under the Registered Designs Act 1949 could enjoy much longer protection under copyright law if there were drawings showing the design. Designs that did satisfy the requirements for registrability could not take advantage of copyright in drawings as a modification to copyright law limited the copyright protection of registrable designs to 15 years only. A requirement for registrability was that a design had eye-appeal. Therefore, functional designs, as opposed to aesthetic designs, would be protected for the full duration of copyright, then being the life of the author plus 50 years from the end of the calendar year during which the author died. This was seen as anomalous and there were concerns that this could have a negative impact on industrial designs, stifling innovation and severely constraining the number of designs available to all manufacturers.

In the end, the House of Lords was left with little option but to do something about this state of affairs, pending legislative action. For example, in *British Leyland Motor Corp Ltd v Armstrong Patents Co Ltd* [1986] AC 577, the defendant declined to take a licence from the claimant to allow it to copy the claimant's exhaust pipes for Morris Marina (later called Morris Ital) but, instead, made exhaust pipes for the spare parts market by copying the shape and dimensions of the original exhaust pipes – a process known as 'reverse engineering'. The claimant alleged that this act infringed the copyright in the original drawings of the exhaust systems. Whether or not the defendant had access to the drawings was irrelevant as then (and as is the case now) copyright could be infringed by indirect copying. The House of Lords had to agree and held that the defendant was responsible for a 'technical' infringement of copyright. However, their lordships refused to allow the claimant to assert its rights under copyright law. They said that car owners had an inherent right to repair their cars in the most economical way possible and, for that purpose, to be able to access a free market in spare parts.

It was not long before copyright and design law were to be transformed. The Copyright, Designs and Patents Act 1988 made significant changes to the Registered Designs Act 1949 (including an increase in the maximum duration of protection to 25 years) and also introduced a new form of legal protection for designs, called the design right. Unlike the system of registered designs, the design right was more akin to a copyright and was free from formalities such as registration. It came into being the moment a design was recorded in a design document, such as a drawing or data stored in a computer, or when an article was made to the design, whichever was the first. The design right was of much shorter duration than copyright and the owner of the design had protection for no more than 15 years from the end of the calendar year during which the design was first recorded or an article was made to the design. If the design was commercially exploited during its first five years, the total period of protection was reduced, leaving a maximum term of ten years during which the design was commercialised. Although the design right is not relevant to computer-generated images, it can provide protection to the shape or configuration of computer hardware and, perhaps more importantly, a modified version of the design right protects the topography of semiconductor products, as described in the following chapter.

Although the design right today is the same as when it first came into force on 1 August 1989, there have been some other significant changes and developments in design law. As a result of a European Directive harmonising registered design law in European Community member states (Directive 98/71/EC of the European Parliament and of the Council of 13 October 1998 on the legal protection of designs, OJ L 289, 28.10.1998 p.28, now extended to the European Economic Area) the Registered Designs Regulations 2001 changed the Registered Designs Act 1949 as from 9 December 2001. These changes can only be described as sweeping in terms of the basic nature of the registrable designs and opens up the way for registration of a wider variety of designs than was possible formerly. Of particular note is that computer-generated graphics and icons now appear to be registrable as designs, providing the other requirements for registration are satisfied.

A further change was the adoption of a European Community Regulation on Community design which came into effect on 1 January 2003. This provides for a two-tier system of protection, one based on registration, the other not. The Community design has a unitary nature and takes effect throughout the European Community. The basic features a design must possess to be protected, whether by registration or not, are equivalent to those for the harmonised design. The unregistered version of the Community design is not, therefore, the same or similar to the United Kingdom's design right which continues as before, unchanged.

There are now four ways in which a design may be protected. They are not mutually exclusive and there is some overlap between them. The potential overlap between the United Kingdom's registered design and the Community design is almost complete and there is some overlap between those forms of protection and the United Kingdom's design right, although this is much less.

The different forms of design protection are described in this chapter. First, the United Kingdom's registered design system as modified by the 2001 Regulations is described. Following this the Community design is looked at. This is likely to become the principle form of protection for designs within the European Community. The position with respect to computer-generated images and icons in the light of the United Kingdom's registered design and the Community design is next considered. Finally, the United Kingdom design right is discussed, and this sets the scene for the following chapter.

Registered designs

Before looking at the attributes of designs deemed to be registrable, the scope of what types of designs may be registrable can be gleaned from the definition of design and its associated definitions. Section 1(2) of the Registered Designs Act 1949, as amended, defines 'design' as being:

> ... the appearance of the whole or part of a product resulting from the features of, in particular, the lines, contours, colours, shape, texture or materials of the product or its ornamentation.

A 'product' is defined in section 1(3) as:

> ... any industrial or handicraft item other than a computer program; and, in particular, includes packaging, get-up, graphic symbols, typographic type-faces and parts intended to be assembled into a complex product.

It is relatively clear that these definitions permit the registration of items of computer hardware, such as a computer keyboard, mouse, mouse mat, casing for a screen or printer and computer desk, providing the other requirements for registration, discussed below, are satisfied. Although computer programs are expressly excluded from the definition of 'product', this does not extend to other forms of software and it is notable that graphic symbols are included in the definition. Typefaces are also mentioned, bearing in mind typefaces are invariably stored in software form nowadays. By looking at the definitions of design and product, there seems to be no insurmountable hurdle to the registration of computer-generated images, typefaces and icons, and this aspect is discussed later in this chapter.

The reference to a 'complex product' is to cover products comprised of two or more replaceable parts allowing the product to be assembled and disassembled. This could allow registration of component parts of a modular system or the design of a paper tray for a printer. However, it must be noted that it is the appearance of the product that is important and the right does not apply to the design of parts that are not normally visible in normal use, for example, 'under-the-bonnet' parts.

Section 1B requires that the design is new and has an individual character. A design is new if it, or a design differing only in immaterial details, has not been made available to the public. The date at which this is tested is usually the date the application to register was made but this may be earlier if the priority of an application to register the design within the preceding six months in a Paris Convention country is claimed. The date may also be changed, in some circumstances, if the design has been modified after filing the application. For example, if the design has been modified so as to significantly alter it, the date may be the date it was modified.

A design has been made available to the public if it has been published, exhibited, used in trade or otherwise disclosed to the public. However, this will be ignored in certain situations, including if the design could not reasonably have become known in the normal course of business to persons carrying on business in the European Economic Area and specialising in the sector concerned or if the disclosure was made in breach of confidence or if the disclosure was made by the designer himself in the 12-month period before filing the application. This latter provision allows a designer to market products made to the design for up to 12 months before applying to register his design without compromising novelty. This is something of a departure for law in the United Kingdom. Under the Registered Designs Act 1949 before the latest amendment, marketing articles made to a design before filing the application to register would prevent the design from being considered to be new and registrable. In terms of patents this still would destroy novelty in the United Kingdom and the rest of Europe. (It is noteworthy that, in the United States, a 12-month period of grace is permitted before filing an application for a patent.)

Whether a design has an individual character is assessed by considering if the overall impression it produces on the informed user differs from the overall impression produced on such a user by any design which has been made available to the public. The degree of design freedom of the author in creating the design is taken into account. Therefore, where the designer has little design freedom, a design in which some small details are different from what has previously been made available may suffice for registration.

Features of the appearance of a product that are solely dictated by technical function are excluded under section 1C. Even though some features may fall within the technical function exclusion, other features of the appearance of a product may be protected as a design can apply to the whole of part of a product. Features of the appearance of a product which relate to interconnections or positioning against other products are also excluded but that does not prevent the registration of component parts of modular systems. Certain emblems are also excluded, such as the Royal arms and national flags.

The author of a design, being the person who created the design or, in the case of a computer-generated design, the person by whom the arrangements necessary to create the design are made, is entitled to be the first proprietor of the design; section 2. However, where the design was made in pursuance of a commission for money or money's worth, the commissioner is entitled to be the first proprietor. In cases where the design was created by an employee in the course of his employment, the employer is so entitled. As with other intellectual property rights, a registered design can be assigned in whole or in part and licences may be granted in respect of it.

Initial registration gives five years' protection which can be renewed for further five-year periods up to a maximum of 25 years. The application fee is, at the time of writing, £60 (only £35 for a design for lace or textiles consisting substantially of checks or stripes). The fee for renewal for a second period of five years is £130 and each subsequent renewal fee increases so that the fee for renewal for the fifth and last period of five years is £450.

The registered proprietor of a design has the exclusive right to use the design and any design which does not produce on the informed user a different overall impression (taking into account the degree of freedom in creating the design); section 7. Use includes making, offering, putting on the market, importing, exporting or using of a product in which the design is incorporated or to which it is applied or stocking such a product for those purposes. Under section 8, any person who does anything within the proprietor's exclusive rights without the latter's consent infringes the right in the registered design. However, there are some exceptions to this, for example, acts done in private for non-commercial purposes, for experimental purposes, for teaching purposes or for making citations (in either case, the use must be fair and the source must be mentioned) or acts in connection with ships and aircraft temporarily in the United Kingdom. The doctrine of exhaustion of rights applies so, for example, a product to which the design has been applied and which has been put onto the market in the European Economic Area by the proprietor or with his consent may be imported and resold without the proprietor's consent without infringing the right in the registered design. The right in a registered design applied to a component part of a complex product is not infringed by reproducing the design to repair the complex product so as to restore its original appearance.

Remedies for infringement are not expressly specified in the Act but will be the usual, particularly an injunction and/or damages. There is a remedy for groundless threats of infringement proceedings under section 26. This is available, except in relation to allegations of making or importing products to which the design has been applied. This remedy is available to any person aggrieved and, typically, could be relevant where a retailer has been threatened with legal action for offering for sale products alleged to infringe the right.

Community design

The Community design regime provides for two forms of protection; a right acquired through registration at the Office for Harmonisation of the Internal Market (Trade Marks and Designs) (OHIM), the registered Community design and an unregistered right which comes into being when the design is made available to the public, the unregistered Community design. In both cases, the design right has a unitary nature and is of equal effect throughout the European Community. It can only be transferred, surrendered or made subject to a declaration of invalidity in respect of the entire Community. The Community design rights are provided for by Council Regulation (EC) No 6/2002 of 12 December 2001 on Community designs (OJ L 3, 5.1.2002, p.1) and OHIM commenced accepting applications for the registered Community design on 1 January 2003. The protection afforded by the unregistered Community design has been available as from 6 March 2002.

The basic features a design must possess for protection are the same for both rights and are the same as for the harmonised national registered design system. Thus, the design must be new and have an individual character and these requirements are evaluated in the same way as for the harmonised registered design. The only difference being in relation to the unregistered Community design where novelty is determined as at the time the design is made available to the public and, of course, for this form of design right there can be no claim to priority of an earlier application to register the design in a Paris Convention country. The definitions of 'design', 'product' and 'complex product' are identical to those in the harmonising Directive. Therefore a design which can be registered as a United Kingdom registered design could also be registered as a registered Community design and will also be subject to the unregistered Community design when first made available to the public. As there is also a 12-month period of grace with the Community design rights, it is possible for the designer to market products to the design before applying for registration. In such a case, the unregistered Community design will take effect as soon as the products are marketed in such a way as to make them available to the public and precede the rights afforded by the registered Community design. The rationale behind this is that it allows a designer to market products made to his design without going through the expense of registering the design. If the designs turns out to be successful, the designer might later decide to go to the trouble of registering the design for the longer protection available for registered designs. In the meantime, he can use the unregistered right to take legal proceedings against anyone who has copied the design without his consent.

The duration of the two Community designs is very different. As with the United Kingdom registered design, initial registration endures for five years and is renewable for further five-year periods up to a maximum of 25 years. The unregistered Community design only lasts for three years from the date the design was first made available to the public. Bearing in mind the geographic scope of the Community designs, the fees are reasonable. Currently, the registration fee is €230 and the publication fee is €120. There are reduced fees for additional registrations. Renewal fees vary from €90 to €180. Applications can be made direct to the OHIM or through the United Kingdom Patent Office which charges a £15 handling fee. The examination process is minimal and there are no provisions for opposition but, once a design has been registered and published, an application for invalidity may be made. There are a number of grounds of invalidity but where the basis is a prior conflicting right, generally only the owner of that prior right is able to bring invalidity proceedings.

Most of the other aspects of the Community design rights are equivalent or similar to those that apply to the harmonised national registered design systems. Although the registered Community design gives the proprietor a monopoly form of protection, as with the United Kingdom registered design, infringement of the unregistered Community design, like the United Kingdom unregistered design right, requires proof of copying. The Community design rights should prove to be very important in terms of computers, telecommunications and information technology, not only in respect of items of hardware but also in respect of images displayed on computer screens, mobile telephones and icons, as discussed in the next section which applies equally to the United Kingdom registered design and the Community design rights.

Computer-generated images and icons

Before the changes to registered designs law, a 'design' was defined in the Registered Designs Act 1949 as being '... features of shape, configuration, pattern or ornament applied to an article by any industrial process ...' and 'article' was defined as '... any article of manufacture and includes any part of an article if that part is made and sold separately'. These definitions, together with the requirement that a design be applied to an article by an *industrial process* appeared to prevent the registrability of computer-generated images, such as computer icons and graphical user interfaces (GUIs). The United Kingdom Designs Registry practice at the time was that a graphic symbol displayed on a computer screen, *per se*, was not an article and, hence, not registrable as a design. However, a distinction was made in one case. In *Suwa Siekosha's Design Application* [1982] RPC 166, icons displayed on digital watches were held to be registrable as the symbols were built into the watches (that is, the code to produce them was in an integrated circuit built into the watch). Nevertheless, this was the exception and the number of registrations for computer-generated images in a wide sense was negligible.

Under the old law, the question came up again in *Apple Computer Inc's Design Applications* [2002] FSR 38. In that case, an application was made to register computer icons as designs. The application was stated to be in relation to a 'set of user interfaces for computer display'. The hearing officer at the Designs Registry considered that applying a design to a computer screen by a computer program did not involve an industrial process and, furthermore, a user interface was not an article. On appeal to the Registered Designs Tribunal, Mr Justice Jacob thought the issue was basically one of semantics and modifying the description of the article to which the design was applied might overcome the objection. A suggestion was 'a computer with an operating system which displays the icons concerned'. Jacob J's view was that, where icons are inherently built into a computer's operating system, the requirement for industrial application would be satisfied, as opposed to the display of icons produced by running a particular computer program. Apple eventually was able to obtain registration of the icons by describing the articles as 'computer display screens with computer-generated icon'.

As a result of the *Apple* case, the position immediately preceding the significant changes made by the Registered Designs Regulations 2001 was that graphic symbols including icons and other forms of GUIs were potentially registrable as designs providing they were produced by the computer's operating system, being permanently and inherently built into the computer (or mobile telephone or other item of hardware for that matter). On the other hand, graphic symbols and images produced by applications software were not registrable, as they were not built into the computer: they were not an intrinsic part of the computer.

The position is very different now. We have seen the definitions of 'design' and 'product' in the harmonising Directive and in the Community Design Regulation. These definitions are considerably wider than under the old law. The new provisions relating to the United Kingdom registered design and the Community design rights clearly permit the registration of images generated on computer screen displays and mobile telephones, digital watches, digital cameras and so on. Even though computer programs are excluded from the definition of 'design', this does not extend to images such as icons generated by running computer programs, whether operating system or applications programs. Providing the other requirements, such as novelty and individual character, are satisfied, there should be no difficulty in registering computer-generated images, icons and even webpage designs. Unfortunately the computer and information technology industry and companies with e-business operations have been very slow off the mark either to appreciate such things can be protected by registration, or if they have, they have failed to see the benefits. At the time of writing there are on the United Kingdom Register 69 registrations for icons (Locarno class 14.02.13) and only eight for interfaces and webpages, etc. (Locarno 14.02.14). A few are scattered about in other classes. ('Locarno' refers to the Locarno Agreement Establishing an International Classification for Industrial Designs and is administered by the World Intellectual Property Organisation. As at 1 January 2003, 41 of the Paris Convention countries use the Locarno classification.) Very few registrations have been made at the OHIM for graphic symbols.

An inspection of those computer icons and screen displays, including webpages, that have been registered in the United Kingdom gives some cause for concern. Many of the icons registered seem very simple or commonplace and it is questionable whether they possess an individual character. Some registrations include numerous representations, for example, showing different variants of a screen display or sequential steps in a series of screen displays. In this way, very strong monopolies are being obtained, relatively easily and at little expense. Unlike the case with trade mark law (and in respect of graphic symbols, the overlap between trade marks and designs is particularly strong) there is no requirement that the design is put to use. There is a danger that speculative designs may be registered in the hope that computer companies and e-commerce organisations may have to 'buy' conflicting registered designs or redesign the images they use. The danger of such conflicts is all the greater because, unlike the case with registered trade marks, it is less likely that searches of registered designs will be made before committing to a particular set of icons or webpage designs.

As was seen in the previous chapter, the law of passing off was effective against those who registered famous names as Internet domain names, hoping to sell them on for a large profit. However, registered design law is different and provides more opportunity for pre-emptive registrations of designs which are not similar to existing designs but which may turn out to be similar to designs later created for use as graphic images. In the *Apple* case mentioned above, Mr Justice Jacob thought that the fact that registration of computer icons and the like as designs under the new law meant that the legislators did not think that registration of icons and other graphic images used with computers, mobile telephones, etc. would lead to a 'floodgates disaster' situation. It remains to be seen whether he was right to so conclude. To give an insight into the dangers that might lie ahead, consider the Windows operating system environment, first invented by the Xerox Corporation at its Palo Alto Research Centre. Had that been registered as a design in the United Kingdom competitors could have been kept out of the field for 15 years (now 25 years), something copyright would not have been able to do effectively providing only the basic idea of such a system was used to develop other Windows systems.

The design right

Like copyright, this right is automatic and does not depend on registration but, unlike registered designs, there is no requirement for the design to relate to the appearance of a product, although if it does, it is not barred from protection by the design right. The result is that there is an overlap with registered designs but not all designs that are registrable are subject to the design right and not all designs in which design right subsists are registrable under the Registered Designs Act 1949. Where there is an overlap, the potentially longer duration of registered designs is the main reason why a design should be registered. Another reason is that a registered design gives a monopoly right while infringement of a design right depends on proof of copying. The design right does not apply to designs created prior to 1 August 1989.

A 'design' in the context of the design right is, by section 213 of the Copyright, Designs and Patents Act 1988:

> ... the design of any aspect of the shape or configuration (whether external or internal) of the whole or part of the article.

The design right applies to all manner of industrial designs whether functional or not and whether visible in normal use or not. A design must be original and section 213(4) states that a design is not original if it is commonplace in the design field in question at the time of its creation. It has been held, in *C & H Engineering v F Klucznik & Sons Ltd* [1992] FSR 421, that this requires a two-stage test. First, is the design original in a copyright sense; that is, did the design originate from the author? If the answer is 'yes', then secondly it must be determined whether the design is commonplace (at the time of its creation). The design, therefore, must be the independent work of the designer which was not commonplace in the relevant field when created.

The test for originality was once more considered in *Ocular Sciences Ltd v Aspect Vision Care Ltd* [1997] RPC 289. Mr Justice Laddie pointed out that the word 'commonplace' was new to English law and could be traced back to the European Community Directive on the legal protection of semiconductor topographies, discussed in the next chapter. He accepted as plausible a definition that any design which is 'trite, trivial, common-or-garden, hackneyed or of the type which would excite no peculiar attention in those in the relevant art is likely to be commonplace'. Nevertheless, that did not mean that a design which is made up of such commonplace features must necessarily itself be commonplace. A new and exciting design could be produced from the most trite of ingredients providing the combination itself is not commonplace.

The *Ocular Sciences* case is also authority for the view that the design right could protect detail differences, which may be too small to be readily distinguished by the naked eye. In that case, it was accepted that, in principle, the design right could apply to details of a range of soft contact lenses, although, in the event, Mr Justice Laddie decided that the designs, as a whole, were commonplace.

There are a number of exceptions to design rights and design right does not subsist in a method or principle of construction. Also excluded are features of shape or configuration of an article which:

- enable the article to be connected to, or placed in, around or against, another article so that either article may perform its function (a 'must-fit' exception); or
- are dependent upon the appearance of another article of which the article is intended by the designer to form an integral part (a 'must-match' exception).

These exceptions are significant for manufacturers and suppliers of spare parts. The former part of the exception applies to 'functional' spare parts which have to be a particular shape to fit another article. An exhaust pipe for a car will fall into this exception. Any piece of computer equipment which has to be fitted to some other equipment, such as a replacement 'card' (printed circuit board containing integrated circuits) which has to be a certain shape, or have a certain type of connector, in order to fit into a computer, will also fall into the first part of the exception.

The 'must-fit' exclusion is directed at rationalising the *British Leyland* case and it allows for the fact that persons who buy items of equipment which eventually may need replacement or additional parts should be able to obtain those parts in a free market at reasonable cost. If a design right monopoly were to be granted to spare parts, manufacturers of cars, washing machines, computers, etc. would be able to control the supply and price of spare parts and might be tempted to charge exorbitant prices for them. However, the *British Leyland* principle, sometimes referred to as a 'right to repair' has been shown to be of very limited scope and it is unlikely that it will be further developed by the courts. In *Canon Kabushiki Kaisha v Green Cartridge Co (Hong Kong) Ltd* [1997] FSR 817, the defendant made replacement toner cartridges for laser printers and photocopying machines. The Judicial Committee of the Privy Council held that this went beyond the concept of repair. In a patents case, the House of Lords confirmed that the concept of repair was a narrow one and did not permit the replacement of so much of a product being the subject-matter of a patent such that it could be said that the effect was that a new product was made; *United Wire Ltd v Screen Repair Services (Scotland) Ltd* [2001] FSR 24. In terms of the design right, the better view is that the *British Leyland* principle is no longer applicable leaving the scope of the right to be determined only in the light of the specific exclusions in the part of the Copyright, Designs and Patents Act 1988 covering design right.

The second part of the exception would apply typically to spare parts such as replacement body panels for cars where the design is dictated by the appearance of the car, but it is unlikely that many computer spare parts will fall into this category, although it could apply in respect of replacement parts for items of computer equipment, having visual significance, intended to replace some worn out or damaged part. A further exception to design right protection is surface decoration, being more appropriately protected by registration as a design.

The surface decoration exception was considered in *Mark Wilkinson Furniture Ltd v Woodcraft Designs (Radcliffe) Ltd* [1998] FSR 63, a case concerning fitted kitchen furniture. It was said, in that context, that the exclusion was not restricted to features lying on the surface which were essentially two-dimensional such as a painted finish but could extend to other features such as small grooves. However, other features might not be excepted where, for example, they themselves were subject to surface decoration. A cornice or recessed door panel might be subject to the right.

With registered designs, the person creating the design is known as the author but, and for no explicable reason, the person creating a design which is subject to a design right is known as its designer. The owner of a design right is the designer unless he creates the design in the course of his employment or has been commissioned to create it. A computer-generated design belongs to the person making the arrangements necessary for the creation of the design. Design right lasts for 15 years from the end of the calendar year in which it was first recorded in a design document (which includes storage in a computer) or an article was made to the design, unless articles have been made available for sale or hire within the first five years, in which case the right lasts only a further ten years.

The result of the provisions relating to duration is that the owner of the right can only have a maximum of ten years to exploit the design commercially. This period will be reduced if the owner fails to market articles made to the design within the first five years. Effectively, and in a commercial sense, the right lasts for ten years with the owner being given a five-year breathing space within which to bring articles made to the design to the market place. The right is further diluted because licences are available as of right during the last five years. This means that anyone can exploit the design during its last five years subject to the payment of a royalty to the design right owner. Failing agreement of the terms of the licence, the Comptroller-General of Patents, Designs and Trade Marks will settle the terms.

Infringement occurs when a person makes articles to the design or makes a design document recording the design for the purpose of enabling such articles to be made. This covers identical articles and articles made to substantially the same design. There are also secondary infringements where a person 'deals' with infringing articles, for example, by importing, selling or hiring. Remedies for infringement are as for copyright but there are no criminal penalties for dealing with infringing articles. In *C &*

H Engineering v *F Klucznik & Sons Ltd* [1992] FSR 421, the defendant claimed his design right in a pig fender, a three-sided box structure, had been infringed. The 'original' part of the design was a round bar welded around the top. Aldous J said the question of infringement involved an objective test through the eyes of a person to whom the design is directed (in this case, a pig farmer). There was no infringement here because the claimant's and defendant's articles were not exactly or substantially the same. Although a design can relate to a part of an article, it seems that the whole article must be looked at when deciding infringement.

Apart from the appearance of computer hardware, the design right is important for the computer industry because a variant of it is used to protect the layout of circuitry within semiconductor products, particularly silicon chips, as described in the following chapter.

Chapter 13

Semiconductor products

Introduction

Integrated circuits, commonly known as 'silicon chips' or, simply, 'chips', are of tremendous importance to the computer industry and to other areas of industry and commerce which rely heavily on information technology. Without the miniaturisation that they bring, the powerful personal computer of today would have remained an impossibility. Integrated circuits are made from layers of materials by a process which includes etching using various 'masks' (templates) which are made photographically. Alternatively, electron beam machines are used. The simplest integrated circuit consists of three layers, one of which is made of semiconductor material. A semiconducting material, in terms of its ability to conduct electricity, is one which lies between a conductor such as copper and an insulator such as rubber. Examples of semiconducting materials include silicon, germanium, selenium and gallium arsenide. A wafer of semiconductor material is coated with a layer of silicon oxide (an insulator) and the electronic components (for example, transistors) are made by chemically doping the semiconductor material with impurities through holes etched through the oxide. Finally, an aluminium coating is applied which is partly evaporated using a mask, leaving behind the interconnections between components formed in the semiconductor layer.

The patterns formed by the processes of etching and/or evaporation of the conductor make the electrical circuitry of the integrated circuit. These patterns represent the circuit design. The processes involved in the making of integrated circuits fall within the province of patent law and the first patents for integrated circuits were filed in the late 1950s, the most important one being developed by Noyce of the Fairchild Semiconductor Corporation in 1959. Licences were readily available and in 1961 the first chips were available commercially. Since the early patents expired some time ago, much of the know-how lies in the public domain. It is essential that the considerable effort that goes into the design and development of new integrated circuits is protected. In some cases, new designs of integrated circuits may be patentable as could be a new process for the manufacture of integrated circuits (which indirectly protects the product derived from using that process). Finally, a computer program product (being a computer program installed on an integrated circuit) could be claimed in a patent application if, when run in a computer, it produces a technical effect.

Semiconductor design right

One view was that integrated circuits were protected by copyright through drawings or photographs as most of the masks used in the manufacturing process were produced photographically and would be protected as photographs. This was uncertain, however, because of the requirement in the Copyright Act 1956 for a non-expert to recognise the circuit as being a three-dimensional reproduction of the drawings or photographs. As a result of a European Directive (Council Directive 87/54/EEC of 16 December 1986 on the legal protection of topographies of semiconductor products OJ L 24, 27.01.1987, p.36) the Semiconductor Products (Protection of Topography) Regulations 1987 were laid before Parliament and came into force on 7 November 1987. These regulations gave a right (called a topography right) in the layout of an integrated circuit. With the advent of the Copyright, Designs and Patents Act 1988, however, it was decided to replace these regulations with an amended version of the new design right by the Design Right (Semiconductor Regulations) 1989, which came into force on 1 August 1989. The new right, referred to hereinafter as the 'semiconductor design right', draws heavily from Part III of the Copyright, Designs and Patents Act 1988 which deals with the unregistered design right but with some differences as far as semiconductor topographies are concerned (see Chapter 12 for a general description of the design right). The manner in which this has been done is most inept and we now have the situation where some sections of the 1988 Act are different depending on whether they are being applied to semiconductors or other designs. References below to the 1988 Act are to the Copyright, Designs and Patents Act 1988 as it applies to the semiconductor design right.

The 1989 Regulations are similar to the 1987 Regulations in several respects: for example, it is the topography of a semiconductor which is protected, being, by regulation 2, a design which is either:

(a) the pattern fixed, or intended to be fixed, in or upon
  (i) a layer of a semiconductor product, or
  (ii) a layer of material in the course of and for the purpose of the manufacture of a semiconductor product, or
(b) the arrangement of the patterns fixed, or intended to be fixed, in or upon the layers of a semiconductor product in relation to one another.

A semiconductor product is defined as:

... an article the purpose, or one of the purposes, of which is the performance of an electronic function and which consists of two or more layers, at least one of which is composed of semiconducting material and in or upon one or more of which is fixed a pattern appertaining to that or another function.

These definitions are not very helpful being somewhat tautologous but despite that it is fairly plain that all original integrated circuits will be covered by the Regulations. If the description of integrated circuits given earlier is now considered, it can be seen that the requirements are met: there are two or more layers (usually three), one layer is made of a semiconducting material and a pattern is fixed upon it for the purpose of performing an electronic function. Normally, the ingenuity which requires protection is in the circuitry represented by the patterns formed by the conducting materials, but the Regulations are wider in the sense that they will apply in situations where the ingenuity lies not so much in the horizontal patterns themselves but in the vertical arrangement of layers.

Incidentally, the printed circuit boards commonly found inside most electronic equipment, ranging from transistor radios to computers, are not protected by these regulations because, although composed of layers (usually two), neither layer is made from semiconductor material. The board is made of insulating material and a conductor which is etched away leaving the circuitry to which electronic components are later attached by solder. Generally, however, printed circuit boards will be protected, through their preparatory drawings, by copyright as artistic works and, as they are intended to be read by the person making the printed circuit board, as literary works. Alternatively, they could be considered to be protected by the design right as a configuration (an arrangement of parts?) when all the components are mounted onto the board. A single electronic component such as a silicon diode or a transistor is not protected because it possesses no topography within the meaning of the regulations. A novel electronic device or component might be patentable in its own right if the other requirements for a patent are satisfied.

Subsistence and ownership

To be protected, the semiconductor topography must be original and it is not original if it is commonplace in the design field in question at the time of its creation (section 213 of the 1988 Act). 'Original' is liberally interpreted in copyright law, but the requirement that the topography is not commonplace is likely to lead to a much narrower interpretation (see the discussion of *C & H Engineering* v *F Klucznik & Sons Ltd* in Chapter 12). The two-stage test of originality and not being commonplace derives directly from the European Directive on the legal protection of topographies of semiconductor products, Article 2(2), which states:

> The topography of a semiconductor topography shall be protected in so far as it satisfies the conditions that it is the result of its creator's own intellectual effort and is not commonplace in the semiconductor industry.

Note the preferred European definition of originality being the creator's own intellectual effort, a similar test to that used in respect of copyright databases and, although not expressly stated in the Copyright, Designs and Patents Act 1988, computer programs. It is arguable that the United Kingdom model of protection for semiconductor topographies is unsatisfactory as the first part of the test remains that of originality not intellectual effort. The traditional United Kingdom approach to originality has been fairly generous, as discussed in Chapter 5 in relation to databases.

Article 2(2) goes on to confirm that where a topography comprises commonplace elements, it may still be protected if, taken as whole, the conditions of originality and not being commonplace are satisfied. The modified version of the design right which applies to semiconductor topographies, like the Directive, does not attempt to define 'commonplace'. In *Ocular Sciences Ltd* v *Aspect Vision Care Ltd* [1997] RPC 289, Mr Justice Laddie accepted counsel's submission that it would be likely to cover designs which were 'trite, trivial, common-or-garden, hackneyed or of a type which would excite no peculiar attention in those in the relevant art'. Although this seems to be a good working definition, equally applicable to semiconductor topographies and other designs protected by the design right, it must be noted that this part of Laddie J's judgment can only be regarded as a helpful guideline as he had already decided that the defendant had not copied the claimant's designs.

Apart from being required to be original (and not commonplace), the design has to qualify for protection. These requirements differ somewhat from those that apply to copyright. Qualification is based on the citizenship or domicile of the creator of the topography (or his employer or commissioner) or the person by whom and country in which semiconductors containing the topography are first marketed.

The qualification requirements are similar to those that apply in respect of the design right but there are a number of differences. In particular, the rule that a commissioned design qualifies by virtue of the commissioner (if he is a qualifying person) is subject to any agreement in writing to the contrary. This proviso is missing from the basic design right model. The same applies to designs created in the course of employment. There is also a change with respect to semiconductor designs which qualify by virtue of the first marketing, in that the person must be exclusively authorised to put the semiconductor products on the market in every member state of the European Community, whereas for other designs the exclusivity relates to the United Kingdom only. There are a number of other differences concerning territorial scope for qualification purposes. Protection is also afforded to semiconductor topography designs to persons from the Isle of Man, the Channel Islands and any colony and to firms or companies formed under the law of Gibraltar and to firms or companies having a substantial business activity in a number of other countries including Finland, Iceland, Japan, Liechtenstein, Norway, Switzerland and the United States of America.

One reason the 1989 regulations were passed was to satisfy the United States as to the protection offered in the United Kingdom, otherwise there might have been some doubt as to whether topographies derived from the United Kingdom would have been afforded protection in the United States.

Ownership of the semiconductor design right is dealt with by amending section 215 of the 1988 Act. The first owner of the right is the designer unless the design is created in pursuance of a commission or in the course of employment in which cases the commissioner or the employer respectively is the first owner of the right, subject to any written agreement to the contrary. If the right arises by reference to the first marketing of the article, such as where a semiconductor topography is designed by a Brazilian in Brazil but is marketed in the United Kingdom by an importer who is exclusively authorised to put articles made to the design on the market in every member state of the European Community, then the importer will be deemed to own the semiconductor design right. By section 214 of the 1988 Act, the designer is the person who creates the design and in the case of a computer-generated design, the designer is the person by whom the arrangements necessary for the creation of the design are undertaken. The recognition of computer-generated topographies was added by the 1989 regulations.

Duration

The duration of the semiconductor design right depends on if and when the topography is commercially exploited. Normally, by section 216 of the 1988 Act, the right endures for ten years from the end of the year in which it was first commercially exploited (anywhere in the world). If the right is not commercially exploited within 15 years of the creation of the topography, however, the right expires 15 years from the time the topography was first recorded in a design document or the time when an article was first made to the design, whichever is the earlier. These rules mean that it might benefit the owner of a topography right for him to sit on that right until such time as it can be exploited to its full potential as long as this is done a reasonable period before the 15 years have expired. Given the speed of development in the industry, however, this is unlikely to be a great advantage as there is a danger that the product will be obsolete before it has been exploited. As with the unregistered design right as it applies to other articles, the semiconductor design right is automatic and does not require registration. Bearing this in mind (and the same applies to the unregistered design right generally and to copyright works) it is worthwhile keeping good records of the development of the topography so that the date it was created can be proved in a court of law. This is to prevent a copier claiming that he was the first to develop the topography in question. By regulation 9 of the 1989 Regulations, licences of right are not available in relation to semiconductors as they are with other designs (such licences are normally available in the last five years of a design right).

Rights and infringement

The semiconductor design right is, by section 226(1) of the 1988 Act as substituted for semiconductor topographies, the exclusive right to reproduce the design by making articles to that design or by making a design document (which includes data stored in a computer) recording the design for the purpose of enabling such articles to be made. A person doing either of the above infringes the right whether he does it in relation to the whole or a substantial part of the topography. There are important exceptions to infringement connected with research, non-commercial or educational purposes. The regulations have one very unusual effect in that it is permissible to make a reproduction of a topography for the purpose of analysing or evaluating that topography or the concepts, processes, systems or techniques embodied in it by section 226(1A) of the 1988 Act as substituted. Furthermore, by regulation 8(4), it is not an infringement of the semiconductor design right to create another original topography as a result of such analysis or evaluation or to reproduce that other topography. Therefore, a form of 'reverse engineering' is positively encouraged allowing the knowledge gained from an inspection of an existing topography to be used in the design of a new topography. In practice, a limiting factor will be the requirement for the new topography to be original and not commonplace. On reflection, this exception is probably justified on the grounds that to provide otherwise might inhibit innovation in this very fast-moving field where the existing technology is being built upon all the time while property rights still subsist in that existing technology. However, this runs counter to basic principles of intellectual property rights; such an activity with respect to a copyright work would probably infringe copyright because any derivative work would contain a copy of a substantial part of the first work. It will really depend on how the word 'substantial' is interpreted in terms of the semiconductor design right. For the reverse engineering provisions to have any real effect, the word 'substantial' would have to be interpreted in a quantitative sense which would run counter to copyright law.

If an infringement of a topography right also infringes copyright, the semiconductor design right is suppressed leaving remedies to be pursued under copyright law only, by section 236 of the 1988 Act. This is the same as with other designs. Regard must be had to section 51 of the Copyright, Designs and Patents Act 1988, however, which removes from the scope of copyright infringement the making of articles to designs recorded in design documents (or embodied in models) unless the design is for an artistic work. It is highly unlikely that semiconductor designs will be considered to be artistic works. Design documents include drawings, photographs and computer data and the effect of section 51 is to remove copyright protection from semiconductor topographies leaving the modified design right with its limited duration as the only form of legal protection, apart from the law of confidence which will protect until, at least, the semiconductor products are made available to the public. Compliance with the European Directive, following pressure from the United States, has had the opposite effect to that intended: it has significantly reduced protection in the United Kingdom from what was potentially available under copyright law.

Remedies for infringement

Remedies for infringement are as for the design right generally and are injunctions, damages and accounts of profits 'or otherwise' (section 229 of the 1988 Act). Additional damages are also provided for as they are for copyright infringement and the unregistered design right generally. Orders for delivery up and destruction are also available. In the case of innocent infringement (if the defendant did not know and had no reason to believe that the semiconductor design right subsisted in the article) damages are not available although other remedies may be, such as an account of profits.

Secondary infringement – for example, where a person imports or deals with infringing copies of semiconductors – does not apply if they have already been marketed in the United Kingdom or any member state of the European Community by or with the licence of the owner of the right or other person entitled to do so.

Summary

The protection of semiconductors by means of a modified version of the design right reflects a pragmatic approach to providing adequate protection without the need to formally apply to register a right. In the context of a very large and important industry designing and manufacturing integrated circuits, one thing stands out as surprising. This form of protection has been available since 1987 and yet there is not a single reported case concerning a dispute over the existence or infringement of the right and the author has been unable to discover any unreported case dealing with these issues. This means that either the Regulations are a model of clarity, which they are certainly not, or that something else is going on. In reality, chip manufacturers seem to prefer to rely on patents to protect their products or the processes by which they are made. Even if the whole of an integrated circuit is not protectable by a patent, in many cases, a certain feature such as a communications protocol might be patentable and should be sufficient to prevent duplication of the integrated circuit by a third party without consent. If this is the case, and there are numerous examples of patents granted in respect of integrated circuits, such as the Pentium 4 processor, then the topography Regulations seem to be unnecessary.

A final point is that one might wonder, given the much wider scope of registered designs, why this right does not apply to the design of integrated circuits. The harmonising Directive and the Community Design Regulation both are expressed as being without prejudice to provisions of Community law or national law relating to, *inter alia*, unregistered designs and this should include the semiconductor topography right. Although providing a separate parallel right could hardly be described as prejudicing such a right, the fact is that registered design law protects the design of the appearance of a product and does not apply to features of designs not visible during normal use.

173

Chapter 14

International implications and summary

International implications

Bearing in mind the international nature of business, the territorial scope of intellectual property rights is a serious issue to those creating and developing computer hardware and software and those in the information technology and telecommunications fields. Some forms of intellectual property rights fare better than others when it comes to their subsistence and enforcement in other countries. With the United Kingdom's membership of the European Community, it is to be expected that there should be some degree of harmonisation with our European trading partners and, for some time, intellectual property legislation in the United Kingdom has been influenced by this. For example, the Patents Act 1977 went some way towards achieving compatibility, and the consolidation of moral rights in copyright law, which is a traditional European concept, reinforces the move towards European trading unity. A steady flow of European Community Directives harmonising intellectual property rights confirms the important role of intellectual property in commercial activity within the Community, as does the introduction of the Community trade mark and the Community design.

On a world-wide scale there are many difficulties, and some countries fail to appreciate the significance of intellectual property. World-wide legal protection of invention and innovation is still a long way from being realised, although countries which include the major producers and users of intellectual property have strong laws protecting the same. There are also signs of growing international co-operation in harmonising and enforcing intellectual property laws.

The GATT TRIPs Agreement (General Agreement on Tariffs and Trade, Trade-Related Aspects of Intellectual Property Rights, 15 December 1993) now administered by the World Trade Organisation goes some way towards establishing a level playing field and continues to assist in the international protection of intellectual property rights. In particular, countries which are parties to the Agreement must be committed to providing national treatment: that is, nationals of other parties must be given treatment no less favourable than that afforded to the party's own nationals. Parties to the TRIPs Agreement, *inter alia*, must comply with the major international conventions protecting intellectual property.

Copyright is subject to two international conventions by which reciprocal protection is granted between members. The conventions are the Berne Convention and the Universal Copyright Convention and the United Kingdom is a signatory to both. This means that most works of copyright protected under the Copyright, Designs and Patents Act 1988 are also protected in the countries which are members of these conventions, which include most of the major developed countries. In some countries, a copyright notice is required and it is for this reason that the familiar copyright symbol © is used. To be effective the symbol must be shown with the name of the copyright owner and the year the work was created though alternatives to the symbol are allowed such as the unabbreviated word 'copyright'.

The territorial scope of patent protection is determined by the application procedure. The applicant may apply for a United Kingdom patent, a European patent to be granted for three or more countries under the European Patent Convention or a 'world-wide' patent for one or more of the member countries under the Patent Co-operation Treaty. Whichever route is chosen, if successful, the applicant will acquire a bundle of national patents. For example, if a person applies through the European Patent Convention for a patent in respect of the United Kingdom, France, Spain and Germany, that person will end up with four separate, though identical, national patents. There is not, as yet, a single patent which is valid and enforceable in a number of countries. However, there are plans to introduce a Community-wide patent which will have a unitary nature and be effective throughout the European Community. These plans, which have been around for many years, have now taken on an urgency in the light of some of the jurisdictional problems associated with the enforcement of parallel patents in different member states.

The more countries for which patent protection is sought the more expensive the operation becomes but the expense may be worthwhile if it is intended to exploit the invention internationally. There is an international agreement, the Madrid Agreement, for the international registration of trade marks and a Protocol to this agreement has been ratified by the United Kingdom, with the result that United Kingdom persons should no longer have to make separate application to each country covered by the Protocol in which they wish to gain registration of their mark. The first countries to ratify the Protocol, which runs alongside and separate from the Madrid Convention, were China, Cuba, Denmark, Finland, Germany, Norway, Spain, Sweden and the United Kingdom. Currently, 68 states are party to either the Agreement or Protocol or both.

Generally, intellectual property rights are territorial in nature. However, there are conventions (Brussels and Lugano) and an EC Regulation on jurisdiction and the enforcement of judgments in civil and commercial matters have a significant impact on jurisdiction, that is, the country in which a legal action can be brought. The Conventions and Regulation are given effect by the Civil Jurisdiction and Judgments Acts of 1982 and 1991, as amended. There is also some United Kingdom legislation allowing enforcement in the United Kingdom of judgments made in some countries outside Europe, particularly applying to Commonwealth countries. In terms of the Conventions and Regulation affecting Europe the basic rule is that a defendant is sued in his home country. However, where a breach of contract or an infringement of an intellectual property right, such as a patent or copyright, is concerned, the action can be brought where the harmful event occurred. Where there is more than one defendant having joint liability in respect of the same action, litigation can be pursued in the country in which any one of the defendants is based. Where a German citizen has a German copyright in a literary work, by virtue of the Berne Convention and the Copyright (Application to Other Countries) Order 1999, as amended, he will also qualify for copyright protection in the United Kingdom. If his copyright is infringed by an English company, he can sue in England. If the English company is a joint infringer with a French company and infringing copies of his work are sold in Germany, he can sue in England, Germany or France.

An exception applies in relation to rights that are subject to formalities such as patents. Where the validity of the right is in issue, as it almost certainly will be in an action for infringement of a patent, the action can only be brought in the country in which the patent is registered. This can lead to a very unsatisfactory situation. It means that if a person holds a number of European patents for the same invention and it is being infringed in some of the countries where the patents are registered, that person may have to embark upon a number of separate actions, one in each country, to enforce his patent. This is very unsatisfactory and is compounded by the fact that some countries take a different view of the application of the Conventions. Furthermore, it exposes the owner of a bundle of patents to additional expense and the possibility of conflicting decisions in different countries. A potential defendant may even be able to bring a pre-emptive strike by commencing an action for a declaration of non-infringement in a country in which an action may take a long time to come to trial.

Some areas of intellectual property discussed in this part of the book have little, if any, international scope and are restricted to the United Kingdom. Prime examples are the law of confidence, as demonstrated by the failure to prevent the publication of the *Spycatcher* book in Australia (and, eventually, also in the United Kingdom), the tort of passing off and the United Kingdom unregistered design right. Other countries have other laws to deal with these rights such as a law of unfair competition.

European Community law and intellectual property

Computer technology and its use has attracted much interest from the Europeans Community. There have been a number of harmonising Directives including those dealing with copyright in computer programs and databases, term of copyright, semiconductor products, rental and lending rights, registered designs law, data protection, safety and product liability. In the field of intellectual property the European Community has plans for further harmonisation of rights throughout the Community and, ultimately, the development of more Community-wide rights such as the Community Patent. In these respects, the EC has taken a very proactive role, guided by the importance of the Single Market which cannot effectively exist if intellectual property rights vary from one member state to another or if they can be used to restrict the free movement of goods or services. The European Community has also taken on the role of policing the exercise of these rights through the Commission and the European Court of Justice, taking its brief from the provisions of the Treaty of Rome 1957 (the EC Treaty) concerning the free movement of goods and services, restrictive trade agreements and abuses of dominant trading positions.

There remain significant differences in the intellectual property law of member states of the European Community. However, where these differences operate so as to discriminate against persons on the grounds of nationality, they are likely to offend against Article 12 of the EC Treaty (formerly Article 6) which states that, within the scope of the Treaty, any discrimination on grounds of nationality is prohibited. In *Collins v Imtrat Handelsgesellschaft mbH* [1994] FSR 166, bootleg recordings of performances by Phil Collins and Cliff Richard were being distributed in Germany. The recordings had been made at performances in the United States and the United Kingdom. German copyright law gave protection to German nationals wherever the recording was made but refused protection to non-Germans. The European Court of Justice held that this was contrary to Article 12 and the discrimination offended Community law. The implications of this case are wide-ranging. Provisions in national legislation which deny protection to nationals of member states which are not parties to an international convention providing for reciprocal protection must now be viewed with extreme suspicion.

A full description of the work of the European Community in relation to intellectual property is outside the scope of this book but the main provisions and effects are summarised below, including mention of the future implications. It should be borne in mind that a number of new member states will join the European Union on 1 May 2004. The new members will be the Czech Republic, Estonia, Cyprus, Latvia, Lithuania, Hungary, Malta, Poland, Slovenia and Slovakia. This will bring the total number of member states to 25.

Note: the European Union was established by the Treaty of Maastricht 1992. It comprises the 'three pillars', being the European Communities (European Community, formerly the European Economic Community, Euratom and the European Coal and Steel Community), a common foreign and security policy, and cooperation in justice and home affairs.

Harmonisation and Community-wide rights

Copyright

Directives on the legal protection of computer programs, the legal protection of databases, the term of copyright, rental and lending right, satellite broadcasting and cable retransmission have all been implemented in the United Kingdom. Directive 2001/29/EC of the European Parliament and of the Council of 22 May 2001 on the harmonisation of certain aspects of copyright and related rights in the information society (OJ 167, 22.6.2001, p.10) still awaits implementation at the time of writing. It was due to be implemented before 22 December 2002. A Directive on authors' resale right (the right to a royalty when an original work of art is resold) is required to be implemented by 1 January 2006 (Directive 2001/84/EC of the European Parliament and of the Council of 27 September 2001 on the resale right for the benefit of the author of an original work of art, OJ L 272, 13.10.2001, p.32).

Patent law

There has been, for some time, a proposal for a Community Patent Convention (CPC). Unlike the European Patent Convention, which effectively gives a bundle of national rights, the CPC will introduce a unitary system applying throughout the European Community. It is likely to be administered by the European Patent Office. Following recent political agreement, it now seems like a Regulation on the Community Patent will be adopted very soon and a Community Patent Court may be set up before too long. There is also a proposal for harmonisation of a utility model form of protection. This will introduce this right which is new to the United Kingdom and which is similar to a patent but quicker and easier to obtain than a patent and subject to slightly less rigorous requirements than a patent. Inventions involving computer programs will be included in the subject-matter which could be protected by the utility model.

Trade marks

The Office for Harmonisation of the Internal Market (Trade Marks and Designs) began accepting applications to register Community Trade Marks (CTMs) on 1 January 1996. This system has been very successful and has attracted a large number of applications. The CTM has a unitary nature and is valid throughout the European Community and it exists alongside national trade mark systems. The requirements for registering a CTM are equivalent to those for the harmonised system of national trade marks in member states.

Design law

Registered designs law has been harmonised throughout the European Community and this required some substantial and far-reaching changes to United Kingdom registered designs law. There has also been the introduction of the Community Design which provides for two-tier protection. First, a design can be registered as a Community Design and protected for up to 25 years maximum. Secondly, there is an unregistered design right protection which lasts only three years after the design was first made available to the public. The fundamental requirements for subsistence of the rights are the same and very similar to the requirements for national registered designs. The United Kingdom's unregistered design right is unchanged and bears little resemblance to the harmonised registered design and the Community Design. Provisions of Community law or national law relating to unregistered designs, trade marks, patents, utility model, etc. are not prejudiced by the Community design. Hence the United Kingdom's unregistered design can continue for the time being as can other forms of protection, such as copyright, in other member states.

EC competition law

One of the main aims of the European Community is to remove internal barriers to trade. The EC Treaty (Treaty of Rome 1957, as amended) imposes obligations and provides rights effective upon and in the United Kingdom by virtue of its membership of the European Community. The European Treaties are given direct legal effect in the United Kingdom by section 2 of the European Communities Act 1972. In terms of the exercise of intellectual property rights, the following provisions of the Treaty of Rome are important:

- Article 12, prohibiting discrimination on grounds of nationality (previously Article 6);
- Articles 28–30, promoting the free movement of goods (previously Articles 30–36);
- Article 81, prohibiting restrictive trade practices (previously Article 85);
- Article 82, preventing the abuse of a dominant market position (previously Article 86).

(*Note*: most of the Articles of this Treaty have been renumbered as a result of the Treaty of Amsterdam 1999; the new numbers and old numbers are indicated.)

These provisions apply only in as much as trade between member states is affected. Although European Community law recognises the *existence* of intellectual property rights it may interfere with the *exercise* of those rights if this offends against the Treaty. For example, the proprietor of a patent may wish to be selective about markets and grant licences to work the patent to different organisations in different member states under different conditions. This would have the effect of segregating and splitting the market and would be likely to attract the attention of the Commission, particularly if one of the licensees objects (perhaps the one having the least advantageous terms in its licence agreement).

The application of the Treaty provisions to actual cases has led to the development of the following principles (the second is a direct consequence of the first):

- *Exhaustion of rights* – where the right owner has put articles into circulation (directly or with his consent) he cannot subsequently use his rights to prevent further sale or distribution in respect of those particular articles. It does not apply to works and other material communicated to the public electronically in digital form.
- *Parallel importing* – where articles have been put into circulation by or with the consent of the right owner, he cannot use his rights to prevent the subsequent import into another EC country even though he may be selling those articles himself in that other country. This removes any temptation to sell articles at different prices in different member states.

The restrictive trade practices provisions obviously control price-fixing agreements and other abuses by cartels but they also control licensing agreements – for example, where the proprietor of a patent attempts to impose onerous terms on the licensee. Also covered are agreements to 'pool' (share) intellectual property rights such as patents and know-how. There are exemptions under Article 81(3), either block exemptions (several have been promulgated) or individual exemptions.

Abuses of dominant positions might include demanding excessively high royalty rates or a refusal to grant licences. However, being in a dominant position, *per se*, does not conflict with Article 82. In *Volvo AB v Erik Veng (UK) Ltd* [1989] 4 CMLR 122, the claimant argued that the defendant had infringed its registered design for front wings for Volvo 200 series cars. It was held that, although refusal to grant licences did not amount to an abuse as such, it could so do if refusal was arbitrary or if prices were fixed at unfair levels or if the right owner stopped making spare parts. However, this would be so only if trade between member states was liable to be affected.

In the absence of full harmonisation of intellectual property rights, determination of the scope of the rights was a matter for national laws but, in exceptional circumstances, the exercise of a national right could amount to an abuse under Article 82. So it was held in *RTE & ITP v Commission of the European Communities* [1995] FSR 530, a case in which the claimants were refusing to grant licences to others to publish listings of television programmes.

Articles 81 and 82 apply where trade between member states is affected or may be affected. On a United Kingdom scale, the Competition Act 1998 contains equivalent provisions that apply where trade within the United Kingdom may be affected by the practice under consideration. Section 2 of the Act prohibits (unless otherwise exempt) agreements by undertakings, decisions by associations of undertakings or concerted practices which may affect trade in the United Kingdom and have as their effect or object the prevention, restriction or distortion of competition within the United Kingdom. Section 18 of the Act prohibits conduct amounting to an abuse of a dominant position in the market if it may affect trade in the United Kingdom.

Apart from action being taken by the European Commission of, in connection with the Competition Act 1998, the Office of Fair Trading, competition law can be used as a defence in court action. In *Intel Corporation v Via Technologies Inc* [2002] EWHC 1159 (Ch), Intel, the world's largest designer and manufacturer of microprocessors, including the famous Pentium central processing unit (CPU) chips and chipsets (a set of microchips that interface the CPU with other devices in the computer), sued Via alleging that, by manufacturing and selling chipsets compatible with the Pentium 4 microprocessor, it was infringing the patents relating to the processor. The patents related essentially to the communications protocols of the Pentium 4. Via had a licence to make and sell products compatible to the Pentium III chip but this did not extend to the Pentium 4. Via alleged that Intel was in breach of competition law Articles 81(1) and 82 of the EC Treaty and sections 2(1) and 18 of the Competition Act 1998 by trying to force Via to enter into restrictive and unfavourable licence agreements, by refusing to licence its patents and, in terms of the existing licence, refusing to lift restrictions that prevented Via from making Pentium 4 compatible chipsets.

All the defences failed and summary judgment was granted to Intel in respect of the competition law issues. One of the terms in the licence agreement required Via to cross-license its patents to Intel on a non-exclusive, royalty-free basis. However, the Intel patents were argued to be far more valuable than the Via patents and it has been accepted that such cross-licences are not anti-competitive if they are non-exclusive and there are no territorial restrictions on the licensee. The refusal to grant a patent licence is not an abuse of a dominant position save in very exceptional circumstances, such as a failure to exploit a patent, or in relation to the protection of public health or national security. Bringing proceedings against a licensor who insists on including terms that are contrary to competition law could be an abuse of a dominant position in limited circumstances but that was not the case here.

Summary

The law has developed, somewhat slowly it might be claimed, to take account of computer technology and to protect ideas and innovation concerning the technology. However, the importance of such protection has been recognised by United Kingdom and Community legislators and the judiciary and, as a result, computers and computer software are reasonably well protected from counterfeiting and piracy. The civil remedies available to owners of intellectual property rights have been supplemented by criminal sanctions, showing the seriousness with which Parliament views these matters. Certainly, without strong protection, the computer industry would seem a poor area in which to invest, and foreign investment and the resulting jobs created would be lost to the United Kingdom.

Although this area of law is diverse and complex, it should be noted that, frequently, these various rights overlap and several different rights may each serve a purpose during the life of a product from inception to marketing. For example, in the case of a new piece of computer equipment, the law of confidence is all important in the early stages as it is being developed and evaluated. Then, as specifications and drawings are produced, the law of copyright comes into play and gives parallel protection. When a patent is granted in respect of the equipment, the law of confidence drops from the scene to be replaced by patent law and, possibly, trade mark law if a registered mark is to be used with the equipment. Design law also may be relevant at this stage.

This parallel and overlapping protection is all the more important in the computer industry. For example, imagine that a new computer has been designed. It is to be sold with and includes software which is hard-wired ('firmware'), resident on integrated circuits inside the computer in addition to software on magnetic disk. The computer has a new type of keyboard and an attractive design embossed on the monitor case which also carries the manufacturer's stylised name. The following rights may be relevant to this computer system:

Patent	Being new, the computer may incorporate some new and patentable inventions.
Copyright	The software on the disk and the programs stored on the integrated circuits (firmware) and all accompanying documentation are protected under copyright law. Any included databases may also be protected by copyright and/or the database right.
Semiconductor regulations	The topography of the integrated circuits containing the firmware.
Trade marks	The stylised name may be registered as a trade mark. Some of the computer-generated images also may be protected by trade mark registrations.
Registered design	The embossed pattern and the overall shape of the equipment may be registered as designs. Icons and other computer-generated images may be registered as designs.
Design right	The new type of keyboard and any other new shapes may fall within the scope of the design right.

Key aspects to be remembered with respect to intellectual property rights are:

- the importance of confidence, especially concerning employees and potential business partners,
- the usefulness of keeping a documented record of the development of an idea or invention so that its origin can be verified, and
- the value, sometimes unexpected, of making drawings.

Finally, although the legal enforcement of intellectual property rights is an expensive business, delay or dalliance can be disastrous and the possibility of obtaining some legal remedies, such as interim injunctions, may be prejudiced. There follows a list of practical suggestions concerning ways in which the protection of intellectual property rights can be maximised.

Practical suggestions

Copyright

1 Those writing and developing computer software should distribute the computer programs in object code form only. Consider embedding the names of programmers or the company name within the program code; this can be extremely useful evidentially if a software pirate denies copying. The same applies to deliberate mistakes and redundant code. Software, as it is written and developed, can be deposited with an independent person (for example, a solicitor or the Stationers' Company) who can verify important dates such as when the software was first written and when it was modified. Written and signed contractual arrangements should be made with freelance workers and consultants dealing with the ownership of the copyright in anything they produce.

2 Lawful users of software may now make back-up copies of any programs they have acquired if necessary to the lawful use of the programs. If the programs are transferred later to another person, all back-up copies must also be transferred. Licensees of software should not assign or transfer their rights if the licence agreement prohibits this. If the agreement allows assignment conditional upon certain matters being complied with, it is essential to make sure that these conditions are met. Software users should operate secure and efficient housekeeping systems to reduce the danger of unauthorised copies of programs being made.

3 Software developers and users of software should clarify any doubts concerning the ownership of any output produced by the use of the computer system in question. The scope of the permitted act of decompilation must be fully understood if decompilation is envisaged. The position as regards error correction of software must be examined and clarified.

4 Keep copies of preparatory materials and a log of development of the software. Retain prototype and preliminary versions of software and record changes and any form of investment in relation to the design, development and modification of databases.

Confidence

5 An air of confidence must be maintained during negotiations between those with new ideas for software, computer systems, etc. and potential manufacturers, investors and the like.

6 Confidence can be reinforced by contractual provision in respect of employees and freelance workers. This may entail a reasonable covenant in restraint of trade.

7 It is essential that any ideas and development work concerning a possible future patent application are kept absolutely secret and confidential.

Patents

8 Obtaining the services of an experienced patent agent is highly recommended if a patent application is being considered.

9 Although a patent is a very powerful form of intellectual property, it is worth considering whether the invention involved can be kept secret indefinitely as an alternative to seeking a patent.

10 It may be possible to obtain a patent for an invention which includes a computer program despite the apparent exception of computer programs from the scope of patent law providing there is some technical effect which is not itself excepted. It needs to be borne in mind that the computer program will be protected by copyright law regardless of the patent situation.

Trade marks and passing off

11 Distinctive names or marks are very powerful marketing devices. Those manufacturing or marketing computer software or hardware are advised to register a distinctive name or mark as a trade mark and not to rely on the law of passing off which requires an established goodwill. Computer bureaux and other persons providing computer services for payment, such as designing websites, can register a trade mark.

Design law

12   Although this is a complex area of the law which has recently undergone substantial changes it can be very useful and registration of designs should be a serious consideration, especially as icons and computer-generated images can now be registered.

13   The fact that, with the United Kingdom registered design and the Community registered design, there is a 12-month period of grace before filing an application to register a design means that the owner of the design only need go to the trouble of registration if it is proving to be commercially viable. In the meantime, he can rely on the Community unregistered design and, where applicable, the United Kingdom design right.

14   Design law can be a useful supplement to other intellectual property rights and has been overlooked by many in the past. Registration gives a monopoly protection for very little cost.

PART TWO

Computer contracts

Contracts for the acquisition and use of computer hardware and software are dealt with in this part of the book. Many such contracts are not sale contracts as such but are licence agreements; this is particularly so with respect to computer software where the owner of the rights subsisting in the software grants licences to customers, giving them permission to use the software in return for a licence fee. For these agreements, the existence and scope of intellectual property rights is of fundamental importance. The acts restricted by copyright may form a substantial part of the licence's subject matter. Contracts for the acquisition of hardware and software are subject to many of the legal constraints on contracts such as the Unfair Contract Terms Act 1977 and those provided for by copyright law.

Following the introductory chapter (Chapter 15), the fundamentals of the law of contract are discussed and related to computer technology. Liability issues related to defective hardware and software are discussed next and it should be noted that, in some cases, liability is not dependent upon the existence of a contractual relationship and, where appropriate, liability for negligence and product liability is discussed. An employer's liability in relation to RSI (repetitive strain injury) caused by long periods of work at a keyboard is also discussed. In subsequent chapters, particular types of computer contracts are described: contracts for the writing of computer software, 'off-the-shelf' software licences, website development contracts and hardware contracts. The summary chapter (Chapter 22) includes a checklist of terms normally to be found in contracts concerning computer hardware and software.

Chapter 15

Introduction to computer contracts

Contracts for the acquisition of computer equipment and software present special problems, many of which flow from the unique nature of computer technology. For example, we cannot see or touch a computer program running in a computer; all we can do is experience its effects through a peripheral device such as a screen or a printer. It may be possible to read a computer program listing and perhaps make some sense of it but, certainly to many of us who have to use computer programs, they take on a quasi-mystical nature as they are, after all, intangible. It is the difficulty in coming to terms with the nature, effects and implications of computer equipment and software that is a direct cause of many of the contractual and other problems associated with computers.

The case of *Brownton Ltd* v *Edward Moore Inbucon Ltd* [1985] 3 All ER 499 provides an example of the financial implications of misunderstandings between the parties to a contract involving computer systems. A firm of commodity brokers sought advice from a computer consultant on the installation of a computer system. The consultant recommended a particular system which was installed in 1978. Unfortunately, the system never worked properly, was quite inadequate for the broker's needs and was eventually scrapped. The consultant had charged over £66,000 for his work and the computer system had cost in the region of £75,000. The broker claimed damages, for breach of contract, of over £250,000 based on the wasted expense and the difference in price between the system obtained and a new system that would be capable of doing the work. Later, the broker submitted better particulars and claimed that an alternative computer system capable of carrying out the work would cost in excess of £1.1m. Eventually, a settlement of around £300,000 was reached.

In another case, discussed in detail in Chapter 17, a lack of understanding of the ORACLE fourth-generation computer language on the part of the client and software developer during the feasibility study for and initial development stages of complex accounting software led to the inevitable result. The software was delivered late and, because it contained a large number of errors, it was unusable. The client was awarded £662,962 in damages (see *The Salvage Association* v *CAP Financial Services Ltd* [1995] FSR 654). The software developer was unable to avail itself of a clause in the contract limiting liability for defects to £25,000.

An example of the difficulties arising from a breakdown of the relationship between a software developer and client is afforded by the case of *Pegler Ltd* v *Wang (UK) Ltd* (unreported) 25 February 2000. The contract was for the replacement of an existing computer system with a new integrated system. The agreed price was approximately £1.2m plus £235,000 per annum for maintenance in respect of the provision of hardware, software and bespoke programming and other services. The judge described the software developer's performance as disastrous and, eventually, the developer ceased to carry out any further performance of the contract. The client sued for nearly £23m in damages. In the end, the judge awarded damages of just over £9m. This was for acquiring an alternative system, lost opportunities, outsourcing, software acquisition, wasted management time and reduced business efficiency.

A hypothetical example can further illustrate the difficulties. A company wants to install a computer system in one of its departments which has previously had to use slow, laborious (but reliable) manual methods. The initial decision to do this is probably based on some vague notion that a computer system will increase efficiency, or perhaps because all its competitors have installed computer systems. The company already may have a mainframe computer and the IT manager might suggest that some potentially suitable software packages be evaluated and that obtaining a ready-made package should be considerably less expensive than writing one from scratch. The first problem is to decide how the available packages should be evaluated and by whom. The people in the company who will use the proposed system ought to be involved in the selection process, but such people are unlikely to have much knowledge of computers and computer software although they may be familiar with word processing and spreadsheet systems running on their desktop computers, e-mail and the world wide web.

The IT manager and other computer professionals, either within the company or brought in from outside as consultants, will have an important contribution to make to the decision. Although they will have an intimate knowledge of computers, they will probably not have a deep knowledge of the particular application of the proposed software. Their priorities will differ. The computer people will want to know how the software will fit in with their portfolio of software, whether it will require additional computer equipment, how well it will be maintained, how portable it is and so on. There may follow a lack of communication and understanding between the computer professionals, the legal advisers, the ultimate users and the supplier of the software resulting in the purchase of a system which is cumbersome, does not provide all the information the users now realise they would have liked and which runs far too slowly to be of any practical use. The software company which supplied the package is not unsympathetic but claims that it was just not given clear and sufficient guidance as to what was expected of the software. The software company may even suggest that the problems will be overcome if new and more powerful equipment is obtained. An allegation that the problem lies with the client's own computer installation might be difficult to refute. It is at this stage that the contract is carefully examined, perhaps for the first time, and the company obtaining the software realises, too late, that as far as it is concerned, the contract is little more than worthless and does not provide adequately for the situation. The client might refuse to make the final payments and the ensuing legal struggle is both predictable and inevitable. IT personnel and independent computer consultants must educate department heads and legal advisers as to the implications and dangers involved in acquiring computer equipment and software. Departmental heads and legal advisers, for their part, must be prepared to ask questions of their computer advisers and, even more importantly, to listen to the answers.

The point of the above story is to demonstrate the importance of the parties to a computer contract knowing precisely what is to be expected in terms of performance and the standards required. The role that the equipment or software is intended to fulfil must be clearly identified and quantified; a comprehensive and precise specification must be drawn up. The lack of, or defects in, specification is probably at the heart of most disputes resulting from the acquisition of computer equipment and software.

The importance of choosing the most appropriate hardware and software should not be underestimated and, as a corollary, a contract which provides a reasonable and fair machinery for identifying responsibilities and resolving disputes needs to be negotiated. A mistake in the choice of equipment or software coupled with a poor contract can be disastrous for a purchasing company. The problems are not all one-sided, however, as it may be that a supplier of equipment or software has to fall back on contractual remedies. If the acquiring company refuses to provide, or is incapable of providing, clear instructions, if it refuses to accept and/or pay for the equipment or software, if it tampers with the programs, misuses them and allows employees to copy them freely, the supplier will need to take action. The company making the acquisition will need to decide:

- how the contract can protect it if the equipment or software fails to perform as it should;
- how it should be maintained and how its staff should be trained; and
- what to do if the software or hardware infringes a third party's copyright or patent.

Other decisions will concern the selection of the software developer or hardware supplier, the form of contract and whether a feasibility study or prototyping work is to be undertaken.

One thing is clear, whatever form of contract is used, and that is that great care must be taken in drafting the contract. Judges interpret contracts strictly and will use certain principles of construction when it comes to resolving inconsistencies and ambiguities. If a contract is silent on a particular matter, judges may if necessary imply terms to give the contract business efficacy on the basis of the presumed intention of the parties. A judge will not, however, write the contract for the parties. There must be, at least, something resembling a concrete agreement between the parties. It is certainly very unwise to use a form of contract designed for one jurisdiction in another, even though both have similar legal systems. In *Andersen Consulting* v *CHP Consulting Ltd* (unreported) 26 July 1991, ex-employees of the claimant set up in business on their own account, providing maintenance for the claimant's computer programs. The claimant argued that a term in their licence agreements prevented maintenance by third parties. Mr Justice Harman refused to grant an injunction in favour of the claimant and strongly criticised the use of an American contract which he described as having odd and inept phrasing. The contract should have been drafted to take account of United Kingdom law; it was simply not good enough to make a few modifications to an American form of contract.

In Chapters 16 and 17, the basic legal consequences of computer contracts will be described. The nature of the contract, contractual and tortious liabilities and the use of exclusion clauses will be considered. Individual terms which may be found in various types of computer contracts will then be discussed in subsequent chapters with a view to avoiding the disasters that await the unwary. Balanced, fair and thorough negotiation is the key to a smooth-running contract and all the relevant contractual terms and mechanisms should be considered and agreed before the parties become committed to the contract. The final chapter in this part of the book (Chapter 22) contains a summary and checklist of terms commonly found in computer contracts.

Chapter 16

Fundamentals of computer contracts

Terms of the contract

Sometimes, it may be difficult to determine whether a contract exists, particularly where there have been long and protracted negotiations. This aspect is discussed in Chapter 18 with some examples where a court has had to determine this in the context of computer contracts. Assuming there is a contract, it is important to know precisely what the terms of the contract are. Of course, in many situations where the whole contract is in writing, this might appear to be an easy matter, providing one is skilled in 'legalese', the technical legal jargon still commonly found in legal documents. But even here, things are not necessarily that straightforward and the law may insert additional terms into the contract or strike out some of the terms apparently agreed upon by the parties to the contract. This is notwithstanding the English tradition of freedom of contract – to the effect that the parties should be free to agree precisely what terms they want in their contract, though this principle has been somewhat compromised by legislation and implied terms.

A particular problem is where the contract is not in writing or is only partly in writing. An example of the latter is where a signed note or memorandum indicates that a contract exists but clearly does not contain all the terms on the face of it. For example, the note may state that Ace Software Ltd agrees to write process control software for Boris Boring and Drilling Co Ltd for the sum of £45,000. On its own such a note would be unenforceable because it lacks certainty. Apart from other missing information, there is no specification or other description of what is required of neither the software nor any time for delivery. In relation to oral contracts and contracts partly in writing, it will be a matter of submitting evidence of the other terms to give the contract sufficient certainty. To overcome some of these difficulties, the law may imply terms into the contract.

The first task is to look at what has been expressly agreed by the parties. The *express terms*, whether oral or in writing, may be the only terms of the contract, although this would be rare. In many cases, the law will imply terms into the contract, particularly as a result of statute. These *implied terms*, such as those implied into certain contracts by the Sale of Goods Act 1979 or the Supply of Goods or Services Act 1982 are particularly important and are discussed later in this and subsequent chapters. Sometimes, the courts may imply terms into a contract. However, this will only be done in limited circumstances as indicated by Lord Pearson in *Trollope & Colls Ltd* v *North West Metropolitan Regional Hospital Board* [1973] 1 WLR 602 where he said (at 609):

> An unexpressed term can be implied if and only if the court finds that the parties must have intended that the term form part of their contract: it is not enough for the court to find that such a term would have been adopted by the parties as reasonable men if it had been suggested to them: it must have been a term that went without

saying, a term necessary to give business efficacy to the contract, a term which although tacit, formed part of the contract which the parties made for themselves.

In other words, the term must be such as is necessary to make the contract effective and must be a term which the parties would clearly have agreed to have included had it been mentioned to them at the time. It is not enough for the term to be one which would be reasonable to include. The above sentiment was agreed with in the Court of Appeal by Sir Iain Glidewell in *St Albans City & District Council* v *International Computers Ltd* [1997] FSR 251 where he held that, in a contract for writing computer software without involving the transfer of property in tangible items such as magnetic disks, the court could imply a term to the effect that the software was reasonably fit for its purpose.

Often, the successful development and installation of software will be possible only if the software developer and client cooperate fully with each other. The case of *Anglo Group plc* v *Winther Browne & Co Ltd* (2000) 72 Con LR 118 gives an example of a duty to cooperate being implied by the court. The client did not want a bespoke system and a standard package was delivered but this meant inevitably that the client's other software systems would have to be modified to fit with the standard system. This required full cooperation between the parties and this was particularly important, as the client did not have the full technical knowledge of a computer professional. The judge said that, in relation to a contract for the supply of a standard computer system, it was an implied term that:

- the purchaser communicates clearly any special needs to the supplier;
- the purchaser takes reasonable steps to ensure that the supplier understands those needs;
- the supplier communicates to the purchaser whether or not those precise needs can be met and if so how they can be met. If they cannot be met precisely the appropriate options should be set out by the supplier;
- the supplier takes reasonable steps to ensure that the purchaser is trained in how to use the system;
- the purchaser devotes reasonable time and patience to understanding how to operate the system;
- the purchaser and supplier work together to resolve the problems which will almost certainly occur. This requires active co-operation from both parties. If such co-operation is not present it is likely that the purchaser will not achieve the desired results from the system.

As well as implying terms into a contract, the law may impact upon the express terms. It may make a term, agreed by the parties, void and unenforceable. Normally, this will be the result of a statutory provision. For example, a term in a software licence which prohibits or restricts the making of a necessary back-up copy of a computer program by a person having the right to use it under an agreement is declared void and unenforceable by section 296A(1) of the Copyright, Designs and Patents Act 1988. The Unfair Contract Terms Act 1977 is important in controlling the use of terms which try to exclude or limit liability for negligence and breach of contract, among other things. Another way the courts will control contract terms is by using the common law: for example, by declining to enforce a term which is in restraint of trade such as where a computer programmer's contract of employment prevents him working for a competitor of his employer for a period of five years without any geographical limitation. A common ploy in some contracts is where the party in the stronger bargaining position inserts some draconian terms and, knowing that the courts may interfere with them, seeks to save as many of them as he can. A 'saving' clause, sometimes referred to as a 'blue pencil' clause, may be worded as follows:

> **In the event that any provision of this agreement is unenforceable but would be enforceable if part of the wording of the provision were to be deleted, it shall apply with the minimum of such deletions being made as required to make the provision enforceable.**

Such terms are unlikely to be met with judicial favour. Judges will not write the contract for the parties and draconian terms may be consigned to the court's waste bin rather than the judge striking out the offending parts. The general rule, however, is that if a term is severable, that is, the contract can stand without it, the term will be deleted, leaving the rest of the contract in force. If the term in question is of fundamental importance to the contract, then the entire contract will be in jeopardy. Of course, the ploy of having draconian terms which may be unenforceable is that they may be accepted at face value by the other party and not tested in the courts. Nevertheless, great care must be taken not to attempt to take away certain statutory rights as to do so may result in criminal prosecution.

BCT Software Solutions Ltd v *Arnold Laver & Co Ltd* [2002] EWHC 1298 (Ch) concerned a contract to purchase software. The quotations submitted by the software developer made reference to developer's new and revised standard terms and conditions which were inconsistent with the terms expressly agreed by the parties. The terms expressly agreed treated the grant of the software licence and on-going maintenance as two separate issues and failure to continue to take and pay for support would not bring the licence to an end. The new standard terms and conditions made the licence to use the software conditional upon the client continuing to pay for support services. The software developer went into receivership and the claimant acquired the intellectual property rights of the software developer and the client informed the claimant it no longer wanted support. The claimant sought damages for the continued use of the software by the client. The court held that, in a case where any of the terms imported into a contract conflicted with those expressly agreed between the parties, the latter would prevail. Therefore, the client could continue to use the software and the claimant was not entitled to damages.

Entire agreement

In negotiations leading up to the formation of a contract, it is easy to make exaggerated claims as to the performance and specification of computers and software and the carrying out of obligations under the contract. Such representations, which may be in writing or oral or both, can prove troublesome later especially if one party's understanding of the representations differs from the others or if they conflict with the formal contractual documents. In some cases, it may be difficult to know whether a letter of intent or a letter setting out the client's requirements or the software developer's recommendations is part of the contract between the parties. To overcome such difficulties (and, in some cases, to prevent being bound by an exaggerated or false claim made earlier) it is common for the formal written contract to include a term to the effect that it represents the entire agreement between the parties. (In terms of the effect of false statements, see the section on misrepresentation later in this chapter.)

In *Watford Electronics Ltd* v *Sanderson CFL Ltd* [2002] FSR 19, a computer software contract was on standard written terms and included an entire agreement clause which added that no statement or representations made by either party have been relied upon by the other in agreeing to enter into the contract. At first instance, the judge considered that the second part of the clause was, in effect, an exclusion clause, excluding liability for misrepresentation and, that being so, subject to the test of reasonableness under section 3 of the Misrepresentation Act 1967 (as amended by the Unfair Contract Terms Act 1977). The Court of Appeal rejected that interpretation saying that section 3 applies only where a party has relied on the representation. Lord Justice Chadwick said that in a case where the parties have acknowledged in the contract itself that they have not relied on any pre-contractual representation:

> ... it would be bizarre ... to attribute to them an intention to exclude a liability which they must have thought could never arise.

Counsel for both parties in *Sam Business Systems Ltd* v *Hedley and Co* [2002] EWHC 2733 (TCC) considered that this part of the judgment in *Watford Electronics* was wrongly decided but did not advance any real argument as to why that was so. In that case, the contract also contained an entire agreement clause but added that it superseded all prior representations, negotiations, etc. (apart from fraudulent misrepresentation). However, by virtue of subsequent conversations and letters between the parties, the judge held that the software developer had waived the entire agreement clause.

The question as to whether an entire agreement clause also serves to exclude liability for false pre-contractual statements is not wholly clear. Obviously, the precise wording of the clause will be important. If it purports to exclude or limit liability for misrepresentation, then it will be enforceable only to the extent that it meets the requirement of reasonableness. If, as in the *Watford Electronics* case, it states that the parties have not relied on any prior representation, perhaps the better view is that it does seek to exclude liability for misrepresentation and is not subject to the requirement of reasonableness. This will, however, need a reversal of that part of the Court of Appeal's judgment in *Watford Electronics*.

Nature of the contract

It is not always easy to separate hardware and software and this fact has been demonstrated on several occasions in the courts. For example, in *Dyason* v *Autodesk Inc* (1990) 96 ALR 57, there was much confusion as to whether a 'dongle', a device required to be inserted into a computer before a program would operate, contained a computer program and in *Gale's Application* [1991] RPC 305, the trial judge (erroneously) drew a distinction between a program on disk and one hard-wired into a ROM chip. Such confusion is largely a result of the difficulty many lawyers have when dealing with a highly technical field such as computer science but it does not stop there. Even if the technological aspects are fully understood, the application of the law to them may still perplex.

Although there is some common ground and some similarity in other provisions, contracts for hardware and software are governed by different legal rules. Computer hardware, if it is sold, will be subject to the Sale of Goods Act 1979 and related consumer protection legislation, whereas an agreement to write software ('bespoke' software) will be within the scope of the Supply of Goods and Services Act 1982. There are other differences, for example, as regards the statutory controls over exclusion clauses. This simple distinction is not always easy to apply in practice because hardware equipment often incorporates software and the contractual position of 'off-the-shelf' software is far from clear. Nevertheless, the classification in terms of the legal nature of the transaction is important and the author's suggested approach is to look at the predominant purpose of the transaction. In other words, did the person acquiring the subject matter think that he was obtaining hardware or software?

Consider a person purchasing a new motor car. Motor cars are goods and the transaction is clearly subject to the Sale of Goods Act 1979, section 2(1), which states:

> ... a contract of sale of goods is a contract by which the seller transfers or agrees to transfer the property in goods to the buyer for a money consideration called the price.

The whole purpose of the transaction is to transfer ownership in the car. Suppose the car is faulty, however, and that fault is traced to a computer program installed in the electronic ignition system. The purchaser would still expect, rightly, to be able to obtain a remedy from the seller under the Sale of Goods Act even though he has not obtained ownership of the copyright subsisting in the computer program. After all, the buyer wanted to acquire a car not a computer program. Therefore, a contract to purchase a computer is a sale of goods contract notwithstanding the inclusion of computer software embodied within the computer. If other software is provided (often referred to as 'bundled') that will usually be subject to a separate, collateral licence agreement.

Contracts for the acquisition of software alone cannot be sale of goods contracts; the title to the software is not normally transferred nor are computer programs or databases 'goods'. The only proviso is that, as far as manuals, disks and packaging are concerned, we might have a collateral sale of goods contract. However, the predominant nature of the contract is the provision of a service, the function of the software being the service in question. This is so even if the copyright ownership is transferred, that is, if the agreement is an assignment and not simply a licence.

The nature of software contracts has long puzzled judges and legal writers. Certainly, in the case of software which is specifically written for a client, it must be a service contract as opposed to a sale of goods contract. Although some writers have focused on the fact that tangible items such as magnetic disks may be provided, suggesting a sale of goods contract, where software is delivered on-line or by loading it onto the client's computer, the nature of the arrangement becomes clearer. The delivery of tangible items in addition to the software has only served to cloud the reality of the transaction.

A case which involved a book gave an indication of the approach preferred by the author of this book. In *Ashley v Sutton London Borough Council* (unreported) 8 December 1994, the appellant, Ashley, brought an appeal against his conviction for an offence under section 14 of the Trade Descriptions Act 1968. The charge was that he had made a statement which he knew to be false as to the nature of services he provided in the course of a trade or business.

Ashley had supplied books by mail order which described a winning strategy to be used with fixed odds gambling and he guaranteed to refund the purchase price if customers were not satisfied. It was argued on his behalf that he had supplied books, not services, and, consequently, could not be guilty under section 14 which only concerns services not goods. The Divisional Court of the Queen's Bench Division held that, although goods were supplied (that is, the books), the essential nature of the contract was the provision of a service – the service of providing information. The book was merely the medium through which the information was imparted and the contract was, therefore, predominantly a contract for services and the appeal against conviction was dismissed. The same can be said in terms of software even more forcefully. It is a copy of the programs and/or data that the customer wants. As in the *Ashley* case, the high price of the information relative to the tangible items delivered confirms this. The fact that software can be transmitted without the need for a tangible carrier reinforces the view that software contracts are service contracts. At best, any tangible items delivered with the software give rise to a collateral sale of goods contract in respect of those items only. To return to the analogy with a book, sale of goods law will give a remedy if the book is physically defective: for example, if it falls apart or has pages missing. It will not give a remedy simply because the plot is not very good or if there are grammatical errors. Such defects relate to the information not the good itself.

Two software cases have reinforced the deceptive simplicity of that approach. In *St Albans City & District Council* v *International Computers Ltd* [1997] FSR 251, Sir Iain Glidewell said that computer programs are clearly not within the meaning of 'goods' for the purposes of the Sale of Goods Act 1979 and the Supply of Goods and Services Act 1982. However, at first instance, Mr Justice Scott-Baker accepted that software was goods within the Sale of Goods Act 1979 (although he did not have to decide the point) because '... it is difficult to see what it can be other than something to which no statutory rules apply ...'. Not a very convincing argument!

As has often been the case, it was a Scots judge who most ably defined the nature of a software contract in the context of a licence for off-the-shelf software. In *Beta Computers (Europe) Ltd* v *Adobe Systems (Europe) Ltd* [1996] FSR 367, Lord Penrose in the Outer House of the Court of Session in Edinburgh had to determine the nature of an agreement to acquire off-the-shelf software. He decided that the supply of such software for a price is a *sui generis* (unique) contract rather than a sale of goods contract or a hybrid contract. He considered the Copyright, Designs and Patents Act 1988 and concluded that the supply of the medium on which the program is stored must be accompanied by an appropriate licence conferred directly or by implication from the acquisition of the software. An essential feature of the arrangement was that the supplier undertook to make available to the purchaser both the medium and the right of access and use of the software.

There are some differences between English and Scots contract law and, at that time under Scots law, it was possible to grant third parties rights under a contract. Nevertheless, the judgment is an excellent analysis of the nature of a software contract and an important feature of the case was that the predominant purpose of the contract – that is, to acquire the right to use the software – would be subjugated if it were classed as a sale of goods contract. Subsequently, in England and Wales and Northern Ireland, the Contracts (Rights of Third Parties) Act 1999 gives third parties a right to enforce a contract if the contract expressly provides that he may or the relevant term of the contract in question purports to confer a benefit on him and the contract does not provide that the third party cannot enforce it. Certain types of contract are excluded such as an employment contract where, otherwise, a third party could enforce the contract against an employee. The third party may be identified in the contract by name or as a member of a class of persons or by answering a particular description. These provisions will facilitate the enforceability of software licences by the copyright owners in the case of off-the-shelf software.

Software acquisition

The most common method of acquiring computer software is by way of a licence which is granted by the copyright owner to the person or company acquiring a copy of the software, giving permission to use the software in return for the licence fee – the 'price'. The licence may be for a fixed, perhaps renewable, period of time or there may be no mention of duration, in which case it can be assumed that the licence will last as long as the software is subject to copyright protection. The copyright owner will prefer to grant a licence because he will want to retain the copyright in the software and be free to grant licences to others. The licence may be exclusive, however, which means that the copyright owner cannot grant licences to others in respect of that software. More usually, the licence will be non-exclusive so that the copyright owner will be free to grant licences to anyone else he wishes to. An exclusive licence might be appropriate in connection with bespoke software written for a client in accordance with the client's requirements, as described in Chapter 18. Sometimes, ownership of copyright will be transferred instead and this form of transaction is called an assignment of copyright but apart from transferring ownership of copyright an assignment, as with a licence agreement, will contain numerous other terms dealing with issues such as liability for defects, permitted uses, etc.

The special nature of computer software and the fact that a copy of software is usually acquired by means of a licence have several legal implications. To begin with, the Sale of Goods Act 1979 does not apply to computer software as such. This Act is very important in the commercial world; in addition to being a very comprehensive regulator of contracts of sale it implies important terms into contracts such as requirements that the goods must match their description, be of satisfactory quality and that the seller has the right to sell the goods. However, 'goods' are defined by section 61(1) of the Act as including:

> ... all personal chattels other than things in action and money.

It seems unlikely, even if the copyright is transferred with the computer programs, that an intangible computer program resident on a magnetic disk or installed on a computer chip is a personal chattel (as opposed to the disk or chip), because copyright is a 'thing in action' like company shares or a money order, to be contrasted with the more tangible 'things in possession' such as motor cars or computers. Copyright is thus excluded from the definition of goods. In any case, a licence cannot be a sale of goods contract as there is no transfer of property. The result of all this is that the terms contained in the Sale of Goods Act which are implied into a contract for the sale of goods will not apply to a computer software contract at least as far as the software is concerned. Any tangible items such as magnetic disks transferred with the software may be subject to a collateral contract (a subsidiary or parallel contract). This may seem unfortunate as these implied terms are a very useful weapon for the buyer and, in the case of consumer sales, the implied terms cannot be excluded or modified at all. In non-consumer sales the implied terms can only be so excluded or modified if the terms purporting to do this are reasonable in accordance with the Unfair Contract Terms Act 1977, sections 5–7. However, service contracts are also subject to statutory implied terms and, as a last resort, the courts would be likely to imply terms on the basis of common law and which, for practical purposes, would be likely to have a broadly similar effect.

Supply of Goods and Services Act 1982

The Supply of Goods and Services Act 1982 implies terms into contracts under which the property (ownership) in goods passes, and also into contracts for the hire of goods and contracts for services (Scotland continues to rely on common law rights). Some of the terms implied by the Supply of Goods and Services Act 1982 are similar to those implied by the Sale of Goods Act. Examples of contracts governed by the Supply of Goods and Services Act are hybrid contracts: that is, those which involve part services and part goods such as a contract for the painting of a portrait. In this particular instance the service is the actual act of painting; the goods are the canvas, frame and paint. The Act also governs a contract purely for services, such as a contract for a hair-cut. Has the Supply of Goods and Services Act any relevance for computer software contracts? As far as 'goods' are concerned, the situation is the same as with a sale of goods contract because the definition of goods excludes things in action of which copyright is an example. The 1982 Act will be particularly relevant, however, if an independent computer firm or a programmer is engaged to write a computer program as this should come within the meaning of 'service'. The draftsmen of the Supply of Goods and Services Act elected not to attempt to define 'service', probably in deference to the very wide variety of services offered both to consumers and to businesses. There is good reason to believe, therefore, that a contract for writing a computer program will fall within that part of the Act dealing with the supply of services – sections 12–16. The fact that goods such as manuals and floppy disks may also be transferred does not prevent the contract from being a contract for the supply of services (section 12(3)).

Expert systems and other types of software, including databases, which provide information or advice could, arguably, be construed as supplying a service and thus fall within the ambit of the Supply of Goods and Services Act 1982. If this view is taken by the courts, bearing in mind that 'service' is not defined in the Act, it will result in the appropriate terms from the Act being implied into a contract for the supply of such computer software systems. The dealer who supplies an expert system may be deemed to be supplying a service (that is, providing the advice available from the system) even though others, such as the experts who provided the knowledge used in the system and the makers of the system, are responsible (in a non-legal sense) for how the system operates. This is because section 12(1) of the Supply of Goods and Services Act 1982 states that a 'contract for the supply of a service means':

> ... a contract under which a person (the supplier) agrees to carry out a service.

It may sometimes be difficult to determine the identity of the supplier where computer software is obtained off-the-shelf. For example, if an expert system is obtained from a dealer, is he the supplier or is it the company which made the expert system? In other words, who is the contracting party? Two possibilities exist:

● either the contract is between the person acquiring a copy of the system (the 'acquirer') and the dealer;

- or it is between the acquirer and the software company, in which case the dealer acts as the company's agent.

The answer to this is of crucial importance because of the doctrine of privity of contract: only the parties to a contract can sue on it, except where covered by the Contracts (Rights of Third Parties) Act 1999 or the equivalent rule in Scotland. If the expert system turns out to be defective the acquirer will need to know who is liable. Apart from contract law there may be liability in negligence which does not depend on a contractual relationship and may even extend to others involved in the development of the system such as the experts who provided the knowledge contained in the system.

If a dealer has been asked to supply a suitable expert system it is possible that, by doing so, he carried out a service. By supplying expert systems, the dealer has enabled the advice-giving service to be performed and in some respects it is similar to the position where a supplier sub-contracts all or part of the work. The customer relies on the dealer to provide a suitable and effective system and, consequently, there is a duty on the dealer to select and recommend an adequate system (see *Stewart* v *Reavell's Garage* [1952] 2 QB 545). Therefore, dealers marketing expert systems should satisfy themselves as to the veracity and reliability of these systems and their suitability for particular customers. Dealers may also wish to consider including appropriate and reasonable exemption clauses in their supply contracts with respect to advice-giving computer systems.

The dealer as agent for the software company is a more likely interpretation if the acquirer specifies the system he wants. Of course, the fact that there will, invariably, be a licence agreement with the software company reinforces the view that the dealer acts as an agent to bring about the contract between the software company and the acquirer. The legal position is far from clear, however, and there is a lack of authority on this point. The situation is much simpler where software is written for and at the request of a client. This is a straightforward service contract between the client and the software developer and is covered by the Supply of Goods and Services Act 1982. This has been confirmed in *The Salvage Association* v *CAP Financial Services Ltd* [1995] FSR 654 in which the Official Referee in the High Court confirmed that a contract to develop new accounting software for a client was a service contract. He went on to imply into that contract section 13 of the Supply of Goods and Services Act 1982.

Section 13 implies a term that the supplier, if acting in the course of business, will carry out the service with reasonable care and skill. This restates the previous position at common law, that a person who holds himself out as being prepared to carry out a service is expected to exercise a level of skill that could be expected of a reasonably competent member of the relevant trade or profession. Therefore, if a firm engaged to write a computer program fails to measure up to the standards that would normally be expected from able computer programmers and the program is defective as a consequence then, *prima facie*, the firm will be liable in contract. It does not matter that the firm's employees tried their best; the question is: does the program meet this objective standard?

In the *Salvage Association* case it was held that there was a breach of section 13 and also a breach of an express term in the contract that the software developer would assign suitably qualified staff to perform the work. The staff originally assigned to write the software were insufficiently experienced in the use of ORACLE, the language in which the software was to be written.

Another term implied by the Supply of Goods and Services Act 1982 concerns the time for performance. Again, this only applies to suppliers acting in the course of business, although a similar term would have been implied at common law. Section 14 states that, in the absence of an agreed time for performance or an agreed formula to determine the time for performance, the supplier will carry out the service in a reasonable time. The Act also says that what is reasonable is a question of fact; that is, it depends on the facts of the case. The case of *Charnock* v *Liverpool Corporation* [1968] 1 WLR 1498 gives an example of an unreasonable time. The defendant garage was liable in damages because it took eight weeks to repair a motor vehicle when a normally competent garage would have taken about five weeks. A contract for the writing of computer programs should have detailed provisions about completion times and all section 14 does is to provide a net to catch those instances where there has been an oversight or when some additional or unforeseen work is required. What is a reasonable time will depend on the nature of the programs and their complexity, taking into account the time required for testing and acceptance.

Section 15 of the Act states that, unless the contract fixes the payment or a method of calculating payment, the supplier will be paid a reasonable amount. Usually, the contract will mention the fee, but this provision might be useful if the supplier takes on additional work at the request of the other party and no mention is made at the time of agreement of the charge for this extra work. It means that the supplier cannot, much as he might like to, charge an unreasonably high price. Comparative fees and prices for writing similar software would provide a good indicator of what is reasonable, although it would be sensible to include a mechanism for working out payment for additional work, such as by including a schedule of rates.

Hardware acquisition

As far as computer equipment (hardware) is concerned, this may be purchased outright or hired. If purchased then the Sale of Goods Act 1979 will apply and terms as to quality, complying with description, satisfactory quality, etc. will be implied into the contract, subject to any valid exemption clauses. There have been some important changes to this Act. The Sale and Supply of Goods Act 1994 replaced the old section 14(2) of the Sale of Goods Act 1979 (which required that goods were of merchantable quality) with a new requirement that goods must be of satisfactory quality. This is stated by section 14(2A) to apply if the goods meet the standard that a reasonable person would regard as satisfactory. Account is to be taken of the description of the goods, the price (if relevant) and all other relevant circumstances. In a welcome tightening of the implied term, section 14(2B) defines the aspects of quality to be taken into account, being:

- fitness for all the purposes for which goods of the kind in question are commonly supplied (this is simply a restatement of the previous law);
- appearance and finish;
- freedom from minor defects;
- safety; and
- durability.

This implied term is a condition in England, Wales and Northern Ireland in consumer sales and applies where goods are sold in the course of business. In terms of sales to non-consumers, it is a warranty rather than a condition if the breach is so slight that it would be unreasonable for the goods to be rejected. In Scotland, it is simply a term, the remedies depending on whether the breach is a material one. For a breach of condition (or a material breach in Scotland), the buyer may reject the goods without prejudice to any claim for damages.

The old requirement that goods must be of merchantable quality caused injustice in a number of cases. It did not appear that the goods had to be durable and the presence of minor defects did not necessarily render goods unmerchantable. For example, in *Millars of Falkirk Ltd v Turpie*, 1987 SLT 66, it was held that an oil leak from the power-steering unit of a new car did not make the car unmerchantable and, in *Bernstein v Pamson Motors* [1987] 2 All ER 220, an engine seizure in a three-week-old car that had covered only 140 miles did not render the car unmerchantable. Only occasionally did the courts seem to take a sympathetic view of the buyer's position: for example, in *Rogers v Parish (Scarborough) Ltd* [1987] QB 933 the Court of Appeal recognised that the buyer of a luxury car such as a Range Rover had a right to expect a vehicle that did not continually break down and suffer from rust.

In the context of computers, the courts also took a fairly narrow view of unmerchantability and in *Micron Computer Systems Ltd v Wang (UK) Ltd* (unreported) 9 May 1990, the High Court considered that the failure of a computer's hard disk was a perfectly normal teething problem and did not give the buyer the right to reject the computer. Of course, the buyer may still have a claim to damages in respect of such a defect. Now, because of the test of satisfactory quality, it is more likely that the buyer of a computer with a faulty hard disk would be able to reject the computer and insist on a refund of the purchase price. The same should apply if the computer has an intermittent but troublesome fault.

If the supplier goes beyond the mere supply of the equipment and carries out some work such as assembling and installing the equipment, the Supply of Goods and Services Act 1982 will apply, as discussed above. If the contract is for the hire of the equipment, then the Supply of Goods and Services Act will apply, whether or not installation or other services are also provided by the supplier. An agreement which is described as a lease or a rental is essentially a contract of hire, and a hire agreement is one under which the possession of the goods passes to the other party but the property in the goods (the ownership) remains with the supplier. 'Hire' does not include hire-purchase agreements, which are covered by the Supply of Goods (Implied Terms) Act 1973 – this Act implies similar terms into the contract as under the Sale of Goods Act 1979. The relevant provisions in the Supply of Goods and Services Act 1982 (sections 6–11) regarding hire agreements include implied terms about the right of the supplier to transfer possession of the goods, that the goods must correspond with their description and implied terms about quality and fitness for purpose (sections 7–10). These terms are equivalent to those in the Sale of Goods Act. Similar provisions for hire contracts in Scotland are in the Supply of Goods and Services Act 1982, sections 11G–11L.

Breach of contract

If a party to a contract is in breach of one or more of its terms, the remedy depends on the status of the particular term or terms which have been broken. The aggrieved party may want to repudiate the contract, treat the contract as discharged by reason of the other party's breach and recover any money he has paid out as well as any other expenses and losses suffered. In the *Salvage Association* case it was held that the client was entitled to repudiate the contract when it became clear that the software developer would fail to meet the extended deadline for delivery of the software. The client was entitled to £662,926 in damages being made up of:

- £291,388 paid under the contract;
- £231,866 wasted expenditure; and
- £139,672 wasted management time.

Alternatively, the injured party might prefer to hold the other party to the contract but would like some compensation for the breach and if the breach concerns a minor term this is usually the better solution. However, the injured party does not always have a free choice as the law lays down rules determining and limiting the scope of remedies.

Traditionally there are two types of terms in contracts: 'conditions' and 'warranties'. The distinction is important because breach of a condition gives the other party the right to repudiate the contract and claim damages. For example, consider a contract to deliver a computer by '1 June at the latest'. If the machine has not been delivered by that date, the buyer can treat the failure to deliver as a breach of a condition and he can cancel the contract as time for delivery is usually construed as being a condition (see *Hartley* v *Hyams* [1920] 3 KB 475). Furthermore, the buyer can claim damages that would be equivalent to the difference in cost of buying another similar computer elsewhere and any other expenses and losses he has been put to as a direct consequence of the breach, with the proviso that he mitigates his losses – that is, he keeps them to a minimum. The buyer may have wanted the computer to expand his business and he will be able to claim the resulting loss in profits, provided the seller knew or should have known of this – that is, it was in the reasonable contemplation of the parties.

On the other hand, a breach of warranty allows the aggrieved party to claim damages only. The contract is still in force and must be completed by both parties. They must both perform the remainder of their agreed duties under the contract. For example, if a supplier has agreed to deliver a computer system and the contract states that the terminals are to be a deep yellow colour but, instead, he delivers a computer with lemon coloured terminals, this will amount to a breach of warranty unless there is some special reason why the deep yellow colour was specified. The buyer will be entitled to damages only and he will still have to pay the purchase price of the computer, although he may be able to set off a sum representing the damages. Damages are assessed on the basis of the damage naturally arising from the breach and in the contemplation of the parties. In the example given, the damages would be likely to be nominal only.

In *Koufos* v *C Czarnikow Ltd* [1969] 1 AC 350, a ship was chartered by sugar merchants to transport a cargo of sugar. The ship owners knew that there was a sugar market at the port of destination but did not know that the merchants wanted to sell the sugar immediately on its arrival. The ship deviated from the agreed voyage and arrived about ten days late; in the meantime the price of sugar had fallen and the merchants lost over £4,000. It was held that this loss should be recoverable from the ship owners because they should reasonably have contemplated that the delay would have resulted in a loss. The ship owners knew there was a commodity market at the destination and that prices would be liable to fluctuate, so that any delay could lead to a diminution of the value of the cargo. Unfortunately, this does not appear to work the other way – the ship owners would not be entitled to any share in a windfall profit if the market value of the cargo increased dramatically and was sold for much more than it would have done had it arrived on time.

How does the basic principle that damages are based on the losses that were within the contemplation of the parties when the contract was made to work in the context of computers? Suppose that you run a computer bureau and carry out ordinary data processing work. You decide to expand the business and buy a more powerful computer to be delivered by a certain date. You tell the supplier that you need the computer to carry out some additional data processing but neglect to inform him that you are negotiating a very lucrative top secret government contract on the basis of having the new computer. If the computer is delivered late, then you would be entitled to damages based on the loss in profits in the normal course of business but you would not be entitled to anything should you lose the government contract. This is simply because the supplier did not know, and could not reasonably be expected to know, of this potential contract. A buyer should therefore consider informing a supplier of all the uses to which the equipment or programs will be put, especially if they are unusual.

The distinction between conditions and warranties is not always clear. Sometimes a contractual term lies in a grey area between the two. If the term is broken, then it will be classified in the light of the facts surrounding the breach and it will depend on the facts as to whether the breach goes to the root of the contract. If it does, then the term will be effectively promoted to the rank of condition with all that that entails; otherwise it will be classed as a warranty. These intermediate terms are called innominate terms and their nature is determined retrospectively, after a breach. The case which paved the way for this approach was *Hong Kong Fir Shipping Co Ltd v Kawasaki Kisen Kaisha* [1962] QB 26, in which it was held that a term implied in a hire contract for a ship that it must be seaworthy was such an innominate term. The nature of the breach determined the nature of the contractual term. For example, if the ship had a 5 degree list and was badly leaking it would be totally unseaworthy and this would be a breach of a condition enabling the hirer to repudiate the contract. However, if the breach concerned some trifling defect, perhaps a mere technicality, which could be put right very quickly and easily, the term would be classed as a warranty. For example, if a word processing program is acquired which is claimed by the supplier to be a 'professional package' and it does not have a built-in thesaurus, this might be considered to be a breach of warranty. It cannot be truly said that the breach goes to the root of the contract if the program has all the other usual features normally found in powerful word processing systems. However, if the package does not include features such as fully-functional paragraph formatting, a spelling and grammar checker, tables and frames this would be more serious and could make the system virtually useless in a business environment. Such a breach would go to the root of the contract and would be a breach of a condition, giving the person acquiring the program the right to cancel the contract and recover the cost of the system plus any direct losses.

This way of looking at terms and not deciding their status until there has been a breach is very useful as it gives a welcome degree of flexibility to contracts, although it could be criticised for introducing uncertainty. There may be some terms, however, which are obviously conditions: for example, if the contract is for the delivery of a particular make of computer, and the seller attempts to deliver a different make altogether, this would clearly be a breach of condition.

What sort of terms in computer contracts could be described as innominate terms? Suppose that a contract is made for the provision of hardware and software for a company's intranet. If the transmission of e-mails is slightly slower than provided for in the contract, that could be regarded as a breach of warranty, something the supplier would be expected to improve. However, if e-mails are continually being lost or corrupted and documents and other material placed on the server cannot be retrieved properly or the portal to the Internet does not function at all, these defects might be treated as breaches of condition, unless they can be overcome within a reasonable time by the supplier of the hardware and software involved.

Sometimes a term can start as a condition, become a warranty and then revert to a condition. In *Rickards* v *Oppenheim* [1950] 1 KB 616, the defendant wanted a body built on his Rolls-Royce chassis and he agreed that the claimant (from whom he had purchased the chassis) could use a sub-contractor to do this specialised work, which should have been completed in March 1948. The work was not complete by that time and, although time for delivery is usually a condition, the defendant did not cancel the contract as he was entitled to do, but continued to press for delivery, thereby waiving his right to cancel. In the end the defendant gave an ultimatum. He said that the car must be ready by 25 July 1948 and that he would refuse to take delivery after that date. The car was not ready by that date, so the defendant bought another car elsewhere and claimed back the price he had paid for the chassis. It was held that when time for delivery is of the essence of a contract for the sale of goods (that is, a condition) and, after the stipulated time has elapsed, the buyer waives his right to cancel by pressing for delivery, converting the term into a warranty, he may later give notice setting a reasonable deadline, once again making the time for delivery a condition of the contract.

It is not unusual for new software to be delivered late. In this case, the client must be careful when granting extensions of time and should bear in mind that he will hope to avoid fudging the issue of the date at which he can repudiate the contract on the grounds of the software developer's late delivery. It is essential that any extensions be agreed in writing with the new date being firmly stated as a condition. If this is not done, the client must allow a reasonable time when delivering an ultimatum to the software developer. It is not satisfactory to allow work to drag on for months and then to suddenly state that the contract will be repudiated if the software is not completed 'by the end of this week'.

It is common to find provisions for late delivery and late payment included in contracts. The contract might state that the supplier will pay £150 per week if he delivers late, or that the buyer will pay interest at 0.75 per cent above the current base bank rate, should he be late in making payment. Predetermined and agreed damages, known as liquidated damages, are frequently found in contracts. 'Liquidated' simply means that the damages or the method of calculating them are fixed and agreed. Liquidated damages are to be distinguished from a penalty. Liquidated damages are a genuine pre-estimate of the loss resulting from the breach, whereas a penalty, which might be out of all proportion to the loss suffered, will not be enforced by the courts. The stipulation of liquidated damages for breach of a particular term contradicts the possibility of that term being a condition. Terms backed by liquidated damages will usually not be regarded as conditions, therefore, unless the scale of the breach is considerable.

In practice, many terms will be innominate terms, in which case it will only be possible to determine whether breach of the term allows a party to repudiate the contract in the light of the actual facts of the breach. A similar approach applies in respect of the terms implied by sections 13–15 of the Sale of Goods Act 1979, as amended by the Sale and Supply of Goods Act 1994, in relation to the sale of goods to non-consumers. Under section 15A of the Sale of Goods Act 1979, in England, Wales and Northern Ireland, if the breach is so slight that it would be unreasonable to reject the goods, it will be treated as a breach of warranty. In Scotland, it depends on whether the breach is deemed to be a material breach.

Provisions concerning the performance of a computer system, how fast the programs work in practice and the degree of compatibility with other equipment are likely to be innominate terms. Terms probably classifiable as conditions from the outset deal with aspects such as the time for delivery and the description of the actual computer concerned. Time for payment is usually treated as being a warranty unless the contract states otherwise or the circumstances suggest a different interpretation (see, for example, section 10(1) of the Sale of Goods Act 1979).

By its very nature, when delivered, bespoke software often contains errors and it may be some time before they can all be traced and corrected. It is a brave software producer who claims that his software is error-free. The contractual position was considered in *Saphena Computing* v *Allied Collection Agencies* [1995] FSR 616. A contract for writing a number of programs was terminated while there were still errors in the programs. The Court of Appeal accepted that software was not a commodity that was handed over once and for all and that it would usually require testing and further modification. It would not, therefore, be a breach of contract to deliver software that might, initially, have a defect in it. Usually, the supplier would have a right and a duty to correct the errors within a reasonable time. In this particular case the client, who had a copy of the source code, could carry out error correction himself but, because he had brought the contract to an end, the supplier would cease to be liable for the remaining errors.

Misrepresentation

If you are negotiating with a salesperson with a view to acquiring computer software, he may make statements regarding the software and its performance. It is not unknown for a salesperson to describe the product in glowing terms and you would expect him to highlight the best features. Sometimes, he can go too far; he may be anxious to make a sale and may make statements which are simply untrue in an effort to try to induce you to buy the product. Some statements are so wild that no one is expected to take them seriously; these are sometimes referred to as advertising 'puff'. Examples abound from the second-hand motor trade: for example, an ageing car may be described as being 'immaculate'. Such statements are not to be taken seriously and the courts would not support a case brought on them. Less extravagant statements, however, if untrue, may give rise to remedies. The standing of the statement needs initially to be determined and it may be elevated to the rank of contractual term if the courts consider on the facts that this was the intention of the parties. If this happens then normal contractual remedies are available to the aggrieved party if the statement turns out to be untrue.

If the statement does not become incorporated into the contract, it is said to be a representation – something said in the course of the negotiations leading up to the contract itself. It may well induce the other party to conclude the contract, in which case a remedy may be available on the basis of misrepresentation if the statement turns out to be untrue. Obviously, if the party, to whom the representation is made, knows that the statement is untrue he will not have any remedy. He has entered into the contract with his eyes open to the true facts; the statement itself will not have influenced him.

There are three forms of misrepresentation:

- fraudulent
- negligent and
- innocent.

If the representation has been made fraudulently (or recklessly, not caring whether or not it is true), then at common law the remedy of rescission is available (setting the contract aside as if it had never been made at all), together with a right to recover any money laid out. Fraud may be difficult to prove; the person making the statement may simply say that he honestly believed, at the time he made it, that it was true. The Misrepresentation Act 1967, as amended by the Unfair Contract Terms Act 1977, made the situation more satisfactory. Rescission is the standard remedy for misrepresentation but this may cause hardship; therefore, in the case of negligent or innocent misrepresentation, a court may award damages in lieu of rescission by section 2 of the Misrepresentation Act. This is important because rescission is an equitable remedy and as such will only be ordered by the courts if the aggrieved party has acted promptly. Formerly, if the aggrieved party had already accepted the goods, the very fact of acceptance would mean that rescission would not be available.

Imagine that a company buys a computer. It is important that this computer is directly compatible with its existing equipment and the supplier confirms in good faith, before the contract is made, that the computer is compatible although the contract itself is silent on the matter. Some weeks after accepting delivery and paying for the computer, it is found that, although the computer works well in every other respect, it is not compatible with the company's other machines and cannot reasonably be made so. Before the 1967 Act, the company acquiring the computer would have no remedy for this innocent misrepresentation, unless it was deemed to be a contractual term, as it would be too late to have the contract set aside. Now the courts would be likely to award damages instead, which might be considerable in our example. The better approach would have been for the company to insist that an express term was inserted into the contract to the effect that the computer to be acquired must be compatible with the existing equipment.

Summary

In this chapter the basic nature, legal environment and implications of computer contracts have been discussed. Apart from the difficulties arising from classifying software contracts the law is relatively well settled. One remaining difficulty is to apply that law to computer technology. For example, how do we set the standards for reasonable care and skill and quality in relation to computer hardware and software? Fortunately, to date, judges have shown themselves reasonably well equipped to do this, though some doubts remain.

Of greater uncertainty is the potential for liability for defective software and this is something which is examined in the following chapter together with a consideration of the effectiveness of exemption clauses, limiting or excluding liability for defective software or, indeed, for breach of contract or misrepresentation. Case law has amply demonstrated the care that must be taken in this respect when drafting computer contracts.

Chapter 17

Liability for defective hardware or software

Introduction

There have been a number of occasions when defects in software have had very serious implications. The term 'safety-critical' is applied to software (and hardware) which is used in situations involving risk to life and limb. For example, in 1992 it was discovered that around 1000 patients at a North Staffordshire hospital had received incorrect dosages of radiation therapy because of an alleged fault in a computer program. Later that same year the London Ambulance's new computer system failed dramatically throwing the ambulance service into chaos and, possibly, resulting in a number of deaths caused by the consequential delays in getting ambulances to their call-out destinations. A flaw in Microsoft's Windows 2000 operating system allowed hackers to penetrate a computer server belonging to the United States Military (*BBC News*, 18 March 2003) and there were rumours that a software bug could cause Patriot missiles to lock onto the wrong target (*InfoWorld News*, 27 March 2003). A software bug was claimed to have caused a radioactive spill at a uranium processing plant in Australia in 2001. The bug was detected and corrected (*ZD Net UK News*, 30 January 2002).

Defects in computer equipment and software can cause all manner of damage. The failure of flight control systems, nuclear power station systems and defence systems could result in major loss of life. The same could be true of software used to design buildings and vehicles. Defects in other systems might result in financial loss only where an expert system is used to provide financial advice. The fact that organisations developing or supplying software or manufacturing and distributing hardware could be liable for the consequences of failure requires them to consider means of reducing or limiting liability and, while practical measures such as quality control and testing are of vital importance, regard must be had to the legal position regarding defects.

The 'Millennium Bug' focused minds in 1999 as regards the potential for disaster caused by 'computer error'. That particular problem was caused by the old (and now clearly perceived to be foolish) convention of only using two digits to store the year of a date. Thus, the date 4 August 1999 would be stored in a form equivalent to 04/08/99. Where a calculation is performed which involves dates, such as in determining the duration of some computer-controlled process or operation, it is obvious that things can quickly go wrong on or after 1 January 2000. The convention of using two digits for the year was a result of a desire to save what was then very expensive computer storage. Additionally, most programmers working in the 1960s and 1970s thought the programs they were writing would become redundant long before the millennium. In those days, in terms of the pace of development of computer technology, the turn of the century seemed a very long way off. In the event, nothing serious seems to have resulted from the Millennium Bug, apart from the considerable expense and work in checking and modifying older software systems.

If a person suffers loss or damage as a result of defective hardware or software, one or more of the following areas of law might provide a remedy:

- contract;
- law of negligence;
- negligent misstatement; or
- product liability.

The basic principles of contractual liability have already been discussed in Chapter 16 and often can provide the simplest route to a satisfactory remedy. If the aggrieved person is not in a contractual relationship with the person responsible for the loss or damage, or does not have the right to enforce the contract as a third party, other areas of law must be looked to for a remedy.

Once the risks and liabilities have been identified, the contract should provide a suitable mechanism for apportioning liability between the parties. As HH Judge Bowsher QC said in *Stent Foundations Ltd v M J Gleeson Group plc* [2001] BLR 134:

> **In all projects, the allocation of the risks of negligence and the duty to insure against those risks is a matter to be considered. Clear allocation of risk may reduce the likelihood of litigation or arbitration ... the parties should be clear and explicit in their contracts so that parties start a project with clear knowledge as to where the risks lie rather than disputing the allocation of risk when the project goes awry.**

Once risk has been allocated, insurance can then be obtained to cover the potential losses resulting from defects and from issues relating to the performance of the contract. This is important as recent case law has amply demonstrated that reliance on contract terms, limiting liability to a relatively small sum, is misplaced.

In this chapter, forms of liability for defects, other than contractual, are examined. The focus is upon the law of negligence, negligent misstatement and product liability. These areas are of particular concern because they impose liability in respect of loss or damage sustained by third parties. Finally, the legal control of exemption clauses and notices, which attempt to exclude or limit liability, is considered.

Negligence

Negligence is part of an area of law known as tort. Basically, a tort is a civil wrong, independent of contract. It imposes legal liabilities on a person who has acted carelessly or unreasonably omits to do something. Under certain circumstances a person will be liable to another for failing to exercise a required duty of care. In the case of consumer goods, such as a chair or television set, if the negligence of the manufacturer causes them to be defective, a person injured as a result will be entitled to damages. A claim in negligence does not depend on the presence of a contract, so if the person injured is someone other than the buyer, that person can still sue. The buyer also should be able to sue, but on the basis of breach of contract if the item is defective and fails to comply with implied terms such as those concerning satisfactory quality and fitness for purpose. To be able to sue in negligence, three essential ingredients must be present:

- a duty of care owed to the injured party;
- a breach of that duty of care; and

● consequential loss – that is, loss which is a direct and natural result of the breach of duty of care.

The landmark case on negligence is *Donoghue v Stevenson* [1932] AC 562, in which the claimant had been bought a bottle of ginger beer by a friend in a café. The bottle was made of opaque glass and so the contents could not be seen. The café owner poured part of the contents into a glass which the claimant drank. The claimant's friend then poured out the rest of the contents and the decomposed remains of a snail came out of the bottle. The claimant suffered shock and severe gastroenteritis as a result of the revolting sight and the fact that she had already swallowed some of the ginger beer. The claimant could not sue in contract because she was not a party to the contract – it had been her friend who had bought the drink. Nevertheless, the House of Lords held that a manufacturer, who sold food or medicine or the like in containers of a nature that the distributor or ultimate purchasers or consumers could not discover the defect by inspection, is under a legal duty to the ultimate purchaser or consumer to take reasonable care that the article is free from any defect likely to cause injury to health. This duty of care is owed to any person who might be contemplated to be injured by the act or omission of the manufacturer (the 'neighbour' or proximity test). Negligence can be thought of as an early form of product liability and has developed over the years to its present wide scope, although this is tempered to some extent by the growth of insurance. It is also limited, to some extent, by policy considerations. This is particularly so where the loss is purely economic or the claim is in respect of nervous shock or if a professional would be exposed to an unlimited number of claims from persons other than those for whom he performed his duties.

What is the significance of the tort of negligence as far as computers and software are concerned? Although it is unlikely that decomposing snails will be found within the workings of computers, it is possible to come across computer 'bugs' and there may still be some further nasty surprises. At first sight it may seem unlikely that computers and computer software could kill or cause serious injury; however, negligent liability does not stop at personal injury but extends to damage to property. Computer equipment runs on electricity so there is always the danger of electrical shock and, if this results from negligence, there is a strong possibility of an action in negligence. But what if a large passenger aircraft has to be fuelled ready for flight? A computer program is used to calculate the amount of fuel required. This is based on information such as the number of passengers, the weight of baggage, the flight distance and prevailing winds, etc. Then, because of a hitherto undiscovered bug in the computer program, less fuel is loaded than required, with the result that the aircraft runs out of fuel over the mid-Atlantic. It is possible that the company writing the computer program was negligent in its testing of the program. The total size of the claims resulting from such an incident might well be enormous, even though the copy of the computer program may have cost a relatively small amount.

Other nightmare scenarios include where an air traffic control system contains a software error which incorrectly records the location of an aircraft or where a railway signalling system contains a fault or where guidance software directs a missile with a warhead to the wrong location. Fortunately, most software errors do not have catastrophic effects but they can have very costly consequences if they are not detected and fixed. A simple error in software to assist self-employed persons to calculate their tax liability for the purposes of self-assessment of tax resulted in many people underestimating their tax liability bringing the possibility of fines from the Inland Revenue (*The Times*, 13 August 1997, p.5). The error was a mistake where pounds and pence were confused. In this case, most of the persons affected would have contractual remedies had they been charged interest on the underpayment on the basis of the licence agreement with the software developer (subject to any valid exclusion or limitation clauses).

The fact that an action in negligence lies without the need for a contract is important both for computer program writers and manufacturers of computer equipment. If a program is licensed by a publisher, the program author could be liable in negligence even though he is not a party to the licence agreement. In the case of computer hardware, a person suffering loss or injury as a result of the negligence of the manufacturer will have a claim in negligence against the manufacturer regardless of the fact that the equipment was bought from a dealer.

There are limitations, however, to the scope of the law of negligence and, as mentioned above, certain ingredients must be present. A person writing a computer program, or a company manufacturing computer equipment, will not necessarily be potentially liable to the world at large in negligence. The person/company will be liable, however, to those whom they could contemplate being adversely affected by any negligent act or omission by them. A further limiting factor is that the claimant bears the burden of proof; he has to show that the defendant was negligent and this is not always easy to do. There may be an exception if the event causing the injury or damage could only be reasonably explained by assuming there had been negligence. This is known as *res ipsa loquitur*, that is, 'the thing speaks for itself'. If you are hit on the head by a pot of paint while walking under a ladder you would not be asked to show the precise act of negligence that caused the paint to fall; it goes without saying that someone had been negligent. This is the exception, however, and normally the claimant must prove the negligent act or omission.

Even if negligence is proved, the amount of damages awarded may be reduced if the claimant has contributed in a causal sense to the negligence. If a computer has been badly made and is an electrical hazard then, if the person who has been electrocuted had tampered with the machine, the damages awarded may be reduced in proportion to the extent of his contribution to the accident. Fortunately, death or personal injury resulting from the use of a computer has been a rare occurrence, but other forms of loss or damage might be more common: for example, in a business context where a computer may be used to assist with decision making, there is a strong probability that a financial loss will be blamed on the computer. However, an action based solely on economic loss is unlikely to succeed under the normal law of negligence due to policy considerations. It may be possible in such a case to base an action on negligent misstatement instead, as described later.

Negligence and RSI

Many office workers spend long periods of time at a keyboard. By doing so, they may risk acquiring some form of cramp or painful condition in their wrists and fingers which is often described as repetitive strain injury (RSI). RSI is not, however, a medical term of precision, but for some time the Department of Health has recognised a condition known simply as PDA4 which is on a list of prescribed diseases for the purposes of industrial injury benefit. It is defined as cramp of the hand or forearm due to repetitive movements, such as writer's cramp. The types of occupations where it can occur are those which involve prolonged periods of handwriting, typing or other repetitive movements of the fingers, hand or arm.

The most important case to date on RSI (or PDA4) in the context of a word processor operator was *Pickford* v *Imperial Chemical Industries Ltd* [1998] 3 All ER 462. The claimant worked for the defendant for a number of years as a secretary and spent around 50 per cent of her time using a word processor. She claimed that, at times, that went up to 75 per cent. Eventually, she complained of pain in both hands and, after consulting a number of doctors and specialists, she commenced proceedings against her employer alleging negligence. She claimed that it was reasonably foreseeable that operating the word processor for long periods without breaks or rest periods would cause the condition and that the employer was negligent in failing to warn her of it and the need to take rest breaks. At the trial, the judge found that the claimant failed to establish the case against her employer but the Court of Appeal overturned that decision by a 2:1 majority. The employer appealed to the House of Lords which allowed the appeal by a 4:1 majority.

The majority in the House of Lords considered that the Court of Appeal was wrong to overturn the decision of the trial judge. All the relevant issues related to findings of fact and an appeal court will interfere with such a finding only in exceptional circumstances as it is the trial judge who has the benefit of seeing and hearing the witnesses including, in this case, a number of expert and lay witnesses. Lord Hope of Craighead made a number of observations as follows:

- PDA4 has two possible causes: one is organic and the other is that its basis is psychogenic (that is, 'it is all in the mind'), the product of conversion hysteria whereby the mind uses the body to escape from an objectionable working situation.
- Medical opinion is divided as to the cause.
- The trial judge rightly decided that the claimant failed to prove that the cause was organic and the defendant did not have to prove that the cause was psychogenic (the burden of proof lay on the claimant).
- The judge was right to hold that PDA4 resulting from typing work was not reasonably foreseeable, in the light of the state of knowledge at the time the claimant developed the condition (that is, in 1988–89).
- The nature of the work meant that the claimant had ample non-typing work to intersperse with her word processing and, consequently, there was no duty on the employer to prescribe rest periods.
- There was no duty on the employer to warn of the dangers of PDA4 – this was particularly so as issuing such a warning might bring about the condition, given that one possible cause was psychogenic.

Although the claimant failed in her claim, that does not mean to say that word processor operators and others who, as part of their work, spend long periods at a keyboard would also fail. In the present case, the claimant failed to prove causation – that is, that her injury was caused by the negligence of the employer. Indeed, the dissenting judge, Lord Steyn, said that among the 'tangled words and imperfect scientific insights' the central proved facts established that the claimant's work caused her disability and this could, had the employer exercised reasonable care, have avoided the occurrence of the disability.

One point to make is that it appears that an action might lie only if the court accepts that the cause is an organic one. If the court finds that it is a result of the mind (psychogenic), any claim is bound to fail. That is somewhat controversial, as to the sufferer the pain and discomfort will probably feel just as real and it might have been brought on by having to work at a keyboard at high speed for intolerable periods. In terms of causation, the injury will be the result of the work.

The case raises the question of what advice an employer should give to an employee about the dangers of working at a keyboard for long periods of time without breaks. To warn specifically of PDA4 might induce it in persons of a nervous disposition. The best approach, as was suggested in the above case, is to tell employees simply to go and see a doctor if unusual pain or discomfort is experienced. To warn word processor operators and the like that if they developed pain they would never work again was, in the words of one expert witness, 'disgraceful'. The defendant had an excellent record with respect to health and safety and gave advice to persons using computers with respect to eye-strain, ensuring that work stations were suitably designed and sited.

Computers have been claimed to be harmful to the health of the operator because of radioactive emissions, although at the present time there does not appear to be any conclusive proof that a real danger to health exists. If a definite association were to be found, however, between the occurrence of skin cancers or miscarriages and the continued use of computer monitors, then computer manufacturers and importers who continued to make or sell equipment giving off such dangerous emissions would be liable. There may also be implications under the Health and Safety at Work etc. Act 1974 if an employer persists in requiring his staff to use such machines. The producer would have to consider fitting some device such as an ionisation screen to absorb the rays and, in the absence of a technological way of overcoming the problem, might be forced to withdraw the product until such time as a solution could be found. As regards computer display screens, there is specific legislation dealing with their use and safety, extending to the ergonomic features of the computer equipment and the desk at which the computer operator sits (Health and Safety (Display Screen Equipment) Regulations 1992). These regulations came into force on 1 January 1993. Nowadays, most screen displays are designed to minimise radioactive emissions. Nevertheless, a good employer should ensure that the equipment and the manner in which it is used is not such as to give operators eye-strain or other injuries.

Negligent misstatement

It is in terms of expert systems or other items of computer software designed to provide advice that the potential for liability for negligence takes on special significance. If the system is used to derive advice for a professional to use in the execution of his duties, the ultimate recipient of the advice may find that he has a right of action against the professional or the system developer (or even the independent experts and knowledge engineers engaged by the system developer). The leading case on tortious liability for negligent advice, referred to as negligent misstatement, is *Hedley Byrne & Co Ltd* v *Heller & Partners Ltd* [1964] AC 465. In that case, the House of Lords concluded that a bank, giving information as to the liquidity of one of its own customers to another bank so that the latter could show the information to one of its customers, could be liable to that customer, even though the first bank did not know the identity of the second bank's customer – the ultimate recipient of the information. The fact was that the bank giving the reference must have appreciated that the information would be shown to a customer of the other bank and this was sufficient to satisfy the 'neighbour test'. Therefore, the required relationship exists where one person holds himself out as an expert and gives advice which is intended to be taken seriously and acted upon even though no contractual relationship exists.

This could have the effect of making the persons and organisations responsible for the creation of expert systems and decision-support systems liable to the ultimate consumers of the advice generated. The experts who provided the rules and facts used by the system, the knowledge engineers who formalised the knowledge, the programmers and analysts responsible for designing the inferencing and interface programs could all find themselves liable if the advice generated by use of the system is incorrect. There are, however, two factors which might negate or reduce liability. The first is whether a duty of care will be imposed and the second is the status of any disclaimer. Although the people involved in the development of the system are directly responsible for the performance and accuracy of the system, they have little control over the way the system will be used or interpreted. Unlike a simple bank reference where the significance and use of the information provided is fairly obvious, the advice obtained from an expert system or decision-support system depends on the interaction between the system and its user. As expert systems are designed for use by persons who have some general understanding of the knowledge domain, it is reasonable to assume that the user will take at least some of the responsibility for the output obtained. However, a professional such as a general medical practitioner who has to seek the advice of a specialist consultant will find it difficult to verify and validate the advice of the specialist and this is true also of expert systems and decision-support systems which contain knowledge beyond that of the user of the system. Lack of control over the use to which the information will be put does not in itself negate liability. The central issue is whether a duty of care will be imposed by law.

In *Caparo Industries plc* v *Dickman* [1990] 2 AC 605, it was held that there are three criteria for imposing a duty of care:

- foreseeability of damage;
- proximity of relationship; and
- the reasonableness or otherwise of imposing a duty of care.

In that case, a company bought additional shares in another company following receipt of audited accounts prepared by the defendant. The House of Lords said that liability for statements, put into general circulation in such circumstances that they might foreseeably be relied on by strangers, would only be imposed when the maker of the statement knew it would be communicated to the person relying on it either as an individual or member of a class and that it would be likely to be relied on for a known purpose. In the present case it was held that an auditor owed no duty of care to the general public nor to individual shareholders who relied on the accounts to buy shares because of a lack of proximity. To hold otherwise would give rise to unlimited liability on the part of the auditor. However, in allowing a claim by the intended beneficiaries of a will which should, but for the negligence of the solicitor acting for the person making the will (the testator), have been prepared before the testator died, the House of Lords, in *White* v *Jones* [1995] 2 AC 207, raised the spectre of widening the scope of persons to whom a duty of care was owed. Two of the five Law Lords dissented on the basis that this could lead to the recognition of an extensive new area of potential liability.

Advice produced using expert systems or other decision-support systems is nearer to the *Hedley Byrne* facts than those of *Caparo* v *Dickman* in which the primary purpose of the information was to comply with a statutory requirement; that is, having the company's accounts audited. Advice flowing from expert systems is intended to be taken seriously and acted upon. If the system is designed to produce advice as to trading in stocks and shares that is precisely the use to which it will be put. Therefore, the law of negligent misstatement ought to apply to such systems.

On the other hand factual software such as a database of vehicles performance lies nearer to the *Caparo* v *Dickman* case. The maker of the database has no clear idea as to the particular uses to which the data will be used, unless it has been sold for a specific purpose. Thus, the maker of the database should not be liable to a third party in respect of a mistake contained within it. He may be contractually liable, however, to the purchaser of a copy of the database. Of course, many computer systems lie between these two extremes.

In the *Hedley Byrne* case, the bank providing the advice was able to escape liability because it had printed a clear disclaimer on the information excluding legal responsibility for the advice. Since the *Hedley Byrne* case, the Unfair Contract Terms Act 1977 was enacted to control, *inter alia*, exclusion or limitation of liability for negligence, whether under contract or tort. As far as business liability for death or personal injury is concerned, it cannot be excluded or limited by a notice or term in a contract. In other cases, the notice or term must satisfy the requirement of reasonableness. Furthermore,

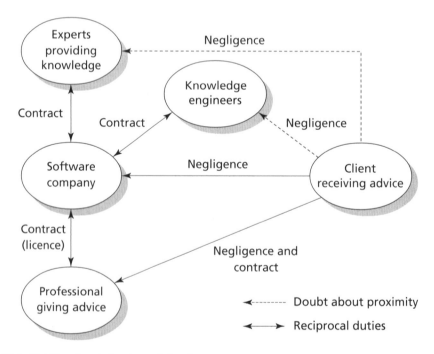

Fig. 17.1 Liability for defective advice from an expert system
Note: For a duty to arise in negligence, owed to the client by anyone other than the person giving advice, it would have to be shown that the client relied on that person's statement rather than on the statement of the person giving advice.

the use of a disclaimer will be effective only if it is clear and unambiguous and drawn to the attention of the person relying on the advice. Figure 17.1 shows the potential liability (tortious and contractual) with respect to incorrect advice derived from a defective expert system. It assumes that the experts and knowledge engineers are consultants to the software company and not its employees (this will be a common arrangement in practice).

The person using an expert system to advise a client will be potentially liable under the laws of contract and negligence. Liability will not be avoided simply because the system has a fault and the same principles apply here as in the case of conventional computer software. It might be important to consider whether it would be reasonable for the person using the system for the purpose of advising others to rely on the system's output. In relation to the exercise of a profession such as medicine, the fact that a person has acted in accordance with practice which is recognised as proper by a responsible body of persons skilled in that profession means that there has been no negligence. In *De Freitas* v *O'Brien* [1995] 6 Med LR 108, however, the Court of Appeal stressed that a responsible body of expert opinion does not have to be a substantial body. A small number of specialists could constitute a 'responsible body'.

Consider an expert system designed to recommend financial investments which is used by a responsible body of financial advisers. If a particular financial adviser uses the system to recommend an investment to a client, the adviser will not be negligent if the system was used in a reasonable and satisfactory manner, even if the advice turns out to be bad retrospectively. The problem is that, until such time as a particular expert system is used by a sufficient number of skilled practitioners (sufficient to be classed as a responsible body), anyone using an expert system is taking a chance should the advice turn out to be wrong, although it must be stressed that the fact that advice is wrong does not inevitably and conclusively mean that there has been negligence. In *Whitehouse* v *Jordan* [1981] 1 All ER 267, the House of Lords confirmed that an error of judgment does not automatically indicate negligence; it depends whether the error would have been made by a reasonably competent professional man professing to have the standard and type of skill that the defendant held himself out to have. If the person using the expert system does not have the degree of skill and knowledge contained in the system he should make this clear to the client and obtain his agreement prior to using the system. The advantage of negligent misstatement over normal negligence claims is that it can be used where the loss has been economic only, although it is not restricted to this.

Liability for indirect statements

Where the original maker of the statement does not directly communicate it to the person relying on it, it appears that for a duty of care to arise, the latter must realise who is the source of the statement. In *Abbott* v *Strong* [1998] 2 BCLC 420, a firm of accountants made statements as to a profits forecast, which were included in a circular sent to shareholders inviting them to subscribe for new shares in a rights issue. It was held that the accountants were not potentially liable for any misstatement to shareholders who subscribed as they had not relied on the accountants' statement. Where a person makes a statement to another person who uses it to advise another but that other does not know of the first person's participation in the advice, then the recipient cannot be said to have relied on the first person. Thus, where a person uses computer software in order to advise a client who believes that the advice comes from the person using the software alone, then any person who has been involved in the development of the software cannot be liable to the client in tort. Of course, this will be different if the client knows that the advice derived from using the software emanates from a person or persons involved in the development of the software, such as in the case of an expert system which contains rules and advice set forward by a particular person.

This approach is based on the concept of reliance. The person originally giving the advice cannot be liable if the ultimate recipient is shown not to have relied on that person but on advice given by another (even if originally given by that person) and can be contrasted with *Hedley Byrne* where it was clear that the recipient of the advice did indeed rely upon the first bank. The recipient's bank was merely the messenger. Thus, if a patient, Tom Cobb, consults a general practitioner, Dr Akerman, in respect of an illness and the doctor uses diagnostic software which includes diagnostic rules and suggested treatment devised by a specialist, Mr Rudge, he will not have a claim against Mr Rudge as he does not rely on him. It is Dr Akerman on whom Tom Cobb relies. It would be different if Dr Akerman first told Tom Cobb that he was going to use a computer system which contained advice from Mr Rudge, a specialist in the field.

The need for reliance does not necessarily require that the recipient of the statement knows the precise identity of the person from whom the advice originated providing that he knew it came from some other person. Reliance as an essential ingredient in an action for negligent misstatement was confirmed by the House of Lords in *Williams* v *Natural Health Foods Ltd* [1998] 2 All ER 577. In that case it was held that a director of a franchisor company (the franchise was in respect of health food shops) was not liable to the franchisees for loss resulting from negligent advice *given by the franchisor company* as there was no evidence that the franchisees believed that the director was undertaking a personal responsibility to them. In the example given in Figure 17.1, if liability for negligent misstatement is to be imposed on anyone other than the professional giving the advice directly to the client, it would be necessary to show that the client relied on any statement made by that person.

Negligent provision of a service and concurrent liability

At first, it was thought that *Hedley Byrne* was limited to negligent statements but it is now apparent that it also applies to the negligent provision of a service. In *Henderson* v *Merrett Syndicates Ltd* [1995] 2 AC 145, discussed later, Lord Goff said that there was no reason why a person should not be liable under the *Hedley Byrne* principle for economic loss which flows from the negligent performance of a service, and this sentiment was approved in *Williams* v *Natural Health Foods Ltd* [1998] 2 All ER 577. The provision of the service must be coupled with a concomitant reliance and will often be set in the context of a contract. This brings into question whether there can be concurrent liability under contract and tort where, for example, a service is provided under a contract.

At one time it was thought that where there was a contract between the parties, that contract would provide the sole basis for the injured party seeking a remedy. At least liability in negligence could not be imposed if it contradicted the express terms of a contract. However, the position was clarified in *Henderson* v *Merrett Syndicates Ltd* [1995] 2 AC 145, where the main issue was whether the defendants (managers of syndicates at Lloyd's) could be liable concurrently in contract and tort to Lloyd's underwriters for the negligent management of syndicates to which the underwriters belonged.

The House of Lords held that such concurrent liability can exist unless the contract itself precludes it. This means that in many cases, the injured party may choose whether to sue on the contract or in tort. Although in many cases the outcome will be the same in practical terms, in some the contractual and tortious duties may be different and the limitation periods may be different. The limitation period is the time within which an action must be commenced, otherwise it will be time-barred. For contract it is six years from the breach (Limitation Act 1980, section 5), while for negligence (and negligent misstatement) generally it is six years from the date the damage occurred (Limitation Act 1980, section 2); although for personal injury cases, the period is three years.

As an example of the above principles, consider a situation whereby Conway Computer Systems Ltd has agreed to maintain for one year the computer system of Willett & Co Ltd, a company with a parcel delivery operation. The contract states that Conway will remedy any defects within 24 hours of being informed by Willett and there is a clause in the contract providing for the payment of £500 per day in liquidated damages by Conway for every 24-hour period in excess of the first such period during which the computer system remains out of action because of a defect. One day, Willett informed Conway of a fault on its computer system. Due to the negligence of its programmers, Conway took 72 hours to remedy the defect. Under the contract Conway is liable to pay £1000 to Willett. However, under the circumstances, Willett's operations were badly disrupted and its total loss was in the order of £15,000. It was reasonably foreseeable that Willett would be so affected by its computer system being inoperable for such a period of time. That being so, the damages arising out of negligence ought to be in the order of £15,000, whereas, under contract, they are only £1000. Although, theoretically, there are concurrent liabilities in contract and tort, it would be highly unlikely that a court would allow Willett to pursue a remedy in tort as the contract has an express limitation on the measure of damages for failure to repair the defect in time. If the limiting clause did not exist, however, it would seem that Willett could be free to chose which route to pursue. This might be advantageous, particularly if the duty of care under the contract is of a lesser standard than that under the tort of negligence.

Product liability

Related to negligence are the product liability provisions contained in the Consumer Protection Act 1987. Under the Act, an ultimate consumer can claim against the producer of a defective product regardless of the lack of a contractual relationship between the consumer and the producer and without having to show the basic requirements for an action in negligence. Part I of the Act deals with product liability and stems from Council Directive 85/374/EEC of 25 July 1985 on the approximation of laws, regulations and administrative provisions of member states concerning liability for defective products (OJ L 210, 07.08.1985, p.29). A 'product' is defined by the Consumer Protection Act as being any goods including electricity and includes a product comprised in another product whether a component part or a raw material or otherwise. A computer would therefore come within the meaning of product but computer software, *per se*, will be outside the scope of this part of the Act.

Although product liability does not appear to apply to software it will apply to a defective product which incorporates software such as a computer-controlled microwave oven. There would seem to be no reason why liability on the basis of product liability should be avoided even if the defect which causes the damage lies within the software. A defect in software controlling a microwave oven or any other product will result in the microwave oven itself being defective.

The producer of a defective product is liable for damage resulting wholly or partly from that defect. Distributors and retailers selling 'own brand' goods can be liable if they can be said to be holding themselves out to be the producer. If a person imports a product, in the course of business, into a country belonging to the European Community from outside the Community in order to supply the product to another, then that importer will be regarded as the producer for the purposes of determining liability by section 2 of the Act. This might have implications for the many companies which import computers made outside the European Community, especially importers who affix their own name to the equipment. If one of these machines is defective and someone is injured as a result, then the importer/distributor will be liable under the Act, apart from any remedies available against him under contract. The Consumer Protection Act also makes a supplier liable if he fails to identify the producer within a reasonable time, having been asked to do so by the claimant.

A defect is defined by reference to the expectation of safety in the product and this relates to property damage as well as death and personal injury. A computer with an exposed unearthed metal chassis would fall short of the expectation of safety.

State of the art defence

An important defence is the 'state of the art' defence contained in section 4(1) of the Consumer Protection Act 1987. This provides that it is a defence in any civil proceedings to show that 'the state of scientific and technical knowledge at the relevant time was not such that a producer of products of the same description as the product in question might be expected to have discovered the defect if it had existed in his products while they were under his control'. This defence would apply, for example, where a product failed suddenly as a result of a form of material fatigue hitherto not widely known amongst producers of such products. The defence as set out in the Act has been criticised as introducing a subjective element as it is a question of whether the producer might be expected to discover the fault, not whether a reasonable producer would be expected to discover the defect. The Directive seems to imply a more objective test as it requires the state of scientific and technical knowledge to be such as to enable the existence of the defect to be discovered. However, in *Commission of the European Communities* v *United Kingdom* [1997] ECR I-2649, the European Court of Justice concluded that the Act validly implemented that part of the Directive and rejected the Commission's argument that the United Kingdom had widened the defence so that the strict liability imposed by the Directive had been turned into mere liability for negligence. As Part I of the Consumer Protection Act 1987 is stated to be intended to comply with the Directive and shall be construed accordingly, it would appear that the courts in the United Kingdom are likely to interpret the 'state of the art' defence on an objective basis.

A possible application of the defence is in the aeronautical industry, for example, where software companies develop sophisticated software for 'fly-by-wire' aeroplanes. Imagine there are two such companies: one is a very large company, Goliath plc, with enormous resources at its disposal whereas the other company, David Software Ltd, is much smaller, being a new entrant into this field, and having proportionally less resources. As a result of considerable research and testing, Goliath is aware of an inherent danger in such software in that it takes a short period of time for the pilot to override the computer software. Consequently, Goliath has incorporated an emergency override command in its software. David Software is not aware of this problem because it has not been published by Goliath and David Software has not carried out sufficient research to detect the problem. If the test in section 4 of the Consumer Protection Act 1987 is subjective, David Software might be able to avail itself of the defence but is less likely to if, as it appears it should be, the test is objective.

The defence is most likely to be relevant in leading-edge technology where new types of products are being developed. This is particularly so where computer technology is being used in process control, traffic control, guidance systems and the like. Consider, for example, the implications of a car with a computer software designed to apply the brakes in an emergency, say if the traffic in front comes to an abrupt standstill. One day a cat runs across the road in front of the car. The software interprets the image of the cat as a stationary object immediately ahead and brings the car to an emergency stop. A lorry following the car runs into the back of it injuring the occupants. Who is liable? The company making the braking system could be potentially liable subject to the state of the art defence (a product includes a product comprised in another product as a component part). The lorry driver, and his employer, may also be liable in negligence.

Extent of liability

Under section 5 of the 1987 Act, the liability covered by Part I of the Act extends to:

- death or personal injury;
- damage to or destruction of any item of property (including land) other than the defective product itself (there is a lower threshold of £275 before a claim can be made) provided that the property:
  - is the type normally intended for private use and consumption, and
  - it is used mainly for the private use or consumption of the person claiming.

Therefore, in dealings between businesses, the product liability part of the Act will only apply to defective products causing death or personal injury. As far as property damage is concerned, the provisions are really aimed at the consumer market, so, if you buy a computer as a present for your aunt and, because of a fault it catches fire and causes £1500 of damage to her house, your aunt will have a claim under the 1987 Act against the manufacturer of the computer for the damage to the house and furniture. Personally, you may have a separate claim against the retail outlet because the computer was not of satisfactory quality under the Sale of Goods Act 1979.

Criminal liability for defective products

Part I of the Consumer Protection Act 1987 imposes civil liability on producers. However, if a person is killed as a result of a defective product and the defect is attributable to the negligence of any person, that person could be exposed to a prosecution for manslaughter. This could even expose a company to prosecution if the negligence of a senior officer of the company is the root cause of the negligence and this is imputed to the company on the basis that the acts of its senior officers are the acts of the company.

Apart from liability for manslaughter resulting from defects in safety critical systems, there are numerous statutes which impose criminal liability and which may be triggered by a computer defect. Examples include the Health and Safety at Work etc. Act 1974, the Food Safety Act 1990 and the Environmental Protection Act 1990. An offence might be committed under the Food Safety Act where a computer is used to calculate cooking times and underestimates safe times because of a defect. A pollution control system run by a computer may result in an offence under the Environmental Protection Act 1990 if toxic substances are released into a stream without treatment because of a software error. The areas where civil and criminal liability may result from the use of defective computer technology are immense and, with the growth of safety legislation and environmental protection law, these areas are increasing rapidly.

The General Product Safety Regulations 1994 impose criminal liability on producers and distributors in respect of products that are not safe. A 'product' means any product intended for consumers or likely to be used by consumers, whether new, used or reconditioned. A 'safe product' is one which, under normal or reasonably foreseeable conditions of use, including duration, does not present any risk or only the minimum risks compatible with the product's use considered as acceptable and consistent with a high level of protection for the safety and health of persons. Amongst other things, account is to be taken of the product's characteristics, presentation (including information given) and categories of consumers at serious risk (for example, children). There is a defence of due diligence.

These Regulations are highly relevant in terms of second-hand computer equipment and any electrical equipment sold to children. In terms of software the same difficulty will apply as identified above – that is, that it is unlikely that software will be deemed to be a product although it is possible that the disks and other tangible items supplied with the software may be so classed.

Exemption clauses

An exemption clause is one which excludes or restricts the liability of a party who is in breach of contract. Exemption clauses can be sub-divided into exclusion clauses and limitation clauses. An exclusion clause gives the party relying on it total exemption for the breach whereas a limitation clause limits liability to a specified amount. An example of an exclusion clause is where a supplier totally excludes his liability under the contract for late delivery if this is caused by circumstances beyond his control such as industrial action. An example of a limitation clause is where a supplier of computer software limits his liability for faulty software to the licence fee he has received for that software.

When people draft contracts they are usually keen to limit or exclude their liabilities and yet wish to ensure that the other party is absolutely bound to perform his part of the contract. Such one-sided contracts were fairly common in the past (they are by no means extinct now), particularly in circumstances where there was an inequality of bargaining power. An ordinary individual buying a product from a supplier who had a monopoly in the product had little choice but to accept the terms imposed on him or manage without it. A golden principle in contract was 'freedom of contract' meaning that the parties should be free to agree whatever terms they wished. This doctrine was acceptable where two powerful companies were negotiating a contract in a free market, but contractually weaker persons suffered. Over the years, however, Parliament and the courts have intervened to mitigate the harshness of the situation and certain terms are now implied into sale of goods and similar contracts, while exclusion clauses have been disapproved of by the courts, especially if such clauses are demonstrably unfair.

The courts developed techniques to limit the effects of exclusion clauses, including the interpretation of an ambiguous clause to the disadvantage of the party seeking to rely on it. For example, in *Andrews Brothers (Bournemouth) Ltd* v *Singer & Co Ltd* [1934] 1 KB 17, the claimant ordered a new Singer car from the defendants. When the car was delivered it was found to have done some 550 miles. The defendants sought to rely on an exclusion clause which stated that liability for terms implied by statute was excluded; one of these terms was that goods must comply with their description. The contract, however, repeatedly described the car as a 'new Singer car'. It was held that, because the car was referred to in the contract as a new car, this was an express term and since the exclusion clause sought to exclude liability for implied terms only, the defendants were liable. The exclusion clause was of no effect for this breach of an express term. The claimant was awarded £50 in damages.

More importantly nowadays, exemption clauses are also controlled by statute. The Unfair Contract Terms Act 1977 limits the extent to which liability can be excluded or limited for breach of contract, or for negligence, or under the terms implied by the Sale of Goods Act 1979 and other legislation containing similar provisions, such as the Supply of Goods and Services Act 1982. Sections 2–4 of the Unfair Contract Terms Act apply to contractual terms or notices which attempt to exclude or restrict liability for negligence and breach of contract. (The equivalent provisions for Scotland are sections 16–18 of the Unfair Contract Terms Act 1977.)

A person may seek to exclude or limit his liability for negligence by means of a notice or a term in a contract. Whether the liability arises in tort or contract, the legal controls are the same and mainly result from section 2 of the Unfair Contract Terms Act 1977. This applies to business liability for negligence whether a breach of a contractual obligation to exercise reasonable care and skill in the performance of a contract or a breach of an equivalent common law duty. Section 2 of the Act prohibits the exclusion or limitation of liability for death or personal injury resulting from negligence, while liability for other loss or damage may only be excluded or restricted in so far as the term or notice satisfies the requirement of reasonableness. Section 11 of the Act provides that a term in a contract is reasonable if it is fair and reasonable to have been included in a contract having regard to the circumstances which were, or ought reasonably to have been, known to or in the contemplation of the parties when the contract was made. In relation to a notice, the test is whether it is fair and reasonable to allow reliance on it having regard to the circumstances. By section 11(4), where the term or notice seeks to limit liability to a specified sum of money, regard must be had to the resources available to the person who would have to meet the liability and how far it was open to that person to take out insurance cover. The burden of proof is on the person claiming that the term or notice is reasonable.

In terms of defective hardware, the basic provisions of the Unfair Contract Terms Act work reasonably predictably but it is in respect of software that doubts were expressed as to the reach of the Act, and this has been the source of some speculation. This is because, as regards England, Wales and Northern Ireland, Schedule 1, paragraph 1 to the Act states that:

Sections 2 to 4 of this Act do not extend to – . . .

(c) any contract so far as it relates to the creation or transfer of a right or interest in any patent, trade mark, copyright or design right, registered design, technical or commercial information or other intellectual property . . .

One view was that the important provisions in section 2 (liability for negligence), section 3 (contractual liability for breach or in relation to performance) and section 4 (unreasonable indemnity clauses) were inapplicable to software contracts because the essence of most software contracts is the granting of a licence to use the software – the creation of a right under copyright law. A number of software companies considered that they could largely ignore the effects of the Unfair Contract Terms Act 1977 and exclude or strictly limit their liability for defects. The courts have taken a more restrictive approach, however, to the scope of paragraph 1 of Schedule 1.

In *The Salvage Association* v *Cap Financial Services Ltd* [1995] FSR 654, the claimant invited tenders for the computerisation of its accounts system. The defendant submitted a successful bid for a feasibility study (strategy study and definition stage) and was awarded the contract in the sum of £30,000. Following this, a second contract was awarded to the defendant to develop and implement the software specified in the feasibility study. The date for completion of the second contract was 18 July 1988 and the contract price was £291,654. The system was to be implemented using ORACLE, a fourth-generation language operating as a relational database management system. In July 1988, the software was declared to be ready for user-training but almost immediately it became apparent that it was unusable and contained a large number of errors that would require substantial work to correct. Many of the errors could be attributed to the fact that the defendant's project team was not sufficiently experienced in the use of ORACLE. Nevertheless, the claimant persevered and allowed additional time for the defendant to complete the work satisfactorily. Several new dates for delivery were agreed but, eventually, it became clear to the claimant that the work was likely never to be completed satisfactorily and, on 13 July 1989, the claimant terminated the contract because of the serious breaches of contract on the part of the defendant.

The claimant argued that it was entitled to reject the system and terminate the second contract and claimed damages of £855,550 (being the sum of £291,388 already paid under both contracts and £564,162 for wasted expenditure resulting from the defendant's breaches of contract). The defendant sought to rely on limitation clauses in its standard form contract which formed the basis of the first contract and, in relation to the second contract, terms which purported to exclude liability except as provided for by the contract and, in any case, to limit liability under that contract to £25,000. The limit in the first contract was £250,000 in respect of physical damage and £25,000 for other loss or damage (except for liability for death or physical injury where there was no limit).

Both contracts contained terms to the effect that the defendant would assign appropriately qualified staff to perform the work and the judge in the High Court held that there was a breach of these terms. Furthermore, the judge implied a term under section 13 of the Supply of Goods and Services Act 1982 to the effect that the defendant would exercise reasonable care and skill and held that the defendant was also in breach of this term. The time for completion of the second contract was extended on a number of occasions but the judge held that time was of the essence and the extensions agreed by the claimant did not alter that simple fact. The claimant's patience had been stretched to the limit and it was entitled to repudiate the contract at the time it did.

If sections 2 and 3 of the Unfair Contract Terms Act 1977 applied to the limitation clauses, they would be upheld only in as much as they met the requirement of reasonableness – otherwise the defendant would probably be able to rely on them. The judge decided that paragraph 1 in Schedule 1 only concerned those provisions in a contract that dealt with the creation or transfer of a right or interest in the relevant intellectual property and did not extend to all the other terms of a service contract simply because the service will result in a 'product' that is subject to intellectual property rights. Thus, terms concerned with aspects of the contract other than those relating to the creation or transfer of an intellectual property right are still subject to sections 2–4 of the Unfair Contract Terms Act 1977. In other words, paragraph 1(c) does not create a blanket exception for software contracts.

As mentioned above, the reasonableness test is expressed in section 11 of the Act. Schedule 2 provides guidelines for the application of the reasonableness test and, though expressed as being applicable only to sections 6 and 7 of the Act, the judge accepted the suggestion of Potter J in *Flamar Interocean Ltd* v *Denmac Ltd (The Flamar Pride)* [1990] 1 Lloyd's Rep 434 that it would be sensible to take the guidelines into account in such cases. He referred also to the judgment of Lord Griffiths in *Smith* v *Eric S Bush* [1990] 1 AC 831 where his lordship identified four matters that should always be considered:

- the relative bargaining power of the parties;
- whether it was reasonably practicable to obtain advice from an alternative source;
- the difficulty and dangerousness of the task to be undertaken – that is, the risk; and
- the practical consequences of the court's decision, the ability of the parties to bear the losses involved and the availability of insurance.

In the present case, the parties were of equal bargaining power but it would have been almost impossible for the claimant to insure to cover the liability excluded by the defendant. The insurance factor was crucial to this case as the defendant itself had recognised the inadequacy of the £25,000 figure in its standard form contracts and it had been raised to £1m at around the time of the first contract. Unfortunately for the defendant, it had not been able to explain convincingly why the higher figure had not been used in its contracts with the claimant. The judge, therefore, held that the terms limiting liability to £25,000 were unreasonable and awarded a total of £662,926 in damages comprising £291,388 (already paid by the claimant), £231,866 for items of wasted expenditure (computer time, wasted computer stationery, payments to consultants and for testing) and £139,672 for wasted management time.

In another important case, *St Albans City & District Council* v *International Computers Ltd* [1995] FSR 686, the judge had to consider the effectiveness of clauses limiting liability in the context of a software 'bug' which caused financial loss to the client. It concerned software used to administer the community charge (poll tax) and has far-reaching implications for software developers, who should look carefully at their standard term contracts and level of insurance cover.

The claimant, a local authority, was responsible for setting the level of and collecting the community charge and invited tenders for the supply of suitable hardware and software to keep a register of charge payers and to carry out additional functions such as raising the necessary bills. The contract was awarded to the defendant in 1988.

Perhaps exacerbated and compounded by unbelievably tight deadlines, an error in the software resulted in the population being over-estimated by some 2966 persons and the community charge was set at too low a level as a consequence. This had a knock-on effect in terms of money flows to and from central government and the total financial loss to the claimant was £1,314,846. The contract was made on the defendant's standard written terms.

Mr Justice Scott Baker accepted that the defendant was under an obligation to provide software that would maintain a reliable database of names entered on to the community charge register, accurately count those names and accurately retrieve and display the population count. Furthermore, the software had to be reasonably fit for its purpose of maintaining and retrieving a reliable register. There was a plain breach of contract because of the erroneous figures produced by the software. Additionally, an assurance made by the defendant's project manager that the figures could be relied upon was a breach of the project manager's contract of service which was part of the overall agreement. This was a negligent misrepresentation and the project manager's obligations were not, as required, exercised with due diligence. A term in the contract that errors had to be notified to the defendant within three months was of no effect because the claimant was unaware of the error and had no way of discovering it.

The judge, in awarding the claimant the full amount claimed, said that the claimant was not at fault in failing to discover the error nor in failing to take different action when it became apparent that there was a problem with the software. He was of the opinion that the defendant had failed to establish that the limitation clauses in the main agreement and the service agreement incorporated in it were reasonable in the circumstances. By section 3 of the Unfair Contract Terms Act 1977, where one party deals as consumer or on the other's written standard terms of business, the other cannot, by reference to any contract term, exclude or restrict any liability for his own breach of contract except in so far as the term satisfies the requirement of reasonableness. The claimant was not dealing as consumer but the judge held that the contract was based on the written standard terms of the defendant even though there had been some negotiation between the parties. He said that it was not necessary for all the terms to have been fixed in advance by the supplier for the contract to be deemed to be on the basis of written standard terms. Some terms, such as those dealing with quality or price, would often be the result of negotiation but that did not necessarily take the contract out of the reach of section 3. In any case, the judge held that either section 6 or 7 of the Unfair Contract Terms Act 1977 also applied.

Sections 6 and 7 deal with implied terms in contracts of sale or hire purchase of goods and other contracts under which the title to goods pass and also require that the reasonableness test be satisfied in relation to terms excluding or restricting liability. Scott Baker J followed the approach of Judge Thayne Forbes in *The Salvage Association* v *CAP Financial Services Ltd* and considered that it would be better for the loss to fall on a large international computer company (which was well able to insure itself against such claims) rather than falling on a local authority. Other factors of particular note were the resources of the defendant and its total insurance cover which was claimed to amount to £50m. The judge decided that the claimant was in a slightly weaker bargaining position than the defendant and, although the claimant knew of the term (indeed, it had complained about its presence in the contract), had received no inducement, and was unable to enter into a similar contract with another without such a term, the defendant had failed to discharge its burden of establishing that the term was fair and reasonable in the circumstances.

The Court of Appeal confirmed that the limitation clause was unenforceable in *St Albans City & District Council* v *International Computers Ltd* [1997] FSR 251. However, the defendant's appeal was allowed in part in that the award of damages was reduced to £685,000. The claim in relation to payments by charge payers was held not to be recoverable as they were under an obligation to pay (otherwise they would get a bonus) and the claimant could simply increase the charge the following year to recoup that loss. This was notwithstanding the fact that some persons would have left the district and some would have moved into the district in the meantime. However, the Court of Appeal confirmed that the claimant could recover for the increased precept payments made to the County Council which it was unable to recover.

The *St Albans* case is very instructive and shows the difficulty that a software company may have in convincing a judge that any term excluding or limiting liability for defective software is reasonable. Here, the defendant's term was deemed to be unreasonable even though the claimant was aware of the term, other software companies had comparable terms and the software was in use while still under development. However, the judge's view that the claimant was in a weaker bargaining position can be criticised. It was a local authority responsible for a population in excess of 100,000 persons, employing professional staff and making use of a respected firm of management consultants to advise on the tender process. The claimant would certainly be in a stronger bargaining position than most small and medium-sized commercial enterprises dealing with a major computer company. Nevertheless, there are important lessons for computer software companies contained within the judgment.

Further developments on exclusion clauses

The *Salvage Association* and *St Albans* cases were important in that they recognised the general applicability of the Unfair Contract Terms Act 1977 to computer contracts including software contracts. In both cases, a fairly robust approach was taken to the question of whether exclusion clauses satisfied the requirement of reasonableness. Both cases indicated that insurance was an important factor and stressed that the Act places the burden of proof to show that an exclusion clause is reasonable in the party seeking to rely on it.

There have been a number of cases subsequently were the reasonableness of exclusion clauses has been under scrutiny. Of course, in contracts that include exclusion clauses, the validity or otherwise of those clauses is a very important issue. If they are valid, they can rob the client to whom software is supplied of a very substantial claim if the software turns out to be defective. If an exclusion clause is invalid, the financial implications can be such as to put the software company out of business or at least put it into serious financial difficulties, especially if it is not insured or is inadequately insured. Apart from the first, the following cases seem to indicate that the courts are taking a more generous view of exclusion clauses, particularly where there is equality of bargaining power and the parties can be said to enter into the contract with their eyes wide open, knowing the implications of what they are agreeing. Surprisingly, it also seems that a failure to have appropriate insurance is fatal to a software supplier seeking to rely on an exclusion clause. After all, insurance can prove expensive, particularly in relation to software development (most if not all insurance companies refused to insure against the Millennium Bug) and this will be passed on to the client by way of increased prices. This could jeopardise the competitiveness of a software developer who takes out a high level of insurance cover as compared to one who takes out no cover or minimal insurance cover.

In *Pegler Ltd* v *Wang (UK) Ltd* (unreported) 25 February 2000, Pegler decided to replace its existing computer systems with a new integrated system. It eventually contracted with Wang to carry out the work for over £1m. Wang's performance was described by the judge as disastrous and, eventually, Wang ceased to carry out further work, abandoning the contract. Pegler terminated the contract and claimed over £22m in damages. The clause in the contract allowing Pegler to terminate did not appear to be subject to Wang's exclusion clauses and Wang sought rectification of the contract so that the exclusion clauses would apply. In such cases, rectification is only possible if it could be shown that the parties were in complete agreement as to the terms but had failed to write them down correctly. Wang failed to adduce convincing evidence that this was the case and the claim for rectification failed and the exclusion clauses were of no effect. However, the judge went on to consider the reasonableness of the exclusion clauses in case of an appeal against his decision.

One of the exclusion clauses excluded liability for indirect, special or consequential loss and the other excluded liability (except in the case of death or personal injury) in respect of actions brought by either party more than two years after the cause of action occurred. Pegler claimed that the contract was on Wang's written standard terms and, therefore, the exclusion clauses were subject to section 3 of the Unfair Contract Terms Act 1977. Wang disagreed, arguing that the contract was the result of a process of negotiation, some important terms of the contract coming from Pegler's own standard terms and conditions. The latter were stated to have precedence over the other terms in case of conflict. The judge said the phrase 'written standard terms' was not confined to written contracts in which both parties use standard forms and he accepted that Pegler was dealing on 'the other's written standard terms' at least as far as the exclusion clauses were concerned, saying that it was not necessary for the whole contract to be on the other's written standard terms of business. That being so, the Unfair Contract Terms Act 1977 applied to the contract and the judge considered the reasonableness of the clauses. The judge analysed the facts in relation to the guidelines in Schedule 2 to the Act, as follows:

- strength of bargaining position – although Pegler was a substantial company it had burnt its boats by accepting the arrangement in principle and allowing work to proceed before the precise terms of the contract were agreed;
- whether the customer had an opportunity of entering into a similar contract with others without having to accept such a term – on the evidence, the judge accepted that all computer companies contract on similar terms as to the exclusion of liability;
- whether the customer knew or ought reasonably to have known of the existence and extent of the term – Pegler was advised by solicitors throughout the negotiation and was aware of the terms on which it was contracting with Wang;
- where a term excludes or restricts liability if some condition was not complied with, whether it was reasonable to expect compliance – to Wang's knowledge, Pegler had been oversold the system: Pegler had every reason to be confident that the system was suitable for its purposes and had been let down disastrously;
- whether goods were manufactured, processed or adapted to the special order of the customer – the overselling included substantial misrepresentations as to the 'fit' of

Wang's standard package to Pegler's requirements and Wang represented its solution as being 'low risk'.

In these circumstances, the judge decided that Wang could not rely on the exclusion clauses. Whilst it might be acceptable to exclude liability for some lapse that was not readily foreseeable, it was quite another thing to exclude liability when, because it had blatantly misrepresented what it was selling, breaches of contract were very likely. In the event, the judge made a total award of damages of £9,047,113.

Sometimes, those responsible for drafting computer contracts write contracts so complex they are bound to contain ambiguities or contradictions. The case of *Kwik-Fit Insurance Services Ltd* v *Bull Information Systems Ltd* (unreported) 23 June 2000 provides an example. Kwik-Fit wanted a new computer system and Bull carried out the work but the contract ran into problems and the system was not delivered on time. Kwik-Fit gave notice requiring the breaches of contract to be remedied within 30 days, but just before the end of that period, Bull withdrew from the project. Soon after, Kwik-Fit wrote to Bull accepting the latter's repudiation of the contract or, alternatively, terminating the agreement. Kwik-Fit claimed damages in excess of £17m, including indirect and consequential losses of over £6m. Bull counterclaimed for over £8m in damages alleging, *inter alia*, that Kwik-Fit failed to state precisely what functionality it required, failed to agree a proper baseline against which the development of the software could be controlled, made changes to the functionality required without going through proper procedures and failed to provide information.

The case involved a number of preliminary issues and the judge had to make some difficult decisions regarding the contract which was very complex, difficult to construe and which conflicted in places. One clause on the contract stated that Bull would not be able to rely on any default of Kwik-Fit in completing agreed tasks or providing information or materials if Bull did not give prompt notice of such failures or breaches by Kwik-Fit. This required consideration of section 7 of the Unfair Contract Terms Act 1977 which applies to miscellaneous contracts under which goods pass and which states:

(1) **Where the possession or ownership of goods passes under or in pursuance of a contract not governed by the law of sale of goods or hire-purchase, subsections (2) to (4) below apply as regards the effect (if any) to be given to contract terms excluding or restricting liability for breach of obligation arising by implication of law from the nature of the contract.**

(2) **As against a person dealing as consumer, liability in respect of the goods' correspondence with description or sample, or their quality or fitness for any particular purpose, cannot be excluded or restricted by reference to any such term.**

(3) **As against a person dealing otherwise than as consumer, that liability can be excluded or restricted by reference to such a term, but only in so far as the term satisfies the requirement of reasonableness.**

The key issue was whether the phrase 'that liability' as used in subsection (3) referred to the specific liability under subsection (2) or the general liability for breach of an implied term under subsection (1). If the latter applied, the test of reasonableness would be available under much wider circumstances. The judge held that the liability in section 7(3) referred back to subsection 2 and was, therefore, not wider and only applied to correspondence with description or sample or quality or fitness for purpose of goods.

That being so, the test of reasonableness did not apply to the clause in question which excluded liability subsequent to a failure to report defaults in performance. The judge said that, consistently with the scheme found elsewhere in the Act, the draftsman of the Act had intended to provide limited protection rather than total prohibition of exclusions in non-consumer cases.

One reason for that sentiment is that businesses and other organisations are expected to be circumspect, to inform themselves and take appropriate advice before committing themselves to important contracts which can seriously affect their operations if they go wrong or fail to deliver the advantages sought. In some cases, the client will have a duty to fully cooperate with the software developer to ensure its satisfactory installation, modification and operation. Failure to cooperate might be a factor in deciding whether an exclusion clause is reasonable.

In *Anglo Group plc* v *Winther Browne & Co Ltd* (2000) 72 Con LR 118 the defendant wanted to replace its outdated computer system and obtained a quote for new hardware and a standard software package from BML Office Computers. The defendant and BML entered a written agreement for the supply of the hardware and software for £64,133 and to pay for this, the defendant entered a lease agreement with the claimant. The contract was one for the transfer of goods (notwithstanding software also was supplied) other than under a sale of goods contract or a hire purchase agreement and, as such, was subject to section 7 of the Unfair Contract Terms Act 1977 which, *inter alia*, makes any terms excluding or limiting liability in a non-consumer contract in respect of correspondence with description or sample, quality or fitness for any particular purpose subject to the test of reasonableness.

After delivery of the equipment and software a number of problems arose, some of which were probably the fault of BML, but others were probably the result of the defendant's reluctance to adapt its working practices. Eventually, the defendant instructed its bank to stop payment of an instalment due to the claimant which then claimed the whole amount of the loan outstanding. The judge held that BML were not in breach of contract and the defendant did not have the right to terminate. The claimant's exclusion clause extended to losses arising from a failure of the equipment to function properly.

The judge held that the exclusion clauses were reasonable. The defendant could have obtained finance elsewhere and was fully aware of the terms and conditions. Although the system was a standard one, its successful implementation would require considerable input from the defendant, and the claimant had not been involved in the negotiations between the defendant and the software supplier. The contractual arrangements were such that the defendant had recourse against the software supplier and financing the acquisition from a finance company rather than buying it direct from the supplier was not a trap (that is, a way of avoiding liability for defects by means of a leasing arrangement).

Another case showing that exclusion clauses may be reasonable where the parties are fully aware of the risks and the allocation of those risks is *Watford Electronics Ltd* v *Sanderson CFL Ltd* [2002] FSR 19 in which the claimant, Watford, sold computers, mainly by mail order. The defendant, Sanderson, supplied software products. Its key product was 'Mailbrain', a marketing package used for mail order operations and which could be used in conjunction with another of its products, 'Genasys' for marketing sales, purchase and nominal ledgers and other accounting operations. A number of contracts were made for the supply of equipment, licences and maintenance agreements in respect of Mailbrain and Genasys and for bespoke modifications to the software and training. Later, after complaints from Watford about performance, further contracts were made for the supply of a Bull minicomputer and a further software licence. All the contracts were subject to similar terms and conditions. After Watford had paid a total of £104,596, it decided to replace the entire system with a new computer system from a third party and claimed damages from Sanderson on the basis of misrepresentation and breaches of implied terms. Sanderson relied on the exclusion clauses in the contracts and an entire agreement clause (discussed earlier in this chapter). The exclusion clauses were of two types. One excluded liability for indirect or consequential losses, whether arising in negligence or otherwise. The second limited liability to the price paid for the equipment or software connected with any claim.

Although Sanderson's written standard contracts had been modified by an addendum which had been negotiated between the parties, it was held that the Unfair Contract Terms Act 1977 applied to the contracts (the Court of Appeal did not even consider this as an issue). At first instance, the judge held that the exclusion clauses were unreasonable in their entirety.

The Court of Appeal disagreed, holding that both forms of exclusion were reasonable. As regards the exclusion of liability for indirect or consequential losses, the court made a number of points. As the parties were of equal bargaining power, the court should be very cautious before concluding that the agreement reached between the parties was not fair and reasonable. In such a case, the parties themselves were often the best to judge this. As a starting point in determining whether exclusion clauses were reasonable in such cases, regard should be had to:

- the significant risk that a customised product might not perform to the customer's satisfaction (there had been some bespoke modification of the software delivered);
- in such a case, there was a significant risk that the customer will not make the profits or savings that it hoped to make and could incur consequential losses;
- those risks which were or ought reasonably to be known or in the contemplation of the parties when the contract was made;
- the software supplier was in a better position to assess the risk that the product would fail to perform to the customer's satisfaction;
- the risk was likely to be capable of being covered by insurance, though at a cost;
- both parties would have known or ought reasonably to have known when the contract was made the identity of the party bearing the risk and that the identity of the party bearing the risk would affect the price the supplier would want or the customer would be prepared to pay.

On the basis of these factors, it was entirely reasonable that the contract should provide that one party only bears the risk of indirect or consequential losses. On the facts of the case, the parties did negotiate as to price and Watford obtained significant concessions. There was also some negotiation as to risk but Watford only obtained a concession that Sanderson would use its best endeavours to allocate appropriate resources to ensure that the product conformed to the specification. A further factor was that the product had been, to some extent, modified to meet the special needs of Watford. Therefore, it was impossible to say that Sanderson took unfair advantage of Watford or that Watford did not properly understand and consider the effect of the clause excluding liability for indirect and consequential losses.

On the issue of the clause limiting liability to the price paid, the Court of Appeal considered that this was also reasonable. An important factor was that section 53(3) of the Sale of Goods Act 1979 sets the damages for breach of a warranty of quality, *prima facie*, at the difference between the value of the goods as delivered and their value had they complied with the warranty.

Failure to acquire appropriate software can sound the death-knell for a business. The fears generated by the Millennium Bug gave an example of the dangers – in that case, of failing to be Year 2000 compliant. The following case shows that failing to take prompt and timely action to replace outmoded equipment and software can result in serious consequences and can put a client out of business, though fortunately it did not do so in the event. In *Sam Business Systems Ltd* v *Hedley and Co* [2002] EWHC 2733 (TCC), the defendant, Hedley, used old DOS-based software for its stockbroking business and was concerned that it was not Year 2000 compliant. In any case, it was about time for Hedley to upgrade its software. The claimant, Sam, specialised in ready-made software, comprising a number of packages, for stockbrokers and banks dealing in stocks and shares and in administering their back-office systems. Sam supplied a new computer software system to Hedley. Problems arose with the software and, eventually, Hedley outsourced its back-office systems to a third party and withheld further payment to Sam which sued for the amount it considered to be outstanding, amounting to over £300,000. (In pre-contractual negotiations, Sam had told Hedley, the whole system would cost no more than £180,000 and Hedley had already paid over this figure.)

Hedley counter-claimed on the basis of misrepresentation and breaches of the licence and maintenance agreements, asking for damages of nearly £800,000 which included money already paid, increased cost of working, additional costs and loss of profit. The licence agreement contained an entire agreement clause (discussed earlier in the chapter) and a clause limiting liability to the fees paid by the client should the software prove to be unacceptable in accordance with the agreement. There was also a deemed acceptance clause and a sweeping exclusion of warranties and implied terms.

The agreements were on Sam's written standard terms, therefore, section 3 of the Unfair Contract Terms Act 1977 applied. Therefore, the exclusion and limitation clauses must meet the requirement of reasonableness and HH Judge Bowsher QC first looked at insurance as a factor. Neither party had insurance to cover the risk. It may have been that Sam thought it did not need insurance cover because of its exclusions clauses and there was no reason for Hedley to have insured against risk of Sam failing to perform properly. Because there was no evidence about the ability of either party to obtain insurance or the cost of such insurance, as a factor it was neutral.

The judge quoted from *Salvage Association* v *CAP Financial Services* [1995] FSR 654 where HH Judge Thayne Forbes QC said:

> Generally speaking where a party well able to look after itself enters into a commercial contract, and with full knowledge of all relevant circumstances willingly accepts the terms of the contract which provide for apportionment of the financial risks in the transaction, I think that it is very likely that those terms will be held to be fair and reasonable. (This was approved by Peter Gibson LJ in the *Watford Electronics* case in the Court of Appeal.)

Although this is a sensible approach, in the context of the present case, it was questionable whether Hedley was well able to look after itself. At the time, there was a lot of panic about Year 2000 compliance. Also, no one at Hedley knew about computers, unlike Sam as its business was computers.

The judge then turned to the guidelines in Schedule 2 to the Act, accepting that they were of general application to the question of reasonableness although only expressed in the Act as being relevant to sections 6 and 7. It seemed that, in the relevant field, it was standard practice to exclude liability, one reason being that the few software suppliers capable of supplying equivalent software knew their client's services intimately. In terms of bargaining power, both Sam and Hedley were small businesses. Hedley had no option but to acquire Year 2000 compliant software very quickly but that was a problem of its own making and it should have woken up to the dangers sooner, as others did. Furthermore, Hedley did not attempt to negotiate the terms of the agreements. Had they done so, Sam might have responded on a take it or leave it basis. However, they might not have done so and might have been prepared to negotiate the terms of the agreements.

There were enormous potential liabilities. If Hedley had not acquired Year 2000 compliant software, it would have been in serious trouble with the regulator and would have gone out of business. Had Sam not excluded liability for warranties, it too could have gone out of business. As it was, Sam had provided that Hedley could get its money back had the system not been acceptable, if Hedley went through the contractual machinery to reject the software. That being so, the judge thought the exclusion clauses in the licence agreement reasonable and, as Hedley had not gone through the proper procedures to reject, it was not entitled to its money back. However, with respect to the maintenance agreement, the judge thought it would be unreasonable for Sam to be paid for putting right a defect for which it had excluded liability under the licence agreement. The judge said:

> Of course, any product, whether it be a motor car, or a washing machine, or computer software, may, after working well to start with, then develop faults and faults arising in that way, provided they did not exist in a hidden form on delivery, would be the proper subject of a maintenance agreement. But no consumer would or should accept liability to pay for rectification of defects existing in goods on delivery even if there was no contractual liability on the part of the supplier to pay damages arising out of those defects.

This is quite surprising and suggests that a software company, having supplied software, cannot charge for corrected defects that were not known about at the point of delivery. This sits uncomfortably with the Court of Appeal's decision in *Saphena Computing Ltd* v *Allied Collection Agencies Ltd* [1995] FSR 616 where the court accepted that it is not necessarily a breach of contract to deliver software which contained a defect. If HH Judge Bowsher QC is correct, this throws into doubt the role and validity of maintenance contracts, unless they go further than correcting latent defects and provide other services, such as enhancements.

Having found the exclusion clauses reasonable (except in respect of the maintenance agreement to the extent that, in effect, it permitted charging the client for inherent defects for which liability was excluded by the licence agreement), Hedley's counterclaim failed. The judge also dismissed Sam's claims for additional work because of the existence of the maintenance agreement and did not allow the claim for a final instalment for the licence of £29,000 payable on completion because completion never took place. The final award to Sam was £7467 plus interest.

The courts' approach to exclusion clauses in relation to computer contracts has changed from its initial position, where it seemed as if it would be extremely rare for such a clause to be seen to be fair, especially as the burden of proof lie on the party seeking to rely on the clause and the feeling that it was the software developer's responsibility to take out an appropriate level of insurance. Now, there seems to be a much more *laissez-faire* attitude, especially as between businesses or broadly equal bargaining power. It also now seems to be recognised that insurance is no longer the key factor and it may be acceptable for a software developer not to insure against the risks of certain losses, such as indirect or consequential losses. The contract is once again seen as a reflection of the allocation of risk between the parties and it should be the one on whom the risk is placed who should insure against it or take the chance that the contract will run smoothly and be performed satisfactorily. The interaction between the amount of insurance cover taken out by a software developer and the price paid by the client is an important factor as is the practice amongst software developers in the same or similar line of business as regards their exclusion clauses.

Fundamental breach

Before the Unfair Contract Terms Act 1977 came into force, the courts developed, somewhat erratically, the doctrine of 'fundamental breach' as a way of curbing the worst excesses of exclusion clauses. *Pinnock Bros* v *Lewis & Peat Ltd* [1923] 1 KB 690 concerned a contract for the purchase of copra cake. When delivered, it was discovered to be poisonous because it had been contaminated with castor oil. It was held that it was not copra cake at all but a substance quite different to that contracted for and, because of this, the sellers could not rely on an exclusion clause purporting to exempt them from liability. Later, it was said that where there had been a fundamental breach of contract – that is, if one party fails to carry out his part of the bargain at all or attempts to render a performance totally different from that contemplated – then the party in breach could not rely on an exclusion clause (see *Karsales (Harrow) Ltd* v *Wallis* [1956] 2 All ER 61). However, the courts later took a more *laissez-faire* attitude to exclusion clauses and fundamental breach on the basis that the parties should be free to agree that there should be no liability under the contract even for a fundamental breach, if that was their desire: see *Photo Production Ltd* v *Securicor Transport Ltd* [1980] AC 827. This case concerned the law before the implementation of the Unfair Contract Terms Act 1977, but the impact of this Act on exclusion clauses was in the minds of their lordships.

Nevertheless, the doctrine of fundamental breach may still have some utility when it comes to controlling exclusion clauses in contracts which do not come within the scope of the Unfair Contract Terms Act – for example, where the breach concerns the grant of the licence itself such as where the licensor turns out not to be entitled to grant the licence or in the context of liability arising outside the course of business. Of course, where a purported licence for the use of software fails because the licensor does not have the right to grant the licence (for example, if he does not own the copyright and does not have the copyright owner's permission to grant licences) then it could be said that the contract will be void on the basis of a total failure of consideration.

Exclusion of liability for misrepresentation

Section 8 of the Unfair Contract Terms Act provides that a clause in a contract which purports to exclude or restrict liability for misrepresentation will only be effective if it satisfies the requirement of reasonableness. The burden of proof is on the person seeking to rely on the clause. If a computer salesperson claims that the computer she is selling will run a particular software package and this claim turns out to be untrue, it will be for the company selling the computer to show that any exemption clause it hopes to rely on passes the test of reasonableness. The test is laid out in section 11 of the Unfair Contract Terms Act 1977 which requires that the term be:

> ... fair and reasonable ... having regard to the circumstances which were, or ought reasonably to have been, known to or in the contemplation of the parties when the contract was made ...

This is a nebulous requirement which also applies to some of the other provisions in the Act. It gives the courts scope to be flexible and to take the facts of a particular case into account. Some indication of the court's approach was given by the decision in *George Mitchell (Chesterhall) Ltd* v *Finney Lock Seeds Ltd* [1983] 2 All ER 737. The claimant bought cabbage seed from the defendant for £192. The seed was defective and the resulting crop was little better than useless. The loss to the claimant, a farmer, was in the order of £61,000. When sued, the defendant claimed to be liable only for the cost of the seed because of a clause in their contract to that effect. Lord Denning (it was his last case) said that the term was not fair and reasonable in the circumstances, although he did say that this was a borderline case. The following were important factors:

- Farmers had no way of knowing or discovering that the seed was defective.
- The defendant seed merchant could have insured against the risk of defective seed but it was unlikely that an individual farmer could so insure.
- The defendants had not relied on the clause but had reached a negotiated settlement in similar prior cases.
- It was likely that the seed merchant or their Dutch suppliers had been negligent.

In a subsequent appeal to the House of Lords, the Court of Appeal's decision was affirmed. It should be noted that, by section 7 of the Unfair Contract Terms Act 1977, liability for defective products under Part I of the Consumer Protection Act 1987 cannot be excluded or limited by any contract term.

Unfair terms in consumer contracts

Individual consumers making contracts for non-business purposes are given greater protection in relation to standard form contracts as from 1 July 1995, by the Unfair Terms in Consumer Contracts Regulations 1994. These Regulations control terms which are unfair and, being contrary to the requirement of good faith, cause a significant imbalance in the parties' rights and obligations under the contract to the detriment of the consumer. To some extent, the Regulations overlap the Unfair Contracts Terms Act 1977 but in some respects, in terms of consumer contracts, they supplement the Act. The nature of the goods or services must be taken into account in assessing the unfair nature of the term in question. Schedule 2 to the Regulations gives a list of things to be taken into account when assessing fairness: the strength of bargaining position, whether the consumer received an inducement to agree to the term, whether the goods or services were sold or supplied to the special order of the consumer and whether the seller or supplier has acted fairly and equitably.

Schedule 3 contains a list of terms that are likely to be regarded as unfair. Some of these would not be effective in any case under English law, an example being a term which allows the unilateral alteration of a term in the contract by the seller or supplier. The provisions do not apply to terms which have been individually negotiated or, if written in plain intelligible language, which define the main subject matter of the contract or are concerned with the adequacy of the price or remuneration. For example, in *Bankers Insurance Company Ltd* v *South* [2003] EWHC 380 (QB), a clause in an insurance contract contained an exclusion clause in relation to claims arising from the use of 'motorised waterborne craft'. Whilst riding a jet-ski, the insured collided with another jet-ski, the rider of which suffered injuries. The court rejected an argument that the exclusion clause was not written in plain intelligible language and, therefore, no assessment of fairness was to be made although the judge did not consider the clause unfair in any case. Where negotiation is in issue, the seller or supplier has the burden of proof in showing that a term was individually negotiated. Where there is any doubt as to the meaning of a term, the meaning most favourable to the consumer will be taken. If a contract contains an unfair term, it will not be binding on the consumer but the contract will continue in existence if it is capable of so doing without the unfair term.

Chapter 18

Contracts for writing software

Introduction

If an organisation wishes to obtain some new computer software, there may be several options open to it. Appropriate software may be available as an 'off-the-shelf' package or the organisation may employ its own computer staff who can develop the software. In other circumstances, it may be advantageous to have the software written or adapted by a software development company – a firm specialising in particular types of computer software. The following example is typical of instances when software will be developed under a contractual agreement.

A company owns a mainframe computer and network of personal computers or terminals. It requires software to automate its accounting and invoicing systems. After reviewing software available off-the-shelf, the company comes to the conclusion that none is ideally suited to its methods of operation and it is neither appropriate nor satisfactory for it to change its methods to suit the available software. Although the company employs a number of analysts and programmers, it decides against asking them to write the software, as they are not sufficiently experienced in the development software that is likely to be used as a platform to deliver the applications software. The company selects an experienced software company to carry out a comprehensive feasibility study which includes development and strategy studies. The software company produces a detailed plan and specification for the work and is awarded the contract to carry out the work following the submission of bids by it and a number of other experienced software companies. We will now turn to the terms and provisions commonly found in a contract for writing computer software. The company commissioning the development of the software will be referred to as the 'client' and the company writing the software will be called the 'software development company'.

Definitions

The very first clause in the contract is likely to deal with a description of the parties to the contract and appropriate definitions relating to the software and the equipment on which the software will be installed. Apart from being a word-saving provision in that the client's full business name can be abbreviated throughout to CLIENT or CUSTOMER, the definitions clause can usefully describe terms such as software and hardware and thus assist with the interpretation and construction of the agreement. Consequently, any expressions defined here should be defined precisely and comprehensively as they will be the key to understanding the remainder of the contract and the scope of the parties' obligations and liabilities under it.

Licence agreement

What will the software development company deliver to the client in return for the payment? On the face of it a set of programs, data files and associated documentation is what will be provided, but will the software development company really hand over ownership of the programs and other software? This will be unlikely and an important term usually states that the software is being licensed; the contract is, first and foremost, a licence agreement. A licence is a permission to do something; in terms of computer software, a licence is a permission to use the software and, without this permission, using the software would be an infringement of the copyright subsisting in it. This is because loading programs and data into a computer's memory is making a copy and copyright can be infringed even if the copy is transient by section 17(6) of the Copyright, Designs and Patents Act 1988.

The software development company will undoubtedly want to retain the ownership of the intellectual property rights in the programs and the documentation, for its business is licensing software and it will want to grant licences in respect of the software, or variants of it or modules contained within it, to others. If it is especially important for the company acquiring the software that it is not made available to others, it should insist on an exclusive licence, which is likely to be much more expensive. Alternatively, ownership of the copyright subsisting in the software could be transferred to the client under an assignment of copyright. In practical terms, there is little difference between an exclusive licence and an assignment of copyright. Where an exclusive licence or assignment of copyright is granted, however, the software development company would be wise to reserve the right to reuse modules in other software or even in the writing of new software to perform similar functions. The drafting of an appropriate and workable clause to allow for this will require a great deal of care and the implications must be thoroughly considered. On the one hand the client may not want its competitor obtaining similar software from the software development company whilst, on the other hand, the latter will not want to unduly constrain its future software development activities.

Important points to check in the licence agreement will include the duration of the licence and its scope (sometimes the licence will be silent on the matter of duration). Because a licence is a permission to do something which would otherwise be unlawful, it does not give any proprietary interest in the software. The implications of this are twofold.

1 The licence should be for a fixed duration or there should be some provisions for termination of the licence. If the licence appears, on the face of it, to be perpetual, this contradicts the nature of a licence and it might even be implied that the agreement is not a licence but an assignment of the copyright and other rights in the software, especially if the rights granted appear to be exclusive. It is more likely, however, in the absence of any express reference to duration, that the licence will endure as long as the copyright subsists in the software. The wording of the agreement as a whole should give a clue as to which interpretation is correct.
2 The licence agreement should state whether the software can subsequently be transferred to a third party. In the absence of any provision covering this aspect, it would appear that the benefit of the licence is transferable, depending on the circumstances (see the following section).

The scope of the licence is very important. Is it permissible to run the software on several computers or just one particular computer? Can it be installed on a server? If the acquiring company is part of a group of companies, can the programs be used throughout the group or just within the one company? Is the licence a single-user licence (if so, can it be used on any computer by the user)? Is it a site licence, a company licence or group licence? Can the software be transferred to another company? Is transfer subject to approval? All these questions should be considered and discussed with the software development company in the light of the contract and the intended uses to which the software is to be put. The possibility of expanding computing facilities and usage in the future must not be overlooked. In this respect, the client should carry out regular audits to make sure that its licensed software is not being used in excess of the licence agreements and to identify whether existing licences are adequate.

Assignment of agreement

It is common for contracts to contain a term dealing with the assignment of the benefit of the contract. That is, the transfer of the right to use the software. For example, in an agreement for the writing of new software by a software development company for a client, there may be a term stating that neither party shall assign the agreement. Sometimes, assignment is permitted providing the other party consents. Note that in this context, we are talking about the assignment of the benefit of a contract rather than the assignment of the ownership of copyright. Terms dealing with assignment are particularly relevant where the performance of the contract will be carried out over a period of time, such as a building contract or a contract for writing new software.

Both parties to a contract enjoy benefits and suffer burdens emanating from the contract. For example, a client for whom software is to be written under a contract may have the benefits and burdens listed in Table 18.1.

Unless prohibited, a party to a contract may assign (that is, transfer) the benefit of the contract but not the burden. The original parties remain liable for their obligations under the contract. In *Linden Gardens Trust Ltd* v *Lenesta Sludge Disposals Ltd* [1993] 3 WLR 408, a building contract contained a term which stated: 'The employer [the client] shall not without the written consent of the contractor assign this contract.' There was a purported assignment of the contract but the House of Lords held that this

Table 18.1 Benefits and burdens in software contract

Benefits	Burdens
1 The services of the software development company in writing the software	1 The obligation to pay the software development company
2 A copyright licence allowing use of the software	2 Providing facilities and information to the software development company
3 The grant of ownership of the property in disks, manuals, etc.	3 Accepting the software after attending testing
4 The services of the software development company in maintaining the software, correcting errors and delivering enhancements	4 The obligation to pay for ongoing maintenance and enhancements

was void. There was some criticism of the drafting of the above term. Lord Browne-Wilkinson said:

> On any basis, clause 17 is unhappily drafted in that it refers to an assignment of 'the contract'. It is trite law that it is, in any event, impossible to assign 'the contract' as a whole, i.e. including both burden and benefit. The burden of a contract can never be assigned without the consent of the other party to the contract in which event such consent will give rise to a novation.

(A novation is where a new contract is substituted for an old one.) Lord Browne-Wilkinson also said, later:

> ... lawyers frequently use those words ['assign this contract'] inaccurately to describe an assignment of the benefit of a contract since every lawyer knows that the burden of a contract can never be assigned.

The House of Lords confirmed that a party to a contract might have good commercial reasons for refusing to grant consent to an assignment. For example, if a software company is providing continuing maintenance of software it might not want to maintain it if the client transfers the software to a third party. As the burden cannot be assigned, the original party remains liable to fulfil his obligations under the contract. For example, if a client transfers the benefit of a software licence to a third party, that original client remains liable for any outstanding payments. Where there is an assignment, the original party, the assignor, might want to consider an indemnity clause to protect himself against any legal action brought by the other party in respect of his obligations under the contract.

It is common for a licence agreement (and the same applies to other forms of agreement such as a maintenance agreement) to state that the benefit of the agreement shall not be assigned without the prior written permission of the other party.

In *Circuit Systems Ltd & Basten* v *Zuken-Redac (UK) Ltd* (1995) 11 Const LJ 201, the defendant rented computer equipment to the first claimant (Circuit Systems) and also entered into a maintenance agreement with it. Both agreements prohibited assignment though, in the case of the maintenance agreement, assignment with written consent was possible. The same day that the first claimant issued a writ against the defendant alleging, *inter alia*, breach of contract and economic duress, the first claimant went into liquidation. The second claimant, Mr Basten (who owned at least 98 per cent of the shares in Circuit Systems) took an assignment of Circuit Systems' rights of action for £1 and was granted legal aid to pursue the claim. It was held that the assignments were not valid and the action was an abuse of process. However, the House of Lords allowed Mr Basten to pursue his claim and, eventually, the case was restarted in the Technology and Construction Court. However, the judge made orders with time limits requiring the claimant to put the statement of case in order (it was very poorly pleaded and unsatisfactory). When the claimant failed to comply the judge struck out the claim, effectively bringing the litigation, which had started in 1988, to an end. The Court of Appeal refused permission to appeal in *Circuit Systems Ltd and Another* v *Zuken-Redac (UK) Ltd* [2001] Build LR 235.

In *Orion Finance Ltd* v *Crown Financial Management Ltd* [1994] 2 BCLC 607, the assignment was subject to consent but the party whose consent was required, Crown, knew that the assignment had been made without consent but failed to draw the other party's attention to this before a lease of computer equipment was registered as a

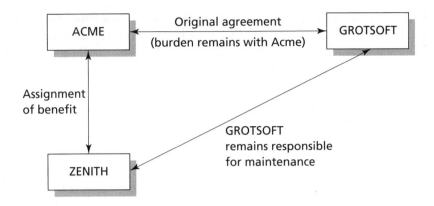

Fig. 18.1 Assignment of benefit of agreement

charge under the Companies Act 1985. Crown was estopped from relying on the lack of consent. Crown's lack of activity was, in effect, a representation that it accepted the assignment as valid.

Under what circumstances might an assignment of the benefit of a contract be appropriate? Consider a client, Acme Manufacturing Ltd, which is a member of a group of companies and which makes an agreement with Grotsoft Ltd, a software development company, for the development, installation and maintenance of stock control software. After a while, because of changes in Acme's manufacturing methods, the software is no longer useful but another company in the group, Zenith Fabrications Ltd, would like to use the software. After seeking Grotsoft's permission as required in the contract, Acme assigns the benefit of the agreement to Zenith and Grotsoft will continue to maintain the software at Zenith's offices for the remainder of the maintenance period. Assuming that Grotsoft will be entitled to a final payment at the end of the maintenance period, this will be payable by Acme which remains responsible for this. In the separate agreement between Acme and Zenith in which the benefit of the agreement with Grotsoft is transferred to Zenith, there is provision for Zenith to refund Acme after it has made the final payment. Figure 18.1 shows the effect of the assignment to Zenith.

If, on the other hand, Acme had wished to hand over the entire contract to Zenith, this would result in a novation (providing Grotsoft agreed to this). The original

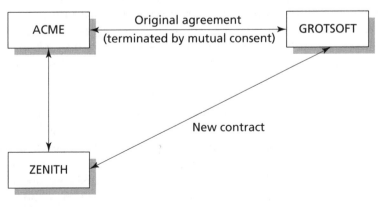

Fig. 18.2 Novation

agreement would be set aside and a new contract between Zenith and Grotsoft would come into existence. If Grotsoft refused to agree to this, however, and Acme indicated that it no longer wanted to proceed with the contract, Grotsoft could sue for wrongful repudiation of contract or anticipatory breach. A novation is shown in Fig. 18.2.

The contract price

As the agreement will be almost certainly in the nature of a licence, the sum payable should be termed a licence fee. This fee is often described as the price, however, and often it will include other things such as training and tangible items such as disks and documentation. The word 'price' will be used, therefore, bearing in mind that this will include a once and for all licence fee which will usually make up the largest portion of the overall price. In some cases, the agreement will not be a licence but, instead, will provide for the assignment of the copyright subsisting in the completed software to the client. Nevertheless, similar considerations will apply as regards the price and many other aspects of the contract.

Wherever possible, the question of price should be tied down precisely. If it comprises a licence fee, maintenance fee, price for any hardware supplied, etc., there should be a breakdown of the constituent costs (in many cases, maintenance will be provided under a separate contract on an annual basis). Apart from anything else, this could be important for tax reasons. In addition, the contract should provide some machinery for calculating the cost of any extra work or services provided other than those which the software development company has agreed to provide as its consideration for the contract. There may be unanticipated problems with the computer equipment, for example, or the client may change his mind halfway through the work and require modifications to be made to the specification. Therefore, the contract should include a list of hourly rates for programmers, analysts and others.

If a lump-sum price is agreed, it should be clear from the contract exactly what this includes: whether maintenance and training are included, whether the price includes the documentation and, if so, how many copies. What about the cost of the media such as magnetic disks and tapes? If the payment is to be made in instalments, when are they due? If they become due following the performance of certain stages of the work, can these stages be clearly identified? For example, the contract might provide for payment of two-thirds of the total price when certain specified programs are operational, usable in practice and acceptable to the client, apart from the fact that further work may need to be carried out. If the client is late in paying, does the contract include provision for charging interest? What if the client shows no intention of paying? It is in the interests of both parties that there should be no ambiguity as far as time for payment is concerned.

It may be that the software development company feels unable to quote a firm price from the start. Perhaps the client's computer equipment is unusual or unfamiliar in some respect. A software development company may refuse point blank to be tied down to a fixed price, particularly if the work involves modifying existing software to run on unfamiliar equipment. If the software development company refuses to quote a fixed price the reason should be ascertained. Is it because the software development company is tackling something beyond its capabilities or are there more acceptable reasons? Is it genuinely difficult even for an experienced company to forecast the amount of work and the timescale because of the complexity of the work? One way round this problem is to ask the software development company or, preferably, a competent and independent consultant, to carry out a feasibility study. This will enable the viability of the project to be determined before the parties are committed, and the actual amount of work involved and the price can be more accurately predicted. If carried through to the writing of a detailed specification, it can form the basis for inviting tenders or quotations from a number of software development companies to carry out the work. The cost of the feasibility study, however, can be a considerable addition to the overall cost of implementing the software though it may prove money well spent in the long run.

Failure to have a feasibility study carried out before the development contract can prove disastrous to any subsequent claim that the software is unsuitable. In *Comyn Ching Ltd* v *Radius plc* (unreported) 29 March 2000, the claimant group of companies wanted to integrate its computer systems and appointed the defendant to carry out the work. There was a misunderstanding as to exactly what was required. During negotiations before the contract was entered into, the defendant twice offered to carry out a feasibility study to assess the claimant's precise requirements. The fee for carrying out the study was only £6930. The claimant refused on both occasions and when it was not satisfied with the system, sued the defendant for damages in excess of £3m. The claimant had little knowledge of computers but decided not to employ a consultant but argued that the defendant owed it a duty of care which extended to investigating the claimant's requirements beforehand without payment. This submission was rejected by the judge who considered the claimant's requirements to be very fluid. He described them as a 'moveable feast'.

If the work involved in writing the software is substantial, the possibility of obtaining quotations by competitive tender should be considered but, if this course is chosen, specialist advice should be sought as to the specification and other aspects of the tender documentation. The company inviting tenders is taking upon itself the responsibility for the feasibility of the project and the quality of the documentation provided to the tenderers. If the specification is inadequate, any software development company awarded the contract will be able to point to this in its defence should the programs fail to be satisfactory, or use the deficiencies as a basis for claiming additional payment. Therefore, this approach can only be recommended for companies who have access to the necessary professional expertise. A major problem with comparing quotations and tenders is that it is unlikely that all those submitting will have put their bids together on the same basis. The chances are that some or all will have modified the specification in some way or another in spite of a request not to diverge from the specification. Some of those quoting may be unable to obtain a particular piece of equipment or software tool and will offer an alternative or they may offer an alternative simply because it is cheaper and they hope this will make their quotation appear more attractive. Although it could be argued that initiative should be rewarded, in fairness to the others quoting, all should be asked to reconsider their quotes in the light of the alternative should it appear to be worthwhile considering. The legal position regarding tenders is discussed in Chapter 21 in relation to hardware and the same principles apply to software.

Specification

Whether the company acquiring the software, an independent consultant or the software development company writes the specification, there are several important points to be made in respect of it. The specification is the main provision in the contract which concerns the performance and capabilities of the software. It should be a detailed description of what the software is, what it will do and how quickly it will do it. The specification may well be contained in a separate document or be an appendix to the contract, but it must be noted that it is of crucial importance, being the yardstick by which the software will be measured in the case of a dispute about the character and performance of the software.

Ideally, the specification will be clear, comprehensive and exactly mirror the client's requirements. Alas, this is not always the case and one of the most common problems is that the client moves the goalposts part way through the work, typically asking for changes to be made to the specification. The client may decide that he requires different or additional reports to be generated, links to other software not envisaged at the outset or the inclusion of additional routines, none of which are mentioned in the specification. Alternatively, some parts of the specification may have to be compromised because of operational and other difficulties not envisaged at the time the specification was written and agreed on by the parties to the contract. For example, the client may want to take advantage of a newly available upgrade to his operating system software which will require changes to the application software being written under the agreement. While changes made to the specification during the performance of the contract may result in the completed software being of a higher standard, more powerful or of increased functionality, the contractual implications of such changes must be catered for in the original agreement.

While the law will imply terms, based on reasonableness, dealing with additional payment and extensions to the time for completion, for example, under the Supply of Goods and Services Act 1982, it is better to build mechanisms into the contract for this purpose. A schedule of rates is a useful addition to a contract to be used for the determination of the additional price to be paid for extra work not included in the original contract because of changes to the specification made part-way through the work. Another term dealing with extensions to the time for completion would also be useful, as discussed later. If the changes are required because of unforeseen problems, then it would be useful to provide a term allowing additional payment if, and only if, a reasonably competent software company would not have anticipated the problem. The use of an independent professional contract supervisor, as advocated at the end of this chapter, will be very useful in dealing with the contractual implications of changes to the specification.

It is useful to include a mechanism for variation orders in the agreement. A basic method is for any variation to the specification or work required to be set out in writing and signed by both parties before the changes are implemented or incorporated in the work programme. The additional cost (or reduction to the overall price) should be agreed by the parties as should the impact on the overall time for completion. It is far better to have agreement before any additional work is done or any other changes made to the planned programme of work implemented and for the consequences of any changes to be thoroughly considered and agreed. Trying to agree additional costs and extensions to the time for completion after the event can often result in acrimonious disputes although it has to be admitted that time pressures sometimes force retrospective action on the parties. At least a schedule of rates provides a safety curtain and a wise software development company will ensure that all the additional or modified work is carefully noted in terms of resources and duration.

If the changes made to the specification are considerable, the contracting parties ought to contemplate whether it would be better to terminate the existing contract and substitute it with another after negotiating a new contract and any settlement under the old contract. This is an example of novation. If the changes made are substantial this is probably the best route. Of course, the costs and liabilities under the original contract which had already been incurred must be dealt with by mutual agreement (otherwise there could be an action for breach of contract). An experienced software development company should not get into a situation such that the original contract has to be substituted by a new one. Where the work to be carried out is particularly difficult or covers new ground, it may be better to make an agreement to build a prototype system first backed by a broad specification, with a view to a subsequent contract to build the finished system backed by a much more detailed and explicit specification, written with the benefit of the experience gained in building the prototype.

The specification will have to address all the technical issues associated with the performance of the software. In particular, the three most important items which the specification should discuss are:

- a detailed description of the tasks the software will perform;
- the equipment on which the software will run and other software with which it will interface; and
- how quickly the software will carry out the operations involved, bearing in mind any networking and concurrent use requirements.

The client may have little knowledge of the mysteries of computer science and will hope to receive some guidance on these matters from the experts writing the programs. Here, as elsewhere, however, the client should contemplate seeking independent advice unless he has his own computer professionals to consult. There are real dangers at this stage of over-optimism by both parties, plain misunderstanding or just a difference in emphasis of priorities. A great number of retrospectively ill-founded assumptions can be made about performance; computer programmers and analysts cannot be expected to know all the intricacies of the client's business, the nature of which may call for very fast information processing.

If the client does rely on the software development company to supply a system that will do a particular job, he can expect that it will bring a certain degree of expertise to bear upon the work and will perform its part of the contract in a workmanlike manner, using reasonable care and skill. Companies in the business of writing computer systems are implicitly holding themselves out to possess a minimum level of skill and experience when it comes to writing their particular type of system, and the courts have long been prepared to imply an appropriate duty in contracts for supplying services, such as in the case of hairdressers, garages and the like. A contract to write or modify computer software is analogous to such contracts; indeed it is a service contract. In *Stewart* v *Reavell's Garage* [1952] 2 QB 545, a customer relied on a garage to reline the brakes on his 1929 Bentley. The garage obtained a quotation from a sub-contractor; the quotation was recommended to the customer who agreed to it. The work by the sub-contractor was carried out in a way unsuitable for Bentley cars and because of this the customer crashed the car, causing £362 worth of damage. It was held that, because the customer had relied on the garage to repair the brakes in a suitable and efficient manner and because the garage owed a duty to provide good workmanship and materials of good quality so that the braking system would be reasonably fit for its purpose, the garage was liable for the faulty work, even though the work itself was carried out by a sub-contractor. The garage had a duty to select and recommend a suitable sub-contractor. The implications of this are very appropriate in the field of software development, given that it is very common for sub-contractors and freelance programmers to be used by the main contractor.

An equivalent duty of care and skill is now implied into service contracts, where the supplier of the service is acting in the course of business, by section 13 of the Supply of Goods and Services Act 1982 or equivalent common law terms in Scotland. We have already seen in Chapter 17 that the courts are willing to imply these terms into contracts for writing software and, indeed, into contracts for feasibility studies for software. Liability for loss resulting from failure to exercise reasonable care and skill can be excluded or limited subject to the controls in the Unfair Contract Terms Act 1977. However, the inclusion of exclusion or limitation clauses would be unlikely to add to the client's confidence in the software development company and, in any case, the courts have shown some reluctance to enforce such terms. The fact that the burden of proof in respect of the reasonableness of an exclusion clause lies with the party seeking to rely on it is another point to bear in mind. Generally, it will be better (and safer) business practice for the software development company to provide a reasonable level of insurance cover against its own negligence and to use that as a basis of any limitation of liability clause. Nonetheless, the expense of arranging insurance is an overhead which will be reflected in the price of the software. A high level of insurance cover could significantly reduce a software company's competitiveness. It should be noted that, by section 2(1) of the Unfair Contract Terms Act 1977, business liability for death or personal injury cannot be excluded or restricted at all.

In terms of computers, if you have a particular computer and approach a company to write software for that computer, the company has a duty to bring a reasonable amount of skill to the task and to supply software that will be fit for its purpose. If your computer is heavily committed to other processing tasks and has little spare processing capacity, you can expect the software development company to use its skill in taking this into account. If it sub-lets part of the work, it is under a duty also to select a sub-contractor capable of carrying out the work in a like manner. The software development company cannot avoid liability for defective software merely because it has asked you to agree to the particular sub-contractor recommended by it. An example of a sub-contract is where a software development company, contracted to write an accounts package, uses another specialist firm or, perhaps, freelance programmers to carry out part of the work. The software development company owes a duty to the client to choose the specialist firm and the freelance programmers carefully.

Other matters to which the specification should address itself include details of any data files and information to be entered to be used by the programs and how they will be entered. Will entry be by keyboard, optical character reader, from magnetic disk, CD or DVD or through a modem? Will the entry be of an interactive nature and can the programs operate quickly enough? What results and reports are expected from the system and is there any likelihood of further reports being required once the programs have become established in use? What files, temporary and permanent, will be created? Is access to be controlled by passwords and, if so, is a hierarchical system of passwords required? With what other software must the new software interact or be interoperable?

The feature of computer systems which lies at the root of many disputes is the speed of operation. Computers work at fantastic speeds, measured in microseconds, but they have a great disadvantage in that the vast majority are designed to process information in serial fashion, a piece at a time. The human brain, because of its massive parallel processing capabilities, can easily outperform a computer and, when given real work to do, computers are anything but fast. Therefore, it is essential that the specification contains information about the speed of the programs in use – for example, response times at the keyboard (two seconds can seem an eternity), the time taken to sort items into ascending or descending order, the time taken to compile and print reports. These timings should indicate the effect of multiple concurrent use of the same files and the fact that the equipment might be carrying out other demanding work at the same time. The specification should also describe the portability of the software – that is, can it be run on other equipment with little effort or will a major 'refit' be needed? The client should ask questions about the effect of a future change of or a modification to his computer equipment or operating system software. Another problem might concern the compatibility of the software with other systems run by the client; can data be easily transferred from the new system to the client's existing computer systems and vice versa?

Time for completion

A contract for writing computer programs and preparing associated documentation is fundamentally different in character from a contract for the sale of goods but is, however, analogous to a building contract. The performance of the contract is not a single event but rather extends over a period of time. This fact alone brings some doubt to any assumption that time is of the essence of the contract. We have already seen that, although time for payment is not usually a condition in a commercial sale of goods contract, time for delivery is. If we enter into a contract with a builder for the construction of a house, however, we would not expect that we could lawfully repudiate the contract if the house was completed a day late and the position is similar with contracts for writing computer software. A delay of a few days might give rise to a claim for damages but would be unlikely to give the client the right to cancel the contract altogether, although if completion is very late the client may be entitled to rescind the contract.

Writing computer software carries with it a degree of unpredictability and the client should be aware of this, especially if he is planning his business operations around a particular completion date. Unexpected problems frequently arise which can add considerably to the overall time for performance, just as construction projects are often delayed because of unanticipated problems with the sub-soil which has to support a new building, requiring extensive changes to be made to the design of the foundations. In *Salvage Association* v *CAP Financial Services Ltd* [1995] FSR 654, however, the judge held that time is of the essence in a contract for writing software, though, in that case, the delay was inordinately long. It is submitted that, if the delivery of the software is late by only a few days, this would not amount to a breach of condition (or a material breach in Scotland) giving the client the option of cancelling the contract. An exception would be where the delivery date was particularly important such as where the software was to be written for some special event such as the launch of a new product at an international exhibition.

In case the software is completed late, it would be sensible to have some contractual provisions to cover this situation rather than arguing about the level of compensation. The usual method of dealing with late completion is to include a term which gives the client a right to liquidated damages. These damages may be quantified as a certain sum of money for every week completion is late – for example, £1500 per week. The sum must be a genuine pre-estimate of the financial losses which the client will suffer as a result of the delay and it must not be in the nature of a penalty. The courts will not enforce a 'penalty clause'. An example of acceptable liquidated damages would be a pre-estimate of the loss of profits arising from the late completion. Sometimes, it may be in the client's interests to offer a bonus for early completion.

It is not always easy to determine when completion has taken place. The software might have been installed on the client's computer and be working in a fashion, but it requires some further work to be carried out. Alternatively, the programs may be finished but the documentation is only available in draft form. It is clear that problems might arise in determining when completion takes place and it is advisable to define completion in the contract. Does it include testing and documentation? What, if anything, does the client have to do to signify his acceptance of the software? What is the effect of completion on payment? Do all outstanding moneys become due? The concept of substantial completion could be used whereby upon substantial completion a large percentage of the agreed price becomes due with the moiety retained by the client until the remaining work has been completed. Of course, substantial completion must be defined if this approach is used.

If completion is late, this will not necessarily be the fault of the software development company. The completion of the work could be late as a result of the inaction of the client in providing information necessary to the continuation of the work or the client might fail to provide on time the facilities required by the software development company. The contract should clearly state what information and facilities the client must provide and when he must provide them. The contract should also contain machinery dealing with extensions to the time for completion as a result of the client's default in his duties under the contract and compensation for the additional expenses incurred. Ideally, the contract should include rates or formulae to help determine such additional costs.

Maintenance of and enhancements to the software

No matter how much skill and care have been put into the writing of the software or how much testing has been carried out, the odds are overwhelmingly in favour of it containing errors or, colloquially, 'bugs'. Some of these bugs might not appear for a considerable period of time and they may be discoverable only under a very rare combination of factors. If a bug does appear this will normally be a breach of warranty and the client can expect that the software development company will correct the error. Naturally, the latter will wish to limit responsibility to correct such errors to a specified period of time. It is therefore important that the contract takes account of the maintenance of the software. A compromise might have to be struck: perhaps the software development company will be happy to rectify errors in the programs and manuals free of charge for a period of time and thereafter they will be prepared to offer this service for a fee. The Court of Appeal in *Saphena Computing Ltd v Allied Collection Agencies Ltd* [1995] FSR 616 has recognised that even when software is delivered there will still be some work to be done. The software will almost certainly contain errors and the software development company will normally be expected to test the software to locate errors and make the necessary modifications. This duty will endure for a period of time though it is difficult to predict how long.

A software development company will usually offer an ancillary contract for maintenance for which the client will have to pay. It would be reckless to eschew a maintenance agreement and the cost of it should be allowed for in the overall budget for the work. However, care needs to be taken to ensure that a maintenance agreement does not simply result in the client paying the software development company for correcting errors that are breaches of quality warranties under the development contract. A maintenance agreement should also provide for enhancements and updates to be made available to the client, which can be very useful because software is continually being developed and having new features added to it. There is likely to be a long-term relationship between the client and the software development company if the software is complex or likely to require ongoing development and enhancement.

Section 50C of the Copyright, Designs and Patents Act 1988 (inserted by the Copyright (Computer Programs) Regulations 1992) allows the lawful user to copy or adapt a computer program for error correction purposes. Terms in a licence agreement prohibiting this are not automatically void under copyright law though they may be subject to other legal controls such as the principle of non-derogation from grant or competition law. Without a copy of the source code (and preparatory materials), however, maintenance of a computer program is, to all intents and purposes, a practical impossibility.

In many cases, the software development company will be unwilling to allow third parties, or even the client himself, to modify the software. The person carrying out the work might do so badly and the software could acquire a bad reputation as a result and this would reflect on the software development company. If the client considers it very important to be allowed to modify the software himself or use the services of a third party providing software maintenance, this should be discussed before the contract is made and a suitable term incorporated. It is highly desirable that the client receives a copy of the source code to facilitate the making of modifications should this be permitted and the contract must clearly provide for this. The contract should also cover questions of copyright ownership in the modifications, the assignment of modifications and whether the software development company has any other rights in respect of them.

In extreme cases, a court may be prepared to order the software company to hand over a copy of the source code. In *Psychometric Services Ltd v Merant International Ltd* [2002] FSR 8, the claimant created and marketed tests to assess job candidates and decided to carry on its business on the Internet. It engaged the defendant to design the websites. The original price was said to be capped at £195,000. The work turned out to be much more complex than originally envisaged and the cap was lifted by the claimant. Eventually, the claimant paid over £700,000 but the defendant claimed a further £960,000 was outstanding. Eventually a software audit was carried out by a third party which indicated that there were serious problems with the software and that it had been written in a substandard fashion. The claimant had lost confidence in the defendant's ability to correct the software effectively and quickly enough and was worried that if the websites did not function properly very soon, the claimant would go out of business. The claimant therefore sought a mandatory injunction requiring the defendant to deliver up the source code to it so that a third party could correct the software. Mr Justice Laddie granted the injunction. This was an interim hearing and the judge had to consider the effects of a wrong decision. He accepted that the claimant would probably go into liquidation if it did not get a copy of the source code and this would mean that the defendant would not get the money it alleged was outstanding. This favoured granting the order to hand over a copy of the source code.

Escrow

It is worthwhile considering what happens if the software development company goes out of business. Will the client be able to maintain and modify the software or find another company to do this for him? If the software development company has only supplied the object code this will be very difficult, if not impossible. A receiver or a company taking over the software development company's business may obtain the source code and design materials and expect to be paid by the client for a copy. If the software development company is taken over, the new parent company might refuse to support the software yet not be willing to make the source code available. Many licence agreements include an escrow clause which is invaluable in such situations – that is, where the client is not given a copy of the source code and other design materials.

Source code escrow describes a situation where the software development company deposits, with an independent person, a source code copy of the programs together with copies of all the documentation and design and preparatory materials essential to the continuing maintenance of the software – in short, all the materials that will enable the client or a third party to take over the maintenance and further development of the software. The independent person (the 'stakeholder') holding these materials is instructed not to divulge them to anyone and to keep them generally secure. If a specified event occurs, such as the software development company going out of business or being unable to continue to support the software, then the stakeholder will release all the materials to the client who will then have all the information he needs to arrange for the software to be supported. Escrow works in the form of a guarantee or as insurance should something unfortunate happen to the software development company or if it fails to maintain the software properly or at all. The stakeholder must obviously be someone who can be absolutely trusted in the performance of his duties under the escrow arrangement and the details of the agreement need to be carefully thought out. It should include terms dealing with the following matters:

- definitions of the source code and other materials subject to the escrow;
- confidentiality of the source code imposed on the escrow organisation and the client should the source code be released under the agreement;
- delivery of updates to the escrow organisation;
- payment details and provisions in respect of late payment;
- a detailed description of the eventualities which will bring about the client's right to obtain the source code;
- an indemnity that the software development company owns the rights in the source code or otherwise has the right to deposit the source code and eventually, if the right

to obtain the source code comes to fruition, that the client will be able to use the source code without hindrance ('quiet enjoyment');
- a system of formal notices requiring the software development company to carry out maintenance by a given deadline subject to the release of the source code;
- termination of the agreement, for example, because of the failure of the client to pay an outstanding fee after receipt of a written demand; and
- the liability of the escrow organisation for loss of or damage to the source code and other materials.

An organisation which provides an escrow service is the National Computing Centre at Oxford House, Oxford Road, Manchester M1 7ED.

The typical mechanism is that an agreement is signed by the client, the software development company and the organisation offering the escrow service. This is a strange tripartite arrangement as shown in Fig. 18.3. A basic rule of English contract law is that there can only be two parties to a contract although, in some circumstances, a third party may be able to enforce a term in a contract. An escrow agreement can be seen as two separate contracts: one between the software development company and the escrow organisation, the other between the escrow organisation and the client. The way the service will be paid for reinforces this analysis. Usually, the software development company will pay a fee upon depositing the materials with the escrow organisation and the client will then pay the periodic fees to the escrow organisation and, if it becomes necessary, a release fee.

The implications of mergers and takeovers will need to be carefully dealt with: the new company might want to carry on business as usual, keeping the source code from the client, for reasons connected with confidentiality. The basic test determining whether to pass on the source code and other materials subject to an escrow agreement should be the permanent inability, for whatever reason, of the software development company to continue to support the software.

Once the event that triggers release of the source code and other materials occurs, the client should act within a reasonable time to seek release. In *CardBASE Technologies Ltd* v *ValuCard Nigeria plc* [2002] EWHC 991 (Ch), the claimant, a supplier of software, granted a non-exclusive licence to the defendant which provided services to banks in Nigeria in respect of smart card computer software. The escrow agreement (with the National Computing Centre as escrow agent) provided for release of the

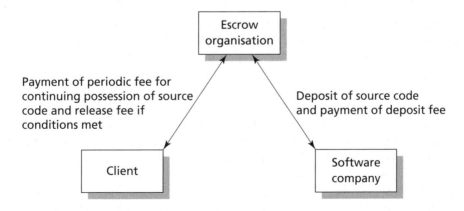

Fig. 18.3 Escrow arrangement

source code under certain conditions including if the software company entered into liquidation or had a receiver appointed or entered into any composition in satisfaction of its debts, or a scheme of arrangement of its affairs, with its creditors. On 18 December 2001, the claimant entered into a scheme of arrangement with its members and creditors. Two days later, the defendant asked for confirmation that the latest version of the source code had been deposited with the escrow agent and, on 10 January 2002, the defendant asked the escrow agent to verify that the newly deposited material was capable of being used to generate the latest version of the software. The verification was carried out on 17 January 2002 and, on 29 January 2002, the defendant served the escrow agent with a declaration of release as required by the agreement.

The claimant sought an order restraining the escrow agent from releasing the source code on the basis of two arguments. First, by exercising the right to have the verification process carried out, the defendant had elected not to exercise its right to release under the escrow agreement. This argument was rejected as it was not inconsistent with release to seek confirmation that the latest version of the source code was suitable for its purpose. It was reasonable for the defendant to exercise this right as a precursor to exercising its right to seek release of the source code. Furthermore, verification after the trigger event was a result of the claimant's tardiness in depositing the latest version of the source code. The second argument was that there was an implied term to the effect that the defendant had to exercise its right to seek release of the source code within a reasonable time of the trigger event and the defendant had failed to do this. The judge accepted that such a term could be implied but the defendant had sought release within a reasonable time of the trigger event. The defendant was entitled to consider its position once the release event occurred and was entitled to satisfy itself that the latest version of the source code had been deposited and was satisfactory. Other factors were that Christmas and the New Year intervened and the defendant had to get certain documents together, including a statutory or notarised declaration. Finally, the claimant could not prove that the delay, such as it was, was prejudicial to it or anyone else. This seems an entirely reasonable decision but it does indicate that a client should act expediently to apply for release once the client becomes aware that an event triggering release has occurred.

Copyright and other intellectual property rights

The contract may impose duties on both parties associated with intellectual property rights. The software development company will be anxious to prevent unauthorised copying of the programs and will want its techniques kept secret. The client will want to be able to use the software with impunity, without interfering with the rights of some third party who might seek an injunction preventing continued use of the software. The client will also be worried about the fact that some of the software development company's staff will have gained a detailed insight into his business. The law of copyright and, to some extent, the law of confidence will give some protection to the software development company should the programs or the ideas contained therein be copied or plagiarised, but problems of proof and evidence make it desirable to place a contractual duty on the client to prevent copying or unauthorised disclosure of methods. This duty will run in parallel to any duties imposed by intellectual property law, but the contractual approach will be useful because it will draw the client's attention to the existence of these rights and the importance of making his employees aware of them and the consequences of infringement.

The client's employees may make, surreptitiously, copies of the programs and pass these on to others. If the software development company discovers these copies, it has remedies available under copyright law to prevent the use of these copies by the recipients and their further transmission to others, but it might be difficult to prove that the copies originated from the client. A unique serial or code number could be embedded in the programs identifying the software as being that given to the client and if the client is made aware of this and the consequences he may be more careful. The contract may state that the licence is to be terminated forthwith should copies of the programs find their way into the hands of third parties without the permission of the software development company. This will not preclude the software development company from seeking remedies for infringement of copyright – a fact which is often expressly stated in software licences.

On the subject of confidentiality, the client will want a term included strengthening and extending the common law duty of confidence. He will want to prevent the software development company's employees divulging details of his business methods and techniques and other confidential information such as client accounts, debtors and creditors. It is inevitable, if the contract is for a substantial amount of work, that the employees of the software development company and any freelance staff they use will be exposed to confidential information. Without such a term in the contract, the client may be lacking legal recourse, especially if the confidential nature of materials involved is not otherwise made clear. The software development company, too, may have worries about confidentiality: it may have developed special techniques for writing and testing software which the client's staff might see when the software is installed and tested. A contractual term imposing a two-way duty in respect of confidentiality should be included in the contract. There may also be data protection issues and the software development company may be required to be under obligations in relation to the security of personal data which must be in writing or evidenced in writing (see Part Five of this book).

Warranties and indemnities

It is usual for a licence agreement to contain a section headed 'Warranties and Indemnities'. Warranties normally found include those relating to the fact that the software development company warrants that it has the right to grant the rights to the client provided for by the agreement and that the client will have 'quiet enjoyment' of the software and the client's use of it will be unaffected by any third party rights. Where, instead of licensing the right to use the software, the agreement is one under which the title to the copyright (ownership) is transferred (that is, an assignment of copyright), the Law of Property Act 1925 used to contain a form of words which would automatically include such warranties in the agreement (although that Act was primarily concerned with rights in or over land, it also had some impact on other forms of property transactions). The person granting the rights would use the term 'As beneficial owner'. Now, as a result of the Law of Property (Miscellaneous Provisions) Act 1994, the phrase used is 'With full title guarantee'. This automatically implies covenants to the effect that the person making the assignment has the right to do so and that the property right transferred is free from all charges and encumbrances and all other rights exercisable by third parties (sections 2 and 3). Other warranties may be given which relate to the performance of the software and its freedom from major defects. These may find their full expression in the specification.

Another aspect of intellectual property rights concerns the possibility that the software might infringe a third party's copyright or other right such as a patent or trade mark. Whether or not the infringement is deliberate will not usually be relevant. The client could have been using the software quite happily for a number of years when the software development company is successfully sued for infringement of copyright by some third party. That third party may then decide to pursue all the clients of the software development company who are using the infringing software and seek injunctions to prevent them continuing to use the software. Even if the client is not troubled in this way by the third party, the software development company will be prevented from continuing to support the software. It may be that the third party will be happy to allow the client to continue to use the software in return for a licence fee. In any case, the client should satisfy himself that there is a term in the agreement with the software development company covering the infringement of intellectual property rights belonging to others. The term should give the client an indemnity against the event of legal action being taken against him as a result of the software infringing third-party rights. The term should be widely drafted so as to include all forms of intellectual property rights such as copyright, patents, designs and trade marks. The costs and implications of suddenly being unable to use an item of software might be quite enormous and it is likely that the software development company will hope to limit its liability under this head, perhaps to the amount of the licence fee. Any term dealing with an indemnity against third party claims should allow the software development company a reasonable time to modify the software so that it no longer infringes the third-party right, if that is a possibility without jeopardising the software's functionality.

Liability

Computer software is widely used to assist in the decision-making processes in business. A decision to engage upon a particular line of action may be based upon an interpretation of the results of running a computer program. For example, a construction company might submit a bid for a motorway contract worth many millions of pounds; the bid total will have been calculated by estimators using computer software. If there is an error in the software, the total might be miscalculated by, say, £1 million. This could mean that the company fails to secure the contract because their bid is too high or, worse still, they win the contract by too great a margin and make a substantial loss.

The software development company will be very keen to limit its liability if the software proves to be defective. The software development company will attempt to limit or exclude its liability for defects by the insertion of a suitably drafted exemption clause – for example, limiting its liability to the cost of replacing the software or remedying the defect. This is unsatisfactory from the client's point of view. Until recently, this way of dealing with liability has been very common but now must be reviewed in the light of recent court decisions such as those discussed in the previous chapter. It is now clear that the controls over exclusion clauses in the Unfair Contract Terms Act 1977 will apply to most terms in software licences, the only major exception, in England, Wales and Northern Ireland, being those terms dealing exclusively with the transfer or creation of intellectual property rights. Thus, section 2 of the Act applies to liability for negligence and section 3 controls attempts to exclude liability arising from the performance of the contract. In some cases, liability cannot be excluded or limited at all – for example, in the case of death or personal injury resulting from negligence. In most other cases, the exclusion or limitation of business liability depends upon the reasonableness of the appropriate term.

A software development company should consider taking out professional liability insurance to a reasonable and affordable level and limit its liability accordingly. Alternatively, the software development company could offer a minimum level of insurance and offer to increase this if the client is prepared to pay the additional premium. How successful this approach will be is difficult to predict but, above all, the software development company must make sure that its liability under the licence and its insurance are matched as far as it is possible to do this and that the client is fully aware of any limitation of liability and agrees to it.

It should be noted that a defect in software does not necessarily and inexorably lead to the conclusion that the software development company has been negligent or has failed to exercise reasonable care and skill. The problem may result from the client's use of the software and the question of how much control the software development company has over the use by the client may be a factor. For example, in the case of a spreadsheet, a mistake may be the result of an incorrect formula entered by the client or the client may be using the spreadsheet software to make calculations requiring extreme mathematical precision. If the software development company has exercised the level of care and skill to be expected from responsible software development companies writing equivalent software, there should be no liability. If a financial loss arises because the software development company and the client have both been negligent, the amount of damages awarded will be reduced on the basis of contributory negligence.

Arbitration

It is prudent to include provision in the agreement for arbitration whereby a dispute between the parties will be referred to an arbitrator, an independent expert, who will rule on the dispute. Arbitration is a commonly used method of resolving disputes without having to go to the courts. The parties to the contract appoint an independent third party who will listen to both sides and then make a ruling. Arbitration is less formal than a court hearing, although the basic rules of evidence and procedure are adhered to, and it has the advantage that the arbitrator, unlike a judge, will be an expert in the technical matters involved. In a dispute involving computer software, the arbitrator would be expected to have considerable knowledge of software engineering and be a leading member of the computer profession. Another advantage of arbitration over a normal court hearing is that arbitration should be, in principle, quicker and cheaper, although this is not always so. Arbitration hearings can be fairly formal involving the calling of expert witnesses.

It is common for arbitration clauses to state that the arbitrator's decision shall be final and binding on the parties, and the courts will not interfere with an arbitrator's decision unless he has erred on a point of law. A court will usually accept the arbitrator's evaluation of the facts of the case as being conclusive. If the contract provides for arbitration, neither party will be able to take a short cut to the courts because a judge will insist that the arbitration procedure is adhered to in the first instance. It must be stressed that the decision of an arbitrator, and any award(s) he makes, is binding upon the parties.

A disadvantage of arbitration is that the arbitrator might not have the depth of legal knowledge of a High Court judge and an arbitrator could be more likely to err on a point of law or procedure. Although a judge will not usually have the technical expertise of an arbitrator, judges by their training and experience have the knack of getting to the kernel of a dispute and are able to concentrate on the important issues without being sidetracked. It must be said, however, that, in practice, arbitration works extremely well and the standard of arbitrators, who belong to the Chartered Institute of Arbitrators, is very high. If an arbitration clause is included in the agreement, the machinery for selecting an arbitrator should also be dealt with, the usual practice being to appoint an arbitrator agreed upon by the parties or, failing such agreement, a person to be nominated by the President of the British Computer Society which holds a register of suitably qualified arbitrators.

Alternative dispute resolution

Taking a dispute to the courts or submitting it to arbitration will plunge the parties into the adversarial contest fundamental to the English legal system. The outcome often will be total success or failure with no half measures even though the decision of the court may be based on the most slender weight in favour of one party on a balance of probabilities. Occasionally, a more attractive route may be that offered by alternative dispute resolution (ADR) where a mediator is appointed to assist and encourage the parties in the negotiation of a settlement to their mutual satisfaction.

The mediator can take an active role and make suggestions for resolving the conflict. However, there is no legally binding obligation on the parties to continue with the process and they may abandon it at any time. The process itself is based on informality and consent. It is said to be a highly successful means of settling disputes with an estimated settlement rate of 90 per cent (Hayward, D, 'Compromising Positions', *Computing*, 8 June 1995, p.31). One technique which may be used is for both sides to make a presentation before senior members of the organisations who will then attempt to negotiate a settlement with the assistance of the mediator. It would be better if the negotiators were not directly involved in the matters leading to the dispute as they are likely to be more objective and more willing to compromise. The following example shows how ADR might present the best course of action.

Imagine that Pickwick Trading has asked Bardell Software to develop and deliver new accounting software. An appropriate contract was made and a detailed specification annexed to it. When the software was delivered it was found to be slightly slower than allowed by the benchmark tests in the specification. Additionally, one particular feature was missing in that the software would not produce annual VAT summary reports as detailed in the specification. The total price is £85,000, 10 per cent of which was payable upon commencement of the work. The time for delivery is three months.

Pickwick has refused to accept the program and has withheld the final payment of

£76,500. Bardell presses for more time to add the VAT report and argues that the speed of the software is so close to that specified as to be of no consequence. The possible outcomes of resolving the dispute by litigation and ADR are discussed below.

Litigation

Bardell sues Pickwick for wrongful repudiation of the contract and seeks damages equivalent to the outstanding sum plus interest and other direct costs. Pickwick submits a defence and counterclaim based on the shortcomings of the program. Pickwick claims the return of the £8500 already paid plus £12,500 in wasted management time, etc. At the court action, the judge holds that Bardell is guilty of a breach of condition and that Pickwick's repudiation was lawful. He awards Pickwick £21,000 plus costs, leaving Bardell to pick up the bill for £31,000 in legal costs also.

This result is unsatisfactory from the point of view of both parties. At the end of it all, Pickwick does not have the program it wanted and will now have to engage another software development company. It may be another six months or so before the program is ready. This could seriously handicap Pickwick's business. Bardell is even less happy as three months' work has been wasted and it has a bill for £52,000. Bardell now thinks that it would have been better had it never heard of Pickwick – a view that is reciprocated by the latter.

Alternative dispute resolution

The contract between Pickwick and Bardell contains a term providing for ADR and a mediator is appointed. After only two days of negotiation the following settlement is reached:

● Bardell will be given two more weeks to complete the software so that it will be capable of producing the VAT report. (Bardell has also agreed to alter a particular screen display because Pickwick has had second thoughts about it for a fee of £3000.)

Pickwick will be given a 5 per cent discount on the total price which it will put towards some additional memory for its computer which should increase its speed of operation.

Pickwick and Bardell will share the mediator's fee of £2500. It is left to the reader to reflect on which is the best solution.

Other ADR techniques are adjudication in which a neutral third party gives a non-binding ruling on the case or certain aspects of the case and expert appraisal in which a technical expert assesses each of the parties' cases for the purpose of assisting negotiations.

ADR is not always appropriate; indeed, it may only be a minority of disputes for which it represents a satisfactory method. There are some drawbacks. It is inappropriate where a point of law is involved, where the issues are very complex or where one party seeks an injunction or court declaration. Although any negotiations will have taken place without prejudice to either party's legal rights, there is danger that subsequent litigation could be influenced by what has been said in abortive negotiations. ADR allows the parties to gauge the strengths and weaknesses of each other's case and could even be used, cynically, as a prelude to litigation. It should be noted, however, that the court will not, under normal circumstances, allow evidence to be given of what has been admitted in negotiations which have been conducted 'without prejudice'. Another factor is that getting involved with ADR could compromise any insurance policy that might be relied upon to pay damages and costs awarded in any court action.

Any ADR clause in a contract must make it clear that anything admitted, said or done in connection with ADR is without prejudice to the legal rights of the parties. The clause should make provision for the appointment of a mediator (who should be skilled in resolving disputes by negotiation), payment of his fees (usually these will be borne equally by the parties) and procedures to be adopted. The Centre for Dispute Resolution, at Princes House, 95 Gresham Street, London EC2V 7NA, provides information and advice about ADR and the procedures to be adopted.

The courts are becoming increasingly keen to encourage parties to consider ADR and a Practice Direction has been published to deal with the impact this may have on legal proceedings and directions given by the judge. See, for example, *Practice Note* [1995] 1 All ER 385 (Queen's Bench Division and Chancery Division); *Practice Note* [1998] 1 Lloyd's Rep 126 (Commercial Court) and *Practice Note* [1999] 2 All ER 490 (Court of Appeal). Further guidance notes send a clear message that parties in dispute really ought to attempt ADR before going to court.

Pulling out of an agreement to submit to ADR may have serious implications in costs if the dispute comes before the courts. In *Leicester Circuits Ltd* v *Coates Brothers plc* [2003] EWCA Civ 290, a dispute arose about the quality of ink supplied by the defendant to the claimant for the manufacture of printed circuit boards. The claimant sought damages of over £600,000 but the parties agreed to mediation. However, just before it was about to start in earnest, the defendant withdrew from mediation, leaving the claimant no option but to commence legal proceedings. The trial lasted for 18 days and judgment was given in favour of the claimant. However, the defendant successfully appealed to the Court of Appeal. Normally, costs follow the result. In other words, the losing party pays the legal costs of the winning party. However, in this case, the Court of Appeal made no costs order for the period between just before the time the defendant withdrew from mediation until the appeal, leaving the defendant to pay its own costs during that period which included the very expensive trial at first instance. The claimant was ordered to pay the defendant's cost before that time and subsequently in relation to the Court of Appeal proceedings.

Other terms

A contract for the writing or modification of software will undoubtedly contain other terms dealing with matters such as the training of the client's staff, termination of the licence and misrepresentation. These will be dealt with in Chapter 19 which covers 'off-the-shelf' software. It is also usual to include a term stating which is the applicable law; this is essential where there is any doubt – for example, where a Scottish and English company are entering into a contract. Entire agreement clauses are common which attempt to limit the terms of the contract to those expressly contained within the formal agreement, thereby attempting to exclude any representations that may have been made in preliminary negotiations. Notwithstanding this, there may still be a remedy for misrepresentation should one party have entered into the contract on the basis of a promise by the other party which turns out to be untrue. Finally, the question of staff poaching is often addressed. This is where one party offers employment to an employee of the other party. The employees of each party will probably be in close contact for some time – for example, because the software is being developed at the client's premises – and this gives each party the opportunity to spot a 'star'. The client may have a vested interest in employing a key member of the software development company's staff who has intimate knowledge of the software written under the contract. Over a period of time, a software development company could find that it has a high turnover of staff. The usual means of countering this threat is for a clause stating that neither party will offer employment (or canvass with a view to offering employment) members of the other party's staff for a period of time, normally six months. In practical terms, there is little to be done beyond this, especially as such terms could be deemed to be in restraint of trade.

Consideration could be given to the use of standard form contracts such as those published by the Chartered Institute of Purchasing and Supply, at Easton House, Easton on the Hill, Stamford, Lincolnshire, PE9 3NZ. These contract forms have been developed to provide a fair balance between the parties' interests and incorporate a great deal of experience in this field. Standard form agreements exist for a variety of hardware and software contracts and can be adapted, if necessary, for a specific contract.

Independent professional supervision

In the case of large important contracts for writing software it may be advisable that the performance of the contract is overseen by a chartered engineer who is a member of the British Computer Society. This person would be responsible for the following aspects:

- ensuring compliance with the specification;
- general supervision;
- determining whether the software is acceptable;
- certifying payments and completion;
- fixing rates for delays or extra work;
- authorising extensions of time for unavoidable delays or additional work; and
- acting as a first-stop informal mediator.

Although it is normal for such a person to be paid by the client, the contract should give certain powers to him as regards determination of the reciprocal rights and duties of the client and software development company. A chartered engineer will remain neutral as between the parties and will help the parties to resolve difficulties amicably and fairly, being particularly good at dealing with the day-to-day minor problems that are bound to occur. This will prevent small problems turning into full blown disputes with the parties breathing fire at each other. This form of contract supervision has been used to great effect for well over 100 years in the construction industry. Should the engineer be unable to bring the parties to agreement concerning a serious difference, the parties could still have recourse to an independent arbitrator or ADR.

Is there a contract?

It is not unusual for work to begin on a contract for the development of software before the precise details of the contract have been properly agreed and formalised. The modern pressures of business life may make it tempting to commence work before the 'legal stuff' has been sorted out but it is a temptation that should be avoided if at all possible. After committing resources or carrying out work, the other party may claim that there is not a contract. Even if it is accepted that there is a binding contract, there may be some uncertainty as to the precise terms of the contract and there is a limit to how much the courts may be willing to imply. Uncertainty itself can be a factor in making a purported contract void and unenforceable.

The case of *Fraser Williams (Southern) Ltd* v *Prudential Holborn Ltd* (unreported) 22 July 1992 provides an example of the dangers and difficulties which might ensue if work begins before a contract is properly in place although, in the event, it was held that there was a valid contract. The claimant submitted a proposal to the defendant to develop software. It was dated 3 March 1989 and was expressed as being 'subject to contract'. Two telephone calls from the defendant on 7 and 9 March 1989 confirmed that the claimant had got the job and a letter was sent from the claimant to the defendant on 10 March 1989 confirming this, though the letter showed that there were still some things to be resolved, in particular how responsibilities would be shared between the claimant and an independent consultant engaged by the defendant in respect of the software. On 13 March 1989 the claimant commenced work and on 5 April it sent a draft contract to the defendant. Subsequently, the claimant raised three invoices which were paid by the defendant, but on 5 May 1989 the defendant informed the claimant that it was terminating the relationship and requested that the claimant vacate the defendant's premises immediately. The claimant complained in writing of the alleged breach of contract by the defendant but the correspondence remained unanswered until, on 27 November 1989, the defendant's solicitor wrote to the claimant asserting that there was no contract between them. It was argued that the letter of 10 March 1989 was merely a letter of intent and, even if it were an acceptance, there was still no contract as the claimant's offer was expressed to be subject to contract.

It was held that there was a binding contract. A number of factors were important, in particular:

- the claimant committed significant resources to the work and this was suggestive that there was a contract – it would hardly have done so otherwise;
- the proposal made it clear that the claimant required a contract to be in force before it commenced work;
- the phrase 'subject to contract' was of very limited effect – the proposal indicated that a contract could come into being in a number of ways by using terminology indicating the existence of a contract such as 'signing of the contract', 'signing the order' and placing a 'firm order';
- the letter of 10 March 1989 was a clear acceptance – it was not expressed as being a letter of intent nor was it stated to be 'subject to contract';
- the issue of shared responsibilities yet to be resolved was deemed to be an administrative matter and did not detract from the contract being sufficiently certain to have effect;
- even if the letter of 10 March 1989 did not create a contract, the subsequent con-

duct of the parties was sufficient – the claimant did some work and the defendant paid for it, and at no time during this period did the defendant seek to redefine the functions of the claimant.

The dangers inherent in embarking on work without a formal contract in place are fairly obvious. In the above case, if the court had held otherwise, the software developer would have found it difficult to obtain any recompense for the work it carried out. One possibility is under a *quantum meruit* (see below). Another difficulty is determining the precise nature and scope of the contractual terms. If, eventually, in the above case, an administrative decision was taken assigning responsibility between the software developer and the independent consultant, it could have been detrimental to the software developer. It could, for example, reduce the total job value for the software developer or increase the amount of work to be completed in an already tight timescale. However, where there is some uncertainty as to the precise terms of the contract, the terms implied by the Supply of Goods and Services Act 1982 or common law may save the contract. Otherwise, if there is a previous course of dealing between the parties, that may provide some clue as to the precise scope of the parties' rights and obligations under the contract. The courts will not, however, write the contract for the parties and, as HH Judge Richard Seymour QC said in *Co-operative Group (CWS) Ltd* v *International Computers Ltd* [2003] EWHC 1 (TCC):

> If satisfied that parties did indeed intend to enter into a binding agreement and sought to do so, it is no part of the function of the court to seek to frustrate that intention. At the same time it is no part of the function of the court to impose upon the parties a contract which they did not, objectively, make for themselves.

In *DMA Financial Solutions Ltd* v *BaaN UK Ltd* (unreported) 28 March 2000, BaaN originally provided training to customers of its accounting software. BaaN decided to outsource its training and wanted DMA to take over this role, as BaaN's authorised training provider. Negotiations began between BaaN and DMA for this purpose. Negotiations went well and both sides seemed confident that there would be final agreement. Eventually, BaaN started closing down its training facilities and DMA began recruiting staff to provide training. BaaN passed on training enquiries to DMA but there was still no formal written contract, as BaaN's lawyers were preoccupied with other matters. Eventually, BaaN's lawyers starting raising objections about what had been agreed by the negotiators and eventually sent DMA its standard form contract which differed in many respects from what had been agreed. After a number of exchanges, DMA's position was that a binding contract existed whilst BaaN, which had changed its mind about outsourcing its training, argued that there was not a binding contract.

As to whether the negotiations resulted in a binding contract before a formal written agreement had been executed, Mr Justice Park thought that three possibilities existed:

1 The negotiations were not intended to result in a contract even if fully concluded until such time as a written contract had been drawn up and executed by both sides. This was equivalent to the usual practice when negotiating to buy a house where the phrase 'subject to contract' was commonly used.
2 The negotiations were such that a contract could exist before the execution of a formal written contract – the negotiations resulted in complete agreement.

3 As 2 above but the negotiations did not get far enough for there to be sufficient agreement for a contract to exist.

The judge said that there was no evidence to satisfy him that, in the computer software industry, it was the generally understood usage that agreements are never binding until they have been drawn up by the lawyers and signed. In this particular case, the phrase 'subject to contract' had not been used during negotiations. All the main terms agreed including the price of $250,000, payable in six quarterly instalments. If some point was not raised in negotiations but was not an essential point, that would not prevent a contract coming into existence. An example was the applicable law for the contract. The fact that this had not been raised did not matter as, although it was certain that BaaN's lawyers would insert such a term in the formal written contract, it was highly unlikely that DMA would have complained about it on the basis it had not been previously agreed. Therefore, the judge held that a valid binding agreement existed between the parties.

The fact that there have been extensive negotiations does not, of course, automatically mean that a contract exists. It depends on whether all the terms considered to be important by the parties have been agreed. In *Co-operative Group (CWS) Ltd v International Computers Ltd* [2003] EWHC 1 (TCC), the claimant alleged that there was a contract between it and the defendant (ICL). It was true that there had been extensive negotiations between the parties and that both expected that agreement would be reached. However, no agreement as to liquidated damages for late delivery had been agreed, amongst other things. CWS had insisted that liquidated damages were included in the contract but ICL was unwilling to accede. The inclusion of liquidated damages in a contract to write software is usually a very important term and failure to agree this was clearly fatal to the argument that there was a valid binding contract between the parties. Some of the negotiators for CWS had been unhappy about ICL's performance on other projects and the judge said that a malevolent influence hung over the negotiations. As there was no binding contract, CWS's claim for repudiatory breach of contract was doomed. CWS had claimed no less than £11m.

As negotiations for a contract to write a substantial software system can proceed over a long period of time, it is sensible for the parties to make it absolutely clear what their position is. The use of a suspensive phrase such as 'subject to contract' on documents created during negotiations should be considered. As parties to drawn out negotiations can run up considerable expenses, this seems the safest approach so that both know exactly where they stand. In some cases, the negotiations could run alongside a feasibility study or the development of prototype systems, which could be subject to a separate contract.

Where it turns out that there is no valid contract – for example, through a lack of certainty as to the terms of the contract – the software developer may be entitled to payment on the basis of the work he has done in pursuance of what he believed was a valid contract. The law will require that the defendant pays the claimant for the 'fruit of his labour'. This is what is termed a *quantum meruit* (roughly translated – as much as he deserves). Of course, the defendant must have agreed to or at the very least acquiesced in the claimant carrying out the work. For example, if a software development company is appointed to write some software for a client but the purported contract between them is so vague and uncertain that it is ruled void, then if the software company has done satisfactory work for the client, it ought to be entitled to payment on the basis of a *quantum meruit*. Nevertheless, it is clearly preferable to have a valid and detailed contract containing all the necessary terms in writing and signed by both parties before the work commences. Writing computer software is sufficiently difficult and unpredictable without adding to the problems by having unsatisfactory legal provision for the work.

Chapter 19

Licence agreements for 'off-the-shelf' software

Introduction

Off-the-shelf software is that which is acquired as a ready-made package; it is mass-produced software usually obtained from a dealer and includes familiar packages such as word processing systems, spreadsheets and databases. It can be described as 'general purpose software'. It may be applications software (word processing, etc.), operating system software (for example, Windows, MS-DOS or Unix) or utility software such as disk management software, software for archiving files or anti-virus software. The contractual nature of transactions involving off-the-shelf software is not absolutely clear. Several possibilities exist:

- a licence agreement with the software publisher;
- a sale of goods contract with the dealer;
- a hybrid licence agreement/sale of goods contract with the software publisher (the dealer acting as the software publisher's agent); or
- a *sui generis* (unique) form of contract.

Before looking further at these possibilities, it must be noted that it is the intangible rights which are dominant in the transaction – for example, the right to use the software. This right requires that the licence of the copyright owner, otherwise the copyright and other rights, such as the database right, subsisting in the software (there are likely to be a number of distinct rights in the software), will be infringed. This is confirmed by section 16(2) of the Copyright, Designs and Patents Act 1988 which states that the copyright in a work is infringed by a person who without the licence of the copyright owner does, or authorises another to do, any of the acts restricted by the copyright. As copying a work of copyright extends to making copies which are transient, it is quite clear that simply operating or running software involves making copies, whether transient or not, and this must have the licence of the copyright owner. Of course, in most cases, the software will be copied from the disk or CD on which it was supplied to the hard disk of the computer of the person acquiring the software. Subsequent copies will be made when the software is used as it will be loaded into the volatile memory (RAM) of the computer. The database right gives the owner the right to prevent extraction and/or reutilisation of the contents of the database.

The fact that a licence is required to use software appears to have been overlooked by a number of persons who have considered the nature of a contract for the existence of off-the-shelf software. Another key fact is the method of delivery of the software. It may be handed over in a box which contains disks or a CD together with printed documentation such as a manual and licence agreement. Increasingly, these days, software may be delivered on-line, with no tangible items being delivered to the person acquiring a copy of the software. Where software is supplied on physical media, in some cases the licence agreement will be exposed on the outside of the package. This is the so-called 'shrink-wrap' licence. The idea is that it enables the person acquiring the software to inspect the terms before opening the package. This is usually backed by a statement to the effect that, if the person acquiring the software does not agree with the terms of the licence, he can return the package unopened to the dealer and recover his payment. Another technique is to have the disks or CD in a sealed package separate to the licence and with a statement that breaking the seal signifies acceptance of the terms of the licence agreement, again, usually backed by a promise that the software can be returned before the seal is broken and any payment refunded. In the case of software delivered on-line, the person acquiring it will usually be required to signify his acceptance of the terms of the licence before the software can be 'downloaded'. Incidentally, the word 'download' has come in for judicial scrutiny and in *R v City of London Magistrates Court, ex parte Green* [1997] 3 All ER 551, it was held that it meant 'transfer from one storage device or system to another', as in the *Concise Oxford Dictionary* which also suggests it applies especially in relation to it being done remotely.

Licence agreement

Where no tangible items are transferred to the person acquiring the software – for example, where the software is downloaded from the Internet – the only contract is a licence agreement. This would also apply where software is specially written for a client and installed on the client's computer from the software development company's disks which are then retained by the latter. If the software is obtained remotely, it is likely that an opportunity will be given to read the licence agreement before the person wishing to obtain a copy of the software is committed to the transaction. Some software is available without cost over the Internet but it must be stressed that its copying and subsequent use must still be licensed by the copyright owner. Even with 'free' software, there are likely to be terms imposed on the person acquiring it, controlling or limiting its subsequent use and copying. For example, it may state that the software is for personal and private use only and must not be further distributed or sold without the permission of the copyright owner. There may also be other rights in relation to the software such as the author's moral rights to be identified as such and to object to a derogatory treatment of the work. (These rights do not apply to computer programs but can apply to other items of software such as a database or document or image in digital form.)

The licence agreement is likely to state what the applicable law is and, in many cases, it will be that of one of the states of the United States of America such as California, New York or Florida. Where this is so, it should be noted that the copyright owner may still enforce his rights in the United Kingdom. The Copyright (Application to Other Countries) Order 1999, amended in 2003, extends the qualification provisions for United Kingdom copyright in the original works to persons and incorporated bodies from a considerable number of other countries. This is to give effect to the international conventions on copyright, in particular, the Berne Copyright Convention. Thus, an American company or citizen of the United States can bring an action for copyright infringement occurring within the jurisdiction of the United Kingdom.

As far as the licence agreement itself, this may be enforced subject to the rules of jurisdiction. The licence may state that not only is the licence subject to the law of a particular country or Federal state but that it is also subject to the sole jurisdiction of that country or state. The rules on jurisdiction are complex and, in relation to bringing an action outside the European Economic Area, leave of the court is required before proceedings can be commenced. Within Europe, the Brussels and Lugano Conventions and the Brussels Regulation on jurisdiction and enforcement of judgments in civil matters apply.

The licence will often be of indefinite duration, with no fixed period being stated, although there may be some provision for termination, such as if the person acquiring it, the customer, contravenes some term in the licence agreement which is stated to terminate it. A term requiring the customer not to transfer the software to a third party could be an example. Strictly speaking, the licence cannot endure longer than the copyright in the software because, when the copyright expires, the software effectively falls into the public domain and can be used freely without requiring permission. Some licence agreements allow the customer to terminate unilaterally simply by destroying all the copies of the programs and documentation, although why he should want to do this is hard to understand. If he no longer requires the software, he may be able to transfer both it and the licence to a third party in return for a payment unless the licence agreement provides otherwise.

Sale of goods contract

We have already seen in Chapter 16 that a contract for the acquisition of computer software is unlikely to be regarded as a sale of goods contract, especially where the predominant purpose of the transaction is the acquisition of the software. It has also been noted that where the software is incorporated into goods such as motor cars and the predominant purpose is the acquisition of the goods rather than the software, then it will be a sale of goods contract. Where off-the-shelf software is obtained, it cannot be a sale of goods contract because to so classify the contract is to trivialise the main purpose of the contract, being the right to use the software. To say it is a sale of goods contract on the basis that some tangible items are handed over is to defy logic and to completely ignore the fact that the use of software requires the licence of the copyright owner. Even so, some writers (and some judges) seem unconvinced and prefer to rely on a familiar and tried and tested area of law to discuss or resolve actual or potential disputes. The convenience of this is that the Sale of Goods Act 1979 implies important terms into sale of goods contracts which give the person acquiring the software some useful rights if it turns out to be defective in some way.

The perceived problem of taking a contract to acquire off-the-shelf software out of the sale of goods arena is not serious as the common law has long since been capable of implying appropriate terms into contracts – indeed, many of the terms implied by the Sale of Goods Act 1979 and the Supply of Goods and Services Act 1982 are derived from terms which were implied under common law. This was recognised by Sir Iain Glidewell in the Court of Appeal in *St Albans City & District Council* v *International Computers Ltd* [1997] FSR 251 where he implied a term into a contract for the transfer of a computer program that the program would be reasonably fit for its purpose, that is, for achieving its intended purpose.

Hybrid contract

This is a possible scenario where the property in tangible items also passes to the person acquiring the software in addition to the right to use it, typically where a person goes into a retail computer shop and buys a software package. There may be two separate contracts: one between the person and the shop owner, being a sale of goods contract; and a licence between the person and the owner of the copyright subsisting in the software.

Consider a situation where George, who wishes to obtain a copy of the ABC spreadsheet software, goes to a computer software dealer, Acme Computers, and asks for a copy of the ABC spreadsheet software. He pays £200 and is given a sealed box. Inside the box is a CD on which the software is recorded, a manual and a licence agreement. There must be a contract between George and Acme Computers on the basis of normal sale of goods law. This will relate to the tangible items. Thus, if the CD is physically damaged and the software cannot be loaded onto George's computer because of this, he will have a remedy under section 14(2A) of the Sale of Goods Act 1979 as the CD is not of satisfactory quality. He will be able to obtain a replacement from Acme Computers or he may return the whole package and obtain a refund of the price he paid.

As between George and the owners of the copyright subsisting in ABC, Lemming Software plc, George must have Lemming's licence to use the software. The problem relates to what the terms of that licence are. It could be that they are those printed on the licence agreement which came with the software but there may be some problems with this as George may not have seen the licence until after he bought the software. A basic rule of English contract law (and many other jurisdictions) is that it is not possible to unilaterally introduce new terms into a contract after it has been made, that is, without the agreement of the other party. If the contract is made at the time George hands over the money in return for the box containing the software, then he will not have seen the licence until it is too late.

Software publishers have tried various methods of giving their licence agreements the force of law. One technique used is to have the licence exposed on the outside of the package, the whole being wrapped in clear plastic, so that the licence may be inspected before the package is opened. This is the 'shrink-wrap' licence. Another technique used is for the licence to be printed on a sealed packet containing the disks or CD with a note to say that breaking the seal signifies acceptance of the terms of the licence. This is usually coupled with a promise that the customer can obtain a refund if he returns the software with the seal unbroken in the event of the customer being unwilling to accept the terms.

Both of the above approaches and variants of them are not without their difficulties as a means of incorporating the terms of the licence into the contract with the customer. The opportunity to read the terms comes after the contract is made because, at the latest, this occurs when the package containing the software is handed over to the customer. In *Olley v Marlborough Court Ltd* [1949] 1 All ER 127, a husband and wife went to an hotel and paid for a room. Their room contained a notice excluding liability for articles lost or stolen unless handed to the manageress for safe custody. A fur coat belonging to the wife was stolen and the hotel sought to rely on the exclusion notice. It was held that the notice was not part of the contract which had been completed at the reception desk when the room had been paid for and the hotel was liable for the loss because of its negligence. There had been insufficient supervision at the reception desk and the thief was able to take the key to the room from behind the desk. However, there are two contrasting cases dealing with tickets: one for a railway excursion ticket, *Thompson v LMS Railway* [1930] 1 KB 41, and one involving a ticket given after hiring a deck chair, *Chapelton v Barry Urban District Council* [1940] 1 All ER 356. In the former, the ticket contained a reference to the conditions in the company's timetable and was held to be validly incorporated into the contract whereas, in the latter case, the exclusion of liability on the reverse of the ticket was deemed to be ineffective as the ticket was considered to be a mere receipt.

The Court of Appeal has suggested that a particularly burdensome term on a delivery note would only be enforced if it had been specifically drawn to the attention of the other party (see *Interfoto Picture Library Ltd v Stiletto Visual Programmes Ltd* [1988] 1 All ER 348). Of course, if the term is in a document signed before or at the time the contract was made, the term will be binding on the party signing whether or not he has read it, providing that he has not been misled by the other party as to its effect. Therefore, to be absolutely sure that the terms in the licence are part of the contract the customer should be asked to sign the licence before the package is handed over. In many situations, however, this is impracticable – for example, where software is acquired by mail order.

If the terms do not become part of the contract by means of any of the ways discussed above, one way in which they might do is by virtue of a previous course of dealing – for example, where the customer previously has acquired software produced by the same software publisher. One final possibility, as a fall-back position, is that the courts will imply appropriate terms based on what is reasonable in the circumstances and necessary to give the contract business efficacy. Custom may be very helpful in this respect and the courts would almost certainly look at what terms have become customary in the trade of software publishing. As noted earlier, the existence of a licence is essential as, without it, the intellectual property rights in the software will be infringed.

A further but less likely possibility is that Acme Computers acts as agent for Lemming Software and, as agent, makes a sale of goods contract and a licence agreement between George and Lemming.

Shrink-wrap licences

This is the fourth mechanism which might be possible and it has a lot to commend it. A Scots judge suggested that contracts for the acquisition of off-the-shelf software of the 'shrink-wrap' licence variety in *Beta Computers (Europe) Ltd v Adobe Systems (Europe) Ltd* [1996] FSR 367 were *sui generis*. Beta, the pursuers (claimants), supplied Adobe, the defenders (defendants), with computer software produced by Informix Software Inc, a third party. It was accepted that Informix owned the copyright subsisting in the software. It had been ordered by Adobe by telephone and was a standard upgrade package suitable for Adobe's computer. The software was delivered with a 'shrink-wrap' licence and the package bore the words 'Opening the Informix S.I. Software package indicates your acceptance of these terms and conditions'.

Adobe claimed that it had the right to return the software without using it and that it had the right to reject it until such time as the package was opened, which it had not been. Beta sued for the price of the software.

Lord Penrose, in the Outer House of the Court of Session, in Edinburgh, reflected upon the legislative framework of the Copyright, Designs and Patents Act 1988 in the context of computer programs. He concluded that the supply of the medium on which the program is stored must be accompanied by an appropriate licence conferred directly or by implication from the acquisition of the software. An essential feature of the supply of off-the-shelf software is that the supplier undertakes to make available to the purchaser both the medium and the right of access and use of the software. In effect, the supplier undertakes that he has the right to communicate the benefit of the use of the software: in other words, that he transfers the benefit of the copyright owner's licence. Lord Penrose said:

> **The supply of proprietary software for a price is a contract *sui generis* ... [it is] unacceptable to analyse the transaction in this case as if it were two separate transactions relating to the same subject matter. There is but one contract ...**

The time such a contract is made is when the conditions imposed by the owner of the copyright were tendered to the purchaser of the software and accepted by the purchaser. Otherwise, there could be no *consensus ad idem* (agreement of the same thing) which is essential for a contract to exist. That being so, the purchaser can reject the software at any time before acceptance by performing the stated act – in this case, opening the sealed package.

Lord Penrose said that if the contract was considered to be a sale of goods contract this would produce the odd result that the dominant characteristic of interest to the parties (the right to use the software) was subordinated to the medium by which it was transmitted to the users.

There is one problem with the decision which may prevent it being fully applicable in other jurisdictions. Scots law is based on Roman law, not common law, and it was held that the contract gave rights to the copyright owner as a third party. This is possible under the Scots law of contract but was not at that time under English law. However, an alternative way of looking at the transaction is that it does not give rights to the copyright owner. Conversely, it is the copyright owner who gives rights to the purchaser of the software. Where there are restrictions in the licence agreement, they simply constrain the rights given to the purchaser rather than giving rights to the copyright owner. In any case, the Contracts (Rights of Third Parties) Act 1999 provides that a third party may enforce a term in a contract under certain circumstances and this would be apt to allow the copyright owner to bring an action for breach of the licence agreement in England, Wales and Northern Ireland.

In the United States, there has been less difficulty with shrink-wrap licences. In the 7th Circuit Court of Appeals, shrink-wrap licences were held to be enforceable; terms did not have to be exposed on the outside of the package containing the software. It was sufficient if there was a notice to the effect that there was a licence agreement inside. Furthermore, the purchaser was entitled to a full refund if, after reading the licence, he did not agree with the terms and conditions (*The Times*, 'Interface Supplement', 10 July 1996, p.6).

Web-wrap licences

Computer software and other works protected by intellectual property rights, such as music and visual works, may be acquired on-line. From the owner of the rights in the software or other works, this has the advantage that the person acquiring it can be presented with the terms of the licence before agreeing to download a copy. This means that question of enforceability, as discussed above in the context of shrink-wrap licences though now at least partly resolved, should not be an issue. The person acquiring the software – or whatever is presented with the licence, often in a separate window – usually has to click a box indicating his assent to the terms. This should be effective to incorporate the terms into the contract, whether or not the person concerned actually takes the trouble to read the terms of the agreement. The fact that assent is indicated by clicking on a box or circle gives these form of licences their alternative name, the 'click-wrap' licence. This method of incorporating terms into contracts is not restricted to software and other intangible things subject to intellectual property rights and is also commonly used in the contracts for the supply of goods and services made on-line.

By incorporating the terms of the licence agreement into the contract is not an end to the matter however. Other information available on the relevant website could give rise to misrepresentation if it conflicts with the terms of the licence and the terms themselves may be subject to legal controls. The fact the licence may be subject to the law of another jurisdiction may not prejudice consumer rights provided for by European Community law, such as those relating to distance selling and electronic contracting (as discussed in Part Three of this book).

Although, on the face of it, there is no real problem with web-wrap licences, there are a number of points that can be made. Unless legally recognised electronic signatures are used, they are not suitable to assign intellectual property rights or to grant exclusive licences in respect of them as there is a general requirement for such agreements to be in writing and be signed by the assignor or owner as the case may be. In some cases, both parties' signatures are required. There seems little doubt that the requirement for writing will be satisfied but there may be difficulties in relation to legal disputes where questions of proof of the agreed terms, the time the contract was made and the fact of assent of both parties may be at issue. Furthermore, certain types of contracts are required to be in writing or by deed.

Typical terms in licences for off-the-shelf software

Usually, licence agreements for off-the-shelf software are not very lengthy. The copyright owner will want to set out the conditions of use of the software and confirm the fact of copyright subsistence and the grant of a licence to the purchaser. The licence may include some warranties and will have to address the impact of the applicable law on the licence. It may also deal with upgrades, user support and termination. Typically, the use may be limited to a single computer or a stated number of computers or users. A term dealing with whether the software and licence can be transferred to another person is also common.

It has been noted in Part One of this book that the Copyright, Designs and Patents Act 1988 makes void and unenforceable some terms in licence agreements which try to prohibit or restrict the permitted acts of decompilation of computer programs and making necessary back-up copies of computer programs. There are some other controls which relate to databases. A form of words which might be used in a licence agreement to restrict decompilation to that permitted under the Act is: 'You may not reverse engineer, decompile, disassemble or otherwise modify or alter the software except as provided for by section 50B of the Copyright, Designs and Patents Act 1988.'

The inclusion of warranties is not universal by any means and where they are given by the copyright owner, they are usually very limited. It may be that they are restricted to the return of the price paid for the software if it fails to perform substantially as stated in the documentation. We have seen that terms excluding or restricting liability for defective software are fairly strictly controlled by the Unfair Contract Terms Act 1977 in the context of bespoke software. However, it is possible that much greater restriction or even exclusion is possible with off-the-shelf software, bearing in mind, of course, that liability for death or personal injury caused by negligence cannot be excluded or restricted by a term in a contract or notice by virtue of section 2 of the Unfair Contract Terms Act 1977. In respect of other types of liability, it would seem reasonable that liability can be restricted or excluded. The main reason is that the software is 'general purpose' and has not been written for a particular client's requirements. Furthermore, the company producing the software has no knowledge of the uses to which end users will put the software. If a person using spreadsheet software to perform some complex financial calculation makes a mistake, that is hardly the software company's fault. However, if there is an inherent defect in the software which is not obvious to a reasonable user, it is a moot point as to whether a clause excluding liability completely would be effective. Until such time as exclusion clauses in off-the-shelf software licences come under judicial scrutiny, it is likely that no warranties will be given or, where they are, compensation for breach of warranty will be limited to the price paid for the software.

If there are no warranties (whether the licence expressly states this or is silent on the point), would the courts be likely to imply any warranties? We have seen in the *St Albans* case that one judge thought an implied term of fitness for purpose would be appropriate. This would seem a sensible approach with off-the-shelf software, the purpose being that for which such software is usually obtained.

Finally, the licence is almost certain to contain an applicable law clause and, possibly, a term stating which courts are to have jurisdiction. A typical formula might be: 'This licence agreement is governed by the laws of England and Wales and any dispute under it is subject to the sole and exclusive jurisdiction of the courts of England and Wales.'

Misrepresentation and dealers' promises

If we accept that a computer software dealer (or mail order supplier) acts as the agent of the copyright owner (usually the software publisher) in bringing about a licence between the software publisher and the customer, this has certain legal implications. The dealer has the authority, express or implied, to bind the software publisher contractually and this should not lead to problems. The dealer may have misled the customer, however, about the nature and performance of the software; he may, deliberately or otherwise, have made false claims which have induced the customer to obtain the software. Alternatively, marketing material published by the software company may contain false or misleading statements. A licence agreement is likely to contain a term to the effect that the software company will not be bound by anything which the dealer says in the pre-contractual negotiations and that the licence itself contains the entire agreement between the parties to the exclusion of anything else. Entire agreement terms are subject to the reasonableness test as stated in section 11(1) of the Unfair Contract Terms Act 1977 by virtue of section 3 of the Misrepresentation Act 1967 (as inserted by section 8 of the former Act). In *Mackenzie Patten & Co v British*

Olivetti Ltd (unreported) 11 January 1984, discussed in more detail in Chapter 21, the buyer of computer hardware claimed, *inter alia*, that he had been induced into entering into the contract on the basis of a salesman's misrepresentation. However, the judge did not need to rule on whether an entire agreement clause in the contract was effective to remove any liability resulting from the misrepresentation as he found for the buyer on the basis of a collateral warranty (a term in a subsidiary contract inducing the party to enter into the main contract).

If the view is taken, contrary to *Adobe v Beta*, that a shrink-wrap licence is ineffective and a licence is implied, this could defeat the copyright owner's preferred choice of applicable law. Some licence agreements contain a term stating that the applicable law is other than English law. It is common to see licence agreements for software from the United States with the law of California or New York designated as the applicable law. If the licence supplied with the software can be disregarded and a licence is implied, that implied licence will most likely be subject to English law (or Scots law as the case may be). In any case the legal maxim *caveat emptor* (let the buyer beware) applies. The vast majority of mass-produced software is of a very high standard but, if the customer is uncertain, it is wise to check with some existing users of the software or in some of the many excellent computer journals and publications which carry out comparative tests on these software packages. It should be borne in mind, however, that sometimes magazines may fail to be truly objective or may omit to test some particular software.

Back-up copies of programs

Making a back-up copy of a computer program infringes copyright unless its making is:

- permitted by the copyright owner;
- within the scope of an implied term; or
- necessary to the licensed use of the program.

Notwithstanding that there may be some doubt as to the contractual status of the licence agreement, as discussed above, it is sensible to check any provisions concerning back-up copies. If making a back-up copy is necessary to the licensed use of the program as provided for by section 50A of the Copyright, Designs and Patents Act 1988, then section 296A of that Act states that any term in a licence agreement which attempts to take this right away is void and unenforceable at law. One way around this would be to prohibit the making of back-up copies while providing a service to replace the licensed copy of the program promptly, perhaps on-line, thereby making the need to take a back-up copy no longer necessary. Even so, it is unlikely that the word 'necessary' will be interpreted in a strict and narrow sense.

In practical terms, a sensible approach to back-up copies is required by both sides. Licensees should guard against the danger of proliferation of back-up copies which can soon become working copies, exceeding the licensed use. If an organisation requires 12 working copies, it should obtain a licence to cover 12 users, not a single-user licence. Users of software should develop a system of software audits to check and monitor the number of copies in use, and information and advice on how to implement software audits can be obtained from the Federation Against Software Theft (FAST). There are a number of other benefits. Regular auditing is part of good practice and quality management and will encourage a responsible attitude towards the use of software. During an audit, some employees might be found to be using old or defective versions of software and any pirated software brought into work by an employee may be discovered and dealt with. The implementation and enforcement of effective software audits also prevents the embarrassment of being raided by software copyright owners who have obtained an Anton Piller Order (now called a 'search order') giving them powers, accompanied by a solicitor, to enter and inspect the computer equipment and remove unauthorised copies of software to be used in evidence in copyright infringement actions.

Integration and upgrades

A person acquiring software should always check how well, if at all, the software will integrate with other software and whether data can be easily transferred to and from the software. Will the software run satisfactorily on the customer's hardware? What is the position if the customer decides to upgrade his equipment or operating system software: will the software still be usable? What if a better version of the software is made available in due course: can the customer trade in his old software or will he have to pay the full licence fee for the new version? These are the type of questions someone contemplating an off-the-shelf system should consider. Even though some of the events described might seem unlikely at the time, they have a nasty habit of becoming relevant later and if a customer is in doubt it is better to err on the side of flexibility. The pace of development in the computer industry shows no signs of slowing down and, as more powerful hardware becomes available, existing software packages will be enhanced in a like fashion and new software applications which were hitherto impossible or impracticable will appear on the market.

Training and support

Training is an aspect which is often overlooked. A computer dealer may offer training under a separate contract between himself and the customer. The quality of the training will obviously be important as will the provision of refresher courses. Many organisations have their own internal training and training videos can usefully supplement this but many organisations will need some external support. Most software publishers provide support, usually by telephone, and it is worth checking with existing users as to the effectiveness of the service. Many such support services leave much to be desired and there seems to be a general inability to deal with anything but the most obvious problems. A typically hard nut to crack is whether the fault is caused by a hardware defect or software fault. A computer dealer may be able to help but, in many cases, a user group may be of more assistance.

A final point concerns 'hotline' support. Will the dealer be prepared to provide an emergency call-out service if there is a problem related to the use of the software, such as trying to interface a word processing package with a new printer? In a case like this, the software itself will not be at fault; it will be a matter of installing the software in the correct manner for the particular printer. A dealer will charge for this type of support and the rate he requires will depend, amongst other things, on the speed of call-out expected by the customer.

Chapter 20

Website development contracts

Introduction

Website development contracts share many features with contracts for the writing of software to a client's specific requirements though there are some additional factors to be taken into account. A great deal of bespoke software is used only within an organisation and, generally, is unseen by the public at large. There are, of course, exceptions to this, for example, where a person goes to a travel agent to book a holiday and sees screen displays and printed reports. A website, however, gives the owner an immediate presence in cyberspace. All manner of things about the owner and his business are laid bare and exposed to the world. As the world wide web is such a powerful marketing tool, it is essential that its design is very carefully thought out and this applies also to the content on the website and its performance. It is not just commercial organisations that have websites, all manner of organisations, such as government departments, local authorities, not-for-profit organisations, professional bodies and private individuals, have them too. It is important also for non-commercial websites to be attractively designed, easy-to-use, informative and up-to-date.

Some organisations and a great many individuals design their own websites. They acquire a suitable domain name and obtain hosting facilities from an internet service provider (ISP). They use a suitable HTML editor to format the content of their webpages, building in links between pages and, possibly, links to other websites, before uploading the files to the host computer. This might be satisfactory if there is sufficient expertise in-house but there are now numerous companies which specialise in website design who can create and maintain very effective websites. Whilst what has been said in the previous chapters in terms of software contracts is still highly relevant, there are a number of particular issues that relate to website design that should be addressed by both the client and the website design company. The purpose of this chapter is to examine those issues and make suggestions as to how they should be dealt with in contractual terms. The first thing to note, however, is that the scope of website development contracts can vary enormously, from the developer simply providing technical support to the complete design, including creating content, registering domain names, uploading and hosting the website, monitoring its use and providing ongoing maintenance and upgrading.

Specification

During initial negotiations, the scope of the work should become apparent. It may be that the development company takes the responsibility for the technical aspects but the client provides all the content for the webpages and updates of the content, perhaps with the development company formatting the content and adding links, meta-tags and the like, uploading it and testing the website works properly. After deciding the scope of the developer's obligations under the contract, the next thing to consider is the specification. It is likely that the website development company has a standard specification but even then, it will probably need some modification to account for the client's particular needs.

The specification will describe the general functionality of the website and the content but will also set out other details such as those set out below.

1 Browser compatibility – different browsers (for example, Netscape Navigator and Internet Explorer) may display webpages differently and some may ignore certain HTML tags or formatting. Whilst it may be tempting to take advantage of the most sophisticated and up-to-date browser, care must be taken as persons accessing the website with a different browser or an older version may lose some of the functionality of the website which might detract from its overall attractiveness.

2 Hosting and bandwidth – the question of where the website will be hosted and who will be responsible for this must be dealt with. It may be that the website developer provides a dedicated server or a shared server to host the website or arranges hosting by a third-party service provider. A further alternative is that the site is hosted by the client using the client's server. Clearly hosting on dedicated servers will optimise performance. The specification also ought to address bandwidth, as this too will affect the speed of transfer of the webpages to the person accessing them.

3 Back-office systems – the developer may also write software to link the website to the client's back-office systems, such as its orders, accounts, marketing and other systems. This work will have to be fully specified and may require some preliminary work to allow the developer to become familiar with the back-office systems and how they can be linked with the website.

4 Search engines – the developer will probably be expected to register the website with appropriate search engines and the client may also want to pay to have certain terms reserved to increase the likelihood of appearing high up on a list of search results. There may also be the possibility of having an advertising banner displayed when the result of a search is displayed.

5 Security – where orders are placed with the client via the website, personal data will be collected from the customer and passed through to the client's back-office systems for further processing. The specification should deal with security measures taken and the encryption of data transferred to appropriate standards, for example, by using public key/private key cryptography.

6 Content – the specification will describe the content and state the overall size, structure, image standards and other features such as program code used on the website. It should be made clear who is responsible for providing the content and for formatting it. If the client is to deliver content to the developer, clear delivery times should be set out. Responsibility for other features, such as the meta-tags to be used on the website, should be set out.

7 The specification must contain a schedule of dates for certain milestones to be reached. It is difficult to generalise, but it is likely that the following milestones will be set out:
- delivery of a prototype and acceptance thereof;
- delivery of content of other data or information if provided by the client;
- development of the website proper;

- testing (including checking that all the links work properly and all text and images are displayed properly);
- acceptance and the date for the site to 'go live'.

8 Maintenance – this is a very important area and may be subject to a separate agreement. It should cover improvements, enhancements, modification and further development to keep pace with changes to browser and search engine technology. Error correction is likely to be an issue (strictly speaking this should not be subject to any separate obligation to pay where the errors are such that they would be seen as a breach of the original development contract). In the first few days and weeks after the website has gone live, it is imperative that the developer responds very quickly to deal with any problems – a typical problem is that the website and the links to the back-office systems cannot cope with the demand. A poorly performing commercial website can result in serious loss of business. A simple error, for example, in the price payable for goods, can have serious repercussions. There have been a number of examples of incorrect prices, for example where a price was shown as £1.00 and not £100. The difficulty with this sort of error is that placing an order is often followed immediately and automatically by an acceptance notice. Amongst other things the specification should deal with the techniques and systems used for placing and accepting orders.

9 If the client's staff will be responsible for uploading new or modified content in the future, they will probably need training and the detail of the training should also be set out in the specification.

10 Data protection – the specification will set out what sort of personal and other data are to be collected and processed. As regards data protection law, the website development company will be acting as the client's data processor and, as such, is required to be under security obligations as required by the Data Protection Act 1998 and these obligations are required to be in, or evidenced in, writing. The specification is an appropriate place to include such obligations, although they may be expressed in the main body of the contract or reference to the obligations in the specification may be made in the main body of the contract.

11 The specification may contain the mechanisms for dealing with legal changes that may affect the website, such as changes in consumer protection law.

Terms

The website development contract will contain many express terms and there will be schedules and annexes, including a fully detailed specification. The express terms will set out the obligations and duties of each party, hopefully in precise details, and also contain terms to deal with difficulties that might arise during the performance of the contract or otherwise, for example, late delivery, breach of warranty and variations. Apart from terms dealing with ownership of the intellectual property rights in the content (formatted and unformatted) and associated works such as computer programs, there are likely to be terms dealing with performance levels and delivery terms, warranties, liability for defects and other breaches of contract and the usual terms concerning arbitration or alternative dispute resolution, applicable law and entire agreement clauses. There may also be a schedule of rates and prices to be used to determine the price payable for any additional work asked for by the client.

Terms will also be implied by law. A website development contract is a contract for services and, as such, terms under the Supply of Goods and Services Act 1982 will be implied. Section 13, the requirement to carry out the service using reasonable care and skill, is particularly important. In some cases this duty may be extended or more clearly defined by express terms, for example, by a term requiring the website development company to assign suitably qualified staff to the performance of the contract. As is the case with software development contracts, and in the absence of an appropriate express term, it is likely that there will be implied into the contract a term imposing a duty on the website development company to correct errors appearing after the website and its content have been accepted by the client; see for example *Saphena Computing Ltd* v *Allied Collection Agencies Ltd* [1995] FSR 616, discussed in earlier chapters. This duty will exist whether or not there is a contractual obligation to maintain the website, though it is difficult to say for how long the duty will endure beyond the client's acceptance of the website. It is not likely to endure for very long if the client takes responsibility for maintenance and further development of the website.

The rights, duties and obligations under the terms implied by the Supply of Goods and Services Act 1982 into contract for services may be excluded, subject to the Unfair Contract Terms Act 1977, providing the terms seeking to exclude or restrict liability is inconsistent with the implied term in question. However, it is unlikely that a term excluding liability for breach of the implied term to carry out the service using reasonable care and skill would ever meet the requirement of reasonableness in the 1977 Act. Incidentally, if hardware is also supplied by the website development company, that does not prevent the contract being a contract for services as confirmed by section 12 of the Supply of Goods and Services Act 1982.

In software development contracts generally, there are usually express warranties to the effect that the developer will not use or incorporate material that infringes third party intellectual property rights. In the absence of an express term, such a term will be implied. In *Antiquesportfolio.com plc* v *Rodney Fitch & Co Ltd* [2001] FSR 23 the client wanted to start advertising and selling antiques over the Internet. It engaged the services of a design consultancy to design the website and carry out other work such as designing business cards. The website was delivered to the client which complained that the content and watermarks used on the website infringed third-party rights and the client commenced proceedings claiming the return of the price already paid of around £37,000 (invoices for a further £31,000 had been submitted by the design consultancy) or, alternatively, £8000 damages assessed at what the client had claimed it had paid another designer to modify the website to overcome the problem.

Mr Justice Neuberger held that there was an implied obligation to carry out the work with reasonable care and skill and there was also an implied obligation to provide the website fit for the purpose for which it had been commissioned. The supply of material that potentially infringed third-party rights was a breach of that obligation. There was a risk that photographs of furniture used in the design of the website infringed copyright. Although, if that was so it was a breach of the implied term, it did not go to the root of the contract and did not entitle the client to treat the contract as repudiated. The judge went on to say that the client still had an obligation to pay money outstanding under the contract subject to a set-off. That is, the client would be allowed to set-off the cost of modifying the website to remove the offending material but the client would have to prove the amount of the set-off. The judge accepted that photographs of single antique items could be the subject of copyright, although he thought the degree of originality was small. He did, however, reject the argument that an outline water-mark or logo made by tracing the outline of a photograph of an antique item could be a work of copyright.

Another common term is that the content, if provided by the developer in whole or in part, will not contain any statement which is defamatory or that could otherwise result in the client being faced with legal action or even criminal prosecution, for example, if the material incited the commission of a criminal offence. Liability for information that is inaccurate and could give rise to liability, for example, for negligent misstatement should also be considered. Other forms of liability could be in the form of trade mark infringement and passing off. Care must be taken to ensure that keyword meta-tags do not infringe trade marks belonging to others, especially as it now seems likely that this can infringe even though the keyword meta-tags are not normally seen by persons visiting a website.

There should be term requiring that the website complies with relevant laws, for example, laws relating to misleading advertising, consumer protection and electronic commerce legislation. In the case of a website targeted at more than one country, this should include a reference to the equivalent laws in all the countries affected. If the website development company will have access to personal data, for example, relating to the client or its staff or customers of the client, the developer will be in the position of being a data processor for the purposes of data protection law. It is a requirement that processors are under obligations relating to security and these obligations must be in, or evidenced in, writing.

A common phenomenon in software development generally which also applies to website development contracts is 'feature-creep'. That is, where part-way through the performance of the contract, the client decides that it wants more features or different or enhanced functionality in respect of the website. There should be a term in the con-tract to cover variations to the contract so that the impact of additional or modified work can be allowed for before the work is carried out. The additional or altered work must be clearly defined and the difference in the price payable under the contract agreed together with any changes to the time for delivery and acceptance of the website. The ideal of having full and informed agreement as to the impact of additional or altered work on the contract before the work in question is started is not always achieved due to factors such as the urgency of getting on with the work or the persons who are in a position to agree such things being tied up with other matters at the time. Trying to reach agreement retrospectively is always more difficult but keeping records of the work in progress and having a mechanism in the contract for pricing additional work should help. The use of an independent professional to supervise the performance of the contract and certify payments due can be extremely helpful in resolving what could prove to be a potential source of conflict.

Feature-creep or failing to agree clearly and precisely what the work will entail at the outset can prove disastrous. In *Psychometric Services Ltd* v *Merant International Ltd* [2002] FSR 8, the claimant was in the business of designing and marketing tests, includ-ing multiple-choice tests for job applicants and a number of companies used these when recruiting new staff. The claimant decided to carry on its business on the Internet and paid a company to carry out a preliminary study and design. Following this, the claimant awarded the contract to design fully three variants of the website to the defen-dant for a price which was initially capped at £195,000. Soon after, the defendant was asked by the claimant to design a further website outside the scope of the original agreement. This was done quickly by the defendant for the price of £20,000. Because of the speed with which it had been written, the software could not be re-used for the main contract. The commercial prospects for the claimant if its websites were fully operational and running properly appeared to be immense but problems arose. It was not clear to the judge whether this was the result of additional requirements asked for by the claimant or because the defendant had underestimated the work involved or because the defendant had not carried out the work properly. The defendant decided that the amount of work it was required to do was far in excess of what had originally been anticipated by the parties and a Variation Letter was signed by the parties lifting the £195,000 cap.

The defendant put in a great deal of effort in further developing the websites and the claimant paid out substantial sums, in the end paying over £700,000 with the defendant charging at an agreed hourly rate of £90 per person-hour. The defendant claimed that it was still owed £960,000. The relationship between the parties broke down and the claimant sought delivery of the source code for the software used for the website which was granted by the court. Mr Justice Laddie thought that, if the source code was not made available to the claimant, it would be likely to go into liquidation and this would cause immense injustice to the claimant if proved right at the full trial. On the other hand, if the order was not granted, the defendant would be unlikely to recover the money it claimed was outstanding and, if the order was granted, the defendant would suffer no loss (all it would have to do was to hand over a copy of the source code) and it would be more likely to recover the outstanding money if it was proved to be right at full trial. It was noted that, if the websites were perfected, the claimant would be in a market-leading and highly profitable business.

Maintenance

It is virtually inevitable that the website will contain errors, whether in the content, HTML code, links, underlying software or in the interaction between the website and the client's back-office systems. It is also a fact of life that the website will require changes over time, whether in the overall look and feel to improve its overall appearance or in the content details, for example, where prices or taxes change. In some cases, the client may take over complete responsibility for future changes and enhancements but it is usual for there to be a maintenance agreement with the website developer. In some cases, it may be a combination of the two, for example, where the client retains responsibility for changing the content with the developer being responsible for the underlying software and more significant design changes.

Without a maintenance agreement, the developer will be under an implied obligation (unless this is express) to correct errors in the software and content if and to the extent that the developer was responsible for creating this. However, if only subject to an implied term, the speed of response might not be as quick as the client might wish for, as the implied term would only require the error to be corrected with a reasonable time. It is certainly better to use express terms to deal with error correction.

Where there is a maintenance agreement it should cover work such as upgrading the website and underlying software, redesigning the website to increase its attractiveness, maintaining links and modifying the content (or converting content provided by the client into HTML format). The agreement should also set out response times and an obligation to make modifications necessary as a result of legislative and tax changes in a timely fashion. For example, if there is a change in value added tax which affects goods or services sold on the website, the appropriate changes to the website must take effect at the same time the tax change comes into effect. As is usual, the date the site was last updated should be shown.

The maintenance agreement should contain appropriate benchmarks to assess the developer's compliance with the obligations in the agreement and relevant warranties. For a commercial website, downtime is very serious and there are likely to be terms dealing with this and the developer's liability if it exceeds a stated period of time. There are also likely to be obligations on the client to inform the developer immediately an error is suspected or in relation to a pending change in prices, legislation or tax. The developer will probably want a term included in the maintenance agreement to cover wasted time and costs, such as where the developer has been asked to deal with a suspected problem which turns out not to exist.

Payment under a maintenance agreement is likely to be on the basis of an agreed annual fee, perhaps payable in instalments with additional payment for upgrades, enhancements and the supply of new content. There may be a formula to work out such additional costs, such as an hourly rate per person engaged on the work with any items of hardware or additional software licences for third party software being supplied at cost plus a percentage uplift. Provision is likely also to be included for the payment of the developer's expenses. However, where the additional work is substantial, it will usually be better to agree the amount of work and payment in advance.

The client may need to consider whether it wants to be able to engage a different developer in the future to maintain and carry out other work on the website design and content. Apart from having clear provisions dealing with termination of the agreement, allowing another developer to take over, perhaps at the end of an annual maintenance period, the original agreement and maintenance agreement should address matters such as delivery of the source code and ownership of copyright and other rights subsisting in the materials.

Domain name, etc.

If the developer registers the domain names for the website, the client may want to ensure that the contract deals with renewal of the domain names as failure to renew in time could result in loss of the domain name. Probably the best solution is for the client itself to register its domain names, if it has not already done so. Alternatively, if the developer registered domain names, it could transfer the name to the client and inform the domain name registry accordingly.

The developer may be responsible for registering the site with search engines and organising pop-up banners to be displayed with a list of search results to enhance the retrieval rates of the site and generally raise its profile. The costs of all this will, of course, be passed on to the client and it may be better if arrangements are made for the client to take over responsibility for recurring fees and costs associated with such things, particularly if the client wants to make it easier to switch to another developer for subsequent maintenance.

Statistics will be generated by the website relating to matters such as number of hits, the 'close rate' (rate of orders compared with number of hits), the 'click rate' (number of clicks on, for example, a web advertisement, compared to the number of visits to the page containing it) and the 'clickstream' (the path used by visitors). These can all provide useful market research information. The website developer should be responsible for producing periodic reports of these statistics and in a form intelligible to the client.

Summary

The precise nature and content of a website development contract will depend, of course, on the requirements of the client, the obligations imposed on the developer and the allocation of risk between them. From what has been discussed in this chapter, it is clear that there are many variables. For example, the client may decide to provide all the content for the developer to format and structure and to provide all the underlying software. Whilst website development contracts have many points in common with contracts for writing software generally, there are some particular issues that are relevant. Unlike back-office computer systems, a website is a window through which the world can see the company, contact it and do business with it. A website is a supreme marketing tool but a slow, unwieldy, badly structured and unattractive website can send out all the wrong messages and be very detrimental to the company's future prospects. It is, therefore, vitally important to bear this in mind when writing the specification and the contract for the design and development of the website. Feature-creep seems to be a particular danger with website development contracts and is likely to be a reflection of the inability of both parties to fully appreciate what the other expects.

It is usual for a website to contain both a privacy policy and a set of terms and conditions. The chances are that these will be written by the client or by the client's legal advisers to be incorporated into the overall design by the developer. Where this is so, and the same goes for any other content provided to the developer by or on behalf of the client, it is important for the client to check that it has been transposed accurately and that the style is appropriate. It is also usual to ensure that anyone placing an order has had an opportunity to read the terms and conditions and privacy policy and has had an opportunity to download them. Obtaining positive assent to the terms and conditions is also important, even though the person placing an order has not bothered to read them. Other issues affecting the design of the website will be how personal data is to be collected, processed and stored. This will be discussed in more depth in Part Five, on data protection law.

Chapter 21

Hardware contracts

Introduction

Computer hardware may be purchased outright or hired. Much of what has already been discussed in relation to computer software contracts, in particular contracts for the writing or modification of software, will apply to contracts for the acquisition of hardware. Very often, the purchase of or hire of computer equipment will include software, such as operating system software, computer programming languages, utility programs or applications programs. These items of software usually will be subject to collateral licence agreements.

Computer software is important; the choice of the software best suited to the client's requirements is critical and when it comes to setting up a computer system in a company or business that has not used computers before to any great extent or where a change in computer equipment is contemplated, the decisions regarding the selection of software are of primary importance. The secondary decision should then be to determine the type of computer equipment which will be most suitable for running this software, not forgetting other important considerations such as future growth, the impact of the computing operations and the future of the software packages and computer equipment. Will the company manufacturing the computer continue to develop and support it in the longer term? Is it an industry standard with a wide range of available software?

If, as is usually the case, the client already has computer equipment and software, this will influence any decisions about obtaining new hardware. Compatibility with the existing equipment will be important and some compromises may have to be made. The aim should be that in three or five years' time the decision will still seem to have been a good choice. Long-term planning is essential, not only in terms of computer equipment but also taking into account the client's business strategy and plans for development and how these will prescribe and influence its computer needs. The client should also consider its internal computer networks (present or potential), links to the Internet and whether it wants to engage in, or extend its, electronic commerce operations.

Performance

The performance of software is directly related to the computer's performance. The speed of operation of the computer will be very important and a contract for the purchase or hire of computer equipment should make reference to this. Information about processing speeds, storage capacities, data transfer and networking capabilities will be paramount. The purchaser must satisfy himself as to the performance of the equipment, bearing in mind the environment in which the equipment will be working.

Simple benchmark speed tests may not provide a very good picture of the computer's performance if it will be used to carry out many different tasks at the same time, with multiple concurrent access to data files. The client should think about the operating system and whether it is a common one able to run a large variety of applications programs. Similar considerations apply to networking hardware and software. Another point which might be relevant is whether there are any limitations on the number of data files the computer will permit to be in use at the same time and whether programs and databases will be installed on a central server or on individual PCs or workstations.

Representations and entire agreement clauses

A salesperson will usually extol the virtues of the equipment he is trying to sell and he will try to convince the would-be purchaser that it is everything he needs. If the equipment turns out to be totally unsuited to the client's needs, the supplier will probably point to a term in the contract of sale which states that the printed agreement represents the entire agreement between the parties and nothing said or done in preliminary negotiations is part of the contract. This ploy may not always work, as the case below demonstrates.

In *Mackenzie Patten & Co v British Olivetti Ltd* (unreported) 11 January 1984, the claimant was a firm of solicitors which wanted a computer to handle its accounts and the defendant company was approached by the claimant with this in mind. Following negotiations with the defendant's salesman, the claimant agreed to obtain one of the defendant's computers under a leasing agreement with a third party. The computer proved totally unsuitable for the claimant's needs and the claimant's staff was incapable of using the computer effectively even following training by the defendant. After hearing expert evidence, the judge decided that the computer was obsolete and not suitable for the claimant's requirements. Indeed, as the claimant firm was a small one, it was questionable whether a computer was needed at all. (Things are much different now; even the smallest firm needs computer technology and, preferably, also access to the Internet.)

The judge held that the claimant relied on the salesman's statements when entering the leasing agreement. The statements were a collateral warranty and, as they were not true, there was a breach of this warranty. There was an entire agreement clause in the contract but this was held to be ineffective as it was stated in terms of a contract of sale and, in fact, the contract entered into by the claimant was a leasing contract. No sale to the claimant took place or was contemplated (the claimant could not afford to buy the computer outright). The contract contained an exclusion clause but the judge held that the defendant had failed to prove that it was reasonable, applying the test in section 11 of the Unfair Contract Terms Act 1977. The judge awarded the claimant the sum of £16,204 which comprised £2661 for payments made under the lease agreement, £12,692 for payments owing under the agreement and £851 interest. A further claim for wasted time in meetings and the like in the sum of £1200 was dismissed by the judge as being both too vague and too remote.

If the entire agreement clause had been found to be effective to exclude the salesman's statements, the claimant would probably have had a remedy under section 2 of the Misrepresentation Act 1967, any attempt to exclude liability being subject to the reasonableness test in the Unfair Contract Terms Act 1977. Hence, suppliers of computer equipment should make every effort to ensure that the would-be purchaser is fully aware of the equipment's capabilities and limitations. The purchaser would be wise to seek independent advice and the supplier, if there is any doubt about the suitability of a particular piece of equipment, would be wise to suggest that such independent advice is sought. In particular, it is unwise to attempt to sell obsolete or unsuitable equipment to a solicitor, although, in the above case, it appears that the solicitor signed the agreement without first reading it thoroughly!

In the context of parties to a contract of equal bargaining power who are assumed to desire commercial certainty and on the assumption that the price paid reflects the risk based on the warranties that have been given, an entire agreement clause which goes on to say that one party did not rely upon any pre-contractual representation of the other will, almost certainly, deprive the first party to succeed in a claim for misrepresentation (*Watford Electronics Ltd* v *Sanderson CFL Ltd* [2002] FSR 19). Such an agreement of non-reliance will not be subject to section 3 of the Misrepresentation Act 1967. Furthermore, an entire agreement clause will deprive any collateral warranty previously given of any legal effect (*Inntrepreneur Pub Co Ltd* v *East Crown Ltd* [2000] 41 EG 209).

For a misrepresentation to have legal effect in the light of an entire agreement clause, according to the Court of Appeal in *Lowe* v *Lombank Ltd* [1960] 1 All ER 611, the statement must be:

- clear and unambiguous;
- such that a reasonable person would expect the other party to understand that he was meant to act on the basis of the representation; and
- the other party had entered into the agreement on the basis that the representation was true.

Businesses and other organisations having the advantage of professional advisers are unlikely to fall within what can only be described as an exception to the basic rule. As Mr Justice Lightman said in the *Inntrepreneur* case:

> The purpose of an entire agreement clause is to preclude a party to a written agreement from threshing through the undergrowth and finding, in the course of negotiations, some (chance) remark or statement (often long-forgotten or difficult to recall or explain) upon which to found a claim ...

Maintenance and upgrades

The contract should state exactly who does what in terms of installation and initial testing. Once the equipment is installed, how well will the supplier support it? Maintenance will probably be provided for by a separate contract, renewable annually, and the client should check this contract to see what it has to say on the point of speed of response to a breakdown. If repairs have to be made to the computer equipment, does the client have to pay for parts or labour or both and is there a minimum call-out charge? The maintenance contract may provide for the loan of alternative equipment while repairs are carried out and, if it does not so provide, it could be worth asking why not. The client should also check whether third party maintenance is a possibility.

Sooner or later the computer equipment will become obsolete as faster, more powerful equipment is continually being developed. This can have one of two consequences. First, the new equipment is better in so many respects and so different that there is no possibility of upgrading the old equipment to the new standards. It is then a matter of making do, standing by the existing equipment, consolidating it and adding improvements when they become available with a view to reviewing the situation in a year or two, when the quality and performance of the new equipment has been fully tested by others. The general acceptance of equipment amongst the computer world is very important. Sometimes, a new computer or processor will catch on and sell in volume and this will then encourage the leading software companies to produce appropriate software for the new machine, making it an even more attractive proposition. Once a new computer attracts the attention of the software companies it is well on its way to becoming established. It is very tempting to stay with the market leaders when buying computer equipment. As the old adage used to go, 'no one was ever fired for buying IBM!'

A second consequence of the announcement of new, improved equipment is that it may be possible to upgrade the existing equipment to those standards, and the new equipment may be in the form of an upgrade. When buying computer equipment, it is worthwhile finding out what the manufacturer's attitude is to existing customers regarding upgrades or new equipment. Will the improved equipment be sympathetically priced as far as existing customers are concerned? Will a generous trade-in be allowed on the old equipment or is there a good second-hand market for the manufacturer's equipment? Does the manufacturer have a history of upwardly compatible machines or does he bring out new equipment that is totally unlike the old equipment? Does he change operating systems continually?

Ideally, the manufacturer should have a policy of building on his past products. It must be borne in mind that there is a dichotomy here for manufacturers. A manufacturer will want to attract new customers and, to do this, the equipment must be up-to-date and make use of the latest technological developments. On the other hand, the manufacturer will owe a moral duty to his loyal customers to maintain some degree of compatibility. The history of computing is one of change and abandoning out-of-date equipment and the person or company considering purchasing a computer or other computer equipment would do well to bear this in mind. There is little that can be done contractually, apart from insisting that the supplier (it will be the supplier and not the manufacturer who will be a party to the contract unless the supplier and manufacturer are one and the same) will continue to support the equipment for a reasonable period of time, regardless of whether it is later withdrawn from the market place.

To provide flexibility, a client may buy computers or other items of hardware on the basis of a contract which includes a buy-back option. If exercised this requires the hardware supplier to buy back the old hardware. The client may then put the payment towards buying new, up-to-date equipment from the hardware supplier or from a third party. Like any other provision in a contract, buy-back options must be clear in their effect. In *Boots the Chemists Ltd* v *Amdahl (UK) Ltd* (unreported) 3 November 2000, Amdahl had supplied Boots with computer processors and upgrades to their existing processors under a contract which contained a buy-back option. Boots could require Amdahl to buy-back two processors, each for over £1m.

Following negotiations, Amdahl wrote to Boots extending the deadline for exercising the buy-back option until mid-August 1995 but the buy-back values quoted were as at August 1996. During August 1995, Boots exercised its option in respect of one of

the processors and this was accepted by Amdahl and Boots bought a replacement processor from IBM. In June 1996, Boots purported to exercise its option in respect of the
second processor but this was not accepted by Amdahl which withdrew its offer to buy-
back the processor. Boots sold the processor elsewhere and sued Amdahl for the difference between the sale price and the buy-back value quoted by Amdahl.

The Court of Appeal accepted that Amdahl's letter was either an offer from Amdahl
or confirmation of an agreement already reached orally for variation of the original
agreement between the parties. This was not dependent upon Boots either upgrading
one processor or retaining the other processor, as had been argued by Amdahl. A further argument that the agreement lacked consideration was unsuccessful. The Court of
Appeal said that the requirement for consideration was satisfied because the variation
to the original contract was capable of benefiting either party. From Amdahl's perspective, a delay in the decision of Boots to exercise its option for a buy-back of the second
processor meant that Amdahl did not have to buy both back in 1995 and, if exercised
in 1996, Amdahl would pay a lesser price. Amdahl also had the benefit of a further
opportunity of persuading Boots to allow Amdahl back as its hardware supplier in
1996. From Boots' point of view, the benefit was the ability to postpone the decision
until 1996 and there was also a detriment in as much as Boots would receive a lower
price if it postponed the exercise of the option.

If the equipment is hired, problems of obsolescence are less important providing the
hirer is not committing himself to an unduly long period of hire. Hiring is often referred
to as leasing; there is no particular significance in this because a lease contract and a
contract of hire are basically the same thing (as opposed to a hire purchase agreement).
The duration of the agreement will be important as will be the presence of any term in
the agreement concerning termination and the relevant circumstances. If a much better
piece of equipment is suddenly available, the hirer may wish to terminate the agreement
quickly so that he can avail himself of the new equipment. The company hiring out the
equipment will obviously want some form of compensation should the hirer want to
return the computer equipment before the normal time and this requires a sensible compromise.

Legal controls

Statutory safeguards are more in evidence when it comes to hardware contracts. For
example, the Sale of Goods Act 1979 will apply because computers or other related
equipment come within the meaning of 'goods'; a computer is a personal chattel. This
means that the important terms such as compliance with description and meeting the
requirement of satisfactory quality will be implied into a contract to purchase a computer. Certain terms implied by the Sale of Goods Act 1979 are implied into all contracts of sale while others only apply where the seller sells in the course of business.
Compliance with description is an example of the former while satisfactory quality is
an example of the latter. Most of the contracts under consideration in this book will be
in the course of business. Similar terms will be implied into hire contracts by the Supply
of Goods and Services Act 1982. Some of these implied terms can be excluded or
limited in the case of a non-consumer sale but only in so far as the exemption clauses
purporting to do this meet the requirement of reasonableness as provided for by the
Unfair Contract Terms Act 1977, sections 6 and 7 (in Scotland, sections 21 and 22 of

the Unfair Contract Terms Act 1977 apply and there the test is whether the term was fair and reasonable to incorporate into the contract).

The fact that the hardware is sold complete with software does not prevent the contract from being a sale of goods contract. For example, in the Australian case of *Toby Constructions Products Pty Ltd* v *Computer Bar Sales Pty Ltd* (1983) 50 ALR 684, the Supreme Court of New South Wales held that the sale of a computer system, comprising both hardware and software, was a sale of goods contract. The contract was primarily one for equipment as the hardware cost was A$12,230 and the software cost was A$2160. This logic was approved of by Scott Baker J in *St Albans City & District Council* v *International Computers Ltd* [1995] FSR 686. Looking at the primary objective of the contract is a sensible approach. After all, the purchaser of a washing machine which turns out to be defective would be surprised to find that the Sale of Goods Act did not apply, even if the defect was traced to the program controlling the washing cycle. Where the balance between hardware and software is more even, however, it may be better to make two separate contracts so that the application of statutory controls is predictable.

In a distributorship agreement, a retailer may sell to the public substantial numbers of computers that are supplied by a large computer manufacturer. If the computers turn out to have some inherent defect, that can be very damaging to the distributor's business as he will have to refund the price paid or pay for repairs to be carried out. By the time the defect comes to light, many thousands of computers with the defect may have been sold. The case of *Time Group Ltd* v *Computer 2000 Distribution Ltd and IBM United Kingdom Ltd* [2002] EWHC 126 (TCC) illustrates the difficulties. During 1994, the second defendant, IBM, sold 20,160 Blue Lightning PCs to the first defendant, as IBM's exclusive distributor of Blue Lightning PCs in the United Kingdom. Later that year, the first and second defendants agreed that the claimant, Time, should take over as exclusive distributor in the United Kingdom. IBM sold over 20,000 Blue Lightning PCs to Time who also bought Computer 2000's surplus stock of over 4000 Blue Lightning PCs. The Blue Lightning PCs were alleged to have two defects, one in a chip on the motherboard, the other was a hard disk fault.

During 1994 and 1995, both Time and Computer 2000 received complaints from customers about the computers and both Time and Computer 2000 sought compensation from IBM. In 1996, IBM and Computer 2000 agreed to settle the latter's claim for £240,394 and the settlement included a term to the effect that Computer 2000 would not pursue any other claims, nor assist any third party in any such claims. Time failed to settle at that stage. Actions were commenced in the United Kingdom against the second defendant but before trial a settlement was reached by which IBM agreed to pay £6m to Time on the basis that it was a final settlement of the claim. The payment was received by Time on Friday 21 July 2000. On Monday 24 July 2000, Time sent Computer 2000 a letter before action and, on 14 August 2000, Time commenced proceedings in the United Kingdom against Computer 2000 for £2.2m. On 16 August 2000, Time brought an action in the United States against IBM's American parent company claiming US$54m. This was dismissed by the Court in New York on the basis of *forum non conveniens* (not the appropriate forum, that is, in the interests of justice, the action should take place somewhere else, the United Kingdom). The settlement Time came to with IBM only referred to the English subsidiary company.

Computer 2000 joined IBM in the action as Part 20 defendants (this is where a person sued as defendant joins another party as defendant on the basis that the other should indemnify the first or make a contribution in respect of any award in damages). The purpose of Time suing Computer 2000 appeared to be so that Time could get a second bite at IBM. This was held to be an abuse of process and the claim and the Part 20 claim were dismissed. Generally, the courts will not allow bringing a second action on issues related to issues in the first action that could properly have been brought up in the first action. HH Judge Bowsher QC said that it was a very serious matter to stop any litigation but he considered it right in this case. He described the actions of the managing director of the claimant as having been 'tricky and devious ... seeking to engineer court procedures as to pressure IBM into making further payment by way of settlement when IBM thought they had achieved finality of settlement on payment of large sums of money'. He ordered the claimant to pay both the defendant's costs and those of the Part 20 defendant.

A final point to consider is that there is a possibility that the computer hardware or the software sold with it infringes some intellectual property right. The hardware itself could infringe a patent, design or trade mark while the software might infringe a copyright or trade mark. The client should make sure that the contract contains a term indemnifying him in case this should happen. If the contract is governed by the Sale of Goods Act 1979, however, there will be remedies available to the buyer if he is prevented from using or is hindered in his use of the equipment because it infringes another person's rights. By section 12(1), there is an implied condition that the seller has the right to sell the goods and, by section 12(2), there is an implied warranty that the buyer will enjoy 'quiet possession' of the goods. However, in a sale to a non-consumer, in England and Wales, a breach of condition may be treated as a breach of warranty only if the breach is so slight such that it would be unreasonable for the buyer to reject them, under section 15A of the Sale of Goods Act 1979.

Section 6 of the Unfair Contract Terms Act 1977 (section 21 in Scotland) provides that section 12 of the Sale of Goods Act 1979 cannot be excluded or restricted by reference to any contractual term. If a company buys a computer and, at the time of the sale, the computer infringes a trade mark or patent, then the seller is in breach of section 12(1) of the Sale of Goods Act 1979. Because this is a condition, the buyer can repudiate the contract and claim back the purchase price, plus damages for any consequential losses he has suffered (provided they are not too remote). In *Niblett Ltd* v *Confectioners' Materials Co Ltd* [1921] 3 KB 387, it was held that because goods, when sold, infringed a trade mark, this entitled the buyer to repudiate the contract. In Scotland the question is whether the breach is a material one.

It may happen that equipment does not infringe a patent when it is sold but does infringe a patent soon afterwards, perhaps because at the time of sale a patent application, made by a third party, was being processed. When the patent is granted, the third party may commence an infringement action against the buyer of the equipment. This occurred in a case involving road marking machines, *Microbeads AC v Vinhurst Road Markings* [1975] 1 WLR 218, where it was held that:

- there was not a breach of section 12(1) because, at the time of the sale, the seller had every right to sell (the patent could not be enforced at that time); but
- the seller was in breach of section 12(2), the implied warranty as to quiet possession, and was liable to the buyer in damages.

There is always a danger that computer equipment or software will infringe a third party's rights (even if it is inadvertent) because of the rapid development of new hardware and software. The remedies in section 12 of the Sale of Goods Act 1979 are useful but it is advisable to make specific contractual provision for the eventuality. For example, in a situation like that in the *Microbeads* case, the buyer may prefer to repudiate the contract rather than being limited to damages only. However, there is a defence to a patent infringement action if a person, in good faith, does the act or makes effective and serious preparations to do the act before the patent's priority date (see Patents Act 1977, section 64).

Tenders

An organisation wishing to obtain computer equipment (the client) may ask a number of suppliers or manufacturers to submit tenders. Each of the companies submitting tenders will be asked for their price to supply the equipment described in a detailed specification. In this way, the bids can be compared on a like-for-like basis and, usually, the one submitting the lowest bid will be awarded the contract to supply equipment complying with the specification. Letting contracts by means of a tendering process is very common and public authorities and many large private organisations make use of this process. In some cases, the organisation will have no other option as it will be laid down in the constitution or articles of association. In some cases, it may be imposed from elsewhere – for example, where the contract value exceeds a particular value, it will have to be open to tenders because of government or European Community regulations.

The contractual status of a tender is that a company submitting a tender is making an offer which can be rejected or accepted by the client as he thinks fit. Indeed, the client can choose not to accept any unless, for example, he has bound himself to accept the lowest. Consequently, the company submitting a tender bears the cost involved in its preparation such as determining which equipment is suitable and calculating the total price. If the hardware is complex, this cost can be considerable. The use of tendering as a means of letting contracts is very common in the construction industry. The convention that the person submitting the tender bears the costs of preparation of the tender is deeply ingrained; that it also applies in the context of computer contracts was emphatically stated in *Comyn Ching Ltd* v *Radius plc* (unreported) 17 March 1997, which concerned a tender for the supply of computer equipment and software. The judge cited a passage from *Keating on Building Contracts*, 6th edn (a leading practitioner text), to the effect that the contractor preparing a tender may incur considerable cost in doing so but there is no implication that he will be paid for this work. Indeed, '... he undertakes this work as a gamble, and its cost ... he hopes will be met out of the profits of such contracts as are made as a result of tenders which prove to be successful!' The judge went on to say 'I see no difference in principle between a building contract and a computer contract.'

Tenders can be requested from a selected list of companies or open tendering can be used – that is, where anyone who wishes may submit a bid. Select list tendering is more usual nowadays and has the advantage that only those companies perceived as being competent are invited to submit bids. However, this may again be subject to rules imposed by government or through the European Community. Sometimes, the rules applicable to the tendering process may differ depending on the classification of the contract. In *Jobsin Co UK Ltd (t/a Internet Recruitment Solutions)* v *Department of*

Health [2001] EWCA Civ 1241, the claimant submitted a tender for the development and management of a website for on-line recruitment to the Department of Health. The claimant was informed that it would not be included in the final shortlist. The issue was whether the services covered by the contract were computer and related services or personnel placement and supply services. The regulations covering the contract differed depending on which it was. The Court of Appeal held that it was the former, which meant that the tender process was defective according to the applicable regulations (the Public Services Contracts Regulations 1993).

The tender process is broadly as follows:

1 A detailed specification is drawn up detailing the functional and performance requirements.

2 If it is to be a select list tender, that list is drawn up and those on it are asked if they are interested in submitting tenders. If open tendering is to be used, an advertisement will be placed in an appropriate newspaper or journal or other publication (for example, the *Official Journal of the European Communities*).

3 To each tenderer, a set of tender documents will be sent comprising the specification (including any drawings and schedules), a form of agreement (so that the tenderer can see what the contractual obligations will be) and, in some cases, a bill of quantities in which the tendering company can write prices or a schedule of rates to be completed or a simple form on which the overall price can be written. The bill, schedule or form will contain a reference to the other documents.

4 A period of time will be allowed and a deadline will be stated for return of the tenders in sealed envelopes – for example, 'no later than noon on 28 February 2000'. Tenders received after this deadline must be rejected (to prevent the possibility of corruption). Of course, nowadays, tenders may be invited and submitted electronically, in which case, care must be taken to ensure confidentiality of the bids before the deadline and that they are opened and compared in circumstances reducing the possibility of corrupt practices.

5 The sealed tenders will be opened after the deadline. This may be before a senior officer and chairman of the appropriate committee in the case of a public authority. Any arithmetic will be checked carefully. (Mistakes can cause all sorts of problems if not picked up and dealt with. If there is a mistake it is usual practice to ask the company submitting that particular tender whether it wishes to stand by its mistake or withdraw the tender.)

6 A letter of acceptance will be sent to the successful company (usually that submitting the lowest bid) and a contract will be executed, typically under seal, as per the original form of agreement.

Tenders can be seen as a very fair means of letting contracts and the system has evolved as a way of reducing the possibility of bribery and corruption. However, tendering is not without difficulties. The client has to make sure that the tender documents are of a high quality, accurately describe the desired equipment and its performance and provide fully for any eventuality. If there are any shortcomings, the successful company may use these as a basis of additional payments and extensions to the time for delivery. A major headache for the client is that the companies submitting tenders, or at least some of them, will wish to make changes to the specification or time for delivery, etc. If this is permitted, it makes comparison of the tenders more difficult. A usual means of trying to maintain some comparability is to ask any company which has expressed a wish to submit on a different basis to submit two tenders, one as per the original tender documents, the other on its preferred specification.

Performance bond

Where hardware is delivered and installed over a period of time, for example, where the hardware has to be built up from numerous components and pieces of equipment and software specifically written for the hardware, it may be wise for the client to insist on a performance bond. This operates to provide a sum of money to the client if the supplier fails to complete the work, typically where the supplier goes into receivership part-way through performing the contract. In such circumstances, it will be more costly to engage a second supplier/developer to complete the work. Of course, the agreement must make specific provision dealing with the ownership of the hardware and when title to it passes to the client, otherwise the receiver may have a claim over it and may seek repossession in order to go towards satisfying the creditors of the supplier.

Performance bonds are usually set at a percentage of the total price agreed for the contract, 10 per cent being a common figure. The bond will usually be arranged with a bank, insurance company or other financial institution. The contract will have to be very precise as to the event when the right to claim the bond is triggered. Standard precedents use a form of words commonly used by lawyers in situations where the supplier goes into receivership, bankruptcy, becomes insolvent or enters an arrangement with its creditors. However, in this context, provision must also be made for the possibility that the supplier simply fails to perform its obligations satisfactorily or effectively or simply abandons the work. This is likely to require formal notice being given to the supplier specifying the alleged breaches of contract and, where remedial, requiring the supplier to remedy the situation within a reasonable time (without prejudice to any remedy the client may seek for damages). Continued failure will trigger release of the bond but usually only after a sworn statement from the client.

Consumer protection – additional safeguards

Some further safeguards apply to sales to consumers, following modifications made to the Sale of Goods Act 1979, the Supply of Goods and Services Act 1982 and the Unfair Contract Terms Act 1977 by the Sale and Supply of Goods to Consumers Regulations 2002. These Regulations, which came into force on 31 March 2003, implement Directive 1999/44/EC of the European Parliament and of the Council of 25 May 1999 on certain aspects of the sale of consumer goods and associated guarantees (OJ L 171, 7.7.1999, p.12).

Satisfactory quality and relevant circumstances

Section 14(2A) of the Sale of Goods Act 1979 states that goods are of satisfactory quality if:

> ... they meet the standard that a reasonable person would regard as satisfactory, taking account of any description of the goods, the price (if relevant) and all other *relevant circumstances* (emphasis added).

The Regulations insert new subsections (2D) to (2F) into section 14 and include in the meaning of 'relevant circumstances' public statements as to specific characteristics of goods made by the seller, the producer or his representative, particularly in advertising or labelling. Thus, any claims made in advertising by a manufacturer of a computer will be included in the relevant circumstances even though a consumer might buy a computer from a retailer, rather than directly from the manufacturer. Therefore, a consumer who buys a computer which fails to perform as stated by a manufacturer may be able to reject the computer and claim a refund of the price even though the retailer did not personally make that statement concerned. This additional implied term also applies, of course, to advertising made by the seller as well. A 'producer' is defined as the manufacturer of goods, the importer of goods into the European Economic Area or any person purporting to be the producer by placing his name, trade mark or other distinctive sign on the goods.

There are some exceptions to this additional implied term and it does not apply if:

- at the time the contract was made, the *seller* can show that he was not and could not reasonably have been aware of the statement – this protects a seller unaware of the statement who is not held responsible for statements made by the producer of the goods that he could not reasonably have been expected to have known about;
- the statement had been withdrawn in public before the contract was made or anything in it that was incorrect or misleading had been corrected in public;
- the decision to buy the goods had not been influenced by the statement.

In all these cases, the burden of proof lies with the seller to show that the exception relied on applies.

These provisions do not prevent other public statements, whether or not the buyer is a consumer (or, in Scotland, whether or not it is a consumer contract) from being relevant circumstances. In other words, the meaning of public statements considered to be relevant circumstances are not limited to the basic definition and exceptions. For example, a statement as to the performance of a computer made in advertising directed at business sales may be a relevant circumstance. This could apply where a consumer sees such advertising and buys the computer from a retailer on the strength of that statement.

If goods fail to meet the requirement of being of satisfactory quality, this will give a buyer who is buying as a consumer the right to reject the goods as it is a breach of condition or, in Scotland, a material breach. This absolute right was modified by the Regulations and sections 48A–48F were inserted into the Sale of Goods Act 1979. Depending on the circumstances, the buyer can require that the goods be repaired or replaced or that there is a reduction in the price. Only if neither of these remedies is appropriate can the buyer reject the goods. The modified rights apply if the goods do not conform to the contract of sale at the time of delivery. This is defined as a breach of any express term in the contract or any breach of the terms implied by sections 13, 14 or 15 of the Sale of Goods Act 1979. (Section 13 requires that goods conform to their description, section 14 requires that goods are of satisfactory quality and fit for their purpose and section 15 applies where sale is by sample and requires that the bulk corresponds with the sample.) Thus, a breach of the condition in section 12(1) that the seller has the right to sell the goods is unaffected by the changes made by the Regulations and the buyer still has an absolute right to reject goods for breach of this condition.

Additional remedies in consumer contracts

An important change is that, if the goods do not conform to the contract of sale at any time within a period of six months from the date the goods were delivered to the buyer, they are treated as not so conforming at the delivery date, giving the buyer these additional remedies. There are two exceptions to this and it does not apply if it is established that the goods did conform at the date they were delivered to the buyer or if the application of that provision is incompatible with the nature of the goods or the nature of the lack of conformity, for example, if the goods are perishable or certain items of clothing or if they are foodstuffs with a 'use by' date that expires within the six-month period.

The Regulations are not clear as to whether the buyer can elect for either repair or replacement but the Directive makes it clear that, if this remedy is available, it is the buyer who can choose whether to have the goods repaired or replaced. Repair or replacement must occur within a reasonable time without causing significant inconvenience to the buyer and the seller must bear any necessary costs including the costs of labour, materials or postage. However, this remedy is not available if repair or replacement is impossible (for example, if the defect is such that repair is not possible or there are no more of those goods available) or if it is disproportionate to the other remedies available, including repair where the buyer has elected for repair rather than replacement or *vice versa*. Disproportionality is defined in terms of the costs imposed on the seller which, compared to the other remedy (whether repair or replacement), are unreasonable taking into account the value the goods had they conformed to the contract of sale, the significance of the lack of conformity and whether the other remedy could be effected without significant inconvenience to the buyer. What is a reasonable time or what is a significant inconvenience to the buyer are to be determined by reference to the nature of the goods and the purpose for which they were acquired. Therefore, if a consumer buys a computer that breaks down a short time after delivery, it might be unreasonable to expect the buyer to wait several weeks for repairs when a replacement can be offered.

The alternative remedies, reduction in price or the right to reject the goods (a right to rescind the contract) are available if the buyer is not entitled to require repair or replacement (for example, if it would be impossible or disproportionate) or if the buyer has elected for repair or replacement and the seller has not done so within a reasonable time and without significant inconvenience to the seller. If a buyer does rescind the contract, he will be entitled to the return of any money paid to the seller. However, if the buyer has used the goods since they were delivered to him, the seller may reduce the reimbursement to take account of such use. Setting off any repayment on account of the use made of goods by the consumer and agreeing the amount by which the price of goods should be reduced if that remedy is chosen could prove to be difficult. In terms of the latter, the Regulations state that the buyer can require the seller to reduce the purchase price of the goods by an appropriate amount. One possibility seems to be that the buyer can leave the seller with the option of either agreeing to the reduction asked for by the buyer or having the buyer rescind the contract and having to reimburse the purchase price.

In terms of conformity with the contract of sale, the Directive states that the buyer may not rescind the contract if the breach is minor but this does not appear in the Regulations. The Sale of Goods Act 1979 has a provision such that, in a non-consumer sale, a breach of condition (under sections 13–15 of the Act) is turned into a breach of warranty (giving a remedy in damages only) if the breach is so slight that it would be unreasonable to allow the buyer to reject the goods. This does not apply, however, to consumer sales.

Risk and delivery

The Sale of Goods Act 1979 contains provisions dealing with who bears the risk of goods being damaged or destroyed. The basic rule in section 20 is that the risk passes along with the property in goods, that is when ownership is transferred to the buyer, it is the buyer who bears the risk. In contracts between businesses and other organis-ations, this is perfectly acceptable and assists in determining who is responsible for insurance of the goods in transit. A modification of that rule is where delivery is delayed through either the fault of the seller or buyer, in which case, the one at fault bears the risk. These provisions are disapplied to contracts for the sale of goods in the case of contracts where the buyer deals as consumer or, in Scotland, consumer contracts. Therefore, in such contracts, the risk stays with the seller until such time as the goods are delivered to the buyer.

Where a seller is authorised or required by the buyer to deliver to a carrier, under section 32 of the Sale of Goods Act 1979, this is deemed to be delivery to the buyer with the necessary implications as to the passing of risk. Again, this is disapplied in the case of sales to consumers and delivery to a carrier in such circumstances is not deemed to be delivery to the buyer.

Meaning of 'consumer' for purposes of Unfair Contract Terms Act 1977

Some of the controls over clauses excluding or limiting liability differ depending on whether the party to the contract under consideration is dealing as a consumer or not. For example, in the case of a person dealing as a consumer, under section 4 of that Act indemnity clauses must be reasonable in the circumstances to be enforceable and liab-ility for breach of sections 13–15 of the Sale of Goods Act 1979 cannot be excluded or restricted by any contract term (in other cases, the term must satisfy the requirement of reasonableness).

The meaning of 'dealing as a consumer' is defined in section 12 of the Unfair Contract Terms Act 1977 which requires that the person is dealing as a consumer if he does not make the contract in the course of a business (nor holds himself out as so doing), the other party does make the contract in the course of a business and, in the case of a contract governed by the law of sale of goods or hire-purchase or other con-tracts under which ownership of goods passes as set out in section 7 of the Unfair Contract Terms Act 1977, the goods are of a type ordinarily supplied for private use or consumption. The Regulation modifies this and the limitation that the goods should be of the type ordinarily supplied for private use or consumption no longer applies where the first party is an individual. Therefore, the greater protection afforded to con-sumers in respect of unfair contract terms applies to consumers buying goods from a business even if the goods are not of the type ordinarily bought for private use or con-sumption.

There is a *caveat* to this and a person is not taken to be dealing as a consumer if the goods are second-hand goods sold at a public auction at which individuals have the opportunity of attending the sale in person or if the buyer is not an individual and the goods are sold by auction or by competitive tender.

Equivalent changes are made to section 25 of the Unfair Contract Terms Act in respect of Scotland.

Consumer guarantees

The status of guarantees given by manufacturers of goods has been something of a grey area where the contract for the sale or supply of goods is not with the manufacturer directly but with, for example, a retailer. As there is no contractual link between the consumer and the manufacturer, it was generally assumed that the guarantee operated as a form of collateral warranty. To some extent, this was alleviated by the Contracts (Rights of Third Parties) Act 1999 but, in line with the Directive, the Regulations put this beyond doubt and state that such guarantees take effect as collateral obligations under the conditions set out in the guarantee and any associated advertising.

The contents of the guarantee and the necessary particulars for making claims must be set out in plain intelligible language and the consumer may apply to have the guarantee made available to him in writing or other durable medium within a reasonable time. Where the goods in question are offered with a consumer guarantee within the territory of the United Kingdom, the guarantee must be written in English. The guarantee must state that the consumer has certain legal rights under applicable law and that these are unaffected by the guarantee (this is in the Directive though not mentioned in the Regulations as law in the United Kingdom already provides for this). Any failure of the guarantee to comply with these conditions does not invalidate it and failure of the guarantor to comply with the terms of the guarantee may result in an enforcement order by injunction or, in Scotland, a compliance order.

Chapter 22

Summary and checklist

Introduction

Many potential pitfalls in contracts for computer software and hardware have been discussed in Chapters 15–21, as were ways in which they can be avoided or at least assuaged by careful consideration of the terms of the contract. The rapid rate of change in the computer industry, whilst bringing great improvements to computer technology, has contributed to the scale of the problems. Tales of incompatibility and abandoned systems are commonplace and the effect of bad decisions coupled with poor contracts can be quite horrendous, in some cases contributing to the downfall of the client's business. Some of the cases described in the previous chapters give a flavour of the pitfalls that await the unwary. Choice of computer equipment and software is a very crucial decision and often is given far too little thought.

When looking at a contract for computer equipment or software, the golden rule is to be suspicious and sceptical. Awkward questions should be asked and their answers sought by reference to the contract. The contract needs to be assessed in the light of such questions as:

- What if the software contains bugs?
- What if the computer breaks down in the middle of the wages run?
- What if the client copies the programs and distributes the copies?
- What if the programs run too slowly to be of any practical use?
- What if the computer becomes obsolete and the manufacturer washes his hands of it?

It is so easy to be over-optimistic when acquiring computers and software and it is essential to have a long, hard look at the contract and be a little cynical about it. Both parties to a contract for hardware or software should be prepared to look at that contract from the other's point of view and be prepared to negotiate an agreement giving a fair balance of responsibilities, rights and liabilities.

The choice of the correct form of agreement is important as is the recognition that the course of action anticipated may affect third-party rights – for example, if third parties suffer loss or damage as a result of defects in the software or the manner in which it is used. Although a contract only gives rights to and imposes duties on the parties to the contract, others may be owed duties under the law of negligence or product liability in addition to having intellectual property or other rights which are affected by the use of the hardware or software.

Website development contracts present additional issues that need to be considered as, not only do they require the writing of software, they also act as an organisation's presence in the global market. The performance and content of the website must be dealt with carefully as these aspects can seriously detract from a website's ability to act as the attractive force that brings in custom apart from causing legal problems associated with infringement of the rights of third parties, defamation and consumer protection law. Some of these points will be explored more fully in Part Three on electronic contracts and torts.

Summary

The previous chapters in this part of the book have considered software and hardware contracts and related issues, such as liabilities to third parties, in addition to looking at the impact of information technology on the formation of contracts and evidence. By way of summary, the following key points are identified.

General points

- Care must be taken in drafting contracts so that the rights and duties, risks and liabilities are precisely defined and equitably shared.
- The nature of the contract needs to be reflected upon as it will affect the legal controls over the terms in the contract.
- Terms will be implied into the contract by legislation, particularly in respect of quality and performance.
- The courts will imply terms into contracts, if necessary, to give effect to the presumed intention of the parties but will not make the bargain for the parties.
- Damages for breach of contract can be high and can include wasted time.
- Liability to third parties can arise through negligence, negligent misstatement or product liability.
- Exclusion clauses are likely to be controlled by the Unfair Contract Terms Act 1977.
- The burden of proof to show that an exclusion clause is reasonable lies on the party seeking to rely on it. Appropriate and carefully written clauses excluding or limiting liability may be acceptable, particularly where the parties are business organisations with approximate parity of bargaining power.
- Failure of an exclusion clause to be effective can be grave and appropriate provision should be made to insure in respect of defects resulting from negligence.
- Only the benefit of a contract can be assigned (transferred) to a third party; the original party remains liable for any burden.
- Appropriate confidentiality and indemnity clauses should be considered, bearing in mind the law of restraint of trade and controls over unreasonable indemnity clauses.
- Provisions should be made for arbitration or alternative dispute resolution.

Contracts for writing software

- These are service contracts subject to the Supply of Goods and Services Act 1982.
- The basis of the contract is a copyright licence or assignment of copyright (transfer of ownership of copyright).
- The specification is particularly important and will define the software, its performance and quality.
- Maintenance of the software must be catered for and associated with this will be whether the client is to obtain a copy of the source code.
- If the client does not obtain a copy of the source code, an escrow arrangement should be entered into by both parties.

- The contract should have provisions to deal with delays, extensions to the time for completion and payment for additional work.
- Issues relating to liability for defects should be addressed.
- Independent professional supervision of the performance of the contract should be considered.

Contract for off-the-shelf software

- Nature of the agreement is uncertain – it may be a hybrid, part licence, part sale of goods, or unique.
- Shrink-wrap licence is inconsistent with the English law of contract and may be ineffective, in which case the terms may be implied by law. Alternatively, the making of the contract may be suspended until the person acquiring the software does an act signifying acceptance, such as by breaking the seal on the package containing the disk or disks on which the software is stored.
- Web-wrap (or click-wrap) licences present fewer problems as the terms of the licence are usually available on the website for inspection before the contract is made and those terms will be incorporated into the contract whether or not the person acquiring the software reads them. There may be other issues, however, such as any material on the website which conflicts with the terms of the licence, controls deriving from consumer protection law and terms implied by law.
- Back-up copies of computer programs may be made if necessary to their lawful use – for example, use by a licensee.
- Training and support must not be overlooked.

Website development contract

- A website development contract is a contract for services and is governed by the Supply of Goods and Services Act 1982 or the equivalent common law terms in Scotland. This will be so even if the developer supplies other things such as hardware.
- The implied term of carrying out the work with reasonable care and skill extends to ensuring that the website is fit for its purpose and does not contain material infringing copyright or other intellectual property rights.
- It is common for the agreement to contain express warranties to the effect that the content, if supplied by the developer, will not infringe third-party rights and will contain no material that is defamatory or otherwise unlawful.
- The specification must be fully detailed and precise and deal with issues such as hosting arrangements, performance levels, browser compatibility and links with back-office systems as well as assigning responsibility between the developer and the client, for example, in respect of provision of content and maintenance.
- Feature-creep is a particular danger in the case of website development contracts and the performance of the contract needs careful supervision.
- Maintenance, error correction, enhancements and upgrading need to be carefully thought out. Where the developer provides these services as part of an ongoing relationship, there must be full cooperation between the developer and the client.
- Domain name registration, maintenance and registration of the website with appropriate search engines need to be fully addressed. The dangers of losing a domain

name through failure to renew means that it is wise for the client to take full responsibility for this.

Hardware contracts

- These are governed by the Sale of Goods Act 1979 if the title to the hardware is transferred to the buyer, even if software is bundled with the hardware.
- If leased or hired, the contract will be subject to the Supply of Goods and Services Act 1982.
- Misrepresentations by a dealer may be dealt with as a collateral warranty or on the basis of the Misrepresentation Act 1967.
- Entire agreement clauses are common.
- There should be an indemnity should the hardware (or bundled software) infringe a third party right.
- Use of tenders as a means of acquiring hardware is common (and for buying computer supplies).

Checklist

Table 22.1 indicates the purpose and relevance of contractual terms to the four types of agreement specifically covered in this part of the book.

Table 22.1 Checklist of terms normally found in computer contracts

Note: * – indicates that this term will normally be present in the particular form of agreement.

Term	Purpose	Type of contract/agreement			
		Software			Hardware
		Bespoke	Off-the-shelf	Website	
Definitions	To clarify and assist with the interpretation of the contract	*	*	*	*
Form of agreement	Describes the nature of the contract, e.g. sale contract, licence or lease agreement	*	*	*	*
Assignment/ transfer	States whether the benefit of the contract can be assigned or transferred to a third party	*	*	*	(if leased)
Items provided	List of items included in the contract, e.g. CDs, manuals, etc. Also, any facilities or information to be provided by the client	*	*	*	*
Price or licence fee	The price to be paid or the method of calculating the price. Instalment details and when they are due	*	*	*	*

Term	Purpose	Type of contract/agreement			
		Software			Hardware
		Bespoke	Off-the-shelf	Website	
Royalties	For third party software or content	*		*	
Specification	Describes in detail the performance, quality and content of the subject matter of the contract	*		*	*
Delivery	Defines the time when the subject matter of the contract will be delivered, completed or made available. Delivery may be made by instalments	*		*	*
Liquidated damages	To quantify the damages payable in the event of late performance of all or part of the contract	*	(only if expressly provided for)	*	*
Acceptance	To define what the client has to do to signify acceptance of the software or hardware. Deemed acceptance may be provided for	*	*	*	*
Use	The scope of the uses to which the client can put the software or hardware. For off-the-shelf software, may limit the number of users	*	*		*
Maintenance	Expresses the duties of the supplier to correct errors in the software or faults in the equipment. May be subject to a separate agreement	*	*	*	*
Enhancements	Outlines whether subsequent improvements to the software or hardware will be available. Enhancements may be available as part of a maintenance contract	*	(upgrades may be available)	*	*
Modifications	States whether the client can modify the software or hardware without recourse to the supplier. If permitted, ownership of rights in any modifications must be dealt with	*	*	*	*

Term	Purpose	Type of contract/agreement			
		Software			Hardware
		Bespoke	Off-the-shelf	Website	
Training	Describes responsibility for training the client's staff in the use of the software. May be a separate agreement with a dealer	*	*	*	
Copyright, etc.	Defines the client's duty to prevent unauthorised copying or transmission of the software or trade secrets relating to the hardware or software	*	*	*	*
Escrow	The machinery for the provision of the source code version of the programs and preparatory materials to the client in the event of the supplier ceasing to support the software	*		*	
Confidentiality	States the supplier's duty not to divulge confidential information concerning the client's business	*		*	*
Liability	To limit the liability of the supplier in the event of defects subject to legal controls such as the Unfair Contract Terms Act 1977	*	*	*	*
Indemnities	To protect the client if the subject matter infringes a third party right such as a copyright or if it contains defamatory material or in respect of claims arising in negligence	*	*	*	*
Staff poaching	To provide contractual remedies should either party offer employment to a member of the other party's staff (taking care that it is not seen as being in restraint of trade)	*		*	*
Termination	Describes under what circumstances the contract can be terminated. There should be provision for termination by either party. If termination is available for a breach of contract, there should be provision to allow the party in breach an opportunity to remedy the breach	*	*	*	(hire contracts)

Term	Purpose	Type of contract/agreement			
		Software			Hardware
		Bespoke	Off-the-shelf	Website	
Legal action	Provision for the other party to assist in or institute any legal action against a third party, for example, who is infringing copyright	*		*	(if contract includes a patent or copyright licence)
Entire agreement	Ensuring that the formal written agreement contains all the terms of the contract and anything else can be no more than a mere representation	*	*	*	*
Arbitration/ ADR	The machinery for settling disputes without recourse to the courts by appointing a suitably qualified arbitrator. Instead, provision may be made for alternative dispute resolution to assist in a negotiated settlement	*		*	*
Applicable law	Denotes the country or state whose law and jurisdiction will be used to settle disputes. Bear in mind that Scots law is different to English law. May also restrict jurisdiction, for example, to England and Wales	*	*	*	*

PART THREE

Electronic contracts and torts

The laws of contract and torts are often grouped together under the description of the law of obligations. Obligations may be contractual, for example, the duties set out in a contract to be performed by the parties to the contract. On the other hand, obligations are imposed outside the context of a contract, such as those imposed by the law of negligence, where the imposition of the obligation is imposed on persons satisfying the 'neighbour' test, as mentioned in Chapter 17. Issues relating to contract and the tort of negligence have been discussed in the previous part of this book as they apply to computer contracts, such as contracts for writing software. This part of the book looks at contract and tort in relation to electronic commerce or e-business.

The initial hysteria surrounding e-business has now subsided and the e-bubble has burst – it is clear that e-business is here to stay. More recently, it has grown in a more balanced way and has gradually increased in significance. So much so that it has attracted a substantial legal response, particularly in Europe. There are a number of reasons why this is so. First, consumer protection is seen as paramount and the nature of the Internet poses real threats to this. Secondly, whilst it is clear that e-business must be regulated, it must be done in such a way so as not to discourage the use of the Internet as an appropriate arena within which to carry out business. This means, for example, that contracts made over the Internet should be legally enforceable and that the terms of the contract can be received in court and not excluded for reasons to do with formalities. Thirdly, harmonisation of laws governing e-business within Europe is desirable so that no member states are disadvantaged compared with others as being a suitable place to establish an e-business operation. Finally, the position of intermediaries, such as internet service providers, for illegal material flowing through their service must be clarified and appropriate defences made available where they are without blame.

The first chapter in this part of the book looks at the nature, content and formation of electronic contracts. It will be seen that the law has gone a long way to providing mechanisms for e-business. The following chapter looks at the performance and breach of electronic contracts and includes a discussion of particular consumer protection legislation. The next chapter covers electronic torts, such as defamation, malicious falsehood and negligent misstatement. The final chapter in this part of the book examines the potential liability of information society service providers for illegal material made available through their services and how that liability is eliminated in 'no-fault' situations.

Chapter 23

Nature, content and formation of electronic contracts

Introduction

Information technology allows and encourages the conduct of many aspects of commercial or business activity by electronic means. Forms of agreement and other contractual documents are likely to be created using a computer and may be transmitted in electronic form anywhere in the world. Standard forms and precedents used by solicitors to draw up agreements, such as a software licence or a will, are now published electronically. Typically, a solicitor acting for a party to a contract will load an appropriate form of agreement into his word processor, make any required modifications and additions, and then either print it out or transmit it to the other party's solicitor. A contractual offer may be made in this way and may be accepted electronically by the other party transmitting his acceptance of the terms of the agreement.

Many transactions are now effected electronically. For example, by the use of automated teller machines (ATMs or cash point dispensers outside banks) and electronic fund transfers (EFTs) transactions are made between financial institutions and even at the point of sale. Most business organisations now exchange data electronically. For example, a large manufacturing company may order components automatically and electronically from its suppliers when stock levels reach a predetermined lower limit. Electronic data interchange (EDI) has the potential to maximise efficiency by reducing repetition and delays, increasing accuracy and permitting the maintenance of minimum stock levels by placing orders for 'just-in-time' delivery. A large proportion of the information flowing between organisations may be handled electronically, including quoting or submitting tenders for work, ordering, scheduling, invoicing and accounting. Land can be bought and sold electronically and the Land Registration Act 2002 includes provisions for e-conveyancing (in force from 13 October 2003).

All of this sounds very good apart, perhaps, from concerns about security but, as expected, there are a number of legal consequences associated with electronic trading.

- The law requires that some contracts are in a particular form – for example, by deed or in writing.
- There may be doubts as to when the contract was made and, if the parties are in different countries, which country's law will apply to the contract.
- The evidential weight of electronic documents must be considered and assessed. For example, will a court admit an electronic signature as proof of a person's consent to a transaction?

To take an example, imagine that Karen, who has a large footwear store in London, wishes to buy 1000 pairs of shoes from Luigi in Milan. Both Karen and Luigi have computers and both use electronic mail. Luigi has a website advertising his shoes. After seeing this, Karen submits an enquiry to Luigi via the website. Further negotiations are carried out using electronic mail. Eventually, Karen transmits a contract for Luigi's approval on Monday at 10.00 am GMT. Later that day, at 2.00 pm GMT, Luigi sends a message to say that he accepts Karen's offer. However, Karen does not read that message until Wednesday as she has to make a trip to Scotland in the meantime. There is a term in the contract to the effect that Karen can terminate the contract if she fails to sell more than 50 pairs of shoes in any one week, returning the remaining stock to Luigi and paying only for those that she has sold. After four weeks, Karen has sold 250 pairs of shoes but 175 pairs were sold in the first week following an intensive advertising campaign. Sales have plummeted since and in the fourth week only 12 pairs were sold. Karen wishes to exercise her right to terminate the contract but the only evidence she has of the numbers sold each week is the record of sales on her computer, entered by her various shop assistants as and when they sold shoes.

The questions that arise in the above scenario related to the use of electronic contracting are:

- Is the contract valid – that is, did the electronically transmitted offer and acceptance create a binding contract? (If so, what would the position have been if Luigi, who did not receive confirmation until Wednesday, had sold the shoes to a third party on Tuesday?) If Karen and Luigi attached or associated their electronic signatures to the contract would this be admissible in a court of law as to the existence of a valid contract?
- If there is a valid contract, when was it made and is it subject to English or Italian law?
- Can a printout of the computer record of sales be used as evidence to prove that Karen sold insufficient numbers of shoes so allowing her to invoke the termination clause?

The main issues relating to electronic contracting concern the legal formalities, the admissibility of electronic signatures, the time that the contract was made, the applicable law and the admissibility of computer evidence in civil proceedings. These are considered below. At the end of the chapter, we will return to Karen and Luigi and advise them accordingly.

Legal requirement as to form

A contract may be made in a number of different forms. For example, a contract may be made by deed, made in writing, evidenced in writing or it may be oral, or it may be a combination of all these. For example, section 4 of the Sale of Goods Act 1979 states that a contract of sale:

> ... may be made in writing (either with or without seal), or by word of mouth, or partly in writing and partly by word of mouth, or may be implied from the conduct of the parties.

An example of a contract implied from the conduct of the parties is given by the case of *Brogden v Metropolitan Rail Co* (1877) 2 App Cas 666 concerning a contract to supply coal. It was held that the conduct of the parties by dealing with each other in accordance with a draft contract could only be explained on the basis that they approved the draft contract and a binding contract came into existence, at the latest, when the claimant supplied the first order of coal placed by the defendant.

Although for some contracts the form used does not matter (as in a sale of goods contract above), occasionally the law requires that a particular form be used. Some contracts must be by deed, an example being a lease of real property (land) for more than three years (sections 52 and 54(2) of the Law of Property Act 1925). A deed is a written document that is signed, sealed and delivered and a contract made by deed is referred to as a contract under seal. This requirement can be traced back to the Statute of Frauds 1677, and was intended to prevent lack of documentation being used as a means of fraud. The formality associated with a deed demonstrates a clear intention to be bound and, therefore, in terms of a contract, there is no requirement for consideration (for example, payment or goods), normally a prerequisite of legally binding contracts.

In recognition of the fact that some flexibility is now required and the traditional form of deed – originally written in beautiful cursive script on vellum with a wax seal attached (or more recently a red adhesive wafer) – is no longer relevant in today's society, the Law of Property (Miscellaneous Provisions) Act 1989 abolished some of the old rules that applied to some deeds. For example, under section 1 of that Act, the requirement for a seal was abolished as was any requirement as to the substance the deed was written on. Now, to qualify as a deed, the instrument must make it clear on its face that it is intended to be a deed (for example, by using a form of words making it clear that it is a deed) and it must be validly executed – for example, signed in the presence of witnesses and delivered (section 1(2) and (3)). The meaning of 'sign' includes making one's mark. It is possible that this could extend to a digital electronic representation of a signature and, because of the other relaxations in the rules, there seems to be no reason why an electronic deed cannot be valid. Nevertheless, because there is still a degree of uncertainty, it would be wise to print out the deed on paper before it is signed before witnesses, although this would then require physical delivery, losing one of the advantages of using information technology.

Relatively few legal documents are required to be by deed. However, some must be in writing. For example, an assignment of a copyright must be in writing and signed by or on behalf of the assignor (section 90(3) of the Copyright, Designs and Patents Act 1988), and regulated consumer credit agreements must be in documentary form and signed (section 61 of the Consumer Credit Act 1974). The same applies to contracts for marine insurance, by section 22 of the Marine Insurance Act 1906, and contracts for the sale or other disposition of an interest in land, which must also incorporate all the terms expressly agreed by the parties (section 2(1) of the Law of Property (Miscellaneous Provisions) Act 1989). Yet other contracts must be evidenced in writing, an example being a contract of guarantee by section 4 of the Statute of Frauds 1677.

For contracts where writing is a requirement it is important to determine whether documents stored magnetically in digital form comply. Fortunately, Schedule 1 to the Interpretation Act 1978 contains the following definition:

'Writing' includes typing, printing, lithography, photography and other modes of representing or reproducing words in a visible form, and expressions referring to writing are construed accordingly.

This would appear to include computer storage. Words stored in a computer may be reproduced on screen or printed on paper. In any case, it is unlikely that a judge would take a restrictive view of this, although the preceding words are somewhat narrow.

Where signatures are required, what has been said earlier in respect of deeds should still hold. The matter is not beyond doubt but there is no logical reason why a person's mark cannot be stored in digital form and affixed to a computer file electronically. The purpose of a signature is to identify the signatory's assent to the document or transaction. This can be done effectively by electronic means, particularly if a form of encryption is used. The stylised handwritten name signatures we are so familiar with are of relatively recent origin. Most of us now have one or more PIN numbers so that we can draw cash from the 'hole in the wall' without the need for any signature. However, use of such facilities is founded on a printed contract signed in the usual way!

If the formalities required by law are not complied with then, at law, the contract will be unenforceable. However, equity may still be available. For example, the party denying that there is a legally binding contract may be estopped from denying its existence and may have to perform his obligations nonetheless. This would be appropriate where that person had behaved in some dishonourable way in the knowledge that the other person was acting to his detriment in the belief that the contract would be binding.

Electronic signatures and electronic communication

Section 7 of the Electronic Communications Act 2000 deals with electronic signatures and related certificates. This came into force on 25 July 2000. An electronic signature is so much of anything in electronic form which:

- is *incorporated* into or otherwise *logically associated* with any electronic communication or electronic data, and
- purports to be so incorporated or associated for the purpose of being used in establishing the *authenticity* of the communication or data, the *integrity* of the communication or data, or both.

Certification of an electronic signature requires that the person whose signature it is has made a statement (whether before or after making the communication) confirming that the signature, a means of producing, communicating or verifying the signature, or a procedure applied to the signature (either alone in combination with other factors) is a valid means of establishing the authenticity or the integrity of the communication or data or both.

Section 7 makes admissible in evidence electronic signatures incorporated or logically associated with a particular electronic communication or particular electronic data and the certification by any person of such a signature. The admissibility relates to the *authenticity* or *integrity* of the communication or data. Authenticity is defined in section 15(2) in terms of the source of the communication or data, the accuracy of time and date, and whether it is intended to have legal effect. Integrity relates to whether there has been any tampering or other modification of the communication or data.

Section 8 of the Act allows the Secretary of State to modify enactments or subordinate legislation or schemes, licences, authorisations or approvals for the purpose of facilitating electronic communications or electronic storage for one or more of a number of specified purposes. These include things required to (or that may) be done or evidenced in writing or otherwise using a document, notice or instrument; things required to (or may) be done by post or other specified means of delivery; things required to (or may) be authorised by a person's signature or seal or is required to be delivered as a deed or witnessed.

These provisions allow the Secretary of State the power to overcome specific requirements in respect of legal formalities to allow for electronic communications or electronic storage to satisfy the requirements. However, this must not compromise the records of things done for their relevant purpose. Changes have been made in a number of cases to facilitate electronic communication in particular including in terms of patents, housing, health, public records and in relation to unsolicited goods or services. The Secretary of State also has the power to make provisions as to the electronic form of electronic communications or storage and conditions for authorisation, manner of proof, provision of criminal offences for making false or misleading statements and other matters.

Part I of the Electronic Communications Act 2000 provides for a register of approved cryptography service providers and regulation of them. However, the government prefers to keep the present voluntary scheme in place and Part I of the Act will only be brought into force if the voluntary scheme proves to be unsatisfactory. In any case, unless Part I is brought into force, it will automatically be repealed on 25 May 2005.

The Electronic Signatures Regulations 2002 deal with the liability of certification service providers in the context of electronic signatures and with certain data protection issues. Members of the public who rely on a certificate and who suffer loss are entitled to damages for any loss as a result of that reliance unless the certification service provider can prove that he was not negligent. This is a useful reversal of the normal burden of proof. There are also data protection issues relating to such certificates and personal data may only be obtained for the purpose of issuing or maintaining the certificate either directly from the data subject or with his express consent. The Secretary of State also has some supervisory powers over certification service providers.

When is the contract made?

The ability to point to the exact time that a contract is made may be important in a number of cases. For example, a contract for the writing of a new item of software may require that the work is completed no later than three months from the date of creation of the contract. A contractual offer for the sale of computer equipment may be expressed as being open for acceptance for seven days only (though such an offer will be binding only if supported by consideration – for example, where the person to whom the offer has been made has paid a fee for the benefit of the 'option').

The normal way that a contract is made is when an offer made by one party is accepted, unconditionally and on identical terms, by the other party. The contract is made the instant that the person to whom the offer is made (the offeree) communicates his acceptance to the person making the offer (the offeror). The first time this rule ran into difficulties was in relation to the use of the postal system, which, as a means of communication, inevitably results in a time lag between making the offer or the acceptance and its receipt by the other party. Typically, problems can arise where the person making an offer revokes that offer before receiving the other's acceptance. A revocation of an offer is effective when communicated to the offeree – that is, when it is actually received by him. If, in the meantime, he posts an acceptance of that offer there is likely to be a conflict.

In *Adams* v *Lindsell* (1818) 1 B & Ald 681, the claimant was a manufacturer of woollen items located in Bromsgrove. The defendant was a wool merchant in St Ives, now in Cambridgeshire, some distance away. The defendant wrote to the claimant making an offer to sell wool to the claimant requiring an answer in the course of the post. Due to the defendant's negligence, the letter was delayed by three days but almost immediately upon receiving it, the claimant wrote back accepting the offer. In the meantime, not having received a reply by the date he expected, the defendant sold the wool to a third party. The claimant successfully sued for breach of contract as the court decided that the contract was made when the letter of acceptance was posted.

This exception to the general rule applies only where it is reasonable to expect communication of acceptance through the post – for example, where the offer is made through the post and there is no stipulation for a different form of communication (see *Byrne* v *Van Tienhoven* (1880) 5 CPD 344). The rule would not apply if the offeror required communication of acceptance by some other method – for example, by telephone, facsimile transmission or by electronic mail.

The postal rule is an exception and where the means of communication being used by the prospective parties is almost instantaneous, the general rule will prevail. Thus, in *Entores Ltd* v *Miles Far East Corp* [1955] 2 QB 327, where offer and acceptance were communicated by telex, it was held that the acceptance took effect not when it was transmitted from Amsterdam but when it was received in London and, accordingly, the contract was subject to English law rather than Dutch law (this manner of determining which law applies has been substantially modified by the Rome Convention, discussed later). The House of Lords approved of this decision in *Brinkibon Ltd* v *Stahag Stahl und Stahlwarenhandelsgesellschaft mbH* [1983] 2 AC 34. In that case, the claimant, an English company, wished to buy a quantity of steel from the defendant, an Austrian company. The claimant sent a telex from London to Vienna, accepting the defendant's offer but the steel was not delivered and the claimant sought damages for breach of contract in England. The House of Lords confirmed that the contract was made in Austria and, therefore, outside the jurisdiction of the English courts. Where the method of communication of acceptance is instantaneous a contract is made when the acceptance is received by the offeror.

The House of Lords went on to stress that this is not a universal rule and the circumstances of a particular case might result in a different outcome. There may be all sorts of variations – for example, where the transmission will be received outside office hours and it is expected that it will be read later or where it is sent to a third party's telex machine or to the agent of the offeror. Lord Wilberforce said:

> No universal rule can cover all such cases; they must be resolved by reference to the intention of the parties, by sound business practice and in some cases by a judgment where the risks should lie.

Brinkibon remains useful in providing a rule of thumb for determining when a contract is made. Some of the other parts of the judgments are, however, of less relevance today because of Conventions and Regulations on jurisdiction, discussed in the following chapter and the Rome Convention, which governs the question of applicable law.

Where an offer and acceptance are to be communicated by electronic mail, the basic rule should prevail, that is, that the acceptance is effective when it is received. Confirmation of receipt and reading is available in electronic mail systems and should be used. Difficulties may arise where the message accepting the offer is not read immediately upon receipt, perhaps because it is received during the night (for example, where one party is in Hong Kong and the other is in England) or the person to whom the receipt is addressed is out of the office for some time. It makes sense in such situations for the parties to stipulate their own rules – for example, that the acceptance is not effective until such time as it is read by the offeror or acknowledged by him. Great care must be taken by any person who has made offers to a number of other persons in respect of the same subject matter. However, where a person wishing to sell an item of computer equipment, for example, places details on the Internet, this will not be deemed to be an offer as such. It is more akin to placing an advertisement in a magazine, which is an invitation to treat – in other words, an invitation to others to make offers to buy the equipment. In *Partridge* v *Crittenden* [1968] 2 All ER 421, Partridge placed an advertisement in the *Cage and Aviary Birds* magazine for the sale of Bramblefinches at £1 5s each. He was prosecuted under section 6(1) of the Protection of Birds Act 1954 for offering for sale a wild bird. His conviction was quashed – he had not offered the birds for sale because the placing of the advertisement was not an offer, merely an invitation to treat.

Bearing in mind the trans-national nature of the Internet, issues of applicable law and jurisdictions should be agreed expressly by the parties to the contract. Although there are Conventions and Regulations that apply in this context, it makes sense to tie things down properly at the outset. Even then, however, there may be some interference, for example, some rules on jurisdiction in consumer contracts cannot be ignored and consumer protection legislation cannot be comprised in Europe by a choice of law clause.

Applicable law

Most contracts contain a term, often at the end of the agreement, stating under which country's law the contract is to have effect. For example, the agreement may state that 'this agreement is subject to the laws of England and Wales'. In Europe, the 1980 Rome Convention on the law applicable to contractual obligations (OJ C 27, 26.01.1998, p.34, consolidated version), given effect in the United Kingdom by the Contracts (Applicable Law) Act 1990, contains rules governing applicable law that apply in all the member states of the European Community. The Convention applies to contracts but there are exceptions, for example, contracts of insurance. The basic rule is in Article 3 and is that the parties are free to choose the law governing their contract, whether in whole or in part. The choice must be expressed with reasonable certainty and they may choose a foreign law or even to vary the choice of law, providing third parties are not prejudiced.

In the absence of choice, Article 4 states that the contract shall be governed by the law of the country with which the contract is most closely connected. There are further rules to determine which this country is. The basic rule is that it is the country where the party who is to effect performance, which is characteristic of the contract, is based. In the case of a contract for the carriage of goods the country whose law applies is generally the country where the carrier has his principal place of business. If the contract involves immovable property (for example, land) it is the country where the land is situated. These rules are just presumptions and do not apply if, in the circumstances, the contract is more closely connected to another country. In some circumstances, consumer contracts are governed by the law of the country in which the consumer has his habitual residence in the absence of any choice of law clause and even if such a clause exists, the consumer cannot be deprived of the consumer protection laws applicable in the country in which he has his habitual residence.

Determining the place where the party is established whose performance is characteristic of the contract in a sale of goods contract should be based on the country where the party responsible for delivering the goods is established, rather than the country of the party who is to pay for the goods. Payment of money is not considered to be the characteristic performance for the purpose of deciding which country's law applies. This was suggested by Professors Giuliano and Lagarde in a Report on the Rome Convention published in the *Official Journal of the European Communities* (OJ C 282, 31.10.1980, p.1). By virtue of section 3(3) of the Contracts (Applicable Law) Act 1990, this Report is to be taken into account in ascertaining the meaning or effect of any provision in the Rome Convention.

In terms of contracts for the supply of goods or services to consumers, a choice of law clause cannot deprive the consumer of mandatory rules of consumer protection in the country where the consumer has his habitual residence:

- if in that country the conclusion of the contract was preceded by a specific invitation addressed to him or by advertising, and he had taken in that country all the steps necessary on his part for the conclusion of the contract, or
- if the other party or his agent received the consumer's order in that country, or
- if the contract is for the sale of goods and the consumer travelled from that country to another country and there gave his order, provided that the consumer's journey was arranged by the seller for the purpose of inducing the consumer to buy.

Otherwise, in a contract for the supply of goods or services to a consumer, in the absence of a choice of applicable law, the law governing the contract is the law of the country where the consumer has his habitual place of residence.

Electronic Commerce (EC Directive) Regulations 2002

Directive 2000/31/EC of the European Parliament and of the Council of 8 June 2000 on certain legal aspects of information society services, in particular electronic commerce, in the Internal Market (OJ L 178, 17.07.2000, p.1, the 'Directive on electronic commerce') was implemented on 21 August 2002 by the Electronic Commerce (EC Directive) Regulations 2002 (apart from one provision relating to 'Stop Now Orders', court orders to prevent activities by traders that contravene European Community consumer protection legislation). As the Regulations closely follow the Directive, references in this section are to the above Directive unless stated otherwise. The part of the Directive concerned with the liability of intermediary service providers in this context is discussed in Chapter 26.

The aims of the Directive are to:

- eliminate the extent to which a member state can control information society services emanating from another member state by co-ordination of certain national laws and by clarification of certain legal concepts;
- lay down a clear and general framework covering certain legal aspects of electronic commerce thus ensuring legal certainty and consumer confidence;
- secure the freedom of movement of information society services;
- secure effective and speedy access to dispute resolution, including by electronic means and injunctive relief.

Scope

The Directive applies in relation to information society services. These are services normally provided for remuneration, at a distance, by means of electronic equipment for processing and storage of data. Processing includes digital compression. Information services within the meaning in the Directive cover a wide range of activities, including:

- on-line contracting including selling goods on-line;
- remuneration other than by those who receive the service such as on-line information or commercial communications or the provision of search facilities for access to and retrieval of data;
- transmissions point to point such as video on demand or provision of commercial communications by electronic mail (but not individual communications by natural persons outside their trade, business or profession including their use for the conclusion of contracts).

The contractual relationship between an employer and employee is not an information society service nor are activities which cannot, by their very nature, be carried out at a distance and by electronic means, such as the auditing of company accounts or medical advice requiring a physical examination of the patient. The definition of information society services refers to Article 1(2) of Directive 98/34/EC of the European Parliament and of the Council of 22 June 1998 laying down a procedure for the provision of information in the field of technical standards and regulations (OJ L 204, 21.07.1998, p.37) amended by Directive 98/48/EC of the European Parliament and of the Council of 20 July 1998 amending Directive 98/34/EC laying down a procedure for the provision of information in the field of technical standards and regulations (OJ L 217, 05.08.1998, p.18). Annex V to the latter Directive gives an indicative list of services which are not provided at a distance, not provided by electronic means, off-line services (for example, distribution of CDs) and services not provided via electronic processing/inventory systems (for example, certain telephony, telex, fax, telephone and telefax services and consultations). Other exclusions include television and radio broadcasting services.

The Directive does not apply to taxation, aspects relating to the data protection Directive (95/46/EC, OJ L 281, 23.11.1995, p.31) and the privacy in telecommunications Directive (97/66/EC, OJ L 24, 30.01.1998, p.1), or agreements or practices governed by cartel law. Nor does it apply in respect of certain activities of information society services, being:

- activities of notaries or equivalent professions to the extent that they involve a direct and specific connection with the exercise of public authority,
- the representation of a client and defence of his interests before the courts,
- gambling activities involving wagering a stake with monetary value in games of chance, including lotteries and betting transactions.

The Directive is also without prejudice to the level of protection already available, in particular, in terms of public health and consumer interests, as established in a number of other Directives. For example, in relation to unfair terms in consumer contracts, distance contracts, misleading advertising, the advertising of medicinal products and advertising and sponsorship of tobacco products.

The Internal Market and law governing service providers

By virtue of Article 3, the requirements for taking up the activity of an information society service provider and pursuing such activities, as laid down in member states' legal systems, are not to be used to restrict the freedom to provide information society services from another member state. Derogation is allowed on the basis of public policy (including the prevention and detection of criminal offences, the protection of minors and the fight against incitement to hatred and violations of human dignity), public health, public security and the protection of consumers including investors. The United Kingdom has taken advantage of all these derogations.

Information service providers established in a member state must comply with the relevant national provisions related to the 'coordinated field'. This includes on-line information, advertising, on-line shopping and on-line contracting, without prejudice to future harmonisation in these areas. The scope of the coordinated field does not extend to national requirements as to safety and labelling of goods, liability for goods, delivery or transportation of goods or rights of pre-emption concerning goods such as works of art. These provisions do not apply in some circumstances, set out in the Annex to the Directive on electronic commerce, including in relation to copyright and industrial property rights and the freedom of parties to choose applicable law.

The recitals make it clear that the concept of establishment is to be determined in accordance with the case law of the Court of Justice. It is not the place where the organisation's website is located (that is, the technology supporting the website) nor where the website is accessible. Rather it is the place where the organisation pursues its economic activity. Where a service provider has several places of establishment it may be difficult to determine which is the place where the service is provided from. In such cases, it will be the place where the provider has its centre of activities for the relevant activities relating to the service in question. This could be relevant where a service provider is a company with a number of subsidiary companies established in other member states.

Services provided by undertakings established in a third country (outside the European Union) are not affected by this Directive but, in view of the global nature of electronic commerce and the desirability of Community rules being consistent with equivalent rules on a broader international stage, the Directive is without prejudice to the results of discussions within international organisations such as the WTO (World Trade Organisation), OECD (Organisation for Economic Cooperation and Development) and UNCITRAL (United Nations Commission on International Trade Law) on legal issues.

Article 4 of the Directive on electronic commerce requires that member states do not make the taking up and pursuit of information society services subject to prior authorisation, except in the context of licensing schemes for telecommunications services not being specifically and exclusively targeted at information society services.

Provision of information by service providers

A key aim of the Directive on electronic commerce is to improve transparency so that, for example, a person accessing information offering goods for sale is fully aware of matters such as the identity of the service provider, price and discounts, etc. or, in the case of an unsolicited communication such as a marketing special offer, the recipient can see it for what it is. Whilst the concept of a provider of an information society service is straightforward, the meaning of 'recipient' is any natural or legal person who, for professional ends or otherwise, uses an information society service, in particular for the purposes of seeking information or making it accessible. This can mean either the provider of information on open networks such as the Internet or a person who seeks information on the Internet for private or professional reasons.

There is a requirement for information society service providers to supply specified information to recipients of the service and to the competent authorities in member states. This requirement is in addition to other information requirements under Community law, for example, the requirement to provide information to individuals if personal data relating to them are being obtained. The minimum information to be given is set out in Article 5 and is:

- the name of the service provider and the geographic address at which the provider is established,
- details of the service provider to enable him to be contacted rapidly and communicated with in a direct and effective manner, including his electronic mail address,
- in cases where the service provider is registered in a trade or similar public register, the trade register and his registration number or equivalent means of identification,
- where the activity is subject to an authorisation scheme, particulars of the relevant supervisory authority,
- VAT number, if applicable,
- in the context of a regulated profession, there is also a duty to provide information about the body or similar institution with which the service provider is registered, the professional title and member state where it has been granted and a reference to the applicable professional rules in the member state of establishment and the means of access to them.

There is a further requirement that where the services refer to prices, they must be indicated clearly and unambiguously and, in particular, indicate whether they are inclusive of tax and delivery costs.

Article 6 requires information to be provided in the case of commercial communications which are defined as those which are directly or indirectly promotional of the goods, services or image of a company, organisation or person carrying on a commercial, industrial or craft activity or exercising a regulated profession. However, this does not extend to information allowing direct access to the activity, such as a domain name or e-mail address, nor to communications relating to goods, services or image compiled in an independent manner, particularly when this is without financial consideration.

The information to be provided in the case of commercial communications must comply with the following conditions:

- the communication must be clearly identifiable as a commercial communication and the person on whose behalf it is made must be clearly identifiable,
- promotional offers (such as discounts, premiums and gifts) and promotional competition and games, where permitted by the member state in which the service provider is established, must be clearly identifiable as such and the qualifying conditions or conditions for participation must be easily accessible and presented clearly and unambiguously.

In cases where member states allow unsolicited commercial communications by electronic mail, as is the case in the United Kingdom, and in addition to any other requirements under Community law, they must be clearly and unambiguously identifiable as such as soon as received by the recipient; Article 7. Furthermore, service providers must regularly consult opt-out registers in respect of natural persons. This is without prejudice to the Directives on the protection of consumers in respect of distance contracts (97/7/EC, OJ L 144, 04.06.1999, p.19 which deals, *inter alia*, with the issue of consent to unsolicited communications) and privacy in telecommunications (97/66/EC, OJ L 24, 30.01.1998, p.1 – see the Telecommunications (Data Protection and Privacy) Regulations 1999, which are due to be replaced by new Regulations on privacy and electronic communications; see Chapter 37).

Commercial communications which are part of, or constitute, an information society service provided by a member of a regulated profession are permitted, subject to compliance with the appropriate professional rules regarding, in particular, the independence, dignity and honour of the profession, professional secrecy and fairness towards clients and other members of the profession. This is in addition to Community Directives relating to the access to, and the exercise of, activities of the regulated professions. Member states and the Commission are to encourage the development of codes of conduct in terms of the information to be provided in accordance with professional rules.

Contracts concluded by electronic means

Article 9 requires that member states ensure that their legal systems allow contracts to be concluded by electronic means and relevant legal requirements do not create obstacles for the use of electronic contracts or deprive such contracts of their effectiveness and validity. The United Kingdom by way of the Electronic Communications Act 2000 seeks to facilitate the use of electronic communications and data storage by encouraging a system of approved cryptography service providers and, in particular, by providing that electronic signatures are admissible in evidence.

Some forms of contract may be excepted from the general principle that there should be no legal obstacles to electronic contracting, should member states wish to do so. These are contracts:

- that create or transfer rights in real estate, except for rental rights,
- that require by law the involvement of courts, public authorities or professions exercising public authority,
- of suretyship,
- governed by family law or the law of succession.

In terms of electronic contracting, Article 10 of the Directive requires certain information to be provided, in addition to other information requirements under Community law. The information must be given by the service provider clearly, comprehensively and unambiguously and prior to the order being placed by the recipient. This does not apply where the parties, not being consumers, agree otherwise. The information to be provided is:

- the different technical steps to follow to conclude the contract,
- whether or not the concluded contract will be filed by the service provider and whether it will be accessible,
- the technical means for identifying and correcting input errors prior to placing the order,
- the languages offered for the conclusion of the contract.

Unless the parties, not being consumers, agree otherwise, the service provider must also indicate any relevant codes of conduct to which he subscribes and how these codes can be consulted electronically. However, the above provisions do not apply to contracts concluded exclusively by the exchange of electronic mail or by equivalent individual communication. Contract terms and general conditions provided to the recipient must be made available in a way which allows him to store and reproduce them.

By Article 11, where the recipient of a service places his order through technological means, the service provider must acknowledge receipt of the order without undue delay and by electronic means. Where the order is for the on-line service itself, the acknowledgement may take the form of the provision of the service itself. The order and acknowledgement are deemed to be received when the parties to whom they are addressed are able to access them. The language of the Article tends to suggest that this does not require that the party actually does access the communication. It seems enough that it is available for the party to access, that is, it is accessible rather than accessed.

There is a requirement that appropriate, effective and accessible technical means are provided to all the recipients to identify and correct input errors prior to placing the order. The above provisions of Article 11 do not apply where the parties, not being consumers, otherwise agree. With the exception of the deemed receipt of order and acknowledgement, these provisions do not apply to contracts concluded exclusively by the exchange of electronic mail or by equivalent individual communication.

However, recital 39 curiously states that this should not enable, as a result, the bypassing of these provisions by providers of information society services in relation to the provision of information and the placing of orders. Reading this with the Article would appear to mean that, in relation to contracts concluded exclusively by the exchange of electronic mail and the like, there is still a duty to provide contract terms and conditions in a manner such that the recipient can store and reproduce them (for example, by recording them in a data file or by printing them out) and the deemed provisions on placing the order and acknowledgement still apply to such contracts.

Model laws

The United Nations Commission on International Trade Law (UNCITRAL) brought out a model law on electronic commerce in 1996, amended in 1998 and adopted by the United Nations in 2001. This has been instrumental in informing the debate as to how legislation should be framed to deal with some of the issues relating to electronic commerce and has certainly been influential in European responses to electronic commerce though not as yet adopted by the European Community. An important definition in the model law is that of a 'data message' being information generated, sent or received or stored by electronic, optical or similar means including, but not limited to, electronic data interchange (EDI), electronic mail, telegram, telex or telecopy.

As at 9 June 2003, legislation based on the UNCITRAL model law on electronic commerce has been adopted in Australia, Bermuda, Colombia, Ecuador, France, Hong Kong Special Administrative Region of China, India, Ireland, Isle of Man, Jersey, New Zealand, Pakistan, Philippines, Republic of Korea, Singapore, Slovenia, Thailand and the State of Illinois in the United States of America.

Some of the main provisions of the model law are as follows.

- Information should not be denied legal effect, validity or enforceability on the grounds that it is contained in a data message. This also extends to information not contained in a data message but referred to in a data message.
- Where there are requirements for writing, these are satisfied by a data message providing the information is accessible so as to be usable for subsequent reference.
- Where there are requirements for signatures, these are satisfied by a data message if the method used to identify the person who sent it and to indicate approval are contained in the data message and that method is as reliable as is appropriate for the purposes, in the light of all the circumstances, including any agreement between the parties.
- Where there are requirements for originality, these are satisfied by a data message if there is a reliable assurance as to the integrity of the information from the time it was first generated in its final form, whether as a data message or otherwise. Further the information must be capable of being displayed when it is required to be presented.
- Formation of the contract – offer and acceptance – may be by data messages unless the parties otherwise agree. There are also rules as to acknowledgement of receipt. If not asked for, this can be by any communications (automatic or otherwise) or by conduct. Any offer may be conditional on the receipt of acknowledgement but otherwise, if acknowledgement is requested within a specified or agreed time (or failing that a reasonable time), a notice may be sent requesting acknowledgement within a reasonable time. If stated conditional upon receipt of acknowledgement it is to be treated as never sent unless acknowledged.
- Despatch of a data message takes place when it enters an information system outside the sender's control (unless otherwise agreed).
- Receipt takes place (unless otherwise agreed) at the time the data message enters the information system designated by the recipient (if sent to an information system other than the one designated, it is deemed to be received when retrieved). If the recipient has not designated an information system, receipt takes place when it enters his information system. It does not matter if, where the party concerned has more than one place of business, the location of the information system is different to that at which the data message is deemed to be received.

The intention is that the model law provides essential procedures and principles to facilitate the use of up-to-date techniques used to record and communicate information in various types of circumstances. It does not, however, set out all the rules and regulations necessary to implement those techniques and is not intended to cover every aspect of the use of electronic commerce. An enacting member state may wish to provide specific laws to build in comprehensive procedures. Other legal issues may be raised, for example, in relation to applicable administrative, contract, criminal and judicial-procedure law.

Summary

The law has developed to take account of the use of information technology in commercial activity and, on a number of occasions, judges have had to deal with modern modes of information transmission such as telex, facsimile machines and computers. As has been shown, there are still some grey areas and those wishing to make full use of new technology to conduct their business must be aware of these areas and make appropriate provision. The strictness of the old rules relating to deeds and written documents was relaxed some time ago and in *Hastie and Jenkerson v McMahon* [1990] 1 WLR 1575, the Court of Appeal accepted that some documents could be validly served by fax. In this case a list of documents was required to be identified by court order and served by the claimant on the defendant. All that was required was a legible copy of the document in question placed in the possession of the party on whom it was served and the fax machine achieved this. Now, under rule 6.2 of the Civil Procedure Rules 1998, documents may be served by a number of methods including by fax or other means of electronic communication providing the appropriate practice direction permits this. Furthermore, where the Rules or a practice direction require a document to be signed, this can be effected by printing the signature by computer; rule 5.3.

To conclude this chapter, it will be useful if we return to consider the position of Karen and Luigi and their contract for shoes. First, is there a valid contract? Karen appears to have made a clear offer by sending a copy of the contract for approval and Luigi has indicated his acceptance of its terms. If the transmission of the contract and Luigi's acceptance have been accurate, there should be a legally binding contract providing all the other requirements are met (for example, that the offer and acceptance were unconditional and that there was clear mutual agreement (*consensus ad idem*)).

The next question to determine is the time that the contract was made. It would seem reasonable to expect that the acceptance became effective when it was first read by Karen on Wednesday, on the basis of the *Brinkibon* case – that is, when it was first communicated to Karen. The Directive on electronic commerce uses the concept of deemed receipt for orders and acknowledgement of orders, being the time the parties are able to access them. Non-consumers can agree otherwise and they are also free to determine how and under what circumstances a binding contract will come into existence. In the absence of any express agreement between Karen and Luigi, it would seem at the latest that the contract came into existence was when Karen first read the acceptance on Wednesday. In any case, it is clear that a contract did come into existence because the parties performed their obligations as if the contract existed, as in *Brogden v Metropolitan Rail*. On the basis of *Brinkibon* the contract would have been subject to English law in the absence of any choice of applicable law by Karen and Luigi. However, this has been overtaken by the Rome Convention and the question is answered by looking at the country where the party whose performance is characteristic of the contract is based. In a sale of goods contract the characteristic performance is the supply of the goods, therefore, it is the law of Luigi's country, Italy, that will be the applicable law. Had a consumer, Mary (who has her habitual residence in England), ordered a pair of shoes direct from Luigi, in the absence of any choice of law clause, the contract would have been subject to English law.

Karen appears to be in a position to reject the remaining shoes on the basis of the contract, providing the relevant term is enforceable under Italian law. Other aspects, such as which country's courts have jurisdiction to hear a legal action, for example, if Luigi wishes to sue for wrongful repudiation of the contract and whether the computer print out is admissible as evidence of the contents of the print out are discussed in the following chapter.

Chapter 24

Performance of electronic contracts and evidential aspects

Introduction

The performance of a contract made electronically has a number of implications that do not generally apply to conventional contracts, although generally, the basic rules of contract apply. We saw in the previous chapter that there are certain requirements placed on information society service providers, particularly in relation to the provision of information prior to the making of the contract and mechanisms to determine the applicable law and when the contract is made. There are further requirements in respect of the provision of information both before and after making the contract in consumer contracts made at a distance as well as the availability of a cooling-off period. These provisions, introduced into the United Kingdom by the Consumer Protection (Distance Selling) Regulations 2000 are explained in this chapter.

If there is a breach of contract that has been made electronically, notwithstanding the applicable law, there are issues relating to jurisdiction and enforcement of judgments obtained in other countries. In the example used in the previous chapter involving Karen and Luigi, say that the shoes turned out to be defective and fell apart after a few days wear. Can Karen sue in the English courts or does she have no option but to commence legal proceedings in Italy? There are Conventions and a European Community Regulation dealing with such issues and other legislation in the United Kingdom providing for jurisdiction on a wider scale.

Where a contract has been made electronically, most, if not all of the contractual documents and other evidence of performance and breach may be in electronic form. A further issue is whether this affects the admissibility of such evidence in court proceedings. In the United Kingdom, stringent and complex rules developed in relation to the admissibility of evidence in civil and criminal proceedings. Fortunately, this has been alleviated in the United Kingdom by the Civil Evidence Act 1995, as will be discussed later.

Other issues, outside the scope of this book, relate to tax liabilities and, particularly, value added tax and customs duties, for example, where goods are ordered on-line from a country outside the United Kingdom.

Distance selling

Because of dangers such as impulse buying on the Internet and credit card fraud, there was a possibility that some member states of the European Community could be tempted to impose restrictive legislation whilst others would wish to encourage electronic contracting by leaving it largely unregulated. Harmonisation to avoid such disparities was the driving force behind the Directive 97/7/EC of the Parliament and of the Council of 20 May 1997 on the protection of consumers in respect of distance contracts (OJ L 144, 04.06.1997, p.19). The Directive has a number of implications for contracting over the Internet and was implemented by the Consumer Protection (Distance Selling) Regulations 2000 which came into force on 31 October 2000.

Definitions and exemptions

A 'distance contract' is one concerning goods or services between a supplier and a consumer under an organised distance sales or service provision scheme run by the supplier who, for the purposes of the contract, makes exclusive use of one or more means of distance communication up to and including the moment the contract is concluded. Thus, right up to and including the time the contract is made, all negotiations and contacts must be by distance communication which includes electronic mail, videotext, videophone, television, radio, videophone and fax as well as more traditional forms of distance selling such as by post (whether or not addressed), telephone (whether with or without human intervention), catalogue and advertising in the press with an order form. The list is contained in Schedule 1 to the Regulations and is not exhaustive, being intended to be indicative only.

A consumer is an individual who is acting for a purpose outside his business and a supplier is a person (an individual or legal person such as a company) who makes the contract in a commercial or professional capacity. An operator of a means of communication is a public or private person whose business involves making one or more means of distance communication available to suppliers. This will include, for example, internet service providers, telecommunications companies, commercial television and radio bodies and postal authorities and bodies.

Certain types of contracts are excluded and the Regulations do not apply to contracts relating to financial services, automatic vending machines, automated commercial premises, in relation to land (whether or not including the construction of a building) but not rental, concluded with a telecommunications operator through the use of a public pay-phone and auction sales. There is an equivalent Directive concerning the distance selling of financial services which is due to be implemented by domestic laws by 9 November 2004 (Directive 2002/65/EC of the European Parliament and of the Council of 23 September 2002 concerning the distance marketing of consumer financial services, OJ L 271, 09.10.2002, p.16).

The provisions in the Regulations that apply to the giving of information, the right of withdrawal and the obligation to execute an order within 30 days do not apply to certain contracts for the supply of perishables and for the provision of accommodation, transport, catering or leisure. Timeshare agreements are exempt from most of the provisions but the Timeshare Act 1992 applies to such contracts and package holidays are exempted from the provisions relating to performance but the Package Travel, Package Holidays and Package Tours Regulations 1992 apply to these.

Provision of information

Certain information must be provided to the consumer before the contract is concluded. This is set out in regulation 7 of the Consumer Protection (Distance Selling) Regulations 2000 and includes information about the identity of the supplier, the main characteristics of the goods or services, the price including all taxes, delivery costs where appropriate, arrangements for payment, delivery and performance, existence of the right of withdrawal where applicable, the cost of using distance communication where other than calculated at a basic rate, the period for which the offer and price remain valid and the minimum duration of the contract in the case of contracts for the supply of goods or services to be performed permanently or recurrently. If the supplier proposes to provide substitute goods or services of equivalent quality or price in the event of those ordered being unavailable, he must also state this and inform the consumer that the cost of returning any such substitute goods will be met by the supplier. The information must be provided in a clear and comprehensible manner, having regard to the principles of good faith in commercial transactions and the principles protecting the interests of those unable to give their consent such as minors. The supplier must make his commercial purpose clear when providing the above information and, where the telephone is used, the supplier must make his identity known at the beginning of any telephone conversation with the consumer.

Regulation 8 requires that written confirmation must be provided (or confirmation in another durable medium which is available and accessible to the consumer). This must be provided in good time, either before conclusion of the contract or in good time thereafter and, in any event, not later than during the performance of the contract in the case of services or at the latest at the time for delivery where goods not for delivery to third parties are concerned. The consumer has a right to cancel the contract in some cases, discussed below, and where this is so, the consumer must be informed of the conditions and procedures for exercising this right, including who will be responsible for returning the goods and the costs of doing so. There is a separate requirement to inform the consumer of the conditions for exercising the right of cancellation where the contract is of unspecified duration or of a duration exceeding one year.

The consumer must also be informed of the geographical address of the supplier to which the consumer may address complaints. Further information, such as that relating to after-sales service guarantees, must also be given. These provisions for providing further additional information do not apply, however, to services performed through the use of distance communication where supplied on only one occasion and invoiced by the operator of the means of distance communication although the geographical address must be divulged nonetheless and the place of business to which the consumer may address complaints.

Right of withdrawal

The consumer has a right to cancel the contract under regulation 10. This is often referred to as the 'cooling-off period'. This period starts the date the contract is concluded (when the contract is made, comes into being) whether it is a contract for the supply of goods or the supply of services. The rules about when the cooling-off period ends are more complex and differ in the case of contracts for the supply of goods or services. They are set out in Table 24.1.

It would be inappropriate to provide for a cooling-off period in respect of everything that can be supplied through a distance contract. For example, if computer software is delivered on-line, the consumer might be tempted to make a copy of the software and then attempt to exercise a right of cancellation. Consequently, regulation 13 contains a number of exceptions to the consumer's right to cancel, being where the contract is for:

Table 24.1 The cooling-off period for distance contracts

Case	Contracts for the supply of goods (regulation 11)	Contracts for the supply of services (regulation 12)
Supplier complies with regulation 8	7 working days beginning the day after the day the consumer receives the goods	(If regulation 8 complied with on or before the day the contract is concluded) 7 working days beginning the day after the day the contract is concluded
Supplier fails to comply with regulation 8 but provides the information required by the regulation within 3 months beginning the day after the day the consumer receives the goods or, in the case of a contract for the supply of services, the day after the day the contract is concluded	7 working days after the day the consumer receives the information	7 working days beginning with the day after the day the contract is concluded
Supplier fails to comply with regulation 8 and fails to supply information within 3 months as above	3 months plus 7 working days after the day the consumer receives the goods	3 months plus 7 working days beginning the day after the day the contract is concluded
Contract provides for goods to be delivered to a third party	Determined as if delivery to third party was delivery to consumer	N/A

- the supply of services where the supplier has informed the consumer that he does not have the right to cancel once the performance of the services has commenced with the consumer's agreement;
- the supply of goods or services the price of which is dependent on fluctuations in the financial market which cannot be controlled by the supplier;
- the supply of goods made to the consumer's specifications or clearly personalised or which by reason of their nature cannot be returned or are liable to deteriorate or expire rapidly;
- for the supply of audio or video recordings or computer software if they are unsealed by the consumer;
- for the supply of newspapers, periodicals or magazines; or
- for gaming, betting or lottery services.

Regulation 14 provides for the speedy reimbursement of sums paid by or on behalf of the consumer. In some cases, the supplier may make a charge but not, for example, where the consumer has a right to reject under implied terms or where a term requiring the consumer to return the goods is deemed to be an unfair term under the Unfair Terms in Consumer Contracts Regulations 1999. Any related consumer credit agreement is automatically cancelled when the consumer exercises his right of cancellation under regulation 15. A duty is imposed on the consumer to retain possession of the goods and to take reasonable care of them until they are restored to the supplier.

Performance of a distance selling contract

The basic rule is that, unless the parties agree otherwise, orders must be executed within 30 days beginning the day after the day the consumer sent his order to the supplier under regulation 19. If the supplier is unable to deliver within that time because of the unavailability of goods and services, the consumer must be informed and any sum paid by or on behalf of the consumer must be reimbursed. Substitute goods or services of equivalent quality and price may be supplied if the contract provides for such a possibility and prior to the conclusion of the contract the consumer was provided with information in a durable form to that effect.

Other provisions

Credit card fraud is a major problem and there are particular risks in relation to distance selling contracts. Under regulation 24, a consumer is entitled to cancel a payment where fraudulent use has been made of his card (including credit cards, charge cards, debit cards and store cards) in connection with a contract governed by the regulation by another person not acting, or to be treated as acting, as his agent. Furthermore, a consumer is entitled to be recredited, or to have all sums returned by the card issuer, in the event of fraudulent use of his card by another person not acting, or to be treated as acting, as the consumer's agent. Where a consumer alleges that any use made of the payment card was not authorised by him the burden of proving that the use was authorised lies with the card issuer, being the owner of the card. These provisions do not apply, however, to an agreement within section 83(1) of the Consumer Credit Act 1974, which confers equivalent protection in relation to regulated consumer credit agreements.

Inertia selling is controlled and the general rule, subject to some exceptions, is that a consumer may treat unsolicited goods as an unconditional gift, the rights of the sender to the goods are extinguished. If the sender makes a demand for payment, or threatens legal proceedings he commits a criminal offence under regulation 24. Any contractual term inconsistent with the regulations is void if and to the extent that it is inconsistent.

Unsolicited e-mails are a growing nuisance and, whilst there are provisions under data protection law to help tackle this problem, at the time of writing there is a Bill before Parliament which will make the sending of unsolicited e-mails a criminal offence. The Consumer Protection (Unsolicited E-mails) Bill 2003, if enacted, will insert a new regulation 24A into the Consumer Protection (Distance Selling) Regulations 2000. The sending of unsolicited e-mails which advertise goods or services, not subject to prior request by or on behalf of the recipient, will attract a fine (the maximum level of which is not yet fixed) based on each and every such e-mail sent. Of course, as many of such unsolicited commercial e-mails originate from outside the United Kingdom and the rest of Europe, this will not be a measure that will finally put an end to such e-mails but at least it will be a step in the right direction.

Evidential status of electronic documents in civil trials

Article 9 of the UNCITRAL Model Law on Electronic Commerce 1996, amended 1998, states that nothing in the application of the rules of evidence shall apply to prevent the admissibility of a data message in evidence on the sole ground that it is a data message or, if it is the best evidence the person adducing it could reasonably be expected to obtain, on the grounds that it is not in its original form. (A 'data message' means information generated, sent, received or stored by electronic, optical or similar means including, but not limited to, electronic data interchange (EDI), electronic mail, telegram, telex or telecopy.)

Putting barriers up to the admissibility of computer documents as evidence of the facts stated therein could seriously prejudice the growth of electronic commerce, for example, making it difficult if not impossible to prove the existence of a contract or the terms of the contract or details of the performance of the contract or determining whether there has been a breach of the contract. Although the rules on the admissibility of computer evidence in civil proceedings were unduly complex, fortunately the civil law has moved on and adopted a far more sensible and realistic approach.

Originally, the best evidence rule insisted that only an original document could be admitted as evidence and copies were not allowed. This could cause significant hardship if the original had been lost or destroyed. The best evidence rule has all but disappeared but remnants of it still remain. The courts have recognised that a rigid adherence to the best evidence rule is inappropriate in the context of the accuracy with which copies of originals may now be made. Lord Justice Lloyd said in R v *Governor of Pentonville Prison, ex parte Osman* [1989] 3 All ER 701:

> We accept that it [the best evidence rule] served an important purpose in the days of parchment and quill pens. But, since the invention of carbon paper and, still more, the photocopier and telefacsimile machine, that purpose has largely gone.

A general exclusion on copies of original documents is no longer fitting. Indeed, in some cases, a document may be unintelligible in its original form without its being converted and displayed on a screen or printed out – for example, in the case of a document stored digitally on a magnetic disk. However, the original must still be produced if it is available. This would not apply where the original had been destroyed or lost.

A long tradition in English law has been the importance of a person giving evidence of what he personally knows or has witnessed with his own eyes. The fact that a witness is confined to matters of which he has personal knowledge and can be examined and cross-examined on those matters is a central plank of the English law of evidence. Second-hand or third-hand evidence is by its nature very unreliable, so much so that it was not allowed to be heard.

There was a rule against admitting hearsay evidence in civil trials (the rule still exists in relation to criminal trials). Hearsay evidence is secondary evidence such as where a witness relates something that was told to him by another person but not directly seen or heard by the witness – for example, where Bill states that Jenny told him that she saw Paul trying to erase a computer program. The rule was quite strict and such evidence would not be admitted at all except in specific circumstances, some of which applied to information stored on a computer. Section 5 of the Civil Evidence Act 1968 (now repealed by the Civil Evidence Act 1995) allowed statements contained in documents produced by a computer to be admitted in civil trials as evidence of any fact stated therein if the evidence would have been admissible as direct oral evidence, but only subject to certain conditions.

Fortunately, the Civil Evidence Act 1995 has effectively swept aside the old rule against hearsay evidence in civil cases. The relevant provisions came into force on 31 January 1997. The new law applies only in respect of cases where proceedings commenced before this date.

Hearsay evidence is admissible under section 1 of the Civil Evidence Act 1995 and is defined as a statement made otherwise than by a person giving oral evidence in the proceedings and includes hearsay evidence of whatever degree. There are certain safeguards as regards notice to be given to other parties.

Although hearsay evidence is now admissible, it may not be given much weight. For example, if it is a document stored on computer which has undergone many alterations that have not been properly recorded or logged, it may carry little weight. Under section 4 of the Act, the weight, if any, to be given to hearsay evidence depends on the circumstances and regard shall be had to whether:

- it would be reasonable and practicable to call the original maker of the statement as a witness,
- the original statement was made at the same time as the occurrence or existence of the matters stated,
- the evidence involves multiple hearsay,
- any person involved has any motive to conceal or misrepresent matters,
- the original statement was an edited account or made in collaboration with another for a particular purpose, and
- the circumstances in which the evidence is adduced as hearsay are such as to suggest an attempt to prevent proper evaluation of its weight.

Hearsay may carry little weight unless it would have been admissible under Part I of the Civil Evidence Act 1968, now repealed. Factors included:

- regularity – whether the computer was regularly used to store or process information, for the purposes of any activities regularly carried out, over a period which includes the time when the document was made;
- consistency – during the relevant period information of the kind contained in the document (or of a kind from which such information is derived) was regularly supplied to the computer in the ordinary course of those activities;
- reliability – the computer was operating properly during the material part of that period (or, if not, any malfunction or breakdown that occurred would not have affected the accuracy of the material contained in the document);
- orthodoxy – the information contained in the document reproduces or is derived from information supplied to the computer in the ordinary course of the activities regularly carried out over the period in question.

Where a number of computers had been used – for example, successively or in a network – all the computers involved were treated as a single computer in determining the purpose of the activities. A person wishing to proffer a computer statement as evidence had to provide a certificate identifying the relevant document and the manner in which it was produced and giving other particulars. The certificate was required to be signed by a person occupying a responsible position in relation to the operation of the relevant device or the management of the relevant activities. It did not matter if the information was supplied or produced without any human intervention by means of appropriate equipment. This covered the situation where a computer was set up to record information and produce documents automatically.

Although the hearsay rule has been relaxed, if not altogether scrapped, the fact that a number of factors determine the weight to be given to such evidence means that it may not always be very influential, if at all. The main advantage flowing from the 1995 Act is that the formal rules under the 1968 Act have gone to be replaced by a welcome degree of flexibility. It will still be important, however, to show that the computer was operating reliably at the time and there is nothing to indicate that the evidence is unreliable. Adherence to the relevant standards applying to security and good computer practice will help in this respect.

Chapter 25

Torts related to electronic information

Introduction

Tort is an area of law in which civil liability may attach to a person independently of the existence of a contract. Areas covered by the law of tort include negligence (including negligent misstatement), defamation, malicious falsehood and nuisance. Tort is a wide-ranging area of law and other torts relate to assault (as opposed to criminal offences relating to assault), trespass to the person, trespass to goods, unlawful interference with contract, passing off, breach of statutory duty and malicious prosecution.

Some torts are outside the scope of this book and some have already been dealt with in appropriate places in the book, for example, in Chapters 11 and 17. This chapter concentrates on torts particularly relevant to the Internet and information placed on websites or transmitted through internet service providers (ISPs). Negligent misstatement has already been dealt with in Chapter 17 in the context of computer contracts but further mention is made in this chapter as appropriate. Defamation is also covered here, including the tort of malicious falsehood and the liability of ISPs and the like as publishers of defamatory information in the context of the publisher's defence. The next chapter looks specifically at the provisions removing liability from information society service providers including ISPs generally for illegal material passing through or stored on their systems. A defence is provided where the provider acts as a mere conduit and in connection with caching and hosting activities under the Electronic Commerce (EC Directive) Regulations 2002.

Negligent misstatement

The fundamentals of an action in negligent misstatement are set out in Chapter 17. To recap, on the basis of *Hedley Byrne & Co Ltd* v *Heller & Partners Ltd* [1964] AC 465, liability can ensue where a statement which proves to be incorrect is made negligently by a person holding himself out as being an expert in the relevant field who intends that statement to be taken seriously. Typically, any person giving advice, whether or not in the course of performing a contract, would attempt to minimise their potential liability by adding a notice or term excluding or limiting his or her liability should the statement turn out to be incorrect. In the United Kingdom, we have seen that the Unfair Contract Terms Act 1977 controls such notices or terms and they will be ineffective in the case of death or personal injury and, in other cases, will only be effective if and to the extent that they meet the requirement of reasonableness as set out in that Act.

Potentially, any information placed on a website which purports to give advice could be actionable under the law of negligent misstatement if it turns out to be incorrect, subject to any valid exclusion or limitation clauses. However, a number of factors may be relevant. If, for example, someone gives advice specifically directed to a particular person or class of persons by e-mail which is intended to be taken seriously and acted upon by that person or persons, then there is no reason why liability in principle cannot ensue should the advice turn out to be wrong and given negligently. The normal rules of negligent misstatement should apply.

Things might be different where information containing advice, whether or not intended to be taken seriously and acted upon, is placed on a website or bulletin board. Cases on negligent misstatement have in the past concentrated on the importance of a special relationship between the giver of the statement and a person who suffers loss as a result of relying on it. Was the advice or information compiled for and directed for the person who relied on it? In other words, is there sufficient proximity between the maker of the statement and the person relying on it; *Caparo Industries plc v Dickman* [1990] 2 AC 605? The importance of proximity and a contemplation that the advice would be relied upon by the claimant has been reinforced in numerous cases after *Caparo*. For example, in *Barings plc v Coopers and Lybrand (No 1)* [2002] 2 BCLC 364, the court stressed the importance of reliance and the question of whether the statement maker had in his contemplation that his advice would be relied upon by the claimant for a particular transaction or class of transactions. Furthermore, the claimant must have, in fact, relied upon the advice before embarking upon the transaction, which resulted in the loss for which compensation is claimed.

This calls into question whether simply posting information on webpages or bulletin boards could result in liability for negligent misstatement. Two situations are possible. The first is where the information is placed there for a general audience. In such a case, it is highly unlikely that liability could result no matter how negligently the advice was compiled. Persons accessing the Internet have become accustomed to the fact that there is a phenomenal amount of information available, some of which is of little or no merit. Most of us have become wary and sceptical of claims made on webpages. The amount of questionable material available has made visitors to websites cautious.

On the other hand, if the advice or information is directed towards individuals or classes of individuals, the situation is less clear. For example, if the information is aimed at potential clients, there is a possibility of finding the necessary proximity. For example, a firm of solicitors may operate a website that provides advice and updates intended to impress existing clients and attract new business. In such a case, it is arguable that the necessary proximity applies not just with the existing clients but also with the potential clients. The firm of solicitors might be well advised to place a disclaimer on the website. In terms of loss or damage other than death or personal injury, it would seem reasonable to do so, provided it was made clear that the information was in a general form and visitors to the site were warned that they should seek professional advice rather than act on the information in what might prove to be an inappropriate context.

Another factor is that negligence is an area of law in which the courts are often influenced by policy considerations. In extending liability for negligence, including negligent misstatement, the courts have been wary of opening the floodgates and imposing liability too widely. This was an important factor in *Caparo Industries plc v Dickman*. A further issue is whether it is feasible to take out insurance to cover a particular form of liability. By too readily making owners of websites liable for negligent misstatement, that could leave them facing an enormous number of claims against which they could find it hard if not impossible to insure.

Owners of websites must also take account of variations in the scope and extent of liability for statements in different jurisdictions. Again, the use of a suitably worded disclaimer could be important.

Defamation

Lord Bingham of Cornhill in his foreword to Collins, M, *The Law of Defamation and the Internet*, Oxford University Press, 2001, said the law of defamation in the context of the Internet would require '... almost every concept and rule in the field ... to be reconsidered in the light of this unique medium of instant worldwide communication'. The issues that arise relate partly from the nature of defamation as a cause of action, differences in national laws on defamation and jurisdictional issues. In terms of traditional forms of publishing, a publisher exerted a great deal of control over where copies of his publications were made available. Publication on the Internet is different in that it is, potentially, publication to the entire world. Factors relevant to intellectual property rights such as where a particular advertisement on a website is targeted seem less relevant for defamatory statements. For trade mark infringement, it is a question of where the website owner actively seeks to attract business; see *Zippo Manufacturing Co v Zippo Dot Com Inc* 952 F Supp 1119 (WD Pa 1997), discussed in Chapter 11. For defamation, the key is more likely to focus on the place where the claimant has a reputation to be harmed by the defamatory statement.

There have been a number of cases of defamation on the Internet. Some of the early cases give a flavour of dangers of being careless or too forthright in making statements available over the Internet. For example, in *Rindos v Hardwick* (unreported) 31 March 1994, the Supreme Court of Western Australia found that a statement made by an academic which seriously denigrated another academic's competence and which also imputed misconduct on his part was defamatory and an award of A\$40,000 in damages was made. (However, judgment was given in default as the defendant did not put in an appearance.) In *Stratton Oakmont Inc v Prodigy Services Co*, 1995 NY Misc. LEXIS 229, the Supreme Court of the State of New York held that the defendant, a service provider, was the publisher of statements on its bulletin board and granted summary judgment against it in respect of libellous statements made on the bulletin board. The statements made claims that the claimant had committed fraudulent acts in relation to a public offering of company stocks. In the United Kingdom, a lecturer accepted undisclosed damages in an out-of-court settlement for on-line statements that were potentially defamatory (Calow, D, 'Defamation on the Internet', *Computer Law and Security Report* (1995) 11(4), p.199). However, following the *Stratton v Prodigy* case, which seemed to impose liability against ISPs who actively checked and screened the content available through its service (deemed to be original publishers) as opposed to those that did nothing (deemed to be distributors subject to a lower 'knowledge' standard), the United States enacted the Communications Decency Act 1996 47 USC §230 which states that 'no provider or user of an interactive computer service shall be treated as the publisher or speaker of any information provided by another information content provider'. This means that the potential liability for defamatory statements made available through an ISP's systems is considerably less in the United States as it is in the United Kingdom, as discussed towards the end of this chapter.

Defamation is something of a rarity in that it is a civil action in which a jury may be sworn in and, if this is the case, it is the jury which decide whether defamation has been made out and, if so, the jury also decides the award. Under section 8 of the Defamation Act 1996, however, the judge may deal with the case summarily where it appears that the case is very clear cut – for example, where the claimant has no real chance of success. Juries have been known to award very substantial damages in defamation actions but there is an argument that damages for injury to reputation should not exceed damages awarded for serious or even catastrophic personal injury arising out of negligence. However, it is not really proper to equate damage to reputation with personal injury. The former has an element of deterrence absent in personal injury cases and, often, defamation is an intentional wrongdoing whereas actionable personal injury is usually the result of negligence. The deterrent effect in defamation should not, however, be so high as to inhibit responsible journalism; *Gleaner Company Ltd* v *Abrahams* [2003] UKHL 55 (Privy Council).

There are two branches of defamation: libel and slander. Generally, libel relates to written statements whereas slander relates to the spoken word. The distinction is important because libel is actionable *per se* – that is, without proof of damage. Except in some cases, slander requires proof of damage. It appears that a defamatory image will be classed as libel rather than slander. In *Yousopouff* v *MGM Pictures Ltd* (1934) 50 TLR 581, the defendant made a film which suggested that the claimant was a Russian princess who had been 'ravished' or seduced by Rasputin. This was held to be libel, not slander.

An image taken from a computer game resulted in a libel action in the House of Lords. In *Charleston* v *News Group Newspapers* [1995] 2 AC 65, a Sunday newspaper carried a photograph which had been taken from a pornographic computer game. It depicted a man and woman who appeared to be engaged in sexual intercourse or other sexual activity. Superimposed on the photographs were images of the heads of the claimants, actors who played Harold and Madge Bishop in the television 'soap' *Neighbours*. The captions ran 'Strewth! What's Harold up to with our Madge?' and 'Porn Shocker for Neighbours Stars'. However, because the text underneath made it clear that the image had been produced as part of a pornographic computer game which had used the images of the claimants without their permission, it was held not to be libellous. The law does not take account of 'a moron in a hurry' – that is, a careless reader, who would not read such a 'disclaimer' and might not realise the true nature of the image, is ignored in determining whether it is libellous. Since that case, the data protection law would almost certainly provide a remedy in that such processing of personal data (and an image from which a living individual can be identified is personal data) has caused substantial distress to the actors concerned.

Before looking further at defamation in the context of the Internet, including considering recent cases in the United Kingdom and elsewhere, the basic nature of defamation is described below.

Basics of defamation

A defamatory statement is one which, when published, tends to lower a person in the esteem of right-thinking members of society generally; or which tends to make them shun or avoid that person. The statement does not have to allege some moral turpitude or wrongdoing on the part of the claimant and it can be defamation to allege insanity or being the victim of a crime such as rape.

It is common to see disclaimers as to the characters portrayed in a film. It is dangerous to publish something containing, for example, a fictional character with a name that might be the same as a real person. In *Hulton & Co v Jones* [1910] AC 20, an article was published by the defendant which was alleged by the defendant to be fictitious. It contained defamatory statements about one 'Artemus Jones', a churchwarden from Peckham. However, and unfortunately for the defendant, by coincidence there was a person with that name who happened to be a barrister living in North Wales. He successfully sued for libel. It was thought that some of his friends and acquaintances might think the article referred to him.

Hulton v Jones was distinguished in *Kerry O'Shea v MGN Ltd* (unreported) 4 May 2001 in relation to images. In that case, the first defendant, the Sunday Mirror published advertisements for the second defendant's internet service which carried the headline, 'Free Internet access for adults only. The world's first free adult ISP.' The advertisements included photographs of females, one of which looked incredibly like the claimant, and was inviting readers to 'see me now' at the website in question. The woman whose photograph it actually was had consented to its publication. The claimant, who was a respectable 24-year-old woman sued for defamation on the basis that persons who knew her would believe it was her photograph in the advertisement. The defamatory meaning alleged was that the claimant was appearing on a pornographic website.

In cases like *Hulton v Jones* were a name was used, it would be possible to discover the existence of the claimant. However, in respect of a photograph, it would be impossible to discover the identity of everyone who was a look-alike or doppelganger of a person whose photograph was to be published or, indeed, whether there was a look-alike. The judge considered the fact that a publisher is subject to strict liability and, subject to the offer of amends procedure in section 2(4) of the Defamation Act 1996, will be liable even if blameless. This could interfere with freedom of expression. Article 10(2) of the European Convention on Human Rights allows restrictions on freedom of expression 'necessary in a democratic society, in the interests of national security, territorial integrity or public safety, for the prevention of disorder or crime, for the protection of health or morals, for *the protection of the reputation or rights of others*' (emphasis added). Mr Justice Moreland concluded that the principle of strict liability should not be extended to look-alike situations as this would unjustifiably interfere with freedom of expression and this would be disproportionate with the legitimate aim of protecting the reputations of others.

For defamation to be actionable, publication is required and it must be to at least one person other than the claimant. It may be by means of words, pictures, visual images, gestures or any other method of signifying meaning. The defendant must either publish the material himself or be responsible for publication. Every repetition of a defamatory publication is a fresh publication and actionable. Thus, if defamatory material is placed on the Internet, every time it is accessed and read by someone, this constitutes a separate defamation. This is certainly the case in some jurisdictions such as England and Australia (though in some states of the United States of America, there is a single publication rule such that only the first publication counts to give rise to a cause of action).

The potential of the multiple publication rule is that thousands or even millions of causes of action could accrue in respect of placing defamatory material on a webpage or a bulletin board. Also, a reasonably foreseeable repetition of a publication by a third party will also bring liability. In *Slipper* v *British Broadcasting Corp* [1991] 1 QB 283, which concerned a film broadcast by the defendant, the claims made by the claimant included damages for reviews of the film in the press. The Court of Appeal refused to strike out these additional claims. In respect of republication it was held that this could be a *novus actus interveniens* (a new act breaking the chain of causation) if it was unauthorised. However, where reasonably foreseeable, the chain of causation was not broken.

There are a number of defences to a defamation action including fair comment, justification (that is, that the statement is true), an offer to make amends and privilege (absolute and qualified).

Defamation on the Internet – special issues

The placing of defamatory material on webpages or sending such material in or attached to e-mails gives rise to a number of issues that relate to the nature of the Internet. One is the multiple publication rule which applies in the United Kingdom and some other places where every time a libel is published causes a new cause of action to accrue. Another area of concern has to do with the global nature of the Internet and may cause courts to question whether they have jurisdiction to hear a defamation claim and, even if they can, whether they ought to on the basis that the courts in some other jurisdiction are a more convenient place to hear and deal with the case. There is also the danger that posting a defamatory statement on a webpage may give rise to concurrent liability in a number of jurisdictions, exposing the person responsible (and, possibly the service provider) to multiple claims in different countries. The position of publishers, as opposed to the author of the defamatory statement is also an issue. A European Directive attempted to deal with this (and other liabilities of service providers in respect of illegal material) and is discussed in the following chapter. However, in this chapter, specific reference is made to the 'publishers' defence' under section 1 of the Defamation Act 1996. The Directive on electronic commerce and legislation made to implement it is of wider significance though may supplement the protection afforded ISPs in respect of defamation.

Multiple publication rule

In the United Kingdom and some other jurisdictions, defamation occurs each and every time the offending statement is published, the 'multiple publication rule'. In others, most notably in many of the states of the United States of America, there is a 'single publication rule' and only the first publication gives rise to a cause of action, although subsequent publications may be taken into account when assessing damages. This is an important distinction as the limitation period for defamation (the time within which legal proceedings must be commenced) is comparatively low. Under section 4A of the Limitation Act 1980, the period is one year from the date that the cause of action arose (although this period may be increased in special circumstances at the court's discretion, for example, where the claimant did not become aware of the facts giving rise to the cause of action until after expiry of the limitation period and he acted expediently once he did become aware). Until 4 September 1996, the limitation period in England

and Wales and Northern Ireland in relation to defamation (and slander of title, slander of goods and other malicious falsehoods) was three years (six years before 1985) and it remains at three years in Scotland.

To take an example of the two rules, say that A writes an article which contains a defamatory statement and it is published in a daily newspaper. Two years later the article is included in a magazine containing interesting articles written over the past five years. Say also that the person defamed, B, was aware of the first publication but took no action at that time. It was only on seeing the second publication in the magazine that she decided to commence legal proceedings against A. If the single publication rule applied, B would be time-barred but if the multiple publication rule applied, she will be able to commence proceedings in respect of the second publication. Thus, if the proceedings were commenced in the State of New York, for example, they would be statute barred but not if the action had commenced in England and Wales.

The multiple publication rule was considered by the Court of Appeal in *Loutchansky* v *Times Newspapers Ltd* [2002] QB 783. In that case, the defendant published, on 8 September 1999 and 14 October 1999, in its newspaper articles alleging that the claimant, who had dual Russian and Israeli nationality, was a Russian mafia boss and involved in international criminal activities. The claimant commenced proceedings in respect of the articles on 6 December 1999. The articles where placed on the defendant's website and were available after 21 February 2000 and the claimant commenced a second action in respect of that publication on 6 December 2000. The defendant claimed qualified privilege, which applies, *inter alia*, where the publisher has a duty to publish and the public had a right to know of the allegations. The judge at first instance rejected that defence in the first hearing and, in respect of the second proceedings relating to the website publication, the defendant argued that this was time-barred as the second proceedings were commenced more than one year after the first publication of the articles in the newspapers.

As regards the qualified privilege point, the Court of Appeal held that the judge had applied the wrong test in deciding that, as the defendant would not be subject to legitimate criticism had it failed to publish, the defence did not apply and this matter was remitted back to the judge for reconsideration. Rather, the test should have been whether there was a duty to publish the material to the intended recipients who had an interest in receiving it. The interest being (*per* Lord Philips of Worth Matravers at para 36):

> ... that of the public in a modern democracy in free expression and, more particularly, in the promotion of a free and vigorous press to keep the public informed ... [the] corresponding duty on the journalist (and equally his editor) is to play his proper role in discharging that function. His task is to behave as a responsible journalist.

The single publication argument was rejected by the Court of Appeal which confirmed that each and every publication causes a fresh right of action to accrue. The basis of this rule is firmly entrenched in English law and goes back to the striking old case, *Duke of Brunswick* v *Harmer* (1849) 14 QB 185, where back issues of a newspaper containing an article libelling the Duke of Brunswick were bought some 17 years after first publication and which were considered to be a separate publication on which the Duke could bring a libel action (the limitation period for libel was six years at that time). Although in the present case, there was some importance in maintaining and publishing archives, that was not as important as contemporary publication. That the multiple publication rule imposed restrictions on giving access to archive material, this was justified as being necessary and proportionate in a democratic society to protect the reputation of others and, consequently, the rule was not in conflict with the right of freedom of expression provided for by Article 10 of the European Convention on Human Rights. In any case, publishing archive material should be possible, even if the content was hotly contested, by adding an appropriate statement or qualification. This had not been done and the Court of Appeal confirmed that qualified privilege could not apply to the internet publication which had been done after the defendant was aware that allegations of defamation had been made in respect of the articles by the claimant.

Jurisdiction and *forum non conveniens*

The basic rule for determining jurisdiction in relation to torts is that it is the place where the harmful event occurred and, for defamation, that is the place where the publication took place. In case of material available on the Internet, if a person has a reputation in a number of jurisdictions and the material is downloaded in at least some of those jurisdictions, it would seem that a cause of action arises in each of them. Three points can be made about that possibility. First, where a libel is disseminated via the Internet does this give rise to a separate cause of action in each country or is there such a thing as a global tort of defamation which can be heard and dealt with by the courts in one country only? Secondly, is there a *de minimis* principle such that if only a few persons in one jurisdiction access the material, the courts will decline jurisdiction? The third point is that, even if a court decides it has jurisdiction, does it decline to hear the case on the basis of the doctrine *forum non conveniens*, that is, that the courts in another jurisdiction should hear the case?

Global tort theory

The global tort theory, convenient as it might be resulting in a single court hearing to resolve the issue of defamation in its entirety, has no place in English law, or for that matter the law in many other countries. It was narrowly rejected by a 3:2 majority in the House of Lords in *Berezovsky v Michaels* [2000] 2 All ER 986, in which a magazine published in the United States contained an article alleging that the claimants, who were Russian citizens, were involved in organised crime in Russia. The magazine had a circulation of 785,000 in the United States, 13 in Russia and around 2000 in England. It was also placed on the defendant's website which was accessed by a number of persons in England and it was accepted that, altogether, around 6000 people had read the article in England. Both claimants had significant connections in England and decided to bring an action for defamation in England.

Counsel for the defendants argued that, on the basis of the United States' single publication rule, in a multi-jurisdiction case on defamation, the correct approach was to treat it as giving a single cause of action and then to decide in which jurisdiction that single cause of action arose. In most cases, of course, that would be the country in which the publisher is established as that would be likely to be the place where the largest amount of publication takes place. That approach was rejected. Whilst it may make sense in the United States because of its federal constitution, it conflicts with the English multiple publication rule, that each publication is a separate tort. In the present case, the claimants had a reputation in England and there had been a significant distribution of the defamatory material in England. Therefore, England was an appropriate place to hear the action and allow service on the United States' defendant.

The global theory also conflicts with the decision of the European Court of Justice in *Shevill* v *Presse Alliance SA* [1996] AC 959. In that case, the court considered the Brussels Convention on Jurisdiction and the Enforcement of Judgments in Civil and Commercial Matters 1968 (now largely replaced by Council Regulation (EC) No. 44/2001 on jurisdiction and the recognition and enforcement of judgments in civil and commercial matters, OJ L 12, 16.1.2001, p.1). The basic rules are, in relation to actions in tort (delict in Scotland), that the defendant is normally sued in the member state in which he is domiciled. However, an alternative is to sue in the place where the harmful event occurred or, in the case of a threatened tort, where the harmful event may occur. A further choice applies where there is more than one defendant domiciled in different member states.

In *Shevill*, the European Court of Justice held that a victim libelled in a newspaper article which had been distributed in several member states may bring an action for defamation either:

- before the courts of the member state where the publisher was established, or
- before the courts of each member state in which the article had been distributed and where the victim claimed to have suffered damage.

The criteria for assessing whether the event was harmful and the evidence required of the existence and extent of the harm alleged were to be determined by the substantive law determined by the national conflict of laws rules of the court concerned. For example, it may be that an action brought before the courts of one member state may be stayed on the basis that it is not the appropriate forum (the doctrine of *forum non conveniens*, see later). The decision does mean, however, that multiple separate actions could be brought in a number of European countries on the basis of the same defamatory statement in a publication distributed in those countries or made available on the Internet.

The decision is particularly important in England and Wales as defamation is actionable *per se*, that is, without proof of damage. Nor is it required that the victim is well-known. If the victim is named in the defamatory statement, that is sufficient to found an action in defamation. The global tort theory has no place in the United Kingdom or in most other jurisdictions. In terms of the United States, the single publication rule makes sense as between the different states of the United States of America but not between different countries.

The Australian High Court has taken a similar stance to the House of Lords and rejected the single publication rule and the consequences of it for jurisdiction. In *Dow Jones & Co Inc* v *Gutnick* [2002] HCA 56, Dow Jones printed the *Wall Street Journal* and Barron's Online (available on WSJ.com). On 28 October 2000, an article 'Unholy Gains' appeared on the website which was claimed by Mr Gutnick to be defamatory of him and he sued in the Supreme Court of Victoria, Australia. The article had suggested that he was a money launderer. WSJ.com was on a server in New Jersey in the United States. Although Mr Gutnick conducted his business outside Australia, it could fairly be said that much of his social and business life was in Victoria. Dow Jones claimed that the publication complained of took place in New Jersey but, at first instance, this was rejected by the judge who considered that the publication also took place in Victoria because it was accessible there. He refused the defendant's application to stay proceedings.

Dow Jones had strongly argued that a distinction should be drawn between internet publishing and traditional publishing. The former was passive as material was made available for would-be readers to actively seek out using web browsers and to download. In relation to traditional publishing such as in a printed newspaper or a broadcast, this was more active as the publisher had to circulate and distribute the information or arrange to have it broadcast.

The High Court of Australia held that it was important that publishers can act with certainty. However, this does not necessarily require singularity in that publishers can act in accordance with a single legal system where the material they publish has an international flavour. Publishing activities that have effects in a number of jurisdictions may properly be said to be the concern of each legal system in which they have such effects. As the tort of defamation is located at the place where the damage to reputation occurs, the claimant must have a reputation in that place and the offending material must be available in a comprehensible form in that place. This could be the case where a person downloads the material in the place where the claimant has a reputation.

The reference to having a reputation is somewhat misleading. A person does not have to be well-known to be defamed and may carry on a very private existence. He may even be a hermit. It is submitted that the requirement to give rise to an action in defamation to X in a particular country, Y, is that the defamatory material is, in fact, made available and is seen by someone who is physically in Y, that X is either domiciled in Y or has some real and significant connection with Y, for example, by having business interests there, family, relatives or others who know him who are domiciled there or that he enjoys a reputation there in that he is well-known and respected in Y.

An argument that this approach would inhibit publishing because a publisher would have to consider the laws of defamation in every country was described by the court as unreal in *Dow Jones* v *Gutnick* because identifying the person about whom the material was going to be published would, in most cases, identify the defamation law to which the claimant would be likely to resort, usually being the law of the country in which that person was domiciled. However, an important factor in that case was that the claimant said that he would only seek redress in Victoria and not bring other actions elsewhere. This may be a useful tactic in encouraging a court to accept jurisdiction.

De minimis rule

The *de minimis* rule (in full *de minimis non curat lex* – the law does not concern itself with trifles) applies in some cases to deprive a claimant of a cause of action. For example, in tort of negligence it is accepted that an action does not arise until damage which is more than *de minimis* is suffered. However, in some areas of law, the rule does not apply and a cause of action might exist no matter how trivial the act or omission concerned. The fact that it is trivial may, of course, be reflected in any remedy granted. For example, an award of damages may be nominal only.

In defamation, if the attack on a person's character is trivial, this may mean that the basic test is not fulfilled and the standing of the person may not be damaged in the minds of right thinking members of society. However, if that test is satisfied, then publication to a single person is sufficient to give rise to a claim in defamation. There is no *de minimis* rule in terms of the number of persons to whom the defamatory statement is published. As Lord Esher MR said in *Whittaker* v *Scarborough Post Newspaper Company* [1896] 2 QB 148:

The amount of the damages in [an action concerning the publication of an article in a newspaper] would not, in my opinion, generally speaking, depend on the number of copies of the newspaper that were published. If a *libel* were a serious one, a jury would give heavy damages, though it were only *published once*. On the other hand, if a *libel* were a trivial or ridiculous one, in respect of which the jury thought that an action ought not to have been brought, they would only give contemptuous damages, though many copies of the libel had been circulated.

It is further acknowledged that there is no need for the act of publication to be a positive act. It is sufficient if a person leaves the offending material in a place where others are liable to see it. As was stated in Milmo, P and Rogers, W V H, *Gatley on Libel and Slander*, 9th edition, Sweet and Maxwell, 2001 (at p.134):

If the claimant proves facts from which it can be inferred that the words were brought to the attention of some third person, he will establish a prima facie case. This is particularly obviously so where the matter is ... distributed ... on the Internet, where in practice it would be impossible to rebut the inference ...

This sentiment was approved by the New South Wales Supreme Court in *Macquarie Bank Ltd v Berg* [2002] NSWSC 1110, in which the claimant alleged that the defendants had placed material on the Internet on a website established in the United States. Solicitors acting for the claimant downloaded the material in New South Wales and this appeared to be sufficient to give rise to a cause of action. However, the case was fraught with procedural difficulties and leave to proceed with the action was given subject to an application to amend the statement of claim and that application itself being granted. The court acknowledged that getting material on a server from outside Australia into New South Wales requires 'pull technology' whereby the operator of a local computer chooses to visit the website to bring the material into jurisdiction. The person who places the material on the server does not choose the destination or the identity of the recipient.

Although a single publication is sufficient to bring a defamation action, a single publication in a particular jurisdiction may, if there exist significantly greater incidences of publications in other jurisdictions, be a reason why a particular court may decline jurisdiction on the basis of *forum non conveniens*, discussed below.

Forum non conveniens

Forum non conveniens is a doctrine by which a court will refuse jurisdiction on the basis that, in the interests of justice and of the parties, the case would be better heard in another jurisdiction. It has been described as a form of self-denial and the court applying the doctrine will stay the action before it (the doctrine also applies to an application to serve proceedings on a defendant outside jurisdiction). The doctrine was adopted only relatively recently in England and its operation was not properly set out until the case of *Spiliada Maritime Corp v Cansulex Ltd (The Spiliada)* [1987] 1 AC 460. This was a case in which the claimants sought to serve proceedings on a defendant based in British Columbia. The claimants had shipped a quantity of sulphur loaded onto their vessels by the defendant. The sulphur was wet when loaded and caused serious corrosion to the vessels. The guidelines set out by Lord Goff in the House of Lords can be summarised as follows:

1 A stay will be granted only if the court is satisfied that there is another court available having a competent jurisdiction which is appropriate for the trial because the

case may be tried there more suitably for the interests of the parties and the ends of justice.

2 The burden of proof rests with the defendant to persuade the court to exercise its discretion to stay in the defendant's favour.

3 The defendant must show that not only is England not the natural or appropriate forum but that there is another forum that is clearly or distinctly more appropriate. In any case, if the connection with the English forum is a fragile one, for example, if he is served with proceedings during a short visit to England, it will be easier for him to show that another clearly more appropriate forum exists overseas.

4 Factors which point to another forum must be considered by the court such as convenience, expense, availability of witnesses, governing law and the places of residence or business of the parties.

5 A stay will almost certainly be refused if the court decides that no such other clearly appropriate forum exists.

6 If the court decides that there is, prima facie, a more appropriate forum, it will normally grant a stay but the claimant, who now bears the evidential burden, may be able to show that circumstances additional to those in 4 above exist such that a stay should be refused. For example, the claimant may be able to show that he will not be able to obtain justice in a foreign court.

As in England, each and every publication is treated as a separate defamation, each will give rise to its own cause of action. In respect of each publication in England, which includes any publication to a person who downloads the material from a website located anywhere in the world, the courts in England clearly have jurisdiction. The 'fragile connection' point in 3 above does not really apply in the context of defamation. It would seem that a stay would only be granted if the claimant has no real connection with or reputation in England.

Another point of interest is that defamatory publications outside England may be actionable in England also. Take, for example, a situation where a person is domiciled in England but is also well-known in a number of other countries, say Eire, Sweden, Australia. A statement which is defamatory of that person is placed on a website located in Brazil. The person defamed will be able to sue in England on the basis of any third party who access the statement in England and on the basis of any persons who access the statement in Eire, Sweden and Australia. In respect of these latter publications, there is an old rule, known as the rule in *Phillips* v *Eyre* (1870) LR 6 QB 1, to the effect that the publications must be actionable as a tort under English law and there is an equivalent civil liability in the other countries where publication took place. This rule was abolished in 1996 for all torts except those relating to defamation to which it still applies (including in Scotland); see section 13 of the Private International Law (Miscellaneous Provisions) Act 1995. Clearly, it is more expedient to the claimant to be able to recover in respect of all the publications in the courts of one country rather than bring several different actions before the courts in different countries.

It is still early days to see how the courts in England and Wales and other common law countries, respond to applications to stay proceedings on the basis of *forum non conveniens*. As each time material is accessed from a website counts as a publication for the purposes of defamation in countries where the multiple publication rule applies, it would seem that the doctrine will have limited application. The situation will be different, however, in the United States where the single publication rule is predominant.

But the wide-scale adoption of that rule would encourage the placing of material that is potentially defamatory on websites located in countries with legal systems which favoured defendants in libel actions, for example, the United States where freedom of expression is paramount.

In relation to cases involving, at least partly, internet publication, the trend seems to be to refuse a stay. In the Australian case of *Dow Jones* v *Gutnick*, no stay was granted on the basis of *forum non conveniens* and, in *Berezovsky* v *Michaels*, the House of Lords confirmed the Court of Appeal decision to overturn a stay granted by the judge at first instance. However, in *Thomas Tracy* v *Niall O'Dowd* (unreported) 28 January 2002, the High Court of Northern Ireland granted a stay in a defamation action. The defendants wrote and published an article which was alleged to be defamatory of the claimant. Publication took place in a New York newspaper entitled *Irish Voice* and, *inter alia*, described the claimant's appointment as American Ambassador to Ireland as being ludicrous, a disaster and would 'turn the Bush White house into a laughing stock with Irish Americans'. The newspaper circulation in America was in the order of 45,000 copies per week but there was no circulation in Northern Ireland. The article appeared also on the newspaper's website where it was available only during the week of publication, no archiving system being used for the website. There was evidence that it was accessed just over 2000 times but only 14 times from the United Kingdom of Great Britain and Northern Ireland.

Although publication to a single person is sufficient to base a defamation action and the jurisdiction in which the tort is committed is prima facie the natural forum for the determination of the dispute, the court stayed the action, holding that the United States was a more appropriate forum, applying the guidelines in *The Spiliada*. Factors favouring the United States as the most suitable forum were:

- the claimant was an American citizen, resident there and carried on business there;
- the defendants resided or were incorporated in the United States;
- the *Irish Voice* was published and circulated only in the United States and the publication of the alleged libel took place almost exclusively in the United States;
- only a tiny proportion of internet accesses were in the United Kingdom and an even smaller proportion were associated with Northern Ireland;
- the thrust of the article was about the appointment of a United States ambassador to Ireland (and not any part of the United Kingdom);
- although the claimant had significant connections with Northern Ireland these paled into insignificance compared with his American connections;
- not all the witnesses referred to on behalf of the claimant said they agreed to give evidence on his behalf.

Factors in favour of refusing the stay were:

- the claimant had a reputation in Northern Ireland with well-known persons there;
- the claimant had an interest in Irish affairs and the problems of Northern Ireland;
- the witnesses referred to lived in Northern Ireland or the Republic of Ireland;
- the defendants had not named any witnesses in any jurisdiction;
- publication to several persons with Northern Ireland connections took place, presumably in Northern Ireland, and;
- the claimant said he was restricting his claim to damage to his reputation in Northern Ireland.

However, the publication in Northern Ireland was minimal and the claimant had a far greater and more substantial reputation on the United States. The judge, in balancing these factors, was of the view that the scales came down clearly in favour of the United States as being the natural forum. He went on to say that, '[i]f a tort had been committed against the claimant in this jurisdiction, it was not a real and substantial one whereas the contrary would be the case in the United States'.

Some criticisms can be made of the decision to stay proceedings. The first is that the judge seemed to be deciding the issue on a balance of convenience. In *The Spiliada*, Lord Goff made it clear that convenience was not the deciding factor. In remarking that the word 'conveniens' was not particularly apt, he said that the question was not one of convenience but of the suitability or appropriateness of the relevant jurisdiction and that a court should be careful not to think that the question at issue was one of mere practical convenience. A further criticism is that the publication in Northern Ireland, albeit of a much more limited nature than was the case in the United States, was nonetheless actionable and it seemed that the claimant would, if the allegation were true, suffer real damage in Northern Ireland for which, although much less than the potential damage in the United States, the claimant may not be compensated for in a court in the United States. It could be even worse for the claimant, for example, if under United States law, the defendants had a defence based on freedom of expression in the context of political or governmental appointments.

E-mails, defamation, malicious falsehood and trespass to goods

As a libellous statement is actionable if published to a single person (other than the person who is the subject of the statement), there is potentially great scope for defamation by e-mail, especially as many of us send e-mails without carefully checking what is contained in them. It can be said that a great many people ought to have a delay on their e-mails, to give them an opportunity to read them through a little later before sending them. The immediacy of this method of sending messages and attached documents, images and the like is one of its strengths but also one of the dangers of the medium.

The use of e-mail to work out a grudge is very foolish, even if the e-mail is sent to only one person or a small number of persons. In *Takenaka (UK) Ltd v Frankl* (unreported) 11 October 2000, defamatory e-mail messages were sent via Hotmail to the claimants. It was accepted that the messages were defamatory and the central issue was whether the defendant had been responsible for sending them. At the time, he was employed by Thames Water and working in Turkey. He had access to the computer from which the e-mails were sent. When informed of the messages, Thames Water agreed to help to trace the culprit but the investigation was described by the judge as ill-conceived and incompetent. The difficulty, of course, is finding whose fingers had been on the keyboard at the relevant times. A lot of forensic work was carried out involving checking access logs of Compuserve and Hotmail and temporary internet files. The judge was of the opinion, on a balance of probabilities that it all pointed to the defendant being responsible for the messages. The alternative explanation was that a third party was in Turkey at the relevant times, had access to the computer which was in the defendant's possession, had a grudge against the defendant and wanted to incriminate him, had a grudge against the claimants, had access to the defendant's password and had the necessary expertise and foresight to carry out the plan. The judge thought that to be highly unlikely. Although the e-mails were not published to many people, in relation to the second claimant they were described as salacious and the judge approved counsel's description that a 'defamatory statement can seep into the crevasses of the subconscious and lurk there ever ready to spring forth its cancerous evil'. He awarded £1000 damages to the first claimant and £25,000 damages to the second claimant. There would be an enquiry into the considerable costs resulting from the extensive and costly litigation needed to track down the defendant.

Malicious falsehood is a tort related to defamation and applies where someone makes a false statement maliciously about, in particular, a person's business. In 1995, rumours started to spread that a competitor, Western Provident Association, was being investigated by the Department of Trade and Industry and that the Association was close to insolvency. The statements had been made by employees of Norwich Union on its internal e-mail system. Western Provident brought an action for malicious falsehood and Norwich Union eventually settled out of court for £450,000.

Another action that might be available in respect of unwelcome e-mails might be that of trespass. There are a number of forms of trespass, which is an ancient form of action deriving from the writ of trespass circa 1215. In the famous old case of *Entick* v *Carrington* (1765) 19 Stat Tr 1029, Lord Camden CJ distinguished between taking away a person's papers and simply reading them saying that '. . . the eye cannot by the laws of England be guilty of trespass'. Also around that time the importance of trespass as an action was summed up by the phrase 'An Englishman's home is his castle', William Pitt, Earl of Chatham (1708–78) said:

> The poorest man may in his cottage bid defiance to all the forces of the Crown. It may be frail – its roof may shake – the wind may blow through it – the storm may enter – the rain may enter – but the King of England cannot enter – all his force dares not cross the threshold of the ruined tenement.

Whether the concept of trespass, which has since been supplemented by statute, applies in relation to electronic information is an important question and could have significant implications in relation to unwanted transmissions of e-mails and electronic advertising materials that are no worse than being of nuisance value, let alone containing defamatory statements.

In terms of the sending of unwelcome e-mails, is this trespass to goods? This action is included in section 1 of the Torts (Interference with Goods) Act 1977 under wrongful interference with goods. It must be a direct interference with goods and it has been said that this would include, for example, moving a chattel or throwing something at it or writing with a finger in the dust on the surface of a car (Keenan, D, *Smith & Keenan's English Law*, 13th edition, Longman 2001, p.481). It could be argued that sending an unwanted e-mail could fall within this tort, whether or not it contains defamatory material. The main questions are whether this would be seen as a *direct* interference, which is an essential ingredient of the tort, and whether sending unwanted e-mails and 'spam' (unsolicited e-mails or junk e-mails) interferes with *goods*, defined in the Act as chattels personal other than things in action and money. The latter would depend on whether the inference was deemed to be in relation to the computer (hardware) or the data (software). However, an analogy may be made to cases on criminal damage to computer data prior to the coming into force of the Computer Misuse Act

1990, where it was accepted that the damage did not have to be tangible, the main point was that tangible goods had been damaged, for example, by being rendered less useful as a result; see, for example, *R* v *Whiteley* (1991) 93 Cr App R 381, discussed in Chapter 30.

The Financial Law Panel chaired by Lord Donaldson of Lymington, in its discussion paper *e-Commerce – Review of Legal Implications*, December 2001, doubted at pp. 11ff whether the tort of trespass could apply to unwanted e-mails and spam but based its view on the paucity of case law and the definition of goods in the Torts (Interference with Goods) Act 1977. However, this was a timid approach and lack of case law is a neutral factor, especially as the United Kingdom approach has been to tackle these and similar problems using the criminal law. It is surely an unlawful interference with a person's computer (hardware) to transmit data or other information (software) to it without consent. This will cause annoyance to the person who has possession of the computer who will have to take action, for example, by erasing the data or information to restore his computer to the state he wants it to be in. Another analogy can be made with sale of goods law. Section 12(2)(b) of the Sale of Goods Act 1979 implies a term into a contract for the sale of goods that the buyer will enjoy quiet enjoyment of the goods. In *Rubicon Computer Systems Ltd* v *United Paints Ltd* (unreported) 12 November 1999, the Court of Appeal accepted that activating a time-lock on a computer subject to a sale contract was a breach of that implied term.

In the United States, the courts have been very willing to apply principles of trespass to unwanted e-mails and the like. For example, in *Thrifty-Tel Inc* v *Bezeneck* (1996) Cal App 4th 1159, the Californian court was happy to accept that electronic signals generated and sent by computer were sufficiently tangible to support a trespass action. In *CompuServe Inc* v *Cyber Promotions Inc* (SD Ohio 1997) 962 F Supp 1015, a District Court in Ohio used the concept of trespass to chattels to grant a temporary injunction curbing the activities of spammers. A number of other cases were to a similar effect.

More recently, the Supreme Court of California made an important distinction in the case of *Intel Corporation* v *Hamidi* (unreported) 30 June 2003. The defendant had been an employee of Intel and had been dismissed following a dispute over compensation for work-related injuries. He later sent six e-mails to thousands of employees of Intel claiming that Intel had adopted abusive and discriminatory practices and he was also critical of Intel's employment and personnel policies and practices. It did not appear that the defendant sent further e-mails to any employee who had asked him not to do so. At first instance, the claim for trespass to chattel was accepted and an injunction was granted in favour of Intel. The Californian Court of Appeal upheld that decision but the subsequent appeal to the Californian Supreme Court was successful in a decision that was split 4:3 in favour of the defendant. One of the majority judges, Kennard J said:

> ... using another's equipment to communicate with a third person who is an authorized user of the equipment and who does not object to the communication is trespass to chattels only if the communications damage the equipment or in some significant way impair its usefulness or availability. ... Intel has not shown that defendant Hamidi's occasional bulk e-mail messages to Intel's employees have damaged Intel's computer system or impaired its functioning in any significant way, Intel has not established the tort of trespass to chattels. This is not to say that Intel is helpless either practically or legally. As a practical matter, Intel need only instruct its employees to delete messages from Hamidi without reading them and to notify

Hamidi to remove their workplace email addresses from his mailing lists. Hamidi's messages promised to remove recipients from the mailing list on request, and there is no evidence that Hamidi has ever failed to do so. From a legal perspective, a tort theory other than trespass to chattels may provide Intel with an effective remedy if Hamidi's messages are defamatory or wrongfully interfere with Intel's economic interests.

Kennard J also alluded to moves to pass laws to deal with such activities and there is at the present time a United States Bill to this effect. Some states have already adopted anti-spam laws such as the State of Virginia.

The Intel case does not say that sending unwanted e-mails and the like can never be trespass but shows that the activity complained of must be of more than nuisance value. It would be trespass, for example, to clog up a computer system with considerable numbers of e-mails, attachments or 'instant messages' or otherwise disrupt the computer system, for example, by sending a computer virus. It would also seem to be trespass if the sender failed to respond to requests from individuals authorised to use the computers to stop sending e-mails.

In Europe, Directive 2002/58/EC of the European Parliament and of the Council on the protection of personal data in the electronic communications sector, OJ L 201, 31.07.2002, p.37 will, when implemented control, *inter alia*, unsolicited marketing by e-mail. The latest date for implementation is 31 October 2003. The Directive and draft Regulations are discussed further in Part Five of this book.

Finally, one possible action in relation to unwanted e-mails in the United Kingdom is to apply for a civil order under section 3 of the Protection from Harassment Act 1997. This can apply where there is a course of conduct which alarms a person or causes distress (clearly more than merely being a nuisance). This was used, in conjunction with a restraining order under section 5 of the Act in a case involving, *inter alia*, offensive messages placed on a website and e-mails sent to staff at a hospital by a person who tried to get the treatment regime for her daughter reinstated; *Chelsea and Westminster Healthcare NHS v Redmond* [2003] All ER (D) 87. Normally, this Act provides for criminal offences but contains civil remedies also.

Internet service providers and defamation

Organisations providing internet access or providing website space or otherwise publishing on-line material created by other persons are potentially liable in a number of ways for the content of the material so made available. Information placed on the Internet (or other electronic publishing medium) may infringe copyright, include a defamatory or negligent misstatement, breach a confidence, be pornographic or be illegal in a number of other ways. This section is concerned with defamatory statements and is written from the perspective of internet service providers (ISPs) but much the same principles apply to others deemed to be publishers of the information. The following chapter looks at the position in relation to illegal information generally and, to some extent supplements this section which is concerned primarily with defamation and the specific 'publisher's defence' in section 1 of the Defamation Act 1996.

Traditional publishers usually include in the formal contract with an author a warranty from the author that the material concerned is not defamatory in any way (a similar warranty will apply in respect of third parties rights such as copyright). In the agreement, the author will be required to indemnify the publisher should the publisher be sued for libel or malicious falsehood and have to pay damages.

Publishing information on the Internet can be done in a number of ways, some of which differ considerably to publishing in paper form under a formal agreement between a publisher and author. For example, an ISP may act as a host, providing a subscriber with space to upload webpages or allow a subscriber to post material on a bulletin board or newsgroup or the ISP may simply act as a conduit through which information is passed, such as by e-mail or through a chat room or by instant messaging.

Liability under defamation flows from the act of publishing the defamatory statement. Therefore, prima facie, it is the person publishing the statement who is liable. Generally, the author of the statement will be considered to have published it as will the publisher himself. However, some specific defences have developed to exclude or limit the liability of publishers who were unaware of the defamatory nature of the statement. Certain defences, such as qualified privilege may apply and, under section 4 of the Defamation Act 1952, the publisher of an innocent defamation (such that the words were not defamatory on their face, the publisher was not aware of the circumstances by which the words might be understood to be defamatory and reasonable care was exercised in the publication of the words) may make an offer of amends, requiring the publication of a suitable apology and correction (as commonly seen in newspapers). A further specific publisher's defence is provided for under section 1 of the Defamation Act 1996 as considered below.

Publisher's defence

Prior to the passing of the Defamation Act 1996, the Lord Chancellor's Department specifically looked at this problem. The 1996 Act has, therefore, a specific defence in which a person can show that he had no responsibility for the publication. The defence came into force on 4 September 1996. Under section 1, the defence applies if a person shows that:

- he was not the author, editor or publisher of the statement complained of,
- he took reasonable care in relation to its publication, and
- he did not know, and had no reason to believe, that what he did caused or contributed to the publication of a defamatory statement.

Under section 1(3) of the Defamation Act 1996, a number of persons are not to be considered authors, editors or publishers if only involved:

(a) in printing, producing, distributing or selling material containing the statement;
(b) in processing, making copies of, distributing, exhibiting or selling a film or sound recording containing the statement;
(c) in processing, making copies of, distributing or selling electronic medium in or on which the statement is recorded, or in operating or providing any equipment, system or service by means of which the statement is retrieved, copied, distributed or made available in electronic form;
(d) as the broadcaster of a live programme containing the statement in circumstances in which he has no effective control over the maker of the statement;
(e) as the operator or provider of access to a communications system by means of which the statement is transmitted, or made available, by a person over whom he has no effective control.

It can be seen that (c) above applies in relation to publishers of computer software on disk or CD-ROM and (e) applies particularly to ISPs and, for example, telephone operators. In other cases, the court may use the above provisions by way of analogy in deciding whether a person is considered to be an author, editor or publisher.

Under section 1(4), employees or agents are in the same position as their employer or principal to the extent that they are responsible for the content of the statement or the decision to publish it.

To determine whether a person took reasonable care, under section 1(5), regard is to be had to:

- the extent of his responsibility for the content of the statement or the decision to publish it;
- the nature of the circumstances of the publication; and
- the previous conduct or character of the author, editor or publisher.

Thus, where an author or publisher has been in trouble before for publishing defamatory material, this is a factor in determining whether he took reasonable care. In other words, a previous history of publishing defamatory material requires the person responsible to exercise greater care to prevent it happening again. This could apply, for example, where a publisher of a web-based journal has previously published articles in the journal that included libellous statements.

The section 1 defence seems to be quite fragile and, once an ISP has been warned that material which contains a statement alleged to be defamatory has been placed on the ISP's server, he should consider whether he should remove it, or disable access to it, immediately. In *Godfrey v Demon Internet Ltd* [2001] QB 201, a subscriber to an internet service, provided by the defendant, made material available through the service which was alleged by the claimant to be defamatory of him. The claimant brought the present action to strike out part of the defence as disclosing no sustainable defence to a libel action, based on the publication of the material by the defendant. After the claimant informed the defendant of his allegation that the material was defamatory, the defendant did not immediately remove the material (although, eventually, it did so).

It was held that the defence did not apply in this case as, at common law, once the defendant became aware that the material contained defamatory statements it could no longer satisfy two of the requirements in section 1(1) – that is, that reasonable care had been taken in the publication and that the defendant had no knowledge or reason to believe that he caused or contributed to the publication of the defamatory statement. Mr Justice Morland pointed out that section 17 of the Defamation Act 1996 states that 'publication' and 'publish' have the meaning they have generally for the law of defamation but 'publisher' is specially defined in section 1. He did accept, however, that the defendant was not a commercial publisher for the purposes of section 1(2), being a person whose business is issuing material to the public, or a section of the public, who issues material containing the statement in the course of that business. Unfortunately for the defendant, for the section 1(1) defence to apply, all three requirements must be satisfied. The defendant's argument that it had played a passive role was not accepted and the judge thought the situation analogous to that of a bookseller who sold a book containing defamatory material.

The significance of this case is that the special defence may be quite limited in its scope. If a person alleges that defamatory material has been placed on the service provider's server, it may no longer be safe to rely on the defence and the ISP ought to consider removing the material immediately. This is quite important as each time an individual accesses the material, there will be a fresh libel. Whether a service provider has no reason to believe that he causes or contributes to the publication must be an objective test based on the reasonable person having knowledge of the facts known to the service provider and which must be coloured by the allegation of defamation.

Consider a situation where an ISP is informed by someone that a statement defamatory of him has been placed on the service provider's server. If the material is not removed immediately, the issue for the court may become one simply relating to the general law of defamation. If the statement is held by the court to have a defamatory meaning, it is highly unlikely that the section 1 defence can apply. For example, if the matter is being decided by a jury and it finds the statement defamatory, it will almost certainly consider that, after being informed of the allegation of defamation, the service provider did indeed 'have reason to believe'. The same probably applies where there is no jury and the case is heard before a judge alone. On the other hand, if the finding is that the statement is not defamatory, that is an end to the matter. Thus, the section 1 defence is likely to be relevant only up to such time as an ISP has been informed of the allegation. If that is so, ISPs would be well advised to remove the material immediately. However, if they respond in that way, that makes freedom of speech vulnerable to persons who simply do not like what is said about them over the Internet without the statements necessarily being defamatory. Given the sensitivity of the issue and the potential of numerous actions for defamation, ISPs are likely to play safe if there is any possibility that the statement complained of may be defamatory. This approach seems to have been the one taken in practice.

An ISP, like anyone else, is subject to data protection law and this may restrict disclosures of personal data relating to subscribers to third parties. In many cases, ISPs and website operators will have an express term in their contract with subscribers confirming that their identity will not be disclosed to anyone else, except where required by law: for example, for the purposes of the prevention and detection of crime. The service providers in *Totalise plc* v *Motley Fool Ltd* [2001] 1 WLR 1233 had so provided. In that case, the claimant was an ISP and the defendants operated websites which included discussion boards. The contracts the defendants had with the subscribers contained a term saying that their identity would not be disclosed. An anonymous contributor to the discussion boards, calling himself 'Z Dust', posted material which was alleged to be defamatory of the claimant company, its officers and directors. The judge at first instance thought that the material was plainly defamatory and that Z Dust was waging an intensive campaign of vilification against the claimant.

The claimant sought an order requiring the defendants to disclose the identity of Z Dust. The defendants eventually barred Z Dust access to their sites. However, the identity of Z Dust was not disclosed on the ground that this would be contrary to the Data Protection Act 1998. The judge had no hesitation in granting the order for disclosure on the basis of *Norwich Pharmacal Co* v *Customs and Excise Commissioners* [1974] AC 133 which gives a court jurisdiction to order a third party to disclose the identity of a wrongdoer. However, he awarded costs against the defendants who had taken a fairly neutral stance on the issue of the granting of such an order. The judge, Mr Justice Owen, said:

> I consider that there is considerable force in Mr Maloney's argument that those who
> operate websites containing discussion boards do so at their own risk. If it transpires
> that those boards are used for defamatory purposes by individuals hiding behind the

cloak of anonymity then in justice a claimant seeking to establish the identity of the individuals making such defamatory contents ought to be entitled to their costs.

The normal rule with costs and *Norwich Pharmacal* orders is that the person applying for the order for disclosure should bear the costs of the application. This was confirmed on appeal to the Court of Appeal which set aside the order for costs, saying that it was legitimate for a party who reasonably agreed to keep information confidential and private to refuse to hand over such information voluntarily.

The United States position

In contrast, the position of ISPs is far more secure in the United States as a result of the Communications Decency Act 1996 47 USC §230 which states that 'no provider or user of an interactive computer service shall be treated as the publisher or speaker of any information provided by another information content provider'. This was a response to fears that ISPs would no longer self-regulate the content of material available through their service as the position, following cases such as *Stratton Oakmont Inc v Prodigy Services Co,* 1995 NY Misc. LEXIS 229, imposing liability on a service provider which checked the content, thereby providing a disincentive to self-regulation. The position seemed to be that service providers which did not check or monitor the information made available through their service would be less likely to be found liable. Clearly, this situation was untenable, hence the change to the law.

The effects of 47 USC §230 were quickly seen. For example, in *Zeran v America Online Inc* (1997) 129 F 3d 327, the claimant complained of alleged defamatory messages posted by an unidentified third party on AOL. He claimed that 47 USC §230 did not assist AOL once it had notice that the material was defamatory. The messages placed on AOL's bulletin board advertised T-shirts containing offensive messages related to the bombing of a Federal building in Oklahoma City. Anyone wanting to purchase a T-shirt was asked to contact 'Ken' at Zeran's home phone number. Zeran received a large number of angry phone calls and a number of death threats. Eventually, AOL removed the posting from the bulletin board. In confirming that AOL could rely on the defence, Chief Judge Wilkinson said of the rationale for the defence:

> The specter of tort liability in an area of such prolific speech would have an obvious chilling effect. It would be impossible for service providers to screen each of their millions of postings for possible problems. Faced with potential liability for each message republished by their services, interactive computer service providers might choose to severely restrict the number and type of messages posted. Congress considered the weight of the speech interests implicated and chose to immunize service providers to avoid any such restrictive effect.

It was also clear from the wording of the statutory provision that Congress intended that the exclusion of liability from ISPs afforded by 47 USC §230 was not to be compromised by state law or conflicting common law. In *Lunney v Prodigy Services Co* (1998) 250 AD 2d 230, an anonymous prankster used the claimant's name to open accounts with the defendant ISP and posted offensive material and sent offensive e-mails under the claimant's name. When the claimant informed the service provider, the postings were deleted and the fraudulent accounts closed. It was held that the defendant was not liable on the basis of prior common law to the effect that publishers are immune from liability for defamation resulting from material transmitted by them, but over which they merely retained passive editorial control, such as a telephone service. The court considered e-mail services to be like a telephone service. However, this defence can be lost if the publisher is guilty of bad faith or malice. But, even where more active editorial control is exercised, such as in the case of electronic bulletin boards, the court accepted that it would be unreasonable to expect an ISP to monitor the countless messages placed on its bulletin boards. Having said that, the court held that it did not need to consider the effect of 47 USC §230 although it did comment that its decision was in harmony with the provision.

The United States acted quickly to protect ISPs against defamation claims when, in practice, they had very little if any editorial control because of the vast amount of information passing through or hosted by the systems. In comparison, the situation in the United Kingdom has left ISPs in an invidious position. Once they have been warned that material is potentially defamatory, they have little option but to play safe and remove it. The publisher's defence in section 1 of the Defamation Act 1996 is too influenced by traditional forms of publishing and fails to properly address the reality of the situation which is that ISPs are unable to check everything going through their systems. Even if they could, should we really expect them to become arbiters of what is or is not defamatory? Fortunately, some of the provisions in the 'Electronic Commerce Directive' described in the following chapter may go some way to alleviating the position.

Defamation and the Internet – the way forward?

In 2002 the Law Commission commenced a study into defamation law in relation to the Internet following a number of concerns raised by on-line publishers and ISPs by developments such as the *Godfrey* v *Demon Internet* and *Loutchansky* v *Times Newspaper* cases, in particular. The main concerns were:

- the scope of the publishers' defence under section 1 of the Defamation Act 1996;
- the potential liability for a defamation action in relation to archive material made available over the Internet;
- the problems of jurisdiction and exposure to claims in foreign jurisdictions and the problem of complying with the laws of every country in which a website could be accessed; and
- the possible exposure to contempt of court resulting from jurors searching the Internet to detect whether an accused person had previous convictions.

These issues and responses by interested parties were set out in a 'scoping report', Law Commission, *Defamation and the Internet: A Preliminary Investigation*, Scoping Study No. 2, December 2002. As far as secondary publishers such as ISPs were concerned it was recognised that the present situation in the United Kingdom was unsatisfactory and a number of possibilities exist such as exempting ISPs from liability as is currently the situation in the United States. Following *Godfrey* v *Demon Internet*, in the United Kingdom service providers were under strong pressure to remove material they have been told was defamatory without considering whether the material was true or whether publication was in the public interest. Another possibility was to extend the innocent publication defence under section 1 of the Defamation Act 1996.

The Law Commission noted that the Electronic Commerce (EC Directive) Regulations 2002, which implemented the 'Electronic Commerce Directive', provided a defence for ISPs and others in relation to acting as a mere conduit, in respect of hosting and caching in respect of 'illegal material' which would include defamatory material but would also cover other forms of illegality, such as obscenity or copyright infringement. This defence (strictly speaking there are three related but slightly difference defences) is discussed in detail in the following chapter. At this stage it can be said that the Law Commission noted that there were two views as to the effect of this defence in the context of defamation. One view was that it simply mirrored the defence under section 1 of the Defamation Act 1996 whilst the other view was that it provided wider protection.

Archives present the spectre of liability arising in years to come, long after initial publication, because of the principle that each publication represents a separate libel. Although the Law Commission had in the past argued that the present one-year limitation period for defamation was possibly too short and could prejudice claimants, the possibility of an action being commenced some years into the future in relation to subsequent accesses to on-line archives could make it difficult for defendants to prepare an effective defence, for example, because witnesses might no longer be available. Clearly, this was an area which demanded further consideration, otherwise the social utility of making archives available could be compromised.

As regards jurisdiction and applicable law, the Law Commission thought that it would be impossible to come up with a solution in the short or medium terms and that further research was required into how this problem is dealt with in other countries. The only realistic longer-term solution might be by way of international treaties. The Law Commission thought it unlikely that on-line publishers, for example, of newspaper archives would be exposed to contempt of court actions. The alleged danger was that a juror might search the Internet and find archive material carrying reports of previous criminal convictions of a person under trial for a criminal offence. Except in exceptional technical legal circumstances, information about an accused's previous convictions is withheld from a jury. It is only after a guilty verdict is returned that details of previous convictions is made available to the court, where it will be taken into account by the judge when fixing the sentence to impose. The Law Commission thought that most jurors were of good sense and would not engage in searching the Internet for previous convictions and, in any case, it thought than internet publishers were already sufficiently protected against 'inappropriate, arbitrary or trivial prosecution. Consequently, no recommendation was made to make changes to the law in this respect.

There is some disquiet about the exposure to liability resulting from innocent publication by internet publishers and the apparent weakness of the publishers' defence under section 1 of the Defamation Act 1996. It seems apparent that some changes are necessary though it is unlikely that the United Kingdom will go as far as the United States has where exemption from liability seems available even if the ISP is in no doubt that the material is defamatory and yet takes no action to remove it. It may be that this will be modified or toned down by subsequent developments in the case law or legislation in the United States. The difficulty for the United Kingdom and other European countries is to strike a balance between protecting the individual whilst maintaining freedom of speech in accordance with the European Convention for the Protection of Human Rights and Fundamental Freedoms, Article 10 of which allows restrictions to be placed on freedom of expression necessary in a democratic society, *inter alia*, for the protection of the reputation or rights of others. It is submitted that the United

Kingdom's pendulum needs to swing back slightly more in favour of freedom of expression otherwise unscrupulous persons may manipulate the Internet to suppress truths or half-truths, the publication of which would be in the public interest.

In terms of the possibility of long-term exposure to defamation actions resulting from material available on archives, perhaps it is time to reconsider the multiple publication rule and, perhaps, replace it with a single publication rule in the context of the Internet. However, this would represent a very substantial change to defamation law in the United Kingdom and its implications would have to be fully explored before such a change, even a partial change, could be contemplated.

Chapter 26

Liability of information society service providers for illegal material

Introduction

Directive 2000/31/EC of the European Parliament and of the Council of 8 June 2000 on certain legal aspects of information society services, in particular electronic commerce, in the Internal Market (OJ L178, 17.07.2000, p.1) was required to be transposed into national law before 17 January 2002. In the United Kingdom, the Directive was implemented on 21 August 2002 by the Electronic Commerce (EC Directive) Regulations 2002. The Directive dealt with a number of issues, such as the obligations of information society service providers to provide information to recipients of their services and competent authorities, in relation to contracts concluded by electronic means and the Internal Market for information society service providers, as described in Chapter 23. The aspects of the Directive with which this present chapter is concerned are those which give defences for information society service providers in respect of illegal information which has passed through their service to a recipient, where such information has been stored temporarily by information society service providers or in respect of illegal activities or information associated with their storage of information where the service provider is not responsible and, if relevant, acts quickly to remove or disable access to the information and, in terms of storage other than certain forms of temporary storage, does not know of the illegal activity or information.

The Directive noted that there were disparities between the laws of member states in relation to the liability of service providers and this could detract from the smooth functioning of the Internal Market. The Directive postulated a number of solutions based on:

- limiting liability where the service provider is a mere conduit and in terms of *caching* (automatic, intermediate and temporary storage) and *hosting* (storage at the request of the recipient);
- the courts or administrative authorities in member states being able to require a service provider to terminate or prevent an infringement or require the removal or disabling of access to information;
- not imposing a proactive duty to look for illegal material (however, member states could, if they wished, impose a monitoring obligation on service providers in specific cases and, in terms of hosting, member states were to be free to impose a reasonable duty of care to detect and prevent illegal activities);
- encouraging the drawing up of voluntary codes of practice;
- setting up procedures for removing and disabling access to illegal information, perhaps on a voluntary basis;
- surveillance, where allowed, subject to the data protection Directive and the Directive on privacy in telecommunications.

As was the case in the description of the other aspects of the Directive, references are made to the provisions of the Directive, which are for all intents and purposes the same as in the Regulations, expect in relation to certain evidential and other aspects specifically covered by the Regulations with no equivalent in the Directive.

Information society services

To remind ourselves, information society services are those normally provided for remuneration, at a distance, by means of electronic equipment for processing and storage of data. Processing includes digital compression. Information services within the meaning of the Directive cover a wide range of activities and include on-line contracting, on-line information services such as on-line newspapers, databases, financial and professional services, access to information through internet service providers (ISPs), search engine providers, on-line marketing and advertising, video on demand and commercial e-mails. It makes no difference if the remuneration is indirect and not paid for by the recipient of the service, for example, where it results from advertising or sponsorship.

Although the precise scope of services covered by the Directive is far from clear, it does not appear to apply to providers of hyperlinks and location tools or to persons who aggregate information from different sources, selecting and compiling the information for subscribers to access. In terms of hyperlinks and location tools, the omission of such service providers from these defences is potentially serious, especially in the context of defamatory material. In an old case, *Hird* v *Wood* (1894) Sol J 234, a placard carrying a libellous statement had been placed on the roadside by a person or persons unknown. The defendant sat by the placard, smoking a pipe and repeatedly pointing to it and attracting the attention of passers-by to the statement. It was held by the Court of Appeal that the defendant was a publisher of the statement.

Activities related to illegal information covered by the Directive

The activities covered by the special defences for information society service providers relate to three forms of activities:

- acting as a mere conduit
- caching and
- hosting.

The scope and extent of the defences vary according to which activity is concerned. Acting as a mere conduit means that the information in question has simply passed through the service provider's network. This would apply, for example, to information passing through a telecommunications network and certain associated forms of temporary storage do not remove the defence. E-mail is outside this activity as e-mails are stored by ISPs and the same applies to websites.

The act of caching occurs where a service provider places information in temporary storage in order to increase the efficient working of the Internet. For example, webpages may be placed in temporary store so that they can be re-displayed more quickly than would be the case if they had to be retrieved from their source again.

Hosting is where the service provider stores information for the recipient of the service. This could apply, for example, where the service provider hosts a website for a subscriber to its services. It could also cover e-mail systems where the e-mails are stored, for subsequent access by the subscriber to the service, bulletin boards and newsgroups.

Mere conduit

The provider of an information society service consisting of the transmission in a communication network of information provided by the recipient of the service or the provision of access to a communication network is not liable as a result of that transmission where the service provider does not initiate the transmission, did not select the receiver of the transmission and did not select or modify the information contained in it; Article 12 of the Directive.

The transmission or access may include the automatic, intermediate and transient storage of the information transmitted provided this is for the sole purpose of carrying out the transmission in the communication network and it is not stored for any longer than reasonably necessary for the transmission.

This exclusion of liability only applies in limited circumstances and will not apply to information stored for any longer or for any other purpose than intrinsically related to the transmission of the information. Thus, a great deal of the services made available by ISPs, such as e-mail, website hosting and newsgroups, all of which involve deliberate storage for other purposes, are not within this exclusion of liability. Where it might apply, for example, is in relation to facsimile transmission, telex or telephonic transmission.

The Directive is silent on the nature of the liability the service provider is exempt from but regulation 17 of the Electronic Commerce (EC Directive) Regulations 2002 states that the service provider shall not be liable for damages or other pecuniary remedy or for any criminal sanction as a result of the transmission. Other remedies, such as an injunction may be possible, for example, an injunction requiring the service provider to block transmissions by or received by a particular person.

Caching

Caching is not directly defined in the Directive but it is clear from recital 42 of the Directive that it refers to temporary storage for the sole purpose of making the transmission of information more efficient, being an activity of a mere technical, automatic and passive nature. The very nature of such storage implies that the service provider has neither knowledge nor control over the information that is transmitted or stored: hence the exclusion of liability. There appears to be some overlap between caching and acting as a mere conduit as the latter extends to incidental automatic, intermediate and transient storage. However, the exclusion of liability for caching must be intended to apply to acts of storage that, albeit temporary, go beyond those covered by the mere conduit defence. The reason is that the exclusion of liability is subject to different conditions. Caching may apply, for example, to the transmission of information which involves storage in volatile computer memory which is not automatically deleted on completion of the transmission but left in computer memory until such time as it is automatically overwritten by other information. Another example is the temporary storage by ISPs of commonly requested webpages, enabling them to be more quickly transmitted to subscribers.

Article 13 of the Directive states that the service provider is not liable where the service consists of the transmission in a communications network of information provided by a recipient of the service where the information is the subject of automatic, intermediate and temporary storage for the sole purpose of making more efficient the onward transmission of the information to other recipients of the service upon their request. Again liability for damages or any other pecuniary remedy or for any criminal sanction resulting from the transmission is excluded, under regulation 18 of the Electronic Commerce (EC Directive) Regulations 2002.

For the defence to apply, there are a number of conditions. First, the service provider must not modify the information transmitted. He must also comply with conditions on access to the information and any rules regarding the updating of the information specified in a manner widely recognised and used by industry. The service provider must not interfere with the lawful use of technology, widely recognised and used in industry, to obtain data on the use of the information. This could apply to access logs and the like. Finally, the service provider must act expeditiously to remove or disable access to the information cached upon obtaining actual knowledge of the fact that the information at the initial source of the transmission has been removed from the network, or access to it has been disabled, or that a court of an administrative authority has ordered such removal or disablement. 'Administrative authority' is defined in neither the Directive nor the Regulations but will include any body having authority to order removal of information or disablement of access. An example is the Office of the Information Commissioner, which has the power to serve enforcement notices requiring, *inter alia*, a data controller to cease certain forms of processing of personal data. This could apply, for example, where a webpage contains sensitive personal data and the conditions for processing such data do not apply. Another example is where a website contains advertising which is subject to a Stop Now Order imposed by the Director General of Fair Trading.

For the purposes of determining whether a service provider has actual knowledge, regulation 22 states that a court shall take into account all matters which appear to the court relevant in the circumstances and, amongst other things, shall have regard to whether the service provider has received a notice and the extent to which the notice includes the full name and address of the sender of the notice, details of the location of the information in question and details of the unlawful nature of the activity or information. The notice may be sent by e-mail and may be sent by any person, whether a recipient of the service, a person claiming to be libelled by the information or by an enforcement authority, being any authority, other than a court, empowered to take enforcement action. The fact no such notice has been received by the service provider does not necessarily mean that he can avail himself of the defence. It could be the case, for example, that concerns about the information have been published in a widely read newspaper.

Hosting

Hosting applies where the service provider stores information which has been provided by the recipient of the service. This could apply to a website hosted by the service provider, information posted on bulletin boards by subscribers and e-mails sent by recipient which are usually stored until deleted by the subscriber. In *Godfrey* v *Demon Internet*, the evidence was that the service provider normally stored information sent to its Usenet service for about two weeks before deleting it. This would certainly fall within the meaning of hosting.

Under Article 14 of the Electronic Commerce Directive, a service provider is not liable in respect of storage if the service provider does not have actual knowledge of illegal activity or information and, where a claim for damages is made, is not aware of the facts or circumstances from which the illegal activity or information would have been apparent or, upon obtaining such knowledge or awareness, the service provider acts expeditiously to remove or disable access to the information. The defence does not apply if the recipient of the service (that is, the recipient who provided the information in question) was acting under the authority or control of the service provider. The provisions for determining whether a service provider has actual notice are the same as those that apply to caching, under regulation 22 of the Electronic Commerce (EC Directive) Regulations 2002.

Again the regulations define the extent of liability excluded in relation to liability for damages or for any other pecuniary remedy (this could, for example, be an account of profits or compensation) or for any criminal sanction. However, in this case, damages may still be recoverable from the service provider if he has objective knowledge, as opposed to actual knowledge as determined in accordance with regulation 22, being where he is aware of circumstances from which it would have been apparent to the service provider that the activity or information was unlawful (note that the Regulations use the term 'unlawful' whereas the Directive uses the term 'illegal', though there is no practical distinction between the words). This form of knowledge should be satisfied if the reasonable person, aware of the same circumstances, would have concluded that the activity or information was unlawful. Information society service providers are under no obligation to monitor the information transmitted or stored, under Article 15 of the Directive.

The requirement to remove or disable access is a concern to ISPs and on-line publishers. ISPs receive numerous requests to remove material, typically by e-mail. Many are not clear or sufficiently specific. The Directive requires member states to encourage the drawing up of codes of practice (not just in relation to these defences) and this would be of some assistance if a code of practice was developed making it clear under what circumstances the notice requirement for determining whether the provider has actual knowledge would be satisfied. Such a code could also set out 'notice and take down' procedures. This is an area mentioned in the Directive in the provisions to re-examine the application of the Directive with a view to adapting it. The problem for service providers is that, without clear guidance, they may find it difficult to decide whether they have been given notice in an appropriate manner and sufficiently detailed to act upon and to decide whether, indeed, whether the activity or information concerned is unlawful. In terms of defamatory material, it is questionable whether these defences add anything to the publishers' defence under section 1 of the Defamation Act 1996.

For unlawful activities (for example, money laundering) or information (such as obscene material or material infringing copyright or information disclosed in breach of confidence) it may be marginally easier, at least in some cases, for the service provider to come to a conclusion as to whether the activity or information is unlawful.

Defamation may still be the most difficult area for the service provider to judge and it is likely that the service provider will simply play safe and remove the information or disable access to it. Old case law shows how easy it is to be liable for a defamatory statement written by someone else. For example, in the Court of Star Chamber (so called because of the star pattern painted on the ceiling of the court) in *Halliwood's Case*, the court noted in (1601) 5 Coke 125b, that it was said that '... if one finds a libel, and would keep himself out of danger, if it be composed against a private man, the finder may either burn it or deliver it to a magistrate'. This indicates the danger of inactivity when it comes to defamatory material. (The Court of Star Chamber existed between 1487 and 1641.) In *De Libellis Famosis* (1605) 5 Coke 125a, Lord Coke pointed out the various ways a libel may be published, including fixing some disparaging object at the party's door. In *Byrne v Deane* [1937] 1 KB 818, a verse written by an unknown person had been left on the notice board of a golf club which had a rule that no notice could be posted on club premises without the consent of the club secretary. The verse was:

> You heard the sound of a merry bell
> Those who were rash and those who were not
> Lost and made a spot of cash
> But he who gave the game away
> May he byrnn in hell and rue the day
> Diddleramus.

There were two copies of the verse, the original and a carbon copy underneath. On the original, the word 'byrnn' had been changed to 'burn' and it was accepted that this was a reference to the claimant, who the person writing the verse must have suspected of informing the police that there was a gaming machine in the club which the police had removed. It was accepted that the defendants, proprietors of the club, by allowing the verse to remain, were responsible for publishing it, though the majority of the Court of Appeal did not consider the verse defamatory of the claimant.

Regulation 20 of the Electronic Commerce (EC Directive) Regulations 2002 states that nothing in regulations 17–19 (the defences) prevents a person agreeing different contractual terms, for example, further limiting or extending the scope of the defences in the context of a contract between a service provider and recipient of the service. Nor are the rights of any person to apply to a court for relief to prevent or stop an infringement of any rights affected. The power of an administrative authority to prevent or stop an infringement continues to apply regardless of regulations 17–19.

Regulation 21 covers the situation where a service provider is charged with a criminal offence in relation to acts of transmission, provision of access or storage within regulations 17–19 but seeks to rely on the defences therein. The service provider is placed under an evidential burden in that he is required to adduce evidence sufficient to raise an issue with respect to the defence. Once he has done this, the prosecution has to prove beyond reasonable doubt that the defence is not satisfied otherwise the service provider can rely on the defence.

Although the service provider is under a general duty to remove or disable access to unlawful information or information relating to unlawful activity, he may be placed under a duty to intercept, retain or store the information under a warrant authorising interception granted under the Regulation of Investigatory Powers Act 2000. In terms of removal of information or disabling access to it, there may also be issues under the

Computer Misuse Act 1990 and the Data Protection Act 1998 and in relation to the right of freedom of expression under the European Convention on Human Rights. Information society service providers should insert terms in their contracts with recipients of their services making it clear that they may take action to remove information or disable access if they have reason to believe that it contains unlawful information or is associated with illegal activity. This may prevent claims from recipients aggrieved at the removal of their information. Two difficulties remain however. The first is that it is probably not possible to contract out of freedom of expression. The second difficulty is that the contract may not be with the recipient, bearing in mind the Directive extends also to services provided for indirect remuneration.

PART FOUR

Computers and crime

Computer technology impacts on criminal law in two ways. It facilitates the commission of existing crimes, such as fraud and theft, but it has also given birth to a new range of activities such as computer hacking and the development and distribution of computer viruses. The criminal law was perceived to be patchy in its application, both to existing and new forms of crime, and this caused considerable concern to the computer industry and financial institutions. Largely as a result of lobbying and pressure from the industry, the Computer Misuse Act 1990 was enacted, having started life as a private member's Bill. The Act closed the loopholes in the prior law and also dealt with questions of jurisdiction and extradition. In particular, it created a new offence of unauthorised access to computer programs or data (hacking), an ulterior intent offence (hacking with intent to commit a further offence) and an offence of unauthorised modification of computer material.

This part of the book concentrates on three areas of criminal activity associated with the use of computers – computer fraud, hacking and damage to programs and data. These have all attracted a great deal of media attention and the nature of these offences and the scope of the criminal law in relation to them are discussed in practical terms. Additionally, the criminal offences available to combat piracy and counterfeiting are described. A further chapter looks at the serious problem of pornography, in particular, child pornography on the Internet and threatening e-mails. One point to be remembered when reading the following chapters is that the actions described will sometimes give rise to liabilities under civil law. For example, if a hacker makes a copy of some of the information stored on a computer system, he may be infringing the copyright subsisting in that information and may also be in breach of confidence if he divulges it to others, depending upon the circumstances. Similarly, a fraudster transferring funds will be guilty of the civil law tort of conversion. If the culprit is an employee who has obtained access to parts of a computer system to which he has no authority to access, then internal action such as a reprimand or dismissal may ensue instead of or as well as a criminal prosecution.

Note that although many criminal offences also apply in Scotland, for example offences under the Computer Misuse Act 1990, there are some significant differences between English and Scots criminal law. Furthermore, where offences do apply in Scotland, there may be differences in their application and scope.

Chapter 27

Nature of computer crime

Introduction

The advent of computer technology has brought many kinds of opportunities and some of these, not surprisingly, are of a criminal nature. Computers may facilitate the commission of 'old-fashioned' crimes such as fraud or counterfeiting or give rise to new mischiefs such as computer hacking and the deliberate erasure of programs or data. Contrary to popular belief, the law is reasonably well equipped to deal with computer crime and was substantially strengthened by the Computer Misuse Act 1990. The biggest stumbling block, in practical terms, is detection and a considerable amount of thought must be given to the security of any computer system as, in this case, prevention is better than cure.

It used to be the case that the greatest threat to a computer system came from within – that is, from employees. One of the largest reported computer frauds ever attempted, which concerned the transfer of $70m, involved an employee of the First National Bank of Chicago. Even when computer crime is detected and the persons involved are prosecuted and convicted, the penalties imposed seem relatively trivial when compared with other forms of criminal activity. In 1989, a teenage bank cashier who transferred nearly £1m into his own and a friend's bank account received only one year's youth custody. However, with the growth of networks and the Internet, things have changed and, the 2002 *CSI/FBI Computer Crime and Security Survey* (conducted by the United States Computer Security Institute with the participation of the San Francisco Federal Bureau of Investigation (FBI) Computer Intrusion Squad, referred to hereafter as the CSI/FBI 2002 Survey) indicated that nearly two-thirds of attacks on the 503 respondents' computer systems came from outside. The average loss for those respondents able to quantify the loss was just over $2m.

The diversity of criminal activities associated with computers is remarkable and has given rise to a whole new vocabulary. Examples are computer hacking, time bombs, logic-bombs, computer viruses and cyber-vandalism. These terms will be defined at the appropriate sections of this part of the book, the purpose of which is to describe the criminal offences associated with computers, what remedies are available at law and to suggest how the threats posed by these activities can be avoided or, at least, minimised. In Chapter 28 the offences popularly described as 'computer fraud' are considered. In Chapter 29 the activity known as hacking is examined together with the aggravated form of hacking where the offender intents to gain access to computer material with the intention of carrying out a further serious offence. This is followed, in Chapter 30, by a discussion of the legal implications when a person erases programs or data from a computer system or leaves a virus on a system which later corrupts or deletes information. Other forms of criminal activity, such as blackmail, forgery and counterfeiting and piracy offences, are discussed in Chapter 31. Computer pornography and harassment are dealt with in Chapter 32 and practical suggestions to prevent computer crime are contained in Chapter 33, which concludes with a summary of offences, their maximum penalties and scope, presented in tabular form.

The scale and nature of computer crime

Stories, often unsubstantiated, of massive computer frauds, widespread hacking and chaotic disruption to computer systems caused by viruses are legend. Cinema films such as *Superman III* and *War Games* fuelled the imagination, and reporting in the media, warning of the Friday 13th virus, for example, adds to this. The 'I Love You' virus released in 2000 was estimated to have had a worldwide economic impact of $8.75bn (CSI/FBI Survey, p.16). However, determining the economic impact is far from an exact science in most cases. A further complicating factor is that discovering the true scale of crime is an impossible task when considering conventional crime because of under-reporting (a great deal of crime goes unreported for a variety of reasons – this is known as the dark figure of crime) and this is even more so when it comes to computer crime. In some cases the crime will remain undetected or it may result in no action or disciplinary action rather than prosecution if the offender is an employee. It is even more so with computer crime and it is unlikely that more than half of computer crimes are reported. It has been rumoured that some financial institutions attempt to cover up the fact they have been a victim of computer crime, fearing that publicity will damage their reputation. In less serious cases occurring in the workplace, employers are more likely to take disciplinary action, which may result in dismissal, than press for the prosecution of the offending employee. In 2002, of the 205 detected instances of computer misuse in the Inland Revenue, there was not a single prosecution. Three staff were dismissed, one downgraded, two given financial penalties and 199 reprimanded; *HC Deb* col 605W, 10 February 2003. Although no details of the individual cases of misuse were given, it is unlikely that all instances fell within criminal offences. A good proportion probably were no more than breaches of internal disciplinary regulations.

Wild, exaggerated figures are sometimes quoted as the total cost of computer crime. In most cases, these can be taken with a pinch of salt because they are purely speculative; there is no foundation for them whatsoever. The best 'guesstimate' for the cost of computer crime in the United Kingdom seems to be in the order of £1.5bn, reputedly mentioned in a yet to be published report. Of course, computer crime has been and remains a very serious issue and, fortunately, some realistic data is available as the Audit Commission for Local Authorities and the National Health Service in England and Wales carry out surveys regularly, for example:

- *Opportunity Makes a Thief: An Analysis of Computer Abuse*, Audit Commission, 1994,
- Audit Commission Update, *Ghost in the Machine: An Analysis of IT Fraud and Abuse*, February 1998 and
- Audit Commission Update, *yourbusiness@risk: An Update on IT Abuse*, 2001.

These surveys give an excellent insight into computer crime and some data have also been available from government departments, though this is lacking in the rich detail of the earlier Audit Commission surveys.

The latest survey covered the three-year period ending 31 December 1999 and, as before, involved both the public and the private sector. The survey was based upon

Table 27.1 Computer misuse (survey based on three-year periods)

Type of misuse	1999 (%)	1996 (%)
Viruses	41	63
Pornography	40	9
Hacking	9	11
Fraud	10	17

Source: Audit Commission Update, *Ghost in the Machine: An Analysis of IT Fraud and Abuse*, 1998 and Audit Commission Update, *yourbusiness@risk: An Update on IT Abuse*, 2001

responses from 688 organisations, reporting a total of 460 incidents. Table 27.1 shows a summary of the results of the surveys for the three-year periods ending 1996 and 1999. Unfortunately, the forms of misuse do not exactly match the legal definitions of offences but the criminal law has changed significantly since the first survey was carried out in 1981. Only the statistics relating to viruses, pornographic material, hacking and fraud are shown and the figures adjusted proportionately to make 100 per cent. It is doubtful that some forms of computer misuse omitted are criminal offences. (The forms omitted are private work, using unlicensed software, invasion of privacy, theft of information and sabotage; these account for around one-quarter of reported cases.) In some cases, precise figures are not given in the surveys and the figures used in Table 27.1 are taken from graphs in the surveys.

Viruses, which were non-existent in the 1987 survey, have fallen back (though many respondents reported multiple attacks) after a high, but pornography has become a major concern. Hacking remains relatively low comparatively but the average cost of dealing with a hacking incident was £6000. Around 40 per cent of hacking incidents came from within an organisation. Although very few cases of sabotage were reported, a new form of sabotage was identified, being 'cyber-vandalism'. In one case, an internet company was brought to a standstill by a hacker who flooded its computer systems with millions of e-mails. Another form of cyber-vandalism is webpage defacement, discussed further in Chapter 30. Government websites seem to be a particular target for this form of activity. Fraud continues to be a problem, usually resulting from the acts of insiders. In one case, a local authority officer took advantage of poor controls and input fictitious invoices to a total of over £15,000. The officer was prosecuted and received a six-month prison sentence.

The HM Treasury, *2001–2002 Fraud Report: An Analysis of Reported Fraud in Government Departments and Best Practice Guidelines*, October 2002 contains some information on computer fraud and theft. Computer fraud in government departments rose from 66 incidents in the previous year to 113 in 2001–02, an increase of 71 per cent. The total value defrauded was fairly small at only £42,000 (compared with £15,300 in the previous year) and though the frauds were of low value, they could lead to significant losses if the lessons were not learnt in terms of security and systems management. Computer fraud accounted for 19 per cent of all reported fraud. There were quite a few cases of theft of computers and computer-related equipment which although accounting for around half the cases of theft of assets, represented 83 per cent of the total losses. In one case, chips worth £226,000 were stolen from a new mainframe computer and around 70 laptops were stolen.

The CSI/FBI Survey noted that 90 per cent of respondents reported computer security breaches in the year of the survey (2000) and 80 per cent reported financial losses.

The total loss of those able and willing to quantify their losses (233 respondents) was a staggering $455,848,000. The number of respondents citing their internet connection as a frequent point of attack has grown to 74 per cent and 40 per cent reported denial of service attacks. The survey also focused on the world wide web. Some 98 per cent of respondents had a web presence, 52 per cent conducted electronic commerce and 38 per cent suffered attacks in the 12 months of the study. The most common forms of abuse were, ranked from highest to lowest, cyber-vandalism, denial of service, theft of transactional information and financial fraud. The survey noted that website defacements of British 'gov.uk' top level domains increased from 9 in 2000 to 43 in 2001.

One thing that is apparent from the surveys is that a significant proportion of perpetrators are not prosecuted and, in many cases, no action is taken or the perpetrator, if an employee, is reprimanded, transferred to other duties or dismissed. In the case of *Denco Ltd* v *Joinson* [1991] IRLR 63, it was held that an employee who used an unauthorised password to gain access to information stored in a computer and which he knew he was not entitled to see was guilty of gross misconduct and could be summarily dismissed from his employment. The employer's security arrangements were criticised by the Employment Appeal Tribunal and the Industrial Tribunal which heard the case first (the employee had argued that he had been unfairly dismissed). In *Pickersgill* v *Employment Service* [2002] EWCA Civ 23, the Court of Appeal dismissed an appeal against the Employment Appeal Tribunal's refusal to hear an appeal on extended grounds by an employee who had been dismissed following, *inter alia*, unauthorised access to the employer's computer system on no less than 70 occasions.

A disregard for basic control safeguards and ineffective monitoring were both highlighted by the Audit Commission as still being prevalent. Recommendations made in the reports, accepting that prevention is better than cure, include:

- carrying out risk analysis reviews;
- developing and implementing secure and controlled environments;
- having rigorously implemented IT security policies;
- giving staff computer awareness training, focusing on risks and precautions to be taken;
- assigning responsibility for security and developing secure access control;
- making sure that the internal audit department has computer audit skills; and
- making the necessary financial commitment to security aspects of an organisation's computer systems.

However, the latest Audit Commission report notes that a failure in basic controls is still a problem and the new risks associated with the upsurge in the use of new technology are not being sufficiently addressed. The report states (at p.20) that 'The key feature about the Internet is not it necessarily presents new risks – rather it provides new and better opportunities for abuse.'

Potential risks are spoof websites inviting orders for non-existent goods or services, getting access to critical or sensitive data, downloading or sending inappropriate information or images, downloading unauthorised software and the ever-present dangers of viruses. In addressing these and other issues, the Council of Europe Convention on Cybercrime (Budapest, 23 November 2001) has been signed by a large number of member states of the Council of Europe and some non-member states, being Canada, Japan, South Africa and the United States. The Convention, claimed to be the first international response to cybercrime, will enter into force when ratified by five states, including at least three member states of the Council of Europe. As at 30 July 2003, there were three ratifications. The main provisions as to the criminalisation of the certain activities committed intentionally require parties to the Convention to adopt legislative and other measures to establish criminal offences in respect of the following:

- illegal access (hacking),
- illegal interception,
- interference with data and systems,
- misuse of devices designed or adapted for committing any of the above and in relation to passwords, access codes and similar data,
- computer-related forgery and fraud,
- child pornography in relation to computer systems, and
- commercial infringement of copyright and related rights by means of a computer system.

Aiding and abetting such activities should also be criminalised and there are provisions for imposing liability on corporations, for example, where the offence is committed for the benefit of a natural person who has a leading position in the corporation. Parties to the Convention must adopt effective, proportionate and dissuasive sanctions. As will be seen in the following chapters, the United Kingdom already provides for the offences within the Convention though some fine-tuning may be required. The Convention contains a great many other provisions, for example, in relation to preservation and disclosure of computer data and traffic data and search and seizure. Jurisdiction will be established in a Party to the Convention if the offence is committed within its territory, on board a ship flying the flag of that Party, on board an aircraft registered under the laws of that Party, or where the offence is committed by a national of that Party, if the offence is punishable under the criminal law where it was committed (the double-actionability rule) or where it was committed outside the territorial jurisdiction of any state. Extradition is also dealt with and the parties to the Convention are required to afford each other mutual assistance.

The need for greater security is ever more urgent now that the threats of global terrorism have been driven home in such an astonishing way. International cooperation on the scale envisaged by the Convention on Cybercrime will prove an important factor in respect of terrorism and computer crime generally. Security is important in all walks of life but is vital in relation to safety critical systems. An awareness of the criminal law and its application to computer technology is an important part of implementing security strategies in a business context and in educating those who work with or have access to computers. Prevention will not, sadly, eliminate computer misuse altogether and the remainder of this part of the book examines the criminal law in relation to computer crime.

The prosecution of criminal offences

Before specific offences are examined, it will be useful to describe, very briefly, the procedure for prosecuting offences, the classification of offences and the different modes of trial.

When a criminal offence has been committed, the normal procedure is for the police to be informed (the police detect very little crime themselves but depend on the public bringing incidents of crime to their notice). The police will then investigate the crime and, if they suspect a particular person or persons of having committed the crime, they may charge the person or persons and then pass the case over to the Crown Prosecution Service which decides whether to prosecute and what charges to bring. The police now have the National Hi-Tech Crime Unit, operating within the National Crime Squad.

In coming to its decision to prosecute, the Crown Prosecution Service uses guidelines which include the possibility of securing a conviction and the public interest. If the decision is made to proceed, the accused will appear before a magistrates' court where, depending on the nature of the offence and other matters, either his case will be dealt with, or he will be committed for trial in the Crown Court. It is possible to bring a private prosecution if, for example, the Crown Prosecution Service declines to act. However, the Director of Public Prosecutions has the power to take over a private prosecution. Other bodies may bring prosecutions such as local authority trading standards officers, the Department of Social Security, the Information Commissioner and HM Customs & Excise. Bringing a private prosecution is, in most cases, an extreme action, but it may be relevant to computer crime if the official bodies fail to take an interest in prosecuting certain behaviour, due perhaps to a lack of understanding of the problems involved or a feeling that the civil law offers sufficient remedies. Though this latter point may be true, it does not have the deterrent effect that a successful criminal prosecution can have.

Criminal offences are heard in either the Crown Court or magistrates' courts. The latter tend to deal with the less serious offences which make up the vast majority of criminal cases. Offences are classified according to how they may be tried. Relatively minor offences, such as exceeding the speed limit, may be tried only in magistrates' courts and these offences are described as being *summary* offences. Serious offences such as murder and robbery can only be tried in the crown court and these are called *indictable* offences. In between these two types of offence, there is a vast number of intermediate offences which can be tried in either a magistrates' court or the Crown Court; these offences, of which theft is an example, are called *triable either way* offences. These may be tried summarily in a magistrates' court or, on indictment, in the Crown Court. Many of the offences which will be described in this part of the book fall into this category; they are offences which are triable either way, an example being the unauthorised modification of computer programs or data. On the other hand, computer hacking (unauthorised access to computer material) is triable summarily only.

When an offence is classified as being triable either way, the choice of mode of trial initially rests with the magistrates. They may decide that the nature of the case is such that it should be tried in the Crown Court: for example, if it is a serious example of the offence. If the magistrates decide that the case can be heard in their court, the accused person can then decide whether to proceed in the magistrates' court, or to elect trial in the Crown Court. Certain other factors are important in deciding on the mode of trial apart from the seriousness of the offence. For example, the magistrates might consider that the accused, if found guilty, is deserving of a punishment greater than they can award (although they can commit a convicted person to the Crown Court for sentence if they feel that their sentencing powers are inadequate in the particular case), or the accused might think he stands a better chance of acquittal before a jury. In one case, a hacker was acquitted by a jury on the basis that he was addicted to hacking even though addiction is not a defence known to English law (see the case regarding Paul Bedworth discussed in Chapter 29)!

The maximum penalties available in magistrates' courts need to be mentioned. Providing the relevant statute does not contain a lower maximum, for a single offence the magistrates may send a person to prison for a term not exceeding six months and/or impose a fine not exceeding £5000. Other sentencing powers are available to the magistrates such as discharging the offender or imposing a probation order or a community service order. In the context of computer crime, the use of imprisonment and fines are the most likely punishments, although other forms of sentence may be appropriate in some circumstances.

Chapter 28

Computer fraud

Introduction

Computer fraud often makes headline news but it is thought that the number of cases of fraud detected and prosecuted is just the tip of the iceberg. Rumours abound about massive frauds which are not reported by the victims (usually large financial institutions) because of a fear of publicity. It does not help a bank's image of solid dependability to have employees prosecuted for computer fraud at regular intervals. All the major financial institutions throughout the world use computers to carry out their business and vast sums of money are transferred by computer (electronic funds transfer). As far as the criminal is concerned, the creation of an account in his own name, followed by instructions via a computer terminal to the main computer to transfer large sums into that account, is much more attractive than walking into a bank with a shotgun. There seems to be a feeling that to commit fraud by using one's own brains to defeat a computer system is something to be applauded and is not really serious crime. However, this form of crime causes great anxiety in the commercial world and is considered by the authorities to be very serious. The maximum penalties available are quite heavy and computer fraud can be dealt with by prison sentences of up to ten years.

Types of computer fraud

The phrase 'computer fraud' is used to describe stealing money or property by means of a computer: that is, using a computer to obtain dishonestly, property (including money and cheques) or credit or services or to evade dishonestly some debt or liability. It might involve dishonestly giving an instruction to a computer to transfer funds into a bank account or using a forged bank card to obtain money from a cash dispenser (automated teller machine).

The types of activities described as computer fraud can be considered to be of two main types: data frauds and programming frauds. In the first type, unauthorised data is entered into a computer, or data that should be entered is altered or suppressed. The main distinguishing factor in this type of fraud is that it is computer data, either input or output data, which is tampered with. Data fraud is probably the most common type of computer fraud (it is the most easily detected) and is relatively easy to carry out. The Audit Commission recognises four types of computer fraud (data fraud is sub-divided into three categories):

- input fraud,
- data fraud,
- output fraud, and
- program fraud.

To these a further form of fraud can be added, credit card fraud over the Internet, a rapidly growing concern. This is where a person uses someone else's credit card details to make a transaction over the Internet. Obtaining the credit card details may involve the interception of a transmission over the telecommunications network (itself a criminal offence under the Regulation of Investigatory Powers Act 2000) or where the criminal has set up a spoof e-commerce website and collected the details from persons, who believing it to be genuine, have ordered goods or services from the website and given their credit card details.

In the latest survey by the Audit Commission (*yourbusiness@risk: An Update on IT Abuse*, 2001), fraud was the fourth most common form of incident reported. Previously, fraud was the second most common activity reported but it has been overtaken by pornographic material and unauthorised use of computer facilities for carrying out private work (though the latter does not necessarily involve a criminal offence). Routine auditing procedures should eventually expose most input, data and output frauds but this is not necessarily true of program frauds which may remain undetected for a long period of time. The sub-species of frauds are described below. Unless otherwise indicated, examples are taken from an earlier Audit Commission report (*Survey of Computer Fraud and Abuse*, HMSO, 1991) which, unlike the later reports, contained substantial detail of individual incidents in an informative and entertaining supplement.

Entry of unauthorised instruction (input fraud)

This is the unauthorised alteration of data prior to it being input into a computer. Typically, an employee preparing data to be entered into a computer by another employee will make incorrect entries on the relevant document or form. The employee who enters the data into the computer may be an innocent agent or, in some cases, may be an accomplice of the first person or conspiring with him. It is an easy form of fraud to attempt and requires no particular computer skills. The only intelligence required to succeed is in knowing the organisation's checking and auditing systems thoroughly and matching the fraud up with any shortcomings in those systems. This is a strong argument for organisations to continually review, modify and enhance their auditing systems.

In one case the perpetrator gave incorrect data input forms to a clerk who then entered the data which related to debits to customer accounts. The perpetrator misappropriated the money concerned – £100,000. His actions were detected by internal audit and he was prosecuted under the Theft Acts 1968 and 1978, sentenced to four years' imprisonment and fined £10,000 (Audit Commission Survey, 1991, Supplement, p.12).

In another case, a local authority officer input fictitious invoices by accessing colleagues computer terminals which had been left unattended. His activities were detected during routine budget monitoring. He received six months' imprisonment and £11,000 of the £15,000 he had stolen was retrieved. Systems were improved and the local authority subsequently instructed staff to sign off when leaving their computer terminals unattended and system time-outs were introduced together with increased supervision (Audit Commission Survey, 2001, p.13).

Alteration of input data (data fraud)

In one case, a box office supervisor cancelled tickets which had been sold and then later resold them, keeping the cash. The box office supervisor falsified the audit trail but this was detected after problems with the software were investigated. The employee was prosecuted under the Theft Acts 1968 and 1978 and given six months' imprisonment (Audit Commission Survey, 1991, Supplement, p.38). In another case reported in the National Audit Office study a member of staff in an employment department entered false data in relation to a claim made by his brother resulting in the brother receiving girocheques to which he was not entitled for a total of £2933. The employee was dismissed and prosecuted and, on conviction, was sentenced to two months' imprisonment (National Audit Office, *IT Security in Government Departments*, HMSO, 1995, p.17).

Data fraud, as defined by the Audit Commission, differs from input fraud in that with data fraud it is the person entering the data into the computer that makes changes to the data. This form of fraud is also fairly common and is easily carried out, but it will be detected if appropriate checking procedures and auditing are adopted. Most organisations using computers are vulnerable to fraud perpetrated by employees preparing data for entry into a computer or authorised to enter data into a computer system and, consequently, care must be taken in the selection of such employees and an effective way of checking systems for the occurrence of fraud should be used, bearing in mind that an audit trail can be vulnerable.

Suppression of data (output fraud)

This particularly applies to output data – for example, printed reports generated by a computer system. These reports may be suppressed simply by tearing them up or not printing them out or, if printed, they may be altered. In either case, the motive will usually be to hide some criminal activity. For example, a person responsible for collecting money for a club might destroy a computer printout, which would indicate that he had kept some of the money collected. Concealing information can be a criminal offence. For example, in *Adams* v *The Queen* (unreported) 4 November 1994, two company directors by the use of offshore companies and bank accounts concealed information relating to secret profits they had made from the company they worked for. One of the directors brought an appeal to the Judicial Committee of the Privy Council against his conviction in New Zealand for conspiracy to defraud. His appeal was dismissed.

An example of this type of fraud is reported in the Audit Commission survey. A cashier who had taken money from her till destroyed daily audit rolls from each printer at her place of work thinking that this would make it impossible to trace her as the thief. Unfortunately for her, she was unaware that a computer file was also used to keep a record of transactions and this identified her as the culprit. She was sentenced to 18 months' imprisonment (Audit Commission Survey, 1991, Supplement, p.25).

Program frauds

The second form of computer fraud (as opposed to fraud involving data in one way or another) is more sophisticated and dangerous, and this is where someone alters a computer program to effect the fraud. Program fraud is much harder to detect than data fraud and reported examples are few and far between. We have to go back to the Audit Commission survey published in 1988 to find a good example. Two computer programmers wrote some stock accounting software and concealed a routine in the software which suppressed certain details in reports generated, in order to reduce value added tax liability (Audit Commission Survey, 1988, p.58). The software was designed for use in video-hire shops and the routine was activated by a special password. The software was sold to 120 shopkeepers although only 12 had been informed of the secret routine. These 12 had defrauded Customs and Excise of £100,000. Each of the programmers was prosecuted and convicted. They were each imprisoned for nine months and were fined a total of £34,000.

Another example of this form of fraud, which was discovered in Germany and made famous in the film *Superman III*, involved the alteration of a program to collect decimal fractions of financial transactions, such as half-cents which were normally rounded down and ignored. Instead, these fractions were placed in an account opened by the perpetrator of the fraud. This is known as a 'salami fraud' because it involves thin 'slices' of money.

Computer programmers, analysts and others involved in the commissioning or alteration of software present another source of danger in that many of them will have detailed knowledge about the security and password systems used and could pass such information on to persons intent on committing fraud. As a result of their knowledge of the computer systems, computer staff are also susceptible to involvement with would-be fraudsters.

Credit card fraud

Buying on-line, or over the telephone, is potentially safer for a fraudster than buying face to face. Apart from physically stealing someone's credit cards, other ways of obtaining credit card details include intercepting a transmission of information containing credit card details, setting up a spoof e-commerce site or hacking into an e-commerce website. In the *CSI/FBI Computer Crime and Security Survey*, 2002 p.5, an example given was that of a software bug in shopping cart software that potentially exposed all customer details on around 4000 websites. All the organisations using the software were warned directly by the FBI but one small e-commerce website failed to receive the warning. The Survey noted at p.6 that: 'credit card information is the single, most commonly traded, financial instrument for attackers. They can sell credit card info, use it to buy computers and equipment, trade it for other information ...' In 2002, the total loss for the 22 respondents able and willing to quantify their losses from fraud was $115,753,000.

In the United Kingdom, VISA reckon that on-line credit card fraud costs retailers about £55m per year. Small and medium-sized businesses are particularly vulnerable and have set up an early-warning scheme, sharing details of credit card scams amongst themselves. One problem of course is that dealing on-line has not carried the same guarantee of payment that usually applies to high street stores where the proper checks are carried out. However, this is now changing and an authentification scheme has been introduced which, provided all the procedures are properly carried out, will guarantee payment to small and medium-sized businesses using e-commerce (Hunt J, 'Beating the Fraudsters at their own Game', *The Guardian*, 31 October 2002).

In Europe, as a result of Directive 97/7/EC of the European Parliament and the Council of 20 May 1997 on the protection of consumers in relation to distance contracts, OJ L 144, 04.06.1997, p.19 (most of the provisions of which were implemented in the United Kingdom by the Consumer Protection (Distance Selling) Regulations 2000) a consumer has a right to cancel a payment involving fraudulent use of his card in relation to a transaction within the provisions or to be re-credited where payment has been made to the fraudster.

The computer as an unwitting accomplice

A computer system might be used to detect information which assists the criminal in the commission of his crime. For example, in the case of *R* v *Sunderland* (unreported) 20 June 1983, Court of Appeal, an employee of Barclay's Bank used the bank's computer to discover a dormant account and then forged the holder's signature to withdraw some £2100. The employee of the bank used the computer in a very simple way to detect an account which had not been used for a long period of time but which had some funds in it, a simple but effective way of stealing money although, eventually, the scheme was discovered when the holder of the dormant account attempted to make a withdrawal and discovered that the account contained less money than it should have done. The employee, who was of previous good character, was sentenced to two years' imprisonment, which was changed on appeal by the Lord Chief Justice who suspended 18 months of the sentence. He said:

> ... other people like bank clerks and bank officials need very little reminding that if they commit this sort of offence they will lose their job and go to prison, albeit for a comparatively short time.

This case illustrates the vulnerability of some computer systems to criminal activities. Of fundamental importance in the design of any computer system is the attention given to passwords and security, audit trails and the controls placed on employees.

Few of the activities described above require a great deal of computer expertise to carry out; often they will be committed by employees on low income engaged to perform relatively menial tasks such as data preparation and entry. Such frauds are fairly easy to detect by careful scrutiny, audits, spot-checks and occasional manual checks. Strong security measures will also have a major deterrent effect, especially if they are performed in a high-profile manner.

Fraud offences

When discussing computer fraud, the word 'fraud' can be a little misleading, and the activities commonly described as computer fraud can involve criminal offences other than those traditionally described as fraud. Fraud comprises a collection of similar offences such as obtaining property or services by deception, false accounting, false statements made by company directors, suppression of documents and income tax fraud including cheating. Most of these offences are covered by sections 15–20 of the Theft Act 1968 and sections 1 and 2 of the Theft Act 1978. Section 15A of the Theft Act 1968, obtaining a money transfer by deception, may also be relevant.

Income tax and value added tax fraud are dealt with by specific legislation such under the Finance Acts although the common law offence of cheating is still available for offences relating to the public revenue. Apart from this exception, cheating was abolished by section 32(1) of the Theft Act 1968. Certainly, some of these offences may be carried out using a computer, but it is with respect to those offences requiring deception that the greatest difficulty lies. Often, the most appropriate offence to charge is theft. Although theft (section 1 of the Theft Act 1968) is not normally considered to fall within the 'fraud' group of offences, there is an overlap between theft and fraud and, depending on the circumstances, a charge of theft might be more likely to lead to a successful prosecution. First, the deception offences will be considered.

Obtaining by deception

At first sight, the offence of obtaining property by deception (section 15 of the Theft Act 1968) seems to be most appropriate to computer fraud as the culprit usually means to obtain someone else's money or other property by a deception or trick – for example, by pretending to have authority to carry out some transaction on the computer such as transferring money. There is no problem stemming from the intangible nature of money, credits or cheques as section 4(1) of the 1968 Act states that property includes money and things in action. Bankers' cheques, money orders and bills of exchange are all examples of 'things in action'. This definition of property applies to the 1968 Act generally and therefore applies to section 15. There are several forms of deception provided for by the Theft Acts of 1968 and 1978 involving the obtaining of property or a pecuniary advantage or services, and the evasion of liability. So far as obtaining property by deception is concerned, section 15(1) of the Theft Act 1968 defines the offence as follows:

> A person who by any deception dishonestly obtains property belonging to another, with the intention of permanently depriving the other of it, shall on conviction on indictment be liable to imprisonment for a term not exceeding ten years.

Dishonesty is an important requirement and this affects the nature of the deception. The Theft Act 1968 further states that the deception can be 'deliberate or reckless', so if a person carelessly causes a computer system to transfer money into his own or a friend's account (an unlikely occurrence if he is no more than careless), he is not guilty of the offence as carelessness is not sufficient in this context, though recklessness is likely to be judged objectively.

In terms of computer fraud, the difficulty with this offence is that it requires a deception and this implies that it is an actual person that is being deceived, not a machine. In *DPP v Ray* [1974] AC 370, Lord Morris said:

> For a deception to take place there must be some person or persons who will have been deceived.

Other case law does not help very much and the question was left open in one case involving an automatic car park barrier (*Davies v Flackett* [1973] RTR 8). Bearing in mind that *DPP v Ray* was decided in the House of Lords, the better view is that the deception must work upon a human mind.

If a person gains access, whether with or without permission, to a bank's computer system and dishonestly instructs the computer system to transfer money from one account into another, then that person is 'deceiving' the computer or computer system: that is, he purports to have the authority to carry out such an act. Even if he has authority to transfer money from one account to another under normal circumstances as an employee would, that authority is nullified by his dishonesty. The main point is that it is the computer which is being 'deceived'. Under normal circumstances, no other human being is involved and, therefore, it would seem that the offence of obtaining property by deception is not made out. It would be different if, before the transfer was made, a message is displayed at someone's terminal requesting confirmation of the transfer. In that case, the other person would be subject to the deception as well as the computer and there should then be no difficulty related to the applicability of the offence of obtaining property by deception or any other offence involving deception.

The notion that a machine cannot be deceived is strengthened by the Theft Act 1978 which defines the offences of obtaining services by deception (services such as hiring a car or providing bed and breakfast) and evasion of liability by deception (such as where a debtor tells a lie to his creditor in order to let him off part or the whole of the debt) because the wording used strongly suggests that the deception must operate on the human mind. For example, section 1(1) states:

> A person who by any deception dishonestly obtains services from *another* shall be guilty of an offence [emphasis added].

This interpretation is reinforced by other language used in the statute. An example of obtaining services by deception in the context of computers is where a person makes an unauthorised use of a system which is normally paid for, such as LexisNexis. The problem of who has been deceived still exists, but if the person has deceived some other person by saying that he has permission to use the terminal used to access the system, then the offence of deception will have been made out under section 1 of the Theft Act 1978. There is a requirement for the services to be subject to payment, so the same act with respect to a 'free' service does not involve the offence – for example, if an unauthorised person dishonestly uses a computer system in a library to locate a particular book.

Obtaining a money transfer by deception

A new offence was inserted into the Theft Act 1968 as a result of the case of *R v Preddy* [1996] AC 815. Charges were brought against the accused persons under section 15 of the Theft Act 1968. They had made over 40 applications for mortgages by making false statements. Their plan was to use the money to buy houses with the intention of reselling them at a profit and redeeming the mortgages. They hoped to make a substantial profit as, at the time, property prices were rising quickly and there was something of a property boom. The lenders said that they would not have lent the money to the accused persons had they known the true motive for obtaining a mortgage. Some of the mortgage advances were made telegraphically or electronically, by electronic funds transfer, while others were made by cheque. The accused were convicted and their appeals to the Court of Appeal were dismissed.

The appeals to the House of Lords were allowed and the convictions were quashed. An account in a bank or building society is classed as a 'chose in action' (thing in action). As regards the telegraphic or electronic fund transfers, it was held that when payment was made from one bank or building society account in credit (the lender's account) to another bank account, the chose in action represented by the credit balance in the lender's account was extinguished or reduced and a new chose in action was created in the borrower's account (or the borrower's solicitor's account). Therefore, the borrower did not get the lender's chose in action. Consequently, the borrower did not obtain 'property belonging to another' as required by section 15(1) of the Theft Act 1968. The account itself, the chose in action, was not transferred to the borrower.

As regards the cheques, the chose in action represented by the cheque never belonged to the bank or building society as when it came into existence it belonged to the borrower – it was made out to the borrower or his solicitor who would then transfer the payment to the person selling the house. As the chose in action belonged to the borrower right from the start, no property belonging to another was obtained by the borrower. Although the cheque itself was a physical object (that is, the paper as opposed to the chose in action relating to the amount it was made out for) and was property belonging to another, the borrower did not obtain it permanently as it would be returned to be bank or building society after presentation to the borrower's bank (or his solicitor's bank). Therefore, even charging these persons with theft of the piece of paper on which the cheque was written would have been doomed to failure.

Section 15A of the Theft Act 1968 was inserted by section 1 of the Theft (Amendment) Act 1996 (it does not apply to Scotland but does to Northern Ireland, see the Theft (Amendment) (Northern Ireland) Order 1997). This provides that a person is guilty of an offence if by any deception he dishonestly obtains a money transfer for himself or another. A money transfer occurs when a debit is made to one account and a corresponding credit is made to another account and the credit results from the debit or the debit results from the credit. Both credit and debit relate to an amount of money and it does not matter if the credit and debit are exactly the same amount or whether the transfer results from the presentation of a cheque or by another method or whether there is a delay in the transfer process. Nor does it matter whether either account is overdrawn before or after the transfer. Under section 15B of the Theft Act 1968, deception has the same meaning as for section 15 and money includes money in currencies other than sterling. The maximum punishment is imprisonment for a term not exceeding ten years on conviction on indictment. It is reasonable to assume that dishonesty is a matter of satisfying the *Ghosh* test, discussed later under the section on theft.

The introduction of the section 15A offence was very welcome. In the light of *Preddy*, anyone who carried out a fraudulent electronic fund transfer could possibly have escaped conviction not only for obtaining property by deception but also for theft as that offence also requires that the property which is stolen belongs to another. The diminution of the victim's bank balance and the corresponding increase in the fraudster's bank balance would not be an obtaining (or, for theft, an appropriation) of property *belonging to another*. The importance of plugging this loophole was reflected in the speed with which the new offence was brought into force. Other offences could be relevant such as under the Computer Misuse Act 1990, and, if two or more persons were involved, the common law offence of conspiracy to defraud, as described below, would be appropriate.

To summarise, an essential element for the deception offences contained in the Theft Acts is that a human being has been deceived. In such a case, the deception could be simply a person claiming to have permission to use a computer system to gain access to a terminal or by pretending to be someone else. Some related offences such as false accounting, where 'deception' is not an element of the offence, should cause no additional problems merely because the offence was committed by or facilitated by the use of a computer system.

Conspiracy to defraud

Generally, a conspiracy is an agreement between two or more persons to carry out an unlawful act. Conspiracy may be statutory or common law. A statutory conspiracy is when a person agrees with another or others to embark upon a course of conduct which will necessarily amount to or involve a criminal offence by section 1 of the Criminal Law Act 1977, as amended. An example is where two persons agree to steal a computer; both will be guilty of a conspiracy to steal the computer even if they do not go on actually to steal it. Statutory conspiracy requires that the proposed act is itself a criminal offence and, in the case of obtaining by deception, difficulties remain relating to the concept of deceiving a machine, as discussed above.

However, at common law, the offence of conspiracy to defraud may be available. It appears that, in this context, 'deceit' is not an essential element of the offence and in *Scott v Metropolitan Police Commissioner* [1975] AC 819, Viscount Dilhorne said:

> ... 'to defraud' ordinarily means ... to deprive a person dishonestly of something which is his or of something to which he is or would or might but for the perpetration of the fraud be entitled.

In other words, it is not necessary to show that a person has been deceived. In the *Scott* case, the accused made an agreement with cinema projectionists to make copies of films being shown in the cinemas and to sell those copies for profit. The original films were borrowed overnight, copied and then returned the next day. It was held that it did not matter that no person had been deceived and the appeal against conviction was dismissed.

The common law offence of conspiracy to defraud is separate and distinct from the fraud offences in the Theft Acts, although in many cases, such as where two or more persons agree to obtain goods or services by impersonating others, the offence of conspiracy to defraud and offences under the Theft Acts will be committed if the course of action is carried through to its conclusion. The maximum penalty for conspiracy to defraud is ten years' imprisonment and/or a fine under section 12 of the Criminal Justice Act 1987.

The consequence is that if two or more persons agree to dishonestly operate a computer, perhaps entering a password they are not entitled to use, to transfer funds to their own accounts, they will be guilty of a conspiracy to defraud even though no human being has been deceived. Of course, a limitation of the scope of this offence is that it requires an agreement between two or more conspirators and it cannot apply when only one person is involved. Nevertheless, the offence is a useful weapon in the fight against computer fraud, especially if the act of transferring the funds in question is not completed and the circumstances are not sufficient to warrant a charge of attempting to steal. In the past, and particularly before the advent of the Computer Misuse Act 1990, the track record of conspiracy to defraud in terms of dealing with computer fraud was very good. Indeed, even now, it may be preferable to use this offence because of its inherent flexibility and freedom from the technicalities of the Computer Misuse Act. In one example, a junior bank clerk, in collusions with others, was imprisoned for five years after pleading guilty to conspiracy after trying to transfer £31 million to a bank account in Geneva (*Computing*, 2 March 1995, p.1).

Conspiring to sell counterfeit computer software and decoder boxes, even on a relatively small scale, resulting in losses hypothetically estimated at £24,000 is almost certain to pass the custody threshold. In *R v Bakker* [2001] EWCA Crim 2354, a computer engineer and serving policeman near retirement set up a business with two others, ostensibly to sell computer systems. The Court of Appeal reduced the sentences imposed at the Crown Court of 6 months and 12 months to 4 months and 8 months respectively. There were some special factors, for example, there was a long delay between arrest and sentencing and the policemen had lost his job, home and wife and suffered health problems.

At one time it was held that conspiracy to defraud and statutory conspiracy were mutually exclusive – that is, if the carrying out of the agreement would result in some offence being committed, however trivial, then a charge of conspiracy to defraud would be bad for duplicity. Section 12 of the Criminal Justice Act 1987 changed that rule and now it does not matter if carrying out the intended acts involves the commission of some other offence. The activities in the *Scott* case did not entail the commission of another offence. The conspirators were infringing copyright in a film, in those days a civil matter only. Now their activities would be a criminal offence under section 107 of the Copyright, Designs and Patents Act 1988 but this would no longer be fatal to a charge of conspiracy to defraud. Indeed, the conspirators could also be charged with a conspiracy to commit a section 107 offence.

Conspiracy is a useful offence where the planned offence has not been carried out or completed. It has become more useful now as it can apply to planned acts or events outside the United Kingdom as a result of the Criminal Justice (Terrorism and Conspiracy) Act 1998. It is a requirement that the act or event would be a criminal offence in the country where it was planned to happen and that the person charged or his agent did anything in the United Kingdom in relation to the agreement before its formation, became a party to it in the United Kingdom or did or omitted anything in the United Kingdom in pursuance of the agreement.

Attempts

To be charged with an attempt, the person involved must have done an act which is 'more than merely preparatory to the commission of the offence' (section 1 of the Criminal Attempts Act 1981). The scope of the law of attempts is uncertain when it comes to computer fraud but it does not apply to conspiracies. It could be argued that a computer fraud which is not completed is an attempt to steal money. However, it depends on how far towards the completion of the theft the fraudster got and whether any of his acts were more than merely preparatory. It has been argued that a criminal attempt occurs when the person concerned carries out an act penultimate to the commission of the offence, that is, the last act before completion. In the end, however, the question is one for the jury to decide being a question of fact.

Consider the case of an employee at a bank who decides, on his own, to transfer money to his own account from a customer's account. First, he switches on a computer terminal. Second, he enters the appropriate password to gain access. Then, he enters the instruction at the keyboard which causes the funds to be transferred. Finally, he draws the money out of the account. The problems arise when the bank employee fails to complete the offence of theft of the money for one reason or another. At what stage in the course of the events described do his actions become more than merely preparatory? A reasonable member of a jury might conclude that the offence of attempting to steal is not made out until the third act has been carried out – that is, the entry of instructions which cause the computer system to transfer the money to the employee's account.

Doubts about the applicability of the law of attempts in the context of uncompleted computer frauds were amongst the reasons why section 2 of the Computer Misuse Act 1990 was enacted. This creates an 'ulterior intent' offence, where someone commits the basic hacking offence with the intention of proceeding to commit a serious offence. Section 2 is discussed in Chapter 29.

Computer fraud as theft

It might seem from the above that, unless a conspiracy or attempt can be proved, a person who dishonestly convinces a computer that he is authorised to do something when he is not in fact so authorised, and makes the computer transfer money into his own bank account, commits an offence only if some other person has been deceived. Unless a human being has been subjected to the deception, it might seem that a charge of obtaining property by deception would not succeed. However, the criminal law is not so easily defeated. Usually, the offence of theft will be committed, regardless of the interposition of a computer. The offence of theft is defined in sections 1–6 of the Theft Act 1968 and section 1(1) states:

> A person is guilty of theft if he dishonestly appropriates property belonging to another with the intention of permanently depriving the other of it . . .

The words 'dishonestly', 'appropriates', 'property' and the phrases 'belonging to another' and 'with the intention of permanently depriving the other of it' all have special legal meanings which are set out in sections 2–6 of the Act. As far as computer crime is concerned, there is no real difficulty arising from the meanings of these words and phrases although the following points should be noted:

(a) the definition of 'property' is very wide and will cover most things that can be stolen with the aid of a computer, but land does not usually come within the meaning of property nor do wild mushrooms or flowers, fruit or foliage on a wild plant;
(b) property is deemed to 'belong to another' if that person has control of it or has any proprietary right of interest in it;
(c) 'appropriation' is the assumption of the rights of the owner;
(d) the 'thief' must intend to permanently deprive the other of the property; usually a mere 'borrowing' of an article is not theft, although it can be if, for example, it is for a very long period of time or if, when it is returned, there is no 'goodness' or value left in the property.

Point (d) above is quite interesting. What is the position if a person gains access to a bank's computer system, draws money from various accounts and puts the money into his own account for a few weeks, collecting interest on the money, and then transfers the money back from whence it came, less the interest earned? Although there has been an appropriation (the person involved has assumed the rights of the owners in respect of the money in the accounts), the account holders have not been permanently deprived of their money; it has merely been borrowed for a few weeks and what has been lost is the interest which the capital would have earned. Clearly, there is no theft of the capital which has been returned intact, but what about the interest – has this been stolen?

A case involving the borrowing of cinema films adds weight to the argument that a person who uses the computer to transfer funds temporarily into his own account does not commit the offence of theft. In *R v Lloyd* [1985] 2 All ER 661, a projectionist at a cinema, in association with two others, removed films from the cinema for a few hours so that they could be copied and then returned the films so that no one would know what had occurred. The pirated copies of the films were then sold, making a considerable profit for the pirates. A charge of theft (actually a conspiracy to steal in this case) was held to be inappropriate. As has been seen in the *Scott* case above, where the facts were very similar, a charge of conspiracy to defraud would have been more likely to secure a conviction.

In the *Lloyd* case, it was obvious that there was no intention permanently to deprive the owners of the films, nor was the copyright in the films stolen (it is not altogether clear whether copyright can be stolen). As mentioned earlier, borrowing can be theft if the period and circumstances are equivalent to an outright taking or disposal by section 6(1) of the Theft Act 1968, and this would be when the 'goodness' or 'virtue' in the thing taken had gone from it. Examples would include when a person borrows a radio battery intending to return it when it is exhausted, or borrows a bus pass intending to return it to the rightful owner when it expires. In the case of the films, however, there was still virtue in them when they were returned; they were still capable of being used and shown to paying audiences, so the pirates' convictions were quashed.

The fact that the owner of the copyright in the films had been deprived of potential 'sales' of the films by the circulation of pirate copies was not relevant to the offence of theft, but would it be relevant in a case of the temporary transferral of funds whilst interest is collected? Although the lawful owner of the money (or other things such as shares and investments) has been deprived of the interest or earnings, it would appear on the basis of *Lloyd* that the law of theft cannot be invoked. Nevertheless, the person borrowing the money could still be deemed to have an intention to permanently deprive the owner by section 6(1) of the Theft Act 1968. This is expressed in terms of treating the thing as one's own to dispose of regardless of the rights of the owner and borrowing or lending may amount to so treating it if, in the circumstances, it is equivalent to an outright taking or disposal. However, it is hard to know whether this would apply to a short-term borrowing without permission as section 6(1) has been described as 'gobbledygook'. Even if it is not equivalent to an outright taking or disposal, the owner may be able to get some relief by obtaining damages for conversion at civil law. Other criminal offences, such as unauthorised access to computer material, discussed in Chapter 29, may also be relevant.

The meaning of 'dishonesty' for the purposes of theft needs also to be considered. The test used, derived from the case of *R v Ghosh* [1982] QB 1053, has two elements:

- First, was what was done dishonest according to the ordinary standards of reasonable and honest people?

- Secondly, did the person involved realise that what he did was dishonest by those standards?

In the example above, where money is borrowed for a period of time for the purpose of collecting interest or as capital for a short-term investment, the second limb of the test could be difficult to prove beyond reasonable doubt as regards the obtaining of interest from the bank. Certainly, the actions as a whole are dishonest and should be criminal and it is likely that a jury would convict on the facts.

What if the money is borrowed for a very short period of time, however, and invested in a high-risk speculation which pays off and the borrower returns the capital and an amount to compensate for lost interest? There has been no intention to permanently deprive the owner of the capital. As far as the interest is concerned, that would seem to be a matter between the owner of the capital and his bank which is contractually bound to pay the interest. However, in *Chan Man-sin v Attorney-General for Hong Kong* [1988] 1 All ER 1, an accountant forged cheques drawn on company accounts and was charged with theft of the debt owed by the bank to the companies. The accountant argued that he had not committed theft because the companies had not been deprived of anything as the bank was contractually bound to the companies to replace the money. The Judicial Committee of the Privy Council rejected this argument because the accountant had purported to deal with company property regardless of the rights of the companies and that was within the meaning of an intention to permanently deprive the companies of their property.

Authority and consent

A person committing fraud may have authority to use the computer system concerned. An employee whose duties include entering data into a computer system may alter the data to effect the fraud. Here, the employee is doing no more than carrying out his duties, albeit fraudulently. However, as discussed in the following chapter, in a controversial case (*DPP v Bignall*), the court suggested that doing something authorised in an unauthorised way may still be deemed to be authorised. Fortunately, this case was effectively overruled soon after in *R v Bow Street Magistrates' Court and Allison (A.P.), ex parte Government of the United States of America* [1999] 4 All ER 1, also discussed in the following chapter.

In other cases, an employee who has permission to use a computer system might do things using the computer in a manner beyond his normal duties. How does the law of theft deal with such cases? The concept of authority or consent is an important one in theft, for how can a person steal something if he has permission to take the thing? In *R v Morris* [1984] AC 320, a case involving label-switching in a supermarket (that is, substituting one price tag with another stating a lower price), it was said that an unauthorised act was required for the appropriation necessary to constitute theft. Switching price labels is obviously not authorised by the supermarket. An employee who attempts to commit a fraud using computers will be doing something outside the scope of his authority to use the computer system: for example, the person employed to input data into a computer system does not have authority to enter false data. If the other elements of the offence are present, such as an intention to permanently deprive, then theft will be committed.

Another case which reinforces and expands this approach is *Lawrence v Metropolitan Police Commissioner* [1972] AC 626. An Italian visitor to England hired a taxi and at the end of the journey gave the taxi driver a £1 note for the fare. The taxi-driver said that this was not enough (the correct fare was just over £0.50) and proceeded to help himself to an additional £6 from the visitor's wallet which was still open. The defence argued that the money had been taken with consent but it was held that the prosecution did not have to prove that the taking of the money was without the victim's consent. This is considerably wider than the *Morris* case and it is difficult to reconcile the two. Even if the narrower view is taken, however, it is difficult to think of a case of computer fraud where the person will not be guilty of theft when he exceeds or otherwise compromises his authority to use a computer system. The fact that the computer system 'consents' to the transaction should not be relevant, as in *Lawrence*, because it is consent obtained by deception. The restriction of deception operating on a human mind should not be relevant in these circumstances. In *R v Gomez* [1992] 3 WLR 1067, the House of Lords confirmed that the wider approach in *Lawrence* is the correct one. Therefore, any assumption of the rights of the owner in respect to any property where it is done with consent obtained by deception can amount to an appropriation for the purposes of theft.

Other offences

Other offences which contain an element of fraud are provided for in the Theft Act 1968 – for example, false accounting (section 17), false statements by company directors, etc. (section 19) and the suppression of documents (section 20). There is nothing special about these offences in terms of computers except that their commission may be carried out with the aid of a computer.

The remaining part of the common law fraud-related offence of cheating is of interest. Cheating was abolished by section 32(1) of the Theft Act 1968, with the exception of cheating with respect to offences relating to the public revenue. If a person makes a false declaration concerning his income tax or value added tax, whether by using a computer or not, he will be guilty of the offence of cheating in addition to any offence under the Finance Acts. This dual liability is useful because there is a higher ceiling on the penalty available for cheating, which can consequently be used for more serious examples of revenue fraud. For example, in *R v Mavji* [1987] 2 All ER 758, the accused had evaded value added tax of over £1m and was charged with cheating; he was sentenced to six years' imprisonment and fined. If he had been charged under the Finance Act 1972, the longest sentence of imprisonment he could have received was two years. In the light of this case, it appears that no deception is required; the omission to make a tax return is sufficient. According to the Theft Acts, it appears that the offence of deception requires a human being to be deceived, but in the case of cheating there is no such requirement. This leads to the conclusion that if a person has a computerised accounts system which incorporates a value added tax report generator, then suppressing or altering computer reports, and consequent failure to submit a return or submitting a 'doctored' return, means that the offence of cheating has been committed and the fact that a computer has been used should not cause any difficulty.

A final possibility is that the fraudster may be prosecuted under the Computer Misuse Act 1990. The section 2 offence is particularly appropriate where the fraud has not been completed, with the advantage that, if there is insufficient evidence of intention, the court or jury (if tried in the Crown Court) can return a verdict of guilty under section 1 (the basic hacking offence). Even the section 3 offence may be applicable (unauthorised modification of computer material) and an example of a conviction for this in relation to fraud is given in the Audit Commission report, 1998. The Computer Misuse Act offences are discussed in the following chapters.

Chapter 29

Hacking – unauthorised access to computer material

The problem in perspective

Computer hacking is the accessing of a computer system without the express or implied permission of the owner of that computer system. A person who engages in this activity is known as a computer hacker and may be motivated by the mere thrill of being able to outwit the security systems contained in a computer. A hacker may gain access remotely, using a computer in his own home or office connected to a telecommunications network.

Hacking can be thought of as a form of mental challenge, not unlike solving a crossword puzzle, and the vast majority of hacking activities have been relatively harmless. Sometimes, the hacker has left a message publicising his feat and this reflects the popular image of a hacker – a young enthusiast who is fascinated by computers and who likes to gain access to secure computer systems to prove his skills to himself or his peers. At worst, this form of hacking is no more than a nuisance although, once it is known that a hacker has entered a computer system, the system manager may have to carry out a significant amount of work to confirm that the hacker has not modified or erased data. Many hackers are motivated by a sense of achievement; the very act of breaking into a computer system using their own mental effort is reward enough for them. There is a danger, however, that such 'innocent' hackers can cause damage to computer systems inadvertently and they may pave the way for other, more malicious, persons.

There is a more sinister side to computer hacking. Many computer systems concern what might be called 'high-risk' activities such as the control of nuclear power stations, defence systems, aircraft flight control and hospital records. These are known as 'safety-critical systems'. The dangers stemming from hacking into these systems are self-evident and the potential for terrorism is worrying. As terrorists are unlikely to be deterred by the criminal law, it is not just a matter of strengthening the law to deal with hackers. The key to overcoming the problems lies with those responsible for computer systems in these high-risk areas and it is essential that they do their utmost to make sure that the systems are as secure as possible. There is something to be said for the view that the enthusiastic young hacker has done the computer industry a great service by highlighting the deficiencies in the security aspects of many computer systems. Rather than subjecting these hackers to criminal proceedings, perhaps the computer industry should consider making use of their skill and expertise. In 1989, the co-founder of the Apple Computer Corporation made a donation to the University of Colorado for a computer hacking scholarship in the belief that it increased knowledge and understanding of computer systems.

Once the hacker has penetrated a computer system he might do one of several different things. He might read or copy information, which may be highly confidential, or he might erase or modify information or programs stored in the computer system, or download programs or data, or he might simply add something, such as a message boasting of his feat. He might be tempted to steal money or direct the computer to have goods sent to him, in which case what has been discussed in Chapter 28 in terms of computer fraud is relevant. By their very nature and relative susceptibility to unauthorised access, computer systems pose different problems to those encountered with information stored on paper. In the days before computers, sensitive information was kept locked away in filing cabinets in locked rooms on the premises of the organisation holding the data. This way the sensitive information was relatively safe from being tampered with or copied. The biggest threat would then come from employees but, burglars and industrial spies apart, persons outside the organisation would find it extremely difficult to gain access to the information. By contrast, information stored on a computer that is linked to a telecommunications system is much more vulnerable. It is analogous to information stored in paper files kept in locked cabinets but left in a public place. It is just a matter of finding the right key to fit the cabinet, and not only can a total stranger try the lock but, often, he can spend as long as he likes trying different keys with impunity until he finds one that turns the lock.

The House of Lords decision in the case of *R v Gold* [1988] 2 WLR 984 highlighted the problem of computer hacking and the ease with which it could be done. After the case, which was taken by many to indicate that computer hacking was not a criminal activity, the computer industry became most dissatisfied with the scope of the criminal law and the perceived lack of haste on the part of Parliament to act. Concern at this position led to the Law Commission Working Paper No. 110, *Computer Misuse* (HMSO, 1988), examining the scope of the law in terms of computer misuse generally and proposing alternative suggestions for legal changes directed at the problem of computer crime.

Emma Nicholson MP, now Baroness Nicholson of Winterbourne, introduced a private member's Bill to combat computer hacking in 1989 but withdrew it after a government promise to legislate in this area. That promise was broken and, in 1990, the late Michael Colvin MP brought in another private member's Bill on computer misuse, which was successfully steered through Parliament and became the Computer Misuse Act 1990. This Act did not restrict itself to computer hacking but also dealt with some other problems such as the law of attempts, unauthorised modification of computer programs and data, as well as addressing problems of jurisdiction and extradition. This chapter deals specifically with the basic hacking offence and ulterior intent offence following a discussion of the decision in *R v Gold*.

The case of *R v Gold*

Two computer hackers gained access into the British Telecom Prestel Gold computer network without permission and altered data. One of the accused also got into the Duke of Edinburgh's personal computer files and left the message:

GOOD AFTERNOON. HRH DUKE OF EDINBURGH

The two accused hackers were journalists who claimed that they had hacked into the network in order to highlight the deficiencies in its security. They were charged under the Forgery and Counterfeiting Act 1981 on the basis that they had made a false instrument within section 1. This states that a person shall be guilty of forgery if he makes a false instrument, with the intention that he or another shall use it to induce somebody to accept it as genuine, and by reason of so accepting it to do or not to do some act to his own or any other person's prejudice.

It was claimed that the false instrument was the CIN (customer identification number) and password. Section 8(1) of the Act states that a false instrument may be 'recorded or stored on disc, tape, sound track or other device'. However, their lordships suggested that 'recorded' or 'stored' connoted a process of a lasting and continuous nature from which the instrument could be retrieved in the future. In this case, the CIN and password were held only temporarily in the computer system while they were checked for validity and, after the check, they were eradicated totally and irretrievably.

The accused had been found guilty at Crown Court – one being fined £750 and the other £600 – but their convictions were quashed by the Court of Appeal and this was confirmed in the House of Lords. In the Court of Appeal, the Lord Chief Justice, Lord Lane, said that the acts of the accused in gaining access to the Telecom Gold files by what amounted to a dishonest trick were not criminal offences. In the House of Lords, Lord Brandon of Oakbrook said:

> The Procrustean attempt to force these facts into the language of an Act not designed to fit them produced grave difficulties for both judge and jury which we would not wish to see repeated. The appellants' conduct amounted in essence, as already stated, to dishonestly gaining access to the relevant Prestel data bank by a trick. That is not a criminal offence. If it is thought desirable to make it so, that is a matter for the legislature rather than the courts. We express no view on the matter.

If the defendants' convictions had been upheld, the only rational interpretation of the effect of section 1 in the circumstances was that the defendants had deceived a computer. Bearing in mind that, in terms of the Theft Act offences, it does not appear to be possible to deceive a machine, the decision in the *Gold* case was eminently sensible.

The basic hacking offence

Section 1 of the Computer Misuse Act 1990 is aimed directly at hackers who gain access to computer programs or data without any further intention to carry out any other act. It says that a person is guilty of an offence if:

- he causes a computer to perform any function with intent to secure access to any program or data held in any computer;
- the access he intends to secure is unauthorised; and
- he knows at the time when he causes the computer to perform the function that this is the case.

The intent does not have to be directed at any particular program or data or at programs or data of a particular kind or at programs or data held in any particular computer. The offence is triable summarily only (that is, in a magistrates' court) and the maximum penalty is imprisonment for a term not exceeding six months or a fine not exceeding level 5 (presently £5000) or both.

Section 17 of the Act contains definitions and other aids to interpretation but the Act does not define 'computer', 'program' or 'data'. Securing access is widely defined as causing a computer to perform any function, altering or erasing a program or data, copying or moving it to a different location in the storage medium in which it is held, using it or having it output from the computer in which it is held, and access to a program includes access to a part of a program. Note that the offence is made out if the hacker simply intends to make access regardless of whether he succeeds but he must know, at the time, that the access is unauthorised. Careless or reckless access will not suffice. Because copying is within the meaning of securing access, potentially it can be an offence under section 1 to make a pirate copy of a computer program or other software or to download an unauthorised copy of a computer program.

The language of section 1 is rather strange at first sight as it speaks of access to programs or data in *any* computer, presumably including the computer being used by the hacker. This has been subject to judicial scrutiny in *Attorney-General's Reference (No. 1 of 1991)* [1992] 3 WLR 432, in which a former employee went to visit his previous employer, a wholesale locksmith, to purchase some articles. While alone (an assistant had temporarily left the room), the ex-employee entered instructions into the computer effecting a 70 per cent discount on the articles he had bought. There was no need for him to use a password. At the trial, the judge said that the wording of section 1 required that a second computer had to be involved. This was rejected on appeal to the Court of Appeal, where it was held that the wording of section 1, given its plain and ordinary meaning, was not limited to the use of one computer with intent to gain access to another computer. The offence was made out even if only one computer was used.

There have been a number of successful prosecutions under section 1 of the Act, the first being in March 1991 when a man was fined £900 for making unauthorised calls to the United States using Mercury Communications equipment. Because 'computer' is not defined, it is likely to be given a generous meaning by the courts and can include equipment which has computer technology built into it although it would not normally be described as a computer.

A tremendous amount of publicity was generated by the acquittal of Paul Bedworth following his prosecution for conspiracy to commit offences under sections 1 and 3 of the Computer Misuse Act 1990 (for example, see *The Times*, 18 March 1993, p.3). The defence counsel argued that Bedworth was addicted to computer hacking and, as a result, he was not capable of forming the necessary intent to commit the offences charged. Although addiction, *per se*, is not a defence to a criminal charge (although it could be a mitigating factor when it comes to sentencing) the jury acquitted him. This raised concerns that the Act was not doing its job and there were calls for it to be strengthened, presumably by watering down the requirement for intention. This is unnecessary and would cause more problems and could result in the imposition of criminal liability on careless, clumsy or inept computer operators who, without meaning to, gained access to material they were not authorised to. The only sensible explanation of the Bedworth decision is that the jury probably felt some sympathy towards the accused. Perverse jury verdicts are not unknown. Two other hackers who had been charged along with Bedworth pleaded guilty and received six-month prison sentences. Altogether, the activities of the three hackers cost the victims hundreds of thousands of pounds.

It is certainly possible for employees to commit the basic hacking offence when using their own computer terminals at work if they intend to gain access to any program or data in respect of which they know they do not have authority to access. The concept of authority is strangely defined in section 17 in terms of being entitled to control access or having the consent of such a person. If the person is not so entitled and does not have the necessary consent, his intended access is unauthorised. Of course, the hacker must know this and the implication is that employers must make it quite clear to employees which programs and data they are entitled to access. This also applies to others such as pupils or students and self-employed consultants. Ideally, a written statement as to access entitlement should be issued.

Authorised access for an unauthorised purpose

An employee may have authorisation to use a computer system as a normal part of his duties to his employer. If the employee subsequently uses the system for an unauthorised use – for example, for his own purposes such as carrying out private work or retrieving information for other purposes unconnected with his employment – does the access become unauthorised for the purposes of the Computer Misuse Act 1990? An example of this form of unauthorised use is given by the Audit Commission. A nurse at a hospital had authorisation to use the patient administration system but used it to search for medical details relating to friends and relatives. She then discussed these details with other members of her family. The nurse was not prosecuted under the Act but given a written warning for this breach of patient confidentiality (Audit Commission, *Ghost in the Machine: An Analysis of IT Fraud and Abuse*, Audit Commission Publications, 1998, p.18).

Where authorised access is used for an unauthorised purpose, is that access authorised? It was held to be so in a surprising judgment in *DPP v Bignell* [1998] 1 Cr App R 1. Two police officers had used the police national computer to gain access to details of motor cars which they wanted for private purposes unconnected with their duties as police officers. They were charged with the unauthorised access to computer material offence under section 1 of the Computer Misuse Act 1990 and convicted at Bow Street Magistrates' Court but their appeals to Southwark Crown Court were allowed and this was confirmed by the Queen's Bench Divisional Court.

The sole issue was whether the access was authorised. The divisional court held that it was, even though the purpose of the access was not authorised. Whether access is unauthorised is defined in section 17(5) of the Computer Misuse Act 1990 in the following terms:

> Access of any kind by any person to any program or data held in a computer is unauthorised if –
> (a) he is not himself entitled to control access of the kind in question to the program or data; and
> (b) he does not have consent to access by him of the kind in question to the program or data from any person who is so entitled,
> but this subsection is subject to section 10.

Section 10 is simply a saving in respect of access carried out for purposes associated with any search warrant, etc.

The court decided that as the police officers were, in fact, entitled to control access to the material within section 17(5) they were authorised to access the computer data even if this was for an unauthorised purpose. As part of their normal duties, the police officers were entitled to access such computer information. But being entitled to access computer material is not the same as being entitled to control access to such material. This is an important and crucial distinction which the court failed to make.

This was a worrying decision which left an unsatisfactory gap in the Computer Misuse Act 1990. The judge drew support for his view of the Act from the Law Commission Working Paper No. 110, *Computer Misuse* (1988), which suggested that it would be undesirable for the hacking offence to extend to an authorised user who is using the computer for an unauthorised purpose. The Working Paper was far from unambiguous and put forward various options for dealing with computer misuse in all its various forms. It went on to give an example of a situation which should not be criminalised: where a word processor operator uses the office computer to produce private correspondence. That is not the type of behaviour at which section 1 of the Computer Misuse Act 1990 was directed and this is confirmed by the White Paper which preceded the Act (Law Com. No. 186, *Criminal Law: Computer Misuse*, 1989). This specifically acknowledged that employees may be liable for the basic hacking offence and stated (paragraph 3.35):

> The thrust of the basic hacking offence is aimed at the 'remote' hacker, but the offence is apt to cover the employee or insider as well. For that reason it is particularly important ... that (in addition to defining 'access' to exclude merely physical access to the computer itself) the *mens rea* of the offence should catch only the case where the employee consciously and deliberately misbehaves.

Fortunately, this aspect of *DPP v Bignell* was soon reversed in the House of Lords. In *R v Bow Street Magistrates' Court and Allison (A.P.), ex parte Government of the United States of America* [1999] 4 All ER 1, the House of Lords considered the concept of authorisation in the context of the Computer Misuse Act 1990. In that case, an employee of American Express in Florida, as part of her duties, was authorised to access specific customer accounts. However, she also accessed other accounts without authority and passed on confidential information, enabling counterfeit credit cards to be made, to a number of persons including Mr Allison. Altogether, as a result of these activities, American Express lost around $1m. Mr Allison was arrested in London in possession of counterfeit credit cards. An application to extradite Mr Allison to the United States was made on the basis of three allegations, the first two which involved a conspiracy to commit offences falling within section 2 of the Computer Misuse Act 1990 – the magistrate refused to commit Mr Allison. The third allegation, unauthorised modification of computer material, resulted in a committal. Then, Mr Allison brought *habeus corpus* proceedings on the basis that none of the offences were extradition crimes. Eventually a question of law of general public importance was certified for the House of Lords being:

> Whether, on a true construction of s.1 (and thereafter s.2) of the Computer Misuse Act 1990, a person who has authority to access data of the kind in question none the less has unauthorised access if
> (a) the access to the particular data in question was intentional,
> (b) the access in question was unauthorised by a person entitled to authorise access to that particular data,
> (c) knowing that the access to that particular data was unauthorised.

Thus, the main issue was whether the employee of American Express in Florida had the requisite authority under the Computer Misuse Act 1990.

The House of Lords confirmed that the offences were extradition offences, being clearly added to the list of extradition offences by section 15 of the Computer Misuse

Act 1990. As regards the issue of authorisation, Lord Hobhouse, with whom the other four Law Lords agreed, criticised *DPP* v *Bignell* in respect of the interpretation of the concept of authorisation. He said that the judge in that case had fallen into error by considering authorisation in relation to programs or data *of a particular kind* (control of the computer at a particular level) when what the Computer Misuse Act required was to consider authorisation in relation to a *particular program or to particular data*. Lord Hobhouse said:

> Nor is s 1 of the Act concerned with authority to access kinds of data. It is concerned with authority to access the actual data involved.

Although the employee had authority to access the kind of data that she accessed, as part of her normal duties, she did not have authority to access the particular data she did access, as such access was made with a view to conspiring with others to commit theft and forgery. This is equivalent to saying that authorisation to access computer material does not extend to accessing computer material for an unauthorised purpose.

Failing to log out of a computer network when leaving the computer is very common. What is the position if someone else comes along later and uses the computer to gain access to material? What if the material accessed could be said to be in the public domain to the extent that it is freely available to anyone with an internet connection? In *Ellis* v *DPP* [2001] EWHC 362 (Admin), Ellis was an ex-student of Newcastle University and a member of the University's Alumni Association. He used non-open access computers at the University to browse websites. The computer had been left logged on by previous users. He had been told by an administrative officer that he did not have permission to use non-open access computers and he said in a tape-recorded interview with a police officer that he had used the computers and that he did not have a password to use them. He also admitted using a computer that had been left logged on to access websites. The Magistrates' Court convicted Ellis on three counts of unauthorised access to computer material under section 1 of the Computer Misuse Act 1990.

A claim that the evidence presented before the magistrates was not sufficient and should, for example, had included direct evidence that the use fell within section 1 and of the lack of authorisation, going beyond the administration officer's and police constable's verbal evidence was rejected by the Divisional Court of the Queen's Bench Division. It was accepted that section 1 of the Computer Misuse Act 1990 was wide enough to encompass the behaviour supported by such evidence as was available. Ellis failed to turn up to the hearing and, consequently, the decision was suspended for 21 days to give him an opportunity to make further submissions. Eventually, he did but they were without merit and the decision was confirmed in *Ellis* v *DPP* [2002] EWHC 135 (Admin). A claim that what he had done was analogous to picking up a discarded newspaper and reading it was rejected (unlike unauthorised access to computer material this is not criminalised in any case) and an attempt to rely on the *R* v *Bow Street Magistrates* case above could not help Ellis as it pointed the other way and weakened his case still further.

The ulterior intent offence

Apart from hacking pure and simple, other problems were identified by the Law Commission. The law of attempts was of uncertain application to computer fraud and it did not seem that a person who obtained services without permission using a computer committed a significant offence. Of course, if two or more persons were involved a charge of conspiracy to defraud might be apposite but, otherwise, there were problems. Section 2 of the Computer Misuse Act 1990 covers these situations and also provides an alternative and, perhaps, better route to conviction where other offences are intended by the hacker. The section 2 offence is described in the Act as unauthorised access with intent to commit or facilitate the commission of further offences. It is a preliminary offence, particularly useful where the offence to which the ulterior intent applies is not completed. Another way of looking at it is to say that it is an aggravated form of the basic hacking offence.

The further offence must be one for which the sentence is fixed by law (for example, murder or high treason) or one for which the maximum sentence is not less than five years. Thus, section 2 applies to theft, blackmail, obtaining property or services by deception, obtaining a money transfer by deception and a great many other offences, all having maximum punishments of five or more years' imprisonment. If the further offence is completed, then that offence or an equivalent will normally be charged but section 2 is useful where, for one reason or another, this is not the case. An example is where a hacker attempts to gain access to a computer with the intention of sending a blackmail message to someone but is not able to get beyond the log-on screen. It is unlikely that a charge of attempted blackmail will succeed because he has not done an act which is more than merely preparatory, but a charge under section 2 will be more likely to result in a conviction providing the necessary intentions and knowledge can be proved – that is:

- the intention to secure access;
- the knowledge that the access is unauthorised; and
- the intention to commit blackmail.

Of course, proving the ulterior intent may be very difficult if the accused has only gone part-way to completing the further offence.

The ulterior intent offence is triable either way and carries a maximum penalty of five years' imprisonment and/or a fine if tried in the crown court. Any person who is tried for a section 2 offence (or a section 3 offence) in the Crown Court can, if found not guilty, be found guilty by a jury of the section 1 offence and sentenced accordingly (section 12). A person can be found guilty of a section 2 offence even if the commission of the further offence is impossible: for example, where a hacker intends to erase details of a debt he owes when the person to whom the debt is owed has already written it off or if the hacker is mistaken about owing the debt in the first place.

The section 2 offence applies whether the accused intends to commit the further offence or whether he intends to facilitate the commission of the offence by another person. A custodial sentence is likely. In *R v Delamare* [2003] EWCA Crim 424, the offender, Delamare, worked for Barclays Bank in Poole. He was approached by an old school-friend, X, to whom he owed a favour, to disclose details of certain bank accounts. A cousin of X put pressure on the offender and he eventually gave in. The cousin of X and another person, who impersonated one of the owners of the bank accounts, were later charged and pleaded guilty to obtaining property by deception and were given community punishment orders. Delamare pleaded guilty to two charges of the section 2 offence and was sentenced to 8 months' detention in a Young Offender Institution. He appealed against his sentence on the grounds of disparity as the others only received non-custodial sentences. The Court of Appeal was not persuaded by the disparity argument. The trial judge had been fully aware of the other sentences and Delamare had acted in breach of trust. Giving the judgment of the Court of Appeal, Mr Justice Jackson said (at paragraph 8):

> **Bank customers must be able to open accounts and to carry on their banking affairs in full confidence that their private details will not be disclosed to outsiders. It must be clearly understood that breaches of trust by bank officials of the kind which occurred in this case are likely to attract prison sentences.**

However, taking into account the guilty plea, his previous good character and the relative youth of Delamare, the sentence was reduced to four months' detention in a young offender institution. As in *Delamare*, it matters not if the further offence is to be committed on another occasion to the authorised access offence.

In *Delamare*, the further offence was carried out by others but again this is not a problem as it is sufficient if the intention is to facilitate the commission of the further offence, whether by the person committing the unauthorised access offence or by any other person. One potential difficulty is where the further offence, as a matter of law, cannot apply. Imagine that a person hacks into a computer with the intention of obtaining a service by entering someone else's details and password. Under section 1 of the Theft Act 1978, it is an offence for a person, by any deception, to dishonestly obtain services from another. The reference to 'another' makes it clear that a person must have been deceived. As that offence carries a maximum of five years' imprisonment, it is one of the ulterior offences for the purposes of section 2 of the Computer Misuse Act 1990. However, if no person has been deceived and the only 'deception' has been that in respect of entering unauthorised information to the computer, it appears that the section 1 offence cannot be made out. If the person succeeds in obtaining the services in question, there is no equivalent offence of theft of a service. This explains why section 2(4) of the Computer Misuse Act 1990 states that a person may be guilty even if the commission of the further offence is impossible. This could apply, for example, where a person intends to steal property by his unauthorised access offence but it turns out that the property actually belongs to him and he mistakenly thinks it belongs to another or if the property does not exist. In such cases, one of the essential elements of the offence is missing. There is some doubt about the offence of obtaining services by deception as being within section 2(4). As one cannot deceive a machine for the purposes of the deception offence, there is no operable deception and, hence, no obtaining of the service by deception. The offence is not just impossible, it is wholly inapplicable. In the case of the theft example, the offence is impossible but it is still applicable as one could say that the offence would have been made out *but for the fact the property no longer belongs to another or no longer exists*. For deception offences, deception is the essence of the offence whereas for theft, the question of whether the property belongs to another, for example, is one of the five elements of the offence which must normally be proved for the offence to be made out.

Jurisdiction

The international character of some computer crime has caused concern about the possibility of criminals escaping prosecution because of jurisdictional issues. For example, in *R v Tomsett* [1985] Crim LR 369, the accused sent a telex from London intending to divert funds from New York to the accused's account in Geneva. It was held in the Court of Appeal that, had the attempt been successful, the theft would have taken place in New York and the English courts would not have had jurisdiction to try the perpetrator. To prevent this type of problem (making it tempting for fraudsters to set up in England to carry out frauds abroad using computers and telecommunications systems), the Computer Misuse Act contains complex provisions relating to jurisdiction and extradition in sections 4–9 (some parts of section 7 and section 8 have been repealed). All that is required is a link with the home country – England and Wales, Scotland or Northern Ireland, as appropriate. That is, the offence must either originate from the home country or be directed to a computer within it: for example, a person from within England attempts to carry out a computer fraud in Sweden or a person from Italy attempts to hack into a computer located in London.

A final requirement is that of double criminality; that is, if the person operates from within any of the home countries intending to commit a further offence under section 2 in a different country, that offence is indeed a criminal offence in that other country as well as in the home country. Of course, in most cases this will not present any problems – most countries recognise theft and fraud.

Conspiracy to commit an offence under the Computer Misuse Act 1990, for example, where two or more persons agreed to release a computer virus, could be tried in England and Wales even if the virus was intended to be placed on a computer outside England and Wales provided the accused or his agent did anything in England in relation to the agreement before its formation, became a party to it in England and Wales or did or omitted anything in England and Wales in pursuance of the agreement, subject to the double criminality rule. This principle has been extended to all offences of conspiracy under section 1 of the Criminal Law Act 1977 and in respect of the whole of the United Kingdom (with necessary modification for Scotland and Northern Ireland) by virtue of section 5–7 of the Criminal Justice (Terrorism and Conspiracy) Act 1998. The act or event planned must also be an offence under the law in force in the other country or territory in which it is planned to take place and it is immaterial how that offence is described in that other jurisdiction.

Other offences associated with hacking

Although it is to be expected that the Computer Misuse Act 1990 will be the main weapon in the fight against computer hacking (and some other forms of computer misuse), certain other areas of criminal law may be relevant. It is possible that these other offences will apply in situations outside the scope of the 1990 Act: for example, there could be a problem in proving that the hacker knew that his access was unauthorised. In such a case, recourse must be had to the pre-existing law and the possibilities are discussed below.

The law of theft

As we have seen, the offence of theft is defined by section 1 of the Theft Act 1968 as a dishonest appropriation of property belonging to another with the intention to permanently deprive the other of it. If a hacker gains access to a computer system without permission and then makes a printout of some information contained therein, has he committed theft? The fact that the owner of the information has not been deprived of it, because the hacker has only made a copy, is fatal to any charge of theft.

In *Oxford* v *Moss* (1978) 68 Cr App R 183, it was held that confidential information does not come within the definition of property for the purposes of theft. The case concerned the 'borrowing' of an examination paper by a student before the date of the examination. Although the authority of the case is weak, having been decided at first instance only, it is likely that it would be followed because the consequences of the decision are fundamentally sensible. After all, the owner still has the information unless the only copy was taken, but this is different from saying that the information is not property for the purposes of the Theft Act. Property is defined as including 'money and all other property, real or personal, including things in action and other intangible property' and it could fairly be argued that confidential information comes within the meaning of 'other intangible property'. A better construction of *Oxford* v *Moss* is that the taking of the examination paper could not be theft because there was no intention to deprive the owner of it permanently. For this reason a hacker who simply reads or copies information has not committed theft. Similarly, in the Scottish case of *Grant* v *Procurator Fiscal* [1988] RPC 41, an employee who offered copies of his employer's computer printouts to a competitor for £400 was acquitted. It was said that there was no authority for the proposition that the dishonest exploitation of the confidential information was a criminal offence.

If the information concerned is copied on to paper belonging to someone else, such as an employer, there will be an offence of theft committed with respect to the paper. Likewise, if a person copies information from a computer on to a disk which belongs to someone else and takes the disk, this would be theft of the disk if the other elements of theft are present such as the intention to permanently deprive the owner of the disk.

If the hacker goes further and not only makes a copy of the information but then, immediately after, goes on to erase the original from the computer system, is this more likely to be viewed as theft? An act of deliberate erasure will almost certainly be an offence under section 3 of the Computer Misuse Act 1990, as discussed in Chapter 30. In terms of theft, there will be a dishonest appropriation of property belonging to another, but is there an intention to permanently deprive the owner of that information? The difficulty here will be if the hacker believes that the owner has another copy of that information, for, if he does so believe, there is no intention to permanently deprive. In the world of computers, back-up copies of programs and data are the rule and it would be very reasonable for the hacker to believe that back-up copies have been made. Therefore, it would appear that unauthorised copying, even coupled with the subsequent destruction of the original, is unlikely to be theft.

There is an offence in the Theft Act 1968 which holds out some promise and that is the offence of dishonestly abstracting electricity. The very act of hacking will result in the host computer (the computer hacked into – accessed without permission) performing work as it retrieves information from its store. If that information is stored on magnetic disks, the disk drive heads will physically move, tracking across the disks, locating and then reading the information which will then be moved into the computer's volatile memory by means of tiny electrical currents. More electricity will be consumed in transmitting the information to the hacker's computer terminal. The total amount of electricity used to perform these acts will be small but, nevertheless, a definite amount will have been used as a result of the hacker's actions.

Section 13 of the Theft Act 1968 describes the offence of abstracting electricity as its dishonest use without due authority, or its dishonest waste or diversion. The offence is committed regardless of the amount of electricity so used and the only difficulty concerns the concept of dishonesty. There is no definition of dishonesty in the Theft Act 1968 for the purposes of section 13, but case law provides some guidance. The test of dishonesty which is used for the offences of theft and obtaining by deception derives from the case of *R v Ghosh* [1982] QB 1053, and there is no reason to doubt that the same test would apply to the offence of abstracting electricity. This test has already been described in the context of fraud in Chapter 28. Ultimately, the test must be resolved by the magistrates or by the members of a jury and whilst they probably consider, objectively, that hacking was dishonest, it might be more difficult to decide whether the accused hacker would realise that what he was doing was dishonest by the ordinary standards of reasonable and honest persons, the second limb of the *Ghosh* test.

Communications offences

Section 1 of the Regulation of Investigatory Powers Act 2000 makes it an offence to intentionally and without lawful authority intercept in any part of the United Kingdom any communication in the course of its transmission by means of a public postal service or public communications system. The interception of a communication in the course of its transmission in a private communications system is actionable under civil law at the suit of the sender or recipient, though this does not apply to the person with a right to control the operation or use of the system or some other person having the former person's consent. Interception of a communication during its transmission by means of a telecommunications system is defined in terms of modifying or interfering with the system or its operation, monitoring transmissions made by means of the system or monitoring transmissions made by wireless telegraphy to or from apparatus comprised in the system so as to make all or part of the contents of the communication available, during its transmission, to a person other than the sender or intended recipient of the communication. Presumably the person modifying, interfering or monitoring may also be the person to whom the communication has been made available. These offences only apply to a case where, for example, a hacker actually intercepts something (for example, the transmission of computer data over the BT network). In most cases, the hacker will initiate the transmission and will cause the sending of the information. This offence therefore applies only to the situation where the hacker is 'eavesdropping': that is, listening in for interesting communications to intercept. The maximum penalty on conviction on indictment is two years' imprisonment and/or a fine.

Section 43 of the Telecommunications Act 1984 makes it a criminal offence to transmit messages which are grossly offensive, indecent, obscene or menacing by means of a public telecommunications system. Similarly, an offence is committed if false messages are sent by a person knowing of their falsity, or persistent use is made of the system for the purpose of causing annoyance, inconvenience or needless anxiety. The Act refers to messages, so if a pornographic diagram or picture is sent by the hacker, the offence might not be applicable. It could be argued, however, that a picture is just another way of conveying a message, in which case section 43 of the 1984 Act would apply. In some cases, there may also be offences under the various statutes covering obscene publications and pornography, particularly in respect of child pornography, as discussed in Chapter 32.

Menacing messages could be linked to the offence of blackmail (see Chapter 30) where the threat itself is transmitted by such means. The threat could concern the computer system – for example, where someone threatens to destroy information stored on the computer system. Alternatively, the threat may be of a less technical nature – for example, a threat to inform the IT manager's wife of his adultery. This offence under the Telecommunications Act will only be committed where a public system is used. It would appear that a hacker who sends just one false message will commit the offence if he knows that the message is false and transmits it for one of the purposes mentioned – for example, to cause annoyance. The same applies if the hacker persistently sends messages, whether true or false, with any of the motives mentioned above. Another possibility is a prosecution under the Protection from Harassment Act 1997, for example, if messages which cause alarm or distress are sent. A course of conduct is required, meaning more than one occasion.

Data Protection Act 1998

This Act is described more fully in Part Five. However, there may be some scope for the Act in terms of computer hacking and therefore this aspect will be discussed briefly here. The Data Protection Act 1998 regulates the use and storage of personal data – that is, information relating to individuals who can be identified from that information.

A 'data controller' is a person who processes personal data and must notify the Information Commissioner if the processing is carried out by automatic means. Failure to notify is a criminal offence, triable either way, carrying an unlimited fine if tried in the crown court, or a fine not exceeding the statutory maximum if tried in a magistrates' court.

If a computer hacker gains access to a computer system on which personal data is stored and then makes a copy of that data which he stores in his own computer, the hacker is guilty of the offence of processing personal data without having notified the Commissioner. There are a number of other offences under the Act, such as obtaining or disclosing personal data without the consent of the data controller or procuring the disclosure of personal data, for which see Part Five of this book.

Chapter 30

Unauthorised modification of computer programs or data

The law before the 1990 Act

Prior to the Computer Misuse Act 1990, damage or erasure of computer programs or data was an offence under the Criminal Damage Act 1971. By section 1(1) of that Act, a person is guilty of an offence if, without lawful excuse, he destroys or damages any property belonging to another. The definition of the offence required that the person intended such consequences to occur or was reckless as to whether property would be so destroyed or damaged. In the case of *R v Caldwell* [1982] AC 341, it was held that whether a person had been reckless was an objective test – that is, whether the course of action undertaken by the accused created what would be an obvious risk of damage in the eyes of the ordinary prudent individual.

One potential difficulty with the Act is that property must be destroyed or damaged and property is defined by section 10 as meaning tangible property. This creates an immediate problem when programs or data stored on magnetic media such as a disk are erased. Programs or data are not tangible in this form, although the disk itself certainly is. The first case to tackle this apparent difficulty was *Cox v Riley* (1986) 83 Cr App R 54, in which the accused erased programs from a printed circuit card used to control his employer's computerised saw for cutting out timber sections for window frames. He was charged with criminal damage but argued that the programs were not tangible property within the meaning of the Act. Nevertheless, he was found guilty on the basis that the printed circuit card had been damaged and was now useless. It would require some work in reprogramming it before it could be restored to its former condition.

The 'mad hacker'

The Court of Appeal had an opportunity to examine the applicability of criminal damage when it heard the appeal against conviction of the self-styled 'mad hacker'. In *R v Whiteley* (1991) 93 Cr App R 381, the accused gained unauthorised access to the Joint Academic Network (JANET) and gave himself the status of Systems Manager. He deleted and added files, changed passwords and deleted audit files recording his activities. He was very skilled and even deleted a special program inserted to trap him. His activities caused serious disruption and he was convicted of damaging computer disks. The Court of Appeal rejected his appeal confirming that the value of the disks had been impaired. The Lord Chief Justice, Lord Lane, said that the Act required that tangible property had been damaged, not that the damage itself should be tangible.

The appeal in *R v Whiteley* had been heard after the Computer Misuse Act 1990 came into force but had to be decided on the basis of the prior law. The 1990 Act provides that, for the purposes of the Criminal Damage Act 1971, a modification of the contents of a computer is not to be regarded as damaging any computer or computer storage medium, unless its effect on that computer or storage medium impaired its physical condition (Computer Misuse Act 1990, section 3(6)). This is to try and remove any overlap between the unauthorised modification offence under the Computer Misuse Act 1990 and the Criminal Damage Act 1971.

Current position under the Criminal Damage Act 1971

It would seem that the 1971 Act no longer applies to damage of programs and data stored in a computer. In R v *Whiteley*, however, the conviction was based on the fact that the state of the magnetic particles on the disks had been altered. These particles, it could be argued, are tangible even if they are not visible. This point may be of academic interest only as it is unlikely that a charge would be brought under the Criminal Damage Act 1971 in respect of damage to programs or data; the 1990 Act would be used instead. There is one occasion, however, when the 1971 Act might be helpful and that is when the accused denies an intention to cause damage because, under the 1971 Act, objective recklessness suffices. It goes without saying that a hacker moving around in a strange computer system without training or the appropriate documentation is being objectively reckless.

Unauthorised modification under the Computer Misuse Act 1990

One of the reasons for the replacement of criminal damage in relation to computer pro-grams and data stored in a computer or on computer storage media was that there were doubts about the logical validity of the approach adopted in *Cox* v *Riley*. Section 3 of the Computer Misuse Act 1990 was intended to put the matter beyond doubt and states that a person commits an offence if:

> ... he does any act which causes an unauthorised modification of the contents of any computer; and at the time when he does the act, he has the requisite intent and the requisite knowledge.

The meaning of 'authority' applies in a way similar to that in relation to the section 1 offence – the modification is unauthorised if the person causing it is not entitled to determine whether the modification should be made and he does not have the consent of any person who is so entitled. Similar considerations in respect of authorisation ought to apply here as in relation to the basic unauthorised access offence, as clarified in R v *Bow Street Magistrates' Court and Allison (A.P.), ex parte Government of the United States of America* [1999] 4 All ER 1. Thus, authorisation to make particular modifications should not extend to a particular modification made in excess of that authorisation, unless it is a natural consequence of making an authorised modification.

'Modification' is extensively defined in section 17, the interpretation section, as the alteration or erasure of any program or data or the addition of any program or data to the contents of a computer. The latter covers situations where someone leaves messages on a computer without authority (a form of computer graffiti perhaps) or the situation where a person introduces a computer virus into the system. It clearly covered the activities of the person who distributed disks claiming to contain advice for the prevention of AIDS; after using one of these disks, data files on the computer were made inaccessible and a message was displayed asking for money in return for a cure. The culprit was arrested in the United States and convicted of blackmail.

For the purposes of section 3, the requisite intent is under section 3(2) an intent to cause a modification to the contents of any computer:

(a) to impair the operation of any computer,
(b) to prevent or hinder access to any program or data held in any computer, or
(c) to impair the operation of any program or the reliability of any data.

It is immaterial whether the intent is directed at any particular computer, program or data or programs or data of a particular kind or at any particular modification or any modification of any particular kind. The requisite knowledge is knowledge that the intended modification is unauthorised.

Adding data to a computer is within the definition of modification. If a person adds information to a computer disk without authorisation does that mean that the person has the requisite intent? If the information is correct it would seem unlikely as that should not impair the operation of the computer, prevent or hinder access to any program or data held in any computer or impair the operation of any such program or the reliability of any such data. This would apply, for example, where an unsolicited e-mail has been sent. Of course, the situation could be different if large numbers of unwanted e-mails were received from the same person which had the effect of clogging up the computer disk or degrading its performance.

If information is added without authorisation and which is factually incorrect to some extent, it appears that it will be easier to find the requisite intent as this will impair the reliability of data held on the computer. In *Re Yarimaka* [2002] EWHC 589 (Admin), the Divisional Court of the Queen's Bench Division rejected an application for *habeus corpus* made by two persons facing extradition to the United States in respect of four charges of blackmail, one offence of conspiracy to commit an offence under section 2 of the Computer Misuse Act 1990 (the ulterior offence being blackmail) and a conspiracy to commit an offence under section 3 of the Computer Misuse Act 1990 in relation to computer material located in New York. Bloomberg LP was a company supplying financial information all over the world and had around 143,000 clients, many of which were financial institutions. Michael Bloomberg founded the company and, at the time of the case, still played an active role as director. In 1999, Bloomberg LP provided database services to a company in Kazakstan, of which one of the applicants for *habeus corpus*, Oleg Zezov, was an employee.

Oleg Zezov and Igor Yarimaka gained unauthorised access to Bloomberg's computer and accessed highly confidential information. E-mails were sent to Michael Bloomberg and the head of security saying that the security of their computer system had been compromised and that they wanted $200,000 or they would inform Bloomberg's clients which would result in a loss of confidence. The e-mails were purported to be from someone named 'Alex'. The United States government claimed that Zezov and Yarimaka offered to show Bloomberg how they had compromised the computer system. Eventually, arrangements were made for Michael Bloomberg to meet Zezov and Yarimaka at a London hotel. The room had been fitted with surveillance equipment by the FBI and Scotland Yard. Zezov and Yarimaka were later arrested. Defence counsel raised a specific argument that section 3(2), defining the requisite intent, did not apply. It was said that the purpose of the offence in section 3 was to confine the offence to those who damaged a computer so that it no longer accurately recorded information fed into it. If accurately fed in information was untrue, that does not impair the operation of any computer, nor does it prevent or hinder access to programs or data. The reliability issue was more difficult for defence counsel to argue. She referred to the Law Commission Report on Criminal Law: Computer Misuse (Law Com. No. 186) which distinguished between people who deliberately erased or altered data and those who did so recklessly. At best the information indicated it came from a source other than its true author. The court rejected this last argument. The fact that information was added which indicated it was from someone other than whom sent it manifestly did affect the reliability of that data, notwithstanding the Law Commission Report. The language of section 3 made this clear, according to Lord Woolf CJ. In the second judgment, Mr Justice Wright said:

> ... obviously in the case of legitimate e-mails such as are invited by the owner of a computer by the publication of his e-mail address, such modification is not a criminal matter, without more, within the meaning of s 3 of the same Act. But if an individual, by misusing or bypassing any relevant password, places in the files of the computer a bogus e-mail by pretending that the password holder is the author when he is not, then such an addition to such data is plainly unauthorised, as defined in s 17(8); intent to modify the contents of the computer as defined in s 3(2) is self-evident and, by so doing, the reliability of the data in the computer is impaired within the meaning of s 3(2)(c).
>
> Those four elements, modification, lack of authorisation, intent and reliability, are the four elements of an offence under s 3.

Thus, sending accurate data may not affect the reliability of any data held in a computer but it will do so if untrue. If any inaccuracy is the result of an honest error on the part of the sender, then, although the reliability of data might be impaired, the person who sent the data cannot have the requisite intent to affect the reliability of data. Of course, even though reliability of data may be affected, or the operation of a computer impaired, or access to programs or data prevented or hindered, the prosecution still have to prove the requisite intent. It is actual intention that must be proved and carelessness or recklessness will not suffice. Where the modification is in the form of a virus or time-bomb or logic-bomb, it may be easy to infer the requisite intent, providing that it can be shown that the accused placed it in the computer deliberately and not inadvertently, such as in a case where someone innocently forwards an e-mail attachment containing a virus in ignorance of its existence.

The section 3 offence is useful in that it deals with the problem of unauthorised modification with precision and is wide enough to cover viruses, time-bombs and logic-bombs as well as dealing with immediate, direct modification. However, the need for the prosecution to prove that the accused possessed both of two states of mind – that is, having the requisite intent and the requisite knowledge – may make conviction less certain, particularly where employees are concerned. There seems to be no justification for narrowing intention in this way and the objective recklessness approach in criminal damage is preferable in this respect.

The offence is triable either way and the maximum penalties in the Crown Court are the same as for the section 2 offence: that is, imprisonment for a term not exceeding five years and/or a fine. The jurisdiction provisions apply to this offence as they do the section 1 offence.

Apart from those mentioned in this chapter specifically, there have been a number of successful prosecutions under section 3. For example, in June 1992 a freelance typesetter tampered with a computer owned by a client thereby denying access to the client. He argued that the client owed him £2000 in fees but was, nevertheless, convicted of an offence under section 3 of the Computer Misuse Act 1990 and given two years' conditional discharge and fined £1650. The judge said that his crime was not particularly serious even though the client claimed to have lost £36,000 in lost business as a result (*Computing*, 18 June 1992, p.2). In December 1993, a nurse hacked into the hospital computer and changed patients' drug prescriptions in a way that was potentially lethal. He was found guilty of two offences under section 3 and sentenced to 12 months' imprisonment. It is possible that a charge of attempted murder or manslaughter is appropriate in such circumstances but it might be difficult to prove the required intention. The same applies to the ulterior intent offence in section 2. The section 3 offence is much simpler as the intention only has to be directed towards the computer or programs or data stored in the computer.

If a prosecution is brought under section 3 it is important that there is sound evidence linking the alleged culprit with the unauthorised modification. In *R v Vatsal Patel* (unreported) July 1993 (see *Computers and Law* (1994) 5(2), p.4), strange things started to happen on a project to write bespoke software. Database tables started to disappear and eventually development work was halted. The accused was a freelance programmer and was a member of the team writing the software and two 'wrecking programs' were found on his computer. One of the programs was named VAT which was the accused's nickname. A trap was set but nothing further happened – although the wrecking programs had been erased in the meantime. A charge was brought under section 3 of the Computer Misuse Act 1990 but, following a trial lasting six days, the jury acquitted the accused. The total losses to the client were in the order of £90,000 and there was a suspicion that the accused had erased the tables in order to prolong his lucrative contract. However, any number of persons could have been responsible for erasing the data and, in addition, there had been problems with the hardware and the development platform itself had been highly unstable. In other words, there was no real proof that the accused was responsible. It was remarked upon that had he been responsible, he would have been unlikely to use his own nickname for one of the wrecking programs.

A person might modify computer records in order to cover up some other criminal or disreputable activity. In *R v Sinha* [1995] Crim LR 68, a doctor at a medical practice in Cardiff was charged with manslaughter and the offence of attempting to pervert the course of justice. A 30-year-old female patient who suffered from asthma consulted the doctor and he prescribed a beta-blocker drug which induced a fatal asthma attack. The doctor later altered the computerised records relating to the patient to remove references to her suffering from asthma. However, although the references were no longer displayed they could still be retrieved from the computer disk. A charge was not brought under section 3 of the Computer Misuse Act 1990. As mentioned previously, because the doctor had authorisation to use the computer and access patient records, there could have been a problem with the issue of whether the modification was unauthorised. The offence of perverting the course of justice is more reliable in this respect and certainly applies to the destruction or concealment of evidence.

Computer viruses

A computer virus is a self-replicating program which spreads throughout a computer system, attaching copies of itself to ordinary programs. Often, by the time the virus is detected, many back-up disks also will have been infected. Rumours abound to the effect that viruses are far more likely to be on disks containing pirated software. There were no reports of computer viruses in the Audit Commission surveys prior to the one undertaken in 1990 where a total of 54 incidents were reported, accounting for some 30 per cent of all reported computer fraud and abuse (Audit Commission, *Survey of Computer Fraud & Abuse*, HMSO, 1991). The next survey showed a massive increase to 261 incidents (Audit Commission, *Opportunity Makes a Thief: An Analysis of Computer Abuse*, HMSO, 1994). In the survey published in 1998, nearly 50 per cent of the organisations surveyed reported problems with viruses (Audit Commission, *Ghost in the Machine: An Analysis of IT Fraud and Abuse*, Audit Commission Publications, 1998). However, this fell to around 30 per cent in the latest survey but this can be explained by a disproportionate increase in the number of cases of pornographic material (Audit Commission, *yourbusiness@risk: An Update on IT Abuse*, 2001)

There are, literally, thousands of viruses and strains of viruses; some are relatively innocuous (though irritating) like the Italian virus which causes a bouncing ball to appear on screen but others are more pernicious and may completely corrupt a hard disk. The 'AIDS' disk mentioned earlier was distributed as part of a blackmail scheme to over 30,000 organisations world-wide. Other recent viruses causing havoc, and considerable expense estimated to run into billions of dollars world-wide, were the 'I Love You', SirCam and Melissa viruses. Obviously, viruses are going to remain a threat in the future but persons responsible for deliberately introducing them into a computer system are clearly guilty of an offence under section 3 of the Computer Misuse Act 1990. This is so even if the perpetrator does not personally carry out the act causing the infection because section 3 states that the person is guilty if he does any act which causes the unauthorised modification and this will include distributing infected disks.

Publishing details of how to write computer viruses could fall within the law of incitement; that is, the person publishing the details could be inciting others to commit a section 3 offence. However, there must be an intention on the part of the inciter to bring about the criminal consequences and this may be difficult to prove, although, in May 1995, an unemployed man who called himself the 'Black Baron' became the first person to be convicted of incitement in respect of computer viruses (*Computing*, 1 June 1995, p.1). He was also convicted of 11 charges under the Computer Misuse Act 1990 and the judge warned him to expect a custodial sentence.

There is also a possibility of a charge as an accomplice but, again, intention must be proved. Obvious doubts about the applicability of the law of incitement and accomplices were confirmed by police fears concerning the then imminent publication of a book revealing virus techniques in 1992 (*The Times*, 12 June 1992). The same difficulties apply in regard to access providers on the Internet, though individuals responsible for posting details of how to write and spread viruses could be liable to prosecution. Bearing in mind the international nature of the Internet, however, jurisdiction and extradition will be problematic in many cases.

Sentencing for section 3 offences

The courts now take offences under section 3 of the Computer Misuse Act 1990 very seriously and custodial sentences seem to be the norm even for first offenders, particularly if the resulting damage is severe. This is probably a reflection of the concerns that are raised by persons making unauthorised modifications to computer material and it is no longer perceived as a youngster's prank. Some sentencing guidance can be gleaned from Court of Appeal decisions in the two following cases involving appeals against custodial sentences though the facts of the cases are very different.

In the first case, *R v Maxwell-King* [2001] 2 Cr App Rep (S) 136, the accused pleaded guilty to three counts of incitement to commit offences under section 3 of the Computer Misuse Act 1990. He was a co-director (with his wife) of a company, MaxKing Interfaces Ltd, which manufactured and supplied General Instrument devices which, when fitted to General Instrument set-top boxes, made it possible for subscribers to cable television services to access all channels provided by the service provider no matter how many the subscriber had paid for. Therefore, subscribers could pay for a minimum of access and, using Maxwell-King's device, receive all channels, thereby depriving the cable television service provider of an average of £14 per month for each device used. The accused, who first got the idea from an American website advertising such devices which also carried a disclaimer, thought that what he was doing was possibly not illegal provided his website advertising also carried a disclaimer and he did not use the devices himself. The business did not prosper. The accused only sold around 30 devices and some of the buyers returned the chips. Apparently, the cable television service providers had developed a 'chip-killer' which damaged chips in such unauthorised devices, although this was disputed by the prosecution. The total turnover was about £600, the profit was minimal and the scheme was ended.

Maxwell-King was sentenced to four months' imprisonment and he appealed against the sentence (his company which was also charged pleaded guilty and no punishment was imposed but it was ordered to pay £10,000 towards the prosecution costs). The Court of Appeal noted that he was of previous good character (described by the trial judge as being of exemplary character) and had high-class character references. He had been entirely forthright and open. However, the Court of Appeal thought what he had done was dishonest and was a form of theft choosing not to take seriously his claim that he thought what he was doing was not illegal. However, this was a first offence, the accused had pleaded guilty at the first opportunity and it was thought that the custodial threshold had not quite been reached. The Court of Appeal distinguished an earlier case, *R v Carey* [1999] 1 Cr App Rep (S) 322, where a custodial sentence was imposed on a man who pleaded guilty to a conspiracy to defraud in relation to the production of some 850,000 counterfeit smart cards and had benefited to the tune of many thousands of pounds. In Maxwell-King, the Court of Appeal thought a fine or community service order might be more appropriate and substituted a community service order of 150 hours for the custodial sentence, adding that the court hoped that he could use his undoubted technical skills in computers in the context of the community service order.

Maxwell-King is hard to reconcile with a later case before the Court of Appeal where, if anything, the criminal intent seems much less. It does, however, reflect the breathtaking scope of acts that might come within the section 3 offence. In *R v Lindesay* [2001] EWCA Crim 1720, the appellant pleaded guilty to three counts of unauthorised modification of computer material contrary to section 3 of the Computer Misuse Act 1990. Lindesay was a freelance software designer and developer who had considerable experience and repute. He had a short contract with a computer firm but was dismissed on the grounds that the firm was not satisfied with his work. There was a dispute about money said to be owed to Lindesay and, about one month later, after a few drinks and acting under an impulse, he used his own internet account to gain unauthorised access to three clients of the computer firm he was in dispute with. Using passwords he had used when working for the computer firm, he deleted some of the contents of the websites of the clients and modified some of the content (for example, modifying recipes on a supermarket website). He also sent e-mails to customers of the supermarket claiming it was going to increase its prices. The total cost of putting things right was estimated at £9000. In sentencing Lindesay to nine months' imprisonment, the trial judge took account of the guilty plea, his openness with the police, his remorse and the high esteem he was held in (a university professor provided a character reference for him). But, in Lindesay's case, the trial judge thought the offence so serious that only a custodial sentence was justified. It was an act of pure unmitigated revenge after a slight. The judge equated what he did to a 'glassing' in a public house by a person who took offence at what someone had said.

The Court of Appeal did not think that the trial judge's analogy with a pub glassing was helpful. But the Court of Appeal considered the gravity of the offence. However real the grievance or impulsive the act of revenge and how inevitable that it would be discovered that it was Lindesay's doing, the fact was that he had used his skill and judgment and his knowledge of his former employer's business to cause a great deal of work, inconvenience and worry to clients of the former employer which were completely innocent. In those circumstances, an immediate custodial sentence was proper and the Court of Appeal could not say that the sentence imposed was excessive, let alone manifestly excessive.

The decision of the Court of Appeal in *Lindesay* can be criticised on a number of counts. First, it completely disregards the decision in *Maxwell-King* (which was not cited and not mentioned in the judgment of the court). *Maxwell-King* was a case involving, as the court found, dishonesty. That element was not present in *Lindesay*. Secondly, the maximum penalty for a section 3 offence is five years' imprisonment and/or a fine. In terms of sentencing practice, it has long been accepted that the maximum penalty should be reserved only for the worst possible conceivable example of the offence. As the section 3 offence covers a whole spectrum of activities, ranging from those that might result in wide disruption to computer systems costing billions of pounds to a silly prank, which can be quickly and easily remedied, nine months in the *Lindesay* case does seem extreme. Perhaps the maximum penalty ought to be reviewed and uplifted, bearing in mind that copyright and trade mark offences, which only damage economic interests, now carry a maximum of ten years' imprisonment. Section 3 offences, on the other hand, can damage economic, security and privacy interests. Finally, although the Court of Appeal thought the glassing analogy 'unhelpful', on the facts of *Lindesay*, it was an outrageous and disgraceful analogy to draw.

Prosecutions under the Computer Misuse Act 1990

Although the amount of criminal activity that falls within the offences under the Computer Misuse Act 1990 must be quite large, there have been relatively few prosecutions under it, although there seems to be a recent upsurge in prosecutions. Table 30.1 shows the statistics for cautions and prosecutions brought under the Act in England and Wales (the figures for Northern Ireland and Scotland are minimal only).

There may be a number of reasons for the relative scarcity of prosecutions under the Computer Misuse Act 1990, these being:

- in many cases, where two or more person were involved, conspiracy charges may have been preferred as an easier option from the prosecution's perspective;
- if, for example, a fraud was brought to fruition, a theft charge was simpler as this was within known and well-explored territory;
- lack of awareness of the offences and their scope and applicability among the police and prosecution authorities;
- the technical nature of the elements of the offences and the potential for misunderstanding as evidenced by some of the early cases;
- in the first few years, the perception that the problems addressed by the Computer Misuse Act 1990 were more imagined that real;
- whether the criminal law should be used to cover up bad security by organisations using computer systems.

How things have changed. The dangers from terrorism and malicious disruption and damage to computer systems now far outweigh the risks associated with computer fraud (though by no means trivial). Computer systems are now on the front line of the war against international terrorism, anarchists and those who wish to impose their views on the rest of the world. It is imperative that the criminal law is given the teeth to tackle these problems head on. In this respect, the Computer Misuse Act 1990, a forerunner in dealing with computer abuse in its time, is now looking dated and in need of some updating to address the problems of the present time. The maximum penalties, in particular, are now looking insufficient in terms of the misuses and attacks we can expect on our computer systems in the near future.

Table 30.1 Cautions and prosecutions under the Computer Misuse Act 1990 in England and Wales

Year	Section 1 offences		Section 2 offences		Section 3 offences	
	Cautions	Prosecutions	Cautions	Prosecutions	Cautions	Prosecutions
Up to 1997	N/K	N/K	1	6	10	34
1998	N/K	6	0	6	0	4
1999	9	6	2	3	7	4
2000	4	8	5	3	15	8
2001	10	9	0	4	10	12
Totals	23	29	8	22	42	62

N/K – figures not known.
Source: *HL Deb*, col WA35, 26 March 2002 and HL Deb, col WA187, 7 January 2003.

We are likely to see a further upsurge in the number of criminal prosecutions under the Computer Misuse Act 1990 and other offences applicable in the context of computer misuse and abuse. Computer systems have now become so established as an essential feature of the modern world that the protection of computer systems in relation to the ever-growing number of attacks and increasing seriousness of some of those attacks is of paramount importance. Such considerations have at last spurred the setting up of a Police National Hi-Tech Crime Unit under the auspices of the National Crime Squad.

A possible change to the Act for the future

It has already been suggested that the Computer Misuse Act 1990, a response to the perceived threats of what now can be regarded computer history, is in urgent need of reform and updating. When the Act came into force, the Internet was a reality and the world wide web had just been conceived but these were in their infancy and the opportunities and threats could only have been dreamt about. The unauthorised modification offences in section 3 of the Act cover such a wide spectrum of activities that the time has come to sub-divide them and assign different criminal penalties in respect of them. Activities such as website defacement and denial of access were unthinkable in 1990 but are now of serious concern. Denial of access can seriously damage a business that transacts on-line. It was with such concerns in mind that the Earl of Northesk introduced into the House of Lords a Bill in 2002, entitled the Computer Misuse (Amendment) Bill 2002. The Bill was designed to protect computer systems against denial of service attacks and would have made it an offence to do any act which causes or is intended to cause directly or indirectly a degradation, failure or other impairment of function of a computerised system or part. An objective standard was used so that the prosecution would not have to prove intention providing it could show that a reasonable person could have contemplated that the act would have caused such an effect.

As denial of service attacks are now a considerable concern in the United States, the Bill would have represented a welcome extension to the Computer Misuse Act 1990. The Bill did not make it through Parliament, however, and an equivalent Bill has not appeared in the current year. Reform of the Computer Misuse Act 1990, bringing it up to date to current concerns and criminal and terrorist activities is now overdue.

Blackmail

Blackmail is a serious offence and is triable only on indictment: that is, in the Crown Court. The offence is provided for in section 21 of the Theft Act 1968 and carries a maximum penalty of 14 years' imprisonment. Basically, a person is guilty of blackmail if, with a view to gain for himself or another or with intent to cause loss to another, he makes any unwarranted demand with menaces. The menaces are not restricted to threats of violence and include threats of action which is detrimental or unpleasant to the person to whom those threats are directed. An example is where a person threatens to reveal someone's previous financial difficulties unless that other person pays him some money. The 'protection racket' provides another example: that is, a shopkeeper's premises will be destroyed unless he makes certain payments.

So far as computers are concerned, a person would be guilty of blackmail who inserted a 'time-bomb' into a computer system and demanded money in return for details of how to disable the time-bomb. If the owner of the computer system has already discovered and removed the time-bomb when the demand is made, it makes no difference; the offence has still been committed. The offence of blackmail will also have been committed even if the computer owner is not worried about the threat because he has a complete, up-to-date set of back-up copies of everything likely to be affected.

Blackmail may be associated with a virus. The fact a virus is present may focus the victim's mind more wonderfully than would be the case with a time-bomb where no harm would be done until a predetermined date. A virus starts its destructive work by immediately spreading throughout a system, corrupting programs and files or filling the computer disk with garbage bringing the system down or seriously degrading performance. If freelance workers feel inclined to leave a virus or time-bomb behind to be used to pressurise a client into paying the agreed fee promptly, they should think again. A university lecturer carried out some consultancy work but when he was paid the client deducted part to pay for the telephone bill the lecturer had incurred. The lecturer retaliated by placing a virus in the client's computer with a message to the effect that he was owed money and that files were being modified and that the sooner the matter was settled, the less damage would be done. He was convicted of attempted blackmail and fined £500 (*Computing*, 8 October 1992, p.2).

The meaning of the word 'unwarranted' can cause problems. A demand is unwarranted unless the person making the demand does so in the belief that he has reasonable grounds for so doing and that the use of menaces is a proper way of reinforcing the demand. In most cases, the demand will plainly be unwarranted on the basis of this test, but there might be circumstances where this was not so. For example, a freelance programmer has carried out a substantial amount of work for a company which, he believes, has substantially and deliberately underpaid him. In order to encourage the company to pay up, the programmer might tell the company that he has entered a computer virus into the computer system and he will not remove it unless the shortfall in his payment is made up. It appears from case law that the accused must be judged by his own standards when it comes to the interpretation of 'unwarranted' and a jury might acquit the programmer if it feels that the programmer genuinely believes that he has reasonable grounds for making the demand and that the means he employs are proper, in his subjective opinion. Although this is somewhat unsatisfactory in that an accused person is being judged by his own moral standards, this is the current state of the law. However, the case discussed above where a university lecturer used a virus as a means of securing payment shows how a jury is likely to react in practice. If the action threatened is of a very serious nature (for example, if it would result in the commission of a serious offence), a jury should be directed that the means cannot be proper.

Bearing in mind the serious nature of blackmail, any victim should not hesitate to inform the police. As with other forms of blackmail, a payment made to a blackmailer in return for not destroying computer data is likely to be followed by further demands in the future. Good security and comprehensive back-up systems are the best defences against this insidious form of crime. At the same time as committing blackmail, the blackmailer may also commit other offences such as unauthorised modification of computer material, basic hacking, abstracting electricity and offences under section 43 of the Telecommunications Act 1984.

Chapter 31

Piracy and related offences

Copyright law

We have already seen that infringement of copyright can give rise to a wide range of civil law remedies such as injunctions, damages and accounts of profits. From a time when the maximum penalty for a criminal offence under copyright law carried a maximum penalty of a fine of £2 per infringing copy, the maximum penalty is now 10 years' imprisonment and/or a fine. (The penalties in respect of illicit recordings of performances have also been increased to a maximum of 10 years' imprisonment and/or a fine.) These substantial increases are a reflection of the fact that Parliament recognises the serious nature of copyright piracy involving money laundering by serious criminal gangs in some cases and that it is analogous to theft, depriving the owners of the copyrights involved of substantial amounts of income. Piracy is an offence of dishonesty which often also involves deception. Although it is true to say that the majority of copyright infringements will be dealt with in a satisfactory manner by the civil law, the criminal penalties available may be more appropriate in some circumstances. One concern, however, is that the mental element required to be proved to secure a conviction is set at a low standard and the prosecution does not even have to prove dishonesty. This has been carried over from the time when the penalties for criminal offences under copyright law were relatively minor and it this aspect of the offences that should be looked at again by parliament. Similar concerns apply to trade mark law (and, in a good number of cases, copyright piracy will also give rise to offences under trade mark law), where the threshold to secure a conviction seems even lower.

Copyright law contains criminal penalties for many of the activities collectively known as 'secondary infringements' giving rise to civil liability. The same standard of knowledge is used for secondary infringements and the equivalent criminal offences, that is, knowing or having reason to believe that the copies are infringing copies. In practice, the prosecution will only have to show that the accused had reason to believe that the copies were infringing copies and this is an objective test. The only difference is that the standard of proof is different. In a civil action, the claimant will win if he can prove the necessary elements for infringement on a balance of probabilities whereas, for criminal liability, the standard is beyond reasonable doubt. The common denominator between the civil secondary infringements and the equivalent criminal offences is that the activities concerned in most cases can be thought of as being of a commercial nature and include the infringements of copyright commonly known as 'computer software piracy' – an example would be importing or selling infringing copies of computer software without the permission of the owner of the copyright in the software, knowing or having reason to believe that they are infringing copies.

The criminal offences under copyright law are not restricted for cases of blatant piracy. In *Thames & Hudson Ltd* v *Design and Artists Copyright Society Ltd* [1995] FSR 153 the Design and Artists Copyright Society Ltd commenced private prosecutions against Thames & Hudson Ltd and its directors for offences under sections 107 and 110 of the Copyright, Designs and Patents Act 1988 on the basis that Thames & Hudson was selling and distributing a book knowing, or having reason to believe, that it contained material infringing copyright. (Section 110 imposes liability on officers of corporate bodies for offences under section 107.) An application by Thames & Hudson for a stay of proceedings until after the civil case had been heard was rejected by the judge who confirmed that section 107 does not differentiate between a reputable company and a pirate. The mental element for the offences is made out if the accused had reason to believe that the copies were infringing copies. The activities which attract criminal penalties are listed in Table 31.1 with the appropriate maximum penalties.

As can be seen from Table 31.1, the scope of these criminal offences is fairly wide and will cover most forms of commercial exploitation. Of particular note is the fact that making an article designed to make copies is a criminal offence, as is being in possession of such a device if the person knows or has reason to believe that the article will be used to make infringing copies for sale or hire or for use in the course of business. This would cover a piece of equipment specifically designed for this purpose but not a computer with CD writer drive or a floppy disk drive. Although the latter can be used for making infringing copies, they are not designed for infringing copyright; they are designed for legitimate uses. The word 'article' is used in section 107(2) but is not defined in the Act in this context. In terms of older technology it would cover, for example, a master for making vinyl records or plate for making prints. In terms of software, it could be very wide. For example, placing an unauthorised copy of a work in digital form on a website, inviting others to make copies, could fall within this offence. However, it only attracts the lighter sentences available in magistrates' courts. The same activity would be more likely to be charged under section 107(1)(e), distributing an infringing copy otherwise than in the course of business to such an extent as to affect prejudicially the owner of the copyright. The only issue here would be whether placing the work on a webpage with such an invitation could be deemed to be distributing the work. Making it available for downloading is not necessarily the same. However, placing material on a webpage has been accepted to be publishing the work even though it waits there passively for people to access and download.

The reason why the criminal law is strong as regards copyright is the ease with which copyright works can be copied and the scale on which it can be done and the ensuing economic harm to copyright owners. In 1998, customs officers in Germany seized £37m worth of pirated software in two warehouses (*Computing*, 13 August 1998, p.4). Various estimates of the losses due to software piracy have been made: in 1990 the losses in Europe alone were estimated at $4.3bn (*Computing*, 9 January 1992, p.3). World-wide losses were once estimated to stand at $12.8bn (*PC Week*, 3 May 1994, p.4). Of course, such figures must be taken with a pinch of salt, but they do give some indication of the scale of the problem. In 2003, the Business Software Alliance estimated that reducing the piracy rate to 15 per cent would increase the United Kingdom's gross domestic product by £10bn (*Computing*, 12 June 2003, p.13). It is a simple matter to copy most computer software, even if it is copy-protected, and, what is more, the investment required to do this and to market and sell the copies is relatively small. In contrast, to copy and sell an invention protected by patent law is likely to involve a substantial investment, requiring the acquisition of factory space, storage, expensive equipment, transport, etc. The scope and magnitude of criminal penalties have been increased and strengthened to cater for the growing ease of copying with the advent of

Table 31.1 Criminal offences and copyright law

Offence (Copyright, Designs And Patents Act 1988)	Classification of offence (see below)
Section 107(1)	
With respect to an article which the person concerned knows or has reason to believe is an infringing copy of a copyright work:	
(a) making for sale or hire	MC/CC
(b) importing into the UK (not for private or domestic use)	MC/CC
(c) possessing in the course of business with a view to committing any act infringing the copyright	MC
(d) in the course of a business:	
(i) selling or letting for hire	MC
(ii) offering or exposing for sale or hire	MC
(iii) exhibiting in public	MC
(iv) distributing	MC/CC
(e) distributing otherwise than in the course of a business to such an extent as to affect prejudicially the owner of the copyright	MC/CC
Section 107(2)	
With respect to an article specifically designed or adapted for making copies of a particular copyright work where the person concerned knows or has reason to believe that it is to be used to make infringing copies for sale or hire or for use in the course of a business:	
(a) making such an article	MC
(b) being in possession of such an article	MC

Classification of penalties:
MC/CC – (triable either way). On summary conviction: imprisonment not exceeding 6 months and/or a fine not exceeding £5000. On conviction on indictment: imprisonment not exceeding 10 years and/or a fine (from 20 November 2002, previously a maximum of 2 years' imprisonment and/or a fine)
MC – (summary trial only, i.e. in magistrates' court). Imprisonment not exceeding 6 months and/or a fine not exceeding level 5 (presently £5,000)

high speed photocopying, video recorders, twin-tape cassette players and computer and digital technology and the massive storage capacities of inexpensive media such as CD and DVD. As a result of the Copyright etc. and Trade Marks (Offences and Enforcement) Act 2002, the maximum penalty for offences under sections 107(1)(a), (b), (d)(iv) and (e) (see Table 31.1) is now 10 years' imprisonment or a fine or both. The penalties in respect of illicit recordings of performances and unauthorised decoders have also been increased likewise. The increased penalties came into effect on 20 November 2002. Further changes to criminal liability in relation to copyright are likely to result from the United Kingdom's implementation of Directive 2001/29/EC of the European Parliament and of the Council of 22 May 2001 on the harmonisation of certain aspects of copyright and related rights in the information society, OJ L 167, 22.06.2001, p.10, discussed in Chapter 8.

The formula used for criminal liability for the copyright offences is that the person concerned 'knows or has reason to believe'. The meaning of this phrase was considered in *LA Gear Inc* v *Hi-Tec Sports plc* [1992] FSR 121, where the Court of Appeal said that the test to apply was an objective one – that is, whether the reasonable man, having the defendant's knowledge of the facts, would have believed that the copy was an infringing copy. Previously, the High Court had gone further saying that the phrase connoted the allowance of a period of time to allow the reasonable man to evaluate the facts and so form a reasonable belief. Although the Court of Appeal said the test was objective, it is not truly so if it takes into account the facts known to the defendant. What if the defendant deliberately turns a blind eye to the facts; he suspects that copies are infringing copies but does not enquire into this?

Where a pirate includes a sign which resembles a registered trade mark on the infringing copies, he also runs the risk of a prosecution under section 92 of the Trade Marks Act 1994. This offence is almost one of strict liability subject only to the accused showing on a balance of probabilities that he believed on reasonable grounds that the use of the sign and the manner in which it was used was not an infringement of the registered trade mark. An argument that this 'reverse persuasive burden of proof' was contrary to the presumption of innocence in a criminal trial under Article 6(2) of the European Convention on Human Rights was rejected by the House of Lords in *R* v *Johnstone* [2003] UKHL 28. In that case, Johnstone was convicted under section 92 of the Trade Marks Act 1994 in respect of bootleg recordings of performances by famous singers and pop groups. He was sentenced to six months' imprisonment and a confiscation order was made of just over £130,000.

The availability of equipment which facilitates copying has not gone unchallenged. In the United States of America, the film industry attempted, unsuccessfully, to prevent the sale of the Sony Betamax video recorder. In the United Kingdom the record industry argued unsuccessfully that the sale of the Amstrad twin-tape cassette machine was an incitement to infringe copyright (see *Amstrad Consumer Electronics plc* v *The British Phonograph Industry Ltd* [1986] FSR 159 and *CBS Songs Ltd* v *Amstrad Consumer Electronics plc* [1988] AC 1013). The way these machines were advertised did nothing to reassure the industry, using phrases such as 'you can even make a copy of your favourite cassettes', and it is true that most purchasers of such machines would use them to make unauthorised copies of music tapes and computer software, especially computer games on cassette tape. In the first Amstrad case above, it was held that supplying machines which would be likely to be used to unlawfully copy pre-recorded cassettes subject to copyright protection was insufficient to make the manufacturer or supplier an infringer of copyright. Neither could Amstrad be said to be authorising infringement of copyright because it had no control over the way its machines were used once sold. In the latter case, it was held that a claim that Amstrad, by its advertising literature, was inciting others to infringe copyright gave no legal remedies in civil law to the relevant copyright owner. In any case, Amstrad had printed a small warning about infringing copyright in its literature.

These two cases illustrate the difficulties in reconciling two distinct objectives – that is, encouraging technical innovation and making it available to the public on the one hand and protecting the interests of those willing to invest in music, films, computer software, etc. on the other hand.

Incitement is a common law offence and, with the exception of incitement to commit murder, is not to be found in Acts of Parliament. This gives the courts some flexibility in applying and interpreting this area of law. Although Amstrad, because of the use of a warning against copyright infringement, was not guilty of incitement, there may be other situations where a conviction might be more likely. For example, in the case of devices and computer software specifically designed to circumvent copy protection, the makers and sellers of such gadgets and software cannot point to legitimate uses unlike the Amstrad and similar twin-tape machines. They are designed to enable persons to make copies of software packages clearly against the wishes of the owners of the copyright in such packages. Indeed, as has been noted in Chapter 4, the Copyright, Designs and Patents Act 1988 specifically provides that civil law remedies should be available against persons responsible for the sale and distribution of such methods of overcoming copy-protection. (These provisions are likely to be expanded and subject to criminal penalties under the imminent implementation of the Directive on copyright in the information society.) It would appear that the criminal law offence of incitement also may be available against such persons.

A pirate who copies or imports copied software with a view to selling it may commit other offences apart from those under copyright law, depending on the circumstances. The Forgery and Counterfeiting Act 1981, the Trade Descriptions Act 1968 and section 25 of the Theft Act 1968 may be relevant. The pirate can also be pursued through the civil courts and the decision to pursue civil or criminal remedies, or both, will depend on the nature and scale of the infringement, the pirate's knowledge of the existence of copyright in the work and whether the pirate has any funds available to pay damages.

The Copyright, Designs and Patents Act 1988 has been used increasingly to prosecute computer software pirates and magistrates and judges are at last taking this form of crime seriously, using custodial sentences more readily. For example, an Oxford computer dealer was imprisoned for six months and fined £5000 for making unauthorised copies of a popular word processing package with the intention of selling them (*Computing*, 11 August 1994, p.3). A few weeks earlier, a brother and sister pleaded guilty to 23 counts of software piracy and offences under the Trade Descriptions Act 1968 and were sentenced to 200 and 100 hours' community service respectively (*Computing*, 23 June 1994, p.14). We can expect longer terms of imprisonment in the future for those involved in piracy on a large scale.

Forgery and Counterfeiting Act 1981

Section 1 of this Act states that:

> A person is guilty of forgery if he makes a false instrument, with the intention that he or another shall use it to induce somebody to accept it as genuine, and by reason of so accepting it to do or not to do some act to his own or any other person's prejudice.

We have seen that the application of this offence to computer hacking has been a failure. If a computer software pirate makes copies of a popular package, however, dressing up the copies to look like the original and then selling them, he may be guilty of the offence contained in section 1 of the Act. It may seem strange to talk in terms of a 'false instrument' in relation to computer software, but section 8 of the Act describes a false instrument as including:

> ... any disc, tape, sound track or other device on or in which information is recorded or stored by mechanical, electronic or other means.

It would seem that every form or method of storing computer software will fall within this definition.

It could be argued that the person who buys a pirate copy of computer software will not be deceived and that he will know that, in the circumstances, the software he is purchasing is an unauthorised copy, especially if the price is considerably lower than usual, but this does not matter. The Act requires that the pirate intends the customer to accept the copy as being genuine and in one sense the copy will be genuine as it will be a direct copy of the computer programs. The programs themselves are the genuine programs. Section 1 requires that someone should accept the false instrument as genuine resulting in that person or another being prejudiced. Therefore, it does not matter if the person buying the copy is not prejudiced – after all he will have obtained a copy which works as well as the genuine article – it is sufficient that someone else has been prejudiced. That someone else is the owner of the copyright subsisting in the programs who will have been prejudiced because he has lost a potential sale as a result of the pirate's activities. If the customer himself believes that the software is genuine, then the pirate can be charged with the offence of obtaining by deception (Theft Act 1968, section 15) which carries a maximum of ten years' imprisonment, the same as under section 1 of the Forgery and Counterfeiting Act 1981. The choice between these two offences will have to be carefully considered in the light of the actual circumstances. In April 1991, a computer dealer was found guilty of obtaining by deception for selling pirate copies of software at the full retail price. He was sentenced to nine months' imprisonment, suspended for two years (*Computing*, 18 April 1992, p.3).

Trade Descriptions Act 1968

By section 1 of the Trade Descriptions Act 1968, any person who, in the course of a trade or business, applies a false trade description to any goods or supplies or offers to supply goods to which a false trade description has been applied, is guilty of an offence. A 'trade description' includes an indication as to the person by whom the goods are manufactured. Therefore, if a computer software pirate makes copies of a software package, without the permission of the copyright owner, in such a way that the copies look like the genuine article, then the offence is committed. A person who sells or offers such copies for sale will also be guilty of the offence. The rationale behind these provisions is to protect the public from being deceived into buying inferior goods rather than protecting the interests of copyright owners. Prosecution is normally undertaken by trading standards officers and the offence carries a maximum of two years' imprisonment and/or a fine if tried in the Crown Court or a fine not exceeding £5000 if the offender is convicted in a magistrates' court. The utility of this offence is that it is appropriate to pirated goods, including computer software, video cassettes, etc. sold in markets, often in the unofficial Sunday markets or car boot sales, which will be monitored by trading standards officers.

The offence can only apply if the copy carries the name or mark of the genuine maker, or a name or mark which is similar (false to a material degree). So a pirate can avoid the consequences of this particular legislation if he takes care to use a different name for the software and its maker and uses packaging which is different. Of course, this does not prevent prosecution for the copyright offences.

Section 25 of the Theft Act 1968

Consider a software pirate travelling by car to a car boot sale with a quantity of pirated software. The police stop him on the way and the pirate copies are noticed. Has he committed an offence? He has not yet sold or offered any of the copies for sale. By section 25 of the Theft Act 1968, he may be guilty of 'going equipped to cheat' and 'cheat' means the same as obtaining by deception (section 15). Therefore, if the pirate intends to sell the software as genuine to obtain payment, he is guilty of the offence. The maximum penalty is three years' imprisonment. It must be noted, however, that the software must look like the genuine article and it must be packaged to look like the real thing so that potential customers will be deceived.

As the penalties for the copyright offences have been increased significantly, it is more likely that prosecutions will be brought for those offences (or the trade mark offences) rather than forgery, trade descriptions or going equipped to cheat. (Note that the forgery and going equipped legislation does not apply to Scotland, where alternative offences are available.)

Chapter 32

Computer pornography and harassment

Introduction

The ability of computer technology to process, store and make available static and moving images with increasing quality and speed has not all been beneficial. It has also enabled persons with abnormal or perverted sexual drives and desires to gain access to and download phenomenal quantities of pornographic material. Much of the material available goes beyond that which has become acceptable in some societies, even liberal societies, and there are grave dangers that the sheer volume of pornographic material will feed depravity and, this in turn, could lead to increases in sexual crimes, particularly against children, both within the United Kingdom and in other countries from which this sort of material originates. Obviously, it is impossible to police the Internet on a world-wide basis but the issues are considered so serious that a number of countries, including the United Kingdom, have taken measures to criminalise the activities of those who intentionally access such material, whether for their own use or for distribution to others. The maximum penalties available have been increased substantially in relation to child pornography.

Another issue covered in this chapter is the position in relation to e-mails that may cause alarm or distress or which threaten violence or involve racial harassment. The Protection from Harassment Act 1997 is a useful piece of legislation dealing with this problem, though it must be said that the Act was not specifically directed at this problem. However, harassment is not defined in the Act and it now seems clear that, although originally designed to combat stalkers and 'neighbours from hell', it can also be very effective in terms of e-mails.

Pornography

There has been considerable publicity about the availability of pornographic material on the Internet and it is clear that the courts treat this form of computer abuse seriously. It is also one of the most reported forms of computer abuse along with viruses. The law is reasonably well provided with relevant offences though there may be difficulties in deciding whether something is obscene. Under section 1 of the Obscene Publications Act 1959, an article shall be deemed to be obscene if its effect is such as to tend to deprave and corrupt persons who are likely, having regard to all relevant circumstances, to read, see or hear the matter contained or embodied in it. By section 2, any person who, whether for gain or not, publishes an obscene article or who has an obscene article for publication for gain (whether gain to himself or another) commits an offence. There may be some difficulty with the requirement for an article but this is defined as any description of article containing or embodying matter to be read or looked at or both, any sound record, and any film or other record of a picture or pictures. There is no reason to doubt that it will include a magnetic disk or other form of electronic storage media.

Publishing obscene material on a website may result in a prosecution under the Obscene Publication Acts. In *R v Perrin* [2002] EWCA Crim 747, the appellant had been convicted of publishing an obscene article, namely a webpage on the Internet, contrary to section 2(1) of the Obscene Publications Act 1959. The webpage contained images of people covered in faeces, coprophilia or coprophagia and men engaged in fellatio and it had been accessed by a police officer who recorded the images onto video tape. The webpage could be accessed free of charge by anyone. Other webpages were only accessible on subscription and the one accessed by the police officer acted as a 'trailer'. The appeal was based on a claim that the conviction breached the right of freedom of expression under Article 10(1) of the Council of Europe Convention for the Protection of Human Rights and Fundamental Freedoms (the 'Human Rights Convention'), that the charge was not sufficiently precise to allow the appellant to regulate his behaviour to avoid committing further offences as required under Article 7 of the Convention, that the trial judge erred in rejecting the argument that the only relevant publication was to the police officer and it was wrong to test obscenity by reference to others who might have access to the material and, finally, the judge failed to make it clear to the jury that it was necessary for a significant proportion of those visiting the site to be affected by it.

The Court of Appeal rejected the grounds of appeal based on the Human Rights Convention, noting that Article 10(2) allows derogation from the right of freedom of expression where necessary in a democratic society, *inter alia*, for the prevention of disorder or crime or for the protection of health and morals. It also said that the Article 7 point added nothing. As regards publication, the Court of Appeal said that this took place when images are uploaded or downloaded from a website. Section 1(3) of the Obscene Publications Act 1959 provides that a person publishes an article when he distributes, circulates, sells, lets or hire, gives, or lends it, or who offers it for sale or for letting or hire; or ... where the matter is data stored electronically, transmits that data. Although some types of publishing are based on another person actually having access to the article (for example, 'sells' or 'gives') other forms of publication, such as 'offers it for sale' do not require actual access by another person. The Court of Appeal refined a test to be applied in such cases, being:

> First, whether any person or persons were likely to see the article, and if so, whether the effect of the article, taken as a whole, was such as to tend to deprave and corrupt the person or persons who were likely, having regard to all relevant circumstances, to see the matter contained or embodied on it.

That being so, the publication in this case was to any person, including vulnerable young persons, who may choose to access it. The jury was entitled, therefore, to look beyond the police officer who had actually accessed the webpage. The failure to give a direction to the jury that it must consider whether a significant proportion of persons who might access the webpage was also rejected. Such a direction was common in terms of traditional forms of publishing, for example, in the form of books or video tape, but was not necessarily appropriate in terms of publishing on the Internet. It would seem, therefore, that there is no need to prove that anyone has accessed pornographic material on a website or that, in fact, anyone seeing it would be likely to be depraved or corrupted. In the present case, it would be implausible that a police officer, working in this area and used to viewing pornographic material would be likely to be depraved or corrupted by what he saw.

The main concern now is child pornography available on the Internet. This is dealt with by section 1 of the Protection of Children Act 1978, as amended, which makes it an offence to take or permit to be taken or to make any indecent photograph or pseudo-photograph of a child or to distribute or show such photographs or pseudo-photographs or to have it in possession with a view to their being distributed or shown by himself to others. It is also an offence to publish or cause to be published an advertisement likely to be understood as conveying that the advertiser distributes or shows such indecent photographs or pseudo-photographs or intends to do so. A person is to be regarded as distributing an indecent photograph or pseudo-photograph if he parts with possession of it to, or exposes or offers it for acquisition by, another person.

Indecent photographs are defined as including data stored on a computer disk or by other electronic means which is capable of conversion to a photograph. Films and video recordings are also covered as are copies and negatives. A pseudo-photograph is an image, whether made by computer graphics or otherwise howsoever, which appears to be a photograph and includes copies of pseudo-photographs and data stored on a computer disk or by other electronic means which is capable of conversion into a pseudo-photograph; section 7 as amended by the Criminal Justice and Public Order Act 1994. It is a defence to a charge under section 1 for the accused to prove that he had a legitimate reason for distributing or showing the photographs or pseudo-photographs or (as the case may be) having them in his possession; or that he had not himself seen the photographs or pseudo-photographs and did not know, nor had any cause to suspect, them to be indecent. The maximum penalty for an offence under the Protection of Children Act 1978 is now 10 years' imprisonment or a fine or both (from 11 January 2001 by virtue of the Criminal Justice and Court Services Act 2000).

Opening attachments to e-mails and downloading images from the webpages were acts of making indecent photographs and would be a criminal offence under section 1 of the Protection of Children Act 1978 unless the person concerned was not aware that the attachment contained or was likely to contain an indecent photograph or pseudo-photograph of a child. So it was held by the Court of Appeal in R v Smith and Jayson [2003] 1 Cr App Rep 212, dismissing the appeals of Smith who received two years' probation and Jayson who was sentenced to 12 months' imprisonment (the sentences were imposed before the increase in maximum penalties). The mental element of the offence is that the act of making should be a deliberate and intentional act in the knowledge that the image made is, or is likely to be, an indecent photograph or pseudo-photograph of a child. Of course, an image simply downloaded to a computer screen is clearly capable of being converted into a photograph.

Simply being in possession of an indecent photograph or pseudo-photograph of a child (without any intention to distribute or show it to others) is also a criminal offence under section 160 of the Criminal Justice Act 1988. The defences are as those under the Protection of Children Act 1978 plus, in addition, where the person accused proves that the photograph or pseudo-photograph was sent to him without any prior request made by him or on his behalf and that he did not keep it for an unreasonable time. The maximum penalty for this offence has also been increased (as from 11 January 2001) and now stands at five years' imprisonment or a fine or both, if tried on indictment in the Crown Court.

In *R v Fellows* (1997) 1 Cr App R 244, Fellows was a computer specialist from Birmingham University who used a university computer to store indecent pictures of children and he printed copies. He also made the data available on the Internet. The Court of Appeal rejected the accused's argument that the computer data did not comprise a photograph for the purposes of the Protection of Children Act 1978. It was claimed that Parliament could not have envisaged data being stored on computer so as to reproduce photographs which could be transmitted anywhere in the world when the relevant legislation was enacted. However, the Court of Appeal held that the images held in digital form were copies of photographs for the purposes of section 1 of the 1978 Act. The authority of an earlier case was accepted in which the court accepted that a video cassette was an article for the purposes of section 1(2) of the Obscene Publications Act 1959; *Attorney-General's Reference (No. 5 of 1980)* (1980) 72 Cr App R 71. In that case, the court found the accused guilty notwithstanding that it was accepted that Parliament probably had not envisaged that video cassettes would become widely available and provide a means of distributing obscene material.

In *Fellows*, Lord Justice Evans said that a computer disk was not a photograph but was a copy of a photograph which made the original photograph or a copy of it available for viewing by a person with access to the disk. Furthermore, under section 7 of the Protection of Children Act 1978, there was no restriction on the form of the copy of an indecent photograph and later, contemporary copies were included. Fellows' appeal, and that of a person who received material from Fellows' archive, were dismissed. Fellows had been sentenced to three years' imprisonment, demonstrating the seriousness with which the courts regard such activities.

Sentencing for child pornography

Sentencing guidelines based on the increased penalties were laid down by the Court of Appeal in *R v Oliver* [2003] 2 Cr App Rep (S) 64. The Court of Appeal adopted a scale suggested by the Sentencing Advisory Panel, with some modification as follows:

- Level 1 – images depicting erotic posing with no sexual activity.
- Level 2 – sexual activity between children or solo masturbation by a child.
- Level 3 – non-penetrative sexual activity between adults and children.
- Level 4 – penetrative sexual activity between adults and children.
- Level 5 – sadism or bestiality.

Having set out the levels, the Court of Appeal made recommendations (as below), stressing that these were guidelines only and not a straightjacket for sentencers. Regard would also need to be given to the present state of prison overcrowding and to public concerns about child pornography.

- Possession for own use of small quantities of material not involving exploitation or abuse of children or small quantities of material in level 1, particularly where downloaded from the Internet, would suggest a fine might be appropriate. A conditional discharge might be suitable if the offender pleaded guilty and had no previous convictions.
- A community sentence might be appropriate where the offender had possession of large quantities of material in level 1 or small quantities of level 2 material, provided

the material had not been distributed or shown to others. A cooperative and motivated offender might be dealt with by a community rehabilitation order with a sex offender programme. The custody threshold might be passed if the material had been shown to others or where there was a large quantity of level 2 material or a small amount of level 3 or above material. Sentences might vary, depending on the circumstances, from six to 12 months' imprisonment.

- A sentence of between 12 months' and three years' imprisonment might be appropriate for possession of large quantities on level 3 or 4 material, even if not shown to others or for showing or distributing large quantities of level 3 material or for producing or trading in material at levels 1 to 3.
- Sentences longer than three years should be reserved for more serious cases, where images in level 4 or 5 had been shown or distributed, where the offender was actively involved in producing material in level 4 or 5, particularly in breach of trust whether or not there was an element of commercial gain or where the offender encouraged or commissioned the production of such images. A higher sentence should be granted if the offender has been involved in more than one of the above activities.
- Sentences approaching the ten-year maximum would be appropriate in very serious cases where the offender has previous convictions for dealing in child pornography or abusing children sexually or with violence.

Aggravating factors, likely to lead to an increased penalty, include whether the images had been shown to children, if there are a large number of images, how the images have been arranged on a computer (might indicate a sophisticated approach to trading in the images or a higher level of persona; interest in the images), whether the images are available on public areas of the Internet and whether they are likely to be found by accident by persons not looking for pornographic material, whether the offender was responsible for the production of the images, whether the children were members of his or her own family, or drawn from vulnerable groups or where the offender was in a position of trust such as being a teacher, the age of the children, whether injury to their private parts was likely, and whether they appeared fearful or distressed.

Sexual grooming of children by e-mail or in chat rooms

There have been a number of worrying cases where adult men have met young children after contacting them initially by e-mail or through internet chat rooms. The dangers are apparent, a paedophile could lie about his age and pretend to share similar interests with a child contacted through a chat room, and arrange to meet the child, intending to engage in sexual activity. The government considered that it was important to introduce a new offence of grooming for sexual activity so that a prosecution could be brought before any sexual activity takes place.

At the time of writing, a Bill is before Parliament, called the Sexual Offences Bill 2002. It deals with a whole range of issues but does include an offence of meeting a child following sexual grooming. The offence can be committed without a meeting having taken place, if the offender travels to any part of the world with the intention of meeting the child. The offender must be aged 18 years or over and must have met or communicated with the child (being under 16 years of age) on at least two previous occasions and the offender must not reasonably believe that the child is 16 years or over

(17 in Northern Ireland). The offence is completed when the offender intentionally meets the child or travels with the intention of meeting the child in any part of the world, though part of the travel must be in England and Wales or Northern Ireland. The maximum penalty for the offence is set at seven years' imprisonment in the Bill. It is clear that the offence is intended to cover communication over the Internet. Thus, the offence can be committed if a person sends two e-mails to a child, arranges to meet the child and then travels to meet the child with the intention of doing anything to or in respect of the child that is a relevant offence, such as rape or sexual assault. Evidence of the necessary intention may be gleaned from the content of the communications or, for example, from objects in the possession of the offender when travelling to meet the child, such as condoms or lubricants.

The e-mails or other communication do not have to have a sexually explicit content and might appear wholly innocent on the face of them, for example, where the offender suggests that he can give the child help with homework or swimming lessons. The grooming offence in the Bill, if it receives Royal Assent, is likely to be in force in the near future, though it may be subject to amendment on its way through Parliament.

Threatening e-mails

We have seen in Chapter 29 that sending a threatening or malicious message by a public telecommunications system, including by e-mail, can constitute an offence under the Telecommunications Act 1984. A much wider piece of legislation was brought in to deal with the problem of stalking and other antisocial behaviour such as that emanating from 'neighbours from hell'. The Protection from Harassment Act 1997 may apply where threatening messages are sent by e-mail or other forms of communication. It provides for criminal penalties as well as a civil remedy.

The relevant provisions of the Act came into force on 16 June 1997. Under section 1, pursuing a course of conduct which amounts to harassment of another, and which the person responsible knows or ought to know amounts to harassment of the other, is an offence. Whether a person 'ought to know' is an objective test based on a reasonable person in possession of the same information. If such a person would think the course of conduct amounted to harassment of the other, that is sufficient. By section 7, references to harassing a person include alarming the person or causing the person distress and a 'course of conduct' must involve conduct on at least two occasions though not necessarily the same conduct. 'Conduct' includes speech.

It can be seen that the offence can be committed relatively easily. Just sending two e-mails which objectively would cause in a reasonable person alarm or distress should be sufficient. For example, if Rodney sends two messages threatening to harm Wendy that should be an offence. The same applies if Rodney makes unwelcome sexual advances of an unpleasant nature to Wendy by e-mail. As it appears that the conduct does not have to be the same variety, Rodney could also possibly commit the offence by sending one threatening e-mail and making one telephone call to Wendy.

Notwithstanding the right of freedom of expression, newspaper articles can amount to harassment under the Act if, for example, they promoted racial hatred of an individual. In *Thomas* v *News Group Newspapers Ltd*, *The Times*, 25 July 2001, two police sergeants had been demoted following a complaint from a black clerk at a police station who was concerned at their treatment of a Somali asylum-seeker and had overheard them make a private remark about the asylum-seeker. *The Sun* newspaper ran a story about it entitled 'Beyond a Joke: Fury as Police Sarges Busted after Refugee Jest'. Several readers wrote in and their letters were published later; a follow-up story was published in *The Sun* which repeated part of the original article. The black clerk, the claimant, was named in the articles. The defendant's appeal against the refusal of a county court judge to strike out the claimant's particulars of claim was rejected by the Court of Appeal which considered that there was an arguable case that the defendant was guilty of harassing the claimant by stirring up racial criticism of her which would cause her distress. It was accepted that the right of freedom of expression did not extend to protect remarks undermining the basic values expressed in the European Convention on Human Rights.

Newspaper articles can cause distress because others who may know the person to whom remarks in an article are directed see the offending article. However, there is no requirement that the remarks are published to third parties. A person may be distressed by telephone calls, letters or e-mails, even if no one else hears or sees them. The case of *R v Norman* [2003] All ER (D) 88 gives an example of how seriously the courts take harassment by e-mail. In that case, a controversial radio broadcaster and journalist received many e-mails from the defendant who had used fictitious names. Eventually, he was traced. A large proportion of the e-mails were racially abusive and referred to the broadcaster's Jewish origin. There were also threats, though not of immediate violence. The defendant was convicted of racially aggravated harassment (an offence under section 28 of the Crime and Disorder Act 1998) and sentenced to 18 months' imprisonment. He appealed on a number of grounds claiming that the judge failed to take into account that the broadcaster was controversial, he was not a vulnerable person and the threats were made by e-mail and not face to face. The Court of Appeal considered that aggravating factors were the length of time over which the e-mails had been sent and the ferocity of their contents. However, mitigating factors were the defendant's previous good character and the fact that he had apologised to the complainant. The Court of Appeal substituted a sentence of 12 months' imprisonment.

The threshold for the offence may be relatively low if the Lord Chancellor's view is accepted. He approved of a description favoured by Lord Russell (*Hansard*, HC Deb, 24 January 1997) to the following effect:

> He said first, it [the conduct] is driving me round the bend. That is harassment. It is a continuation of the matter. Secondly it was unwelcome: that is an important criterion. He said that the activity went on and on. That makes for a course of conduct. He also said 'I did not want it'. Those are the elements of harassment.

The offence is triable in the magistrates' courts only and carries a maximum penalty of imprisonment for a term not exceeding six months and/or a fine not exceeding level 5 on the standard scale.

A more serious form of the offence is covered by section 4 of the Act. This is where the course of conduct causes another to fear violence on each occasion. The person pursuing the course of conduct must know or he ought to know that the other person will fear violence. Whether a person ought to know is based on an objective test – whether a reasonable person with knowledge of the same information would think it would put the victim in fear of violence. The offence is triable either way and, on conviction on indictment in the Crown Court, the maximum penalty is imprisonment for not more than five years and/or a fine.

In terms of the civil remedy, an actual or apprehended breach of section 1 is sufficient to give a right of action. The use of the word 'apprehended' makes it clear that it is the victim's perception which is important. Damages are available and there is provision also for injunctions, for example, prohibiting the person responsible from continuing the conduct.

There are some specific defences to the offence of harassment and it does not apply to a course of conduct if the person who pursued it shows that it was pursued for the purpose of preventing or detecting crime, that it was pursued under any enactment or rule of law or to comply with any condition or requirement imposed by any person under any enactment, or that in the particular circumstances the pursuit of the course of conduct was reasonable. For the section 4 offence the defences are the same except the last one which is to the effect that the conduct was reasonable for the protection of the person pursuing the conduct or another or for the protection of his or another's property. Note that the burden of proof is on the person responsible for the conduct (this will be satisfied on a balance of probabilities – the usual criminal standard of proof, beyond reasonable doubt, does not apply to defences).

Finally, a software pirate will be unlikely to maintain a claim of harassment in respect of legal and associated action against him by or on behalf of the owners of the copyrights alleged to have been infringed. In *Tuppen* v *Microsoft Corp Ltd, The Times,* 15 November 2000, the claimants alleged that the defendants, Microsoft and their solicitors, had harassed them by suborning the police to raid the home of one of the claimants, by conducting oppressive litigation, by suborning witnesses into lying and by telephoning the claimants late at night. The judge struck out this claim saying that the purpose of the Protection from Harassment Act 1997 was to prevent stalking, anti-social behaviour by neighbours and racial harassment and that, apart perhaps from the telephone call to each of the claimants (an isolated incident), none of the defendants' behaviour came anywhere near falling under the Act. However, the judge was a little too narrow in describing the behaviour sought to be controlled by the Act, as some of the cases mentioned above show. Furthermore, although conducting a course of litigation would not normally amount to harassment, there is no reason why it might not be in extreme cases, for example, where several law suits with no chance of success are made against an individual. In the *Tuppen* case, the allegations that the police and witnesses had been suborned (incited to do something by bribery) were very serious allegations and, as far as the law report indicates, with nothing whatsoever to support such allegations.

Chapter 33

Computer crime – concluding remarks

Suggestions to prevent or minimise criminal activities

There are several things which the owner or operator of a computer system can do to prevent or minimise the possibility of criminal activities being successfully perpetrated against the computer system or the data or software stored therein. The main principle is to avoid complacency; it would be a very brave IT manager who considers his system so secure that it is safe against criminals and malicious employees. To some extent, strong security can foster complacency and can even present the would-be criminal with an enjoyable challenge. However, the golden thread running through the suggestions below is that security is a most important means of protection and great care must be taken to develop a strong, yet workable system of passwords and hierarchical access. Persons using the computer system should only be able to obtain access to those parts of the system which they will use. Different modes of access might be appropriate for different operators. For example, if the computer system contains a database, some users will only need to view and inspect the data, while some will be allowed to add to the data; yet others may be entitled to delete or edit the data or parts of the data. The scope of access granted to various people should reflect their responsibilities and be no more than is necessary for them to carry out their duties. Access will be by way of passwords and passwords which are easy to guess such as car registration numbers, spouse's names, etc. should be avoided. Passwords need to be changed frequently and the use of a two-password system, one password or identifier unique to each user and another for his level of access, should be considered.

A log of access to the computer system must be kept which notes user identification and times of ingress and egress, and these must be checked with users periodically. Furthermore, it must be made as difficult as possible for ordinary users to enter the computer's operating system. It is wise to invest some time and effort in making computer systems secure, appointing specialist staff or consultants for this purpose. Although this will require financial commitment it should be remembered that the consequences of poor security can be dire, not just in terms of direct costs but also in relation to the costs associated with detection and prosecution and in validating that a system is now free from viruses. With this general advice in mind, some more suggestions, related to specific criminal threats, are described below.

Fraud and theft

At one time it could be claimed that the largest threat to an organisation of fraud and theft was from employees. Whilst employees still pose a serious threat, there has been a significant increase in fraud on e-commerce sites by criminals using stolen or forged credit card data. Often, the details have been captured via computer networks and from insecure websites or even spoof websites.

In terms of employees, training is important and their attention must be drawn to the fact that security is taken seriously and incidents will be reported to the police. Less serious incidents may still result in internal disciplinary procedures being initiated. Employees should be made aware of the details of those procedures and associated regulations and the possible penalties. This will help reinforce a culture of compliance if done sensitively. An effective system of audits should be adopted including spot checks and systems for double-checking (including manual systems). These systems should be varied from time to time as variety is the criminal's greatest enemy and someone considering using the computer to commit a fraud will usually do so only after they have become familiar with the systems in operation. Changes will frustrate attempts to do this. Spot checks should be carried out on accounts chosen at random and on any unusual transactions – for example, sudden movement in an account that has been dormant for some time.

As regards supplier/sub-contractor accounts and wages systems, it must be ensured that any new accounts are genuine and that they have performed the work for which they are being paid. An IT manager must learn to behave like an external auditor with his own computer systems and to use a high profile when it comes to checking that everything is as it should be.

In terms of e-commerce fraud by outsiders, the systems in place now for guaranteeing payment to retailers should be extended to organisations doing business on the Internet, providing appropriate security standards are adopted. However, a great deal of fraud already goes on in the conventional retail arena and security is likely to be enhanced here soon. In France, for example, a person presenting his credit card at a retail outlet is also required to enter the PIN number. An experiment is already underway in the United Kingdom to adopt this system, but it might be more difficult to persuade consumers that it is safe to submit their PIN numbers on-line.

Hacking

Obviously, security is very important here too. The location of passwords must be carefully considered: are they in a text file stored on the computer which can be easily inspected by a person working in the operating system? Some form of code for any passwords which must, of necessity, be stored on the computer system should be considered. If a computer system is being installed or expanded, the need for linking that system with a telecommunications system must also be carefully considered. Is it essential to have remote access to the system? Would it be feasible to have computers at branch offices which are updated by being sent new copies of the data on disk or tape from time to time? Security needs to be made a high-profile matter at branch offices.

Educating employees should be seen as a priority. The need to take care of their passwords and change them frequently should be stressed. It may be better if the software is designed so that password changes are forced on employees after a period of time. Employees should be made aware of the dangers of accessing software they are not entitled to access and they should be given express instructions as to what they can and cannot access and what they are allowed to do where they have access.

As far as external hackers are concerned, the problem is likely to remain and all that can be done is to continually review and update security measures. The dangers posed by hackers is now very serious in the current climate of terrorism. An example of the potential for disasters was indicated when an unemployed computer programmer from Hornsey, London allegedly hacked into nearly 100 military computers in the United States, including at the Pentagon, the United States' Army research facility and a Naval base. His alleged activities went on for a year up to March 2002 and the United States government has applied for extradition; *The Times*, 13 November 2002.

Unauthorised modification (including time-bombs and viruses)

The danger here can come from hackers, employees, freelance programmers and sub-contractors. Employees who have been dismissed or have been given notice of termination of their employment represent a significant threat of damage to a computer system for such a person may seek revenge. If an employee has been given notice to leave his employment, or has been dismissed, that employee should be denied access to the computer system and should perhaps be given salary in lieu of notice. Passwords and security generally will need to be reviewed and changed depending on the employee's familiarity with the computer system. It should be borne in mind that the employee may have found out a considerable amount about the computer system during his employment – perhaps more than he should know for the purpose of performing his duties. It is worthwhile keeping a separate set of back-up copies of important programs and data in write-protected form. For example, when a new software package has been obtained the original disks need to be write-protected immediately and duplicates made which can be used as working copies.

Again, it needs to be clear that security is taken seriously and that the computer system is constantly being monitored. A potential source of computer viruses is pirated software which is to be avoided at all costs as should any software of doubtful pedigree. If a computer is attended to by a maintenance engineer, his diagnostic disks should be checked to ensure that they are write-protected for, if not, he may have collected a virus on his rounds which could be passed on to any computer. We have all seen the havoc that some viruses have caused, such as the 'I Love You' (it is understandable that few could resist opening that e-mail) and the SirCam virus. The acquisition of suitable anti-virus software is a must and should be updated as new versions are available in an effort to keep up with the ever-increasing number of viruses. Executable files, images and attachments must not be downloaded by remote access, especially on the Internet, unless they are known, positively and absolutely, to be free from viruses. Particular caution should be exercised with unsolicited e-mails and their attachments and the cunning used by those who distribute viruses to make the attached file look innocuous or from a familiar source.

Intellectual property offences

So far as these offences are concerned, little can be done in terms of prevention apart from pursuing the pirates ruthlessly and using the full weight of the civil law as well as the criminal law. Users should be educated about the important benefits of using genuine software such as support and the availability of updates. Care must be taken to prevent employees copying software and distributing it as this could breach the terms of the employer's licence agreement, allowing the licensor to revoke the licence and claim damages. Really serious economic harm can be done by piracy of computer software, music and film. Making and distributing bootleg recordings is also a serious problem. With the Internet, the dangers of wide scale distribution of music and film (and more recently books such as the Harry Potter books) are grave and highlighted by the activities of Napster, a peer-to-peer file sharing operation, recently closed down (but is alleged to have just started up again in a new format). The recent increases in the penalties available for copyright piracy show how seriously governments take this form of criminal activity. Powers of trading standards officers have also been enhanced to fight this problem. Further help in the form of civil liability and criminal penalties may come with the implementation of the Directive on copyright in the information society.

Pornography and harassing e-mails

Pornography is a problem that has attracted a great deal of attention by governments in many countries and is now, in the United Kingdom, where children are involved, subject to very heavy maximum penalties. Individuals should be aware of the seriousness of pornography (and we are not talking of *Playboy* centrefolds or 'Page 3 girls' here) and the dangers they run if they deliberately and intentional download such material, particularly if it is child pornography. As far as employers are concerned, they should make staff aware that downloading pornographic material will not be tolerated and, in appropriate cases, the police will be informed. Employers are likely to make the downloading of any images that are 'glamorous' or sexually explicit a disciplinary offence and this is to be encouraged as, if it is condoned, it could lead to the downloading of more objectionable material.

Guidance should also be given by employers about the dangers of sending e-mails that could fall within the Protection from Harassment Act 1997, bearing in mind that the threshold for the causing alarm or distress offence does not seem to be particularly high. There are always dangers of a senior member of staff bullying juniors or engaging in sexual or racial harassment and typically nowadays this could include e-mail messages. Everybody, whether in the workplace or elsewhere, ought to reflect that it is all too easy to send e-mails in anger and in haste. Do it twice and a criminal offence might be committed. The instant form of communication that e-mail is makes one wonder whether some of us ought to have a delay on our e-mail transmission to allow us to read them again a little later before sending them.

Audit Commission recommendations

The Audit Commission reports, *yourbusiness@risk: An Update on IT Abuse*, 2001, *Ghost in the Machine: An Analysis of IT Fraud and Abuse*, 1998 and *Opportunity Makes a Thief: An Analysis of Computer Abuse* (HMSO, 1994), contain many recommendations to improve security on the basis that prevention is better than cure. All persons having responsibility for the management of computer installations of whatever size would do well to read the reports. The latest report shows that poor supervision of staff is still the biggest problem, followed by inadequate access controls and inadequate or insufficient training of staff. A lack of monitoring and checking (including monitoring internet access) were also problems as was the lack of firewalls and virus detection software. Poor password control is still an issue but less so than it once was.

E-mail and internet abuse have come to the fore and have resulted in significant numbers of staff being subject to disciplinary action.

The development of a security ethos is seen as a key action and the reports identify a number of characteristics as being important in terms of an IT security policy; these are summarised below:

- an IT security which fits in with business strategy;
- a clear statement by management of the importance it places on IT security;
- a statement of staff responsibilities to protect the investment in IT and in respect of the computer data they use;
- a statement of the relevant legislation confirming that it will be enforced (this applies not only in terms of computer crime but also software piracy and data protection law);
- a statement indicating the steps taken by management to encourage and enforce high security standards;
- the steps taken to minimise computer abuse (adequate division of duties, secure password systems, etc.);
- the procedures relating to the acquisition of new hardware and software to ensure completeness and accuracy of data processing;
- the internal control mechanisms for monitoring that the policy is working and being adhered to; and
- the role of internal audit and other monitoring agencies in the organisation.

The reports recommend the use of codes of practices such as that applying to the National Standard on Information Security Management ISO/IEC 17799 (formerly BS 7799). The standard proposes ten key controls over information, including having an information security document, education and training, allocating responsibilities as to security, reporting incidents, having virus controls in place, controls over copying software, data protection and complying with security policy. It is of some concern that the number of organisations adopting the standard seems to have fallen to only 15 per cent. The 1998 Audit Commission Report suggested a checklist of questions that should be asked by management, which include questions as to 'all risks', fraud, viruses, sabotage, private work, theft of data and software, the Internet, hacking, illicit software and misuse of personal data. The questions include individual issues such as whether:

- management has issued an IT security policy and, if so, whether this is known to all staff,
- regular audit and security reviews are carried out of all key systems,
- staff are instructed not to use externally acquired disks,
- procedures are clear when disgruntled employees resign,
- risks posed by the Internet have been reviewed and steps taken to prevent access to the Internet for unauthorised and improper purposes,
- records of internet sites visited are regularly reviewed,
- attempts at password guessing are monitored,
- staff are aware of the Data Protection Act and have been warned against misusing personal data.

The seriousness of computer misuse cannot be overstated and the consequences of poor controls and procedures can be very costly. As more reliance is placed on IT systems, it is vital that effective and workable security policies are established and reviewed regularly and implemented in an effective manner. The importance of good security can be put into perspective when one reflects on the annual UK budget for information technology spending, which was reported to be in the order of a staggering £26bn (Audit Commission, *Ghost in the Machine: An Analysis of IT Fraud and Abuse*, Audit Commission Publications, 1998, p.3).

Organisations should develop their own code of practice and ensure that it filters down to all departments. Probably the most important aspect is raising staff awareness and obtaining the commitment and support of staff at all levels in developing and maintaining secure computer systems. Good security will come from delegation of responsibilities and developing an ethos of mutual commitment rather than by the imposition from on high of time-consuming and awkward procedures with little explanation of their importance and rationale.

An interesting feature of the Audit Commission report of 2001 is that it shows statistics of preventative and control measure taken in respect of the Internet. Of the survey sample, 76 per cent monitored internet activity and only just over half monitored e-mail activity. Just over half banned access to specific websites and 30 per cent reviewed out of hours access to websites. Seven per cent admitted that they applied no preventative measures at all to internet activity. Finally, the report stated (at p.28):

> There must be a reliable and secure IT network underpinning internet use. If the network is not fully protected then the organisation will undoubtedly face major risks and may well find itself unable to survive. The network infrastructure must:
> - be resilient,
>   - capable of providing a 24 hours a day, seven days a week service;
>   - capable of maintaining a service when power failures occur;
> - identify users,
>   - prevent unauthorised access attempts; and
> - monitor activity;
>   - report unusual occurrences.

Summary

It has been shown that a wide variety of criminal offences can be committed using or involving computer technology. Other offences may also be carried out. For example, murder or manslaughter can be committed by interfering with a safety-critical system such as an air traffic control computer or a hospital computer monitoring the treatment of patients. Of course, some offences are not relevant to computer technology and it would be difficult to envisage a situation where rape could be carried out using a computer (though it could be associated with sexual grooming). However, given the ingenuity of the criminal mind, there are certain to be other forms of crime which will be attempted in the future.

The criminal law is now quite strong in relation to all forms of computer crime following the enactment of the Computer Misuse Act 1990 and changes to pornography laws. On the whole, the legal environment in the United Kingdom has struck a reasonable balance between the interests of industry and commerce and the private individual. At least we do not execute computer hackers as happened in China a few years ago. Although the Computer Misuse Act has been welcomed by many in the computer industry and financial institutions, the presence of stronger laws should not be seen as a substitute for strong security measures and effective systems of auditing. Those organisations which store confidential information concerning individual members of the public or which have safety-critical systems have a moral duty (and in some circumstances a legal duty) to protect their computer systems from criminal activities, whether perpetrated from outside the organisation or within it.

Finally, the fact is that only the minority of offences result in prosecutions. Of the 537 reported incidents in the Audit Commission report published in 1994 only 58 of the culprits were prosecuted. The 1998 survey indicated 510 incidents reported by 900 organisations. In terms of all IT fraud and abuse around 20 per cent resulted in dismissal and/or prosecution. As regards computer fraud over 40 per cent of detected incidents led to prosecutions. The 2001 Audit Commission study showed that the average value of detected computer frauds was £36,000 and of the 688 organisations taking part, 460 reported that they had suffered some form of computer abuse over the three years of the study. One welcome sign is that judges seem to be more prepared to take computer crime seriously and a number of offenders have been imprisoned. This now seems to be the most likely outcome where fraud, large-scale piracy or a serious case of hacking is involved. Other penalties imposed include large fines, suspended sentences and community sentences.

Table 33.1 gives a summary of offences together with their maximum penalties and some comment concerning their scope. It should be noted that, in most cases, a fine is also possible in addition to or instead of a prison sentence. Of course, subject to the maximum penalty, the courts have a full range of other disposals available to them such as probation orders, community sentences, fines and absolute or conditional discharges and may also make compensation orders. Note that some of the offences do not apply in Scotland where broadly equivalent offences apply. Unless otherwise stated, the offences, in the case of adults, are triable either in the Crown Court or magistrates' courts.

Table 33.1 Summary of offences

Offence	Description	Maximum penalty	Comment
Fraud/theft related s 15 Theft Act 1968	Obtaining property by deception	10 years	Difficulty with respect to machine being deceived (requires a human to be deceived)
s 15A Theft Act 1968	Obtaining a money transfer by deception	10 years	Designed for, but not restricted to, 'mortgage frauds'; applies to electronic funds transfers as well as cheques
s 1 Theft Act 1968	Theft	7 years	Will cover most cases involving computer 'fraud'
ss 17, 19 and 20 Theft Act 1968	False accounting, etc.	7 years	No particular difficulties with computer technology

Offence	Description	Maximum penalty	Comment
s 2 Computer Misuse Act 1990	Basic hacking plus ulterior intent	5 years	Useful for attempts and not restricted to fraud
Conspiracy to defraud	Common law	10 years	2 or more persons. Triable in CC only
Cheating	Common law	Imprisonment and/or fine without limit	Only available for Inland Revenue and VAT frauds
Hacking and damage s 1 Computer Misuse Act 1990	Basic hacking offence	6 months	Triable only in MC. Search warrants available from circuit judge
s 13 Theft Act 1968	Abstracting electricity	5 years	May be difficult with respect to 'knowledge'
s 1 Regulation of Investigatory Powers Act 2000	Interception of communication during its transmission through a public telecommunications system (or through a public postal service)	2 years	Suitable for computer 'eaves-dropping'
s 43 Telecommunications Act 1984	The transmission of grossly offensive, indecent, obscene or menacing messages	6 months	Can only be tried in MC. Must be by public telecommunications system
s 3 Computer Misuse Act 1990	Unauthorised modification of computer material	5 years	Replaced criminal damage in relation to programs and data
s 21 Theft Act 1968	Blackmail	14 years	Unwarranted demand with menaces. Triable in CC only
Intellectual property related s 107 Copyright, Designs & Patents Act 1988	Secondary infringement generally making pirate copies for sale or 'dealing' with pirate copies, etc.		See Table 31.1 for penalties
s 1 Forgery and Counterfeiting Act 1981	Making a false instrument	10 years	Requires someone to believe it to be genuine
s 1 Trade Descriptions Act 1968	Applying false trade description, etc.	2 years	Trade description includes an indication of the manufacturer of the goods
s 92 Trade Marks Act 1994	Applying a registered trade mark, etc. without consent	10 years	It is a defence if the person concerned reasonably believed that the use did not infringe

Offence	Description	Maximum penalty	Comment
s 25 Theft Act 1968	Going equipped to cheat	3 years	'Cheat' has same meaning as 'obtaining by deception'
Other s 21 Data Protection Act 1998	Processing personal data without having notified	fine	Strict liability; failure to notify changes is also an offence subject to a due diligence defence
s 55 Data Protection Act 1998	Obtaining, disclosing or procuring the disclosure of personal data without the consent of the data controller	fine	Some defences apply. Selling such data is an offence. For further offences under the Data Protection Act, see Part Five of this book
Obscene Publication Acts 1959 & 1964 (s 2 of the 1959 Act as amended)	Publishing obscene article or having obscene article for publication for gain	3 years	Would apply with respect to a computer disk containing pornographic images or information but some doubt about transmission over network
s 1 Protection of Children Act 1978	Taking, or permitting to be taken, an indecent photograph or pseudo-photograph of a child, distributing, showing or being in possession with intent to distribute or show such a photograph	10 years	Making a photograph or pseudo-photograph includes downloading an image to a computer screen or cache
s 160 Criminal Justice Act 1998	Possession of an indecent photograph or pseudo-photograph of a child	5 years	'Pseudo-photograph' covers computer graphics images and covers data stored on disk or electronically
s 1 Protection from Harassment Act 1997	Pursuing a course of conduct which causes alarm or distress on at least two occasions	6 months	A course of conduct (more than one occasion); could include sending threatening e-mails. Triable in MC only
s 4 Protection from Harassment Act 1997	Pursuing a course of conduct causing another to fear violence on at least two occasions	5 years	Course of conduct as for s 1 offence
Incitement (in the context of computer abuse)	Encouraging, persuading, suggesting, proposing to someone to commit a criminal offence	At the court's discretion if tried in CC	Could apply particularly to material posted on the Internet, for example, describing how to make a bomb, how to write a computer virus

Note: CC = Crown Court, MC = magistrates' court.
Unless otherwise indicated, offences can be tried in either a Magistrates' Court or in the Crown Court in the case of an adult.

PART FIVE

Data protection

Computer technology heightened fears about a society of the kind portrayed in George Orwell's *1984*, because of the power of computers in terms of information processing. Even now, there remains a feeling shared by some that computers undermine human skills and that the growth of computer technology heralds the dawn of an austere and coldly logical society. Certainly, the power of computers can be misused and there needs to be a system of checks and balances to prevent abuse of this power. In particular, computers raise concerns about individuals and their privacy.

Until recently there was no general right to privacy under English law although some legal remedies may be available in some circumstances, such as an action for breach of confidence or publishing defamatory material, or the limited protection afforded by the Data Protection Act 1984. Things have changed enormously. The United Kingdom finally got round to bringing the European Convention on Human Rights into force on 4 November 2000 (the full title of the Convention is the Convention for the Protection of Human Rights and Fundamental Freedoms, agreed by the Council of Europe at Rome 4 November 1950). Another Council of Europe Convention is the Convention for the Protection of Individuals with regard to Processing of Personal Data, Strasbourg, 28 January 1981. This latter Convention, which in its Preamble refers to the importance of protecting individuals' rights and freedoms, especially the right of privacy in respect of transborder flows of personal data, can be seen as either supplementary to the Human Rights Convention or as an application of that Convention in a specific context.

The Strasbourg Convention justified and underpinned subsequent developments in data protection law. It was the basis of the United Kingdom's Data Protection Act 1984 (now replaced by the Data Protection Act 1998). The European Directive on data protection, from which the 1998 Act derives its force, can be seen as an updating of the Strasbourg Convention in line with the Human Rights Convention. Theoretically, there should be no conflict between the two though, in some cases, litigants may choose the Human Rights Convention on which to base their grievance. Under section 2 of the Human Rights Act 1998, primary and secondary legislation must, as far as it is possible to do so, be given effect in a way compatible with rights under the Human Rights Convention. This is retrospective. Thus, if a provision of the Data Protection Act 1998 is in conflict with the Human Rights Convention or, for example, a decision of the European Court of Human Rights, the Act should be interpreted in the light of the Convention. If it cannot be interpreted in accordance with the Convention and there is a clear conflict, a court (in England and Wales, the House of Lords, the High Court or the Court of Appeal) may make a declaration of incompatibility under section 4 of the

Human Rights Act 1998. It would then be for Parliament to consider modifying the legislation.

The Data Protection Act 1984, in line with the Strasbourg Convention, only applied to automatically processed personal data. The European Directive on data protection made significant changes to the model of data protection and even extended to certain forms of manual processing, basing its legitimacy on the Human Rights Convention and two of the key features of that Convention, being the right to privacy under Article 8 and the right of freedom of expression under Article 10. Balancing these two, sometime contradictory rights, has not proven easy. Both of the rights contain derogations, for example, both rights can be suppressed in the interests of national security if prescribed by law and necessary in a democratic society.

Data protection law can be truly said to be voluminous with the Data Protection Act 1998, which is a large and complex piece of legislation and around two dozen statutory instruments made under it. The Act and the statutory instruments have been subject to modifications and the whole must be interpreted in line with the data protection Directive and the Human Rights Convention, where applicable. There is also a great deal of guidance on data protection law and, taken altogether, it is easy to criticise the breathtaking size and scope of data protection law as taking a sledgehammer to crack a walnut. Most reasonable organisations in the public and private sectors would, as a matter of course, adopt effective and fair systems for their data processing activities, as this is largely a reflection of good practice. However, the dangers posed by the processing of personal data, which may be unfairly processed, inaccurate, out-of-date or disclosed in a harmful way, are very serious. Furthermore, the reality is that, for the majority of organisations and persons processing personal data, compliance is not onerous and there may be savings available, for example, by destroying or erasing old, irrelevant and inaccurate data and ensuring that good levels of data security are adhered to, including processing by contractors and by sub-contractors.

Readers may be a little confused by some of the terminology which has changed. Originally, the person responsible for data protection was known as the Data Protection Registrar (Eric Howe was the first Registrar). Following the 1998 Act, the position became known as the Data Protection Commissioner (Elizabeth France was in position as this and the following change took place). Following the introduction of the Freedom of Information Act 2000 (being brought into force in stages), the position is now known as the Information Commissioner. The present incumbent is Richard Thomas, the third to be responsible for data protection law in the United Kingdom. A tribunal set up originally under the 1984 Act as the Data Protection Tribunal is now known as the Information Tribunal. Other changes in terminology will be noted in relevant places in the following chapters.

Note: Unless otherwise mentioned, all statutory references in this part are to the Data Protection Act 1998, as amended.

Chapter 34

Introduction and background to the Data Protection Act 1998

Introduction

Data protection law affects everybody. Most persons process information about individuals, even if it is simply name, address and telephone number. Many do this by computer and only those who use a computer for little more than straightforward word processing will fail to be regulated under data protection law, whether or not they are required to notify their processing activity under the Data Protection Act 1998. A great many people have manual filing systems containing information relating to individuals. These may be in the form of a card index system or even a simple address book. Until the 1998 Act, data protection law did not apply to manual processing but it now applies to certain types of manual filing systems. Even if we do not process personal information, it is almost certain that numerous organisations and persons are processing personal information relating to us. Indeed, there can be very few persons who are not affected by data protection law as being the subject of data processed by others. The identities of some of those who process our personal data are easy to guess such as employers, health providers, banks, local authorities, government bodies and creditors. Others who process personal data relating to us are less easy to know specifically in advance, such as marketing organisations.

Data protection law has two main influences. First, those who process information concerning individuals are subject to a regulatory framework within which they can process personal data lawfully. Secondly, as individuals we all have rights under data protection law, enhanced by the 1998 Act and, in some cases, supplemented or strengthened by the Human Rights Convention. As this area of law has changed, the rights of individuals are given more prominence and a key phrase is 'transparency of processing'. Individuals should be better informed as to who is processing data relating to them, what the purpose of the processing is and what other processing activities are involved. They also have a right to more information than before in response to a request for access and greater rights to control processing activity. As we shall see, transparency of processing is often compromised, to a greater or lesser extent.

There are many horror stories about people who have had information wrongly attributed to them and stored on computer. For example, a man with an impeccable character and without any convictions at all was arrested and charged with driving whilst disqualified because of incorrect information stored on the Police National Computer. Details about the disqualification had been entered against his name by mistake. He lost his job and had his car impounded. It took him four months to trace the man to whom the previous conviction related and whose name was very similar before he could clear his name (*The Times*, 8 May 1990, p.4). A more recent example, though of less serious consequences, was the case of *Ogle* v *Chief Constable of Thames Valley Police* [2001] EWCA Civ 598. The claimant had been disqualified from driving for four years following drink-driving offences but this was subsequently reduced on appeal to two years. Unfortunately, the reduction of the ban was not recorded on the Police National Computer and, some time after the two years had expired, the claimant was arrested for driving whilst disqualified by a different police authority and he was detained for two and half hours before being released. However, as the claimant had previously accepted a settlement of £950 for wrongful arrest, his later attempt to re-open the case on the basis of a claim for distress under the Data Protection Act 1984 was rejected.

Another problem has been the lack of control of organisations who pass on personal information to others, resulting in many people having been inundated with unsolicited mail, faxes and e-mails. A more sinister aspect of computer-stored information is a direct result of the powerful processing capacity of computers and the ability to use computers to target certain groups of individuals or to build profiles about our preferences and spending habits. There are also serious issues associated with the processing of sensitive personal data stored on computers or in structured manual files and the collection, storage and disclosure of sensitive personal data needs to be subject to special safeguards and should only be processed in limited circumstances.

As computer technology becomes progressively powerful and more use is made of computers, the dangers are set to increase. Numerous concerns have been expressed in the past by the Information Commissioner and others. For example, some data may be very sensitive and may cause considerable harm if its use is not strictly controlled such as data relating to genetic information or illnesses and diseases. Other concerns flow from the use of 'white data' showing that a person has a good credit record and the activities of private investigators has caused concern in the past and continues to do so. Other issues relate to the balance between freedom of speech and individuals' right to privacy, two areas of apparently diametrically opposed interests always very difficult to reconcile. Nor is computer technology the only threat. The Economic League was an organisation which retained details of individuals who had been active trade unionists or members of the Communist Party. All this data was kept on paper. The Data Protection Act 1984 had no effect upon such data processing – it had to be by automatic means. Structured manual files can pose just as many problems as automated processing activities.

The Data Protection Act 1984 received the Royal Assent at an appropriate time in Orwellian terms. It was designed to control the storage and use of information about individuals stored and processed by computer. Control of processing was provided for by a system of registration with penalties for failing to register and for acting beyond the scope of the registration. Additionally, the Act introduced a set of *Data Protection Principles*, derived from the Council of Europe's Convention for the protection of individuals with regard to automatic processing of personal data, which must be followed by persons who store or process information, using computers, about living persons. Computer bureaux providing services to those who process such information were also controlled and were required to register under the 1984 Act. Individuals, about whom information is stored on computer, were given rights of access and a right to have inaccurate records corrected or deleted. Under certain circumstances, individuals had a right to compensation.

The history leading up to the 1984 Act was relatively long and there were several Parliamentary Bills, Reports and White Papers concerning privacy and data protection. The Lindop Report (*Report of the Committee on Data Protection*, Cmnd 7341, HMSO, 1978) was important in respect of moves towards legislation. The final impetus was provided by the Council of Europe's Convention for the protection of individuals with regard to automatic processing of personal data, signed by the United Kingdom in 1981 and ratified in 1987. The convention included principles for data protection and proposed a common set of standards. In 1982, a White Paper was published, outlining the Government's intentions (Cmnd 8539) and following this a Bill was introduced in the House of Lords. However, this failed to become law because of the general election of 1983 and a new Bill was introduced after the election and eventually received the Royal Assent in July 1984. The Data Protection Act 1984 was implemented in stages, the last of which mainly concerned individuals' rights of access and which came into effect on 11 November 1987.

In this chapter, following a brief discussion of the Data Protection Directive, the catalyst for the current model of data protection law throughout the European Economic Area, the background to the Data Protection Act 1998 is described. Next the *Data Protection Principles* are stated and there follows a look at the definitions contained in the Act. The work of the Information Commissioner is then considered, followed by material on the Information Tribunal and the Working Party set up under the Data Protection Directive.

The Data Protection Directive

In the context of a Single European Market, it is essential that there should be no barriers to the transfer of information between member states. The principle of freedom of movement of goods and services has been largely achieved and it would be unthinkable if, in this age of information technology, the same freedom of movement did not apply to computer data. However, not all the member states complied with the European Convention for the protection of individuals with regard to automatic processing of personal data. Being conscious of the possibility that member states of the European Community could erect barriers to the flows of computer data on the basis of insufficient protection for individuals in other member states, the Commission worked towards a Directive laying down a basic framework for the protection of personal data whilst stressing the freedom of movement of personal data. The argument is that, if all member states adhered to a reasonable standard of protection of personal data, there should be no barriers to the movement of personal data within the Community. The other countries in the European Economic Area (EEA) – Norway, Iceland and Liechtenstein – also agreed to comply with the Directive so, effectively, there are no barriers to the free movement of personal data throughout the EEA.

A proposal for a Directive on the protection of individuals in relation to the processing of personal data was published in 1990 (COM(90) 314 final – SYN 287, OJ C 277, 05.11.1990, p.3) and provided a complex system differentiating between the public and private sector as was then the position in some countries such as the Netherlands. A further proposal was published in 1992 (COM(92) 24 final – SYN 393, OJ C 311, 27.11.1992, p.38). The distinction between the public and private sector disappeared but this particular proposal was perceived by data users as being unduly restrictive and extremely onerous to comply with. Particular concerns were directed at the extension of data protection law to manual files, the requirements to inform data subjects and, in some cases, the need to seek data subjects' consent to processing. A survey carried out for the Home Office in the United Kingdom indicated that compliance would cost the

625 organisations included in the survey at least £2bn (*Costs of implementing the Data Protection Directive: Paper by the United Kingdom,* Home Office (1994)) whilst the Department of Health estimated that it would be necessary to inform every member of the population that it held personal data concerning them and that this would cost over £1bn (*Draft EC proposed Directive on data protection: analysis of costs,* Department of Health (1994)).

The Commission responded to some of the concerns of data users and changes were made to reduce the financial burden whilst retaining the principle of protecting the individuals' rights of privacy. Furthermore, a survey carried out for the Commission by the author of this book and a number of colleagues at Aston University and the University of Leiden indicated that the above costs were exaggerated. Eventually, the Directive was adopted in July 1995 although the United Kingdom abstained in the vote. The full title of the Directive is Directive 95/46/EC of the European Parliament and of the Council on the protection of individuals with regard to the processing of personal data and of the free movement of such data, OJ L 281, 23.11.1995, p.31. In this and the remaining chapters in this part of the book it will simply be referred to as the 'Data Protection Directive'. In December 1999, the Commission decided to take five member states to the European Court of Justice for failing to implement the Directive, these being France, Ireland, Germany, Luxembourg and the Netherlands. At the time of writing, only France has failed to implement the Directive but the preparatory work is well under way.

Model of data protection under the Directive

The Directive has, under Article 1, the twin aims of protecting privacy in the context of processing personal data and providing for the freedom of movement of personal data. Article 1 states:

1 **In accordance with this Directive Member States shall protect the fundamental rights and freedoms of natural persons, and in particular their right of privacy, with respect to the processing of personal data.**
2 **Member States shall neither restrict nor prohibit the free flow of personal data between Member States for reasons connected with the protection afforded under paragraph 1.**

In other words, providing member states have complied with the requirements of the Directive there must be freedom of movement of personal data throughout the Community, at least no barriers can be erected on the grounds of privacy concerns.

Although the Directive marks a significant change in data protection law, it has at its heart data protection principles in Article 6. These derive from the European Convention for the protection of individuals with regard to automatic processing of personal data, supplemented by a Protocol to the Convention. The data protection principles provide a common link between the new law and that under the 1984 Act. Thus, fair and lawful processing must be ensured, personal data must be processed only for specified purposes, the data must be adequate, relevant and not excessive, they must be accurate and up-to-date and not kept in a form which permits identification of the data subject for longer than necessary. Nevertheless, and reflecting the changes to data protection law, the mechanism of protection under the Directive is, it is fair to say, more complex than that under the Data Protection Act 1984. It is shown in Fig. 34.1.

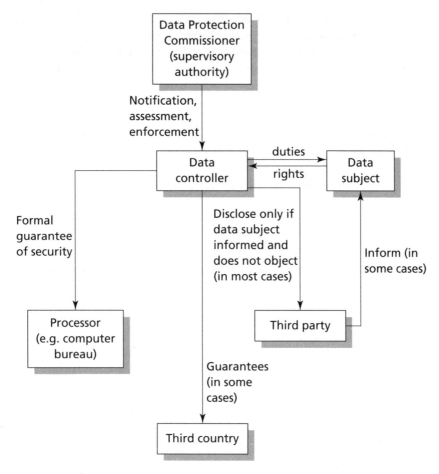

Fig. 34.1 Model of data protection under the Data Protection Directive

Although the definitions used in the Directive and the Data Protection Act 1998 are described below, for the purposes of understanding the diagram, suffice it to say that the data controller is the person who decides the purposes and manner of processing, the processor is a person who processes personal data on behalf of the data controller, the data subject is the individual to whom the personal data in question relate, a third country is a country outside the EEA. The Information Commissioner is responsible, amongst other things, for supervising compliance with the Act and a third party is any person other than a data controller, processor or employee or agent of either.

Data controllers are required to notify their processing activities to the supervisory authority (the Information Commissioner in the United Kingdom). Where the processing in question is likely to pose specific risks to rights and freedoms, the processing operation must be examined before it can commence. The Directive permits exemption from or simplification of notification where the processing is unlikely to affect the rights and freedoms of data subjects or where an 'in-house' data protection official (data protection supervisor) is appointed. Data controllers can only process personal data if they fall within one of a number of conditions. One of a further number of conditions must be satisfied where the personal data are 'sensitive', for example, relating to racial or ethnic origin, health, political or religious beliefs. Further duties are imposed on data controllers to inform data subjects. Data subjects are given rights of access and rights to object to processing and to prevent processing in some cases. They are also given certain additional rights in respect of automated decision taking and rights of rectification, erasure or blocking of data, the processing of which does not comply with the Directive.

Security obligations are imposed on a data controller and, where a data controller engages a processor, such as a computer bureau or a company to provide IT facilities management services, equivalent security obligations must be imposed on the processor. This must be by contractual means or by some other legal act and be in writing or equivalent form. Transfers to countries outside the EEA may be allowed only under certain conditions if the country in question does not have adequate protection for personal data.

The Directive also applies to structured manual files which, because of their structure, make it easy to access personal data belonging to a particular individual. However, there are a number of important derogations and options provided for in the Directive which allow for its impact to be lessened somewhat. Particularly important are the derogations allowing member states to delay the implementation of the Directive to processing already under way at 24 October 1998 (the date the Directive should have been implemented into domestic law) and to further delay the impact of certain parts of the Directive on manual processing.

A feature of the Directive is that the definitions used are fairly wide. For example, it is clear that personal data can include image data or sound data. The definition of processing is breathtakingly wide, including:

> ... collection, recording, organisation, storage, adaptation or alteration, retrieval, consultation, use, disclosure by transmission, dissemination or otherwise making available, alignment or combination, blocking, erasure or destruction.

The presence of the word 'storage' indicates that simply being in possession of personal data is processing for the purposes of the Directive.

To summarise, issues flowing from the Directive which caused particular concern were:

- the extension of data protection law to some manual files,
- the requirement to inform data subjects on collection of data or otherwise,
- the possibility of data subjects objecting to processing,
- having to seek data subjects' consent to processing in some cases,
- the introduction of conditions for processing to proceed,
- possible constraints over transfers of personal data to countries outside the EEA,
- security of processing of personal data, and
- controls over automated decision making.

In the remainder of this chapter and the following two chapters, the provisions of the Data Protection Act 1998 will be examined. Where appropriate, the provisions of the Directive will be discussed though, generally, it must be noted that the 1998 Act appears to be a reasonably faithful implementation of the Directive. The United Kingdom took advantage of many (though not all) of the derogations and options available in the Directive. Of course, mention will also be made of the 1984 Act where appropriate and particularly where the new law is significantly different. Some of the cases mentioned in this and following chapters were decided under the 1984 Act. Some are no longer relevant: for example, *R v Brown* [1996] 1 AC 543, an unsatisfactory decision under the 1984 Act by the House of Lords which has been overtaken by the wider definition of processing. But others remain very valuable in determining the scope of the new law: for example, *Innovations (Mail Order) Ltd v Data Protection Registrar* (unreported) 29 September 1993, concerning fair processing. Cases under the 1984 Act will only be discussed where they are still relevant or for comparative purposes only.

The Data Protection Act 1998

The Data Protection Bill was introduced in the House of Lords in January 1998. During its passage through the Lords and, later, through the House of Commons, it underwent many changes. For example, as first printed, the Bill had no specific provisions for transitional arrangements, the list of conditions for processing sensitive data were inadequate and there were no controls over enforced subject access (although this aspect still has not been brought into force). The Act finally received the Royal Assent on 16 July 1998. Some provisions came into force immediately, being primarily concerned with the definitions under the Act and the arrangements to make Regulations under the Act. The remaining provisions of the Act came into force on 1 March 2000, apart from section 56 making enforced subject access an offence. This section is dependent upon certain provisions of the Police Act 1997 coming into force but because of subsequent changes, it now looks unlikely that section 56 of the Data Protection Act 1998 will come into force in the immediate future, if it ever does. There was no express provision in the Directive concerning enforced subject access. No fewer than 24 statutory instruments have been made under the Act and the Act has itself already gone through numerous modifications. The statutory instruments and changes will be mentioned in this and the following chapters if appropriate.

Before looking at the Data Protection Principles, the definitions and other provisions of the Act, it must be noted that the Act is not the only source of constraints and controls on the collection, processing and use of personal data. Other areas of law may be highly relevant. For example, a person holding personal data may have an obligation of confidence not to disclose the data or a fiduciary duty in relation to them. Disclosure may be allowed only in a limited number of situations as is the case in banking where rules concerning when personal data may be disclosed were laid down in *Tournier v National Provincial* [1924] 1 KB 461. In that case, it was held that disclosure of confidential information could proceed where the interests of the bank required disclosure. However, it is an old case and it is arguable whether it would be applied without modification in the present climate of greater respect for individuals' rights and freedoms. Disclosure may otherwise be lawful if the individual consents or where the disclosure is in the public interest or where it is required by law. The laws of copyright and defamation may also restrict the use and disclosure of information relating to individuals.

The Data Protection Principles

The Data Protection Principles are at the root of data protection law and they are contained in Part I of Schedule 1 to the Act. Part II of the Schedule provides interpretation of the Principles. The Principles appear much as before although there are some important differences. They are as follows.

1 Personal data shall be processed fairly and lawfully and, in particular, shall not be processed unless –
   (a) at least one of the conditions in Schedule 2 is met, and
   (b) in the case of sensitive personal data, at least one of the conditions in Schedule 3 is also met.
2 Personal data shall be obtained only for one or more specified and lawful purposes and shall not be further processed in any manner incompatible with that purpose or those purposes.
3 Personal data shall be adequate, relevant and not excessive in relation to the purpose or purposes for which they are processed.
4 Personal data shall be accurate and, where necessary, kept up to date.
5 Personal data processed for any purpose or purposes shall not be kept for longer than is necessary for that purpose or those purposes.
6 Personal data shall be processed in accordance with the rights of data subjects under this Act.
7 Appropriate technical and organisational measures shall be taken against unauthorised or unlawful processing of personal data and against accidental loss or destruction of, or damage to, personal data.
8 Personal data shall not be transferred to a country or territory outside the European Economic Area unless that country or territory ensures an adequate level of protection for the rights and freedoms of data subjects in relation to the processing of personal data.

Whilst these are very similar to those under the 1984 Act, Principle 8 is new and reflects concerns about transfers of personal data to countries that do not have adequate protection. Furthermore, the first Principle now refers to conditions for processing. Again this is new. Of course, the first Principle is without a doubt the most important – that processing shall be fair and lawful – and it could be said that the rest of data protection law merely fleshes this out and provides the detail of just what fair and lawful processing is.

There have been a number of cases on the Data Protection Principles under the 1984 Act, particularly in respect of the first Principle and these are discussed in depth in the next chapter. Some of the other Principles have also exercised the Data Protection Registrar (as the Information Commissioner was then known) who was quite active at the time of the introduction of the Community Charge ('poll tax') following concerns that a number of local authorities were collecting unnecessary information about persons and that the information was excessive in terms of that required for the purposes of the Community Charge. In *Rhondda BC* v *Data Protection Registrar* (unreported) 11 October 1991, the Tribunal upheld the Registrar's interpretation of the fourth Principle (third Principle under the 1998 Act) and confirmed the enforcement notice issued against the officers in charge of collecting information. They had been asking for individuals' dates of birth. In *CCRO of Runneymede BC* v *Data Protection Registrar* (unreported) 1990, Data Protection Tribunal, information relating to the type of property in which the poll tax payer resided was deemed excessive.

The seventh Principle is concerned with security (it was the eighth Principle under the 1984 Act) and, following a number of thefts of computers from doctors' surgeries, the Data Protection Registrar warned general practitioners to review their security arrangements otherwise they could be in breach of that Principle (*The Times*, 2 December 1992, at p.3). The worry here was that the information stored could be used to blackmail individuals. One criticism of the 1984 Act (and the same applies to the 1998 Act) is that there was no express requirement to report the 'theft' of personal data and a spate of 20 such thefts over a six-month period could be just the tip of the iceberg.

The Principles and their interpretation will be discussed in greater depth in the following chapters. It is considered to be useful, however, to let readers have sight of them now and to stress that it is the Principles which underpin the new law, as they did, in slightly different form, under the 1984 Act.

Definitions

The definitions are very significant and they set out the scope of the new law. The most important definitions are contained in section 1 of the Act. Some are similar to those under the 1984 Act, though others are much wider. First, the definition of data is given.

'*data*' means information which–
(a) is being processed by means of equipment operating automatically in response to instructions given for that purpose,
(b) is recorded with the intention that it should be processed by means of such equipment,
(c) is recorded as part of a relevant filing system or with the intention that it should form part of a relevant filing system,
(d) does not fall within paragraph (a), (b) or (c) but forms part of an accessible record as defined by section 68, or
(e) is recorded information held by a public authority and does not fall within any of the paragraphs (a) to (d).

The meaning in (e) was added by the Freedom of Information Act 2000 and will apply on 30 November 2005 or such earlier date as may be appointed by order by the Secretary of State. This is in relation to a right of access to unstructured personal data held by public authorities, not yet in force.

Data within (a) and (b) above are those which are being or are to be processed by automatic means; in other words, computer data. Data within (c) are those in structured manual filing systems ('relevant filing system' is defined below). These are the data to which data protection law has been extended by the Act. The inclusion of such data was seen as one of the most costly provisions in the new law to implement.

Accessible records within (d) above are health records and certain educational and local authority records; these are caught by the new law even if they are processed manually and are not structured within the meaning required for a relevant filing system. The inclusion of such data is to incorporate the effect of the Access to Personal Files Act 1987 within the new law. This Act gave a right of access to certain local authority files, such as social services files and housing files, and is repealed in full. Access to health records which was covered by the Access to Health Records Act 1990 is also included in the new law. Where local authority files or health records are processed by computer, they are treated in the same way as other data under the 1998 Act.

Automatically processed data are treated somewhat differently than data in relevant filing systems within (c) above and accessible records within (d) above. In particular, only automatic processing need be notified unless specifically exempt (although, in rare cases, manual processing may be subject to a preliminary assessment before processing can proceed). There are also provisions delaying parts of the new law specifically directed towards manual processing.

'*personal data*' means data which relate to a living individual who can be identified–
(a) from those data, or
(b) from those data and other information which is in the possession of, or likely to come into the possession of, the data controller,
and includes any expression of opinion about the individual and any indication of the intentions of the data controller or any other person in respect of the individual.

There was some doubt as to whether the Directive intended to restrict personal data to living individuals but the 1998 Act puts this beyond doubt. The definition confirms that it is not necessary for all the identifying data to be subject to the processing activity. It is enough for there to be further information which the person processing the data has or will obtain and which, together with the data being processed, is sufficient to identify an individual. For example, a computer database may not include names but might, instead, operate on individuals' national insurance numbers. If the person processing the data also has a card index which contains national insurance numbers and the names of the individuals to whom they belong, that is sufficient for the data being processing by computer to be classified as personal data.

Personal data now include expressions of opinion and any indication of intentions. The latter was expressly excluded from the meaning of personal data under the 1984 Act. However, some of the exemptions from the subject access provisions compensate for this change. In any case, it might be difficult to distinguish between an expression of opinion and a statement of intention. 'The performance of Joe Bloggs as a sale executive indicates that it is unlikely that he will be promoted in the near future' is an example.

'*relevant filing system*' means any set of information relating to individuals to the extent that, although the information is not processed by means of equipment operating automatically in response to instructions given for that purpose, the set is structured, either by reference to individuals or by reference to criteria relating to individuals, in such a way that specific information relating to a particular individual is readily accessible.

The requirement is that personal data are easily accessible because of the structure, such as in the case of a *pro forma* application form. This is confirmed in the Directive and recital 15 thereto, which emphasises ease of access by virtue of structure. Clearly a card index system where each card bears an individual's name on the top, the cards being stored in name order, will be a relevant filing system. It would appear that a file relating to a specific individual containing, for example, only correspondence to and from that individual will not be deemed to be a relevant filing system. The Home Office view was that some internal structure also is required. However, it is possible that a simple address book set out in alphabetical order is caught by the new law. If this contains name, address, telephone number and e-mail address it is at least arguable that it is a relevant filing system as it enables ease of access to information relating to any particular individual. Furthermore, it probably will have some form of internal structure: for example, it may have two columns, the left-hand column containing a name followed below by an address; the right-hand column might have telephone numbers and the like. Fortunately, if a simple address book is a relevant filing system, as such it does not have to be the subject of formal notification to the Information Commissioner, as we shall see. Note that accessible records in the definition of data are caught by the new law even though they are not processed automatically, nor intended to be processed automatically, and are not structured.

'*data controller*' means ... a person who (either alone or jointly or in common with other persons) determines the purposes for which and the manner in which any personal data are, or are to be, processed.

Data controllers are the equivalent to 'data users' under the 1984 Act. Note that there may be two or more data controllers in respect of a single collection of personal data: for example, where an association of builders mutually share and are responsible for a central database of sub-contractors and suppliers. The significance of the phrase 'jointly or in common with other persons' is that if two or more data controllers agree between themselves as to the purposes and manner of processing, then they determine these matters jointly. However, if two or more data controllers have access to a central database, say a data warehouse, but they each have their own individual purposes and manner of processing, then they determine these matters in common. For example, Company A has a data warehouse (a massive collection of data relating to individuals where the information has been obtained from a number of sources). Company A uses this to extract information relating to creditworthiness of its customers. Company A also allows Company B to access the data warehouse. Company B has its own computer programs which are used to identify potential customers for a marketing campaign and to print out envelopes with the selected persons' names and addresses.

As before, under the 1984 Act, a '*data subject*' is simply an individual who is the subject of personal data. He is the person to whom the personal data relate or refer.

'Processing' is very widely defined (much more than under the 1984 Act) and, in relation to information or data, means:

obtaining, recording or holding the information or data or carrying out any operation or set of operations on the information or data, including–
(a) organisation, adaptation or alteration of the information or data,
(b) retrieval, consultation or use of the information or data,
(c) disclosure of the information or data by transmission, dissemination or otherwise making available, or
(d) alignment, combination, blocking, erasure or destruction of the information or data.

Obtaining, recording, using or disclosing data extends to the information contained within the data and it is immaterial if the processing or inclusion in a relevant filing system takes place outside the EEA.

The definition extends to 'holding' personal data (the Directive uses the term 'storage' instead). This means that simply being in possession of personal data will be processing for the purposes of the Act. Even if the data are stored in structured paper files kept as archive material in a dusty basement, the person responsible will be processing those data. Under section 1 of the 1984 Act, a data user was defined as being a person who holds personal data. Holding data was then defined in terms of the data being part of a collection processed or intended to be processed by automatic means and the person holding the data alone or jointly or in common with others controlled the contents and use of the data. The definition also extended to data which were not at the time in a form ready for processing. Although 'holding' is not defined in the 1998 Act, one view is that, if the data are in a store and not subject to current processing activity, there must be an intention to process the data in the future. Given the very wide definition of processing, there would be little point in keeping data without having such an intention. This would probably be a breach of the fifth data protection Principle.

The definition of processing covers every conceivable use of data and its width is enhanced because the operations referred to are not intended to be exhaustive owing to the insertion of the word 'including'. The House of Lords case of *R v Brown* [1996] 1 AC 543, heard under the 1984 Act, shows the importance of having a wide definition of 'processing'. In that case, a police officer worked in his spare time with a friend in their debt collection agency. The agency was engaged by a third party to recover a debt. The police officer used the police national computer to obtain information concerning the debtor. He denied that he had used the computer for non-police purposes and said that he accessed the data because he had noticed that the debtor's car was without a tax disc. Furthermore, he claimed that he had only accessed the data and had not 'used' it subsequently. He was convicted at first instance for an offence under section 5(2)(b) of the Data Protection Act 1984 which made it an offence to hold or use personal data for a purpose which had not been registered.

The police officer's conviction was quashed by the Court of Appeal and this was confirmed in the House of Lords, which dismissed the appeal by the Crown by a 3:2 majority. The majority confirmed that the word 'use' must be given its ordinary dictionary meaning and simply retrieving the information in computer readable form from the database was not using the information so recorded. The minority judges thought that the word 'use' should be liberally interpreted so as to achieve the purpose of the Act otherwise there would be a serious gap in the law. It is as well that the 1998 Act has consigned this unfortunate decision to history.

The definition of 'processing' takes on special significance when we look at the meaning of a '*data processor*' which is:

> **any person (other than an employee of the data controller) who processes data on behalf of the data controller.**

A computer bureau, processing data on behalf of a data controller, will certainly be a data processor. However, unlike the old law, computer bureaux do not have to register under the 1998 Act. But, as the meaning of processing is very wide, it is worth considering the types of persons who will be classed as processors under the present law. There follow some examples (it is assumed that the persons involved are not employees of the data controller – they may be self-employed, freelancers or independent organisations):

- persons collecting data, such as market researchers accosting individuals in a shopping precinct,
- mail order catalogue agents,
- a small IT company providing data entry services,
- a company providing disaster recovery services or other back-up services,
- a company engaged to carry out database quality control by verifying, checking and, where necessary, correcting inaccurate information,
- a person engaged to prepare reports for a client, using the client's database,
- an internet service provider which provides webpages or e-mail services to a client who includes personal data on those webpages or e-mails,

- a company providing IT facilities management services to a client who has 'out-sourced' his IT function,
- a company engaged to remove and destroy old computer printout or archived files containing personal data.

The significance of being classified as a processor is that the entity must be subject to security obligations which are at least evidenced in writing.

Further definitions are contained in sections 2 and 3 and elsewhere in the Act. A very important definition is that of '*sensitive personal data*' which are, by virtue of section 2 of the Data Protection Act 1998, personal data consisting of information as to:

(a) the racial or ethnic origin of the data subject,
(b) his political opinions,
(c) his religious or other beliefs of a similar nature,
(d) whether he is a member of a trade union ...,
(e) his physical or mental health or condition,
(f) his sexual life,
(g) the commission or alleged commission by him of any offence, or
(h) any proceedings for any offence committed or alleged to have been committed by him, the disposal of such proceedings or the sentence of any court in such proceedings.

Sensitive data are treated somewhat differently from other personal data. As far as all personal data are concerned, they can only be processed if one of a list of conditions in Schedule 2 to the Act is present. For sensitive personal data, there must *also* be present a condition from a list of further conditions in Schedule 3. These are considered further in the following chapter.

The Act contains comprehensive provisions aimed at protecting freedom of speech. There is an obvious tension between this and the powers of the Information Commissioner which are severely constrained where processing is for the special purposes, defined in section 3 as any one or more of the following:

(a) the purposes of journalism,
(b) artistic purposes, and
(c) literary purposes.

Further definitions are buried away in section 70. They include:

'*recipient*', in relation to any personal data, means any person to whom the data are disclosed, including any person (such as an employee or agent of the data controller, a data processor or an employee or agent of a data processor) to whom they are disclosed in the course of processing the data for the data controller, but does not include any person to whom disclosure is or may be made as a result of, or with a view to, a particular inquiry by or on behalf of that person made in the exercise of any power conferred by law.

This is relevant in terms of notification of processing activity as recipients must be described in the particulars notified to the Information Commissioner. Note that employees and agents of the data controller and any data processor must be mentioned. The latter part of the definition is intended to excuse the notification of recipients who cannot easily be predicted but to whom personal data may be required to be disclosed by law. A particular example is where a government department makes a particular

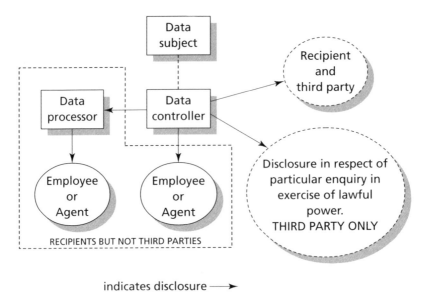

indicates disclosure ⟶

Fig. 34.2 Persons involved in processing activity

one-off enquiry to a local authority where the person concerned is based. However, in practice, generic descriptors are used in notifications to the Information Commissioner, obviating the need to expressly identify each particular recipient.

'*third party*', in relation to personal data, means any person other than–
(a) the data subject,
(b) the data controller, or
(c) any data processor or other person authorised to process data for the data controller or processor.

The relevance of the identity of third parties is that, under certain circumstances, where data are disclosed to a third party, there is an obligation to inform data subjects of this. For example, where data controller A sells a copy of his customer list to data controller B, he should inform all the data subjects concerned unless they are already aware that this would happen.

Now that the main definitions have been introduced, it is useful to reflect on the identity of the various persons involved in data processing and this is set out in Fig. 34.2.

Application of the Act

The Data Protection Act 1998 applies to the United Kingdom and extends to Northern Ireland. By section 5, except as otherwise provided for by or under section 54 (which concerns the Information Commissioner carrying out designated functions to enable the government to give effect to any international obligations of the United Kingdom), the Act applies to a data controller in respect of any data only if:

(a) the data controller is established in the United Kingdom and the data are processed in the context of that establishment, or
(b) the data controller is established neither in the United Kingdom nor in any EEA

[European Economic Area] State but uses equipment in the United Kingdom for processing the data otherwise than for transit through the United Kingdom.

In the last case, the data controller must nominate a representative established in the United Kingdom. Thus, an English company processing data in connection with its business operations is subject to the 1998 Act. A Spanish company which engages a French company to process personal data on its behalf will be subject to the Spanish implementation of the Data Protection Directive under Spanish law. An Australian company using the services of a computer bureau situated in Scotland and using equipment situated there will be subject to the United Kingdom Act and must nominate a representative in the United Kingdom. In this case, it can be expected that it will be the Scottish company which will be the representative. Of course, in the latter case, the Australian company must notify the Information Commissioner of the processing activity carried out in Scotland. If a Brazilian company transfers personal data to Japan via a computer situated in the United Kingdom, the United Kingdom Act will not apply unless the data are processed in the United Kingdom for any purpose other than the purpose of transit to Japan. This latter point is particularly important in terms of transmission via public telecommunications systems including by e-mail and the Internet. It obviates the need for the data controller to notify in all the member states of the EEA if the data is likely to pass through any or all of them (which it is by the nature of transmission over the Internet).

Role of the Information Commissioner

The Information Commissioner is required to act in an independent manner and is appointed by Her Majesty by Letters Patent. Apart from duties, responsibilities and powers under the Data Protection Act 1998, the Information Commissioner now also has duties and powers in relation to privacy in telecommunications (soon to be extended to privacy and electronic communications) and increasing duties under the Freedom of Information Act 2000, as parts of that Act are gradually being brought into force. In terms of the Data Protection Act 1998, the role of the Commissioner can be seen as being concerned with the following major functions:

- consultation and dissemination of information,
- investigation,
- intervention,
- enforcement, and
- cooperation.

Consultation and dissemination of information

As required by the Data Protection Directive, the Commissioner must be consulted as regards administrative measures and regulations relating to the protection of individuals' rights and freedoms with regard to the processing of personal data. Thus, under section 67 of the Data Protection Act 1998, the Lord Chancellor shall consult the Commissioner before making an order under the Act (except for an order bringing parts of the Act into force) or before making any regulations under the Act except for the notification regulations.

Under the 1984 Act, the Data Protection Registrar was very active in the dissemination of information concerning the Act and compliance with it. This included advertising and the publication of an excellent set of guidelines, written in plain English. Anyone interested in seeing these and other reports and information should visit the Information Commissioner's website at http://www.dataprotection.gov.uk/ which also gives access to the register and is well worth the time taken to visit. Under the 1998 Act, the responsibility for the Commissioner to disseminate information continues and is extended.

As before, the Commissioner is given general duties to promote good practice by data controllers and to promote observance of the Act. This includes the dissemination of information about good practice and about other matters within the Commissioner's functions under the Act. The Commissioner may give advice to any person as to any of those matters.

As before, there is a duty to lay a report before Parliament annually. Other reports may be placed before Parliament as must be codes of practice ordered to be prepared by the Lord Chancellor who may direct the Commissioner to draw up and disseminate codes of practice after consultation with trade associations, data subjects or persons representing data subjects. The order will describe the personal data or processing to which the code is to relate and may also describe the persons or classes of persons subject to the processing. The Commissioner may also draw up codes of practice where he considers it appropriate.

A further function is that the Commissioner will disseminate Community findings as regards the adequacy of protection for personal data in third countries (countries or territories outside the EEA) and decisions under Article 31(2) of the Directive made for the purposes of Article 26(3) or (4) as regards measures to be taken in respect of adequacy of protection in third countries and contractual clauses considered to offer sufficient safeguards and such other information relating to processing of personal data outside the EEA. So far, Switzerland, Hungary, Canada and Argentina have been designated countries having adequate protection.

Investigation

The Information Commissioner has wide-ranging powers of investigation aimed at determining that processing complies with the Data Protection Principles and whether there has been otherwise any contravention of the Act. The powers of investigation are exercised through:

- information notices,
- special information notices, or
- powers of entry and inspection.

Before looking at these individually, it should be noted that any individual who considers that he is directly affected by any processing may, under section 42, apply to the Commissioner for an assessment as to whether or not it is likely that the processing has been or is being carried out in compliance with the Act. The Commissioner must, upon receipt of such a request, make such assessment, providing he has been furnished with sufficient information to identify the person making the request and the processing in question. The Commissioner may take into account the following factors to determine the manner of the assessment:

- the extent to which the request appears to the Commissioner to raise a matter of sub-stance,
- any undue delay in making the request, and
- whether the person making the request is entitled to make a subject access request.

The Commissioner shall notify the person whether an assessment has been made as a result of the request and any view formed or action to be taken, having regard in particular to any exemption from subject access enjoyed by the data controller. In particular, a request for an assessment may cause the Commissioner to serve an information notice. For the year ending 31 March 2003, the Commissioner received 10,230 requests for assessment under the Act (most in the form of complaints). In most cases, advice was given to the individual making the request (Information Commissioner, Annual report and accounts for the year ending 31 March 2003, HC727, 2003, pp.96–97).

Information notices

An information notice may be served as a result of a request for assessment from an individual or if the Commissioner has reasonable grounds for suspecting that the data controller has contravened or is contravening any of the Principles. The notice requires the data controller to furnish the Commissioner with information relating to the request within the specified time and in such form as may be specified. The notice must include a statement that the notice has been served in response to a request from an

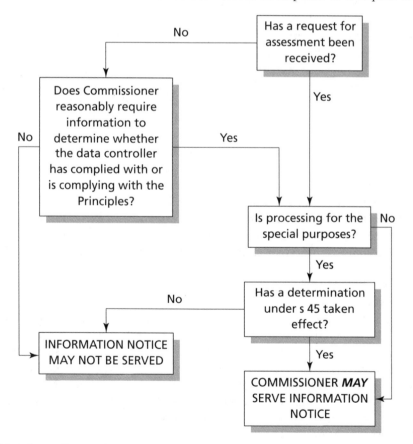

Fig. 34.3 Information notice

individual if that is the case or, otherwise, with a statement that the information requested is regarded to be relevant in determining whether the data controller has complied or is complying with the Principles, together with reasons why the information is regarded as relevant. The notice must also contain particulars of appeal.

Normally, the time to reply should not be less than the time during which an appeal may be brought, being 28 days, except where the Commissioner considers that the information is required as a matter of urgency where the time limit can be seven days. The Commissioner must state the reasons why the information is required as a matter of urgency. The data controller is excused from providing information which is privileged or would reveal evidence of an offence other than an offence under the Act.

Information notices may not be served on a data controller in respect of processing for the special purposes (journalism, artistic or literary expression) unless a determination has been made and has taken effect under section 45 where it appears to the Commissioner that the personal data are not being processed only for the special purposes or are not being processed with a view to publication by any person of any journalistic, literary or artistic material which has not previously been published by the data controller. This provision is intended to prevent undue interference with freedom of speech. Figure 34.3 shows when an information notice may be served by the Commissioner.

Section 45 determinations are important also in respect of special information notices and enforcement notices, as described later. The Commissioner must serve on the data controller notice of the determination which must include particulars of the right to appeal and which must not take effect until the end of the period for an appeal or, if an appeal is pending, until the appeal has been determined or withdrawn. Thus, if processing is for the special purposes only or with a view to publication, the Commissioner's powers are curtailed until a determination has taken effect. Note that publication can be by any person – presumably this includes the data controller and of any personal data not previously having been published by the data controller. Thus, if the data controller has already published material including the personal data in question, he cannot rely on the restrictions to the Commissioner's powers if he is now processing the data with an intention that he should re-publish it. Even so, the Commissioner would still need to make a determination under section 45. In the year up to 31 March 2003, four preliminary enforcement notices were served, one of which led to an information notice, and one further information notice was served. No information notices had been served in previous years (Information Commissioner, Annual report and accounts for the year ending 31 March 2003, HC727, 2003, p.100).

Special information notices

These notices relate to processing for the special purposes (journalism, literary and artistic purposes). These provisions are, in many respects, similar to those for information notices. Under section 44, the notice may be served if the Commissioner has received a request for assessment from an individual under section 42 (the Act is silent on whether there must be, on its face, an issue in the request relating to the special purposes) or if the Commissioner has reasonable grounds for suspecting that, in a case where proceedings have been stayed under section 32, the data are not being processed only for the special purposes or with a view to publication for the first time by the data controller.

A stay under section 32 shall be ordered by the court where the data controller claims, or it appears to the court, that the processing is only for the special purposes

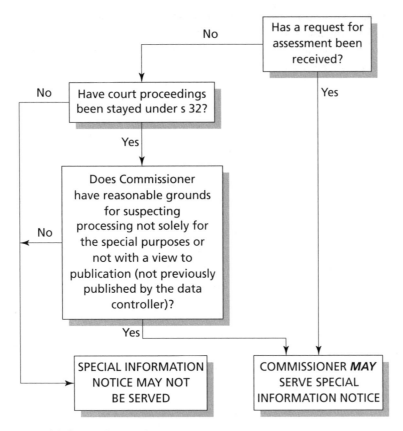

Fig. 34.4 Special information notice

and with a view to publication by any person of any journalistic, literary or artistic material which, at the time 24 hours immediately before the time of the claim, had not previously been published by the data controller.

The proceedings referred to in section 32 are in relation to subject access, processing likely to cause damage or distress, automated decision taking or rights in relation to inaccurate data. The stay applies until the Commissioner makes a determination under section 45 or the data controller withdraws the claim.

Unless the notice is sent after a request for assessment is made, the notice may only be sent where a data controller has used the exemption under section 32 (special purposes) as a shield in any proceedings to obtain a stay. The purpose of the notice is to obtain information to determine whether the exemption for the special purposes does indeed apply. Figure 34.4 shows when a special information notice may be served.

Entry and inspection

The Information Commissioner has powers of entry and inspection, which are very similar to those under the 1984 Act. The powers are contained in Schedule 9 to the Data Protection Act 1998 and can be exercised by him after obtaining a warrant from a circuit judge who will grant the warrant if he is satisfied by information supplied by the Commissioner on oath that there are reasonable grounds for suspecting that a data controller has contravened or is contravening any of the Data Protection Principles or that an offence under the Act has been or is being committed. If the processing is for the special purposes, a warrant must not be issued until a determination under section 45 has taken effect. The warrant must be executed within seven days of the date of its issue.

A judge must not issue a warrant (except if satisfied that the case is urgent as discussed below) unless he is satisfied that the Commissioner has given the occupier of the premises in question seven days' notice in writing demanding access and such access was demanded at a reasonable time and was unreasonably refused or although entry was granted the occupier unreasonably refused to comply with a request to permit the Commissioner or his officers or staff to do anything within the powers of entry and inspection, and the occupier, after such refusal, has been notified of the intended application for a warrant and has had the opportunity to be heard by the judge concerned. However, where the case is urgent and the judge is also satisfied that to comply with the above provisions would defeat the object of entry, he may issue a warrant without those preconditions being present.

A warrant will permit the Commissioner or his officers or staff executing the warrant to use such force as is reasonably necessary to enter and search the premises within seven days, to inspect, examine and operate any test respecting any data processing equipment on the premises and to inspect and seize any documents or other materials (presumably including items such as magnetic disks and tapes) which may be evidence of an offence or contravention of the Data Protection Principles. Warrants are not available in the case of personal data which are exempt from any provisions of the Act under the national security provisions under section 28. In the year to 31 March 2003, five search warrants were obtained by the Information Commissioner (Information Commissioner, Annual report and accounts for the year ending 31 March 2003, HC727, 2003, p.98).

Intervention

The Data Protection Directive requires that the supervisory authority shall have effective powers of intervention. This requires the Information Commissioner to carry out a preliminary assessment of processing operations likely to pose specific risks to the rights and freedoms of individuals. The types of operations concerned will be specified by the Lord Chancellor and such processing must not proceed until the Commissioner has made the assessment to ensure that the processing will comply with the Act: section 22. In the normal course of events, the Commissioner should inform the data controller of the results within 28 days of notification by the data controller. The period can be extended for a further period not exceeding 14 days.

It is unlikely that a preliminary assessment will be required in many cases. Indeed, the Directive states in recital 54 that the amount of processing likely to pose specific risks should be very limited. The Home Office indicated that it might apply in the case of genetic data, data matching (that is, where personal data from different sources are matched to find any discrepancies which might indicate that the person concerned is involved in fraudulent applications for credit) and processing by private investigators. The key should be whether the particular description of processing is likely to cause substantial damage or substantial distress to data subjects or to otherwise significantly prejudice the rights and freedoms of data subjects. Processing may not proceed until the 28 days (as extended, if applicable) has expired or the data controller has received a notice from the Commissioner permitting processing. At the time of writing, no orders have been made under section 22.

Another form of intervention is that the Commissioner may require a data controller to rectify, block, erase or destroy inaccurate data as part of an enforcement notice and the Commissioner may also require the data controller to inform third parties to whom the data have been disclosed, having regard, in particular, to the number of persons who would have to be notified.

Enforcement

The Information Commissioner has two ways of enforcing the new data protection law. One is through enforcement notices, the second is by bringing a prosecution under the Act. In England and Wales and Northern Ireland, prosecutions normally will be brought by the Commissioner. Otherwise a prosecution may be brought by or with the consent of the Director of Public Prosecutions (or Director of Public Prosecutions for Northern Ireland). Presumably, in Scotland, prosecutions are brought by or with the leave of the Procurator Fiscal. The offences, of which there a several, are set out in the following chapter.

Under section 40, if the Commissioner is satisfied that the data controller has contravened or is contravening any of the Data Protection Principles, he may serve a notice requiring the data controller to take or refrain from taking specified steps within a specified time and/or refrain from processing after a specified time:

- any personal data,
- personal data of a specified description, or
- for a specified purpose or purposes or in a specified manner.

As mentioned above, where an enforcement notice relates to a breach of the fourth Data Protection Principle (in that the data are inaccurate), the Commissioner may, if reasonably practicable, require the data controller to notify third parties to whom the data have been disclosed. Regard is to be had to the number of persons who would have to be notified. The court also has similar powers in respect of inaccurate data that record accurately information provided by the data subject or a third party.

In deciding whether to serve the notice, the Commissioner is to consider whether the contravention has or is likely to cause any person damage or distress. The provisions as to the service of enforcement notices are subject to restrictions as regards processing for the special purposes (journalism, literary and artistic purposes). Here, the provisions envisage that a court must give leave to serve the notice. In particular, the notice shall not be served unless a determination under section 45 has taken effect and the court has granted leave for the notice to be served. Such leave will only be granted if the Commissioner has reason to suspect a contravention of substantial public interest and, except in cases of urgency, the data controller has been given notice in accordance with the rules of court for the application to the court for leave to serve the notice. Figure 34.5 shows when an enforcement notice may be served.

Enforcement notices cannot take effect until the period for appeal has expired (28 days) or pending an appeal unless the case is a matter of urgency, in which case the time for compliance is seven days. An enforcement notice may be cancelled or varied by the Commissioner. This may be done on the Commissioner's own initiative or following a written application by the data controller after the period for appeal has expired where he can show by reason of a change in circumstances that some or all of the provisions

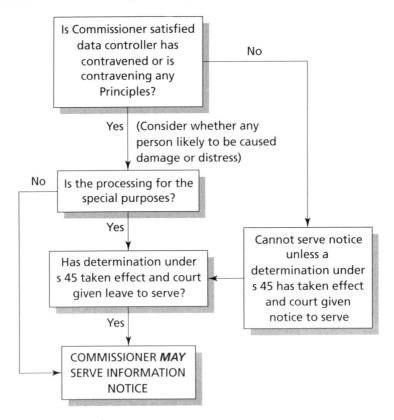

Fig. 34.5 Enforcement notice

of the notice need not be complied with to ensure compliance with the data protection principles: section 41.

Under the 1984 Act, in *British Gas Trading Ltd v Data Protection Registrar* (unreported) 24 March 1998, the Data Protection Tribunal held that the Registrar was right to serve an enforcement notice under the 1984 Act rather than accept an undertaking from British Gas Trading Ltd. Under the 1984 Act, there were other forms of enforcement, by de-registration notices and transfer prohibition notices. These find no direct equivalent under the 1998 Act. The Information Commissioner had developed a preliminary notice with the approval of the Information Tribunal. This system continues to be used and, in the year to 31 March 2003, three preliminary enforcement notices were served, one of which led to an enforcement notice, and four further enforcement notices were served (Information Commissioner, Annual report and accounts for the year ending 31 March 2003, HC727, 2003, p.100). The preliminary enforcement notice can be seen as a useful 'Yellow Card' system.

Cooperation

All the supervisory authorities in the EEA are required to cooperate with each other in respect of exchanging all useful information and to the extent necessary for the performance of their duties. Furthermore, each member state shall designate a representative of its supervisory authority (or a joint representative if the member state has more than one supervisory authority, unlike the United Kingdom) to be a member of the

Working Party set up under the Data Protection Directive, discussed later in this chapter.

Cooperation is also implicit in the drawing up of codes of practice, which may be required by the Secretary of State or may be developed as a result of the Information Commissioner's own initiative. Another provision is that the Commissioner can, with the consent of the data controller, assess processing for the observance of good practice. The Commissioner may, with the consent of the Secretary of State, charge for this service. This is not to be confused with requests for preliminary assessments which will be required in specified cases posing risks to rights and freedoms of data subjects before processing can commence.

Where an individual is an actual or prospective party to proceedings under one of a number of provisions, being in respect of:

- a failure to comply with a subject access request,
- a failure to cease processing likely to cause substantial damage or substantial distress,
- a failure to comply with the provisions on automated decision taking,
- an application to have inaccurate data rectified, erased, blocked or destroyed, or
- the compensation provisions,

that individual can apply to the Commissioner for assistance where the processing relates to processing for the special purposes (that is, journalism, artistic or literary expression). The Commissioner shall provide assistance where it appears to him to involve a matter of substantial public interest under section 53. The assistance provided may be in the form of legal advice or assistance from a solicitor or counsel or assistance during proceedings. The Commissioner has a first charge on any costs or award in respect of the expenses in providing assistance.

The Commissioner will continue to be the designated authority for the purposes of Article 13 of the Council of Europe Convention for the Protection of Individuals with regard to Processing of Personal Data, Strasbourg, 28 January 1981, and will be the supervisory authority for the purposes of the Data Protection Directive. Orders may be made for the Commissioner to cooperate with the European Commission and supervisory authorities in other EEA states and to carry out data functions to enable the government to give effect to international obligations in the United Kingdom.

The Tribunal and appeals

The Information Tribunal (formerly known as the Data Protection Tribunal) is the first line of appeal from notices served by the Commissioner or a determination by the Commissioner under section 45. It also has jurisdiction to hear appeals against information and enforcement notices under the Freedom of Information Act 2000. The Tribunal is made up of:

- a chairman appointed by the Lord Chancellor after consulting the Secretary of State (being a lawyer of at least seven years' standing),
- such number of deputy chairmen as determined by the Lord Chancellor (also being lawyers of at least seven years' standing), and

- such number of other members appointed by the Lord Chancellor (being persons representing the interests of data subjects and persons making requests for information under the Freedom of Information Act 2000, persons representing the interests of data controllers and persons representing the interests of public authorities).

The functions of the Secretary of State are, as regards Scotland, transferred to the Scottish Ministers. Under section 48, a person may appeal to the Tribunal on grounds related to the following:

- enforcement, information or special information notices,
- a refusal by the Commissioner to cancel or vary an enforcement notice,
- where a notice contains a statement that the notice must be complied with as a matter of urgency within seven days, the Commissioner's decision to include the statement or the effect of the inclusion of the statement as regards any part of the notice, or
- a determination under section 45.

The Tribunal may:

- allow the appeal,
- substitute another notice if it considers that the notice is not in accordance with the law,
- where it involved an exercise of discretion by the Commissioner, rule that the discretion ought to have been exercised differently,
- cancel or vary a notice,
- rule on a statement made by the Commissioner that compliance is required as a matter of urgency,
- cancel a determination of the Commissioner.

The Tribunal may review any determination of fact on which the notice in question was based. Appeals from the Tribunal on a point of law go to the High Court in England or Wales, the Court of Session in Scotland or the High Court of Justice in Northern Ireland, depending on the appellant's address. Detailed procedures before the Tribunal are set out in the Information Tribunal (Enforcement Appeals) Rules 2000, as amended, and the Information Tribunal (National Security Appeals) Rules 2000, also as amended. These latter rules apply to appeals against claims to exemption on the basis of national security under section 29 of the Data Protection Act 1998.

The Working Party

A Working Party on the Protection of Individuals with regard to the Processing of Personal Data ('the Working Party') was established under Article 29 of the Data Protection Directive. It is an independent body with an advisory status. The Working Party is composed of a representative from the supervisory authority of each member state. Where a member state has more than one supervisory authority (for example, where one looks after the public sector and another looks after the private sector), a joint representative is nominated. A representative of the authority or authorities established for the Community institutions and bodies and a representative of the

Commission are also members of the Working Party. A chair is elected every two years and decisions are taken by a simple majority of representatives of supervisory authorities. The Working Party considers items placed on its agenda by the chairman, either on his own initiative or at the request of a representative of the supervisory authorities or at the request of the European Commission.

The brief of the Working Party is set out in Article 30 of the Directive and is to:

- examine any questions covering the application of national measures implementing the Directive so as to contribute to the uniform application of such measures;
- give the Commission an opinion on the level of protection afforded in the Community and in third countries;
- advise the Commission on any proposed amendment to the Directive, on any additional or specific measures to safeguard rights and freedoms with regard to the processing of personal data and to advise on any other proposed Community measures affecting such rights and freedoms;
- give opinions on codes of practice drawn up at Community level.

Furthermore, the Working Party must inform the Commission if it finds disparity between the laws of member states in respect of the protection of individuals with regard to the processing of personal data. It may, on its own initiative, make recommendations on all data protection matters. An annual report, which will be made public, is to be drawn up dealing with the protection of natural persons with regard to the processing of personal data within the Community and in third countries. The Commission must inform the Working Party of the action it takes in response to its opinions and recommendations. This is to be done in a report forwarded to the European Parliament and the Council and will also be made public.

The Working Party has published numerous opinions and press releases, most recently covering issues such as on-line authentication systems, 'Who is' directories, the level of data protection in Guernsey (it concluded that it did have adequate protection for the purposes of transfers to third countries), transfers of passenger data to the United States and e-government.

Chapter 35

Data controllers and the Data Protection Act 1998

Introduction

It is upon the data controllers, those who process personal data, that the main burden of data protection legislation falls. In spite of some changes to the text of the 1992 proposal for a Directive and the significant use by the United Kingdom of derogations permitted by the Directive as adopted, costs of implementing the new law are not insignificant. The financial memorandum to the Data Protection Bill put the figures as shown in Table 35.1.

Although these figures are high, there is a great deal that data controllers can do to ease the burden of complying with the new law. By understanding data protection law, data controllers are in a much better position to develop systems and procedures to minimise the financial impact of compliance.

The purpose of this chapter is to explore the model of data protection law under the 1998 Act from the perspective of the data controller. The discussion will involve further consideration of the Data Protection Principles which, with their interpretative provisions, are very important. Some of these latter provisions contain some of the most important and potentially onerous elements of the Directive. First, the notification requirements will be described. From a data controller's point of view, this is arguably of most immediate impact. This will include a look at the requirements to provide data subjects with information when data are obtained from them and in other cases. Following this, the constraints on processing activity are discussed. These include the conditions for processing which cannot proceed unless one of the conditions applies for normal data and, in the case of sensitive data, a further condition also is satisfied. These conditions were new departure for the United Kingdom except in so far as processing was required to be fair under the 1984 Act.

The security provisions are, to some extent, similar to those under the 1984 Act but there are important requirements where data processors are engaged. Following the discussion of security, the exemptions are described. Although a number of exemptions are similar to those under the 1984 Act, there are some important differences. Some exemptions under the 1984 Act disappear including the 'word processing' exemption and those relating to unincorporated members' clubs and mailing lists. There are some new exemptions such as the exemption in respect of processing for the special purposes

Table 35.1 Financial impact of the new law

Sector	Start-up costs (£m)	Annual recurring costs (£m)
Central government	90	46
Local government	104	29
Private sector	836	630
Voluntary sector	120	37

(journalism, literary or artistic expression) and in respect of confidential references. Next there is a brief look at enforcement from the data controller's viewpoint. This builds up on the description of the Information Commissioner's functions in the previous chapter. The offences under the Act are then described in summary, as many will have already been covered in this chapter. Finally, the complex, though important, transitional provisions are discussed. One advantage of studying these is that some aspects of the transitional arrangements show how the new law differs from that under the 1984 Act. Two transitional periods were provided for, the first of which ended on 23 October 2001 which applied to 'eligible data' (data in respect of which processing was already under way before 24 October 1998 – the latest date the Directive should have been implemented by domestic law). The scope of the first transitional period is still described as it does indicate how different the 1998 Act is to the 1984 Act.

Notification and informing data subjects

The Data Protection Act 1998 exempts from notification all manual processing of data, that is data that are part of a relevant filing system or accessible record as defined in section 1. Unless exempt, all automated processing must be notified. However, even if required to be notified, processing may still be subject to a preliminary assessment where it poses specific risks and the Lord Chancellor has made the appropriate order requiring such assessment before processing can commence. Exemption from formal notification to the Information Commissioner is not all good news as the data controller must still furnish information to any person making a written request, as we shall see later. Further exemption from notification is possible by order of the Lord Chancellor. So far specific exemptions have been made under the Data Protection (Notification and Notification Fees) Regulations 2000. These apply to staff administration; accounts, marketing and public relations; accounts and records, and in the case of non-profit organisations. The exemptions are not absolute and only relate to specified purposes, data subjects, types of personal data and disclosures. Partnerships are allowed to register under the name of the partnership and the governing body and head teacher of a school may register in the name of the school.

Under section 4(4) a duty is placed on every data controller, unless exempt, to comply with the Data Protection Principles. This applies whether or not he has notified his processing activities. Section 17 states that personal data must not be processed until registered, except in the case of manual processing which is not subject to a preliminary assessment (which will usually be the case) or if the processing is of a particular description to be exempted by notification regulations or if the sole purpose of the processing is the maintenance of a public register – for example, the electoral roll. Unless exempt from the notification requirements, section 18 requires data controllers wishing to be included in the register to notify the 'registrable particulars' together with a general description of security measures. The information to be contained in the registrable particulars is set out in section 16(1), being in relation to a data controller:

(a) his name and address,
(b) if he has nominated a representative, the name and address of the representative,
(c) a description of personal data being or to be processed by or on behalf of the

data controller and of the category or categories of data subject to which they relate,

(d) a description of the purpose or purposes for which the data are being or are to be processed,

(e) a description of any recipient or recipients to whom the data controller intends or may wish to disclose the data,

(f) the names, or a description of, any countries or territories outside the European Economic Area to which the data controller directly or indirectly transfers, or intends or may wish directly or indirectly to transfer, the data.

Where the data controller is a public authority (as defined in the Freedom of Information Act 2000), there must also be a statement to that effect. Under regulation 11 of the Data Protection (Notification and Notification Fees) Regulations 2000, the Information Commissioner may also include other information in the register entry such as the registration number, the date the registration is treated as having been made, the date it falls or may fall to be removed and information to assist individuals communicate with the data controller regarding subject access requests. As regards security measures, data controllers have simply to check a number of boxes indicating, for example, that they have a security policy, train staff and adhere to BS7799, the British Standard on Information Security Management.

Where relevant, a statement must also be included of the fact that the notification does not extend to personal data being processed, or intended to be processed, but not subject to notification. This will apply to manual processing exempt from notification where the data controller has not chosen to notify such processing. For example, if a data controller has a computer database containing personal data, he must notify that. If he also has a card index system processed manually, that will be exempt from the notification requirements. The data controller may choose not to notify his card index system and, if he so chooses, he must include a statement in his notification of his automatic processing that he also processes personal data not subject to notification. This simply flags the fact that there is other processing being carried on and a person alerted to that fact may wish to obtain further information from the data controller in respect of such processing, as discussed below. Alternatively, the data controller may decide to notify his manual processing also, in which case he need not provide a supplementary statement. The rationale is that of transparency of processing. Individuals should be able to see what processing is being carried out by consulting the register and, if alerted to the fact that there is non-notifiable processing also going on, he can find out what that is also. Notification lasts for 12 months, although the mechanism is included to modify this period.

Under section 19, the Information Commissioner maintains a register of data controllers, available for public inspection free of charge. Certified copies may be obtained for a prescribed fee, currently £2, under the Data Protection (Fees under section 19(7)) Regulations 2000. The general description of security measures is not available to the public. The register is available for public inspection at the Information Commissioner's website at: http://www.dataprotection.gov.uk/

One significant difference in the register is that, under the 1984 Act, data users could have more than one register entry. The 1998 Act only allows one entry per data controller. This could ease the task of individuals carrying out subject access requests.

Failure to notify is an offence of strict liability. Even if the person processing personal data had never heard of data protection law, he will be guilty of the offence. There is a further duty on the data controller to notify changes in the registrable particulars by virtue of section 20. However, failure to notify any changes is a criminal offence which is subject to a due diligence defence.

The basis of a due diligence defence is that, generally, liability is strict unless the accused makes out a defence. Such a statutory defence presumes that the fault is the responsibility of another person and that the accused has exercised due diligence to prevent the wrongful act from occurring. One way a data controller may prove that he has exercised due diligence is to show that he had installed systems or procedures aimed at preventing the wrong occurring. This might be by training employees or agents as to the importance of data protection law and providing them with clear information as to what the scope of their duties was. In terms of failing to notify changes, a data controller might escape liability if he can show that clear instructions had been given to an employee responsible for data protection within the data controller's business.

Requirement to provide information to any person on request

Where a data controller has not notified his processing activity because he is not required to do so and has chosen not to do so, he must still be in a position to supply information equivalent to the registrable particulars (as per (a) to (f) above) to any person who submits a written request for such information. The information must be provided within 21 days of the written request otherwise the data controller commits an offence, subject to a due diligence defence under section 24. No charge can be made for providing this information and the person making the request does not have to be a data subject in relation to the data controller.

The main implication of this provision is that it may suit a data controller to notify processing which he is not required to notify and the Information Commissioner will accept such notifications. A further point is that, if a data controller has not notified all his processing which is within the scope of the Act, he ought to consider implementing a procedure for dealing with such requests although, for many data controllers, they are likely to be quite rare.

Preliminary assessment (prior checking)

In cases, to be specified by the Lord Chancellor, processing will be subject to a preliminary assessment by the Information Commissioner (known as 'prior checking' in the Directive) and the processing must not proceed until the Commissioner has made a preliminary assessment to ensure that it will comply with the Act: section 22. Where a preliminary assessment is required, in the normal course of events, the Commissioner should inform the data controller of his assessment within 28 days of notification by the data controller. The period can be extended for a further period not exceeding 14 days. No distinction is made between automatic and manual processing for a preliminary assessment. The Lord Chancellor will, by order, detail the descriptions of processing for which preliminary assessment is required. It is likely to be required in relatively few cases where it appears to the Lord Chancellor that a particular description of processing is likely to cause substantial damage or substantial distress to data subjects or to otherwise significantly prejudice the rights and freedoms of data subjects. Processing genetic data, data matching, endangered life databases and other sensitive processing operations are potential candidates for preliminary assessment. Processing may not proceed until the 28 days (as extended, if applicable) has expired or the data controller has received a notice from the Commissioner permitting processing. Otherwise a criminal offence of strict liability is committed. As yet no orders have been made under section 22.

The preliminary assessment provisions contain no power for the Commissioner to prohibit processing. The intention is that they enable the Commissioner to give a view on whether the processing is likely to comply. It will then be up to the data controller to decide whether or not to proceed. Of course, if the Commissioner considers the processing unlikely to comply with the Act, he may use his powers of enforcement if the data controller decides to go ahead.

Data protection supervisors

In some member states, a system of internal data protection supervisors is in place. In-house officials oversee compliance with data protection law. The Directive provided the opportunity for other member states to adopt such a system which should permit the exemption or simplification of notification and allow internal preliminary assessments to be made, reducing the time delay in introducing new forms of sensitive processing. Under section 23 of the Data Protection Act 1998, the Lord Chancellor is given the power to make orders providing for personal data supervisors. They are to be responsible in particular for monitoring, in an independent manner, the data controller's compliance with the Act. There are likely to be duties imposed on personal data supervisors owed to the Commissioner who may be given functions in respect of them. No order has been made under section 23 as yet and it may be some time before we see data protection supervisors in the United Kingdom. Perhaps when they are brought in, the first place they may be allowed is in the public sector.

Informing data subjects on collection and in other cases

The provisions on interpretation of the Data Protection Principles require that, for the first Principle, the method of obtaining the data and whether the person from whom they were obtained was deceived or misled as to the purpose or purposes of processing are factors in determining whether the processing is fair (although data obtained or supplied under statutory authorisation is automatically deemed to be fairly obtained). Transparency is obviously important here and the individual should know what personal data relating to him are to be used for. This principle of openness is developed further in the interpretative provisions which place further duties on data controllers to provide specific information to an individual on collection of personal data and in other cases, especially where the data are disclosed to a third party.

These obligations to inform data subjects are derived from Articles 10 and 11 of the Data Protection Directive and have no equivalent under the 1984 Act, except as developed by case law such as in *Innovations (Mail Order) Ltd* v *Data Protection Registrar*, 29 September 1993 before the Data Protection Tribunal (now Information Tribunal). In that case, Innovations operated a large mail-order business, advertised through catalogues, newspapers and television. It also had a lucrative business selling its customer lists to other retailers and service providers (an activity known as 'list trading'). Customers ordering goods from Innovations were not told of the list trading activity at the time they placed their orders. It was only when they received a written acknowledgement of their orders that they were informed by way of a notice on the rear of the acknowledgement form. The notice informed customers that they could have their names removed from the lists if they applied formally, sending in details of their name and address.

The Data Protection Registrar (now Information Commissioner) took the view that this was a breach of the first Data Protection Principle, as the data were not being obtained fairly because customers ought to have been informed at the time the data were collected and not later. An enforcement notice was served on Innovations which appealed to the Tribunal. The Tribunal agreed with the Registrar and said that the question as to whether data had been fairly obtained related to the time of the obtaining and not a later time. If a purpose for which the data are intended to be used is not obvious at the time of obtaining the data, the data subject must be told of that non-obvious purpose at *that* time. If the data user does not inform the data subject at the time of collection of the data, the data subject's express consent must be sought before any non-obvious processing can be commenced.

This approach was adopted again by the Tribunal in *British Gas Trading Ltd v Data Protection Registrar*, 24 March 1998. British Gas Trading had inherited a large number of its customers from the previous bodies which made and supplied gas. When it wanted to send marketing material to all its customers, British Gas Trading inserted a note to that effect when it sent out gas bills and statements. The note informed customers that they could opt out of receiving such marketing material by writing in. The Tribunal held that this was not fair processing. A number of factors in the case are important and instructive:

- at least some of the marketing material related to services or products that were not directly related to gas or gas appliances (for example, the 'Goldfish' credit card);
- customers should be able to object without having to perform a positive act like writing in – they should be able to signify consent or otherwise at the time data were collected from them, 'there and then';
- new customers could be informed and given an opportunity to object when completing a contract form, for example by ticking the 'opt-out' box.

An argument that the processing was also unlawful, for example, by being in breach of confidence or contract, were rejected by the Tribunal. This case was followed by *Midlands Electricity plc v Data Protection Registrar*, 7 May 1999. Midlands Electricity had sent a little magazine to domestic customers with their quarterly bills. Some of the material in the magazine had nothing to do with energy such as advertisements for holidays and mobile phones. As with the *British Gas* case, many of Midlands Electricity's customers had been inherited from the previous public utility. An enforcement notice had been served on Midlands Electricity requiring compliance as a matter of urgency. The Tribunal agreed that the notice was valid but that the requirement that it be complied with as a matter of urgency in seven days was removed and the Tribunal gave Midlands Electricity around 18 months to comply (it had to redesign its database to include a field to record whether individuals objected and to consult its customers as to whether they were happy to receive the booklet). A number of other interesting points arose from the decision:

- it was accepted that processing of personal data was involved as commercial customers received a different magazine;

- no evidence of damage or distress caused to customers was found by the Tribunal;
- the Tribunal accepted that including information about energy saving was not unfair, nor was advertising gas supplies, bearing in mind diversification in the energy market – advertising other products and services not related to energy supplies or appliances such as cookers and electric fires was unfair if the positive consent to this had not been obtained;
- obtaining consent in the case of new customers would be easy by use of the ubiquitous 'tick-box' – in terms of existing customers, consent could be sought when the customer returned a document, such as a direct debit mandate.

These cases show that, although there was no specific duty in the 1984 Act to inform individuals of non-obvious uses at the time the data were collected, the duty arose as a direct consequence of the requirement that processing must be fair. However, the duty under the 1998 Act is much more extensive.

Inform on collection

Part II of Schedule 1 to the Data Protection Act 1998 requires that, where the data are obtained from the data subject, the data controller must ensure, so far as is practicable, that the data subject has or is provided with the 'relevant information' or *has made it readily available to him*. The relevant information to be provided is:

- the identity of the data controller (and representative, if any),
- the purpose or purposes of the processing (but see below on the second Data Protection Principle),
- any further information, having regard to the circumstances in which the data are or are to be processed to enable such processing in respect of the data subject to be fair.

The White Paper, *Data Protection: The Government's Proposals* (Home Office, Cm 3725, 1997) which preceded the Bill suggested that it would be the controller who would decide whether further information was required to be given, though the Act is silent on this point. The second Data Protection Principle requires that data shall be obtained only for one or more specified and lawful purposes and not further processed in an incompatible manner. The interpretation provisions for this principle allows the purpose to be specified either by notification to the Commissioner or in a notice given to the data subject for the purpose of informing him, as above. This means that, where the data controller has notified his processing to the Commissioner (which he must do in the case of automatic processing, unless exempt), the data controller will not have to separately provide this information to the data subject. As the purposes of processing are amongst the registrable particulars, this information will be publicly available where processing is notified. Thus, the data subject can, by consulting the data protection register, find this information out himself.

Unless further information is deemed to be required to ensure fair processing, all the data controller will have to do is to identify himself to the data subject, unless a non-obvious use is envisaged or disclosure to a third party is possible. *Innovations, British Gas Trading* and *Midlands Electricity* are likely to remain good law under the 1998 Act. Certainly, if the data are to be used for marketing purposes, this is likely to be a situation where further information must be given. However, it should be noted that the Tribunal in *British Gas Trading* accepted that what is or is not obvious may change over time as consumers become more aware of diversification of business activity carried out by a company or group of companies.

Inform in other cases

Other cases will cover the situation where the data have not been obtained directly from the individual concerned. For example, it might be that the data are disclosed by the data controller who obtained the data from the data subject in the first place and now chooses to disclose them to a second data controller. Another example is where a data controller generates for himself data relating to the data subject.

In cases other than where the data are being obtained directly from the data subject, the data controller must ensure so far as practicable that, *before the 'relevant time' or as soon as practicable thereafter*, the data subject has or is provided with the relevant information or *has it made readily available* to him. The requirement to provide information does not apply where its provision would involve a disproportionate effort or where the recording or disclosure is necessary to comply with a legal obligation to which the data controller is subject (other than a contractual obligation) together with such further conditions as may be prescribed by Regulations. Although many data controllers will be tempted to claim 'disproportionate effort' it will probably apply in limited circumstances only. It might apply where a large number of individuals would have to be informed and the processing is non-sensitive. It probably will not apply where the proposed use to be made of the data could trigger one of the rights of data subjects to object to processing – for example, where the purpose is direct marketing or involved automated decision taking.

Some conditions must be satisfied if the data controller seeks to rely on the exclusion of the requirement to inform the data subject. These are stated in the Data Protection (Conditions under Paragraph 3 of Part II of Schedule 1) Order 2000. Articles 4 and 5 of the Order contain the conditions. Where the recording or disclosure is necessary to comply with a legal obligation to which the data controller is subject, where this is not a function conferred on the data controller under any enactment or by court order, Article 4 applies as it does also to the disproportionate effort situation. Article 5 only applies to the disproportionate effort exclusion. Article 4 is to the effect that the requirement to provide information applies in any case if the data subject has informed the data controller by written notice that he requires such information to be given to him. Article 5 requires that the data controller records his reasons for believing that providing the information would involve a disproportionate effort. This could be the case, for example, where there are large numbers of data subjects to inform. However, processing must still be fair and it is submitted that the disproportionate effort excuse would only apply in innocuous situations or in circumstances where it would be reasonable for a data subject to be aware that such a transfer of personal data relating to him and subsequent processing activity was likely. An example where disproportionate effort could apply is where a copy of a customer database is sold to another company to use for marketing purposes, bearing in mind that data subjects have an absolute right to object to direct marketing. The fact that it might be costly to inform data subjects cannot be the sole reason why information should not be provided to data subjects.

It should be noted that the exception to providing information where a disproportionate effort is involved does not apply to the situation where data are being obtained from the data subject. An example of where the recording or disclosure is required by law is in the field of employment law, especially in the context of official returns and disclosures to the Inland Revenue and Department of Social Security or in a case where disclosure of the personal data in question has been ordered by a court.

The information to be provided is exactly as applies in relation to obtaining data from the data subject. The 'relevant time' is when the controller first processes the data or, where disclosure to a third party within a reasonable period is envisaged:

- if it is in fact disclosed to such a person within that period, the time of disclosure,
- if during that period the data controller becomes or ought to become aware that the data are unlikely to be disclosed to such a person within that period, the time he does become or ought to become so aware, or
- in any other case at the end of that period.

Presumably, the disclosure referred to must be envisaged by both the data controller and the data subject. If it is not envisaged by the data subject, the provision of information in the second and third cases would seem fairly pointless.

The need to provide information on first processing could apply where data have been disclosed to a third party and the third party now processes the data (bearing in mind the very wide definition of 'processing'). As in all cases, the data controller is excused where the data subject already has the information or has it made *readily* available to him. It would seem that, in the latter case, it may be permissible to require the data subject to perform some positive task such as making a request for the information though it must be *readily* available. Where data are disclosed to a third party, it may be that the first data controller is in a position to inform the data subject that this will happen. If he does inform the data subject of the identity (at least) of the third party, then the third party may be excused because the data subject already has the requisite information.

For example, consider two data controllers, Andrew and Barbara. Andrew obtained data from Clarence and, at the time, provided information as required. If disclosure to a third party within a reasonable period was envisaged, when Andrew discloses the data to Barbara, Andrew must inform Clarence no later than that time that the data have been disclosed. When Barbara first processes the data, she must inform Clarence of her identity (at least), unless to do so would involve a disproportionate effort or where the recording or disclosure is required by law. However, if Andrew previously

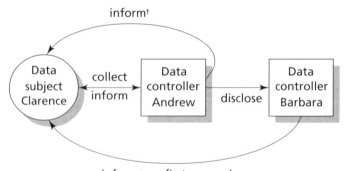

inform* on first processing

†Unless Clarence (data subject) already has information or has it readily available

*Unless Clarence already has information or has it readily available or where required by law (but not contractual obligation) or where it would involve a disproportionate effort

Fig 35.1 Informing data subjects

informed Clarence that the data would be disclosed to Barbara (or perhaps even if he told him that the data might be disclosed to data controllers of a generic description within which Barbara would fall), then Barbara is excused providing this information and, if required to ensure processing is fair, the further information if Andrew also informed Clarence of it. Figure 35.1 shows the working of these provisions. It assumes that disclosure by Andrew within a reasonable period was envisaged and that the disclosure does in fact take place.

The Lord Chancellor may by order impose conditions as to the processing of any general identifier (for example, an identity number) should, of course, such an identifier be introduced in the United Kingdom. This may include further obligations to inform data subjects.

Constraints on processing

The Data Protection Act 1998 introduced conditions for processing personal data. Personal data cannot be processed unless one of the stipulated conditions applies and, in relation to sensitive personal data, a further condition also applies. This seems much more restrictive than under the 1984 Act which effectively only required that processing complied with the Data Protection Principles. The conditions for processing are listed in Schedules 2 and 3 of the Act and are intended to specify the circumstances when processing is deemed to be lawful and fair for the purposes of the first Data Protection Principle. At first sight they can appear restrictive because, if not within the conditions, processing is not allowed at all, unless otherwise exempt or outside the scope of the Data Protection Act 1998. The conditions for processing personal data are central to the controls over processing contained in the Data Protection Directive (Articles 7 and 8). As expressed in the Act, the first Data Protection Principle states:

1 Personal data shall be processed fairly and lawfully and, in particular, shall not be processed unless –
   (a) at least one of the conditions in Schedule 2 is met, and
   (b) in the case of sensitive personal data, at least one of the conditions in Schedule 3 is also met.

The conditions are examined further below.

Conditions for processing 'normal' data

'Normal' personal data are those not defined as sensitive personal data in section 2 of the Act. The conditions in Schedule 2 are:

1 The data subject has given his consent to the processing.
2 The processing is necessary for the performance of a contract to which the data subject is a party or for taking steps at the data subject's request for entering into a contract.
3 The processing is necessary for compliance with any legal obligation to which the data controller is subject, other than a contractual obligation.
4 The processing is necessary to protect the vital interests of the data subject.
5 The processing is necessary for the administration of justice, for the exercise of any functions of either House of Parliament, for the exercise of functions conferred on

any person under any enactment, for the exercise of any function of the Crown, a Minister of the Crown or government department, or for the exercise of any other functions of a public nature exercised in the public interest by any person.

6 (1) The processing is necessary for the purposes of the legitimate interests pursued by the data controller or by the third party or parties to whom the data are disclosed, except where the processing is unwarranted in any particular case by reason of prejudice to the rights and freedoms or legitimate interests of the data subject.

(2) The Lord Chancellor may by order specify particular circumstances in which this condition is, or is not, to be taken to be satisfied.

The last provision sensibly allows for the list of conditions to be modified. However, and this is so important, if the data controller cannot fit within one of these conditions, then he may not process personal data unless otherwise exempt.

A number of points can be made about these conditions:

- The data subject's consent is not stated to be express or explicit (unlike the case with sensitive data) and it would seem reasonable that it may be implied or result from failing to object, having been given the opportunity, for example, by failing to tick a box on a form.
- The word 'necessary' appears in all the other conditions – this is unlikely to be taken in a strict sense such as it being absolutely essential: it is a question of proportionality and depends on the importance of the goal sought to be achieved as accepted by Lord Woolf CJ in *R (on the application of Ellis)* v *Chief Constable of Essex Police* [2002] EWHC 1321 (Admin) adapting the test of Lord Steyn in *R* v *Secretary of State for the Home Department, ex parte Daly* [2001] 2 AC 532 in respect of the European Convention on Human Rights in relation to the right of privacy under Article 8. Lord Woolf noted the acceptance of counsel that the effect of Article 8 was the same as the combined effect of section 29 and Schedules 2 and 3 of the Data Protection Act 1998 (section 29 is the exemption that applies to processing for the prevention or detection of crime).
- An example of the vital interests of the data subject could be where his present address is disclosed to an appropriate authority after it has been discovered that he has been in contact with someone with a contagious disease or where he is using a defective and dangerous implement. Perhaps the main reason for this condition is that it is needed to back up an equivalent though inconsistently wider condition in Schedule 3.
- The fifth condition will apply to a great deal of processing in the public sector, including but not restricted to central and local government. The Freedom of Information Act 2000 extended the condition to the exercise of functions of the Houses of Parliament.
- Most commercial organisations will be able to rely on the second or sixth condition (although the data subject's consent may still be required to ensure processing is fair generally). There is, however, a slight difference to the language used in the Directive which speaks of the legitimate interests being 'overridden by the interests for fundamental rights and freedoms of the data subject which require protection under Article 1(1)' (being in particular the right to privacy in relation to processing of personal data) – the Data Protection Act 1998 seems slightly more restrictive; the European Court of Justice gave some guidance in *R* v *Minister of Agriculture, Fisheries and Food, ex parte*

Fisher, Case C-369/98, 10 October 2000, saying that it requires a balancing of the legitimate interests of the data controller and the data subject. In that case, the Minister refused to disclose details of crops grown in previous years to farmers who had recently purchased a farm. The information was required for an official return and penalties were imposed for errors in making the returns. The farmers could not complete the returns properly without such information.

- It is a little difficult to say just what 'legitimate interests' are – one view is that they cover any activity that is lawful while another is that they cover activities within the organisation's powers, that is, the organisation is acting *intra vires* (within its powers). Certainly discharging duties imposed by law is included.
- Some flexibility is introduced by empowering the Lord Chancellor to specify what is or is not within the 'legitimate interests' form of processing – although this power is not mentioned in the Directive it could prove to be important as the requirement for conditions is new to the United Kingdom and the practical application of the sixth condition may be unpredictable.

In most cases data controllers should find that they satisfy at least one of the above conditions and, in practice, this requirement will not prove restrictive. It is difficult to think of a form of processing that falls outside all the conditions and would yet be deemed to be fair and lawful. Where the personal data are sensitive, the data controller must satisfy one of the conditions in Schedule 2 above as well as one of the conditions in Schedule 3, discussed below.

Conditions for processing 'sensitive' data

'Sensitive' personal data are defined in section 2 of the Data Protection Act 1998 and include data relating to racial or ethnic origin, political opinions, religious or other similar beliefs, trade union membership, physical or mental health or condition, sexual life and data relating to offences (including proceedings, disposal of such proceedings or the sentence of any court). The conditions in Schedule 3 have been extended as a result of the Data Protection (Processing of Sensitive Personal Data) Order 2000.

The conditions contained in Schedule 3 were originally as follow.

1 The data subject has given his explicit consent to the processing.
2 The processing is necessary for employment law rights or obligations (subject to potential modification by the Secretary of State).
3 The processing is necessary to protect the vital interests of the data subject or another where consent cannot be given by or on behalf of the data subject or the data controller cannot reasonably be expected to obtain the consent of the data subject or the processing is necessary to protect vital interests of another person in a case where consent by or on behalf of the data subject has been unreasonably withheld.
4 The processing is carried out subject to appropriate safeguards by a non-profit-making body or association which exists for political, philosophical, religious or trade-union purposes – processing must be carried out with appropriate safeguards for the rights and freedoms of data subjects and relate only to individuals who are members or have regular contact in connection with the body's or association's purposes and which does not involve disclosure to a third party without the consent of the data subject.

5 The information contained in the data has been deliberately made public by the data subject.

6 The processing is necessary in respect of legal proceedings, legal advice and legal rights.

7 The processing is necessary for the administration of justice, the exercise of any functions by either House of Parliament, the exercise of functions conferred by or under any enactment, the exercise of any functions of the Crown, a Minister of the Crown or a government department (the Secretary of State may exclude this condition in specified cases or require further conditions to be satisfied).

8 The processing is necessary for medical purposes (includes preventative medicine, medical diagnosis, medical research, provision of care and treatment and management of healthcare services) and is undertaken by a health professional or a person under a duty of confidentiality equivalent to that owed by a health professional.

9 The processing of sensitive personal data consisting of information as to racial or ethnic origin when it is necessary for the purpose of identifying or keeping under review the existence or absence of equality of opportunity or treatment between persons of different racial or ethnic origins, with a view to enabling such equality to be promoted or maintained, and is carried out with appropriate safeguards for the rights and freedoms of data subjects.

10 The Lord Chancellor may by order allow sensitive data to be processed in other circumstances.

The last provision allowing the list of conditions to be extended has already proved useful and the Data Protection (Processing of Sensitive Personal Data) Order 2000 added the following conditions to the list:

1 Where processing is in substantial public interest and is necessary for the purposes of prevention or detection of any unlawful act (or failure to act) and must necessarily be carried out without the explicit consent of the data subject being sought so as to prejudice those purposes.

2 Where processing is in substantial public interest and is necessary for the discharge of any function designed to protect members of the public from dishonesty, malpractice, or other improper conduct by, or unfitness or incompetence of, any person or mismanagement in the administration of, or failures in services provided by, any body or association, and which must necessarily be carried out with the explicit consent of the data subject being sought so as to prejudice the discharge of that function. These first two conditions also extend to processing for the special purposes with a view to publication where the data controller reasonably believes such publication is in the public interest.

Further conditions cover processing in relation to confidential counselling, in the context of insurance and occupational pensions, equal opportunity monitoring in the context of religious beliefs or physical or mental health, political opinions where processing is by a political party, processing in the substantial public interest for research purposes or where necessary by a constable in the exercise of functions conferred by law.

The Data Protection (Processing of Sensitive Personal Data) (Elected Representatives) Order 2002 allows processing by certain elected representatives in relation to requests made by individuals, whether the data subject or another, to take action on behalf of the data subject or another.

A 'health professional' is defined in section 69 and includes, *inter alia*, registered practitioners such as doctors, dentists, opticians, pharmaceutical chemists, nurses, midwives or health visitors, chiropractors, clinical psychologists, child psychotherapists or speech therapists, music therapists employed by a health service body or a scientist employed as head of department of such a body.

These conditions are fairly extensive and the following points can be made in respect of them:

- where the data subject's consent is relied upon it has to be explicit and it should be informed consent – failing to tick a box on a form will not be good enough;
- what has been said above in relation to the word 'necessary' ought also to apply here though the proportionality test will have a higher threshold;
- vital interests in this context will include situations where an individual is unconscious and disclosure of his blood group is required so that he can be given a life-saving blood transfusion;
- certain types of non-profit-making bodies are included as much of the personal data such bodies will be processing will fall within the definition of sensitive data and it is plainly important for them to process such data belonging to their own members or others having regular contact (note that the condition does not necessarily relate only to registered charities): disclosure requires the consent of the data subjects and it is likely that express consent should be obtained;
- conditions relating to legal proceedings and justice, functions of the Houses of Parliament, legally imposed functions and government functions are as expected but note that the Lord Chancellor has the power to exclude some of these in particular cases or require further conditions;
- processing for equal opportunity monitoring (race, ethnicity, religious belief, physical or mental health or condition) is not specifically mentioned in the Directive but it does allow member states to include other conditions allowing processing where there is substantial public interest subject to satisfactory safeguards;
- in the Data Protection Act 1998, there was no condition allowing processing of personal data relating to criminal offences such that, for example, commercial organisations which grant credit could process such data – hence the additional condition allowing processing for the prevention or detection of crime.

Data controllers who intend to process sensitive data must ensure that they fall within one of the conditions above in addition to one of the conditions in Schedule 2. In some cases, to be specified in the future, the intended processing may fall within the requirement to have a preliminary assessment carried out by the Information Commissioner and, in other cases, where the data controller is unsure, he could consider approaching the Commissioner for guidance or consulting a representative body such as a trade association. Guidance notes have been published to further assist the data controller in deciding whether he can process the sensitive data in question. Furthermore, the Commissioner may, with the consent of the data controller, individually assess the processing for good practice. A fee can be charged for this service if the Lord Chancellor so provides.

Further provision for processing health data is provided for separately under the Health Service (Control of Patient Information) Regulations 2002, made under section 60(1) of the Health and Social Care Act 2001. Confidential patient information relating to patients referred for the diagnosis or treatment of neoplasia may be processed for medical purposes including the surveillance and analysis of health and disease, monitoring and auditing of health and health related care provision and out-comes, planning and administration of the provision made for health and health related care, medical research approved by research ethics committees, provision of information about individuals who have suffered from a particular disease or con-dition where the information supports an analysis of the risk of developing that dis-ease or condition and is required for counselling and support of persons concerned about the risk of developing that disease or condition. Processing may only be under-taken by persons approved by the Secretary of State and is authorised by the person who lawfully holds the information.

A person who processes such confidential patient information must inform the Patient Information Advisory Group and make available information required by the Secretary of State to assist in the investigation and audit of that processing. This is because the provisions in the Regulations must be considered annually.

Under section 60(4) of the Health and Social Care Act 2001, the processing con-cerned must not be inconsistent with provisions made by or under the Data Protection Act 1998. The underlying aims of processing under the Regulations is that it is in the interests of improving patient care or in the public interest.

Constraints on processing may be imposed in particular cases. Regulation 5 of the Electronic Signature Regulations 2002 imposes further constraints of certification-serv-ice-providers, being persons who issue certificates or provide other services in respect of electronic signatures. They are not allowed to obtain personal data for the purpose of issuing or maintaining that certificate otherwise than directly from the data subject or after the explicit consent of the data subject, and may not process such personal data to a greater extent than is necessary for the purpose of issuing or maintaining that cer-tificate, or to a greater extent than is necessary for any other purpose to which the data subject has explicitly consented. An exception is made where the processing is necess-ary for compliance with any legal obligation, to which the certification-service-provider is subject, other than an obligation imposed by contract.

Data subjects and their exercise of rights to prevent processing

Although data subjects are given some new rights under the Data Protection Act 1998 and the rights they enjoyed previously have been enhanced, in the past individuals have not generally exercised their rights to any great extent directly against the data con-troller. Of course, it is impossible to verify precisely how frequently data subjects made use of their rights (for example, no figures are published on how many data subjects sought to gain access to personal data relating to them); it is reasonable to assume that a much larger proportion of individuals complained to the Information Commissioner in preference to bringing a personal action before a civil court against a data controller.

Subject access requests, with some exceptions, do not seem to be made in large vol-umes (this may be because it was possible to charge the data subject up to a maximum £10 in respect of the request). One exception is in relation to data held by credit refer-ence agencies (where the maximum fee is £2 if the required information concerns financial standing only) which, under the old law, was dealt with under section 158 of the Consumer Credit Act 1974. As regards individuals, these requests have been brought within the scope of the Data Protection Act 1998 although the right to have wrong information corrected is still dealt with under the 1974 Act.

In most cases, where a data controller is processing safely within the Data Protection Principles and the processing activities carried on are not particularly sensitive, the data controller should not experience a great deal of activity from data subjects exercising their rights. That being so, the basic rights are stated briefly below but they are described in more detail in the following chapter which focuses on data subjects.

The following rights, which existed under the 1984 Act, are enhanced or improved:

- right to subject access (more information should be given now),
- right to compensation available in respect of damage or distress caused by *any* contravention of the new law,
- rights of rectification and erasure (extended to blocking and destruction and somewhat widened in scope).

Of course, the rights are considerably expanded when one takes into account that the 1998 Act extends also to certain manual files (relevant filing systems and accessible records and unstructured recorded information held by public bodies).

The new rights granted to data subjects are:

- rights to be informed, as discussed above,
- a right to prevent processing likely to cause substantial damage or substantial distress,
- a right to prevent processing for purposes of direct marketing, and
- rights in relation to automated decision taking.

Apart from the concerns about the requirement to inform data subjects, data controllers expressed some anxiety about the possibility of data subjects objecting to certain forms of processing and being able, in some cases, to require the data controller to stop processing personal data relating to them. The reality is less burdensome. In particular, fair and lawful processing will rarely cause substantial damage or substantial distress. The mail, fax and telephone preference schemes are quite effective at preventing (or at least reducing the amount of unsolicited marketing material or calls an individual receives) and the rights in the context of automated decision taking are considerably reduced in a contractual situation or where authorised or provided for by legislation.

Although the rights of data subjects should not prove too onerous for data controllers, they must ensure that they have systems and procedures in place to recognise and comply with data subjects' requests to the extent they are required to do under the Data Protection Act 1998 and subordinate legislation.

Transfers to third countries

Many data controllers transfer personal data to other countries for processing activities. The Act contains provision that apply where personal data are being transferred to a country outside the European Economic Area (EEA). As mentioned earlier, the rationale behind the Data Protection Directive is that, by providing a level playing field in terms of effective protection for rights and freedoms of individuals, particularly with respect to their right of privacy in relation to processing personal data, there can be no barriers to freedom of movement of personal data throughout the EEA. However, problems may occur where a data controller wishes, as many do, to have personal data processed elsewhere and the country to which he wants to transfer the personal data for processing has no specific data protection laws or, if such laws exist, they fail to meet the European standards and safeguards. A transfer does not have to be permanent and the language of the Directive suggests that permitting access to personal data, for example, on a website is within these provisions.

The eighth Data Protection Principle requires that personal data must not be transferred to a country or territory outside the EEA unless it ensures an adequate level of protection for the rights and freedoms of data subjects in relation to the processing of personal data. The interpretative provisions in Part II of Schedule 1 state that an adequate level of protection is one which is adequate in all the circumstances of the case, having regard in particular to:

(a) the nature of the data,
(b) the country or territory of origin of the information contained in the data,
(c) the country or territory of final destination of that information,
(d) the purposes for which and period during which the data are intended to be processed,
(e) the law in force in the country or territory in question,
(f) the international obligations of that country or territory,
(g) any relevant codes of conduct or other rules which are enforceable in that country or territory (whether generally or by arrangement in particular cases) and
(h) any security measures taken in respect of the data in that country or territory.

Thus, adequacy depends on a number of factors and it will not be possible to say that a particular country does not have an adequate level of protection in all cases. It might be possible to say the opposite, however, where a country embraces a model of data protection law which is, to all intents and purposes, a mirror image of that in Europe. There are no restrictions on such countries and those already declared to have adequate protection are Switzerland, Hungary, Canada and Argentina. Recently, it has been accepted that the data protection law in Guernsey also meets the requirements for adequacy of protection.

Even if a particular country or territory does not have an adequate level of protection in terms of the particular transfer envisaged, it may still be possible to make that transfer. The European Community legislators have at least adopted a sense of reality and accepted that there may be good reasons why a data controller might validly wish to transfer data to such a country. The approach taken is to allow the transfer subject to a condition being satisfied; the purpose of the conditions is to try to overcome the danger of inadequate protection. Thus, the eighth Data Protection Principle does not apply to data within Schedule 4 (except by order of the Lord Chancellor), being where any one of the following conditions is present:

1 The data subject has given consent to transfer.
2 The transfer is necessary for the performance of a contract between the data subject and data controller or for taking steps at the request of the data subject with a view to his entering into such a contract.
3 The transfer is necessary for the conclusion of a contract between the data controller and a third person entered into at the request of the data subject or in his interests, or is necessary for the performance of the contract.
4 The transfer is necessary for reasons of substantial public interest (the Lord

Chancellor may specify circumstances in which a transfer is or is not covered by this).

5 The transfer is necessary with respect to legal proceedings, legal rights or obtaining legal advice.

6 The transfer is necessary to protect the vital interests of the data subject.

7 The transfer is part of the personal data on a public register and any conditions subject to which the register is open to inspection are complied with by any person to whom the data are or may be disclosed after the transfer.

8 The transfer is made on terms of a kind approved by the Commissioner as ensuring adequate safeguards for the rights and freedoms of data subjects.

9 The transfer has been authorised by the Commissioner as being made in such a manner as to ensure adequate safeguards for the rights and freedoms of data subjects.

In relation to the eighth condition above, the Information Commissioner may approve terms which ensure adequate safeguards or authorise transfer as being made so as to ensure adequate safeguards. In any proceedings under the new law, questions as to whether the eighth Principle has been met are to be determined in accordance with any finding made by the European Commission under Article 31(2) of the Directive as to transfers of the kind in question. In the main, safeguards are likely to come from approved contractual terms. There are obligations to inform the Commission to the European Communities as to authorisations granted and the Commission has agreed standard contractual clauses that are deemed to offer sufficient safeguards.

Security

The seventh Data Protection Principle requires that appropriate technical and organisational measures are taken against unauthorised or unlawful processing of personal data and against accidental loss or destruction of, or damage to, personal data. Security was an important aspect of data protection law under the 1984 Act and is continued under the 1998 Act with additional emphasis on the relationship between the data controller and a processor (under the 1984 Act, computer bureaux also had to comply with the security requirements). Factors influencing the level of security include the state of technological development, the cost of implementation, the potential harm of unauthorised processing or accidental loss, destruction or damage and the nature of the data. That being so, a prudent data controller will continually review his security arrangements and monitor technological improvements to security measures available.

Data controllers must take reasonable steps to ensure the reliability of staff having access to personal data. They must choose processors who provide sufficient guarantees as regards technical and organisational measures and take reasonable steps to ensure compliance with those measures. Where a processor is engaged, the processing must be carried out under a contract made or evidenced in writing under which the processor is to act only on the instructions of the data controller and which imposes equivalent security obligations on the processor. Data controllers are required to take reasonable steps to ensure that the processor complies with the security measures. Although processors do not have to notify the processing they perform on behalf of others, this mechanism is designed to make sure that they are aware of the importance of security and, in the event of a failure on the part of the processor, he will be liable for breach of contract.

Exemptions

The Data Protection Act 1998 contains a large number of exemptions from parts of the Act. There are some significant differences compared with the exemptions under the 1984 Act. Reference to the section on the transitional provisions illustrates the differences in this respect as specific provision had to be made to deal with these differences in respect of automated processing already under way at the time the new law should have come into force (at the latest 24 October 1998).

First, it should be noted that there are some multiple exemptions from the 'subject information provisions' and the 'non-disclosure provisions', as follows:

- 'subject information provisions' meaning the first Principle, in as much as it requires compliance with Part II, paragraph 2 of Schedule 1 (providing information to the data subject on collection or in other cases) and section 7 (subject access),
- 'non-disclosure provisions' meaning the first Data Protection Principle (but not with respect to the requirement that one of the conditions in Schedule 2 is met and, for sensitive data, one of the conditions in Schedule 3 is also met), the second to the fifth Data Protection Principles, section 10 (the right to prevent processing likely to cause damage or distress) and section 14(1) to (3) (right of rectification, etc. in relation to inaccurate data) *to the extent that they are inconsistent with the disclosure in question.*

Except as provided for in the exemptions, the subject access provisions are unaffected by any enactment or rule of law prohibiting or restricting the disclosure, or authorising the withholding of information.

The exemptions, some of which are set out in Schedule 7, are numerous. Under section 38, the Lord Chancellor is given the power to make further exemptions to the subject information provisions and the non-disclosure provisions if he considers further exemption is necessary to safeguard the interests of data subjects or the rights and freedoms of any other individual. This is a basis for exemption in the Directive. Some of the exemptions are outside the scope of the Directive in any case, such as those relating to national security or processing by an individual for a purely personal or household activity: Article 3(2).

It should be noted that a general principle is that exemption from the relevant provisions of the Act is available only in as much as compliance would prejudice the purpose governed by the exemption or if the particular exemption is required for the purpose concerned. For example, exemption is granted from the subject access provisions for the purposes of the prevention or detection of crime. However, if subject access can be granted without prejudicing these purposes (or other exempted purposes), then it must be granted. The exemptions are not generally blanket exemptions and require a value-judgment by the data controller as to whether an exemption is available in a particular circumstance.

All the exemptions are listed in Table 35.2 and then most of the exemptions are described in more depth.

Table 35.2 Exemptions under the Data Protection Act 1998

Description	Exemption provided from	Notes
National security, s 28	● all the Principles ● Parts II, III and V (rights of data subjects, notification, enforcement) ● s 55 (offences of unlawful obtaining, etc. – see later)	The exemption must be required for the purpose of safeguarding national security but a certificate signed by a Minister of the Crown (being a Cabinet Minister, the Attorney General or, in Scotland, the Advocate General for Scotland) to that effect is conclusive (as it was under the 1984 Act) – there are provisions for any person affected to appeal to the Tribunal In Schedule 6, para 6 the Tribunal's jurisdiction shall be exercised *ex parte* by the Chairman or a Deputy Chairman – subject to rules made under para 7 for regulating the exercise of the right of appeal
Crime and taxation, s 29	● 1st Principle (except to the extent which it requires compliance with conditions in Schedules 2 and 3 – thus the conditions still apply) ● s 7 (subject access) ● all only to the extent to which application of those provisions would be likely to prejudice matters in s 29(1)	Only for purposes of prevention/detection of crime, apprehension/prosecution of offenders or assessment/collection of any tax or duty or any imposition of a similar nature (s 29(1)) Data processed for purpose of discharging statutory function where information obtained for any purpose mentioned above are exempt from subject information provisions to the same extent Data disclosed for purposes of crime or taxation are exempt from non-disclosure provisions if those provisions would be likely to prejudice those purposes Where the data controller is a government department, local authority or other authority administering housing or council tax benefit, data are exempt from s 7 (subject access) if the exemption is required in the interests of a system of risk assessment for taxation or crime where the offence involves unlawful application for or claim in respect of public funds

Description	Exemption provided from	Notes
Health, education and social work, s 30	Exemptions from subject access provided for by the Data Protection (Subject Access Modification) (Health) Order 2000, the Data Protection (Subject Access Modification) (Education) Order 2000 and the Data Protection (Subject Access Modification) (Social Work) Order 2000. These exemptions apply where access to the information would be likely to cause serious harm to the physical or mental health or condition of the data subject or any other person. Exemptions from the subject information provisions apply in the case of processing by courts in relation to certain types of reports in family proceedings	Leaves it to the Lord Chancellor to make orders – three have been made as noted in the preceding column. The exemptions may cover, for example, where a doctor does not want to allow a patient access to his file if it shows the patient is terminally ill and the doctor considers this knowledge would be harmful to the patient
Regulatory activity, s 31	● subject information provisions	If likely to prejudice proper discharge of function covered (to protect public, charities, persons at work (as appropriate)) functions are: ● financial loss resulting from dishonesty, malpractice, unfitness, incompetence of persons concerned in banking, insurance, investment or other financial services or management of bodies corporate ● financial loss resulting from the conduct of a bankrupt ● dishonesty etc. by professional persons ● misconduct or mismanagement in administration of charities ● in respect of protecting property of charities ● in relation to health and safety at work Exemption is extended to others such as the Parliamentary Commissioner for Administration, Health Service Commissioner, Office of Fair Trading, etc.

Description	Exemption provided from	Notes
Journalism, literature and art, s 32	● all the Principles (except 7th – security measures) ● s 7 (subject access) ● s 10 (right to prevent processing likely to cause damage or distress) ● s 12 (automated decision taking) ● s 14(1)–(3) (rectification etc.)	An important exemption protecting freedom of speech Where personal data are processed for the special purposes the exemption applies if: (a) processing is with a view to publication by any person of journalistic, literary or artistic material, (b) the data controller reasonably believes it is in the public interest, having regard to the special importance of freedom of expression, (c) the data controller reasonably believes, in all the circumstances, that compliance with the provision is incompatible with the special purposes Codes of practice may be designated by the Lord Chancellor and taken into account in determining reasonableness of public interest belief. A number of codes designated by the Data Protection (Designated Codes of Practice) (No 2) Order 2000 include those of the Broadcasting Commission and the Press Complaints Commission Provision for the court to stay certain types of proceedings if data controller makes a claim that special purposes exist and he has not published the material in the preceding 24 hours – the stay is subject to the claim being withdrawn or the coming into effect of a determination by the Commissioner under s 45

Description	Exemption provided from	Notes
Research, history, statistics, s 33	• such further processing not incompatible with Principle 2 (purpose for which obtained) • may be kept indefinitely notwithstanding Principle 5 • s 7 (subject access) – if processed in accordance with relevant conditions and results not made available in any form identifying any data subject	Research purposes includes statistical or historical purposes 'Relevant conditions' are: (a) the data are not processed to support measures or decisions with respect to particular individuals, and (b) are not processed in such a way that substantial damage or substantial distress is or is likely to be caused to any data subject Personal data will still be treated as processed for research purposes where disclosure is to any person for research purposes, to the data subject or person acting on his behalf, at the request or with consent of data subject or person acting on his behalf or where person making disclosure has reasonable grounds for believing any of the above disclosures apply
Manual data held by public authorities, s 33A	• 1st, 2nd, 3rd, 5th, 7th and 8th Principles • 6th Principle, except for the right of access under s 7 and the right of rectification, etc. under s 14 • ss 10–12, rights to object to processing and right in relation to automated decision taking • s 13 (right to compensation) except where it relates to damage caused by a contravention or section 7 or the 4th Principle • Part III (notification) • s 55 (offences of unlawful obtaining, etc.)	Applies to personal data within (e) of the definition of data under section 1(1). Where the personal data relate to appointments and removal, pay, discipline, superannuation and other personal matters in relation to employment or service in the armed forces, the Crown, local authorities, etc. further exemption from the remaining principles and the remaining parts of Part II (rights of data subjects) is given

Description	Exemption provided from	Notes
Information available to public by or under any enactment, s 34	• Subject information provisions • 4th Principle • s 12A (rights in relation to exempt manual data) – applies until 23 October 2007 • s 14(1)–(3) (rectification, etc.) • non-disclosure provisions	If the data controller is obliged by or under any enactment (other than one contained in the Freedom of Information Act 2000) to make the information available to the public whether by publicising it, making it available for inspection or otherwise, whether on payment of a fee or not
Disclosures required by law or in connection with legal proceedings, etc. s 35	• non-disclosure provisions	Where disclosure required by or under any enactment, rule of law or by court order or if necessary for legal proceedings, obtaining legal advice or establishing, exercising or defending a legal right
Parliamentary privilege, s 35A	• 1st Principle (except to the extent which it requires compliance with conditions in Schedules 2 and 3 – thus the conditions still apply) • 2nd, 3rd, 4th and 5th Principles • s 7 (subject access) • s 10 (right to prevent processing likely to cause damage or distress) • ss 14(1)–(3) (rectification, etc.)	If the exemption is required to avoid an infringement of the privileges of either House of Parliament (will not come into force until 30 November 2005 unless the Secretary of State appoints by order an earlier date)
Domestic purposes, s 36	• all the Principles • Parts II and III (rights of data subjects and notification)	Processed by an individual only for that individual's personal, family or household affairs (including recreational purposes)
Miscellaneous exceptions in Schedule 7		
Confidential references by data controller, para 1	• s 7 (subject access)	Applies to references in respect of education, employment or appointment of data subject to any office (actual or prospective) or the provisions of services by the data subject (actual or prospective)
Armed forces, para 2	• subject information provisions	If likely to prejudice the combat effectiveness of any of the armed forces of the Crown
Judicial appointments, honours, para 3	• subject information provisions	To assess suitability for judicial office or as a QC or the conferring by the Crown of any honour or dignity

Description	Exemption provided from	Notes
Crown employment, etc., para 4	● subject access provisions (by order of the Lord Chancellor – Data Protection (Crown Appointments) Order 2000 – lists the appointments, includes the Poet Laureate, Astronomer Royal, Lord-Lieutenants and Archbishops and other positions in the Church of England)	Processing to assess any person's suitability for: (a) employment by/under the Crown, (b) any office to which appointments are made by Her Majesty, by a Minister of the Crown or a Northern Ireland Authority
Management forecasts, para 5	● subject information provisions	For purposes of management forecasting or planning to assist the data controller in the conduct of any business or other activity where complying would be likely to prejudice that conduct
Corporate finance, para 6	● subject information provisions	Underwriting in respect of issues, advice to undertakings on capital structure, industrial strategy and related matters, advice and services in relation to mergers and acquisitions of undertakings and underwriting such matters Where compliance could affect the price of an instrument in relation to investment services or if exemption required to safeguard important economic or financial interest of UK Lord Chancellor may specify by order circumstances in which exemption is or is not taken to be required or matters to be taken into account in determining whether required for safeguarding important economic or financial interest of UK (see the Data Protection (Corporate Finance Exemption) Order 2000 – matters are the orderly functioning of financial markets and the efficient allocation of capital within the economy – data are, *inter alia*, those the data controller reasonably believes would affect a decision to deal in, subscribe to or issue an instrument)

Description	Exemption provided from	Notes
Negotiations, para 7	• subject information provisions (to extent would prejudice negotiations)	Records of intentions in relation to any negotiations with the data subject if likely to prejudice those negotiations
Examination marks, para 8	• s 7 (subject access)	Simply postpones the time for compliance in cases where application made before examination results are announced Time for compliance is 5 months after request or 40 days after results announced, whichever is the earlier If based on the 5-month period, there is a duty to supply details at the time the request was made together with subsequent versions
Examination scripts, para 9	• s 7 (subject access)	Personal data recorded by candidates during academic, professional or other examination
Legal professional privilege, para 10	• subject information provisions	Information in respect of which a claim to legal professional privilege (or, in Scotland, to confidentiality of communications) could be maintained in legal proceedings
Self-incrimination, para 11	• s 7 (subject access)	But not in respect of offences under this Act, though such information is not admissible in criminal proceedings

National security

This exemption is provided under section 28 and applies if it is necessary for the purpose of safeguarding national security. The exemption is very wide-ranging and is from all the principles, the rights of data subjects, notification and enforcement. Furthermore, the offences in section 55 in respect of unlawful obtaining, etc. do not apply if this exemption applies. A certificate signed by a Minister of the Crown who is a member of the Cabinet, the Attorney-General or, in Scotland, Advocate General, is conclusive evidence that the exemption is required. The need for this exemption is plain but the certification arrangements mean that there is little control over the scope and application of this exemption. However, there is provision for an appeal against a certificate to the Information Tribunal. Any appeal will be held before the Chairman and/or deputy Chairmen as designated by the Lord Chancellor and proceedings normally will be held *ex parte*, that is, without hearing the person appealing against the certificate. There are special procedures in respect to an appeal brought under section 28 which are set out in the Information Tribunal (National Security Appeals) Rules 2000.

Crime and taxation

This applies if the personal data are held for the purpose of the prevention or detection of crime, the apprehension or prosecution of offenders or the assessment or collection of any tax or duty or imposition of a similar nature. Under section 29, the exemption is from the first Data Protection Principle and the subject access provisions. However, the conditions for processing under the first Principle (in Schedules 2 and/or 3) still apply. Exemption is also given in respect of the non-disclosure provisions in relation to processing for the prevention or detection of crime. The exemption applies only in as much as the provision in question would be likely to prejudice any of the purposes covered by the exemption.

The case of *R v Chief Constables of C and D, ex parte A, The Times*, 7 November 2000 illustrates the operation of the prevention or detection of crime exemption. A local authority asked one police force to obtain information about a job applicant from another police force and to disclose the information to the local authority. It was required for a child access vetting enquiry as the job involved working with children. The information sought related to previous police investigations into allegations of inappropriate behaviour with children. The job applicant applied for judicial review of the decision taken by the police forces to disclose the information to the local authority after an offer of employment by the local authority was withdrawn. He claimed, *inter alia*, that the disclosures were a breach of the Data Protection Act 1984 and/or the Data Protection Act 1998. The court held that the 1984 Act was not applicable as the information was processed manually. As regards the 1998 Act, it was held that the processing clearly fell within the framework of the 1998 Act and the Data Protection (Processing of Sensitive Personal Data) Order 2000 (which added processing for the prevention or detection of crime in the substantial public interest to the list of conditions in Schedule 3). Therefore exemption from the non-disclosure provisions applied.

The exemption under section 29 also applies to anyone discharging a statutory function who has obtained the data from a person who held the data for any of the above purposes but here the exemption is from the subject information provisions. An example might be personal data held by the police which has been given to the Crown Prosecution Service which is considering whether to prosecute the individual concerned. As a judgment has to be made by the data controller as to whether any of the purposes covered would be prejudiced by compliance, a subjective and qualitative element is brought into the practical application of the exemption. This can be criticised as it will be the data controller who decides this, subject only to a challenge by an aggrieved person. Further exemption is granted, from the non-disclosure provisions where the disclosure is for any of the above purposes and where compliance would prejudice any of those matters.

An example of the latter is where a local authority, empowered under section 163 of the Criminal Justice and Public Order Act 1994 to use video surveillance in order to promote the prevention of crime, discloses copies of CCTV footage to the media in order to facilitate this purpose. In *R v Brentwood Borough Council, ex parte Peck* [1998] EMLR 697, an applicant for judicial review complained when the local authority disclosed a video showing him walking down the High Street, Brentwood, with a knife. He later attempted suicide by slashing his wrists but this was not caught on video. He was not charged by the police. The video was shown on television. His face had been masked at the request of the local authority but this proved to be inadequate and some of the applicant's friends and neighbours recognised him, from his distinctive hairstyle and moustache. The application was dismissed, Mr Justice Harrison confirming that the statutory provisions above empowered the local authority to take the actions it had, including distributing the footage. Furthermore, it had not acted irrationally and had not known of the objection until the video had been broadcast. The Court of Appeal refused leave to appeal and Peck brought an action before the European Court of Human Rights on the grounds that his right of privacy under Article 8 of the Human Rights Convention had been breached and he had no effective domestic remedy as required by Article 13 of the Convention; *Peck v United Kingdom*, 23 January 2001. The Court unanimously held that there had been a violation under both Articles and awarded him €11,800 for non-pecuniary damage plus costs.

The facts of Peck happened before the Data Protection Act 1998 and the Human Rights Act 1998 came into force, hence the finding of the Court of Human Rights that Peck had no effective remedy under domestic law. Now, operators of CCTV systems have to comply with the Data Protection Act 1998 and must comply with the conditions for processing, though in the context of processing for the prevention or detection of crime, the remainder of the first Data Protection Principle does not apply. Furthermore, the processing must be viewed in the light of the European Convention for the Protection of Human Rights and Fundamental Freedoms and the Human Rights Act 1998 requires that so far as it is possible to do so, primary and subordinate legislation must be read and given effect in accordance with the Convention. The Act also states that it is unlawful for a public authority to act in a manner incompatible with the Convention. A claim by the United Kingdom government that the decision could undermine the right of freedom of expression under Article 10 was rejected by the European Court of Human Rights as the local authority and the media could have achieved their objectives by ensuring that Peck's identity was properly concealed. Note that, under the 1998 Act, personal data can extend to visual data (this is confirmed by the Directive) and accepted as uncontroversial by Mr Justice Lindsey in *Michael Douglas v Hello! Ltd* [2003] EWHC 786 (Ch) in relation to photographs taken surreptitiously at the wedding of Michael Douglas and Catherine Zeta-Jones.

Where the data controller is a lawful authority (government department, local authority or other authority administering housing benefit or council tax benefit) and the personal data consist of a classification of the data subject as part of a risk assessment system, exemption from the subject access provisions is granted. This applies only with respect to the purposes of assessment of tax, duty or similar imposition or the prevention or detection of crime, apprehension of offenders or where the offence concerned involves any unlawful claim for payment out of, or any unlawful application of, public funds where the processing is for any of those purposes.

Under the 1984 Act, the Data Protection Registrar had a long-running dispute over the scope of the equivalent exemption with the Halifax Building Society. It all started when an individual complained to the Registrar that he had not received all the information he was entitled to in pursuance of a subject access request. The Society had withheld data which it considered to be 'system security data' on the basis that the crime prevention exemption applied to the data. The Data Protection Registrar issued an enforcement notice and the Society appealed to the Tribunal. After many meetings and discussions and the issue of a preliminary notice in respect of the complainant (with which the Society complied), an agreement was reached between the Halifax Building

Society and the Registrar. The agreement was to the effect that the Society would not normally give details of transactions on the data subject's account, card number, computer terminal and location of the automated teller machine. However, as part of the agreement (*Agreement in the Enforcement Action against the Halifax Building Society*, 6 January 1992), the Society agreed to inform any person making a subject access request of this fact and that all other information had been made available: for example, details of address, financial circumstances, balance and the Society's views (if appropriate). The data subject would also be informed that the Society would consider requests for other information if there was a genuine need for the data subject to see it. Finally, the Society agreed to inform data subjects that they are entitled to complain to the Data Protection Registrar (now Information Commissioner) if not satisfied with the Society's response.

In relation to prevention and detection of crime, exemption is also given from the non-disclosure provisions. In *James Martin (Application for Judicial Review)*, 20 December 2002, allegations of sexual abuse of a child had been made against the applicant for judicial review in the High Court of Northern Ireland. A Health and Social Services Trust retained information about these allegations. The applicant was never charged with a criminal offence. Later, a social worker divulged information about the allegations to the applicant's new partner who had three children. The applicant and his new partner separated soon after. The applicant claimed that the retention, processing and disclosure of the information was in breach of his right to privacy under Article 8 of the Human Rights Convention and a breach of data protection law.

Article 8(2) contains a derogation from the right of privacy in accordance with the law and where necessary in a democratic society, *inter alia*, for the prevention or detection of crime. The first issue then was whether the processing by the Trust was in accordance with the law. The judge had no hesitation in accepting that the processing fell within the exemption and, therefore, the processing met the requirement of legality. The judge then went on to consider whether the Trust was justified to act as it did and he concluded it was justified. The Trust had reasonable cause to suspect that the new partner's children could be harmed and an assessment was made based on the facts and circumstances of the particular case and a pressing need for disclosure was established. Furthermore, the Trust had no blanket policy of disclosures in such cases.

Offender naming schemes are sometimes used by the police under the Crime and Disorder Act 1998. Essex police wished to introduce such a scheme, under which a photograph and name of a convicted offender would be displayed together with details of the offences committed and the sentence he was serving (only offenders with at least 12 months' imprisonment were to be selected). The first offender selected objected arguing that his right to privacy under Article 8 of the Human Rights Convention would be breached by the scheme in *R (on application of Ellis) v Chief Constable of Essex* [2003] EWHC 1321 (Admin). In terms of preventing and detecting crime, the actions of the police had to be proportionate. The scheme was a genuine initiative and in the public interest but more care had to be taken in appraisal and monitoring of the scheme and the effect on the offender's family must also be taken into account. There also had to be a structured assessment of the risks in the light of further information and appropriate professional advice. Only when that had been done could it be said whether the potential benefits of the scheme were proportionate to the intrusion on an offender's right to privacy. The offender also claimed a breach of the Data Protection Act 1998 but it was accepted that the combined effect of section 29 and Schedules 2 and 3 of the Act was the same as under Article 8 of the European Convention for the Protection of Human Rights and Fundamental Freedoms. Lord Woolf CJ, said that counsel accurately stated that

> ... under the 1998 Act, in order to establish the legality of the Scheme it has to be shown that the inclusion of a selected candidate is necessary for the discharge of the duty cast upon the police to formulate and implement policies designed to reduce crime and disorder. The reference to 'necessary' in this context requires that the action on behalf of the police should be a proportionate response in precisely the same way it is described by Lord Steyn in Daly [R (on the application of Daly) v Secretary of State for the Home Dept [2001] 2 AC 532].

It now seems tolerably clear that the impact of the Data Protection Act 1998 in relation to the exemption for the prevention or detection of crime is, to all intents and purposes, identical to that under Article 8 of the European Convention for the Protection of Human Rights and Fundamental Freedoms. Indeed, data protection law has it roots in the Convention and can be seen as protecting privacy in the context of processing personal data. In any event, the Act must be construed, as far as possible, to be interpreted and given effect in a manner compatible with the Convention.

Health, education and social work

Section 30 of the Data Protection Act 1998 empowers the Lord Chancellor to make orders concerning exemptions from subject access in the context of health, education and social work. Three such orders have been made:

- the Data Protection (Subject Access Modification) (Health) Order 2000,
- the Data Protection (Subject Access Modification) (Education) Order 2000, and
- the Data Protection (Subject Access Modification) (Social Work) Order 2000.

In respect of health, exemption is from the subject access provisions under section 7 to the extent that compliance with the request would be likely to cause serious harm to the physical or mental health or condition of the data subject or any other person. Where the data controller is not a health professional, he may not withhold the information covered by the subject access request unless he has consulted a health professional, whom he thinks appropriate, on the question of whether to withhold the information. Where a person (such as a person having parental responsibility) is lawfully entitled to seek access on behalf of the data subject, the data controller must consider any expectation of confidentiality of the data subject and any wishes of the data subject as regards disclosure to that other person.

There is also exemption from the subject information provisions where processing is carried out by a court under specified circumstances, for example, where the data consist of information supplied in a report or other evidence provided by a local authority, Health and Social Services Board or Trust or probation officer in certain proceedings involving child care or criminal proceedings in relation to a child.

In terms of education, exemption from subject access is granted where disclosure of information in an educational record would be likely to cause serious harm to the physical or mental health or condition of the data subject or any other person. Where a person making a subject access request on behalf of a child for whom he has parental responsibility or on behalf of a person incapable of managing his own affairs, having been appointed by the court to manage those affairs, there is a further exemption from subject access. This is to the extent that the information indicates that the data subject, being a child or incapable of managing his own affairs, is or has been the subject of child abuse or is at risk of child abuse and complying with the request would not be in the data subject's best interests. There is also an equivalent exemption from the subject information provisions in the case of processing by a court as applies in respect of health records. Educational records are defined in Schedule 11 to the Data Protection Act 1998. In England and Wales it is any record of information processed by or on behalf of the governing body or by a teacher at a local education authority maintained school or a special school as defined in section 6(2) of the Education Act 1996. The information must relate to any person who is or has been a pupil of the school and originated from or was supplied by an employee of the local education authority or a teacher or other employee of a special school or voluntary aided, foundation or foundation special school.

There is a general exemption from the subject information provisions for social work. For some particular forms of social work, there is also an exemption from the subject access provisions except the requirement to inform the data subject whether the data controller is processing personal data relating to the data subject. It applies to the extent that access would be likely to prejudice the carrying out of social work by reason of the fact that serious harm would be likely to be caused to the physical or mental health or condition of the data subject or any other person. Where, as in relation to health and educational records, a person is entitled to make a subject access request on behalf of the data subject, that request shall not be complied with to the extent that the access would disclose information provided by the data subject, or obtained as a result of an examination or investigation, in the expectation that the data concerned would not be so disclosed or where the data subject has expressly indicated that they should not be so disclosed. The Order applies to social work set out in a Schedule to the Order, including social services work, data processed by a probation committee and by education authorities exercising their functions in relation to ensuring children of school age receive efficient education.

Any overlap between the Orders is removed. The Education Order does not apply to personal data within the Health Order and the Social Work Order does not apply where the Health or Education Orders apply.

Prior to the equivalent provision to the health exemption under the 1984 Act, it was accepted that there was no common law right of access to health data. In *R v Mid-Glamorgan Family Health Services, ex parte Martin* (unreported) 29 July 1994, a patient had been refused access to his health records going back to before 1990 on the basis that it would be detrimental for the patient to see those records directly. An offer was made to disclose the records conditionally to a medical expert appointed by the patient but was not accepted. The patient claimed that there was a right of access at common law. However, the Court of Appeal refused to grant access on the 'best interests' principle, denying that there was such a common law right.

Regulatory activity

This exemption from the subject information provisions covers a wide range of regulatory activities in order to protect the public from dishonesty, malpractice and the like by persons involved with financial services, carrying on any profession or other activity or in relation to charities. It also extends to health and safety at work. A complete list is given earlier in Table 35.2. Under section 31, the function is one conferred by or under any enactment, any function of the Crown or a Minister of the Crown or a government department or any other function of a public nature which is exercised in the public interest. This latter category is potentially very wide ranging.

Further exemption is available from the subject information provisions in respect of statutory functions of the Parliamentary Commissioner for Administration, the Commission for Local Administration, the Health Service Commission and other public bodies. The exemption also applies to certain functions of the Director General of Fair Trading.

In all cases, the exemption is only available where the application of the subject information provisions would be likely to prejudice the proper discharge of the relevant function. The purpose of the exemption is to prevent, for example, a person under investigation by the Charity Commissioners for the misapplication of the property of a charity discovering that his activities are being investigated. He could find out by carrying out a subject access request or because, under normal circumstances, he is required to be informed of the disclosure of personal data relating to him to the Charity Commissioners.

Journalism, literature and art

This is an important and wide-ranging exemption protecting freedom of speech. Under section 32, exemption is from all the Data Protection Principles (except the seventh on security measures), and most of the rights of data subjects including subject access. We have seen in the previous chapter how the Information Commissioner's powers are severely constrained in relation to the purposes of journalism and artistic and literary purposes (the special purposes). Indeed, in a court action in relation to the data subjects' rights or compensation, a claim by the data controller that he is processing only for the special purposes with a view to publication of material not previously published by him at a time 24 hours before he makes that claim, proceedings must be stayed until the Commissioner makes a determination under section 45 as to whether the special purposes do apply or the claim is withdrawn. The same applies if it appears to the court that the special purposes apply.

For the exemption to apply, the processing must be undertaken with a view to publication of any journalistic, literary or artistic material and the data controller must reasonably believe that publication is in the public interest, having regard in particular to the special importance of the public interest in freedom of expression. Furthermore, the data controller must reasonably believe that compliance with the exemption in question is incompatible with the special purposes. In making a determination as to the data controller's belief that publication is in the public interest, regard may be had to his compliance with any relevant code of practice designated by the Lord Chancellor for this purpose. Under the Data Protection (Designated Codes of Practice) (No. 2) Order 2000, the codes are those of the Broadcasting Standards Commission, Independent Television Commission, Press Complaints Commission and the Radio Authority and the Producer's Guidelines of the British Broadcasting Corporation. As noted previously, the Lord Chancellor can order the Commissioner to prepare and disseminate codes of practice after consultation with trade associations and data subjects or persons representing data subjects.

The scope of the section 32 exemption came up for consideration in *Naomi Campbell* v *Mirror Group Newspapers* [2002] EWHC 499 (QB). The defendant had published newspaper articles which showed that the claimant, contrary to her previous false assertions, was addicted to drugs and attending meetings of Narcotics Anonymous. The articles included details of those meetings and a photograph of her leaving a meeting in Chelsea. She brought an action against the defendant for breach of confidence and for compensation under section 13 of the Data Protection Act 1998. At first instance, Mr Justice Morland in looking at the wording of the exemption under section 32 thought that the exemption only applied up to the time of publication and did not provide a defence thereafter. The wording states that processing is undertaken *with a view to publication.*

Having found that the section 32 exemption applied only up to the time of publication, the judge awarded damages for breach of confidence and under section 13 of the Data Protection Act 1998 of £3500 including £1000 aggravated damages. As the exemption did not apply post-publication, the judge found that the defendant could not rely on the conditions for processing data in Schedules 2 and 3 to the Act. The legitimate interests condition did not apply as the processing was unwarranted intrusion into the claimant's right of privacy. In terms of Schedule 3 (accepting that the data relating to treatment for drug addiction were sensitive personal data) the appropriate condition for processing was disclosure in the substantial public interest in connection with the commission of any unlawful act, etc. for the special purposes with a view to publication where the data controller reasonably believed publication would be in the public interest. Publishing details of the therapy (rather than simply the fact that she was having therapy) was not in the substantial public interest and the disclosure was not in connection with the commission of a criminal offence but, rather, the claimant's attempts to avoid committing criminal offences related to controlled drugs. Therefore, the processing by the defendant was in breach of the Act and the claimant was entitled to compensation under section 13 for substantial distress for a contravention of the Act by the data controller. Where the contravention relates to processing for the special purposes compensation is available for substantial distress in the absence of substantial damage. The total award could be seen as fairly small and may have been coloured by the behaviour of the claimant. The judge described her as lacking in frankness and having lied on oath.

Mirror Group Newspapers appealed against the decision of Morland J and, in *Naomi Campbell* v *Mirror Group Newspapers* [2002] EWCA Civ 1373, the Court of Appeal found for the defendant on both the breach of confidence issue and the section 32 defence, holding that it did apply to post-publication also. As far as the breach of confidence point, the Court of Appeal accepted that publication of the details of treatment and the photograph were acceptable as they provided credibility to the story, showing that the claimant had lied to the public when she said she did not take drugs. A claim that publication of hard copies of newspapers was outside the scope of processing for the purposes of the Data Protection Act 1998 was rejected by the Court of Appeal which said that an act carried out at the instigation of the data controller which is linked to the automated processing of personal data, such as obtaining or using (as defined in section 1(1)), should fall within the scope of the Act.

On the section 32 point, the Court of Appeal considered the Directive and the whole of section 32, which all agreed was ambiguous. The Court of Appeal thought that, if section 32 only applied up to publication, section 32(1)–(3) would be unnecessary (the main provisions for the exemption) as section 32(4) and (5) contains the provisions requiring the court to stay proceedings where the data controller claims to be within the special purposes or it so appears to the court. If the exemption only applied to pre-publication processing, section 32(4) and (5) would prevent anyone obtaining a 'gagging' order (that is, an interim injunction preventing publication) and the defence in section 32(1)–(3), with its test of reasonable belief that publication was in the public interest and the requirement to consider designated codes of practice, such as that of the Press Complaints Commission, would be irrelevant. Furthermore, the wording of the Directive and references to Hansard supported that view. The exemption was not restricted to pre-publication processing but was, therefore, of general application.

The relevant provision in the Directive is Article 9 which states that exemption or derogation may be provided if necessary to reconcile the right to privacy with the rules governing freedom of expression. This reflects the balancing act in Article 10 of the European Convention for the Protection of Human Rights and Fundamental Freedoms, paragraph 1 of which provides a right of freedom of expression subject to derogation necessary in a democratic society in paragraph 2. Of course, if section 32 gave exemption only up to the time of publication, then the freedom of the press could be seriously prejudiced for fear of an award of substantial damages. As the Court of Appeal said, if this was the case, Naomi Campbell would also have been able to obtain compensation for a story that simply mentioned the facts that she was a drug addict, contrary to her earlier claims, and was having treatment.

Of course, section 32 only applies to processing under the Data Protection Act 1998 and does not affect any right to relief for breach of confidence or defamation, in appropriate cases. In *Michael Douglas v Hello! Ltd* [2003] EWHC 786 (Ch) the judge held that the reliance on the section 32 exemption as a defence was unsustainable as the judge held that the defendant has adduced no credible evidence of a reasonable belief that publication was in the public interest. Mr Justice Lindsay also said that what was interesting to the public was not necessarily in the public interest as many judges have also said previously. In that case, he held that some of the defendants were in breach of confidence by publishing photographs of the wedding of Michael Douglas and Catherine Zeta-Jones taken surreptitiously and that the claim to compensation under the Data Protection Act 1998 was also made out. However, in respect of the latter, he said he would make a nominal award only as this was not a separate route to recovery. The award was left over for another hearing but it can be expected that the claim for breach of confidence will attract substantial damages. (In an earlier hearing in the Court of Appeal, *Michael Douglas v Hello! Ltd* [2003] EWCA Civ 139, it was held that there was a good arguable claim that a transmission by ISDN line to London of the photographic data was processing other than for the purposes of transit through the United Kingdom, and therefore subject to the 1998 Act.)

Research, history and statistics

In many cases, data processed for statistical or research purposes only will not be within data protection law as the data will be anonymous and, therefore, not personal data within the meaning in section 1(1). However, where the data remain personal data because they contain identifiers or the data controller has or may obtain other data which, together with the research data, allow individuals to be identified, section 33 allows some useful exemptions. These apply where the relevant conditions are present, being that the data are not processed to support measures or decisions with respect to particular individuals and are not processed so as to cause, or be likely to cause, substantial damage or substantial distress to any data subject. These conditions will usually be easily satisfied. If the data are being used to support measures or decisions affecting particular individuals, it may be that other exemptions are relevant – for example, in the case of research data relating to health which are now being processed to identify persons who have been exposed to some virus in the past and are now in need of an urgent inoculation.

The first exemption is simply to the effect that further processing only for research purposes is not to be regarded as incompatible with the purposes for which they were obtained, otherwise this could be a breach of the second Data Protection Principle. The fifth Principle requires that personal data are not kept for longer than is necessary and exemption from that requirement is granted in that data processed only for research purposes can be kept indefinitely. A further exemption is from the subject access provisions but only if the results of any research or any resulting statistics are not made available in a form identifying any data subject.

The exemptions are not lost merely because the data are disclosed to any person for research purposes only, to the data subject or a person acting on his behalf or at the request of, or with the consent of, the data subject or a person acting on his behalf. Nor are the exemptions lost if the person making the disclosure has reasonable grounds for believing any of these apply in the circumstances.

Sometimes research data will have been rendered anonymous by the stripping out of personal identifiers. Where this has been done, it is unlikely that the Data Protection Act 1998 applies to the data, unless the data can be later reconstituted to identify individuals or where the research data contain some entries from which an individual can be identified, for example, because the data are very unusual. In *R v Department of Health, ex parte Source Informatics Ltd* [2001] QB 244, Source Informatics Ltd attempted to persuade general practitioner doctors and pharmacists to transfer data showing the prescribing habits of doctors. The intention was that the data would be made anonymous before being supplied to Source Informatics. Processing this data would produce information about prescribing habits and trends which would prove valuable to pharmaceutical companies. The doctors and pharmacists taking part would, for a fee, download onto disks details of the quantity and identity of drugs prescribed. The Department of Health issued a policy document warning of the complex legal and policy issues and advising against such disclosures. Source Informatics sought declaratory relief in respect of the policy document arguing that disclosure after the data had been rendered anonymous would not constitute a breach of confidence.

The Court of Appeal did not consider that the planned action would involve a breach of confidence providing the identity of the patients was protected. The sole issue was the patients' right of privacy. Patients had no proprietary interest in the information and no right to control what happened to it subsequently providing his privacy was not put at stake. Thus, participation in the scheme by doctors and pharmacists would not expose them to a serious risk of successful breach of confidence actions. In terms of data protection law, the court said it was premature to try to make a definitive ruling on the data protection Directive (the 1998 Act had not been passed at the time the action accrued) but the view seems to have been that it would be unlikely to contravene the new law. Simon Brown LJ said (at paragraph 45):

the anonymisation of data is, in my judgment, unobjectionable here under domestic law, so too, I confidently suppose, would it be regarded by other member states.

It would appear, that supplying a copy of a database containing personal data that has been made anonymous would be acceptable. However, data subjects have rights under the Data Protection Act 1998 which include rights of compensation for breaches of the Act and, if processing was previously underway because of the data subject's express consent, it is more doubtful whether providing an anonymised copy would be within the Act. This could then take processing outside the conditions for processing. Whether removal of identifiers would also be regarded as an unauthorised erasure or loss of personal data is another point to bear in mind.

Information available to the public

This applies where the data consist of information which the data controller is required to make available to the public, whether by publication or making it available for inspection or otherwise and whether or not a fee is charged. The exemption is from the subject information provisions, the fourth Data Protection Principle (accuracy and kept up to date), the right of rectification within section 14(1)–(3) and the non-disclosure provisions. Clearly where information has to be made available, full application of these provisions would be unnecessary. The type of information that will be within this exemption includes the electoral roll, copies of birth, marriage and death certificates and copies of specifications for patents.

Two copies of the electoral roll are now prepared. A full register is only available to credit reference agencies and, in other cases, an edited version is made available. In *R (Robertson)* v *Wakefield Metropolitan Borough Council* [2002] QB 1052, Mr Justice Maurice Kay held that supplying a copy of the full register for the purposes of direct marketing without giving individuals an opportunity to object was contrary to section 12 of the Data Protection Act 1998 and a number of provisions of the European Convention for the Protection of Human Rights and Fundamental Freedoms. The offending parts of the Regulations that provided for copies to be made available was repealed and replaced by the Representation of the People (England and Wales) (Amendment) Regulations 2002. The provisions now allow electors to choose not be included in the edited version of the electoral role. Further challenges were made against the new provisions, the first applicant, Robertson claimed that they did not go far enough but that was rejected by Kay J. A claim from a company offering an on-line credit reference service claimed that the new provisions went too far was rejected in *I-CD Publishing Ltd* v *Secretary of State* [2003] EWHC 1761 (Admin) as the company did not fall within the requirements for credit reference agencies to have access to the full register. The judge also refused to grant a declaration that, if the company changed its operations in certain ways, it would fall within the requirements.

Disclosures required by law or in connection with legal proceedings, etc.

Other exemptions in the main body of the Act are disclosures required by law or made in connection with legal proceedings or for the purpose of obtaining legal advice or otherwise necessary for the purposes of establishing, exercising or defending legal rights: section 35. A related exemption is in Schedule 7, paragraph 10, being exemption from the subject information provisions on the basis of legal professional privilege.

Thus, there can be no barrier to disclosing personal information in connection with legal proceedings. For example, Andrew, who is a self-employed accountant, wishes to sue Brenda (one of his clients) for non-payment of accountancy fees. Andrew has a meeting with his solicitor, Carolyn, and provides her with information about Brenda and the work he did for her. Andrew is a data controller under the Act. Naturally, his notification does not mention such a disclosure but section 35 grants him exemption. As the meeting between Andrew and Carolyn is privileged, neither has to give Brenda any information about it. For example, there is no need to inform Brenda that Carolyn now has personal data relating to Brenda and, of course, any subject access request made by Brenda to Carolyn can be ignored with impunity.

Under the 1984 Act, the question of disclosure of data where the data user was exempt from registration came up for consideration in *Rowley* v *Liverpool City Council* (unreported) 24 October 1989. The judgment amply demonstrates the complexity of that Act (the new Act is no less complex), and Lord Justice Woolf in the Court of Appeal said of the 1984 Act:

> ... it is right to say straightaway that the act is a complex enactment in which it is difficult to find your way about unless you are very familiar with it indeed.

In that case, the claimant brought an action against her former employer for personal injury and she had made an application for discovery (disclosure to a party in legal proceedings) of information including details of three 'comparative earners'. She wanted details of payments made to three persons employed in a similar capacity to help work out what she would have been paid had she not had to stop working because of her injury. The defendant refused claiming that such disclosure was prohibited by the Data Protection Act 1984.

The defendant was exempt from registration because the data related to payroll and is similar to the equivalent provision under the 1998 Act. Section 32(2) of the 1984 Act made it a condition of the exemption that the data are not disclosed except in limited circumstances relating to payroll and accounts. However, section 34(5) of the 1984 Act, in similar though not identical lines to the equivalent provision in the 1998 Act, allowed disclosure if required by law or in the course of legal proceedings and, therefore, the disclosure requested did not contravene the Act. Disclosure was allowed in two ways: first, because it was in the course of legal proceedings in which the defendant was a party and, secondly, in compliance with an order of the court.

The working of the section 35(1) exemption is much simpler in many cases. For example, in *Guyer* v *Walton (Inspector of Taxes)* [2001] STC (Special Commissioners' Decisions) 75, Guyer was a solicitor who claimed he did not have to provide evidence such as his clients' ledger and cash book, copies of invoices and receipts and bank statements, cheque stubs and building society passbooks. The Revenue contended that it required such information to follow discrepancies in information provided by Guyer in his self-assessment form. Guyer claimed that the documents were not reasonably required, that he owed a duty of confidentiality to his clients, that the documents asked for were subject to legal professional privilege, that disclosure would be a breach of the right to privacy under the European Convention for the Protection of Human Rights and Fundamental Freedoms and that disclosure of the documents would be in breach of the Data Protection Act 1998. In rejecting all those submissions, the Special Commissioner noted that, as far as data protection law was concerned section 35(1) gave exemption from the non-disclosure provisions where, *inter alia*, this was required by law. Disclosure was required by law as the Revenue had, in accordance with and as provided for by section 19A of the Taxes Management Act 1970 served a written notice requiring provision of documents, as specified in the notice, that are reasonably required for the purpose of determining whether a tax return is correct.

An order of a court requiring disclosure also falls within this exemption from the non-disclosure provisions. In *Anderson* v *Halifax plc* [2000] NI 1, the widow of a deceased man sought information from the Halifax concerning the withdrawal of £60,000 from his account with the Halifax by her husband just before his death which he had given to an unknown person. The deceased had been suffering from cancer and the heavy doses of painkillers had made him confused and his behaviour became irrational. His widow was his personal representative and applied to the court for an order for disclosure after the Halifax had refused to disclose the information sought on the grounds of confidentiality and that it would be contrary to data protection law. The court held that the appropriate remedy would be one of tracing and, being broadly equitable, within the discretion of the court. The order for disclosure was granted.

Domestic purposes

The Data Protection Directive does not apply to processing by a natural person in the course of a purely personal or household activity. Thus, section 36 of the Act exempts from all the Data Protection Principles, the rights of data subjects and the requirements as to notification of personal data processed by an individual for that individual's personal, family or household affairs. This also extends to recreational purposes. The Information Commissioner may still exercise his powers of enforcement in the context of such processing if it is believed that the individual concerned is processing in such a manner as to exceed the scope of this exemption. If this is so, then the exemption will be lost to that extent. In particular, an individual who is otherwise employed but who carries on some private work in his spare time may be required to notify.

Schedule 7 exemptions

For no particular reason, a further set of exemptions is tucked away in a Schedule to the Act. All of these exemptions are listed earlier in Table 35.2, but the following are notable and discussed in more detail.

Confidential references

This exemption is from the subject access provisions only and is given under paragraph 1 of the Schedule. It applies where the reference is given or intended to be given by the data controller for the purposes of the education, training or employment (actual or prospective) of the data subject or the appointment or prospective appointment of the data subject to any office or the provision or prospective provision by the data subject of any service. The reference must be given or be intended to be given in confidence. There is no distinction between the person by whom the reference is given and the person who receives it. Both will be data controllers for the purpose of this provision *if and only if* the personal data are within the scope of the Act.

To take an example, consider Harold, an employee of the Peak Accountancy Practice who now seeks employment with Flaky Financial Services. Flaky has requested a reference from Peak, which is in the form of a letter hand written by Paul, Peak's managing director. This letter is unlikely to be within the meaning of data for the purposes of the Act. It is not automatically processed nor intended so to be and is not a relevant filing system nor an accessible record. Both Peak and Flaky can refuse Harold access to it. However, if the letter is produced on a word processor by Paul, it will be within the Act but Peak can refuse Harold access to it providing it is given in confidence. Flaky is under no obligation to grant access, whether it is confidential or not, because Flaky is not processing the data automatically. If the reference is made out on a pro forma document, then both Peak and Flaky must provide access (unless it was given in confidence) providing the reference is recorded as part of or with the intention that it should form part of a relevant filing system. This will be so if Peak and Flaky keep a file of references given or received.

Management forecasts and negotiations

These two distinct exemptions are discussed together here as they may overlap and often both will apply in the context of business planning and strategy and relationships with employees. Both exemptions are from the subject information provisions. In both cases, the exemption only applies if and to the extent that compliance would be likely to prejudice the activity or negotiations, as appropriate. Both of these exemptions are new and the 1984 Act had no direct equivalent.

The first applies to personal data processed for the purposes of management forecasting or management planning to assist the data controller in the conduct of any business or other activity: paragraph 5. No further guidance is given but this could apply, for example, where a company is carrying out a feasibility study on some new proposed venture. It might involve personal data relating to present and potential employees and other individuals such as investors. The company may wish to gather information on individuals who are candidates for 'head-hunting' to lead the new venture. Alternatively, a company may be considering closing down some of its activities which, if carried out, will affect numerous employees. Fulfilling a subject access request could destroy the secrecy of such forecasting or planning and cause serious prejudice.

Paragraph 7 deals with negotiations with the data subject and records of intentions in respect of such negotiations by the data controller. Under the 1984 Act, statements of intentions in respect of individuals were outside the definition of personal data and, therefore, outwith the scope of the Act. This is not so under the Directive and statements of intention are personal data, providing the other requirements are met. It was thought important to grant exemption from the subject information provisions – after all, an intention is not a reality until it is carried out and the data controller may change his mind. The sort of things covered will include an intention to promote an employee or provide some person with a particular service. The exemption is not limited to negotiations between employers and employees and can apply in any context.

Examination marks and examination scripts

The exemption for examination marks is similar to that under the 1984 Act and gives exemption from the subject access provisions though it can only act to delay subject access. Under paragraph 8 of Schedule 7, the marks or other information must be held for the purpose of determining the results of an academic, professional or other examination or enabling such determination or in consequence of the determination of any such results. In the case of an undergraduate, such information might include the marks he obtained in each subject by examination (including assessed coursework) and the details of the degree classification to be awarded to the student. 'Examination' includes a process for determining the knowledge, intelligence, skill or ability of a candidate by reference to his performance in any test, work or other activity. The normal period for responding to a subject access request is 40 days. Where the period of 40 days is used below, it is to be taken to be 40 days or such other period as may be prescribed.

Normally, a data controller must comply with a data subject request within 40 days but, in respect of examination marks, the data controller does not have to respond until either the end of five months after the request has been received or 40 days after the day the results are announced (published or made available or communicated to candidates), whichever is the earlier. If the request is complied with more than 40 days after it was made, the response by the data user must include all the information held at the time of the request *and* subsequently.

The following dates provide an example of the workings of these provisions:

1	Student sits examination	4 June 2003
2	Marks entered on a computer	27 June 2003
3	Student makes subject access request	2 July 2003
4	Results published	23 July 2003

Normally, the request must be complied with within 40 days from the request at the latest; that is, within 40 days of 2 July, which gives 11 August as being the latest date for compliance. However, in the case of examination marks, the request must be complied with by the earlier of five months after the request (2 December 2003) or 40 days after publication (1 September 2003). Therefore, the data controller must supply the data by 2 September. But, unlike other subject access requests which may take account of amendments, in this case the information supplied must include that held on 2 July (the request date) *and* must also include any subsequent amendments up to the date of reply. Consequently, a data controller holding examination marks must be careful to make sure that he retains copies of the personal data prior to any amendments or deletions so that he can provide all this information. For example, if the student's degree classification is changed, perhaps from a lower second honours degree to an upper second honours degree after mistakes have been found in the marking, the response must show this fact indicating the marks before and after correction. This requirement could prove very embarrassing to the data controller.

The exemption that applies to examination scripts is new and is granted in respect of the subject access provisions. The meaning of 'examination' is as above and the exemption relates to personal data consisting of information recorded by candidates during an academic, professional or other examination. As the 1984 Act only applied to automatically processed personal data, there was no real need for such an exemption under that Act as most examinations were handwritten, though this is changing rapidly: for example, by the use of multiple-choice tests performed on computers. Of course, the last thing most students want is access to their examination scripts.

Offences

The offences in section 55(1) – without the consent of the data controller, obtaining or disclosing personal data or procuring the disclosure to another person and the associated offences relating to selling or offering to sell data obtained in contravention of section 55(4) and (5) – are the equivalent to those inserted into the 1984 Act by section 161 of the Criminal Justice and Public Order Act 1994. Section 55 is, however, wider and is not restricted to procuring, selling and offering to sell. The 'procuring' offences only came into force on 3 February 1995 but there were a number of successful convictions in respect of them. For example, in July 1998, a father and son were found guilty at Horseferry Magistrates Court of a number of offences under the 1984 Act. The father operated a private investigation company and his son, who worked for the National Westminster Bank, passed on details of individuals from the bank's database to his father. The son was convicted of two charges of unauthorised disclosure and fined £500 for each. The father's company was charged with being an unregistered data user and with two charges of unlawful procuring of personal data and two charges of unlawful sale of personal data, and was fined a total of £5000. The father was convicted of four charges of consenting or conniving with the offences committed by his company and was fined £500 for each.

The utility of the unlawful obtaining, disclosure, procuring and selling offences is clear. Apart from widening the ambit of them, there is also a change to the state of mind required of the accused (known as the *mens rea* to lawyers) as, before, it was 'knowing or having reason to believe' whereas now, for the offences in section 55(1), it is 'knowingly or recklessly'. A person behaves 'recklessly' if the risk of the relevant act or omission transpiring would be obvious to a reasonable man, whether or not the person responsible for the act or omission thought about the possibility of the risk. It is, therefore, an objective test. The seriousness of the risk is not a factor to be taken into account. There are two leading cases on the meaning of recklessness, both decided in the House of Lords on the same day. In the first, *R v Caldwell* [1982] AC 341, a case on criminal damage, Lord Diplock described the test of recklessness in terms of a real risk of the relevant harmful consequences which would be apparent to the ordinary prudent individual. The accused would be reckless if he gave some thought about the risk and decided to ignore it or if he failed to give any thought to it at all. However, in *R v Lawrence* [1982] AC 510, a case of reckless driving (this offence no longer exists and has been replaced by dangerous driving), Lord Diplock spoke of *serious* harmful consequences.

The fine distinction between these two judgments (that is, the inclusion of the word 'serious' in *Lawrence*) has exercised the mind of many law students and academics which was not resolved until the case of *Data Protection Registrar v Amnesty International (British Section)* (unreported) 8 November 1994. Amnesty International was charged with offences under section 5(2)(b) and (d) of the 1984 Act after exchanging its mailing lists with another charitable body. The offences were holding data for purposes other than those mentioned in the register entry and disclosing data to a person not described in the register entry (there are no offences directly equivalent to these under the 1998 Act). One of the subscribers to Amnesty International complained after receiving a request for money from the other charity. The exchange of the list was outside the scope of Amnesty's registration. There had been no fee charged for the list and the stipendiary magistrate accepted that Amnesty International honestly believed it was acting in accordance with its registration. The stipendiary found that Amnesty International had not been reckless because the disclosure of the list did not cause a serious harmful consequence, relying on Lord Diplock's judgment in *Lawrence,* and dismissed the case. The Data Protection Registrar (now the Information Commissioner) appealed by way of case stated on a point of law.

The Divisional Court of the Queen's Bench Division allowed the appeal, confirming that, taking the two speeches of Lord Diplock together, it is not a prerequisite of recklessness that serious harm should result. Lord Justice Rose said that in order to prove recklessness for the purposes of section 5(2) of the Data Protection Act 1984:

(a) there must be something in the circumstances that would draw the attention of the ordinary prudent individual to the possibility that his act was capable of causing the kind of mischief that section 5(2) is intended to prevent and the risk of that mischief occurring was not so slight that an ordinary prudent individual would feel justified as treating it as negligible, and

(b) before doing the act, the accused either failed to give any thought to the possibility of there being such a risk or having recognised that there was such a risk, he nevertheless went on to do it.

Although the offences involved are not in the 1998 Act, this case is important authority for the meaning of recklessness for the offences in the 1998 Act, for which recklessness will suffice for the mental element of the offence. In some circumstances it might be easy to infer that a person has been reckless. For example, in R v Rees, 20 October 2000, the appellant, a Detective Inspector of the Warwickshire Constabulary was accused of procuring the disclosure of personal data without the data controller's consent and also of aiding and abetting a sergeant to misconduct himself in public office. He had asked a police sergeant in the same police force to disclose to him information held on the Police National Computer. The sergeant had previously pleaded guilty to misconduct in public office and data protection offences and was sentenced to three months' imprisonment. The appellant had been found guilty and sentenced to nine months' imprisonment. His appeal against conviction was dismissed. The Court of Appeal thought that it was inconceivable that an experienced detective sergeant could not be aware of the requirements under the Data Protection Act 1998.

The offences under the 1998 Act are summarised in Table 35.3. The table contains the section number and a description of the offence, the state of mind required of the accused and whether there are any specific defences. Note that many of the offences are strict liability, that is to say that ignorance of the offence will not excuse.

All the offences, apart from those relating to warrants in Schedule 9, are triable either way: that is, either on indictment in the Crown Court or summarily in a magistrates' court. They are punishable on conviction on indictment by a fine or, on summary conviction, by a fine not exceeding the statutory maximum: section 60. Offences in relation to warrants are summary only and punishable on conviction with a fine not exceeding level 5 on the standard scale. There are also provisions for forfeiture, destruction or erasure of documents or other material, subject to persons other than the offender being heard as to why the order should not be made.

Section 61 applies the usual provisions with respect to offences committed by a body corporate where it is proved that the offence was committed with the consent or connivance or was attributable to any neglect on the part of any director, manager, secretary or similar officer or person purporting to act in such a capacity. If this is so, that person as well as the body corporate is liable to prosecution. This also applies where the affairs of the body corporate are managed by its members. They are treated as directors for the purposes of this provision. In England and Wales, no proceedings for an offence under the Act can be brought except by the Information Commissioner or by or with the consent of the Director of Public Prosecutions: section 60.

Table 35.3 Offences under the Data Protection Act 1998

Section	Description	State of mind (mens rea)	Defences
21(1)	Processing personal data without having notified where this is required under s 17	Strict liability	None
21(2)	Failing in the duty to notify changes in the registrable particulars or in the measures taken to comply with the security requirements under the seventh Principle	Strict liability	Where the person charged can show that he exercised all due diligence to comply with the duty
22(6)	Carrying on assessable processing unless notification has been received from the Commissioner	Strict liability	None. No order has yet been made specifying processing subject to a preliminary assessment
24(4)	In a case where processing has not been notified (because it was not required and the data controller has chosen not to notify), failing to provide relevant particulars to any person on request within 21 days	Strict liability	Where the person charged can show that he exercised all due diligence to comply with the duty
47(1)	Failing to comply with an enforcement, information or special information notice	Strict liability	Where the person charged can show that he exercised all due diligence to comply with the duty
47(2)	In purported compliance with an information notice or special information notice, making a statement which is false in a material respect	Knowing that the statement is false in a material respect or recklessly making such a statement	None

Section	Description	State of mind (mens rea)	Defences
SECTION 55 OFFENCES. Note that the s 55 offences below do not apply in relation to processing for the purposes of national security under s 28 and to manual data within the definition of data in s 1(1)(e) processed by public authorities under s 33A			
55(1) and (3)	Without the consent of the data controller – (a) obtaining or disclosing personal data or the information contained in personal data, or (b) procuring the disclosure to another person of the information contained in personal data	Knowledge or recklessness required	Does not apply where the person shows: (a) that the obtaining, disclosing or procuring – (i) was necessary for the purposes of preventing or detecting crime, or (ii) was required or authorised by or under any enactment, by any rule of law or by the order of a court, (b) that he acted in the reasonable belief that he had in law the right to obtain or disclose the data or information or, as the case may be, to procure the disclosure of the information to the other person, (c) that he acted in the reasonable belief that he would have had the consent of the data controller if the data controller had known of the obtaining, disclosing or procuring and the circumstances of it, or (d) that in the particular circumstances the obtaining, disclosing or procuring was justified as being in the public interest
55(4)	Selling personal data by a person who has obtained the data in contravention of s 55(1)	Strict liability	None

Section	Description	State of mind (mens rea)	Defences
55(5)	Offering to sell personal data if: (a) the person has obtained the data in contravention of s 55(1), or (b) he subsequently obtains the data in contravention of s 55(1) Note: offering to sell includes an advertisement indicating that personal data are or may be for sale	None – but require the past or future commission of an offence under s 55(1)	The defences that apply to the s 55(1) and (3) offences do not apply to this offence
55 (7)	Section 1(2) does not apply for the purposes of this section; and for the purposes of this and the above offence (s 55(4)), 'personal data' includes information extracted from personal data		
56(5)	Requiring a person to supply a relevant record (enforced subject access) in connection with: (a) the recruitment of another person as an employee, (b) the continued employment of another person, or (c) any contract for the provision of services to him by another person or Requiring a person to supply a relevant record as a condition of providing or offering to provide goods, facilities or services A relevant record is one relating to convictions or cautions or in relation to certain types of benefit	Strict liability	But not where required or authorised by or under any enactment, rules of law or by court order, or where the requirement is justified as being in the public interest. This provision is not yet in force and is unlikely to be brought into force in the foreseeable future

Section	Description	State of mind (mens rea)	Defences
59(3)	The disclosure of information obtained or furnished under the Act which relates to a living individual or business and has not previously been available to the public from other sources by a present or past Information Commissioner, member of the Commissioner's staff or an agent of the Commissioner	Knowledge or recklessness as to the contravention	None
61(1)	Where an offence under this Act has been committed by a body corporate and is proved to have been committed by or with the consent of, connivance of, or to be attributable to any neglect on the part of any director, manager, secretary or similar officer of the body corporate or any person who was purporting to act in any such capacity, he as well as the body corporate shall be guilty of an offence and be liable to be proceeded against and punished accordingly	Consent, connivance or neglect (the latter would seem to be based on an objective test)	None
Schedule 9, para 12	Intentionally obstructing a person in the execution of a warrant issued under this Schedule, or failing without reasonable excuse to give any person executing such a warrant such assistance as he may reasonably require for the execution of the warrant	Intention or not having reasonable excuse as the case may be	None

The number of prosecutions remains relatively low. In the year ended 31 March 2003, there were a total of 80 convictions, most of which were under the 1998 Act. There were 33 convictions under section 55(1) of obtaining personal data without the consent of the data controller, one conviction, also under section 55(1), for disclosing personal data without the consent of the data controller and 20 convictions under section 55(4) for selling personal data obtained in contravention of section 55(1). There were a small number of convictions under the 1984 Act. The Information Commissioner also administered 11 cautions (Information Commissioner, Annual report and accounts for the year ending 31 March 2003, HC727, 2003, pp.100–103).

Transitional provisions

Because the new law marks such a sea change in the regulation of processing of personal data, there is need for comprehensive transitional provisions. Additionally, these make full use of the derogations permitted in the Directive, allowing the application of the law to pre-existing processing to be delayed for up to three years for automatic processing and up to 12 years for manual processing.

Schedule 8 to the Data Protection Act 1998 contains the main transitional provisions. There are two transitional periods as follows:

'the first transitional period' means the period beginning with the commencement of this Schedule and ending with 23rd October 2001; and
'the second transitional period' means the period beginning with 24th October 2001 and ending with 23rd October 2007.

The first period applies to automated processing already underway and also deals with the exemptions under the 1984 Act which are no longer available. The second period relates only to manual files (relevant filing systems and accessible records). Processing for historical research already underway, whether automated or not, is separately provided for and there is no time limit for such processing.

To understand the scope of the transitional provisions, it is vital to look at the meaning of processing already underway. A particular issue is whether automatically processed personal data which were subject to processing on 23 October 1998 lose the advantage of the exemptions if new personal data are added subsequently. Three possibilities exist.

1 The collection of personal data as a whole continues to be able to take advantage of the transitional provisions.
2 The collection of personal data as a whole is now caught by the new law and the exemption is lost.
3 The new personal data must comply with the new law in all respects but the pre-existing data do not have to.

The Directive is somewhat ambiguous on the point and is couched in terms of 'processing already under way'. However, the Data Protection Act 1998 seems clearer but, potentially, less generous to data controllers. The exemptions in the Act under the transitional provisions are expressed primarily in terms of 'eligible data'. These are defined in the following terms (emphasis added): 'personal data are "eligible data" at any time if, and to the extent that, they are at any time subject to processing which was already under way immediately before 24th October 1998'. Eligible automated data are eligible data processed or to be processed by automatic means and eligible manual data are simply eligible data which are not eligible automated data. Two points can be made about the definition of eligible data.

1 There is no express requirement that the data are being processed by or on behalf of the data controller. Simply the fact that they are subject to processing by any data controller should suffice; that is, data that exist before 24 October 1998 are eligible data.

2 The phrase 'if, and to the extent that,' implies that data created on or after 24 October 1998 are not eligible data and subject immediately to the new law. This suggests that the third alternative interpretation above is the correct one. However, if this is so, the scope of some of the transitional provisions is seriously prejudiced.

Another unresolved issue is what the effect is of commencing some new processing activity in respect of pre-existing personal data. If a strict interpretation is taken of the definition of eligible data, it would appear, at least to that extent, that the personal data will no longer be eligible data.

The two transitional periods will now be examined in greater depth together with other transitional provisions relating to research data and the requirement for a preliminary assessment.

The first transitional period

This applied to automated processing and manual processing until 24 October 2001 and has now expired. It remains of some interest because it indicates some of the major differences between the 1984 Act and the 1998 Act. The provisions differed for automatic data and manual data.

Manual data

Eligible manual data, other than data forming part of an accessible record, were exempt from the data protection principles and Parts II and III of the Act during the first transitional period. Parts II and III of the Act contain the rights of data subjects and the notification requirements respectively. However, if the manual data consist of information relevant to the financial standing of the data subject and the data controller is a credit reference agency, the exemption was limited. It did not extend to the right of access of data subjects (section 7 as modified by section 9) and there was a right to rectification, erasure, blocking or destruction of inaccurate or incomplete data and a right to require the data controller to cease holding exempt manual data in a manner incompatible with the data controller's legitimate interests (it was the data controller's legitimate interests that are relevant, not those of the data subject). These latter rights are provided by section 12A of the Act, which was inserted into the Act by the Act itself and available until 24 October 2007.

Where the data were part of an accessible record, whether eligible data or not, the exemptions were largely subject to the same rights of data subjects as applied to credit reference agencies. Thus, pre-existing and new data contained in accessible records such as health records, educational and certain local authority records had exemption from the Principles (except in so far as the sixth Principle in as much as it related to subject access under sections 7 and 12A), other rights of data subjects (such as the rights to prevent processing) and the notification requirements. The complexity of this could be explained by the fact that the 1998 Act incorporated some provisions of other legislation allowing access to personal data such as the Consumer Credit Act 1974 (access to credit reference agencies data) and the Access to Personal Files Act 1987, which was repealed in its entirety by the Data Protection Act 1998.

Eligible automated data – general exemption

Data protection law under the 1998 Act is significantly different to that under the 1984 Act. As well as applying the possibility in the Directive not to make processing already under way subject to the new law for three years, the transitional provisions had to cope with a number of differences between the two Acts, particularly in respect to a number of exemptions under the 1984 Act that were no longer available.

Paragraph 13 of Schedule 8 to the Act gave general exemption to all eligible automated data and was intended generally to place such data in the same position as applied under the 1984 Act. The exemptions are as set out below (bearing in mind that, nevertheless, the Principles under the 1984 Act still applied to such processing).

- The data controller did not have to provide data subjects with information when data were obtained from him and in other cases.
- There was no need for any of the conditions for processing in Schedule 2 to be present nor, in the case of sensitive data, any of those in Schedule 3.
- There was no obligation to impose security obligations on processors in writing or evidenced in writing.
- The provisions controlling transfers of personal data to third countries not having an adequate level of protection did not apply.
- The requirement to give additional information in response to a data subject request compared to that required under the 1984 Act (such as a description of the data, the purposes of processing, and recipients) did not apply.
- The data controller was exempt from the right of data subjects to prevent processing causing or likely to cause substantial damage or substantial distress, the right to prevent processing for the purposes of direct marketing and the rights of data subjects in respect of automated decision taking.
- The enhanced rights of data subjects to compensation did not apply and are restricted to those under the 1984 Act.

Eligible automated data – particular exemptions

Other exemptions for automated processing were needed because some of the exemptions under the 1984 Act disappeared. For the purposes of the Data Protection Act 1984, processing had to be by reference to the data subject. An express exception was where processing was performed only for the purpose of preparing the text of documents (the 'word processing' exception). Paragraph 5 of Schedule 8 extended the benefit of this exemption for a further three years for eligible automated data.

An important exemption under the 1984 Act which disappeared and which was relied on by many data users under the 1984 Act was in respect of processing for payroll and accounts. The exemption was not total but was from the registration requirements and the rights of data subjects. This was continued for a further three years until 24 October 2001 (note that under the 1998 Act there is exemption from notification in respect of payroll and accounts). Eligible automated data processed for payroll or accounts were exempt from the Data Protection Principles and Parts II and III (data subjects' rights and notification) during the first transitional period. However, the data could not be processed for any other purpose, although the exemption was not lost by any processing for any other purpose if the data controller could show that he had taken such care to prevent it as in all the circumstances was reasonably required. The burden of proof to show this was so was imposed on the data controller.

Certain disclosures were also permitted, such as to any person by whom the remuneration or pensions are payable; for the purpose of obtaining actuarial advice; or for the purpose of giving information as to the person in any employment office; or for use in medical research into the health of, or injuries suffered by, persons engaged in particular occupations or working in particular places or areas. The data subject (or a person acting on his behalf) could also request or consent to the disclosure either generally or in the circumstances in which the disclosure in question is made. The exemption still applied if the person making the disclosure had reasonable grounds for believing that the data subject requested or consented to the disclosure. Further disclosures were permitted which include the purpose of audit or for the purpose only of giving information about the data controller's financial affairs.

Unincorporated members' lists and mailing lists also had an exemption under the 1984 Act. The transitional provisions extended this for a further three years. The exemption was, as before, from the Data Protection Principles and Parts II and III of the Act. The conditions that applied to unincorporated members' clubs and mailing lists under the 1984 Act, such as the requirement to ask data subjects whether they objected to the processing of personal data relating to them, still applied during the transitional period.

A further exemption under the 1984 Act was from the subject access provisions where the data were solely for back-up purposes, for example to replace data on a computer in the event that they were accidentally erased or corrupted in some way. This also was continued until 24 October 2001.

The second transitional period

The second period applies only to manual processing and is a partial derogation for 12 years, until 24 October 2007, and applies to eligible manual data and accessible records, whether eligible or not. It does not apply to eligible manual data processed only for the purposes of historical research for which there is separate provision. The exemption is from the first Data Protection Principle (except to the extent to which it requires compliance with the requirements to inform data subjects when the data are obtained from the data subject or in other cases), the second, third, fourth and fifth Data Protection Principles, and section 14(1)–(3) which contains the basic rights to rectification, blocking, erasure and destruction. Of course, there is no requirement generally to notify manual processing (except where the processing is assessable). Data subjects still have a right of access to such data and a right to be informed in accordance with the first Principle. Although exemption is granted in respect of some of the rights of rectification under section 14(1)–(3), this is of little consequence as the processing is subject to section 12A instead which grants similar rights in addition to a right in relation to processing not in accordance with the legitimate interests of the data controller.

Even though the new law will not fully affect manual records until 24 October 2007, some data controllers could still find it difficult and expensive to comply fully after that date. This is a particular problem where an organisation has a significant amount of archived data which it wants to retain, for example, for future research purposes or for defending legal claims. During the lead up to the Directive, the Council and Commission made a joint statement to the effect that, in certain circumstances:

> at the end of the 12 year transitional period, controllers must take all reasonable steps relating to the requirements of Articles 6, 7 and 8, which do not prove impossible or involve a disproportionate effort in terms of cost.

The manual data exemption does not prevent individuals exercising their right of subject access, their right to prevent processing and their rights to compensation. The security obligations also apply and data controllers need to review this aspect in relation to manual files. For example, are manual files kept in secure locations and is access to them restricted to those having a genuine need to use or access them?

Specific provision has been made for partial exemption during the second transitional period for personal data within the meaning of data in section 1(1)(e) processed by public authorities. The exemption is from the fourth Data Protection Principle and section 14(1)–(3) containing some of the rights of rectification, etc. This will come into force on 30 November 2005 unless the Secretary of State by Order appoints an earlier date.

Processing for historical research (partial derogation)

This exemption is indefinite in time. After 23 October 2001, eligible manual data processed only for the purpose of historical research in compliance with the 'relevant conditions' and relevant automated data which are processed only for the purpose of historical research, in compliance with the relevant conditions, and otherwise than by reference to the data subject, are exempt from the first Data Protection Principle (but not as regards informing data subjects), the second, third, fourth and fifth Data Protection Principles, and the rights of rectification, blocking, erasure and destruction under section 14(1)–(3).

The relevant conditions are those specified in section 33 and are that the data are not processed to support measures or decisions with respect to particular individuals and that they are not processed in such a way that substantial damage or substantial distress is, or is likely to be, caused to any data subject.

Other eligible automated data processed only for the purpose of historical research in compliance with the relevant conditions are exempt from the first Data Protection Principle to the extent to which it requires compliance with the conditions in Schedules 2 and 3 (the conditions for processing). This more limited exemption applies where, in spite of the other conditions being present, the data are processed by reference to the data subject.

In respect of these exemptions, personal data are not to be treated as processed otherwise than for the purpose of historical research merely because the data are disclosed:

(a) to any person, for the purpose of historical research only,
(b) to the data subject or a person acting on his behalf,
(c) at the request, or with the consent, of the data subject or a person acting on his behalf, or
(d) in circumstances in which the person making the disclosure has reasonable grounds for believing that the disclosure falls within paragraph (a), (b) or (c).

Section 12A does not apply to eligible manual data processed for historical research.

If the relevant conditions are not met, the exemption for eligible automated data is of the more restricted variety and applies only in respect of the first Data Protection Principle but subject to the conditions for processing.

Chapter 36

Data subjects' rights

Introduction

This chapter looks at the Data Protection Act 1998 from the perspective of data subjects. We have seen how the Act impacts upon data controllers, and many individuals as well as organisations in the public and private sectors (ranging from central government departments to sole traders) will be classed as data controllers, even if they do not possess a computer. But we are all data subjects. There can be very few, if any, persons in respect of whom someone, somewhere, is not processing personal data relating to them in a manner within the new law. As information processing becomes more powerful, there is a growing need to protect the rights of individuals in that context, because of the threats to privacy and freedom. The 1998 Act significantly developed and expanded the rights of data subjects. An example of the differences in data subjects' rights compared with those under the 1984 Act was given by Mr Justice Gray in *Lord Ashcroft* v *Attorney General* [2002] EWHC 1122 (QB) where, in a preliminary hearing, he noted that a claim for damages under the 1984 Act could only be made under section 23 where there had been loss of personal data, destruction without the authorisation of the data user or disclosure or access to personal data without such authority. A breach of a Data Protection Principle did not, *per se*, give rise to a claim in damages. The position under the 1998 Act is entirely different and a breach of the Principles or indeed any of the requirements of the Act does give rise to a claim in damages if the data subject suffers damage as a result. A claim for distress also can be made where damage has been suffered or, where the breach relates to processing for the special purposes, a claim for distress can be made in the absence of damage.

In addition to the pre-existing rights of subject access, rectification or erasure of personal data and compensation for damage and distress, all of which have been enhanced, further rights became available under the 1998 Act being a right to prevent processing likely to cause substantial damage or substantial distress, a right to prevent processing for purposes of direct marketing, and rights in relation to automated decision taking. Data controllers also have a duty to provide data subjects with information. This is described in the previous chapter.

Data subjects may approach the Information Commissioner for an assessment, usually expressed as a complaint about a processing activity rather than a request for assessment. In some cases, individuals may be granted assistance such as the payment of legal fees. As far as enforcing their rights, data subjects may apply to a court for compensation or to ask the court to order the data controller to do something required, such as comply with a subject access request, or to refrain from doing something – for example, to comply with a notice from a data subject requiring the data controller to cease processing which is causing substantial damage to the data subject or another person. Figure 36.1 shows the relationship between the data subject, the Commissioner and the courts.

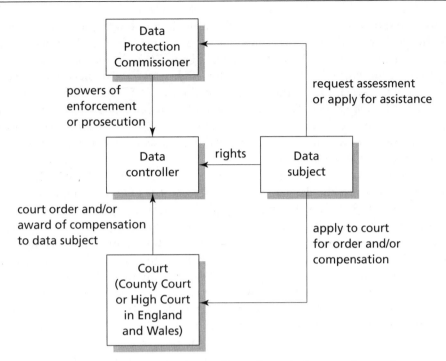

Fig. 36.1 Relationship between the data subject, Commissioner and court in respect of data subjects' rights

Right of access

The data subject's right of access is fundamental to the policing of data protection law by individuals. By seeing what personal data relating to a particular individual a data controller is processing, that person may, with the knowledge of other factors such as the purposes of the processing, take a view on whether the processing is fair and lawful or otherwise within the Data Protection Principles. In particular, individuals are likely to be concerned to satisfy themselves that their personal data are correct and not excessive. This may be important where the granting of credit or obtaining employment or services could depend on the data and considerable damage can be done if it is incorrect – for example, by falsely indicating that a person has a criminal record, has a county court judgment against him for debt, is an active member of an extreme political group and so on.

A statutory right of access is essential as there is no common law right to access. In *R v Mid-Glamorgan Family Health Services, ex parte Martin* (unreported) 29 July 1994, a patient had been refused access to his health records going back to before 1990 on the basis that it would be detrimental for the patient to see those records directly. An offer was made to disclose the records conditionally to a medical expert appointed by the patient but this was not accepted. The patient claimed that there was a right of access at common law. However, the Court of Appeal refused to grant access denying that there was a right of access under common law.

There may be a right of access under the European Convention for the Protection of Human Rights and Fundamental Freedoms, in particular as a result of Article 8, which provides that everyone has the right to respect for his private and family life, his home and his correspondence. The Convention was brought into law in the United Kingdom under the auspices of the Human Rights Act 1998, the main provisions of which came into force on 2 October 2000. In *McGinley & Egan* v *United Kingdom* (unreported) 9 June 1998 in the European Court of Human Rights, two ex-soldiers had witnessed nuclear testing carried out by the United Kingdom in 1957 and 1958 at Christmas Island in the Pacific Ocean. They later suffered health problems which they thought were caused by their exposure to radiation and they lodged claims for war pensions. These were turned down and the government did not disclose documents indicating the radiation levels at the time.

The Court held that access to the documents would have either allayed their fears or allowed them to assess the danger to which they had been exposed and this raised an issue under Article 8. Although Article 8 was primarily a negative undertaking by, for example, protecting a person against arbitrary interference by public authorities, it went beyond that and could give rise to positive obligations (also recognised in *Gaskin* v *United Kingdom*: see later). Those obligations required a balance between the interests of individuals and the general interest of the community. Where a government was engaged in a hazardous activity which might have adverse consequences on the health of those involved, Article 8 required that an accessible and effective procedure was in place to enable such persons to seek all relevant and appropriate information. However, there was no breach of Article 8 in the present case as the ex-soldiers had failed to avail themselves of an appeal under rule 6 of the Pensions Appeals Tribunals (Scotland) Rules 1981 which would have allowed them to apply for an order for disclosure of the relevant documents. The existence of that procedure meant that the United Kingdom had fulfilled its obligations under Article 8. (Note that the United Kingdom ratified the Convention in 1951 but did not bring it into direct effect until the Human Rights Act 1998 came into force.)

There is a close relationship between data protection law and the Human Rights Convention, which is expressly mentioned in the data protection Directive. The right of privacy under Article 8(1) including the permissible derogations from it in Article 8(2) and the balancing with the right of freedom of expression form a significant basis for data protection law. Theoretically, there should be no conflict between the Data Protection Act 1998 and the Convention rights. If there is, it should be resolved in favour of the Convention rights as required by the Human Rights Act 1998.

A right of access was available under the 1984 Act but was limited simply to a statement from the data user (now data controller) as to whether he was processing data relating to the applicant and, if so, to access the data. Various rules existed to deal with the situation where access to the data would reveal information relating to another identifiable individual and the 1998 Act has provisions to deal with this situation but with some significant changes.

Sections 7–9 and 9A of the Data Protection Act 1998 deal with data subjects' right of access. (Section 9A applies to unstructured files, within the meaning of data in section 1(1)(e), processed by public authorities but will not be brought into force until 30 November 2005 unless the Secretary of State by Order appoints an earlier date.) Section 7 of the Data Protection Act 1998 provides:

(1) Subject to the following provisions of this section and to sections 8 and 9 [sections 8, 9 and 9A], an individual is entitled –
  (a) to be informed by any data controller whether personal data of which that

individual is the data subject are being processed by or on behalf of that
data controller,

(b) if that is the case, to be given by the data controller a description of –
   (i) the personal data of which that individual is the data subject,
   (ii) the purposes for which they are being or are to be processed, and
   (iii) the recipients or classes of recipients to whom they are or may be disclosed,

(c) to have communicated to him in an intelligible form –
   (i) the information constituting any personal data of which that individual is the data subject, and
   (ii) any information available to the data controller as to the source of those data, and

(d) where the processing by automatic means of personal data of which that individual is the data subject for the purpose of evaluating matters relating to him such as, for example, his performance at work, his creditworthiness, his reliability or his conduct, has constituted or is likely to constitute the sole basis for any decision significantly affecting him, to be informed by the data controller of the logic involved in that decision-taking.

Normally the data controller has to comply within 40 days and may charge a fee up to the maximum of £10 (there are differences in respect of requests to credit reference agencies and in respect of educational records and health records, as discussed later). Notwithstanding the maximum period for complying with a subject access request, the data controller has, under section 7(8), a duty to act promptly. However, the data controller does not have to comply until he has received the request in writing and the fee, if there is one. Under section 7(3), where the data controller reasonably requires further information from the individual making the request to identify him and locate the relevant data and has informed the individual accordingly, he does not have to comply unless he is provided with that further information. Data controllers must be careful to satisfy themselves as to the identity of the person making the request and to ensure their employees and agents also appreciate the importance of this. There have been numerous examples of employees disclosing personal data to persons posing as the data subject.

Much more information is required than under the 1984 Act, although much of this additional information would be available to a data subject who examined the register entry, except for the description of the logic involved in any automated decision taking. A person making a subject access request is entitled to a copy of the information constituting the personal data of which that person is the data subject in permanent form unless the supply of such a copy would be impossible or would involve a disproportionate effort or if the individual agrees otherwise; section 8(2). Making permanent copies may be very expensive in certain cases, such as in the case of X-ray plates or where there is a substantial amount of paper files involved. In assessing whether provision of a copy in permanent form would involve a disproportionate effort, factors that may be relevant, in the Information Commissioner's view, are the cost, length of time to make the copies, the difficulty in making copies and the size of the data controller's organisation. All these factors should be balanced with the effect on the data subject. Where the information is not intelligible without an explanation, such explanation must accompany the information.

As individuals may not realise that they are entitled to more information than was the case previously, the Act allowed the Lord Chancellor to make regulations in particular cases so that a request for some of the above information may to be treated as a request for other information required to be given. The Data Protection (Subject Access) (Fees and Miscellaneous Provisions) Regulations 2000 state that a request for information under section 7(1)(a), (b) or (c) is to be treated as a request for all the information under those provisions, though not to information under section 7(1)(d) unless there is an express intention to that effect. A request for information under section 7(1)(d) (that is, in respect of the logic in any automated decision taking) is to be treated as extending to other information under any provision of section 7(1) only if there is an express intention to that effect. A subject access request therefore should be made in terms of 'all the information under section 7(1)(a) to (d)'.

To overcome the problem of 'nuisance' subject access requests, made at frequent intervals by the same person, under section 8(3), the data controller can refuse to comply with a subsequent identical or similar request by a particular individual unless a reasonable interval has elapsed. In determining what a reasonable interval is, regard should be given to the nature of the data, the purposes of the processing and the frequency with which the data are altered; section 8(4). So, for example, where data are being updated and modified on an ongoing basis, fairly frequent requests may be deemed reasonable. The information to be given must be as it was when the request was received apart from deletions or amendments which would have been made notwithstanding the request. Therefore, if the data are inaccurate and in breach of the fourth Data Protection Principle, the data controller must not deliberately correct the data because a subject access request has been made. However, if the data controller systematically checks the validity of the personal data as part of the management of his processing activity and, as a result of such checking, an inaccuracy is detected and corrected between the time the subject access request is made and the time when it is complied with, then the data controller need give access to the data as corrected only. As noted in the exemptions in the previous chapter, if the data are evidence that the data controller has committed an offence other than one under the Act, he is excused compliance with the subject access request to the extent that such evidence would be revealed.

Where the processing is by automatic means and has constituted or is likely to constitute the sole basis for any decision significantly affecting him, in evaluating matters relating to the data subject such as his performance at work, creditworthiness, reliability or conduct, the data subject has the right to be informed of the logic involved in that decision taking, as mentioned above. However, this does not apply if, or to the extent that, the information constitutes a trade secret under section 8(5). 'Trade secret' is not defined but it would seem sensible to apply the meaning used in the law of breach of confidence, although it is not particularly clearly defined there. Perhaps it would be reasonable to consider a 'trade secret' here to be information the disclosure of which would harm the data controller's legitimate interests, be of benefit to a competitor or expose the data controller to a serious risk of fraud.

The provisions in the Data Protection Act 1998, dealing with the situation when compliance with a subject access request would disclose information relating to another identifiable individual, took account of a case before the European Court of Human Rights, *Gaskin* v *United Kingdom* (1990) 12 EHRR 36. The applicant for subject access claimed he had been ill treated while a child in care of the local authority. He sought access to confidential records concerning him and his care from Liverpool City Council, which was required to keep such records. The City Council decided to give

Gaskin access provided the persons who contributed to his file consented. Only 19 out of 46 of the contributors gave their consent and the relevant documents were released to him. However, the remainder, where the contributors refused consent or could not be traced, were not disclosed to him. It was held by the European Court of Human Rights that this was a breach of his right to respect for his private and family life under Article 8 of the European Convention for the Protection of Human Rights and Fundamental Freedoms. Although the United Kingdom could not be said to have interfered with his private life, there could be circumstances where an inherent positive obligation arose in respect for private life. Whether such an obligation arose in a particular case was a matter of balance and, on the basis of proportionality, required that an independent authority decided whether access should be granted or denied if a contributor to such records withheld consent or did not answer. That had not happened in *Gaskin*, hence the breach of Article 8.

Under section 7(4)–(6) of the Data Protection Act 1998, to comply with the request, the data controller must be satisfied that the other person (including a person who is the source of the information) has consented to the disclosure of his personal data to the person making the request. Otherwise, access can be given where it is reasonable in all the circumstances to comply without the consent of the other. In determining whether it is reasonable in all the circumstances to comply without the consent of the other, factors that may be taken into account are any duty of confidentiality owed to the other, any steps taken by the data controller to gain the consent of the other, whether the other is capable of giving consent and any express refusal of consent by the other individual.

In other cases such as where it would not be reasonable to comply, lack of consent does not excuse a data controller altogether where he can provide the access to the applicant's data without disclosing the identity of the other individual – for example, by omitting the name or other identifying particulars. This may be done by suppressing the identifying information from a computer printout which is handed to the person making the subject access request or, in the case of manual files caught by the new law, by masking the relevant information when making a photocopy to give to the person making the request.

As mentioned above, the basic time period for complying with a subject access request is 40 days and the maximum fee that may be charged is £10. The Data Protection (Subject Access) (Fees and Miscellaneous Provisions) Regulations 2000, as amended, in a case where the subject access request is limited to information relating to financial standing, give the maximum fee as being £2 (as it was previously under section 158 of the Consumer Credit Act 1974) and the maximum period for compliance is seven working days. For health records, being accessible records within the meaning of the Act, the maximum fee that can be charged is £50 if a permanent copy is provided. However, where the record has been at least partially created within the 40-day period immediately prior to the request, and no permanent copy is requested, no fee may be charged. For educational records, being accessible records for the purposes of the Act, the maximum period for compliance is 15 school days if the data controller's address is in England and Wales. Where a copy is provided in permanent form, there is a sliding scale of maximum fees in the Schedule to the Regulations, ranging from £1 for fewer than 20 pages to £50 for 500 pages or over. If the information includes material in another form to writing on paper, the maximum fee is £50, regardless of how many paper pages are also involved. This could apply, for example where the data are in the form of a photograph or on video or CD. Where health or educational records are processed by automatic means (or intended to be so processed) within section 1(1)(a) or (b), these special provisions do not apply.

Credit reference agencies

Under section 9 of the Data Protection Act 1998, an application to a credit reference agency is taken to be limited to financial information relating to the data subject unless a contrary intention is expressed. The data controller must include a statement of the data subject's rights under section 159 of the Consumer Credit Act 1974 (a right to have wrong information corrected), to the extent required as prescribed. Section 62 of the Data Protection Act 1998 modifies section 158 of the Consumer Credit Act 1974 and the right under that section to obtain a copy of a file applies only in relation to partnerships. For other individuals the right to a copy of the file is under section 9 of the 1998 Act, although the right of correction of wrong information remains under section 159 of the 1974 Act.

Enforced subject access

Enforced subject access was perceived as an abuse of a data subject's right of access by the Data Protection Registrar under the 1984 Act and remains a concern of the Information Commissioner under the 1998 Act. This occurs where, for example, a potential employee requires a job applicant to provide a copy of his police file showing whether the data subject has been convicted or cautioned in relation to any offences. The dangers of leaving enforced subject access uncontrolled were clearly seen in *R v Chief Constable of 'B', ex parte R* (unreported) 24 November 1997, Queen's Bench Division.

R, who was 29 years old at the time, wanted to travel to a foreign country to teach English to adults and, to do so, he had to apply for a visa. He was required by the Consulate General of the country concerned to provide a certificate of his prosecution and conviction history. Unfortunately, R had a conviction for a minor offence of theft committed when he was 19 years old for which he received a conditional discharge and was ordered to pay compensation. However, the conviction was a 'spent conviction' under the Rehabilitation of Offenders Act 1974, the effect being that by virtue of section 4 of that Act, he was treated in law as a person who had not committed or been charged with or prosecuted for or sentenced for the offence. The time after which a sentence is considered spent depends on what the sentence was. The purpose is that a person who has not re-offended will not be prejudiced by an unwarranted disclosure of the fact of the offence to a third party. The Chief Constable to whom R applied for subject access provided a statement to the effect that R had 'no citeable convictions' but this was not on the standard form issued under the Data Protection Act 1984 and as required by the Consulate General. This form would show R's spent conviction.

The Code of Practice for Data Protection used by the Association of Chief Police Officers generally requires 'reportable' offences to be retained for 20 years, even though they may be spent convictions. However, the Data Protection Act 1984 contained no discretion to exclude some information from being provided under a subject access request and, according to Lord Justice Laws, section 21 of that Act clearly required all the information constituting the personal data to be supplied. Any conflict with the Rehabilitation of Offenders Act 1974 was removed by section 26(4) of the 1984 Act which stated that the subject access provisions apply notwithstanding any enactment or rule of law prohibiting or restricting disclosure or withholding information. The judge expressed sympathy for R whom he described as having lived down his conviction, gaining a series of academic and professional qualifications and generally leading an exemplary and productive life. The judge said it was little comfort to R that enforced subject access under the new law is intended to obviate the problems he had encountered but it came too late for R. Of course, in other situations, enforced subject access can be important such as where a person applies for employment in a position of trust or authority where children or other vulnerable persons are involved.

In a late amendment to the Bill, provisions were added to prevent enforced subject access, in specified cases. Section 56 of the Act sets out the situations where enforced subject access is prohibited, being in relation to:

- the recruitment of another as an employee,
- the continued employment of another person,
- any contract for the provision of services by another person, or
- the provision of goods, facilities or services to any person (this extends also to the supply of a relevant record by a third party).

The prohibition applies in relation to 'relevant records', being those showing convictions and cautions where the data controller is a chief officer of police or the Secretary of State. Also included is subject matter relating to the Secretary of State's functions under section 92 of the Powers of Criminal Courts (Sentencing) Act 2000 (detention of young persons for long periods of time for grave crimes), the Prison Act 1952, under the Social Security Contributions and Benefits Act 1992, the Social Security Administration Act 1992, the Jobseekers Act 1995 or in relation to certificates of criminal records under Part V of the Police Act 1997 (all with necessary amendments for Scotland and Northern Ireland). Even if the record simply states that the data controller is not processing data relating to a particular matter, this is still to be taken as relating to that matter. For example, if the information provided under the subject access request states that the person concerned has no convictions or cautions, this will still be deemed to be within the prohibition.

Contravention of the enforced subject access provisions will be a criminal offence of strict liability. However, this will not apply where the access is authorised or required by law or court order or justified as being in the public interest. The latter will not include the ground that it would assist in the prevention or detection of crime – there must be some other public interest involved. Section 56 has not yet been brought into force, and it may be some time before it is.

Enforced subject access in relation to health records is also controlled but not by way of imposing criminal liability. Rather, it is a matter of making any such requirement void in contractual terms. Under section 57, any term or condition in a contract is void in as much as it purports to require the supply of, or producing to another person of, a record, copy or part of a record consisting of information contained in any health record as defined in section 68(2), which is a record consisting of information relating to the physical or mental health or condition of an individual made by or on behalf of a health professional in connection with the care of that individual. 'Health professional' is widely defined in section 69. The provisions relating to enforced subject access to health records were brought into force on 1 March 2000, when much of the remainder of the Act was brought into force.

Right to prevent processing likely to cause substantial damage or substantial distress

This right was introduced by the Data Protection Act 1998 and had no direct equivalent under the 1984 Act, although processing which had the potential to cause damage or distress might have been caught by the first Data Protection Principle in particular and dealt with by the powers of enforcement under the Act. The right to prevent processing likely to cause substantial damage or substantial distress is a considerable improvement to the rights of the data subject in that it empowers individuals to require the data controller to stop or not commence processing that has certain consequences for the individual concerned or another. This right is backed by the power of the court to order compliance.

A data subject can require the data controller to cease or not to begin processing for a specified purpose or in a specified manner on the ground that, for specified reasons, it is unwarranted as causing or being likely to cause substantial damage or substantial distress to him or another: section 10(1). However, a limitation is that this right does not apply to processing under conditions 1–4 in Schedule 2, being processing where the data subject has given consent, where it is necessary in relation to a contract, where it is necessary for compliance with a legal obligation or where it is to protect the vital interests of the data subject. The Lord Chancellor may add further exceptions to the right. It can apply to the other conditions for processing 'normal' data (such as processing necessary for the legitimate interests of the data controller or a third party to whom the data are disclosed) and to all the conditions for processing of 'sensitive' data in Schedule 3 and the additional conditions provided for by Regulations.

The data subject has to give notice in writing to the data controller, specifying the purpose or manner of processing objected to and the reasons why he or another is likely to be caused substantial damage or substantial distress. Within 21 days, the data controller must give a written notice stating that he has complied with the data subject's notice or intends to do so or stating why he considers the notice unjustified to any extent and the extent, if any, to which he has complied or intends to comply.

If the data controller does not comply with the data subject's notice in whole or in part, the data subject may apply to a court for an order requiring the data controller to comply with the notice. The order will be granted if the court considers the notice justified to any extent and the data controller has failed to comply to that extent. Any failure by a data subject to exercise this right (and the right to prevent processing for the purposes of direct marketing under section 11(1)) does not prejudice any of the other rights of the data subject. An application to the court might include a claim for compensation under section 13, discussed later.

Curiously, the heading to section 10 does not contain the word 'substantial' referring only to the right to prevent processing likely to cause damage or distress. Furthermore, the word 'substantial' does not appear in section 13, which provides a right to compensation for damage or distress. The data protection Directive does not use the word 'substantial' and gives the data subject a right to object 'on compelling legitimate grounds relating to his particular situation': Article 14. The implications of all this is that, for example, a data subject will be able to obtain compensation for damage which is insufficiently substantial to give rise to the right to prevent such processing. Alternatively, or additionally, the right to compensation might apply where the data controller has already ceased the processing operation concerned. For example, this could be where a disclosure to a third party has already been made which has caused substantial damage or distress to the data subject.

Right to prevent processing for purposes of direct marketing

The European Commission perceived direct marketing, the sending of junk mail or faxes, as a particular problem. It was decided that an individual ought to be able to prevent it in a case where the marketing material is addressed specifically to the individual. Anonymous advertising material is not affected. This is material not addressed to specific persons, such as advertising inserts in newspapers and magazines or which is simply pushed through letterboxes in a blanket mailing. In any case, such advertising campaigns of that nature do not require the processing of personal data of the recipients.

The Directive gives individuals an absolute right to prevent processing for the purposes of direct marketing and it also requires that member states ensure that individuals are aware of this right. Thus, under section 11 of the Data Protection Act 1998, a data subject has a right, by giving written notice, to require a data controller to cease within a reasonable time in the circumstances or not to begin processing his personal data for the purposes of direct marketing. 'Direct marketing' is defined in the Act as meaning the communication by any means of any advertising or marketing material which is directed at particular individuals. The data controller must give the data subject a written notice within 21 days of receipt of the data subject's notice stating what steps he has taken or will take to comply. Again, the court has the power to order the data controller to comply, following an application by the data subject and if satisfied that the data controller has failed to comply with the data subject's notice.

There is an exception to the right in the case of processing of certain types of data held by a telecommunications provider. The type of data could include telephone number, address, type, starting time and duration of call, sums payable, etc. (all set out in the Telecommunications (Data Protection and Privacy) Regulations 1999). The type of processing is in respect of marketing telecommunications services but only if the subscriber consents. It is unclear what the position is if the subscriber, having given consent, later withdraws it. It would seem sensible to conclude that the right under section 11(1) of the Data Protection Act 1998 would then extend to such processing. Soon the 1999 Regulations will be revoked and replaced by some new Regulations, presently in draft form and entitled the Privacy and Electronic Communications (EC Directive) Regulations 2003, which will extend data protection and privacy in to the field of e-mail and the Internet. These changes are discussed further in the following chapter.

In the United Kingdom, the presence of the mailing preference system (MOPS), the Telephone Preference Service and the Fax Preference Service already allows individuals to indicate that they do not wish to receive marketing material. Organisations which send out marketing material are informed from time to time of persons who do not wish to receive such material. Furthermore, if individuals are careful to make sure that they always tick the ubiquitous 'no marketing' box on forms and the like, this should prevent a great deal of marketing material being sent to them. However, even if advantage is taken of the above scheme and the no marketing box is always ticked, some marketing material may still get through. In such cases the right to prevent marketing under the Act will prove useful, though it does require the data subject to be proactive.

It may be that the right to prevent processing for the purposes of direct marketing might go further than was originally thought. At first reading, it might seem that the right has to be exercised by an individual after he has received the offending marketing material. Under the 1984 Act, cases such as *Innovations (Mail Order) Ltd v Data Protection Registrar*, 29 September 1993 and *British Gas Trading Ltd v Data Protection Registrar*, 24 March 1998 showed that unfettered marketing activities could be in breach of the first Data Protection Principle, which required that personal data be processed fairly and lawfully. Individuals should be allowed to object to marketing at the time data were first collected from them and not later. Such developments did not, however, give the individual a right to prevent marketing, as a breach of the Principles could only be dealt with by the Data Protection Registrar (now the Information Commissioner) exercising his enforcement powers. However, by marrying the underlying rationale behind these and similar cases with the right under section 11, it is not a giant leap to accept that the right might not be confined to the ability to put a stop to further marketing from a data controller who has already sent some unsolicited marketing. It might be a right not to be sent unsolicited marketing material at all unless the individual concerned has expressed positive consent. Certainly in terms of the Regulations in the telecomms sector, soon to be extended to electronic communications, the notion of positive consent applies.

There is also some authority for the scope of the right to prevent processing for the purposes of direct marketing in the case of *R (Robertson) v Wakefield Metropolitan District Council* [2002] QB 1052. In that case, Mr Justice Kay held that the supply of the electoral register for the purposes of direct marketing without previously giving individual electors the opportunity of objecting was unlawful, being contrary to section 11 of the Data Protection Act 1998, Article 8 of the European Convention for the Protection of Human Rights and Fundamental Freedoms (the right to privacy) and Article 3 of the First Protocol to the Convention (the right to free elections). If this view is of general application, and there is no reason to doubt this, the impact of Article 8 of the Convention on section 11 of the Data Protection Act 1998, is to only allow the sending of unsolicited marketing material if the data subject has consented or, at least, having been given an opportunity to object, has chosen not to do so. If this is so, it has serious implications for organisations involved in list trading for marketing purposes.

One small provision in the Data Protection Act 1998 might compromise this wider view of the right. Section 10(6) states that, if a data subject does not exercise his right to prevent processing likely to cause substantial damage or substantial distress or his right to prevent processing for the purposes of direct marketing, this does not affect his other rights under Part II of the Act (the Part dealing with data subjects' rights). This suggests that the right is only available in cases where the data subject has taken positive steps to exercise it. However, this interpretation may be contrary to Article 8 of the Convention. It should be remembered that the right to privacy is subject to derogations in Article 8(2) but none of these could fairly be said to apply in the context of direct marketing.

Automated decision taking

Another concern in the lead up to the Directive was automated decision taking where the decisions had or could have significant impacts on data subjects. There are obvious dangers where decisions are taken dogmatically on the basis of a number of factors without any discretion that could be used in particular cases. We have already seen the apparent unfairness of decisions to grant credit being influenced on the credit record of the previous occupant of the house or flat presently occupied by the applicant for credit in *Equifax Europe Ltd* v *Data Protection Registrar*, 28 February 1992, Data Protection Tribunal (now Information Tribunal). In that case, a credit reference agency was using personal data relating to the financial status of individuals by reference to the current or previous address of the data subject together with financial information relating to *any other individual who had been recorded as residing at any time at the same or a similar address*. The use of such third party data was deemed to be unfair by the Data Protection Registrar (now Information Commissioner) although, in the event, the Tribunal did not revoke the enforcement notice but substituted its own on much narrower terms: for example, allowing the use of such third party data if there appeared to be a financial relationship or dependence between the applicant and the third party.

A mechanical and predetermined decision-making process can bring unsatisfactory decisions. It could be because a factor which is a good statistical predictor is built into the logic of the decision process. The data subject's postal code is a good example but says nothing about any particular data subject. Another example is where the data subject has a foreign-sounding name. The controls over automated decision taking are aimed at overcoming decisions that are unfair in a particular case. The Directive took a fairly severe approach and permitted such decision taking only in the context of contracts or, subject to safeguards, where national legislation specifically allowed it.

Section 12 of the Data Protection Act 1998 deals with automated decision taking and takes advantage of the Directive permitting it in cases other than contract. The provisions are targeted at decision taking which significantly affects an individual and which is:

> based solely on the processing by automatic means of personal data in respect of which that individual is the data subject for the purposes of evaluating matters relating to him such as, for example, his performance of work, his creditworthiness, his reliability or his conduct (section 12(1)).

Note that the definition is not exhaustive. Decisions in the context of contract or specifically permitted under legislation (known as 'exempt decisions') are treated somewhat differently to other forms of automated decision taking. In the latter case, the data subject has the right to prevent automated decisions being taken in respect of him or to require a data controller to reconsider such a decision. In terms of 'exempt decisions', the data controller must take steps to safeguard the legitimate interests of the data subject.

Exempt decisions

The precise meaning of 'exempt decisions' is given in section 12(4)–(7), being where:

- the decision is taken in the course of steps taken to consider whether to enter into a contract with the data subject or with a view to entering into such a contract or in the course of performing such a contract, or is authorised or required by or under any enactment, and
- the effect of the decision is to grant a request of the data subject or steps have been

taken to safeguard his legitimate interests (for example, allowing him to make representations).

These may be added to by the Lord Chancellor, though none have been added as yet.
However, the conditions that either the data subject's request is granted or steps have
been taken to safeguard the data subject's legitimate interests do not automatically
apply to any further types of decision added by the Lord Chancellor although, of
course, any Regulations adding to the list of exempt decisions may make specific provisions for safeguards.

As an example of an exempt decision, consider an individual, Herbert, who has
applied for hire purchase to buy a used car. The hire-purchase company, Grabbitt &
Co Ltd, use an automated decision system on a computer which is based on a credit
scoring formula. If Grabbitt & Co accepts Herbert's application and a hire-purchase
contract is duly executed, there is no further requirement under these provisions. (Of
course, if Grabbitt & Co want to disclose personal data relating to Herbert to another
company, say for marketing purposes, Herbert should be told this, preferably by having
a 'tick box' on the hire-purchase application form.) However, if Grabbitt & Co turns
down Herbert's application, steps must be taken to safeguard his legitimate interests
and, as the Act suggests, this will probably be by allowing him to make representations,
that is, to respond to the failure to be granted credit. It may be that some years ago
Herbert had a court judgment against him for debt and he has been open about this
when completing the application form (or Grabbitt & Co have found out from a credit
reference agency that he has been in default of a loan). Herbert might now want to say
to Grabbitt & Co that he is a much better credit risk nowadays and that his default was
at a time when he lost his job and he has since repaid the amount outstanding in full.

The Act is silent on what, if anything, the data controller should do in response to
representations made by a data subject but a reasonable data controller ought seriously
to consider any representations made by an individual and, in appropriate circumstances, reconsider the decision, perhaps by personal review rather than by automated
decision taking.

Non-exempt decisions

As mentioned above, where the decision itself is not an exempt one, data subjects have
far greater rights and can even prevent automated decision taking in respect of them
where the decisions, based solely on automated decision taking, significantly affect
them and are for the purpose of evaluating matters such as performance at work, creditworthiness, reliability or conduct. This is where the right not to be subject to a
decision taken by automated means finds expression in the Act. However, probably the
greatest proportion of automated decision taking within section 12 of the Data
Protection Act 1998 will be in respect of contracts and will be exempt decisions. Other
exempt decisions may be specifically authorised by or required by legislation. An
example might be an automated system to determine social security payments.

It is not an easy matter to think of examples of automated decision taking which will
be outside the realms of contract. One possible hypothetical candidate is where a
doctor in a local NHS Trust hospital uses an automated system to decide on priority
for operations where there is a long waiting list. Being an NHS Trust hospital, there is
no contract between the patient and the hospital, or for that matter, between the
patient and the doctor. Indeed, there are probably several other potential areas where

the public sector confers benefits on individuals outside a contract. Some, such as the social security example quoted above, may be specifically provided for by legislation and thus become exempt decisions.

In respect of automated decision taking which is not exempt, under section 12(1) the data subject is given a right to prevent such decisions by serving a written notice on the data controller. There is no mention of any time limit for the notice to take effect nor that it has to be reasonable. It would seem that the intention is for the notice to take immediate effect. As with direct marketing, this right is absolute but does not, of course, apply to exempt decisions.

Where no notice has been served by the data subject, further safeguards are provided. Under section 12(2), the data controller is required to notify the data subject that the decision was taken on the basis of automated decision taking as soon as reasonably practicable. The data subject then has the opportunity to ask the data controller, by written notice, to reconsider the decision or take a new decision by other means within 21 days of receipt of the notice. Within that period, the data controller must serve a written notice on the data subject stating what steps he intends to take to comply with the data subject's notice. These rights of data subjects are backed by court powers to order compliance by the 'responsible person', being the person taking the decision in respect of the data subject. The use of the term 'responsible person' presumably is used to include the situation where the decision taking is actually carried out on behalf of a data controller by a processor, such as a computer bureau. Any court order does not affect the rights of any person other than the data subject or the responsible person.

A final point is to note that these provisions apply only where the decision is based *solely* on processing by automatic means. The word 'solely' should not be taken in a strong sense. For example, simply having the person operating the automated decision-taking software confirm or ratify the decision in an unquestioning way will not take the decision taking outside the controls on automated decision taking. Simply 'rubber-stamping' the result is not enough to escape the provisions. It would be different, however, if some aspects of the decision were actively reviewed by a human being.

Compensation

Individuals are entitled to compensation from the data controller for damage resulting from a contravention of *any* of the requirements in the Act. Although similar in operation, this is much wider than under the 1984 Act as it extends to any contravention of the Act, whereas before it was available only in respect of inaccurate data, loss of data, unauthorised destruction of data or unauthorised disclosure of or access to the data. Now, under section 13 of the 1998 Act, compensation is available for any contravention causing damage to the data subject. Under the 1984 Act compensation was also available for distress suffered by the data subject but it appeared that this applied only where the data subject had also sustained damage. Under the 1998 Act, compensation for distress is available generally where there is also damage or where the contravention concerns processing for the 'special purposes' (journalism, artistic or literary expression).

Examples of situations where the data subject should be able to claim compensation for damage and/or distress under the 1998 Act are given below.

Andrew has been turned down for employment because a reference given by a former employer taken from Andrew's personnel file contained a statement that Andrew had been subject to disciplinary action for dishonesty when, in actual fact, Andrew had been cleared of the charge following an appeal within the company's disciplinary procedures. He may now have a claim for compensation for damage and, possibly, depending on the circumstances, for distress.

Brenda is a famous singer who had an illegitimate child some years before she became famous. A local newspaper published details of this last week, including the identity of the child (who was unaware of the identity of Brenda or even that the child was adopted), and today the newspaper has sold the story to a national television company which intends to broadcast details in a documentary on single mothers. Brenda (and her child) may have a claim for distress as such processing may not be able to rely on the exemptions for the special purposes. The publication and broadcast would be permissible only if the data controller reasonably believes that it is in the public interest: see section 32. If this is not so, and it may not be so because the information published probably goes beyond what is required in the public interest, the exemption for processing for the special purposes will be lost.

Colin is a self-employed management consultant. He recently submitted a quotation to carry out an in-depth management analysis for Fizkin plc, a large manufacturing company. However, the managing director of Fizkin has spoken to the company secretary of Pipkin Trading Ltd who told him that Colin used to be a member of the Communist Party. Colin used to carry out consulting work for Pipkin. Fizkin turns down Colin's quotation and tells him that the company has discovered from Pipkin that he has a dubious political background. Colin made a data subject access request to Pipkin and the printout from the computer file indeed shows that Colin was a member of the Communist Party when he was a student many years ago. Colin should have a claim for compensation for damage because, although the information is correct, it is probably in breach of the third Data Protection Principle in that the data relating to him held by Pipkin are excessive in relation to the purposes for processing (keeping information about consultants, their work, payments to them, etc.). It is also likely that there is a breach of the first Data Protection Principle as it is likely in the circumstances that none of the conditions for processing sensitive personal data (which such information is) apply to the processing.

Deborah recently went into hospital to have a toe amputated. Her details were sent to the hospital from her general practitioner and the hospital added further information. Her general practitioner failed to note that, in the last year or so, Brenda has developed an allergy to a certain type of anaesthetic. The information was kept in a structured paper file (a 'relevant filing system'). Unfortunately, the junior doctor entering information into her file made a mistake and this was not spotted by the surgeon. The wrong toe was amputated and, as a result, Brenda is more severely disabled physically than she would have been had the correct toe been amputated in the first place. She has also suffered minor brain damage as a result of being given an anaesthetic to which she is allergic. Brenda should have a claim to compensation for damage and possibly also for distress because the data were in breach of the fourth Data Protection Principle in that that they were inaccurate and not kept up to date (the allergy was not mentioned). Of course, Brenda will also have a claim for damages on account of negligence, apart from data protection law, and it is most likely that this will be her main claim. However, there is nothing in the Data Protection Act to suggest that full compensation cannot be given for the breaches of duty imposed by the Act.

The right to compensation is tempered by the existence of a defence similar to that under the 1984 Act, being where the data controller can prove that he took such care as was in all the circumstances reasonably required to comply with the requirement which has been contravened. Of course, compensation can only be awarded to an individual who goes to court. There are no powers for the Information Commissioner to award compensation. A data subject seeking compensation has to go to either the county court or High Court (in England and Wales). Choice of court will depend, to some extent, on the amount of compensation sought.

Rights in relation to inaccurate data

Fundamentally, the rights of data subjects in respect of personal data that are inaccurate are similar to those under the 1984 Act. However, there are some changes and the scope of the right is widened somewhat. There is also the possibility now that any court order may require that third parties to whom the data have been disclosed are informed of the inaccuracy. Another change is that, under the 1984 Act, the rights where limited to rectification or erasure. Under the 1998 Act, reflecting the fact this Act also covers certain types of manual data, rights relating to blocking and destruction are added. 'Blocking' is defined neither in the Act nor in the Directive but it would seem reasonable to assume that it means suppressing the data without erasing them. For example, in a computer database, data may be suppressed from a particular form of processing or a 'flag' may be set indicating that data relating to a particular person are no longer to be processed even though they are not deleted permanently. 'Destruction' clearly is applicable in relation to manual data.

Under section 70(2), data are inaccurate if they are incorrect or misleading as to any matter of fact. This is an identical definition to that under the 1984 Act. There are two forms of control in the 1998 Act, contained in section 14. The first relates to data that are inaccurate. The second relates to serious contraventions of the Act causing damage to the data subject. As with compensation, the data subject must apply to the court for an appropriate order for rectification, blocking, erasure or destruction. However, it should be noted that the Commissioner may also require rectification, blocking, erasure or destruction of inaccurate data as part of an enforcement notice.

Inaccurate data

Inaccurate data may be ordered by a court, on application by the data subject, to be rectified, blocked, erased or destroyed, if the court is satisfied that they are inaccurate. This extends to other data which contain an expression of opinion about the data subject which is based upon such inaccurate data: section 14(1). Paragraph 7 of Part II of Schedule 1 (interpretation of the Data Protection Principles) states that it is not a contravention of the fourth Principle (data shall be accurate and, where necessary, kept up to date) if the data accurately record information given by the data subject or a third party where:

- having regard to the purpose or purposes for which the data were obtained and further processed, the data controller has taken reasonable steps in the circumstances to ensure the accuracy of the data, and
- if notified by the data subject of his view that the data are inaccurate, the data indicate that fact.

Thus, where this is the case, the court may instead of ordering rectification, etc. require a supplementary statement of the true facts. If data accurately record information received or obtained from the data subject or a third party but paragraph 7 of Part II of Schedule 1 does not apply (for example, where the data controller has *failed* to take reasonable steps to ensure accuracy), the court may instead of ordering rectification, etc., make an order to secure compliance with or without a further order for a supplementary statement of the true facts.

The court may also order the data controller to inform third parties to whom the inaccurate data have been disclosed of the rectification, blocking, erasure or destruction.

Rectification, etc. in the case of any contravention of the Act

Under section 14(4), the court has an additional and general power to order rectification, blocking, erasure or destruction of data where the data subject has suffered damage *by reason of any contravention of the Act* in circumstances which entitle him to compensation under the Act where there is a substantial risk of further contravention in respect of those data in such circumstances. This could apply, for example, where data are accurate but excessive in breach of the third Data Protection Principle. In such a case, the court may order erasure of the excessive data. The difference between this provision and the right of rectification, etc. under section 14(1) is that the latter applies only where the data are inaccurate.

In addition to the order above and as with inaccurate data, a court may, where it considers it to be reasonably practicable, order the data controller to notify third parties to whom the data have been disclosed of the rectification, blocking, erasure or disclosure. Regard is to be had, in particular, to the number of persons involved. The data protection Directive requires third parties to be notified unless it proves impossible or involves a disproportionate effort. This provision also applies in relation to inaccurate data described above. To some extent, the ease with which third parties can be notified will be a reflection of how well the data controller keeps records of disclosures. With the use of electronic mail and a good audit trail of disclosures, notifying third parties could be quite an easy matter even if there are a large number to be informed. This could be important from the point of view of third parties as, until they have rectified, blocked, erased or destroyed, third parties will probably be in breach of the Data Protection Act 1998 and vulnerable to an action for compensation.

Jurisdiction and procedure

Under section 15, jurisdiction is conferred, in England and Wales, on the High Court or a county court. In Scotland, it is the Court of Session or the sheriff court. Where there is an issue as to whether a data subject is entitled to subject access under section 7 (including information as to the logic in any automated decision taking), the data subject or his representative will not have access to the information unless and until the court determines the matter of right of access in favour of the data subject. If this were not so, the ordinary rules of discovery in court proceedings could defeat the subject access exemptions where litigation is under way.

Summary

We have seen that the rights of data subjects have been significantly improved by the Data Protection Act 1998. However, rights are only any good if the persons to whom they are given are aware of them and prepared to exercise them. There are no statistics to indicate how much use has been made of the rights mentioned above but it is unlikely that many persons have been prepared to go to the expense and worry of a court action. For the aggrieved data subject, there is an alternative route to obtain a data controller's compliance with the Act and that is by asking the Information Commissioner. Any individual who considers that he is directly affected by any processing may, under section 42, apply to the Commissioner for an assessment as to whether or not it is likely that the processing has been or is being carried out in compliance with the Act. There is also a right to apply to the Commissioner for assistance where the processing relates to processing for the special purposes.

Individuals generally will not use their right to access to personal data unless something appears wrong: for example, where they have been denied credit. Numerous requests are made to credit reference agencies. Other areas where subject access requests are often made is in connection with health or social records, typically from persons contemplating a claim for negligent treatment or care. The fact that the data controller can charge a fee, up to a prescribed maximum, will deter all but the most curious from carrying out subject access requests simply for the sake of it. The right to prevent processing for the purposes of direct marketing is likely to be used by a proportion of data subjects, but the other rights are very important in the minority of cases where there are problems, in particular the right to compensation. Quite often, a claim to compensation will be added to a claim of a breach of the right to privacy under Article 8 of the European Convention for the Protection of Human Rights and Fundamental Freedoms. Of course, the rights of data subjects are somewhat compromised by the exemptions from the subject information and non-disclosure provisions, described in the previous chapter. Furthermore, because of the use of generic descriptors in notifications under the Act, the principle of transparency of processing is undermined. Unless a data subject knows who is processing personal data relating to him, this further weakens the value of the subject access provisions and the remedies that depend on subject access as a means of verifying whether or not there is or has been a contravention of the Act.

Chapter 37

Privacy in electronic communications

Introduction

The advent of new technological developments in the telecommunications sector, such as the ability to capture information such as a caller's telephone number or to see the number from which an incoming call is made before deciding whether to answer, brought concerns about privacy. Another issue was the growing use of telephones and facsimile machines ('faxes') for marketing purposes. There is nothing more irritating than seeing your fax machine churning out unsolicited advertising material, tying up the machine and using your paper. Other concerns related to the use and storage of personal data relating to customers of telecommunication service providers, automatic call forwarding and information made available in directories, whether in paper or software form. Security and the prevention of unlawful eavesdropping are other privacy issues.

The stimulus for change and greater protection for individuals' rights to privacy came about by way of a European initiative. Directive 97/66/EC of the European Parliament and of the Council concerning the processing of personal data and the protection of privacy in the telecommunications sector, L 24, 30.01.1998, p.1, was implemented in the United Kingdom by the Telecommunications (Data Protection and Privacy) Regulations 1999, as amended.

Since that time, further concerns have surfaced about the use of the Internet for communications, such as e-mail. With a global technology, serious threats to privacy are raised and, accordingly, a further European Directive has been adopted, which replaces Directive 97/66/EC and extends the protection afforded by it to other forms of electronic communications. Directive 2002/58/EC of the European Parliament and of the Council concerning the processing of personal data and the protection of privacy in the electronic communications sector ('Directive on privacy and electronic communications') OJ L 201, 31.07.2002, p.37 is required to be transposed into national laws before 31 October 2003. Already, the Department for Trade and Industry has published a draft statutory instrument, the Privacy and Electronic Communications (EC Directive) Regulations 2003. As these Regulations may be modified before being laid before Parliament, in this chapter, the focus is on the Directive itself, with a brief overview of some of the aspects of the draft Regulations but only to the extent that they provide more detail or add further provisions (and then not exhaustively). Of course, the Regulations must accord with the provisions in the Directive, which must be accurately transposed into United Kingdom law.

The recitals to the Directive on privacy and electronic communications make it clear that it supplements the data protection Directive and is aimed at '... protecting the fundamental rights of natural persons and particularly their right to privacy, as well as the legitimate interests of legal persons' in the context of subscribers (whether natural or legal persons) to publicly available electronic communications services. A legal person is a body such as a company, firm or other organisation, for example, a public authority or charity. The Directive does not require member states to extend the protection afforded to natural persons under the data protection Directive to legal persons. It is intended that the protection of personal data and privacy should be the same whatever form of technology is used in publicly available electronic communications services, for example, whether analogue or digital voice telephony systems, mobile telephones or the Internet. As far as non-public communications services are concerned, the recitals to the Directive on privacy and electronic communications recognise that the data protection Directive applies to these. Harmonisation is also important to avoid obstacles to the internal market for electronic communications.

Broadcasting over a public communications network, being intended for a potentially unlimited audience, is outside the scope of the Directive, except to the extent that an individual subscriber or user can be identified, for example, in the case of video-on-demand services.

In terms of the Internet, the recitals stress the fact that terminal equipment and information stored on them are part of the users' private sphere and, under the European Convention for the Protection of Human Rights and Fundamental Freedoms, need protecting from devices that can enter the user's terminal such as spyware, web bugs and hidden identifiers which can gain access to information stored in the terminal or store information there or trace the user's activities, such as the addresses of websites visited by the user. Such devices should only be used for legitimate purposes and then only with the user's consent. Cookies are seen as a legitimate and useful tool. They can be used to analyse the effectiveness of a website and advertising and in verifying the identity of users engaged in on-line transactions. These should only be used, however, where clear and precise information is provided about the purposes of cookies and similar devices and users should have a right to refuse to have them stored on the equipment they are using. The fact that access to a particular website may be prevented in the absence of informed consent is seen as acceptable.

Other aspects of the Directive relate to security and confidentiality, traffic and billing data, identification of calling and connected lines, location data (for example, in connection with the use of a mobile phone), automatic call forwarding, directories, unsolicited marketing material and technical features and standardisation.

The Directive on privacy and electronic communications

The definitions are important to consider. Some are contained in the Directive but others are in Directive 2002/21/EC of the European Parliament and of the Council of 7 March 2002 on a common regulatory framework for electronic communications networks and services OJ L 108, 24.04.2002, p.33 ('the framework Directive'). First, the definitions contained in Article 2 of the Directive on privacy in electronic communications are listed:

(a) 'user' means any natural person using a publicly available electronic communications service, for private or business purposes, without necessarily having subscribed to this service;
(b) 'traffic data' means any data processed for the purpose of the conveyance of a communication on an electronic communications network or for the billing thereof;

(c) 'location data' means any data processed in an electronic communications network, indicating the geographic position of the terminal equipment of a user of a publicly available electronic communications service;

(d) 'communication' means any information exchanged or conveyed between a finite number of parties by means of a publicly available electronic communications service. This does not include any information conveyed as part of a broadcasting service to the public over an electronic communications network except to the extent that the information can be related to the identifiable subscriber or user receiving the information;

(e) 'call' means a connection established by means of a publicly available telephone service allowing two-way communication in real time;

(f) 'consent' by a user or subscriber corresponds to the data subject's consent in Directive 95/46/EC [the data protection Directive];

(g) 'value added service' means any service which requires the processing of traffic data or location data other than traffic data beyond what is necessary for the transmission of a communication or the billing thereof;

(h) 'electronic mail' means any text, voice, sound or image message sent over a public communications network which can be stored in the network or in the recipient's terminal equipment until it is collected by the recipient.

The relevant definitions from the framework Directive are as follow (renumbered from the Directive so as to be consecutive with those above):

(i) 'electronic communications network' means transmission systems and, where applicable, switching or routing equipment and other resources which permit the conveyance of signals by wire, by radio, by optical or by other electromagnetic means, including satellite networks, fixed (circuit- and packet-switched, including Internet) and mobile terrestrial networks, electricity cable systems, to the extent that they are used for the purpose of transmitting signals, networks used for radio and television broadcasting, and cable television networks, irrespective of the type of information conveyed;

(j) 'electronic communications service' means a service normally provided for remuneration which consists wholly or mainly in the conveyance of signals on electronic communications networks, including telecommunications services and transmission services in networks used for broadcasting, but exclude services providing, or exercising editorial control over, content transmitted using electronic communications networks and services; it does not include information society services, as defined in Article 1 of Directive 98/34/EC [any service normally provided for remuneration, at a distance, by electronic means and at the individual request of a recipient of services], which do not consist wholly or mainly in the conveyance of signals on electronic communications networks;

(k) 'public communications network' means an electronic communications network used wholly or mainly for the provision of publicly available electronic communications services;

(l) 'subscriber' means any natural person or legal entity who or which is party to a contract with the provider of publicly available electronic communications services for the supply of such services.

The definitions are fairly straightforward and not particularly controversial. It is important to note that in most cases, the protection of privacy applies to users of electronic communication services as it does to subscribers. Therefore, where the user and subscriber are different such as where an employee is using his employer's computer to send or receive e-mail messages or where a student is using a university computer to buy goods on-line, in most cases the rights to privacy apply also to that person as it does the subscriber. One difference is that a user can only be a natural person, that is, a living individual, whereas a subscriber can be either a natural person or a legal person such as a limited company or other organisation. The definition of value added service is important because some of the provisions of the Directive also apply to services which 'piggy-back' on the basic electronic communication service, for example, the provision of information as to congestion or weather or about the best contract for a mobile phone. A number of organisations provide information about different tariffs for telephone services and the like and indicate typical savings available by changing service providers. Location data are particularly relevant in the context of mobile phones as it is possible to find the geographic location of a mobile phone and this information could prove very important, for example, if it is important to trace the person using the mobile phone because he is injured or being attacked. Recital 14 to the Directive gives examples of location data, being data referring to longitude, latitude and altitude of the user's terminal equipment, to the direction of travel and the level of accuracy of the location information.

Security and confidentiality

The provider of a publicly available electronic communications service must take appropriate technical and organisational security measures, if necessary, in conjunction with the provider of the public communications network under Article 4. Factors to be taken into account are, as for the data protection Directive, the state of the art, cost of implementation and the risk. Where there is a particular risk of a breach of security, the provider of a publicly available electronic communications service must inform subscribers of this risk and any possible remedies including the costs involved. Where the risks lie outside the scope of the measures to be taken, the service provider must inform subscribers of any possible remedies together with an indication of the likely costs involved. Recital 32 states that where a service provider subcontracts processing, the subcontracting and subsequent processing shall be in accordance with the security obligations imposed on data controllers and processors by the data protection Directive. In particular, this means that the contract between the service provider and the subcontractor must impose the appropriate security obligations on the subcontractor and be at least evidenced in writing.

Article 5 requires that confidentiality of communications and related traffic data by means of a public communications network and publicly available electronic communications services must be ensured by national legislation. Listening, tapping, storage or other kinds of interception or surveillance must be prohibited except where such restriction is authorised by law and is a necessary, appropriate and proportionate measure in a democratic society to safeguard national security, defence and public security, or for the prevention, investigation, detection and prosecution of criminal offences, or of unauthorised use of the electronic communication system, as referred to in Article 13(1) of the data protection Directive. The Regulation of Investigatory Powers Act 2000 prohibits interception of communications and provides for surveillance in certain circumstances under carefully regulated conditions. However, recording of communications and related traffic data in the course of lawful business practice for the purpose of providing evidence of commercial transactions or other business communications which are legally authorised are unaffected. This could apply, for example, where an individual takes out car insurance over the telephone.

As regards storing information on or gaining access to information stored on a subscriber's or user's terminal equipment, this is only allowed where the subscriber or user is provided with clear and comprehensive information in accordance with the data protection Directive about, *inter alia*, the purposes of processing and an opportunity to refuse such processing must be given. However, this does not prevent technical storage or access for the sole purpose of facilitating the transmission of a communication over an electronic communications network, or as strictly necessary to provide an information society service explicitly requested by the subscriber or user.

Traffic and billing data

Providers of public communications networks and publicly available electronic communications services need to process data relating to calls for the purpose of billing their customers. A considerable amount of information may be collected by the service provider and will include the subscriber's number, the number called, the date, start time, finish time, duration of the call, the call rate and the charge cost. Other information may be involved such as the data volume, the tariff class and data identifying the telephone exchange.

By virtue of Article 6, providers of public communications networks and publicly available electronic communications services must erase or make anonymous traffic data relating to subscribers and users when it is no longer required for the purposes set out in the remainder of the Article or when authorised by law and is a necessary, appropriate and proportionate measure in a democratic society to safeguard national security, defence and public security, etc.

Traffic data necessary for billing and interconnection payments may be processed up to the end of the period when the bill may lawfully be challenged or payment pursued (this is the limitation period for contracts, usually being six years from the date of breach of contract under section 5 of the Limitation Act 1980 but provision has to be made for legal proceedings already underway at the end of that period). With the consent of subscribers and users, as appropriate, processing may be carried out by publicly available electronic communications service providers of such traffic data, to the extent and for the duration necessary, for marketing their own services or value added services (which, according to recital 18 to the Directive, may include advice on the cheapest tariff packages, route guidance, traffic information, weather forecasts or tourist information). Information as to the type of traffic data processed and the duration of such processing must be given prior to obtaining consent. Any consent given to processing for such marketing purposes may be withdrawn at any time.

Processing of traffic data within Article 6 must be restricted to persons acting under the authority of the provider of the service or network, as the case may be, handling billing or traffic management, customer enquiries, fraud detection, marketing the provider's own services or providing a value added service. Furthermore, the processing must be restricted to that necessary for the purposes of such activities.

The above provisions are without prejudice to the possibility of competent bodies being informed of billing or traffic data under applicable legislation for settling disputes. The competent body in the United Kingdom for these purposes will be OFCOM, the Office of Communications.

Subscribers are given a right to receive non-itemised bills under Article 7. Where itemised bills are sent out, this could conflict with the right of privacy of calling users and called subscribers (outlined below). To reconcile this problem member states must, by national provisions, for example, ensure that 'sufficient alternative privacy enhancing methods of communications or payments are available to such users and subscribers'.

Presentation and restrictions of calling and connected line identification

Article 8 of the Directive concerns calling line and connected line identification and apply where calling line or connected line is offered. The provisions are that:

- a calling user must be able, using a simple means and free of charge, to prevent the presentation of calling line information on a per-call basis and a calling subscriber must be able to do this on a per-line basis;
- a called subscriber must be able, using a simple means and free of charge, to prevent the presentation of calling line information on incoming calls (why a subscriber would want to do this is unclear although it could be relevant where the subscriber is a company and it wants to prevent employees selectively declining to answer calls from, for example, awkward customers);
- where calling line information is presented prior to the call being established (that is, prior to connection) a called subscriber must be able, using simple means, to reject any incoming call for which calling line information has been prevented by the calling user or subscriber (an individual called at home late in the evening may prefer not to answer a call where calling line information has been suppressed);
- a called subscriber must be able, simply and free of charge, to eliminate the presentation of calling line information to the calling user (this would prevent the automatic capture of the subscriber's telephone number, say, by a commercial organisation);
- the elimination of the presentation of calling line identification by a calling user (on a per-call basis) or calling subscriber (on a per-line basis) must also apply to calls to third countries and the other provisions must also apply in respect of calls coming from third countries (that is, from outside the European Community).

Member states are obliged to ensure that, where presentation of calling and/or connected line information if offered, providers of publicly available electronic communications service publicise this and the possibilities of suppression as set out above.

As complete suppression of calling line information could hinder the tracing of persons making malicious or threatening calls, providers of public communications network and publicly available electronic communications service may override the elimination of presentation of calling line information in two cases and the procedures for doing must be transparent: Article 10. First, elimination of presentation of calling line identification may be overridden on the application of a subscriber requesting the tracing of malicious or nuisance calls, on a temporary basis. This will allow the storage of the data identifying the calling subscriber to be made available in accordance with national law. The second case applies to overriding the elimination of calling line information on a per-line basis for organisations dealing with emergency calls as recognised in member states including law enforcement agencies, ambulance services and fire brigades and other organisations dealing with emergency calls for the purpose of responding to such calls.

Location data other than traffic data

It is now possible to locate the geographic position of a mobile phone with some degree of accuracy. Clearly, the misuse of location data could serious compromise privacy, particularly if a person using a mobile phone does not want the other person to know his location at a particular time. Under Article 9 of the Directive, where such data can be processed, they may only be processed if they are made anonymous or with the consent of the user or subscriber, as appropriate, to the extent and for the duration necessary for the provision of a value added service. Thus, for example, a person with a mobile phone may want an up-to-date weather forecast for the place where he is. By simply calling a number, a forecast may be sent back immediately in the form of a text message.

Again the concept of informed consent is used, the user or subscriber being given information as to the type of location data and any other traffic data to be processed, the purposes and duration of processing and whether the data will be transmitted to a third party for the purpose of providing a value added service. Consent may be withdrawn at any time. Where consent has been obtained in respect of location data other than traffic data, there must be an opportunity to temporarily refuse such processing, using a simple means and free of charge, for each connection to the network or for each transmission or communication.

Processing must be restricted to persons acting under the authority of the provider of the public communications network or publicly available electronic communications service or of a third party providing a value added service. In the latter case, processing must also be restricted to that necessary for the purposes of providing a value added service.

The second form of exception under Article 10 also applies to location data. The temporary denial or absence of consent of a subscriber or user for processing of location data may be overridden for the purpose of responding to emergency calls. This could cover a case where, for example, the owner of a mobile phone, who has not consented to processing of location data, lends his phone to a friend who makes an emergency call after breaking his leg whilst walking on wild moor land and is unable to give an accurate location.

Automatic call forwarding

A lot of persons make use of call divert services, for example, by diverting calls to their mobile phone to their home or office telephone. This can be quite a useful service, for example, if a person is at a concert and wants to divert calls to his home answer phone or to his partner's phone. Such diversions can, however, be intrusive and prejudice the right to privacy, for example, where a business call is forwarded to a person's home late in the evening. To prevent unwelcome call forwarding by third parties, Article 11 of the Directive gives every subscriber the right to prevent automatic call forwarding by a third party to his terminal, using a simple means and free of charge.

However, this provision and those on the elimination of presentation of calling and connected line identification, and Article 10, do not apply to subscriber lines connected to analogue exchanges unless compliance is technically possible and does not require a disproportionate economic effort. Such cases must be notified to the European Commission.

Directories

Directories of subscribers to public communication services, such as telephone directories, may seem innocuous enough but may still contain information that can threaten privacy or even safety. If the directory is available electronically, especially on-line, it may be an easy matter to find the name of a subscriber and address from a telephone number only (which may have been captured through calling line identification). Under Article 12 of the Directive, subscribers must be informed, free of charge and before they are included in a directory personal data, of the purposes of a printed or electronic directory of subscribers available to the public or obtainable through directory enquiry services. They must also be told of possible further usages based on search functions in electronic versions of directories. Subscribers must be given the opportunity to decide whether their personal data are to be included and, if so, to what extent. They must also be given the opportunity to verify, correct or withdraw such data free of charge.

Member states may require that for any purpose of a public directory, other than a search of contact details of persons based on their name and, where necessary a minimum of other identifiers, the additional consent of subscribers must be sought. It is likely that specific consent will be required for inclusion in an electronic directory where searching by number alone is possible. It may be possible to still include an entry for a person but to suppress the search by number facility for that person. Member states must also ensure that the legitimate interests of legal persons are also sufficiently protected with regard to their entries in public directories.

Unsolicited communications

Most people find unsolicited calls from organisations trying to sell something intrusive and a nuisance. It can be very irritating to go and answer the telephone whilst in the middle of cooking a meal, reading a book or performing some other enjoyable activity only to find that it is someone 'cold-calling', trying to get you to buy double glazing, financial services or whatever. By subscribing to the Telephone Preference System, these cold-calls can be reduced to a minimum, if not eliminated altogether. Another way to reduce them is to be 'ex-directory', though this defeats the usefulness of telephone directories as a source of information and may prevent a welcome telephone contact. Things have become far worse now with marketing by e-mail and the possibility of text message marketing.

Controls over unsolicited communications are provided under Article 13 of the Directive. The use of automatic calling machines which operate without human intervention, fax machines, electronic mail for the purposes of direct marketing is only allowed where subscribers have given prior consent. However, where a natural or legal person has obtained from its customers their electronic contact details for electronic mail (e-mail address) in the context of the sale of a product or service, they may still use this for direct marketing of its own similar products or services providing the customer is clearly and distinctly given the opportunity to object, free of charge and in an easy manner when the contact details are collected and on each subsequent occasion if the customer has not initially refused such use. Member states must also ensure that the legitimate interests of legal persons are sufficiently protected with regard to unsolicited communications.

Technical features and standardisation

If different member states adopt different technical features to comply with the Directive, this will work against the common market by impeding the placing of equipment on the market and the free circulation of telecommunications equipment. The basic rule, expressed in Article 14, is that there shall be no mandatory requirements for specific technical features imposed on terminals or other electronic communication equipment which could impede the placing of such equipment on the market and the free circulation of such equipment in and between member states. Where the provisions of the Directive can only be implemented by requiring specific technical features in electronic communications networks, member states are under a duty to inform the European Commission accordingly. Where required, the Commission will ensure the drawing up of common European standards in respect of such technical features in accordance with Council Decision 87/95/EEC on standardisation in the field of information technology and communications (OJ L 36, 07.02.1987, p.31).

Specific aspects of the draft Regulations

The draft Regulations (and it must be emphasised that they are, at the time of writing, a draft and may be modified somewhat before they are laid before Parliament) restate the Directive but add more detail where appropriate and make specific provision for matters left to member states. For example, the Directive on privacy and electronic communications does not mention compensation for breaches of the provisions in the Directive but the data protection Directive does so provide and states that the data controller shall not be liable if '... he proves he is not responsible ...'. The draft Regulations spell this out in more detail, saying that the service provider has a defence to any claim to compensation if he proves that he has '... taken such care as in all the circumstances was reasonably required to comply [with the requirements of the Regulations]'. Compensation is only available for damage and not for distress. Other points of interest in the draft Regulations of interest are listed below.

1 The period of time traffic data can be kept takes into account, where proceedings are brought within the limitation period, the time when those proceedings are determined and the time allowed for an appeal, and if an appeal is brought, the time until the conclusion of the appeal. This could be a considerable time, for instance, in a matter involving Community law, where an application for a preliminary reference is made to the European Court of Justice.

2 The processing of traffic data for billing and, where allowed, for value added services is restricted to the activities of management of billing or traffic, customer enquiries, the prevention or detection of fraud, the marketing of electronic communication services or the provision of a value added service.

3 Emergency calls, allowed the overriding of elimination of calling or connected line identification is limited to 999 calls, or in Europe, 112 calls.

4 In relation to the termination of automatic call forwarding, other communications providers are required to comply with reasonable requests from the subscriber's provider to assist in the prevention of the calls being forwarded.

5 Where a term in a contract between a subscriber and the provider of an electronic communications service or between such a provider and the provider of an electronic communications network is inconsistent with draft Regulations that term is void, to the extent that it is inconsistent.

6 Exemption is granted in connection with requirements imposed by or under any enactment or by court order, where the provision in question would be likely to prejudice the prevention or detection of crime or the apprehension of offenders or if required in respect of legal proceedings, necessary for obtaining legal advice or exercising or defending legal rights.

7 Part V of the Data Protection Act 1998 (the Part on enforcement) and Schedules 6 and 9 (dealing with the Information Tribunal and the powers of entry and inspection) apply with modification.

8 OFCOM (Office of Communications) or any person aggrieved by an alleged contravention of the Regulations may ask the Information Commissioner to exercise his enforcement functions, which are exercisable in any case in the absence of such a request.

9 OFCOM is required to comply with any reasonable request from the Information Commissioner for technical advice relating to electronic communications.

10 Section 11 of the Data Protection Act (the right to prevent processing for the purposes of direct marketing) is disapplied in the context of the electronic communications as the draft Regulations provide broadly equivalent, and possibly more effective, rights.

Summary

Telecommunications and other forms of electronic communications, such as e-mail and the Internet pose specific risks in relation to data processing that do not apply to other forms of data processing operations. The Directive and the Regulations, when in force address these specific risks as does the Data Protection Act 1998 and subordinate legislation made under it which applies to processing of personal data generally. However, this lacks the specificity necessary in the context of electronic communications; hence the Directive on privacy and electronic communications. Without these new provisions, it could mean that the application of data protection law would, in the context of processing for the purposes of electronic communications, be unpredictable and could be subject to different interpretations in different member states. The Telecommunications (Data Protection and Privacy) Regulations 1999 and the Telecommunications (Data Protection and Privacy) (Amendment) Regulations 2000 have already proved useful in a number of respects including the fight against unsolicited marketing by fax and a number of enforcement notices have been issued by the Information Commissioner under the 1999 Regulations. During the year ending 31 March 2003, the Information Commissioner received no less that 1771 complaints of breaches under the Telecommunications Regulations (Information

Commissioner, Annual report and accounts for the year ending 31 March 2003, HC727, 2003, p.96).

The 1999 and 2000 Telecommunications Regulations will be revoked when the new Regulations come into force, hopefully in Autumn 2003, and extend the protection to other areas such as unsolicited commercial e-mails as well as providing further safeguards to privacy as set out in this chapter. In relation to unsolicited e-mails, this will require cooperation between internet service providers and the Information Commissioner, who has said that he intends '. . . to explore the possibility of identifying sources of authoritative and regularly updated advice for internet users on the practical steps they can take to minimise the chances of receiving unsolicited e-mails' (Information Commissioner, Annual report and accounts for the year ending 31 March 2003, HC727, 2003, p.38). An important aspect of the Information Commissioner's responsibilities will be raising awareness of the new regime amongst the general public, providers of electronic communication services and those using such services, whether for personal or business use.

Chapter 38

Summary of data protection law

It would appear that the concerns of data controllers over the costs of implementing the Data Protection Act 1998, which were perceived by some organisations as enormous, have not been realised to anything like the extent feared. It is probably fair to say that there have been costs, in some cases significant costs of compliance, but then there are likely to have been some benefits also. Data controllers had to undertake a complete review of their data processing activities in the light of the substantial changes to the law, including the application of data protection law to certain forms of manual filing systems and records. Apart from the obvious benefit of no barriers to the freedom of movement of personal data throughout Europe on the grounds of privacy concerns, the exercise gave data controllers the opportunity to undertake a critical assessment of their processing activities, giving them valuable information that could be used to improve efficiencies and modernise and streamline their processing of personal data. For example, out-of-date or excessive data could be identified and erased. The opportunity could also be taken to look at the collection or sourcing of personal data and disclosures and transfers. Systems could be put into place to ensure that the subject information requirements were complied with and the rights of data subjects respected in the most efficient and least expensive manner.

The greater profile data protection law was given by the data protection Directive and the 1998 Act has gone some way towards developing a culture of respect for individuals' rights of privacy and has set the right to privacy under Article 8 of the European Convention for the Protection of Human Rights and Fundamental Freedoms in a data processing framework. The data protection Directive also sought to deal with the right of freedom of expression under the Convention. As interpreted by the courts, a reasonable balance seems to be achieved thus far and the importance of codes of practice, such as the Press Complaints Commission's code, are instrumental in determining whether the publisher's defence under section 32 of the Data Protection Act 1998 can be relied upon in a specific case. In the past, there has been no general right of privacy in the United Kingdom, and intrusions into the right of privacy were dealt with in a piecemeal and unsatisfactory nature. Now, it can be said that there is a right of privacy of general application and a specific right in relation to processing personal data. The balance in the Convention with freedom of expression is clearly evident and this area of law is fast developing in the United Kingdom. Given the impetus from the Human Rights Act 1998 and the Data Protection Act 1998, the law of breach of confidence is itself evolving into a further guarantor of privacy as witnessed by the *Michael Douglas v Hello! Ltd* case. It is still early days yet in the United Kingdom but the protection of privacy, subject of course to the derogations permitted in the Convention, already seems well established and there is a wealth of case law before the European Court of Human Rights to help with further developments.

Where there are allegations of breaches of data protection law, there will usually also be associated claims made in respect of a breach of the right of privacy under Article 8 of the Convention and of a breach of confidence. Bearing in mind that personal data can extend to image or voice data and the increasing likelihood (now verging almost on certainty) that such forms of data will be processed by automatic means, the role of data protection law seems assured as a means of protecting privacy notwithstanding the other remedies that might be available. Early indications are, however, that where claims are made that Convention rights have been breached or that there has been a breach of confidence, only a nominal award is likely for the data protection claim if the other claims attract substantial damages. This can limit the utility of a claim for compensation under section 13 of the Data Protection Act 1998.

Practical steps for data controllers

Data controllers and processors should, if they have not already done so, develop a data protection or privacy policy. The policy should be made available to employee and agents and to persons who are or will be data subjects in relation to the data controller. Where the data controller collects personal data through a website or by e-mail, the data protection policy should be accessible for reading before any data are collected. Particular steps data controllers should contemplate are:

- reviewing processing activities and checking them against the Data Protection Principles and the register entry at reasonable intervals, notifying any changes to the Information Commissioner promptly;
- consideration of the appointment of a data protection official, a person for ensuring compliance with data protection law and keeping himself informed of latest developments and guidance from the Information Commissioner. He will also be involved in designing systems and procedures for compliance and training employees and raising awareness. Larger organisations may have a data protection department;
- the allocation of responsibilities amongst employees for compliance with data protection law:
- in particular, checking and, if necessary, modifying forms and other documentation, for example, to ensure compliance with data protection law to provide individuals with information and in relation to obtaining the data subject's consent (in some cases, the simple tick box approach, where failure to tick the box indicates consent, will probably not suffice and express consent may be required);
- carrying out a review of responses to subject access requests and procedures put in place to comply with requests for the equivalent of the registrable particulars in respect of processing that does not need to be, and has not been, notified;
- setting up procedures to deal with the rights of individuals; for example, in relation to automatic decision taking, it may be important to provide the individual with a right to be heard if his request is not complied with or if he requires the decision to be taken again or taken by other means, depending on the purpose of processing;
- developing software, in particular databases, to include fields to enter data subject's wishes, where the data subject has opted-out of receiving direct marketing material or exercised his right to prevent processing to the extent it is likely to cause damage or distress or his right to prevent decisions being taken in relation to him by automatic means where applicable;
- keeping records of disclosure and transfers and having procedures to deal with inac-

curate data including informing third parties if this would not result in a disproportionate effort;
- making sure that contracts with processors (bearing in mind the very wide definition
of processing) contain written guarantees of data security and integrity and stressing
their security obligations which have to be in line with those imposed on the data
controller, and also monitoring the processor's compliance with those obligations;
- regularly review security arrangements and regularly monitor technological developments in security measures with a view to implementing them;
- taking account of the fact that transfers of personal data to some countries outside
the European Economic Area may be permitted only in certain circumstances such
as where there are contractual guarantees as to adequacy of data protection or where
the individuals to whom the data relate have consented to the transfer; considering
using approved contractual clauses which may be used to permit transfers to countries outside the European Economic Area that do not have adequate protection for
personal data, and keeping up to date with developments in respect of transfers to
third countries;
- regularly monitoring the Information Commissioner's website for guidance at
www.dataprotection.gov.uk and watching for relevant codes of practice for data
protection in relevant forms of business or other activity published, for example, by
trade associations;
- considering the impact of the forthcoming Regulations on privacy and electronic
communications, especially in the field of telecommunications and electronic commerce.

Although the changes brought about by the Data Protection Act 1998 are very welcome for individuals, with its emphasis on protecting rights and freedoms, in particular, with respect to privacy of personal data, there are still a number of worrying
aspects. Data protection law, like many laws, looks fairly ineffective when faced with
controlling the Internet but, hopefully the changes to privacy in relation to electronic
communications will help. The nature of the Internet makes it important to consider
individuals' rights especially the requirement for consent, apart from the perspective of
the Directive on privacy and electronic communications, which should also be taken
into account. It is common to see employee data on organisation's websites. Express
consent should be obtained for this. Also, filling in an electronic form is not the same
as filling in a paper form and it might be easier in the former case to fail to spot the opt
out for marketing. That being so, perhaps it might be safer to seek positive consent to
direct marketing material. This will soon be the position as regards unsolicited e-mail
marketing except in the case of a company which has provided a product or service to
a consumer but even then, the consumer must be given, clearly and distinctly, the
opportunity to object, in an easy manner and free of charge. Further considerations in
respect of electronic commerce are the provision of information about the uses to which
data collected will be put and the option to disable cookies.

Other issues in relation to data protection law include the processing of genetic data,
disclosures of financial information relating to persons who have a good credit record
(white data) and the operations of private investigation agencies. The 1998 Act allows
for preliminary assessment of processing where it is likely to pose specific risks and this
is certainly so with respect to genetic data. The Lord Chancellor may by Order specify
forms of processing to be subject to a preliminary assessment but has not done so as

yet. A serious concern at the moment is the retention of personal data in the form of genetic data in a DNA sample or fingerprints by the police where the individual concerned has not been charged with an offence or has been acquitted.

This concern came to the fore in *R (on application of S and Marper)* v *Chief Constable of South Yorkshire* [2002] 1 WLR 3223. Two persons had been charged with unrelated offences. The police lawfully took DNA samples and fingerprints. One was acquitted and the case against the other was discontinued. The retention of such data would have been an offence where the individual was unconvicted but this was changed by section 64(1A) of the Police and Criminal Evidence Act 1984, as inserted by the Criminal Justice and Police Act 2001. In accordance with that statutory provision, the Chief Constable decided to retain the data notwithstanding that they had not been convicted. The individuals applied for judicial review of that decision arguing that it was contrary to the European Convention for the Protection of Human Rights and Fundamental Freedoms, in that their right to privacy under Article 8(1) had been breached and it also discriminated against them contrary to Article 14. The Court of Appeal held that the retention of the data did not breach the applicants' Convention Rights as the interference was justified by Article 8(2) which allows such interference as is necessary in a democratic society in the interests of, *inter alia*, the prevention of disorder and crime. In any case, as the data had been lawfully collected, this reduced the interference significantly and the risks outweighed the benefits of achieving the aim of preventing and detecting crime. As regards the Article 14 claim, harmful consequences would flow only if the DNA sample or fingerprints matched someone alleged to be responsible for an offence. It was wrong to consider the 'pool' of persons for the purposes of discrimination, all those which were innocent including those who had been suspected of an offence but not convicted. Lord Justice Waller said that the relevant pool was the latter group from whom samples had been taken lawfully. Those persons were treated alike and there was no discrimination between them. (This case may be appealed to the House of Lords.)

Other forms of processing which may give rise to unease are:

- data matching, where personal data from different sources relating to a particular individual are compared, for example, in order to try to detect a possible fraudster if the information is contradictory;
- the use of an 'impaired life' database by insurance companies;
- lifestyle databases where data is collected, often from different sources, to build up a picture of a person's lifestyle: this can be extremely useful in targeting marketing material or providing a 'better' service to consumers, for example, when booking accommodation through a travel agent who has a record that the person concerned likes golf and is a vegetarian non-smoker;
- data warehousing, where massive amounts of data are collected from numerous sources with all the inherent dangers of inaccuracies;
- health data of a sensitive nature.

With the 1998 Act and associated legislation and the implementation of the Telecommunications (Data Protection and Privacy Regulations) 1999, as amended, soon to be replaced by the Privacy and Electronic Communications (EC Directive) Regulations 2003, the United Kingdom has gone a long way down the path of formal regulation of the processing of personal data. Issues for the future include the problems of transfers to countries having inadequate data protection law. This has caused many

United States organisations to adopt *International Safe Harbor Privacy Principles*, issued by the Department of Commerce and raise a presumption of adequacy for the purposes of transfers from Europe to the United States, which has a very different approach to data protection compared with Europe (including self-regulation).

A final factor is the creeping implementation of the provisions of the Freedom of Information Act 2000 which, *inter alia*, extends data protection law to unstructured files in the possession of public authorities. The relevant provisions of the Act should be fully in force during 2005. Some parts already in force include a duty imposed on the Information Commissioner to promote the following of good practice by public authorities and a requirement for the Lord Chancellor to issue codes of practice on the discharge of public authorities' functions under the Act and records management.

Selected bibliography

General

Akdeniz, Y, Walker, C and Wall, D, *The Internet, Law and Society*, Longman, 2000.

Butterworths *E-Commerce and Information Technology Law Handbook*, 2nd edn, Butterworths, 2003.

Edwards, L and Waelde, C (eds), *Law & the Internet*, 2nd edn, Hart Publishing, 2000.

Gringras, C, *The Laws of the Internet*, 2nd edn, Butterworths, 2002.

Lloyd, I J, *Information Technology Law*, 3rd edn, Butterworths, 2000.

Reed, C and Angel, J (eds), *Computer Law*, 5th edn, OUP, 2003.

Computers and intellectual property

Bainbridge, D, *Intellectual Property*, 5th edn, Longman 2002.

Bainbridge, D, *Cases and Material on Intellectual Property*, 2nd edn, FT Pitman Publishing, 1999.

Bainbridge, D I, *Software Copyright Law*, 4th edn, Butterworths, 1999.

Cornish, W R, *Intellectual Property: Patents, Copyright, Trade Marks and Allied Rights*, 4th edn, Sweet and Maxwell, 1999.

Garnett, K and Davies, G, *Copinger and Skone-James on Copyright*, 14th edn, Sweet & Maxwell, 2002.

Intellectual Property Institute, *The Economic Impact of Patentability of Computer Programs*, March 2000 available at: http://europa.eu.int/comm/internal_market/en/indprop/studyintro.htm

Laddie *et al*, *The Modern Law of Copyright and Designs*, 3rd edn, Butterworths, 2000.

Patent Office, Guidance, Law and Legal Decisions, Annual Reports and other useful information at www.patent.gov.uk

Phillips, J and Firth, A *Introduction to Intellectual Property Law*, 4th edn, Butterworths, 2001.

Computer contracts

Bainbridge, D I, *Software Licensing*, 2nd edn, EMIS Professional Publishing, 1999.

Berwin, S and Singleton, S, *Tolley's e-contracts*, Butterworths, 2001.

Bond R, *E-Licences and Software Contracts*, 2nd edn, Butterworths, 2002.

Chissick, M and Kelman, A, *Electronic Commerce: Law and Practice*, 3rd edn, Sweet and Maxwell, 2002.

Institute of Purchasing and Supply, *Standard Form Contracts* (various), available from the Institute at Easton House, Easton on the Hill, Stamford PE9 3NZ.

Morgan, R and Steadman, G, *Computer Contracts*, 6th edn, Sweet & Maxwell, 2000.

Rennie, M T, *Computer and Internet Contracts and the Law*, Sweet and Maxwell, 1994 (with CD updates).

Electronic contracts and torts

Collins, M, *The Law of Defamation and the Internet*, Oxford University Press, 2001.

Hammonds Suddard Edge, *E-Commerce – a Guide to the Law of Electronic Business*, 3rd edn, Butterworths, 2002.

Law Commission, *Defamation and the Internet: A Preliminary Investigation*, Scoping Study No. 2, December 2002

Milmo, P and Rogers, W V H, *Gatley on Libel and Slander*, 9th edition, Sweet and Maxwell, 2001.

Prosser, W L, 'Interstate Publication' (1953) 51 *Michigan Law Review*, 959.

Radin, M, Rothchild J and Silverman, G, *Internet Commerce*, Sweet & Maxwell, 2002.

Computers and crime

Audit Commission, *Ghost in the Machine: An Analysis of IT Fraud and Abuse*, Audit Commission Publications, 1998.

Audit Commission, *Opportunity Makes a Thief: An Analysis of Computer Abuse*, HMSO, 1994.

Audit Commission, *Survey of Computer Fraud and Abuse 1987*, HMSO, 1988.

Audit Commission, *Survey of Computer Fraud and Abuse 1990*, HMSO, 1991.

Audit Commission Update, *yourbusiness@risk: An Update on IT Abuse*, 2001.

Computer Security Institute, *CSI/FBI Computer Crime and Security Survey*, 2002.

HM Treasury, *2001–2002 Fraud Report: An Analysis of Reported Fraud in Government Departments and Best Practice Guidelines*, October 2002.

Law Commission, *Computer Misuse* (Working Paper No. 110), HMSO, 1988.

Law Commission, *Criminal Law: Computer Misuse* (Law Com. No. 186), Cm 819, HMSO, 1989.

National Audit Office, *IT Security in Government Departments*, HMSO, 1995.

Data protection

Bainbridge, D, *The Data Protection Act 1998*, EMIS Professional Publishing, 1999.

Bainbridge, D, *The EC Data Protection Directive*, Butterworths, 1996.

Carey, P, *Data Protection in the UK*, Blackstone Press, 2000.

Charlton S, Gaskill S and Sterling, J A L, *Encyclopedia of Data Protection*, Sweet and Maxwell, 1988 (looseleaf, updated).

Information Commissioner, Guidelines, Annual Reports and other useful information, available from the Information Commissioner's website at www.data protection.gov.uk

Jay, R and Hamilton, A, *Data Protection Law and Practice*, 2nd edn, Sweet & Maxwell, 2003.

Report of the Committee on Data Protection, *The Lindop Report*, Cmnd 7341, HMSO, December 1978.

Index